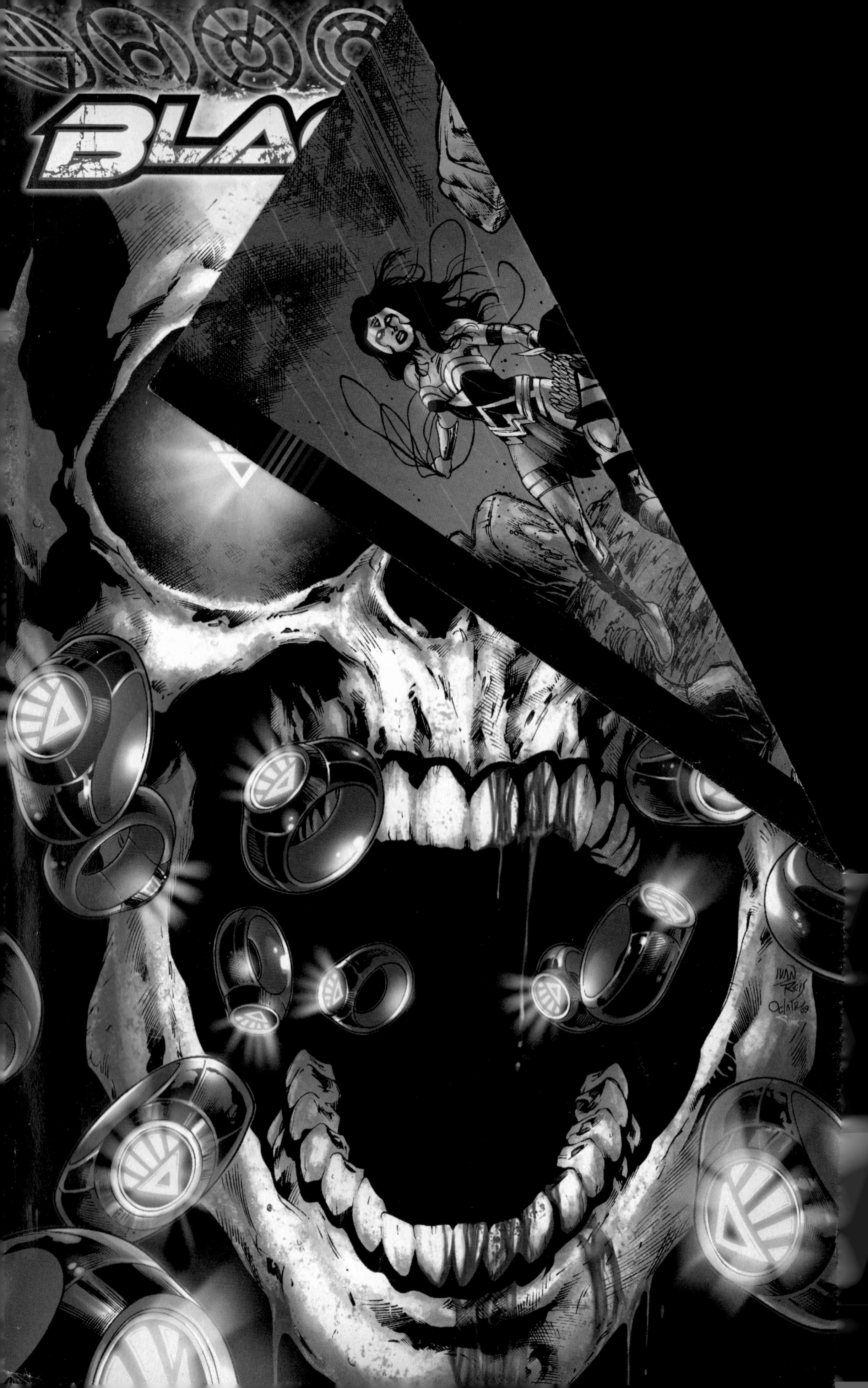
BLA
IVAN REIS

ACKEST NIGHT

GEOFF JOHNS
WRITER

IVAN REIS
PENCILLER

OCLAIR ALBERT
INKER

ROB HUNTER   PROLOGUE
JULIO FERREIRA   PART TWO
JOE PRADO   PARTS THREE–EIGHT
ADDITIONAL INKS

ALEX SINCLAIR
COLORIST

NICK J. NAPOLITANO
LETTERER

IVAN REIS & OCLAIR ALBERT
with **ALEX SINCLAIR**
COVERS

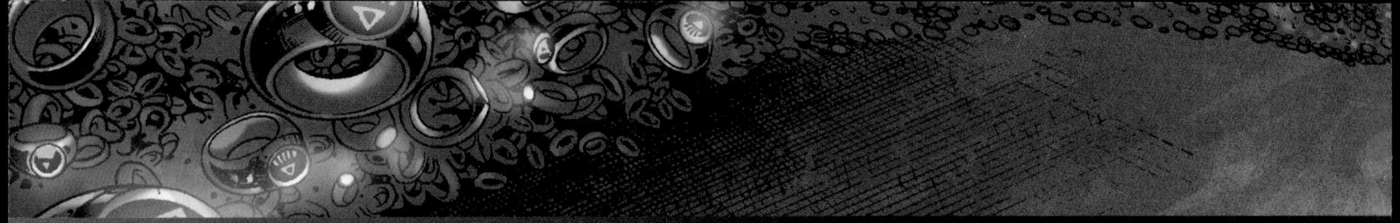

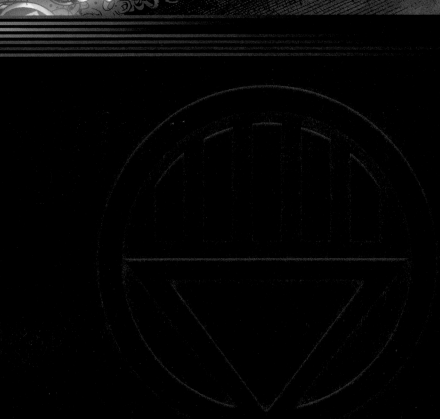

Eddie Berganza *Editor-original series* / Adam Schlagman *Associate Editor-original series*
Bob Harras *Group Editor-Collected Editions* / Sean Mackiewicz *Editor*
Robbin Brosterman *Design Director-Books* / Curtis King Jr. *Senior Art Director*

DC COMICS / Diane Nelson *President* / Dan DiDio and Jim Lee *Co-Publishers*
Geoff Johns *Chief Creative Officer* / Patrick Caldon *EVP–Finance and Administration*
John Rood *EVP–Sales, Marketing and Business Development* / Amy Genkins *SVP–Business and Legal Affairs*
Steve Rotterdam *SVP–Sales and Marketing* / John Cunningham *VP–Marketing*
Terri Cunningham *VP–Managing Editor* / Alison Gill *VP–Manufacturing* / David Hyde *VP–Publicity*
Sue Pohja *VP–Book Trade Sales* / Alysse Soll *VP–Advertising and Custom Publishing*
Bob Wayne *VP–Sales* / Mark Chiarello *Art Director*

Cover by Ivan Reis with Rodolfo Migliari

DC COMICS 1700 Broadway, New York, NY 10019 A Warner Bros. Entertainment Company

Printed by RR Donnelley, Salem, VA, USA. 6/9/10. First printing.

HC ISBN: 978-1-4012-2693-0
SC ISBN: 978-1-4012-2953-5

SUSTAINABLE FORESTRY INITIATIVE
Certified Chain of Custody
Promoting Sustainable Forest Management
www.sfiprogram.org

Fiber used in this product line meets the sourcing requirements of the SFI program. www.sfiprogram.org NFS-SPICOC-C0001801

INTRODUCTION

by Donald De Line

It's 2 am, and I'm standing in a deserted alleyway in New Orleans. Ominous shadows fall across the brick buildings—not the kind of neighborhood where you want to find yourself alone at night. But thankfully, I'm not. Cast and crew buzz about, preparing for the shot, making final adjustments, getting everything just right. With lights rigged, cameras set and actors positioned, our director Martin Campbell shouts *action*. For the first time we see Ryan Reynolds as Hal Jordan embrace his destiny. Wielding the iconic ring, he wreaks havoc against a dark force. I think to myself: "Geoff is really going to love this!"

To give a little context, we are on day two of shooting the motion picture *Green Lantern*. It took a lot of hard work to arrive at this moment, and I must say it feels great to see the cameras rolling. It is a complex and difficult endeavor bringing a story of this scope to life, and we would never be here if not for our creative partner and comic book godfather, Geoff Johns, whose GREEN LANTERN: SECRET ORIGIN is the touchstone for our film. Along with SECRET ORIGIN, Geoff's vision for Green Lantern gave us REBIRTH and then SINESTRO CORPS WAR, but these two series were merely setting the stage for this seminal work: BLACKEST NIGHT.

During my career in film, I've seen how difficult it can be to bring a fresh interpretation to an intellectual property rich in history and tradition. In the case of Green Lantern, we are talking about a character that has been in existence for some 70 years. Yet Geoff has pulled off this feat with aplomb. BLACKEST NIGHT is a groundbreaking culmination of his efforts with artist Ivan Reis. The eight-issue series has taken Green Lantern to unprecedented places, breathing new life and energy into the storied mythology. The result of Geoff and Ivan's vision is something special that the devoted Green Lantern fan base—as well as future generations of Green Lantern fans—can embrace.

In BLACKEST NIGHT, Geoff and Ivan have preserved the signature qualities that made us fall in love with Green Lantern in the first place. At the same time, the series weaves a complete narrative that repositions Green Lantern at the forefront of the DC Universe. Not content with rejuvenating merely the Green Lantern Corps, Geoff creates a story

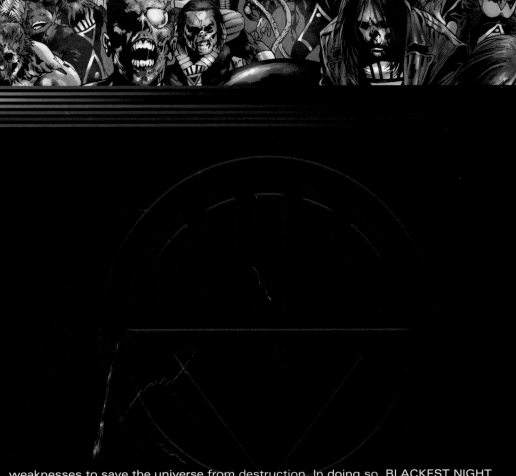

weaknesses to save the universe from destruction. In doing so, BLACKEST NIGHT
embraces certain lesser-known characters, giving them exciting new identities.
By bestowing rings on these characters, for both good and evil, Geoff has brought
the Green Lantern universe into uncharted territory.

From an artistic standpoint, BLACKEST NIGHT features the brilliant work of Ivan Reis,
whose visceral illustrations imbue the world with a newfound gravitas. Ivan's detailed
artwork is terrifyingly lifelike, and is masterfully applied in introducing the black rings
and raising the Black Lanterns. Beyond that, BLACKEST NIGHT is striking for the
manner in which it grounds the characters with an emotional veracity upon seeing their
loved ones and enemies raised from the dead. Heavy stuff, indeed, but the best work
challenges you to ask difficult questions, while at the same time it thoroughly
entertains. Geoff and Ivan have taken the vast Green Lantern mythos and given it their
own spin, creating a series that is well deserving of the Eisner Award nomination.

When you consider Geoff and Ivan's careers on the whole, it is hard not to be
impressed, and yet there's no reason to think their work won't continue to reach new
heights moving forward. From a narrative standpoint, Geoff has taken this high-concept,
cosmic idea and with the characters that we know and love, grounded it in reality.
Making these extraordinary personalities relatable is the hallmark of great superhero
writing. Above all, Geoff has earned our trust as an authority on all things Green Lantern.

Back on set, we are now three weeks into production. As we finish up Abin Sur's
fateful crash scene, I get a buzz on my BlackBerry. It's Geoff, and he's just seen some
early footage:

"Really, just blown away by it all."

The feeling's mutual, Geoff.

Donald De Line is a producer on the *Green Lantern*
motion picture. He has also produced the films *The Italian
Job*, *Body of Lies*, *Observe and Report* and *I Love You, Man.*

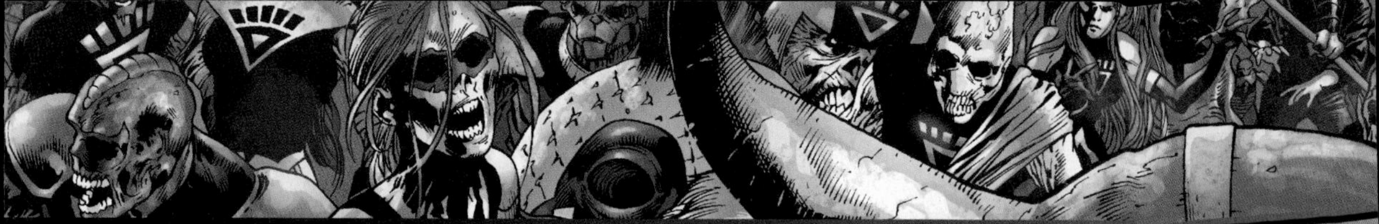

THE STORY SO FAR...

Billions of years ago, the self-appointed Guardians of the Universe recruited thousands of sentient beings from across the cosmos to join their intergalactic police force: the Green Lantern Corps.

Chosen because they are able to overcome great fear, the Green Lanterns patrol their respective space sectors armed with power rings capable of wielding the emerald energy of willpower into whatever constructs they can imagine.

Hal Jordan is the greatest of them all.

When the dying Green Lantern Abin Sur crashed on Earth, he chose Hal Jordan to be his successor, for his indomitable will and fearlessness. As the protector of Sector 2814, Hal has saved Earth from destruction, even died in its service and been reborn.

Thaal Sinestro of Korugar was once considered the greatest Green Lantern of them all.

As Abin Sur's friend, Sinestro became Jordan's mentor in the Corps. But after being sentenced to the Anti-Matter Universe for abusing his power, Sinestro learned of the yellow light of fear being mined on Qward. Wielding a new golden power ring fueled by terror, Sinestro drafted thousands of the most horrific, psychotic and sadistic beings in the universe, and with their doctrine of fear, burned all who opposed them.

When the Green Lantern Corps battled their former ally during the Sinestro Corps War, the skies burned with green and gold as Earth erupted into an epic battle between good and evil. Though the Green Lanterns won, their brotherhood was broken and the peace they achieved was short-lived. In its aftermath, the Guardians rewrote the Book of Oa, the very laws by which their corps abides, and dissent grew within their members.

Now Hal Jordan will face his greatest challenge yet, as the prophecy foretold by Abin Sur in his dying moments finally comes to pass...

The emotional spectrum has splintered into seven factions. Seven corps were born.

The Green Lanterns. The Sinestro Corps. Atrocitus and the enraged Red Lanterns. Larfleeze, the avaricious keeper of the Orange Light. Former Guardians Ganthet and Sayd's small but hopeful Blue Lantern Corps. The Zamarons and their army of fierce and loving Star Sapphires. And the mysterious Indigo Tribe.

As the War of Light ignited between these Lantern bearers, the skies on every world darkened. In Sector 666, on the planet Ryut, a black lantern grew around the Anti-Monitor's corpse, using his vast energies to empower it.

The first of the Black Lanterns, the Black Hand, has risen from the dead, heralding a greater power that will extinguish all of the light—and life—in the universe.

Now across thousands of worlds, the dead have risen, and Hal Jordan and all of Earth's greatest heroes must bear witness to Blackest Night, which will descend upon them all, without prejudice, mercy or reason.

PROLOGUE: DEATH BECOMES US

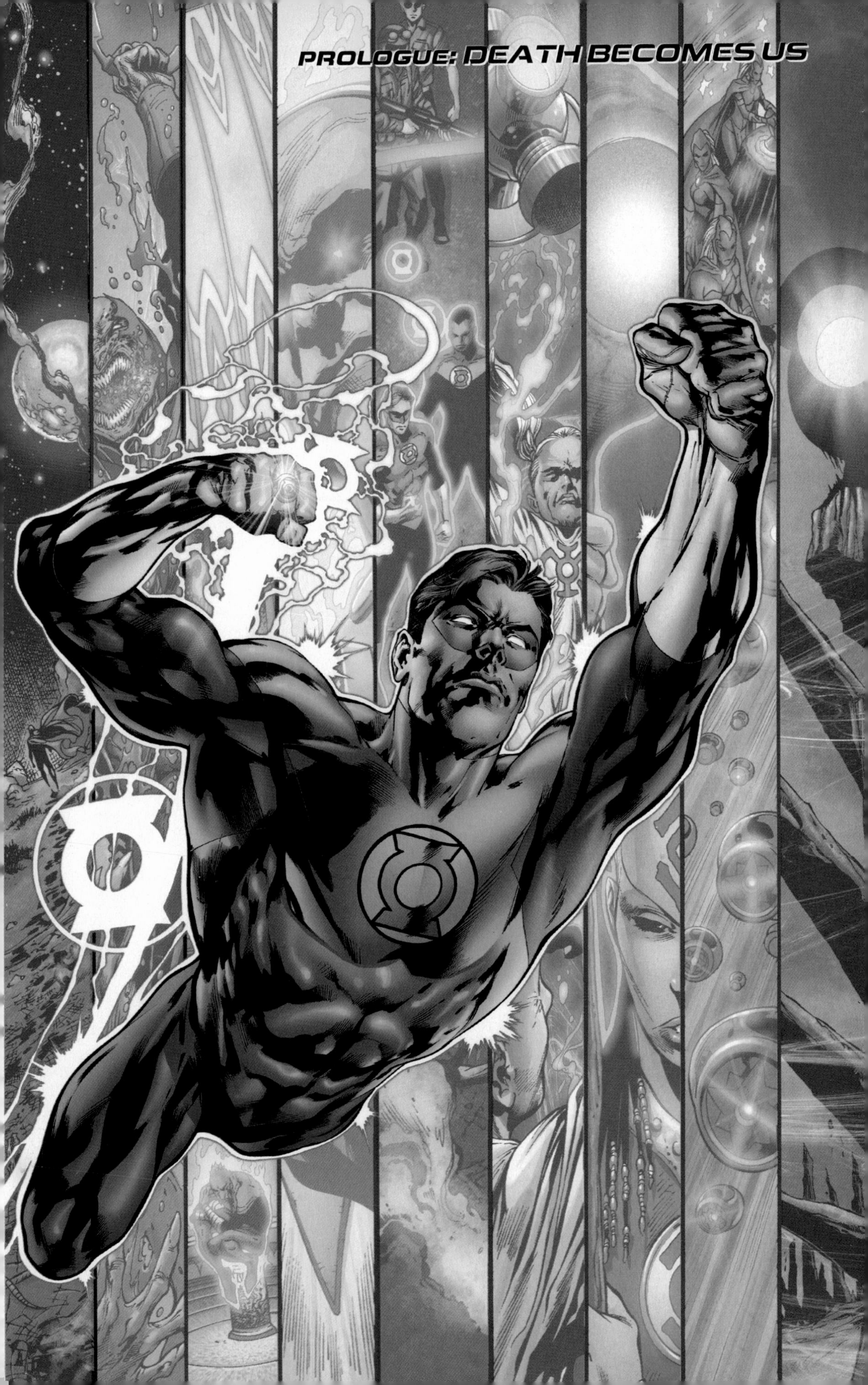

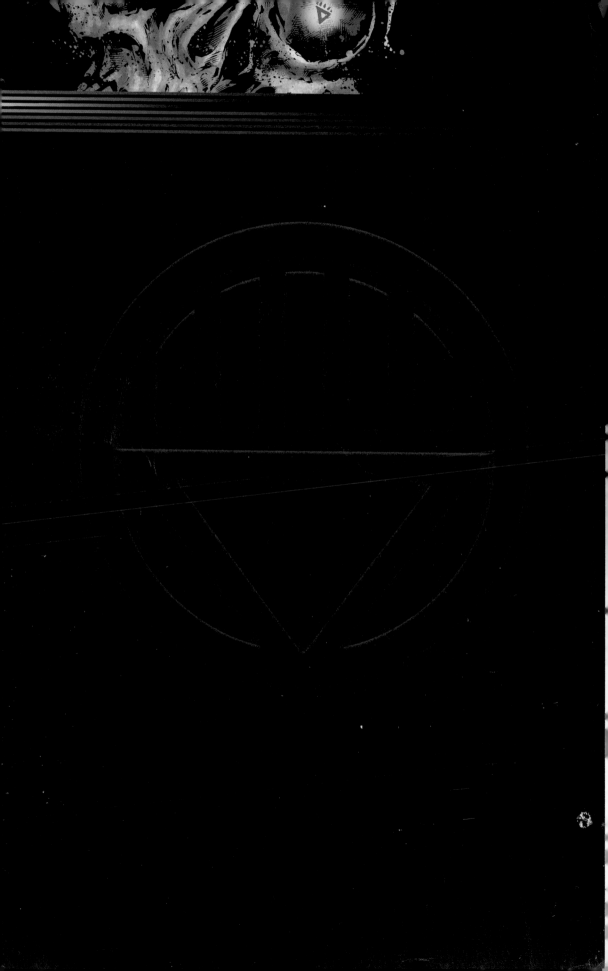

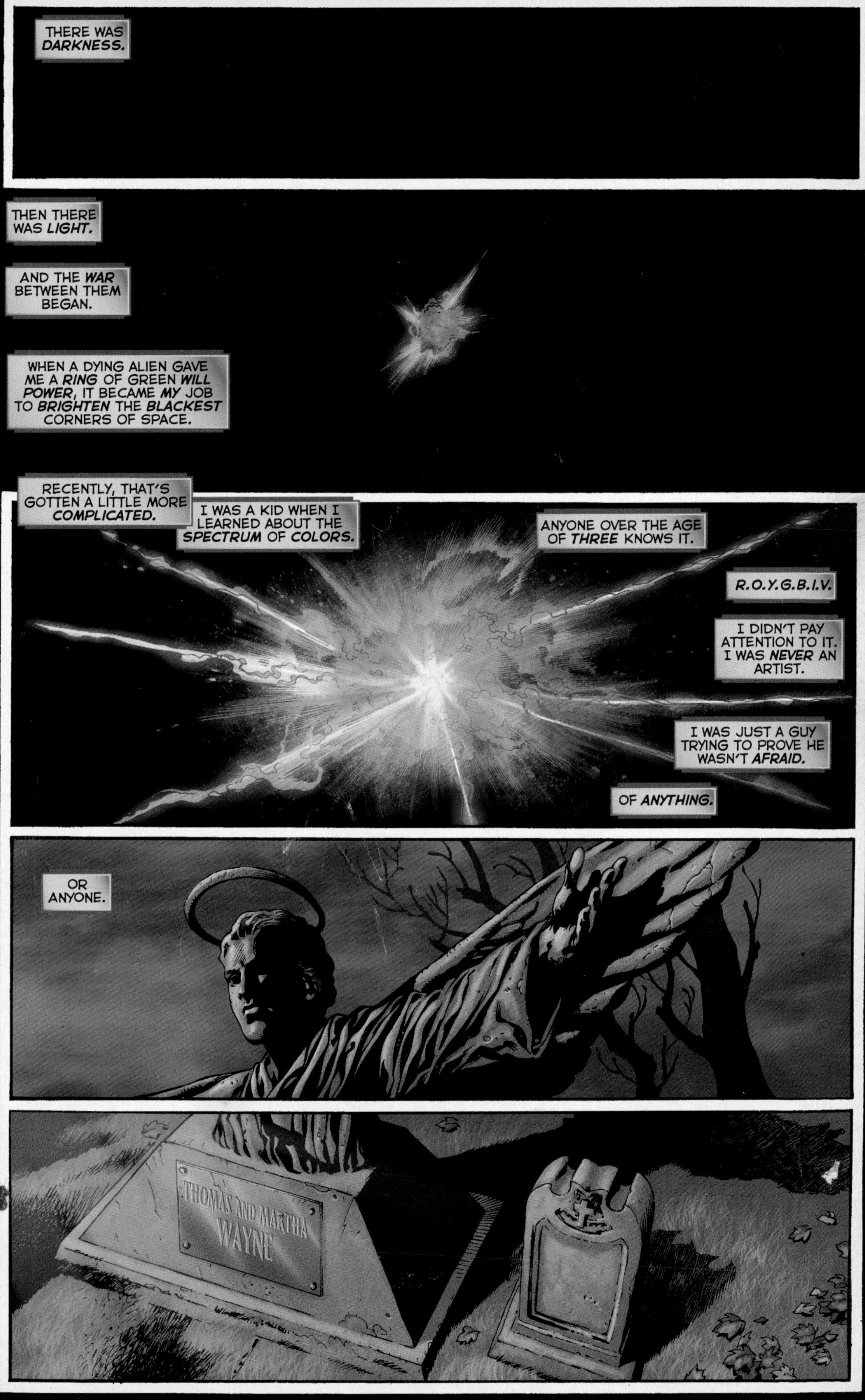
THERE WAS DARKNESS.
THEN THERE WAS LIGHT.
AND THE WAR BETWEEN THEM BEGAN.
WHEN A DYING ALIEN GAVE ME A RING OF GREEN WILL POWER, IT BECAME MY JOB TO BRIGHTEN THE BLACKEST CORNERS OF SPACE.
RECENTLY, THAT'S GOTTEN A LITTLE MORE COMPLICATED.
I WAS A KID WHEN I LEARNED ABOUT THE SPECTRUM OF COLORS.
ANYONE OVER THE AGE OF THREE KNOWS IT.
R.O.Y.G.B.I.V.
I DIDN'T PAY ATTENTION TO IT. I WAS NEVER AN ARTIST.
I WAS JUST A GUY TRYING TO PROVE HE WASN'T AFRAID.
OF ANYTHING.
OR ANYONE.
THOMAS AND MARTHA WAYNE

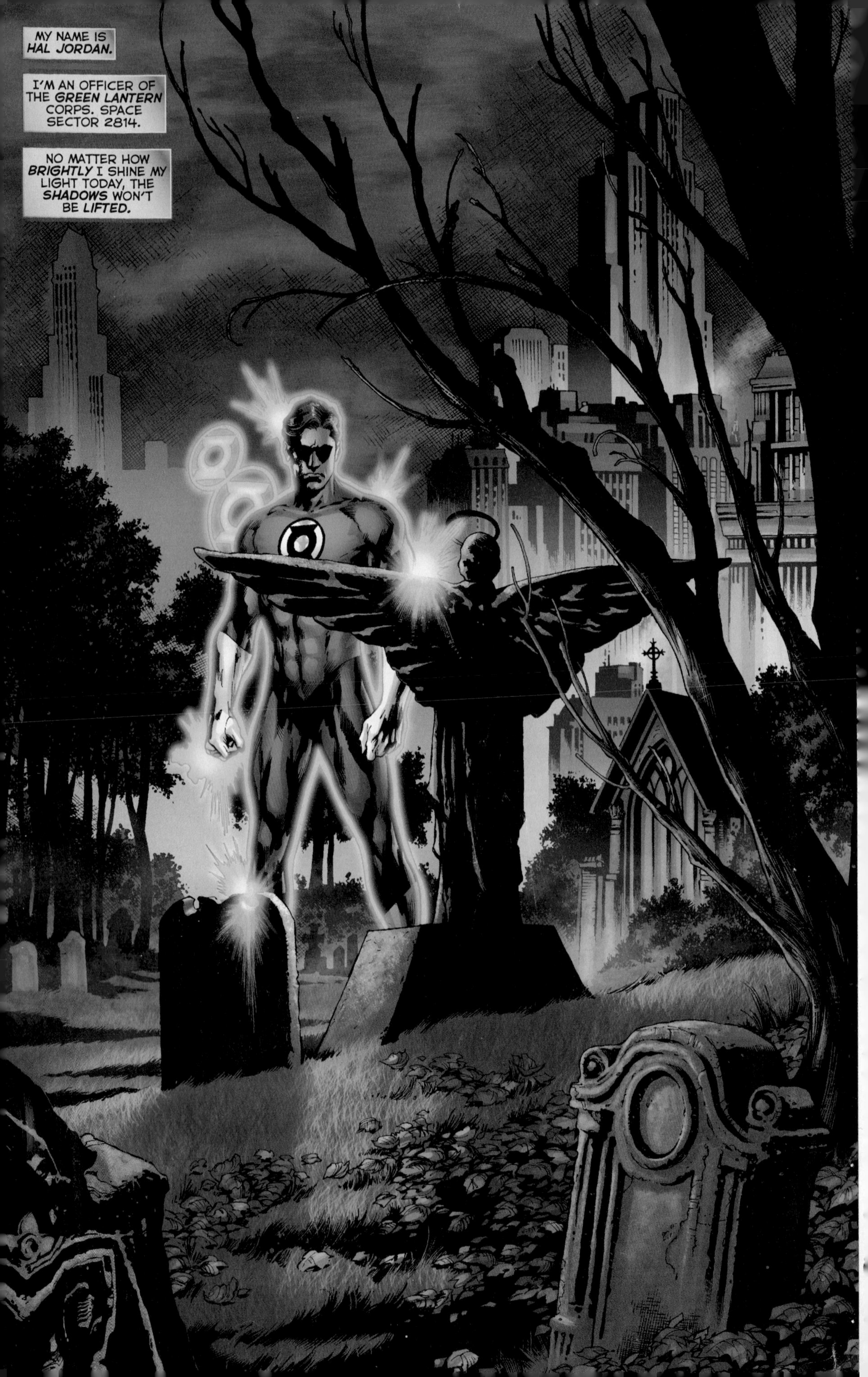
MY NAME IS HAL JORDAN.
I'M AN OFFICER OF THE GREEN LANTERN CORPS. SPACE SECTOR 2814.
NO MATTER HOW BRIGHTLY I SHINE MY LIGHT TODAY, THE SHADOWS WON'T BE LIFTED.

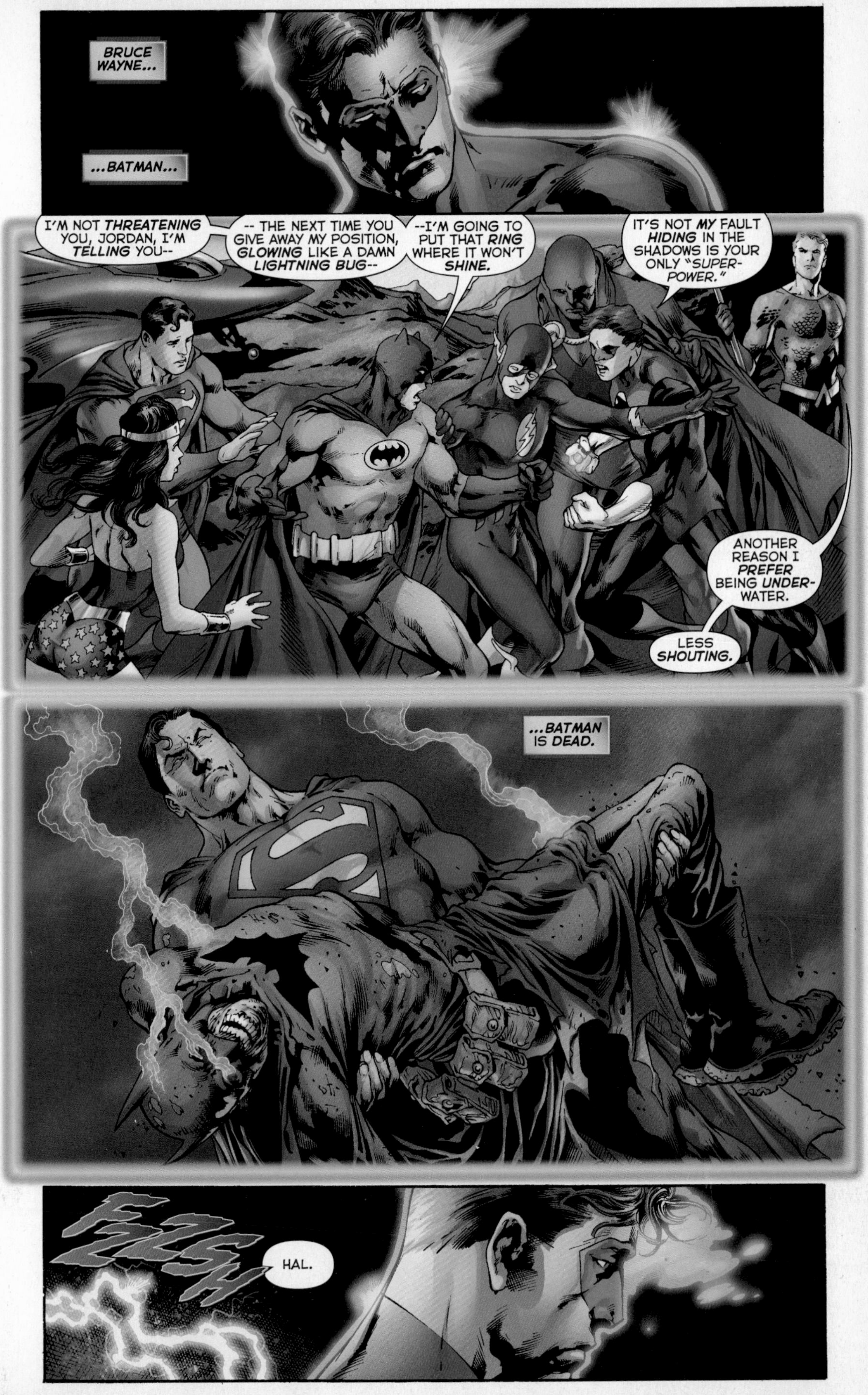
BRUCE WAYNE...
...BATMAN...
I'M NOT THREATENING YOU, JORDAN, I'M TELLING YOU--
-- THE NEXT TIME YOU GIVE AWAY MY POSITION, GLOWING LIKE A DAMN LIGHTNING BUG--
--I'M GOING TO PUT THAT RING WHERE IT WON'T SHINE.
IT'S NOT MY FAULT HIDING IN THE SHADOWS IS YOUR ONLY "SUPER-POWER."
ANOTHER REASON I PREFER BEING UNDER-WATER.
LESS SHOUTING.
...BATMAN IS DEAD.
FZZSH
HAL.

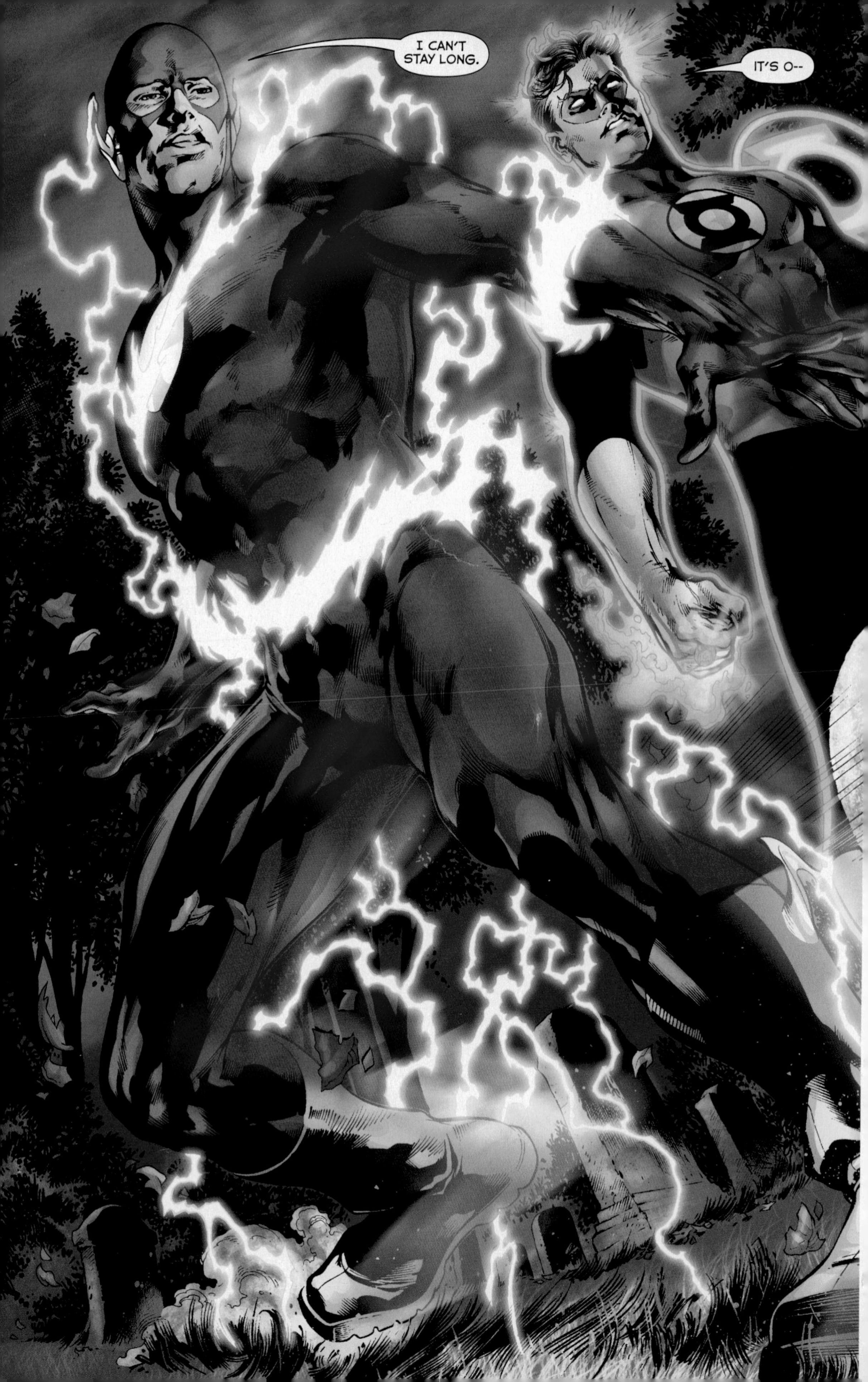
I CAN'T STAY LONG.
IT'S O--

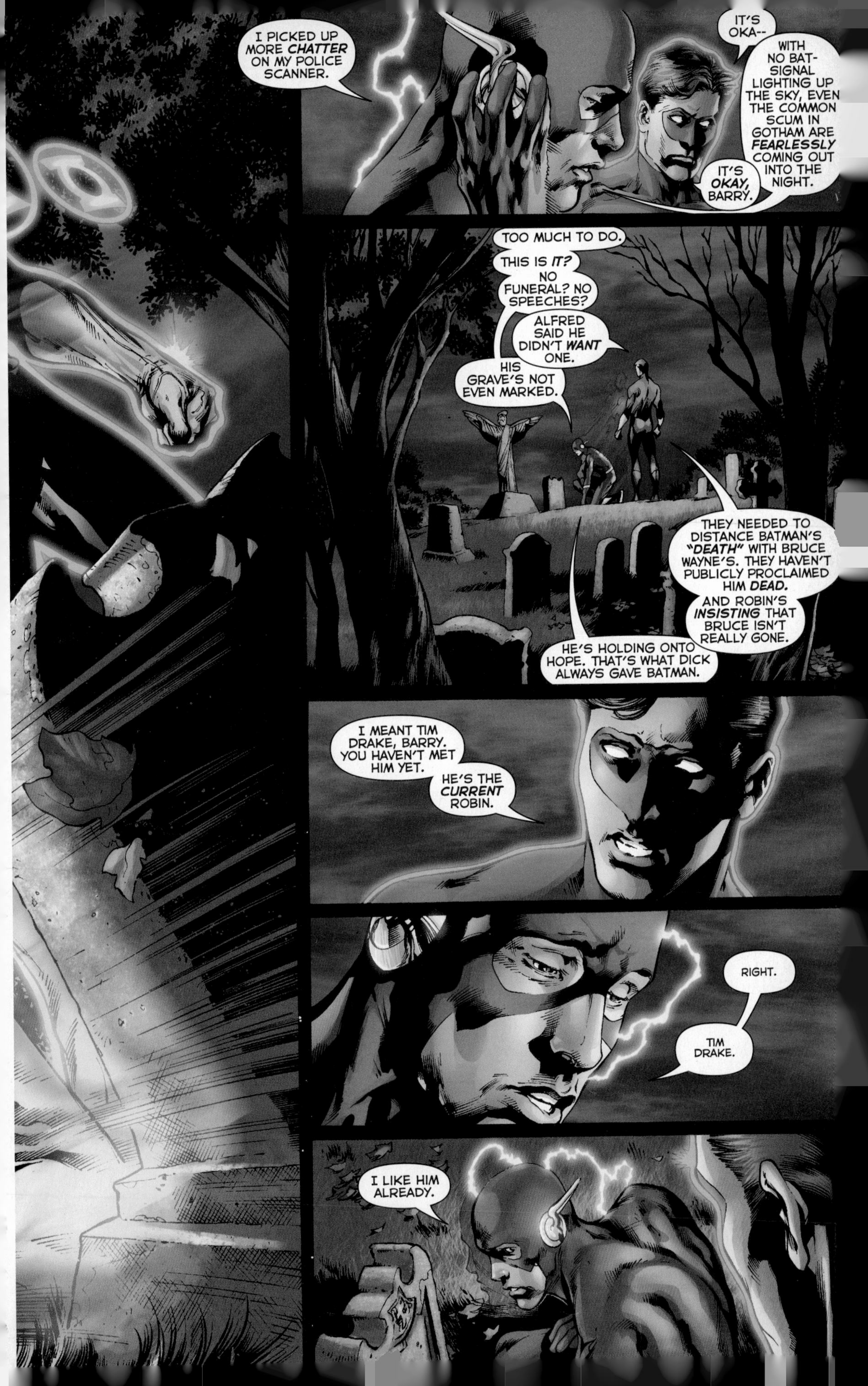
I PICKED UP MORE CHATTER ON MY POLICE SCANNER.
IT'S OKA--
WITH NO BAT-SIGNAL LIGHTING UP THE SKY, EVEN THE COMMON SCUM IN GOTHAM ARE FEARLESSLY COMING OUT INTO THE NIGHT.
IT'S OKAY, BARRY.
TOO MUCH TO DO.
THIS IS IT?
NO FUNERAL? NO SPEECHES?
ALFRED SAID HE DIDN'T WANT ONE.
HIS GRAVE'S NOT EVEN MARKED.
THEY NEEDED TO DISTANCE BATMAN'S "DEATH" WITH BRUCE WAYNE'S. THEY HAVEN'T PUBLICLY PROCLAIMED HIM DEAD.
AND ROBIN'S INSISTING THAT BRUCE ISN'T REALLY GONE.
HE'S HOLDING ONTO HOPE. THAT'S WHAT DICK ALWAYS GAVE BATMAN.
I MEANT TIM DRAKE, BARRY. YOU HAVEN'T MET HIM YET.
HE'S THE CURRENT ROBIN.
RIGHT.
TIM DRAKE.
I LIKE HIM ALREADY.

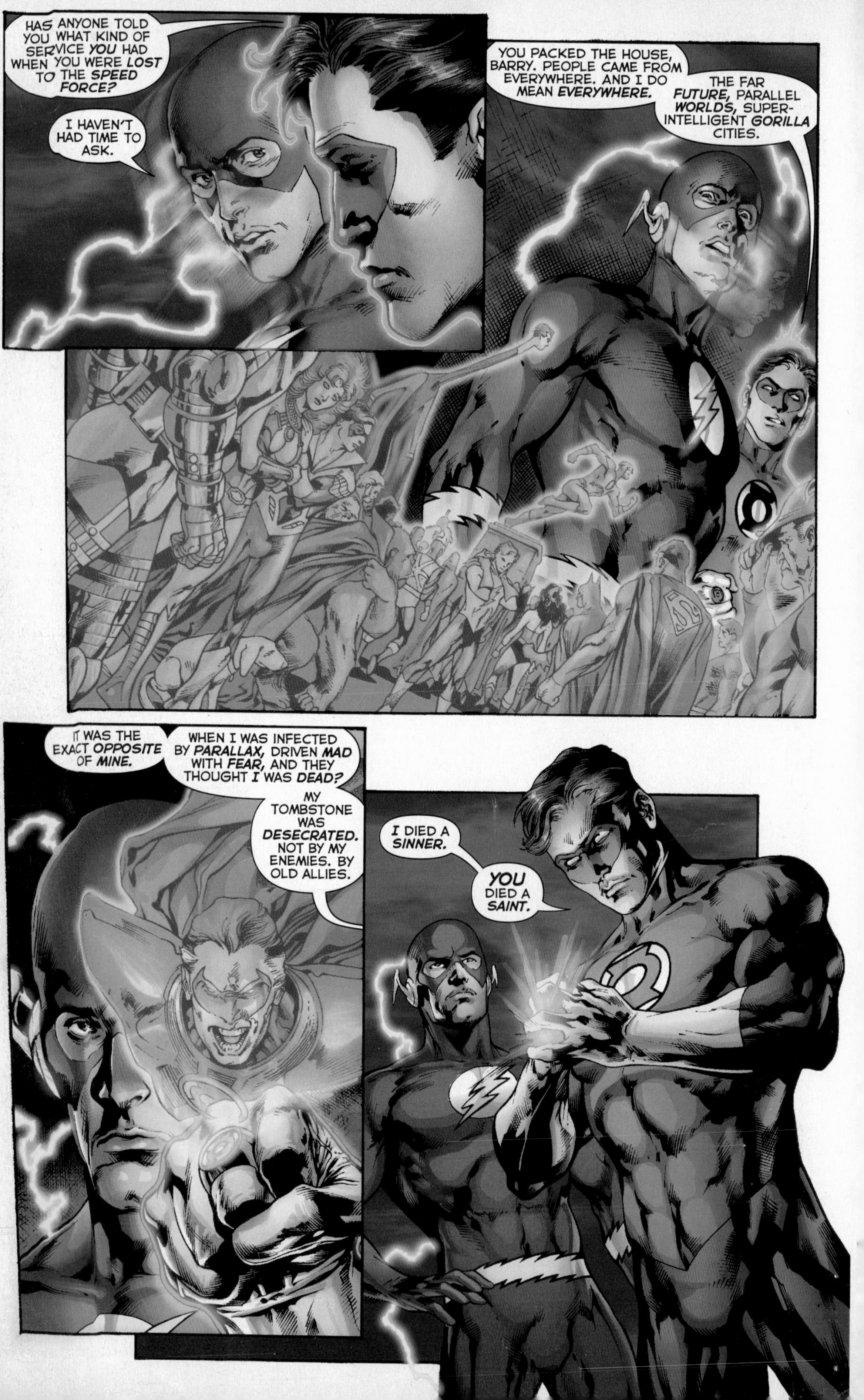
HAS ANYONE TOLD YOU WHAT KIND OF SERVICE YOU HAD WHEN YOU WERE LOST TO THE SPEED FORCE?
I HAVEN'T HAD TIME TO ASK.
YOU PACKED THE HOUSE, BARRY. PEOPLE CAME FROM EVERYWHERE. AND I DO MEAN EVERYWHERE.
THE FAR FUTURE, PARALLEL WORLDS, SUPER-INTELLIGENT GORILLA CITIES.
IT WAS THE EXACT OPPOSITE OF MINE.
WHEN I WAS INFECTED BY PARALLAX, DRIVEN MAD WITH FEAR, AND THEY THOUGHT I WAS DEAD?
MY TOMBSTONE WAS DESECRATED. NOT BY MY ENEMIES. BY OLD ALLIES.
I DIED A SINNER.
YOU DIED A SAINT.

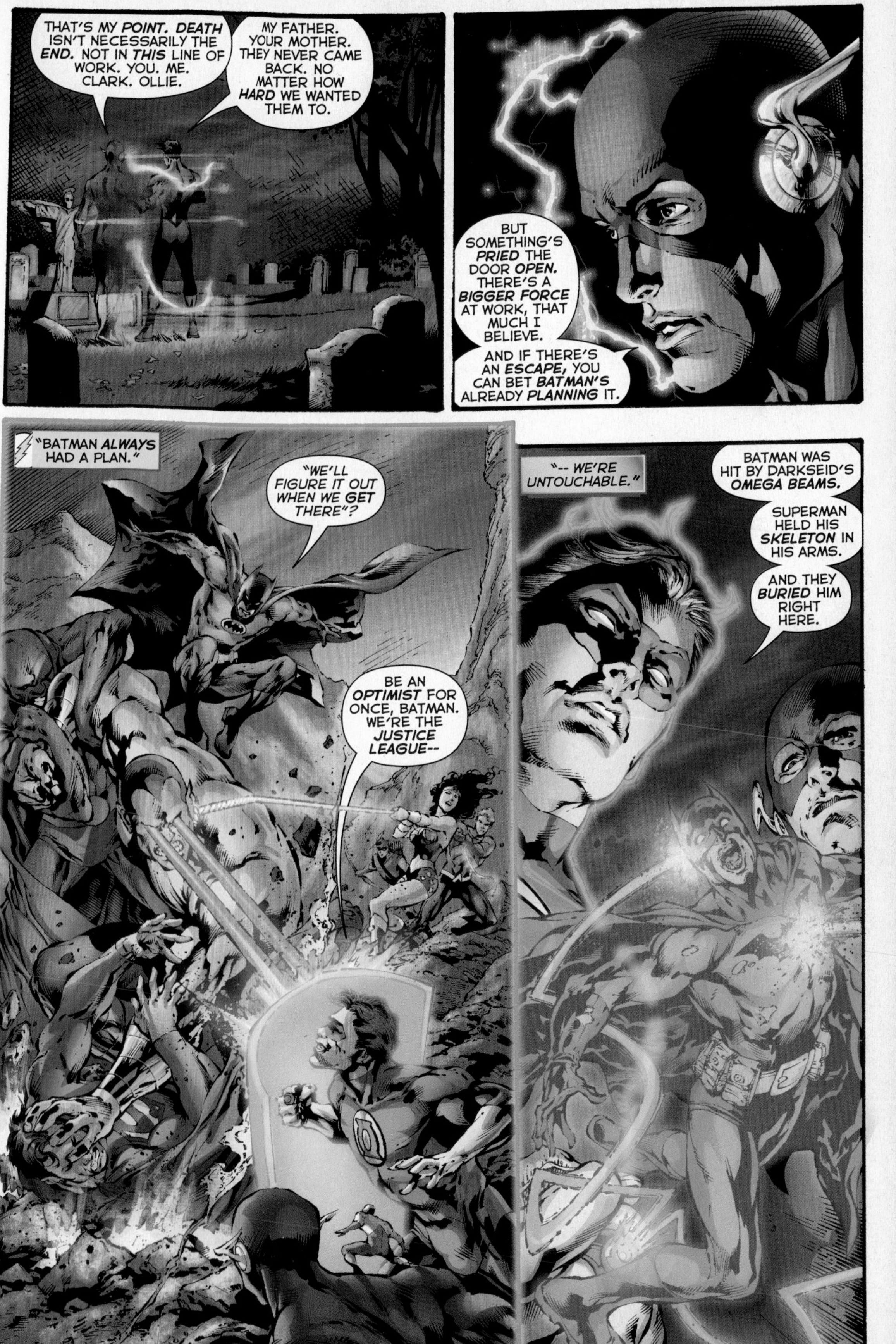
THAT'S MY POINT. DEATH ISN'T NECESSARILY THE END. NOT IN THIS LINE OF WORK. YOU. ME. CLARK. OLLIE.
MY FATHER. YOUR MOTHER. THEY NEVER CAME BACK. NO MATTER HOW HARD WE WANTED THEM TO.
BUT SOMETHING'S PRIED THE DOOR OPEN. THERE'S A BIGGER FORCE AT WORK, THAT MUCH I BELIEVE.
AND IF THERE'S AN ESCAPE, YOU CAN BET BATMAN'S ALREADY PLANNING IT.
"BATMAN ALWAYS HAD A PLAN."
"WE'LL FIGURE IT OUT WHEN WE GET THERE"?
BE AN OPTIMIST FOR ONCE, BATMAN. WE'RE THE JUSTICE LEAGUE--
"-- WE'RE UNTOUCHABLE."
BATMAN WAS HIT BY DARKSEID'S OMEGA BEAMS.
SUPERMAN HELD HIS SKELETON IN HIS ARMS.
AND THEY BURIED HIM RIGHT HERE.

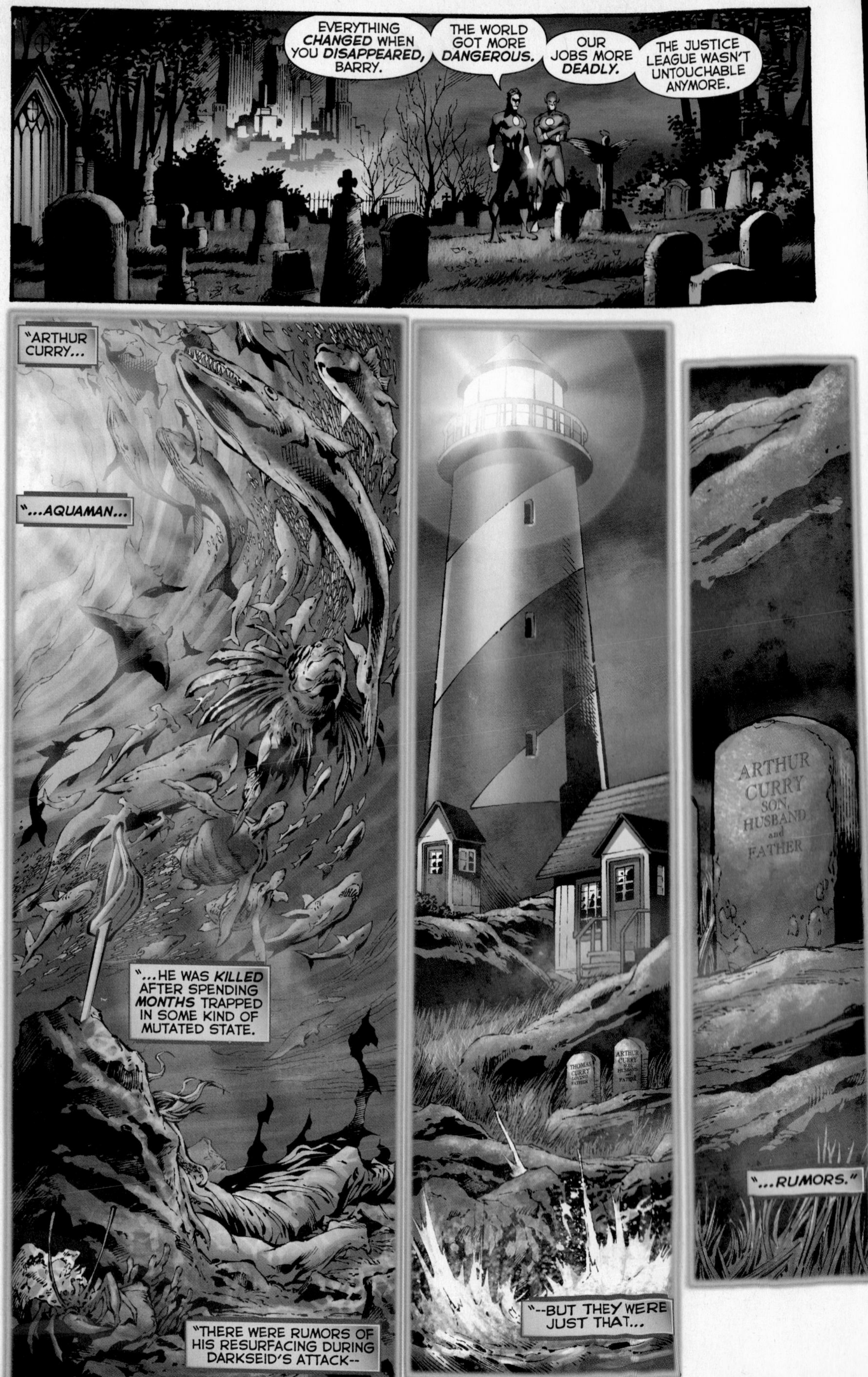
EVERYTHING CHANGED WHEN YOU DISAPPEARED, BARRY.
THE WORLD GOT MORE DANGEROUS.
OUR JOBS MORE DEADLY.
THE JUSTICE LEAGUE WASN'T UNTOUCHABLE ANYMORE.
"ARTHUR CURRY...
"...AQUAMAN...
"...HE WAS KILLED AFTER SPENDING MONTHS TRAPPED IN SOME KIND OF MUTATED STATE.
"THERE WERE RUMORS OF HIS RESURFACING DURING DARKSEID'S ATTACK--
"--BUT THEY WERE JUST THAT...
ARTHUR CURRY SON, HUSBAND and FATHER
"...RUMORS."

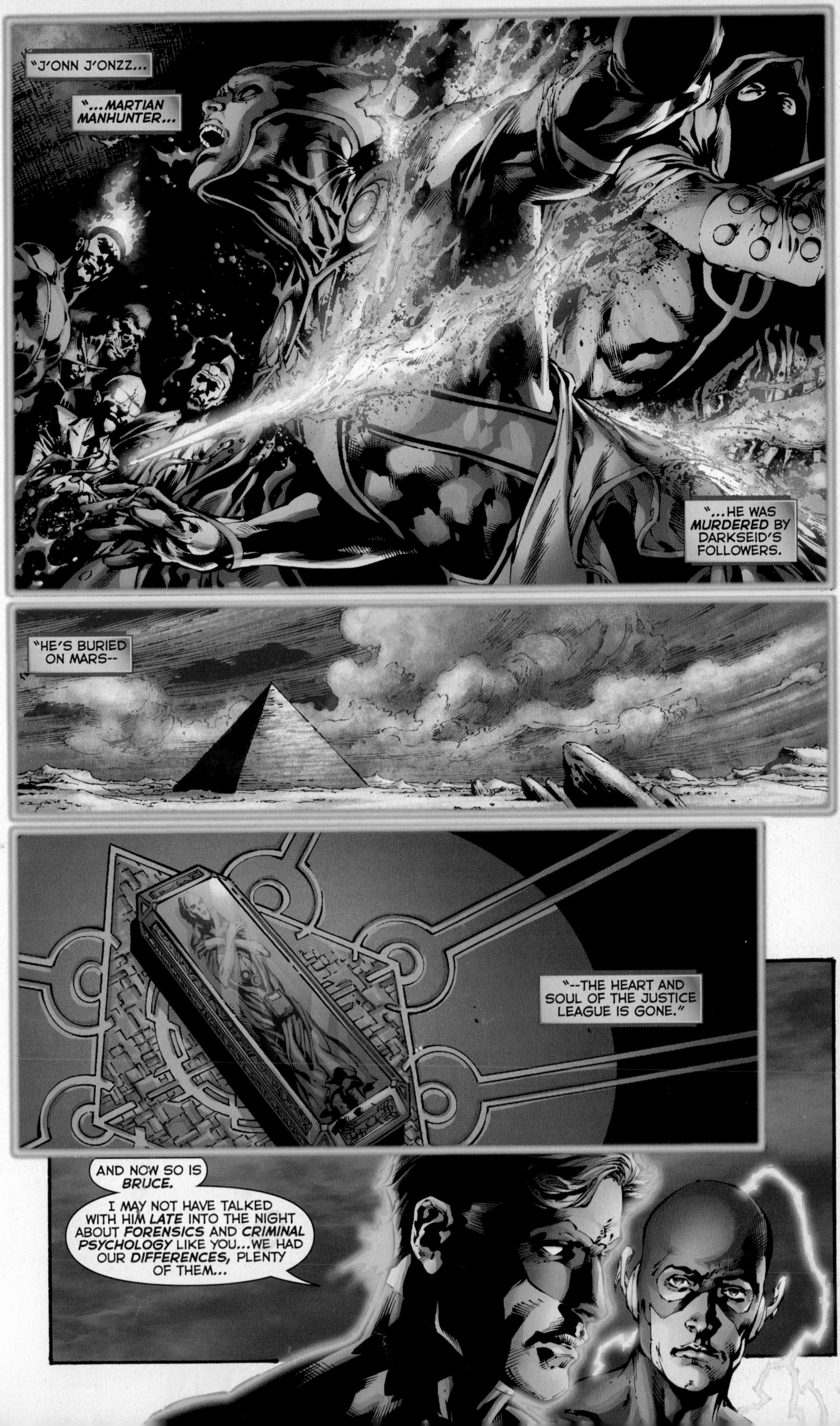

"J'ONN J'ONZZ...
"...MARTIAN MANHUNTER...
"...HE WAS MURDERED BY DARKSEID'S FOLLOWERS.
"HE'S BURIED ON MARS--
"--THE HEART AND SOUL OF THE JUSTICE LEAGUE IS GONE."
AND NOW SO IS BRUCE.
I MAY NOT HAVE TALKED WITH HIM LATE INTO THE NIGHT ABOUT FORENSICS AND CRIMINAL PSYCHOLOGY LIKE YOU...WE HAD OUR DIFFERENCES, PLENTY OF THEM...

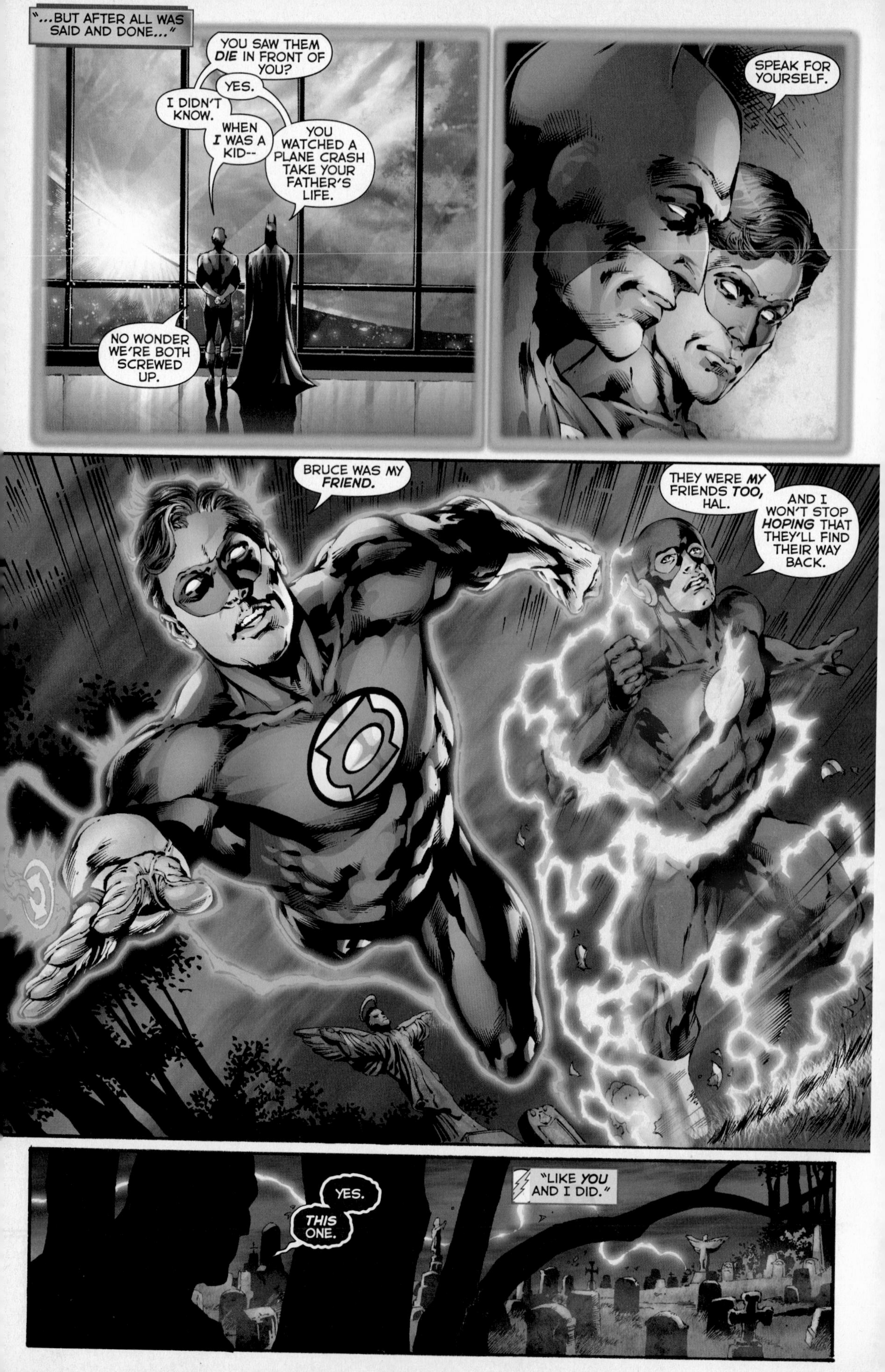
"...BUT AFTER ALL WAS SAID AND DONE..."
YOU SAW THEM DIE IN FRONT OF YOU?
YES.
I DIDN'T KNOW.
WHEN I WAS A KID--
YOU WATCHED A PLANE CRASH TAKE YOUR FATHER'S LIFE.
NO WONDER WE'RE BOTH SCREWED UP.
SPEAK FOR YOURSELF.
BRUCE WAS MY FRIEND.
THEY WERE MY FRIENDS TOO, HAL.
AND I WON'T STOP HOPING THAT THEY'LL FIND THEIR WAY BACK.
YES. THIS ONE.
"LIKE YOU AND I DID."

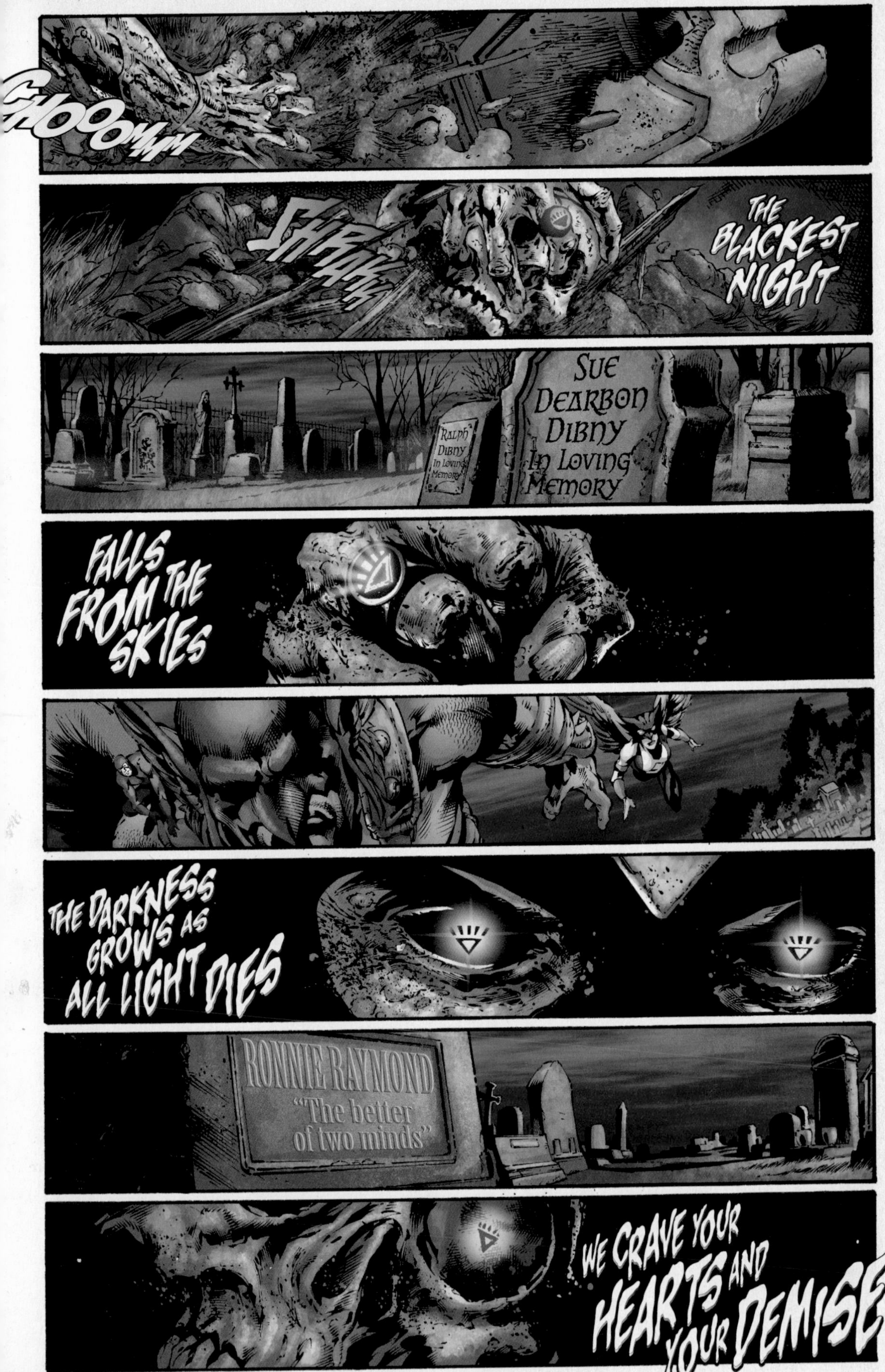
CHOOOMMM
SHRAKK
THE BLACKEST NIGHT
SUE DEARBON DIBNY In Loving Memory
RALPH DIBNY In Loving Memory
FALLS FROM THE SKIES
THE DARKNESS GROWS AS ALL LIGHT DIES
RONNIE RAYMOND "The better of two minds"
WE CRAVE YOUR HEARTS AND YOUR DEMISE

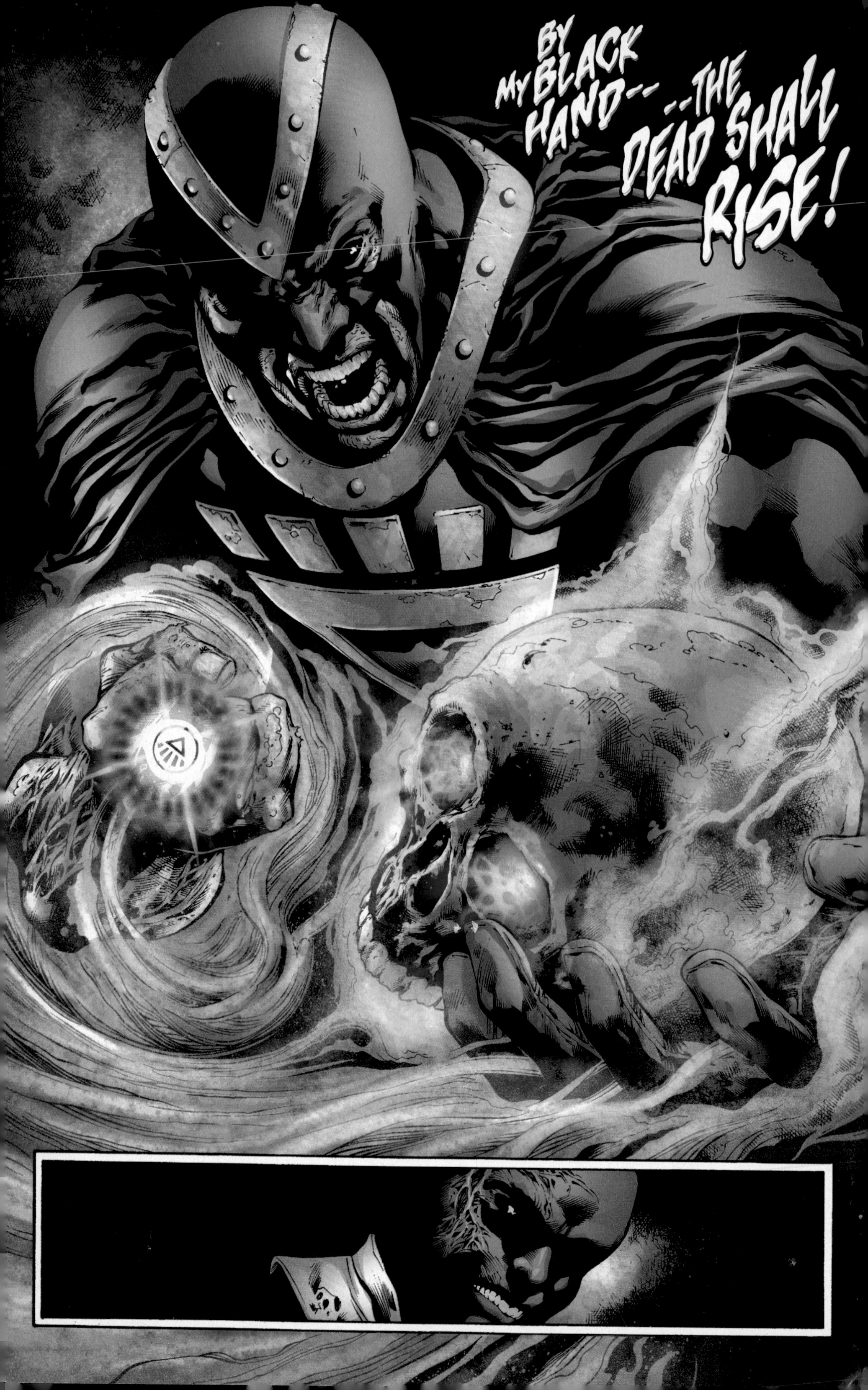
BY MY BLACK HAND--
--THE DEAD SHALL RISE!

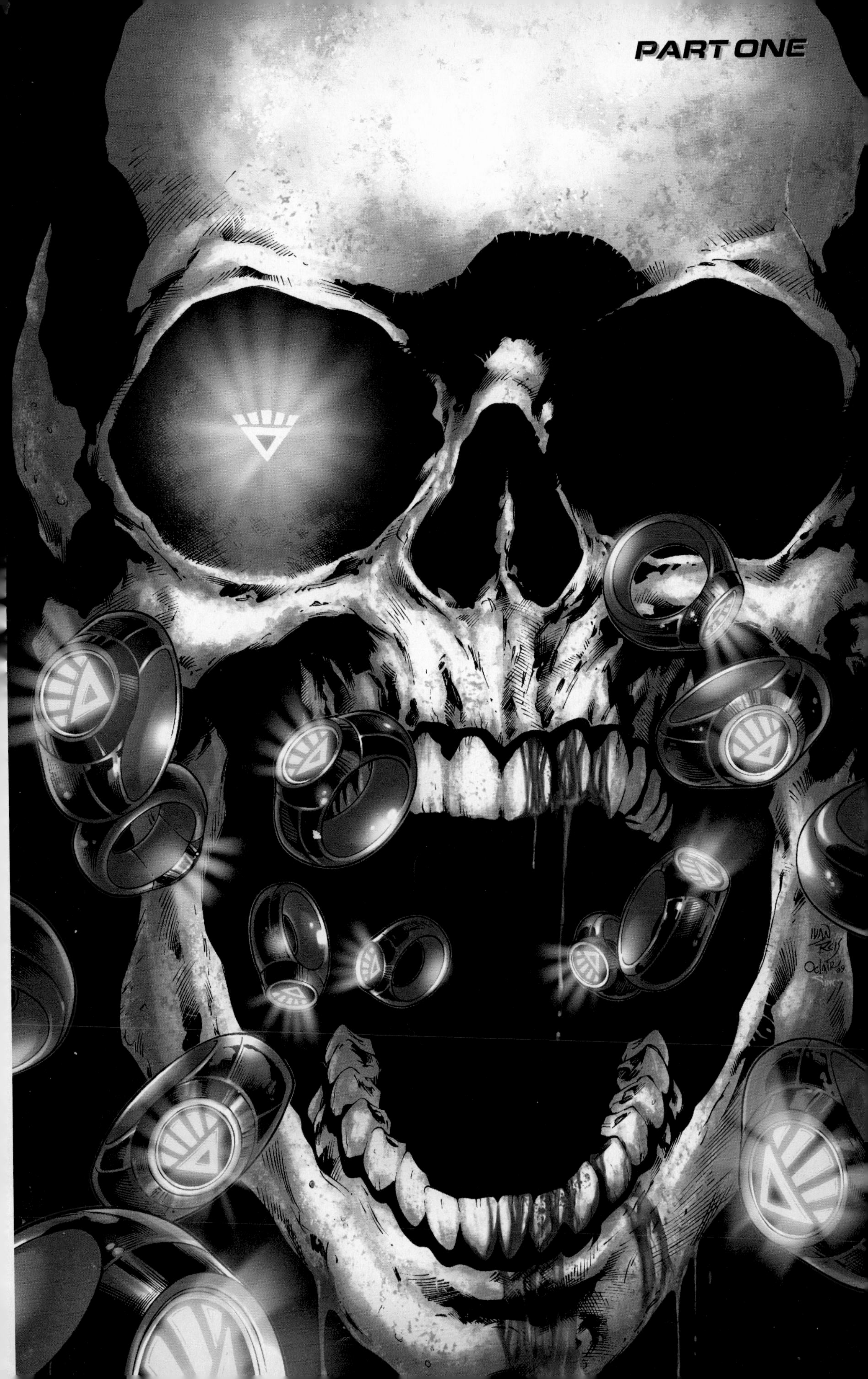
PART ONE

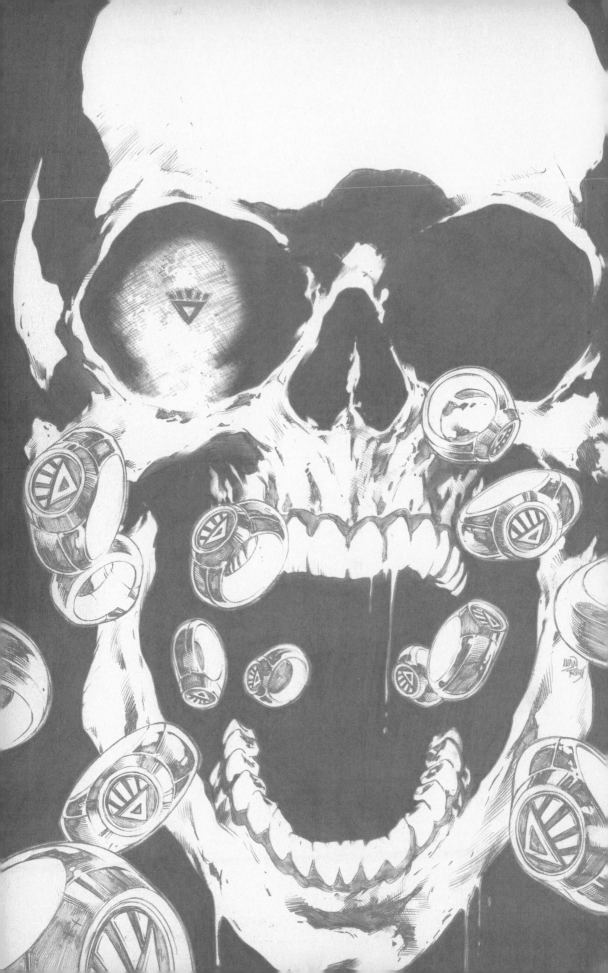

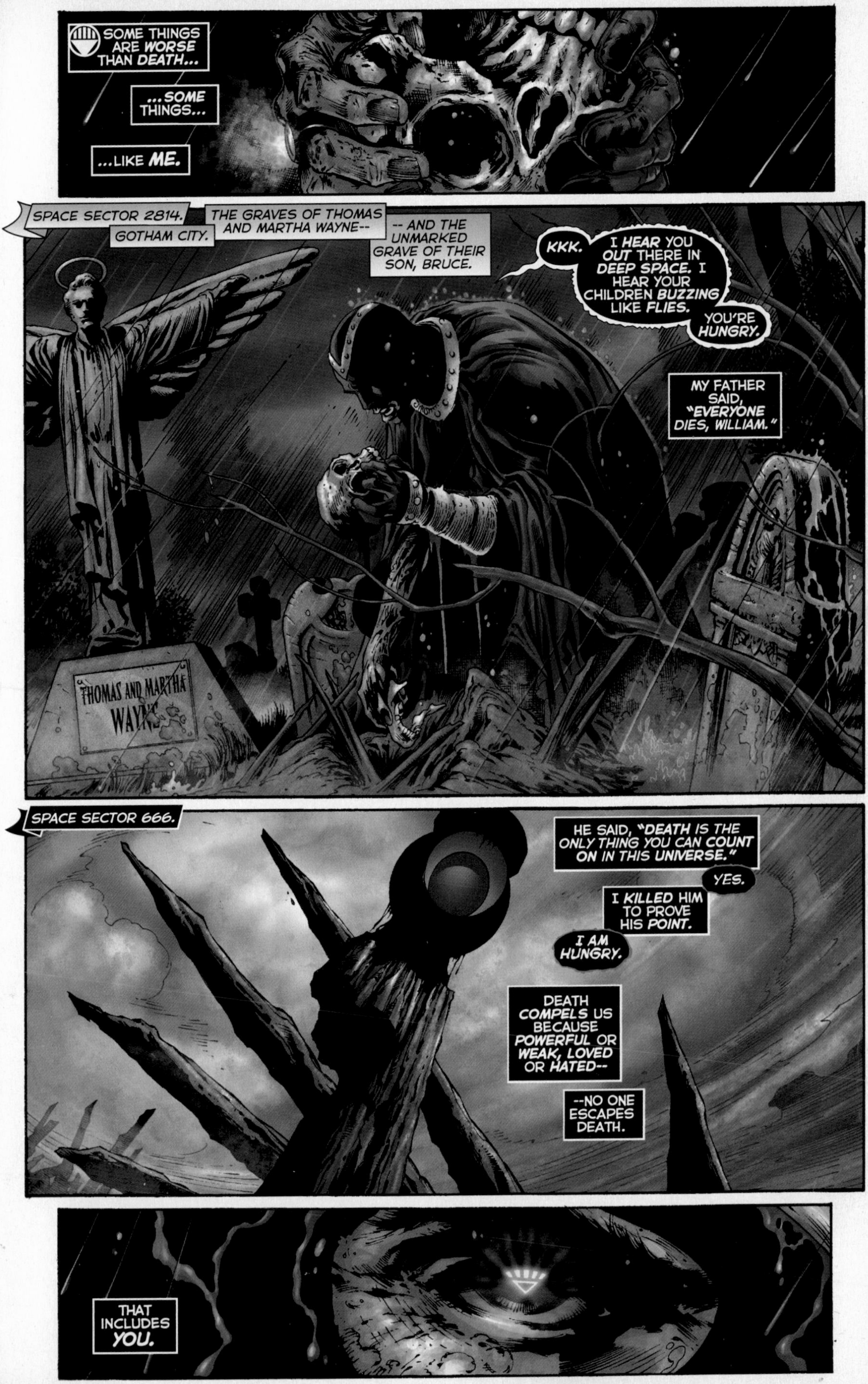
SOME THINGS ARE WORSE THAN DEATH...
...SOME THINGS...
...LIKE ME.
SPACE SECTOR 2814.
GOTHAM CITY.
THE GRAVES OF THOMAS AND MARTHA WAYNE--
-- AND THE UNMARKED GRAVE OF THEIR SON, BRUCE.
KKK.
I HEAR YOU OUT THERE IN DEEP SPACE. I HEAR YOUR CHILDREN BUZZING LIKE FLIES.
YOU'RE HUNGRY.
MY FATHER SAID, "EVERYONE DIES, WILLIAM."
THOMAS AND MARTHA WAYNE
SPACE SECTOR 666.
HE SAID, "DEATH IS THE ONLY THING YOU CAN COUNT ON IN THIS UNIVERSE."
YES.
I KILLED HIM TO PROVE HIS POINT.
I AM HUNGRY.
DEATH COMPELS US BECAUSE POWERFUL OR WEAK, LOVED OR HATED--
--NO ONE ESCAPES DEATH.
THAT INCLUDES YOU.

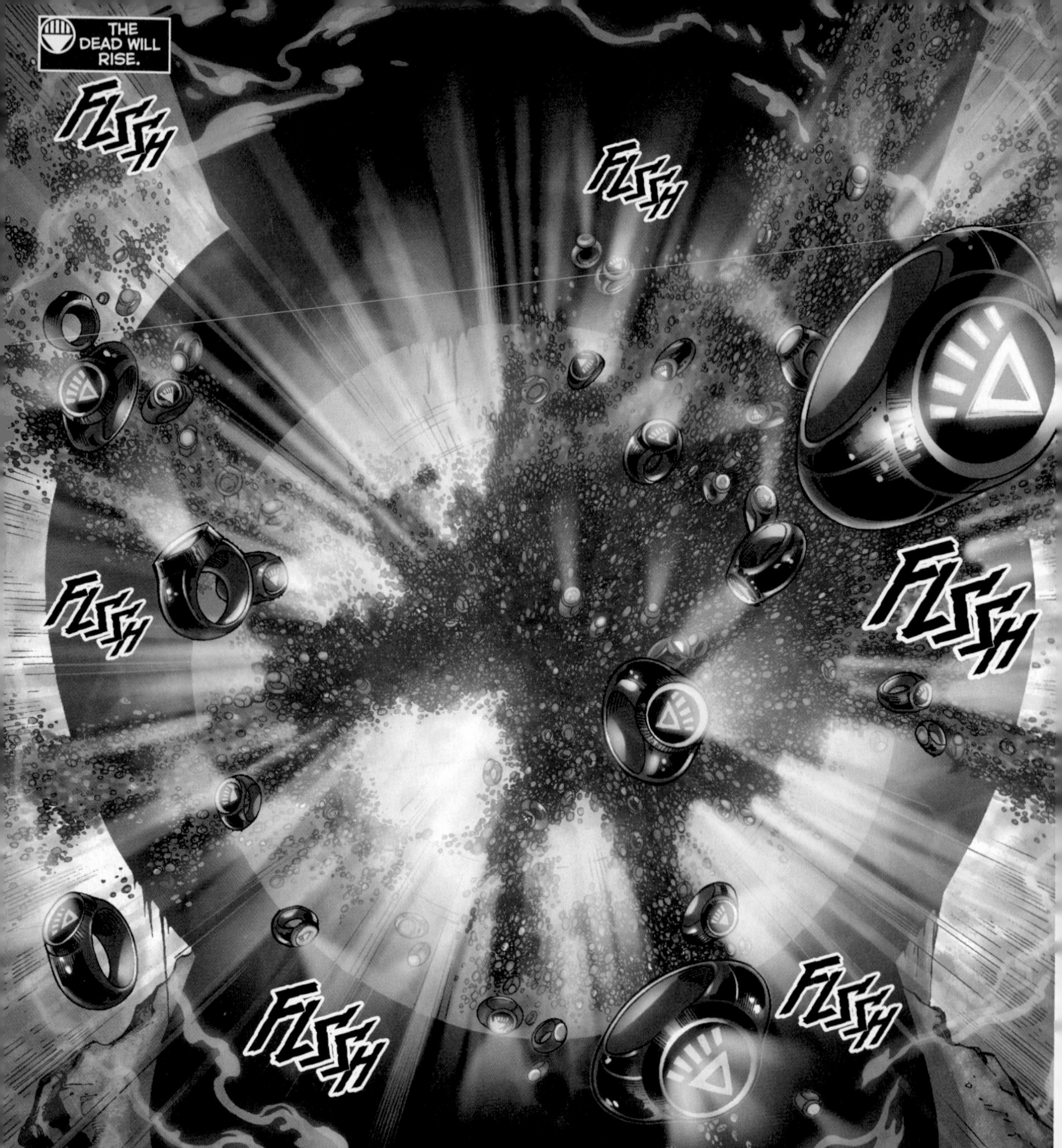
THE DEAD WILL RISE.
FLSSH
FLSSH
FLSSH
FLSSH
FLSSH
FLSSH
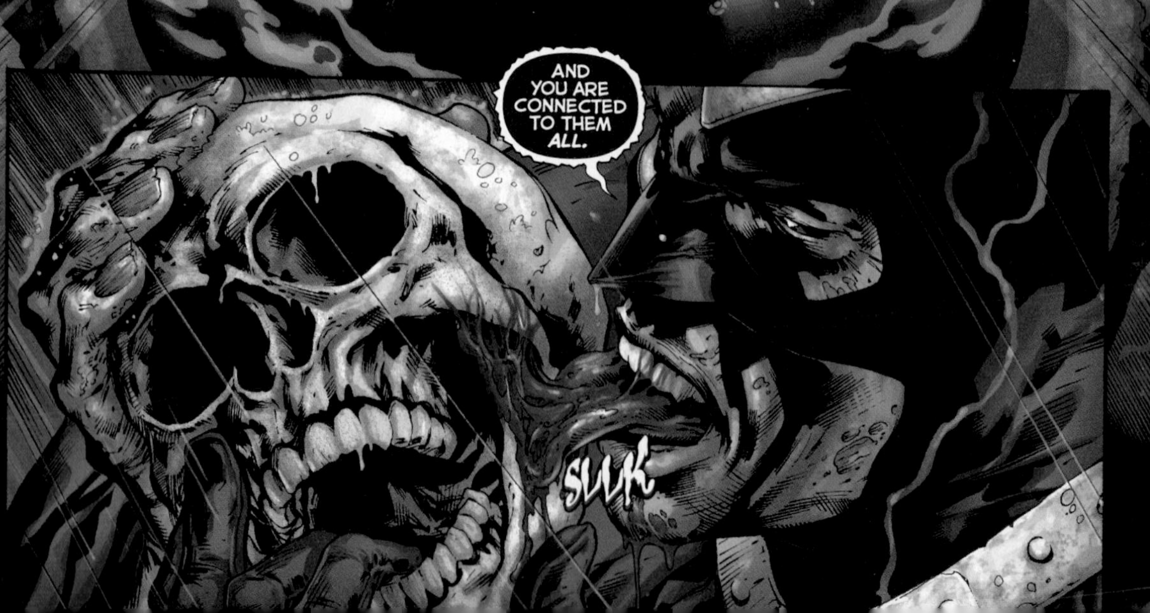
AND YOU ARE CONNECTED TO THEM *ALL.*
SLUK

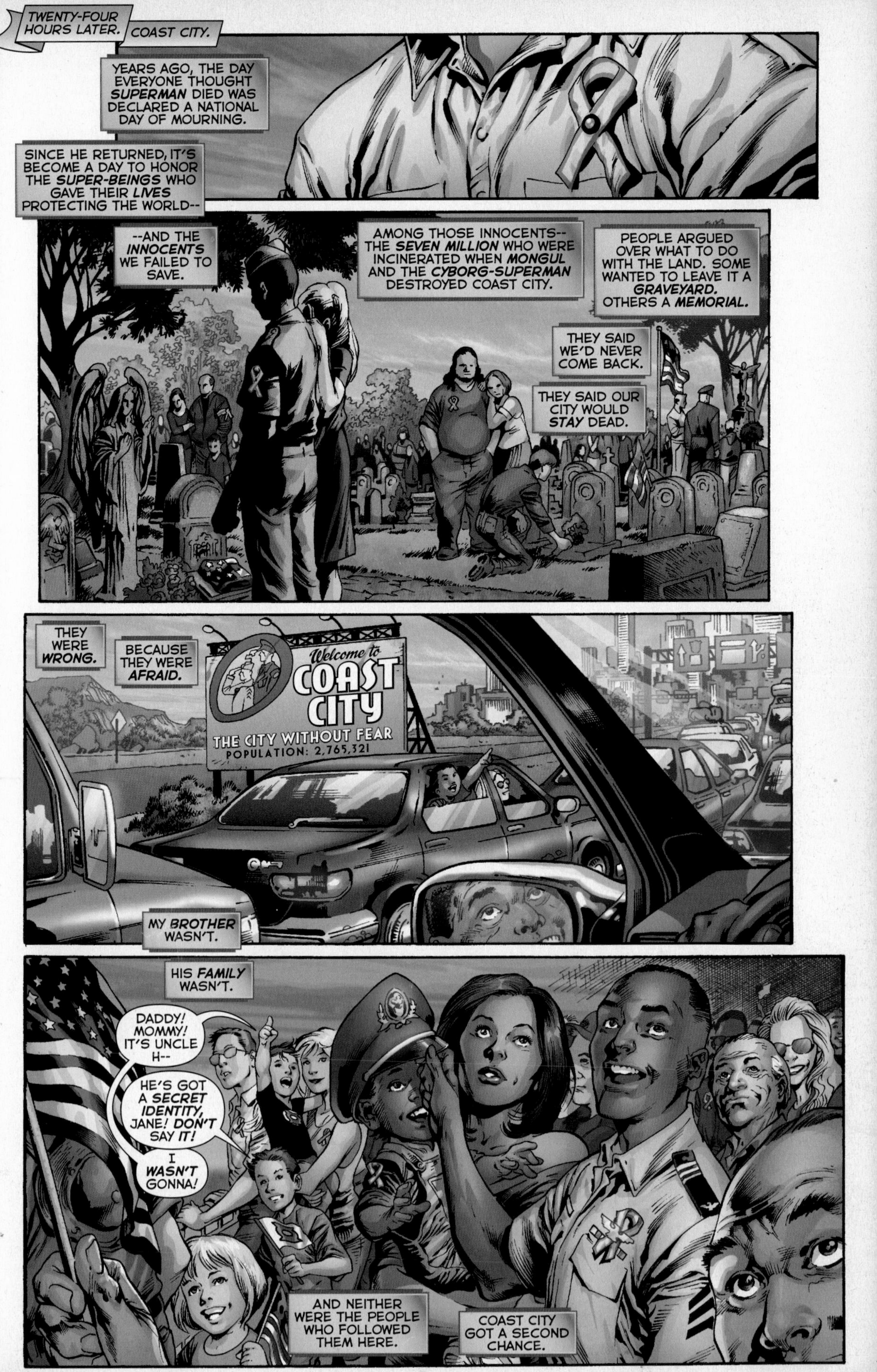
TWENTY-FOUR HOURS LATER.
COAST CITY.
YEARS AGO, THE DAY EVERYONE THOUGHT SUPERMAN DIED WAS DECLARED A NATIONAL DAY OF MOURNING.
SINCE HE RETURNED, IT'S BECOME A DAY TO HONOR THE SUPER-BEINGS WHO GAVE THEIR LIVES PROTECTING THE WORLD--
--AND THE INNOCENTS WE FAILED TO SAVE.
AMONG THOSE INNOCENTS-- THE SEVEN MILLION WHO WERE INCINERATED WHEN MONGUL AND THE CYBORG-SUPERMAN DESTROYED COAST CITY.
PEOPLE ARGUED OVER WHAT TO DO WITH THE LAND. SOME WANTED TO LEAVE IT A GRAVEYARD. OTHERS A MEMORIAL.
THEY SAID WE'D NEVER COME BACK.
THEY SAID OUR CITY WOULD STAY DEAD.
THEY WERE WRONG.
BECAUSE THEY WERE AFRAID.
Welcome to COAST CITY
THE CITY WITHOUT FEAR
POPULATION: 2,765,321
MY BROTHER WASN'T.
HIS FAMILY WASN'T.
DADDY! MOMMY! IT'S UNCLE H--
HE'S GOT A SECRET IDENTITY, JANE! DON'T SAY IT!
I WASN'T GONNA!
AND NEITHER WERE THE PEOPLE WHO FOLLOWED THEM HERE.
COAST CITY GOT A SECOND CHANCE.

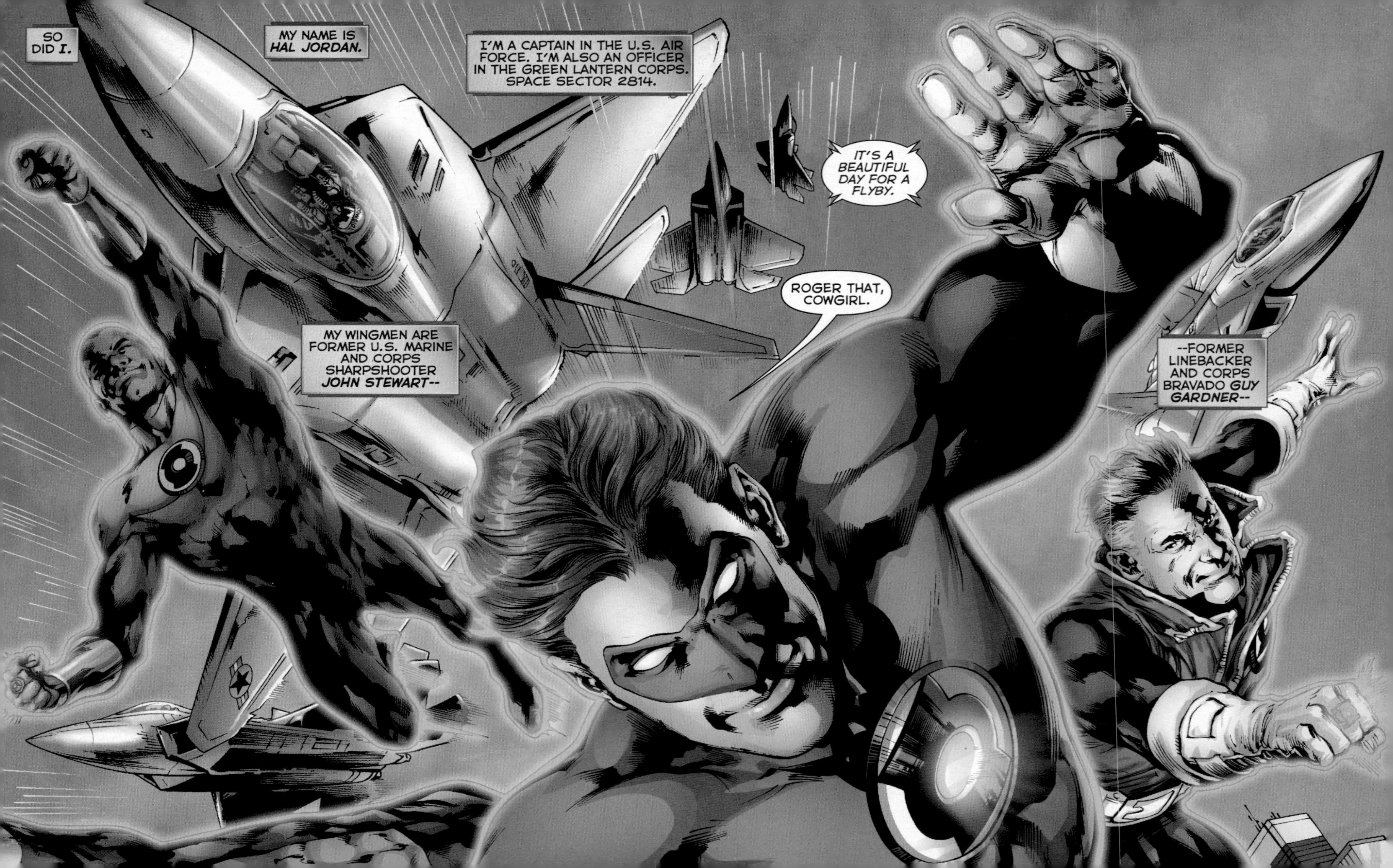
SO DID *I*.
MY NAME IS *HAL JORDAN.*
I'M A CAPTAIN IN THE U.S. AIR FORCE. I'M ALSO AN OFFICER IN THE GREEN LANTERN CORPS. SPACE SECTOR 2814.
IT'S A BEAUTIFUL DAY FOR A FLYBY.
ROGER THAT, COWGIRL.
MY WINGMEN ARE FORMER U.S. MARINE AND CORPS SHARPSHOOTER *JOHN STEWART*--
--FORMER LINEBACKER AND CORPS BRAVADO *GUY GARDNER*--

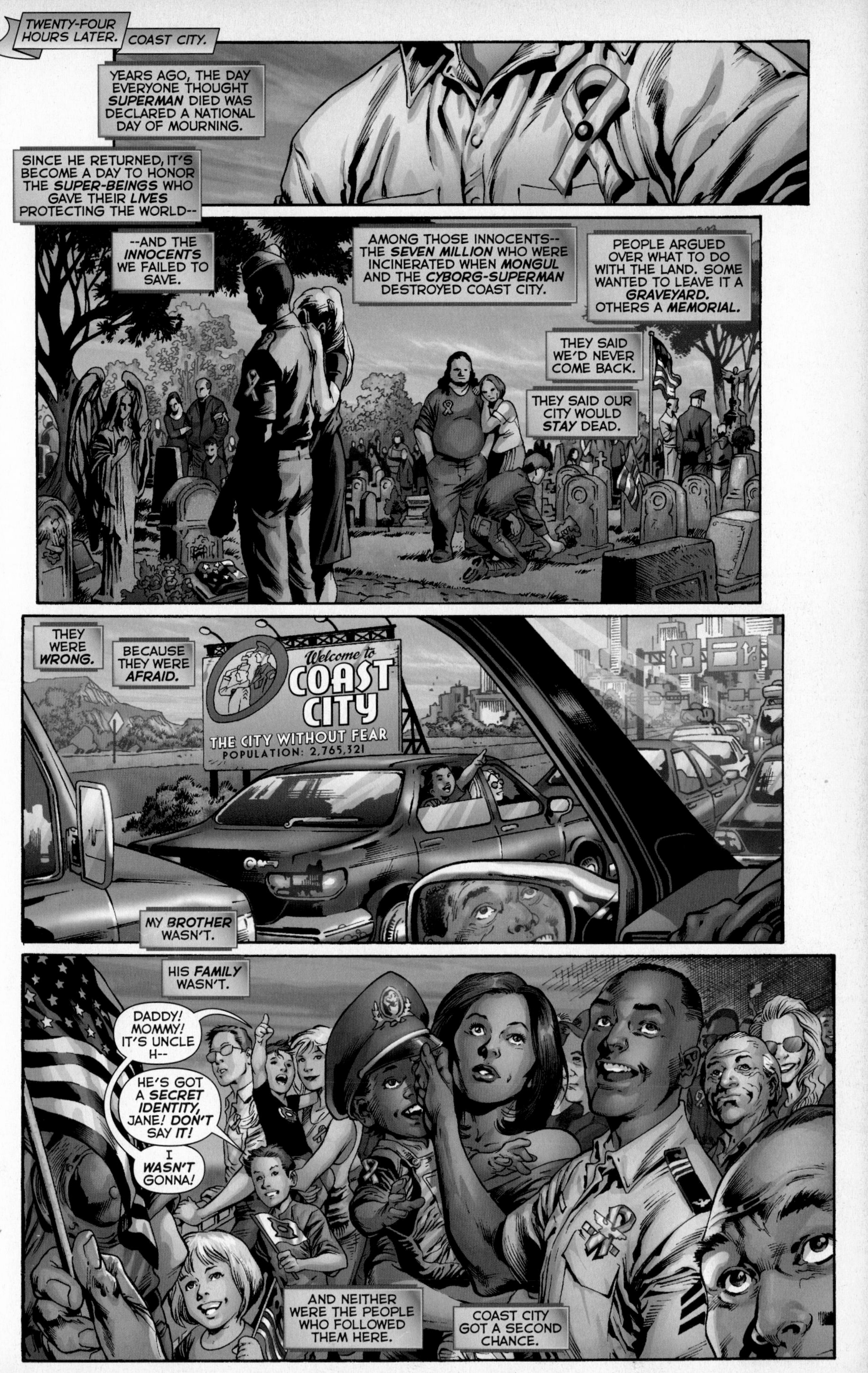
TWENTY-FOUR HOURS LATER.
COAST CITY.
YEARS AGO, THE DAY EVERYONE THOUGHT SUPERMAN DIED WAS DECLARED A NATIONAL DAY OF MOURNING.
SINCE HE RETURNED, IT'S BECOME A DAY TO HONOR THE SUPER-BEINGS WHO GAVE THEIR LIVES PROTECTING THE WORLD--
--AND THE INNOCENTS WE FAILED TO SAVE.
AMONG THOSE INNOCENTS--THE SEVEN MILLION WHO WERE INCINERATED WHEN MONGUL AND THE CYBORG-SUPERMAN DESTROYED COAST CITY.
PEOPLE ARGUED OVER WHAT TO DO WITH THE LAND. SOME WANTED TO LEAVE IT A GRAVEYARD. OTHERS A MEMORIAL.
THEY SAID WE'D NEVER COME BACK.
THEY SAID OUR CITY WOULD STAY DEAD.
THEY WERE WRONG.
BECAUSE THEY WERE AFRAID.
Welcome to COAST CITY
THE CITY WITHOUT FEAR
POPULATION: 2,765,321
MY BROTHER WASN'T.
HIS FAMILY WASN'T.
DADDY! MOMMY! IT'S UNCLE H--
HE'S GOT A SECRET IDENTITY, JANE! DON'T SAY IT!
I WASN'T GONNA!
AND NEITHER WERE THE PEOPLE WHO FOLLOWED THEM HERE.
COAST CITY GOT A SECOND CHANCE.

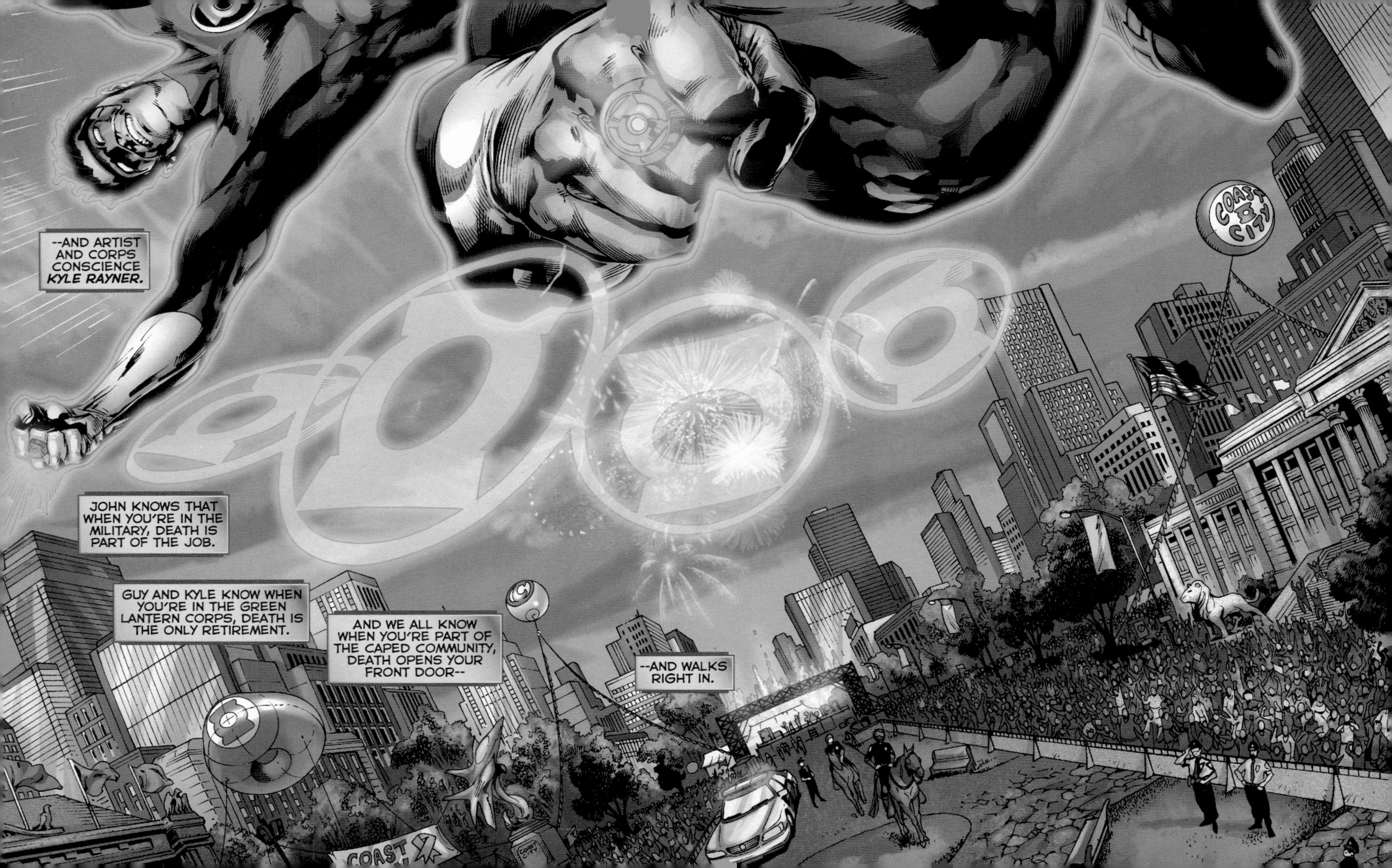
--AND ARTIST AND CORPS CONSCIENCE *KYLE RAYNER.*
JOHN KNOWS THAT WHEN YOU'RE IN THE MILITARY, DEATH IS PART OF THE JOB.
GUY AND KYLE KNOW WHEN YOU'RE IN THE GREEN LANTERN CORPS, DEATH IS THE ONLY RETIREMENT.
AND WE ALL KNOW WHEN YOU'RE PART OF THE CAPED COMMUNITY, DEATH OPENS YOUR FRONT DOOR--
--AND WALKS RIGHT IN.
COAST CITY
COAST

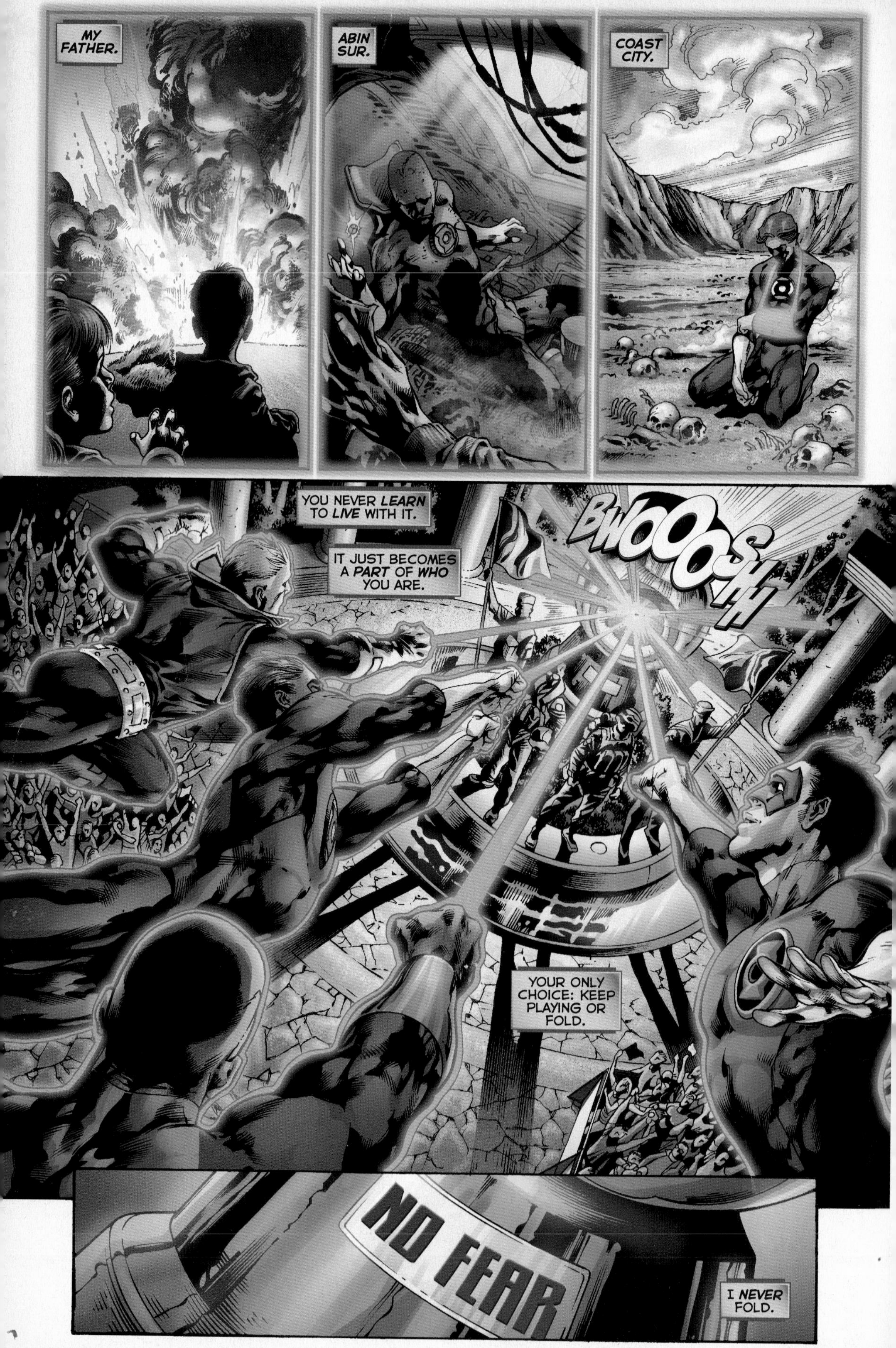
MY FATHER.
ABIN SUR.
COAST CITY.
YOU NEVER LEARN TO LIVE WITH IT.
IT JUST BECOMES A PART OF WHO YOU ARE.
BWOOOSHH
YOUR ONLY CHOICE: KEEP PLAYING OR FOLD.
NO FEAR
I NEVER FOLD.

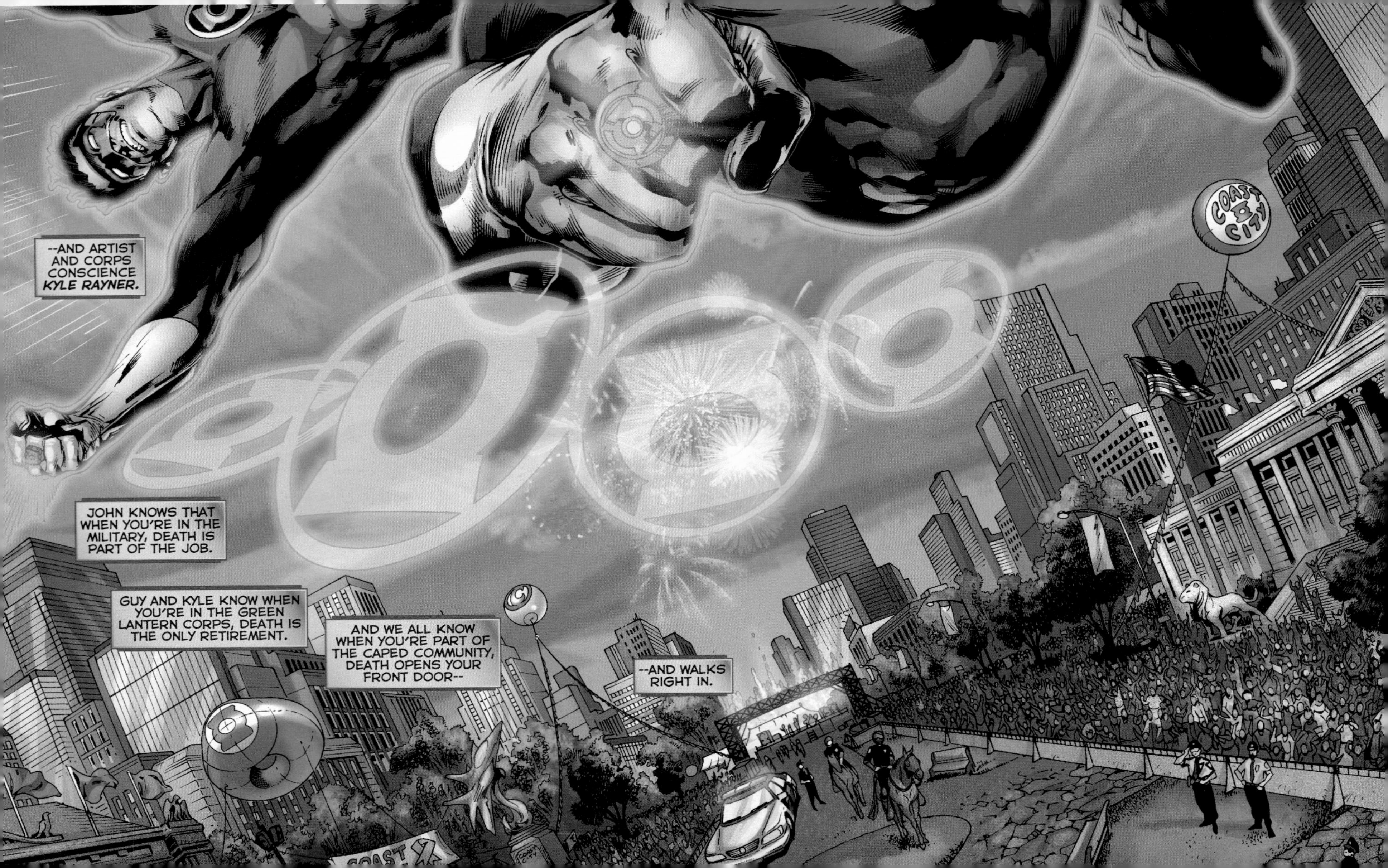
--AND ARTIST AND CORPS CONSCIENCE *KYLE RAYNER.*
JOHN KNOWS THAT WHEN YOU'RE IN THE MILITARY, DEATH IS PART OF THE JOB.
GUY AND KYLE KNOW WHEN YOU'RE IN THE GREEN LANTERN CORPS, DEATH IS THE ONLY RETIREMENT.
AND WE ALL KNOW WHEN YOU'RE PART OF THE CAPED COMMUNITY, DEATH OPENS YOUR FRONT DOOR--
--AND WALKS RIGHT IN.
COAST CITY

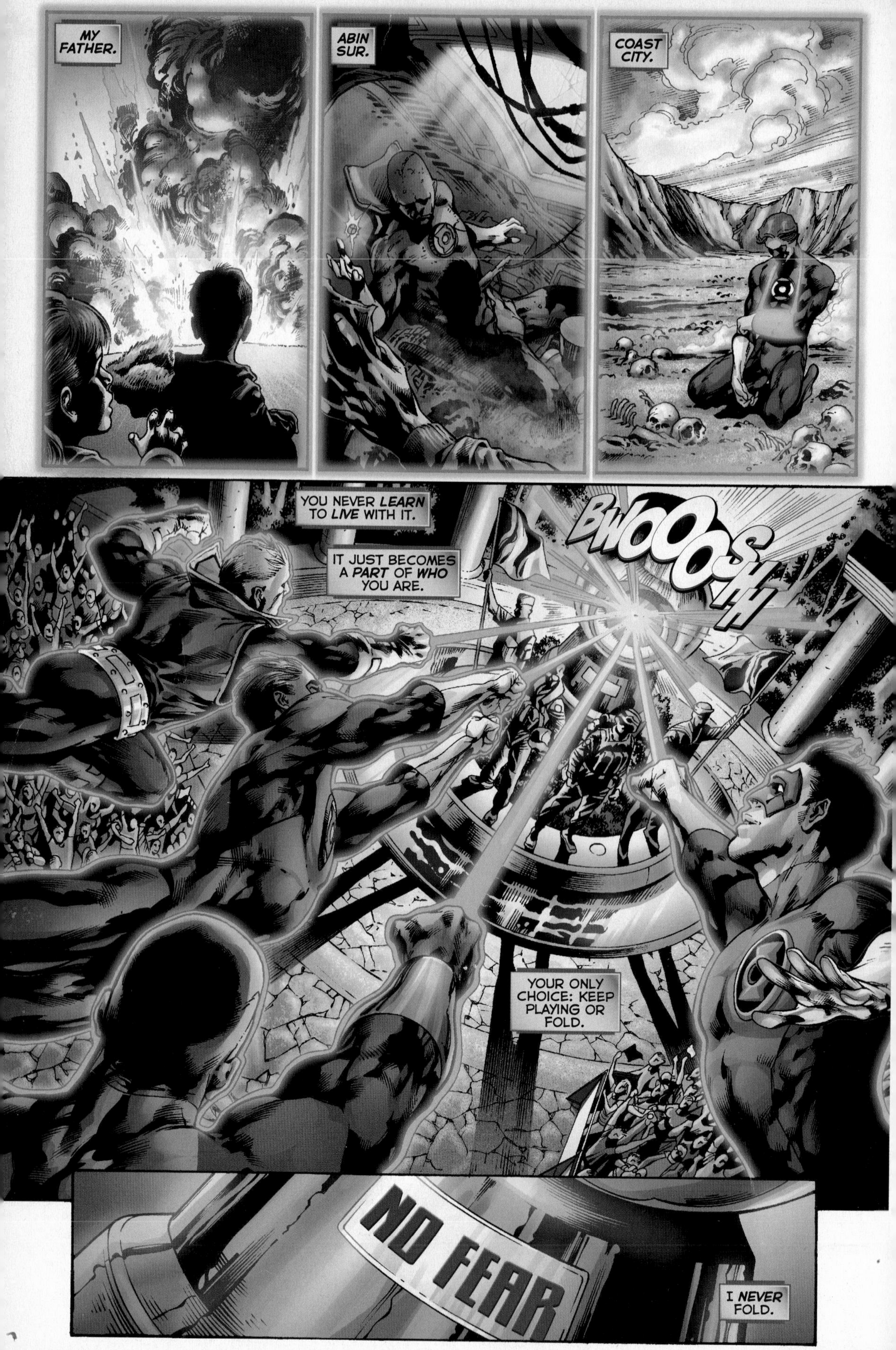
MY FATHER.
ABIN SUR.
COAST CITY.
YOU NEVER LEARN TO LIVE WITH IT.
IT JUST BECOMES A PART OF WHO YOU ARE.
BWOOOSHH
YOUR ONLY CHOICE: KEEP PLAYING OR FOLD.
NO FEAR
I NEVER FOLD.

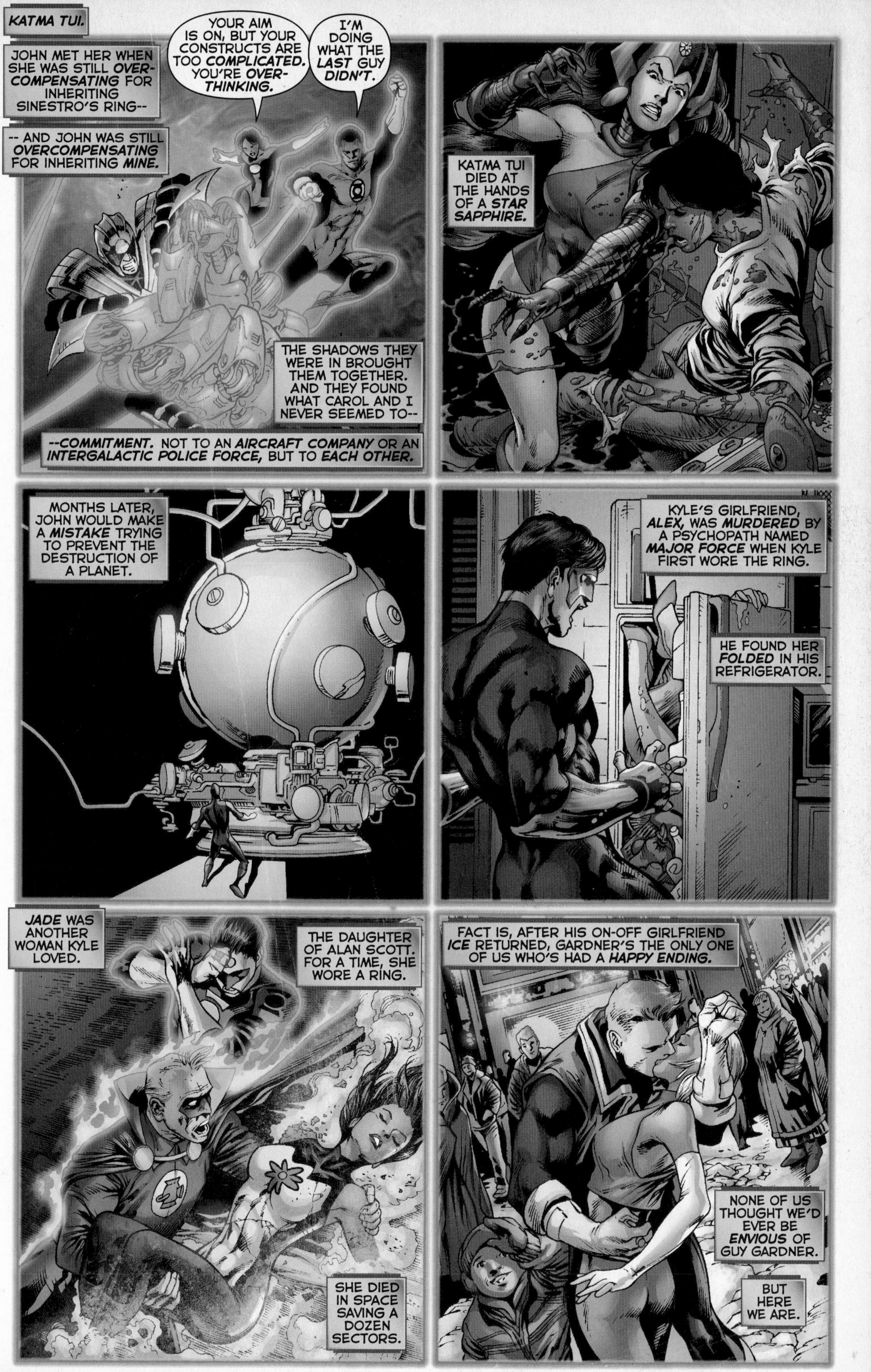
KATMA TUI.
JOHN MET HER WHEN SHE WAS STILL OVER-COMPENSATING FOR INHERITING SINESTRO'S RING--
-- AND JOHN WAS STILL OVERCOMPENSATING FOR INHERITING MINE.
YOUR AIM IS ON, BUT YOUR CONSTRUCTS ARE TOO COMPLICATED. YOU'RE OVER-THINKING.
I'M DOING WHAT THE LAST GUY DIDN'T.
THE SHADOWS THEY WERE IN BROUGHT THEM TOGETHER. AND THEY FOUND WHAT CAROL AND I NEVER SEEMED TO--
--COMMITMENT. NOT TO AN AIRCRAFT COMPANY OR AN INTERGALACTIC POLICE FORCE, BUT TO EACH OTHER.
KATMA TUI DIED AT THE HANDS OF A STAR SAPPHIRE.
MONTHS LATER, JOHN WOULD MAKE A MISTAKE TRYING TO PREVENT THE DESTRUCTION OF A PLANET.
KYLE'S GIRLFRIEND, ALEX, WAS MURDERED BY A PSYCHOPATH NAMED MAJOR FORCE WHEN KYLE FIRST WORE THE RING.
HE FOUND HER FOLDED IN HIS REFRIGERATOR.
JADE WAS ANOTHER WOMAN KYLE LOVED.
THE DAUGHTER OF ALAN SCOTT. FOR A TIME, SHE WORE A RING.
SHE DIED IN SPACE SAVING A DOZEN SECTORS.
FACT IS, AFTER HIS ON-OFF GIRLFRIEND ICE RETURNED, GARDNER'S THE ONLY ONE OF US WHO'S HAD A HAPPY ENDING.
NONE OF US THOUGHT WE'D EVER BE ENVIOUS OF GUY GARDNER.
BUT HERE WE ARE.

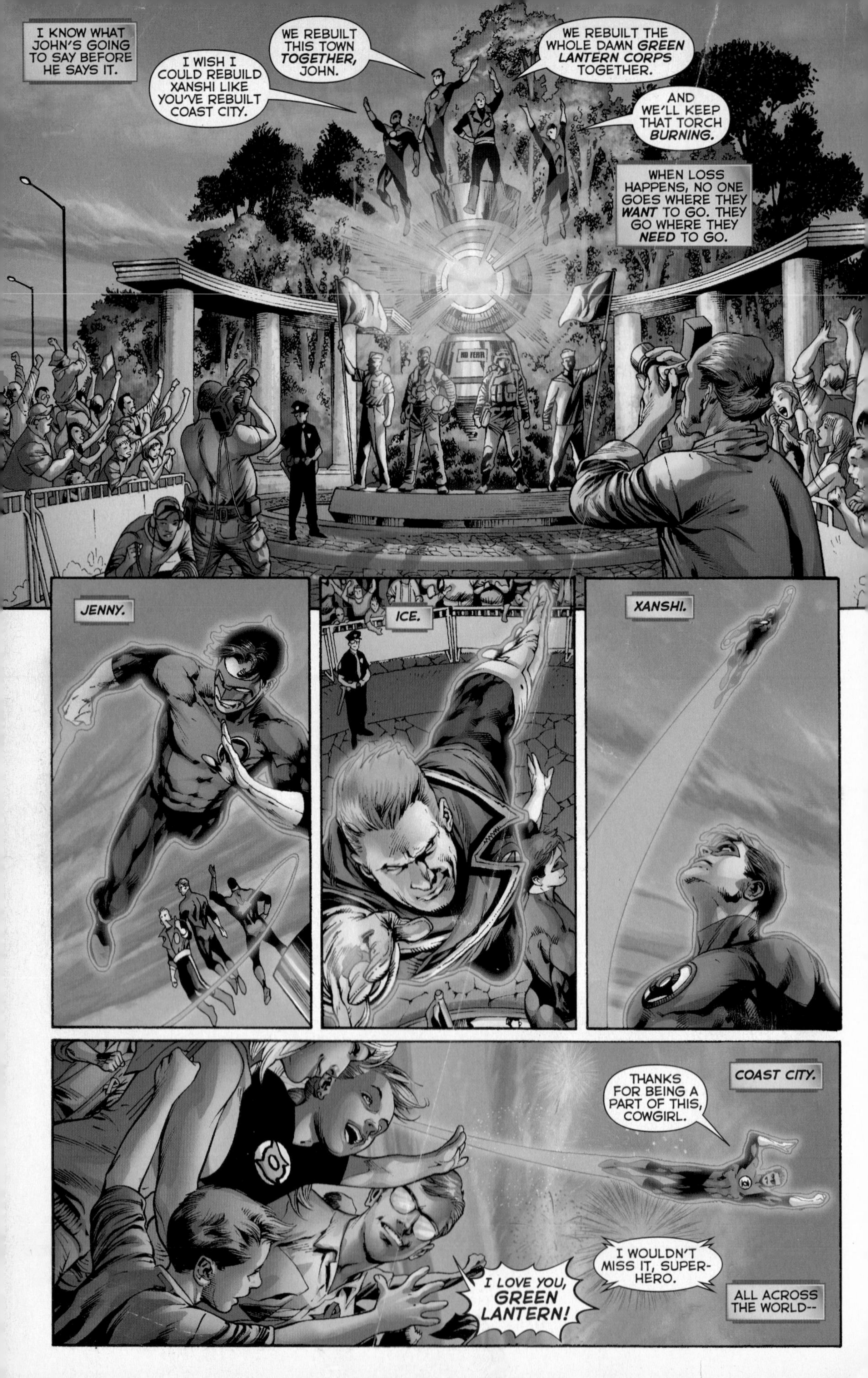
I KNOW WHAT JOHN'S GOING TO SAY BEFORE HE SAYS IT.
I WISH I COULD REBUILD XANSHI LIKE YOU'VE REBUILT COAST CITY.
WE REBUILT THIS TOWN TOGETHER, JOHN.
WE REBUILT THE WHOLE DAMN GREEN LANTERN CORPS TOGETHER.
AND WE'LL KEEP THAT TORCH BURNING.
WHEN LOSS HAPPENS, NO ONE GOES WHERE THEY WANT TO GO. THEY GO WHERE THEY NEED TO GO.
NO FEAR
JENNY.
ICE.
XANSHI.
COAST CITY.
THANKS FOR BEING A PART OF THIS, COWGIRL.
I LOVE YOU, GREEN LANTERN!
I WOULDN'T MISS IT, SUPER-HERO.
ALL ACROSS THE WORLD--

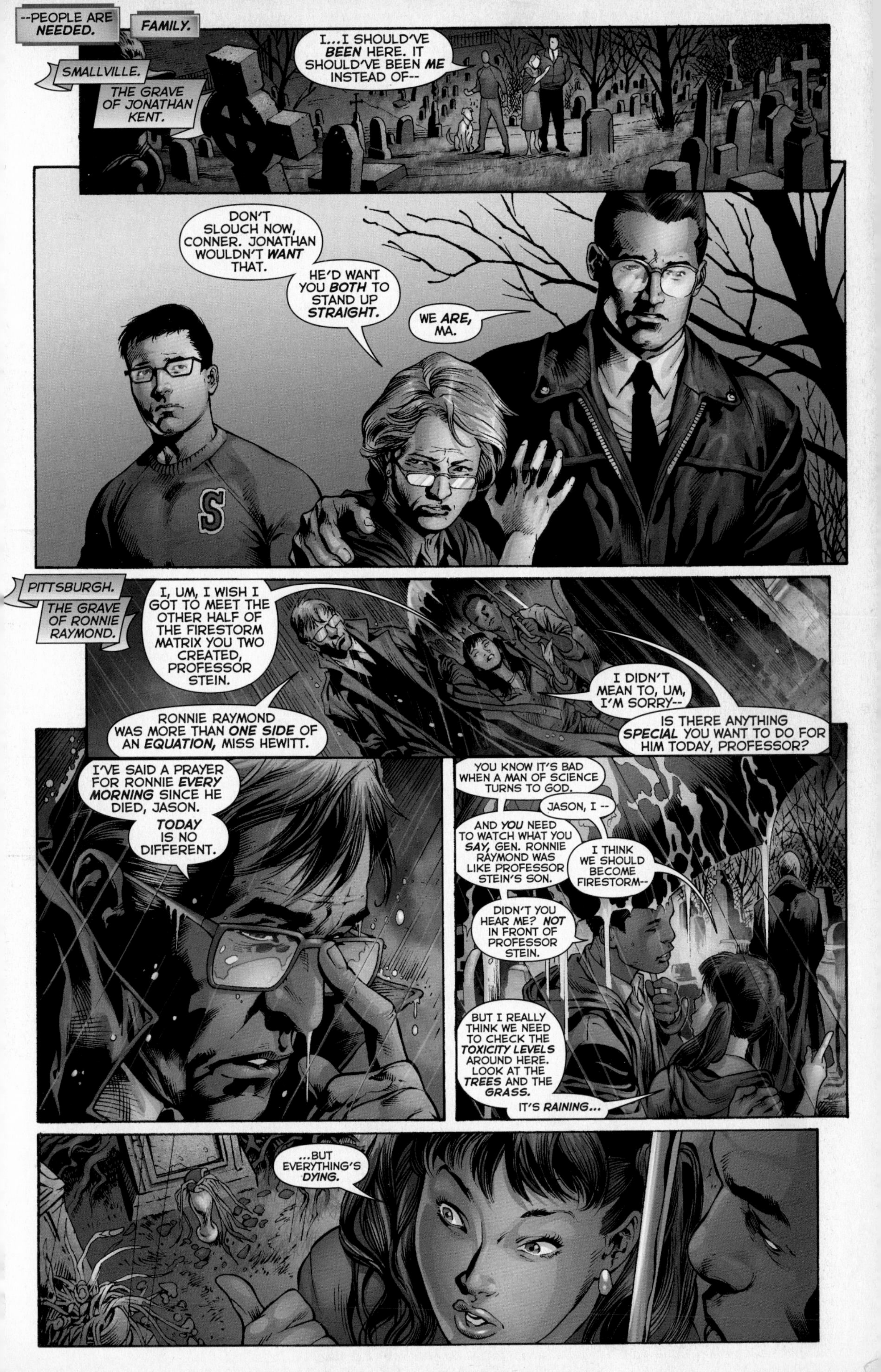
--PEOPLE ARE NEEDED.
FAMILY.
SMALLVILLE.
THE GRAVE OF JONATHAN KENT.
I...I SHOULD'VE BEEN HERE. IT SHOULD'VE BEEN ME INSTEAD OF--
DON'T SLOUCH NOW, CONNER. JONATHAN WOULDN'T WANT THAT.
HE'D WANT YOU BOTH TO STAND UP STRAIGHT.
WE ARE, MA.
PITTSBURGH.
THE GRAVE OF RONNIE RAYMOND.
I, UM, I WISH I GOT TO MEET THE OTHER HALF OF THE FIRESTORM MATRIX YOU TWO CREATED, PROFESSOR STEIN.
RONNIE RAYMOND WAS MORE THAN ONE SIDE OF AN EQUATION, MISS HEWITT.
I DIDN'T MEAN TO, UM, I'M SORRY--
IS THERE ANYTHING SPECIAL YOU WANT TO DO FOR HIM TODAY, PROFESSOR?
I'VE SAID A PRAYER FOR RONNIE EVERY MORNING SINCE HE DIED, JASON.
TODAY IS NO DIFFERENT.
YOU KNOW IT'S BAD WHEN A MAN OF SCIENCE TURNS TO GOD.
JASON, I --
AND YOU NEED TO WATCH WHAT YOU SAY, GEN. RONNIE RAYMOND WAS LIKE PROFESSOR STEIN'S SON.
I THINK WE SHOULD BECOME FIRESTORM--
DIDN'T YOU HEAR ME? NOT IN FRONT OF PROFESSOR STEIN.
BUT I REALLY THINK WE NEED TO CHECK THE TOXICITY LEVELS AROUND HERE. LOOK AT THE TREES AND THE GRASS.
IT'S RAINING...
...BUT EVERYTHING'S DYING.

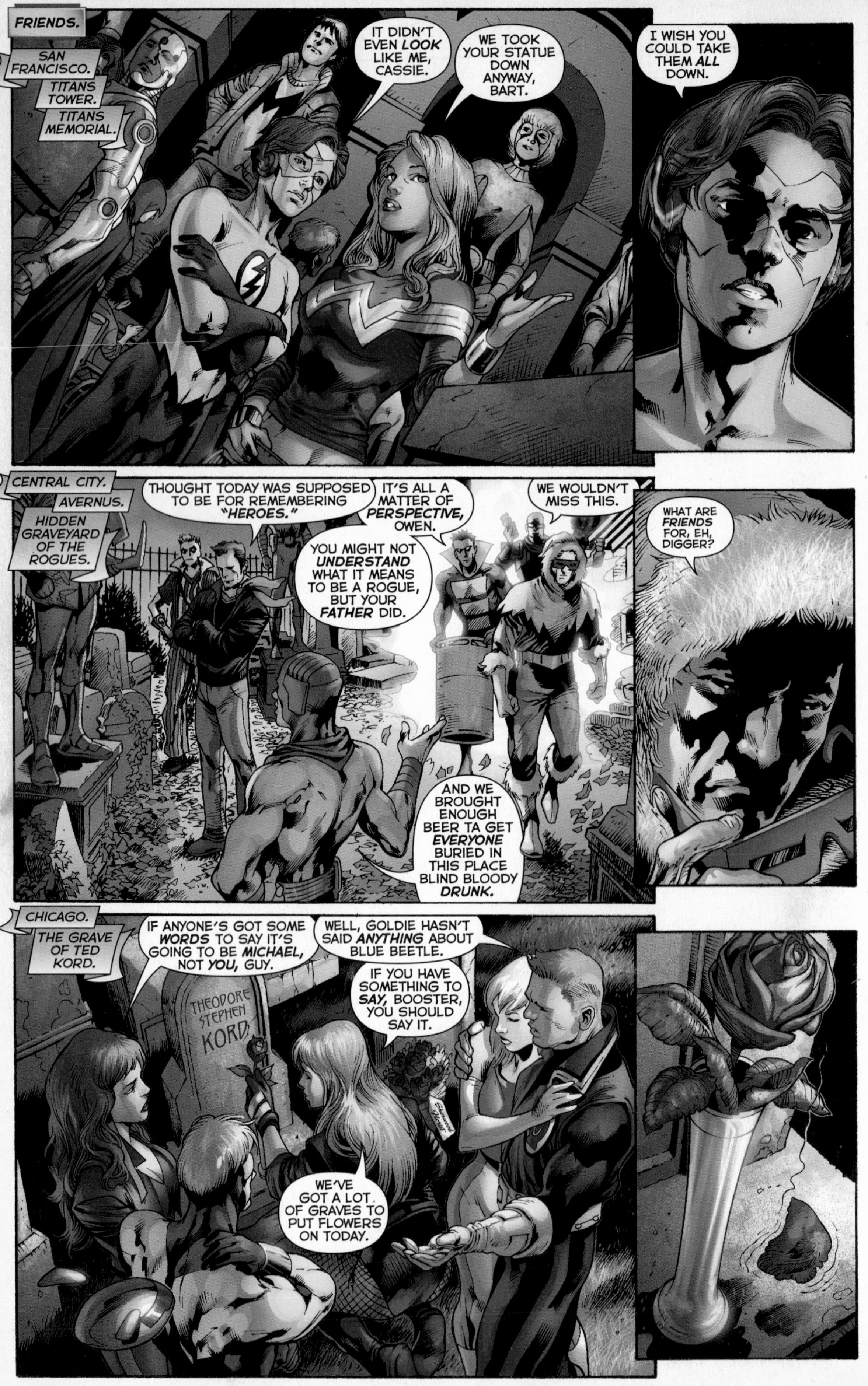
FRIENDS.
SAN FRANCISCO.
TITANS TOWER.
TITANS MEMORIAL.
IT DIDN'T EVEN LOOK LIKE ME, CASSIE.
WE TOOK YOUR STATUE DOWN ANYWAY, BART.
I WISH YOU COULD TAKE THEM ALL DOWN.
CENTRAL CITY.
AVERNUS.
HIDDEN GRAVEYARD OF THE ROGUES.
THOUGHT TODAY WAS SUPPOSED TO BE FOR REMEMBERING "HEROES."
IT'S ALL A MATTER OF PERSPECTIVE, OWEN.
YOU MIGHT NOT UNDERSTAND WHAT IT MEANS TO BE A ROGUE, BUT YOUR FATHER DID.
WE WOULDN'T MISS THIS.
AND WE BROUGHT ENOUGH BEER TA GET EVERYONE BURIED IN THIS PLACE BLIND BLOODY DRUNK.
WHAT ARE FRIENDS FOR, EH, DIGGER?
CHICAGO.
THE GRAVE OF TED KORD.
IF ANYONE'S GOT SOME WORDS TO SAY IT'S GOING TO BE MICHAEL, NOT YOU, GUY.
WELL, GOLDIE HASN'T SAID ANYTHING ABOUT BLUE BEETLE.
IF YOU HAVE SOMETHING TO SAY, BOOSTER, YOU SHOULD SAY IT.
THEODORE STEPHEN KORD
WE'VE GOT A LOT OF GRAVES TO PUT FLOWERS ON TODAY.

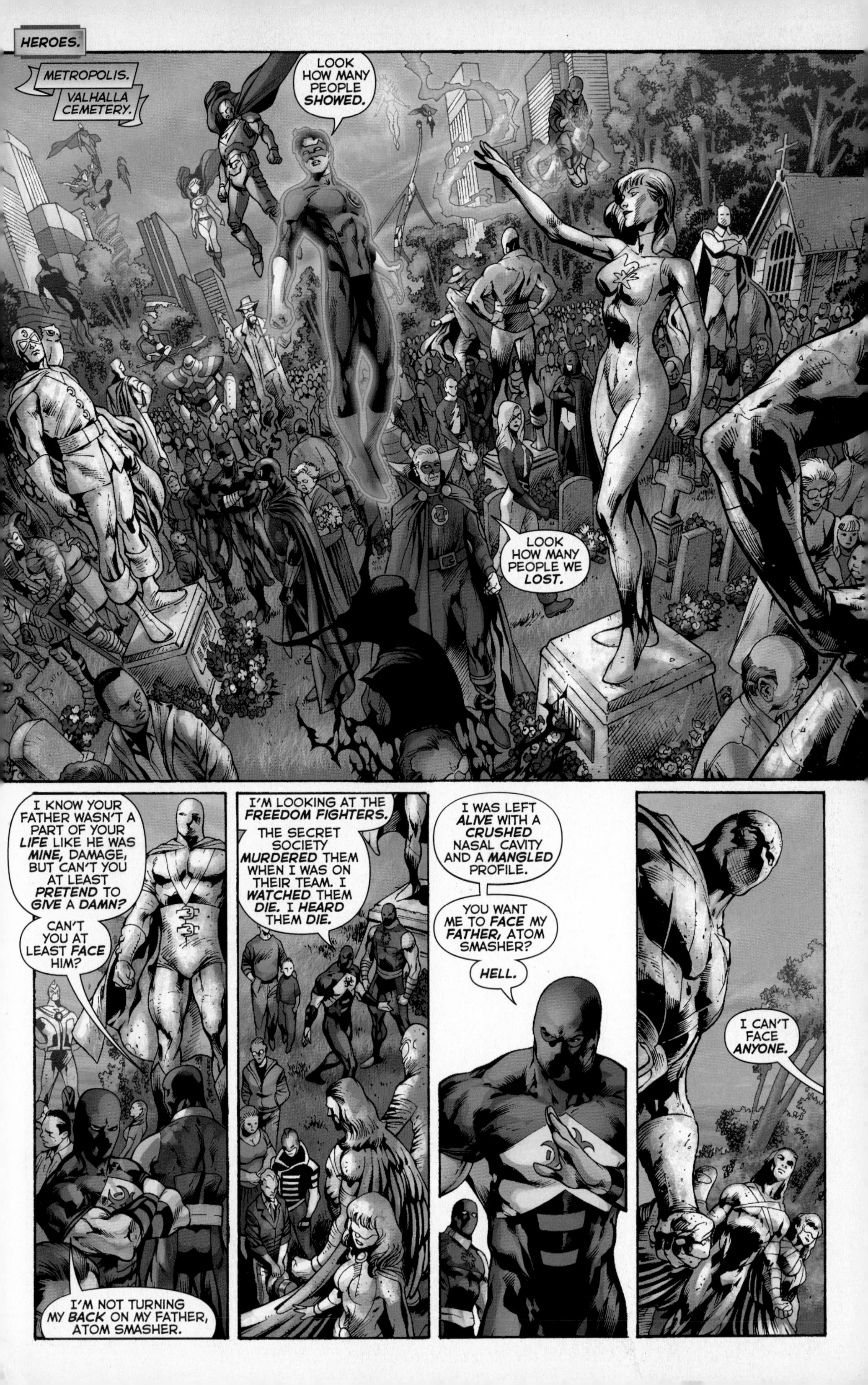
HEROES.
METROPOLIS.
VALHALLA CEMETERY.
LOOK HOW MANY PEOPLE SHOWED.
LOOK HOW MANY PEOPLE WE LOST.
I KNOW YOUR FATHER WASN'T A PART OF YOUR LIFE LIKE HE WAS MINE, DAMAGE, BUT CAN'T YOU AT LEAST PRETEND TO GIVE A DAMN?
CAN'T YOU AT LEAST FACE HIM?
I'M NOT TURNING MY BACK ON MY FATHER, ATOM SMASHER.
I'M LOOKING AT THE FREEDOM FIGHTERS.
THE SECRET SOCIETY MURDERED THEM WHEN I WAS ON THEIR TEAM. I WATCHED THEM DIE. I HEARD THEM DIE.
I WAS LEFT ALIVE WITH A CRUSHED NASAL CAVITY AND A MANGLED PROFILE.
YOU WANT ME TO FACE MY FATHER, ATOM SMASHER?
HELL.
I CAN'T FACE ANYONE.

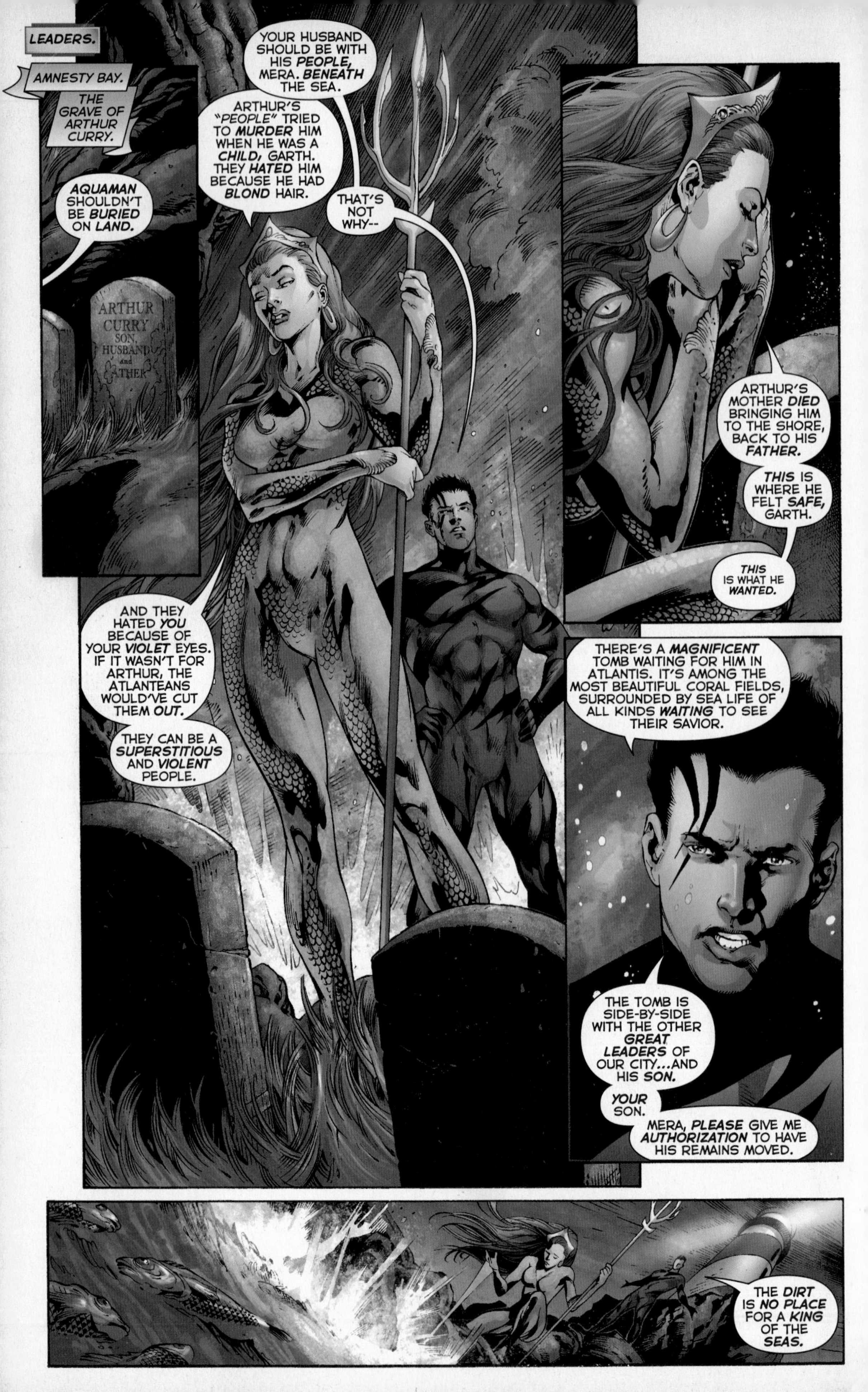
LEADERS.
AMNESTY BAY.
THE GRAVE OF ARTHUR CURRY.
AQUAMAN SHOULDN'T BE BURIED ON LAND.
ARTHUR CURRY SON, HUSBAND and FATHER
YOUR HUSBAND SHOULD BE WITH HIS PEOPLE, MERA. BENEATH THE SEA.
ARTHUR'S "PEOPLE" TRIED TO MURDER HIM WHEN HE WAS A CHILD, GARTH. THEY HATED HIM BECAUSE HE HAD BLOND HAIR.
THAT'S NOT WHY--
AND THEY HATED YOU BECAUSE OF YOUR VIOLET EYES. IF IT WASN'T FOR ARTHUR, THE ATLANTEANS WOULD'VE CUT THEM OUT.
THEY CAN BE A SUPERSTITIOUS AND VIOLENT PEOPLE.
ARTHUR'S MOTHER DIED BRINGING HIM TO THE SHORE, BACK TO HIS FATHER.
THIS IS WHERE HE FELT SAFE, GARTH.
THIS IS WHAT HE WANTED.
THERE'S A MAGNIFICENT TOMB WAITING FOR HIM IN ATLANTIS. IT'S AMONG THE MOST BEAUTIFUL CORAL FIELDS, SURROUNDED BY SEA LIFE OF ALL KINDS WAITING TO SEE THEIR SAVIOR.
THE TOMB IS SIDE-BY-SIDE WITH THE OTHER GREAT LEADERS OF OUR CITY...AND HIS SON.
YOUR SON.
MERA, PLEASE GIVE ME AUTHORIZATION TO HAVE HIS REMAINS MOVED.
THE DIRT IS NO PLACE FOR A KING OF THE SEAS.

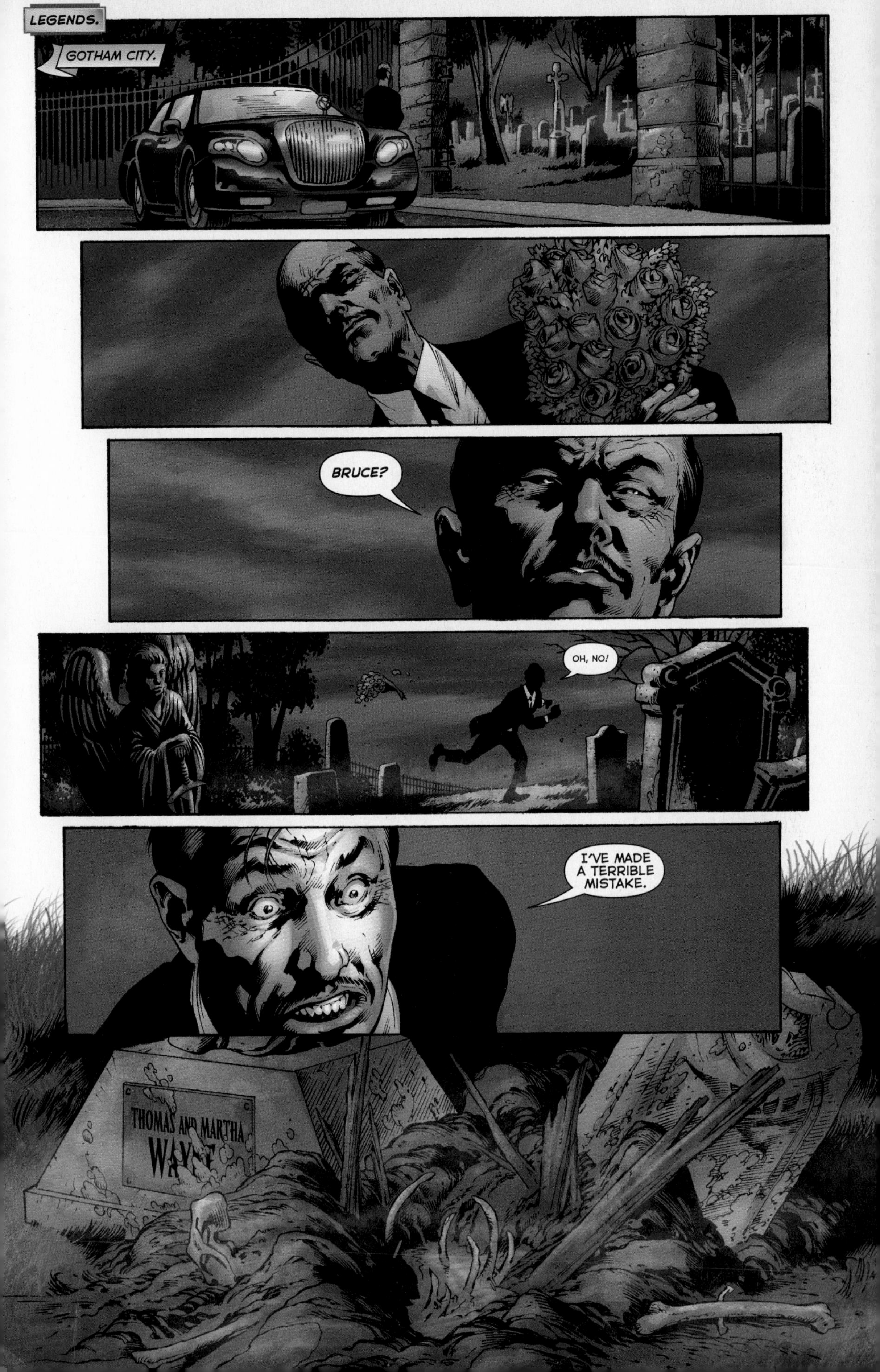
LEGENDS.
GOTHAM CITY.
BRUCE?
OH, NO!
I'VE MADE A TERRIBLE MISTAKE.
THOMAS AND MARTHA

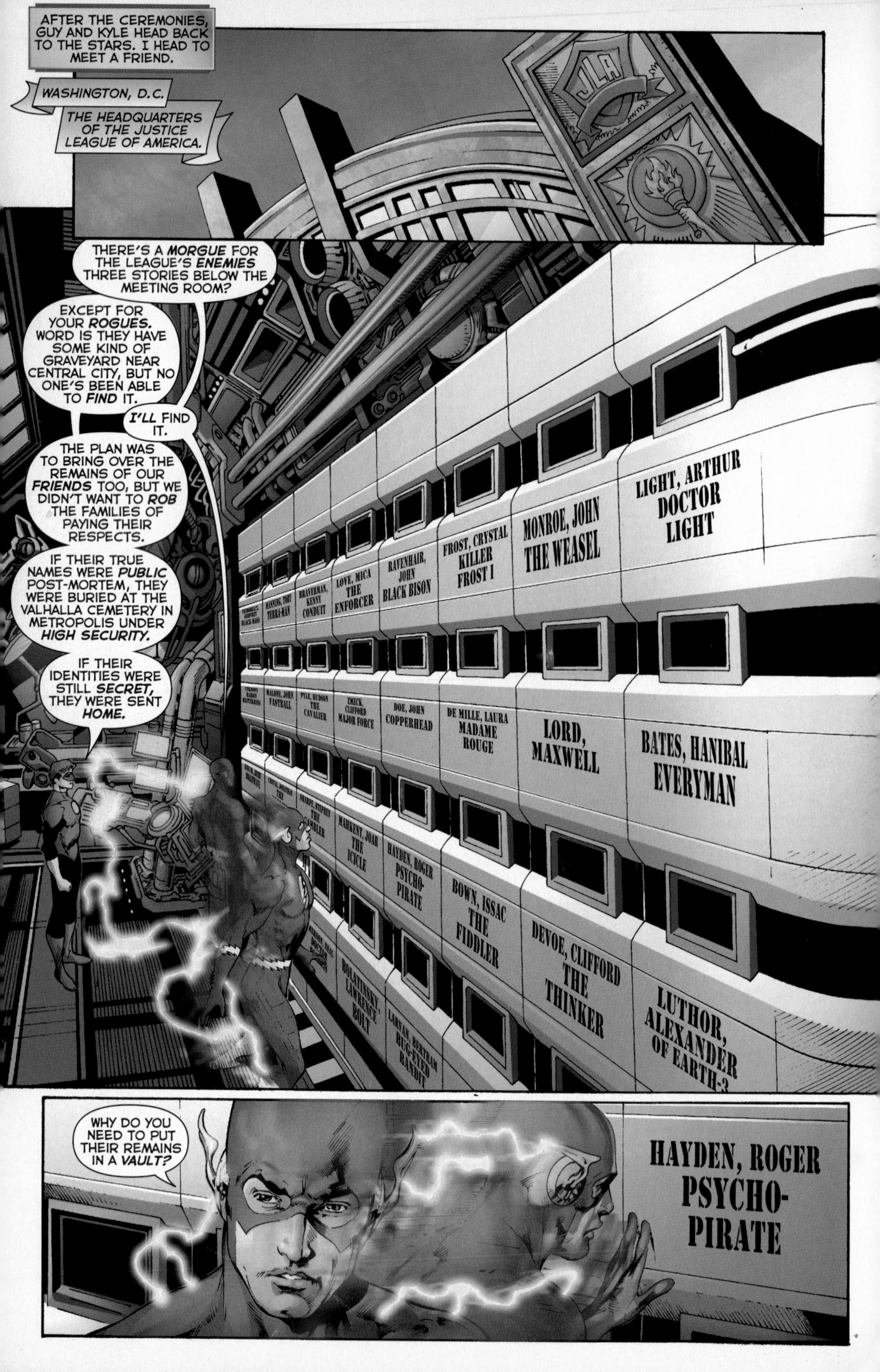
AFTER THE CEREMONIES, GUY AND KYLE HEAD BACK TO THE STARS. I HEAD TO MEET A FRIEND.
WASHINGTON, D.C.
THE HEADQUARTERS OF THE JUSTICE LEAGUE OF AMERICA.
JLA
THERE'S A *MORGUE* FOR THE LEAGUE'S *ENEMIES* THREE STORIES BELOW THE MEETING ROOM?
EXCEPT FOR YOUR *ROGUES.* WORD IS THEY HAVE SOME KIND OF GRAVEYARD NEAR CENTRAL CITY, BUT NO ONE'S BEEN ABLE TO *FIND* IT.
I'LL FIND IT.
THE PLAN WAS TO BRING OVER THE REMAINS OF OUR *FRIENDS* TOO, BUT WE DIDN'T WANT TO *ROB* THE FAMILIES OF PAYING THEIR RESPECTS.
IF THEIR TRUE NAMES WERE *PUBLIC* POST-MORTEM, THEY WERE BURIED AT THE VALHALLA CEMETERY IN METROPOLIS UNDER *HIGH SECURITY.*
IF THEIR IDENTITIES WERE STILL *SECRET,* THEY WERE SENT *HOME.*
MANNING, TOBY TERRA-MAN
BRAVERMAN, KENNY CONDUIT
LOVE, MICA THE ENFORCER
RAVENHAIR, JOHN BLACK BISON
FROST, CRYSTAL KILLER FROST I
MONROE, JOHN THE WEASEL
LIGHT, ARTHUR DOCTOR LIGHT
MALONE, JOHN FASTBALL
PYLE, HUDSON THE CAVALIER
ZMECK, CLIFFORD MAJOR FORCE
DOE, JOHN COPPERHEAD
DE MILLE, LAURA MADAME ROUGE
LORD, MAXWELL
BATES, HANIBAL EVERYMAN
MAHKENT, JOAR THE ICICLE
HAYDEN, ROGER PSYCHO-PIRATE
BOWN, ISSAC THE FIDDLER
DEVOE, CLIFFORD THE THINKER
LUTHOR, ALEXANDER OF EARTH-3
BOLATINSKY, LAWRENCE, BOLT
WHY DO YOU NEED TO PUT THEIR REMAINS IN A *VAULT?*
HAYDEN, ROGER PSYCHO-PIRATE

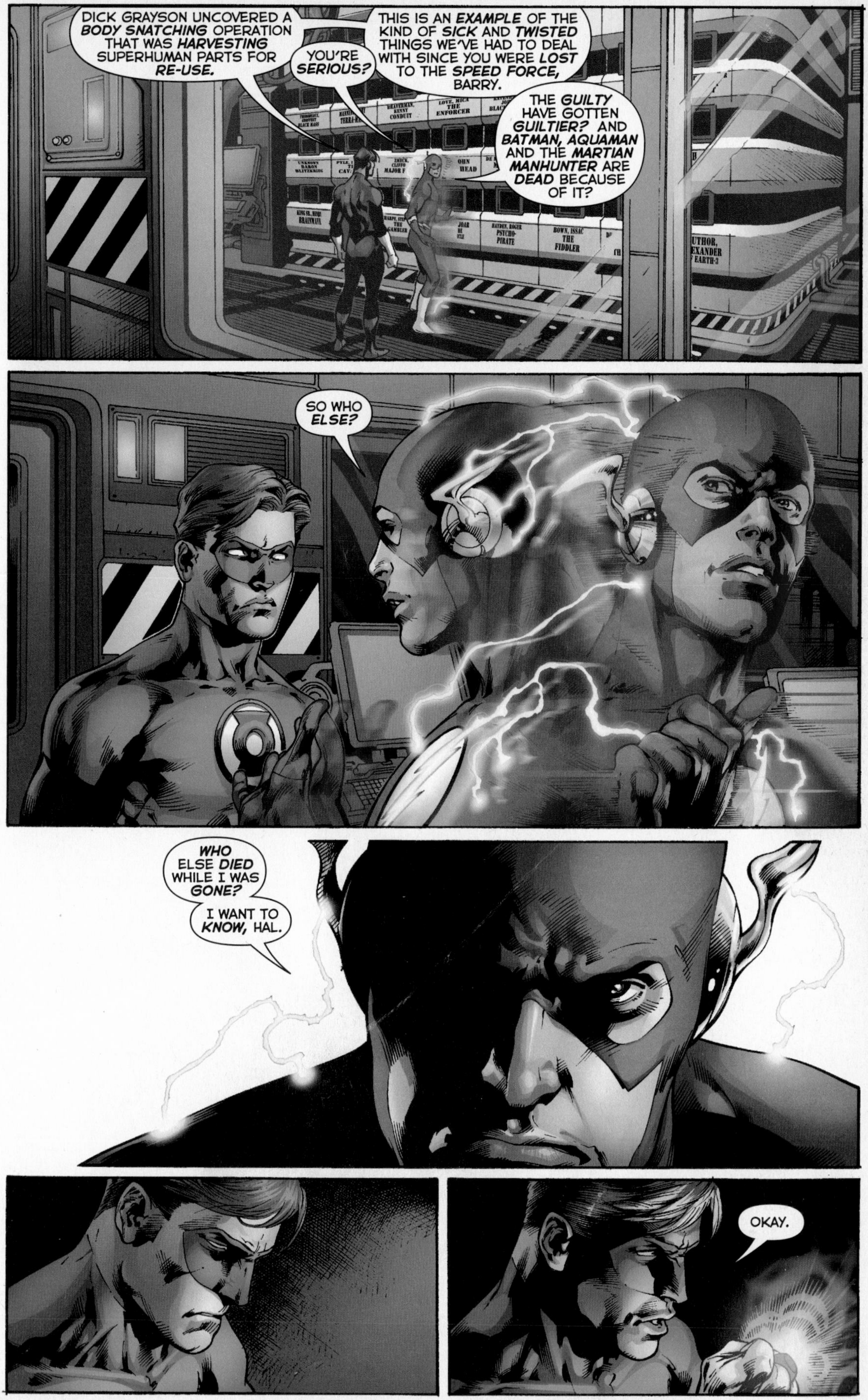
DICK GRAYSON UNCOVERED A BODY SNATCHING OPERATION THAT WAS HARVESTING SUPERHUMAN PARTS FOR RE-USE.
YOU'RE SERIOUS?
THIS IS AN EXAMPLE OF THE KIND OF SICK AND TWISTED THINGS WE'VE HAD TO DEAL WITH SINCE YOU WERE LOST TO THE SPEED FORCE, BARRY.
THE GUILTY HAVE GOTTEN GUILTIER? AND BATMAN, AQUAMAN AND THE MARTIAN MANHUNTER ARE DEAD BECAUSE OF IT?
SO WHO ELSE?
WHO ELSE DIED WHILE I WAS GONE?
I WANT TO KNOW, HAL.
OKAY.

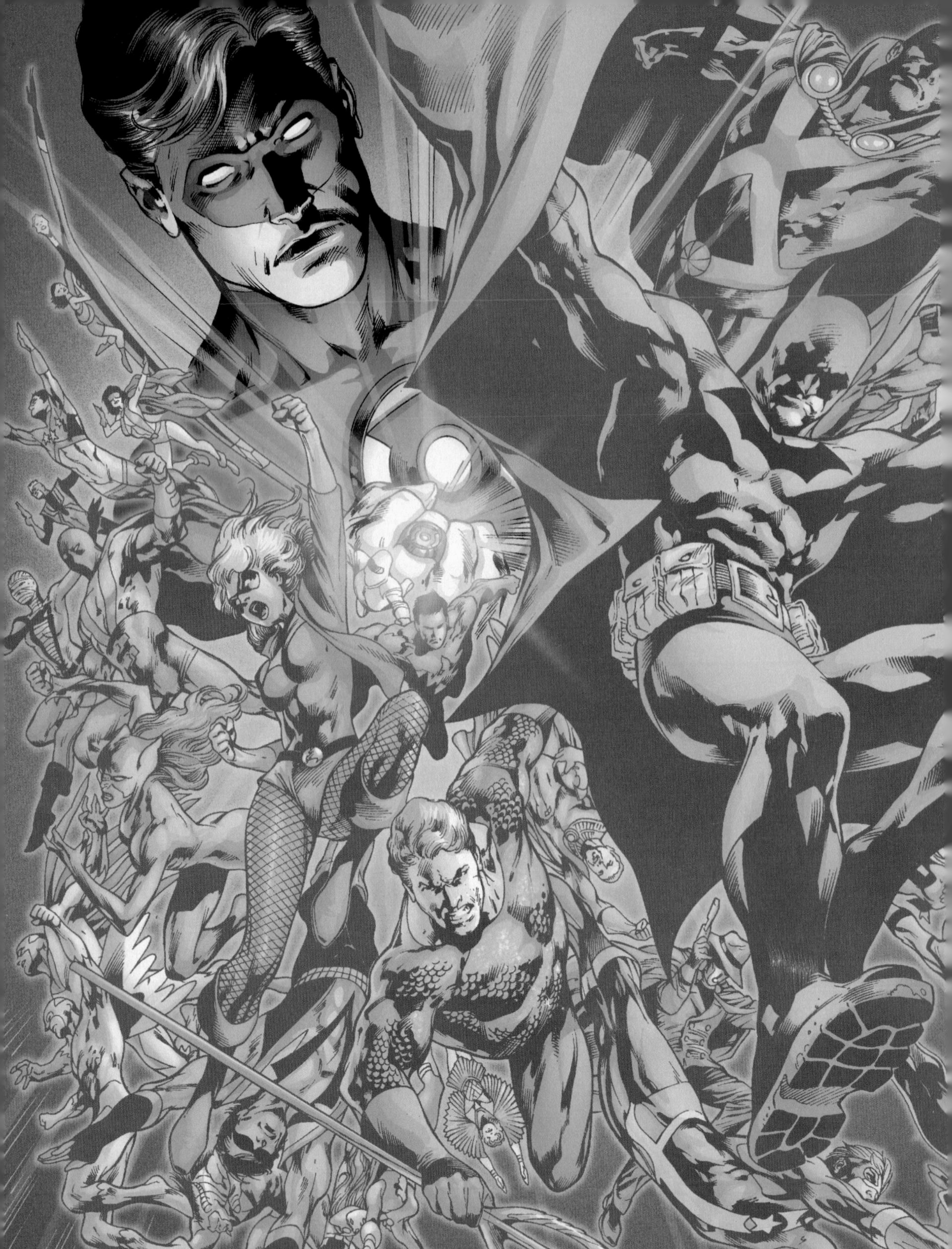

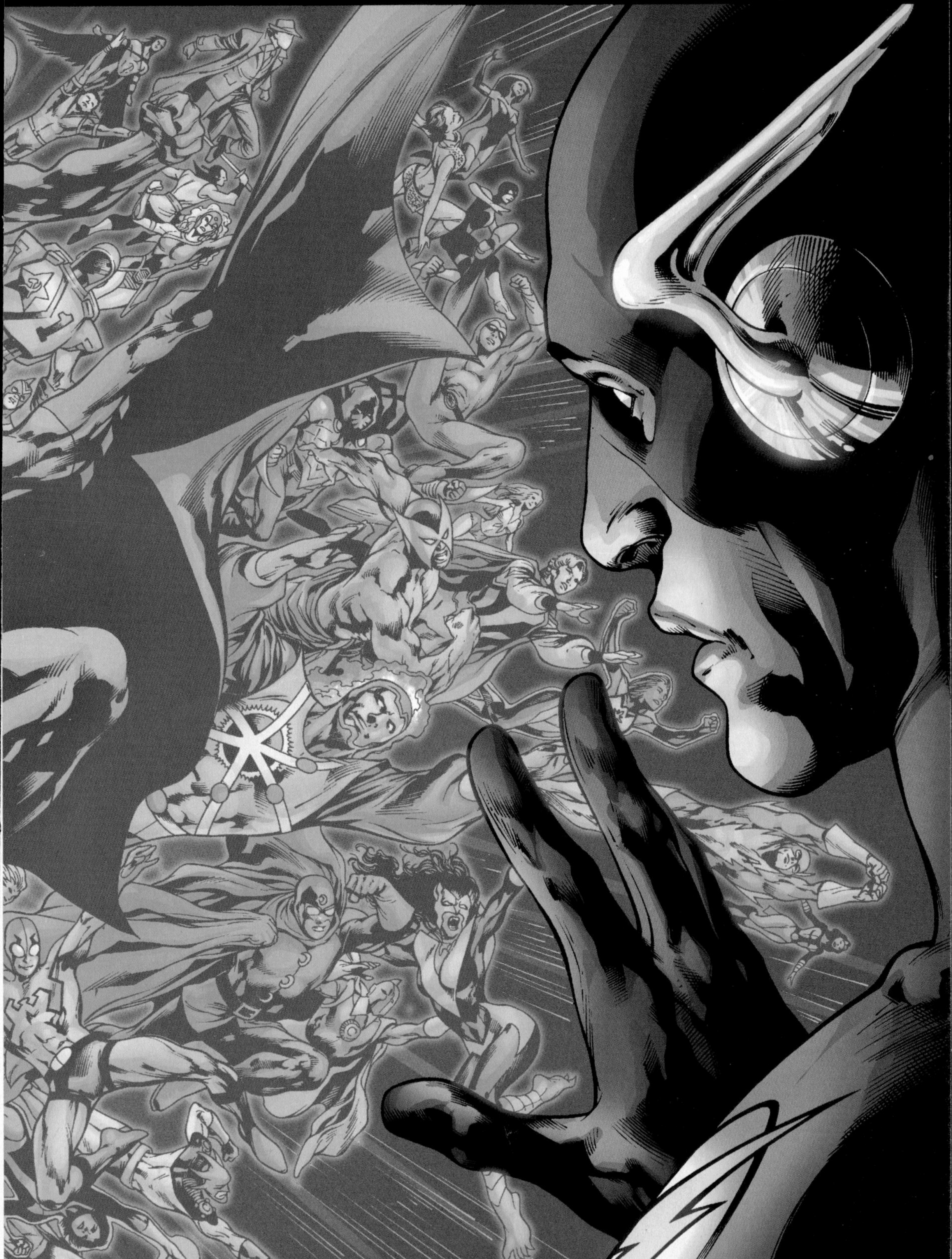

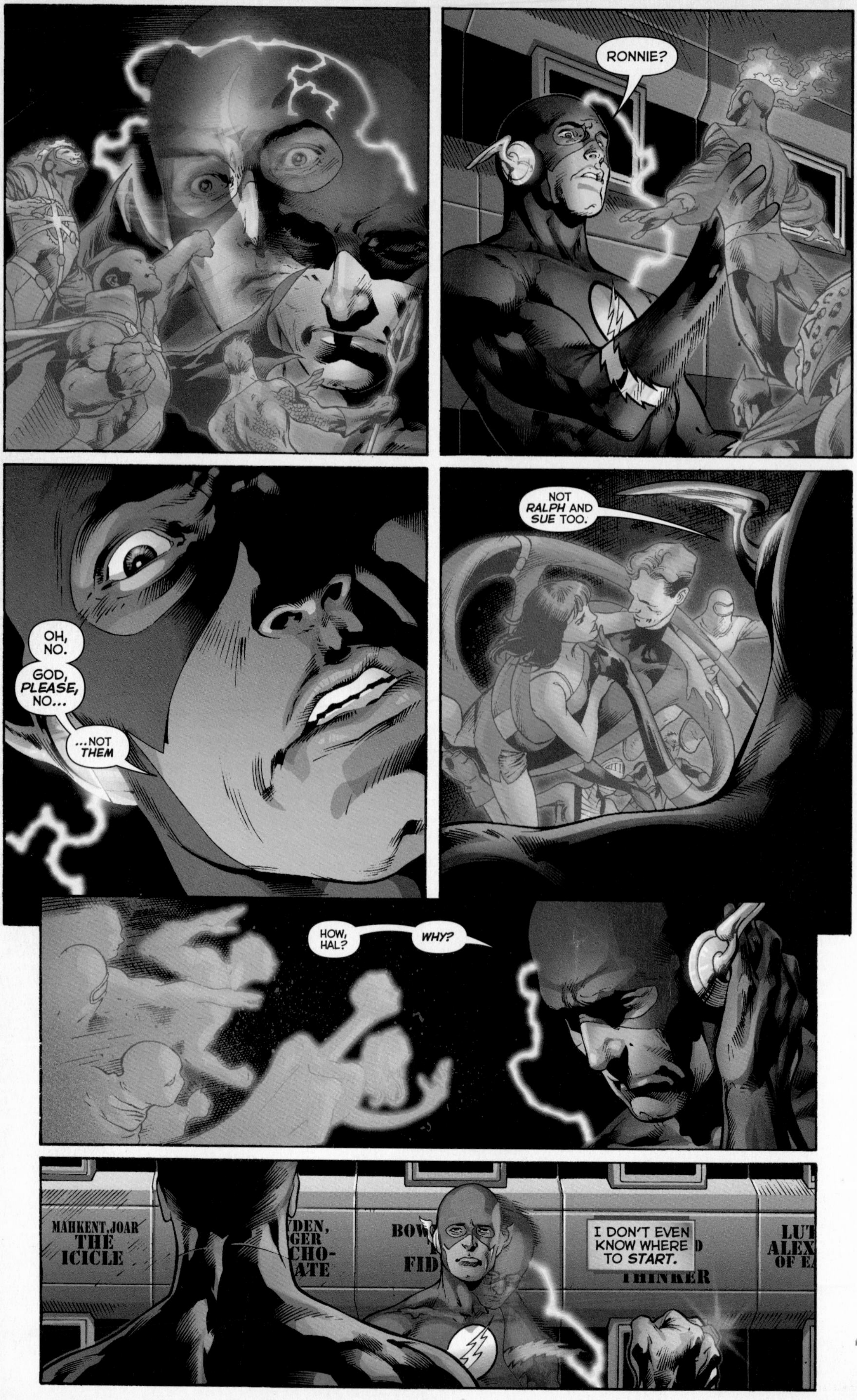
RONNIE?
OH, NO.
GOD, PLEASE, NO...
...NOT THEM
NOT RALPH AND SUE TOO.
HOW, HAL?
WHY?
MAHKENT, JOAR THE ICICLE
I DON'T EVEN KNOW WHERE TO START.

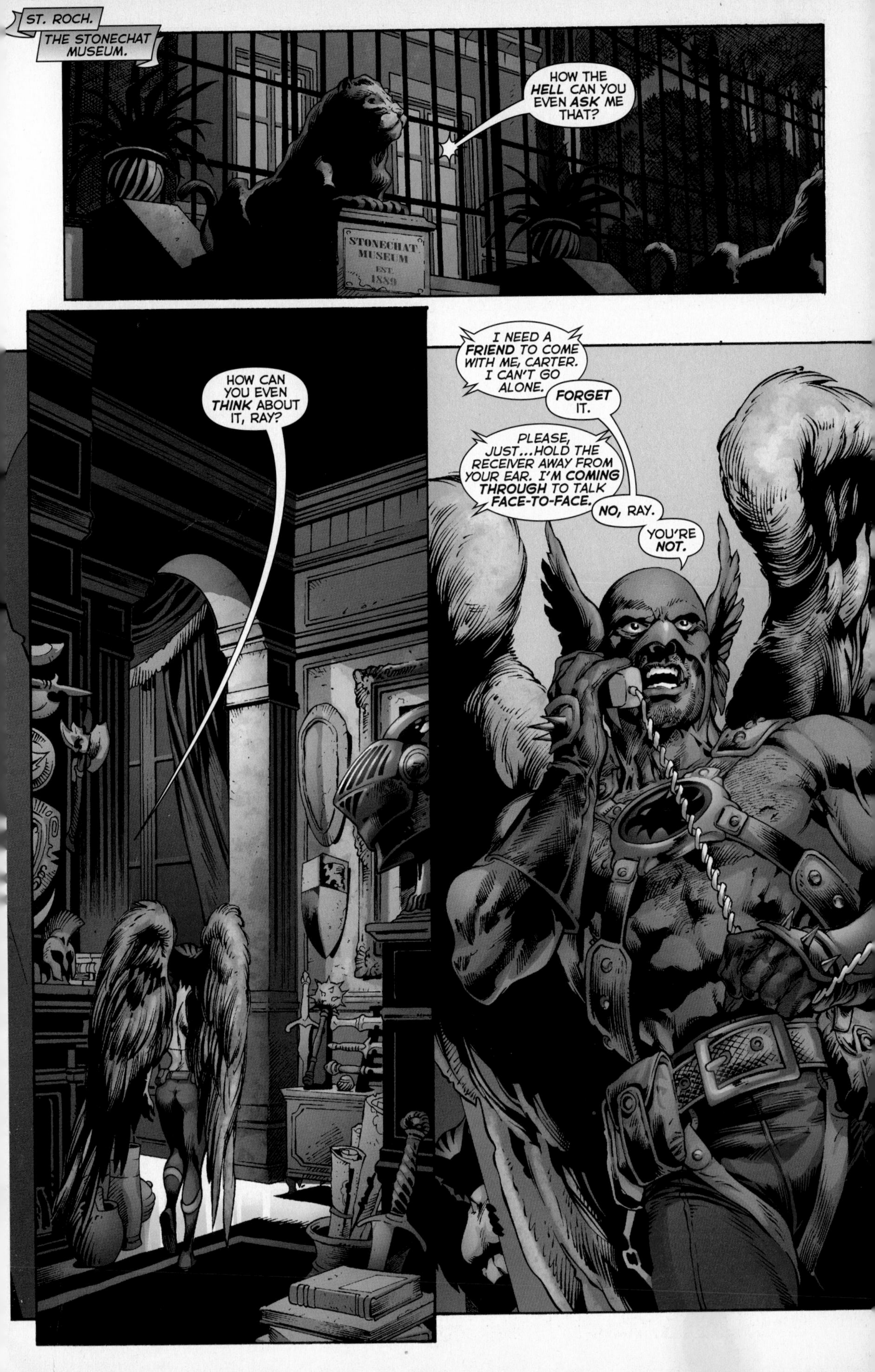
ST. ROCH.
THE STONECHAT MUSEUM.
HOW THE HELL CAN YOU EVEN ASK ME THAT?
STONECHAT MUSEUM EST. 1889
HOW CAN YOU EVEN THINK ABOUT IT, RAY?
I NEED A FRIEND TO COME WITH ME, CARTER. I CAN'T GO ALONE.
FORGET IT.
PLEASE, JUST...HOLD THE RECEIVER AWAY FROM YOUR EAR. I'M COMING THROUGH TO TALK FACE-TO-FACE.
NO, RAY.
YOU'RE NOT.

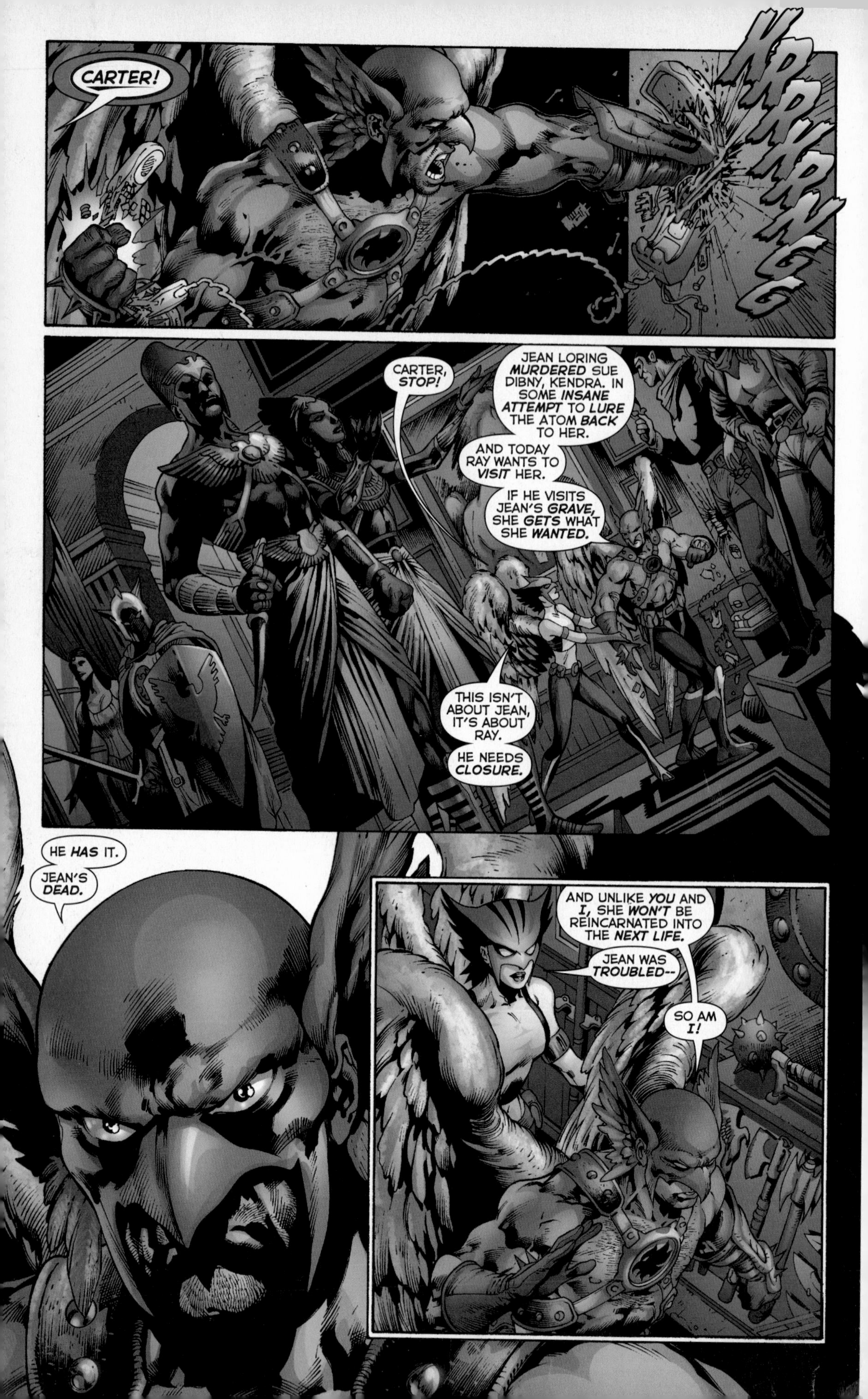
CARTER!
KRRKRNG
CARTER, STOP!
JEAN LORING MURDERED SUE DIBNY, KENDRA. IN SOME INSANE ATTEMPT TO LURE THE ATOM BACK TO HER.
AND TODAY RAY WANTS TO VISIT HER.
IF HE VISITS JEAN'S GRAVE, SHE GETS WHAT SHE WANTED.
THIS ISN'T ABOUT JEAN, IT'S ABOUT RAY.
HE NEEDS CLOSURE.
HE HAS IT.
JEAN'S DEAD.
AND UNLIKE YOU AND I, SHE WON'T BE REINCARNATED INTO THE NEXT LIFE.
JEAN WAS TROUBLED--
SO AM I!

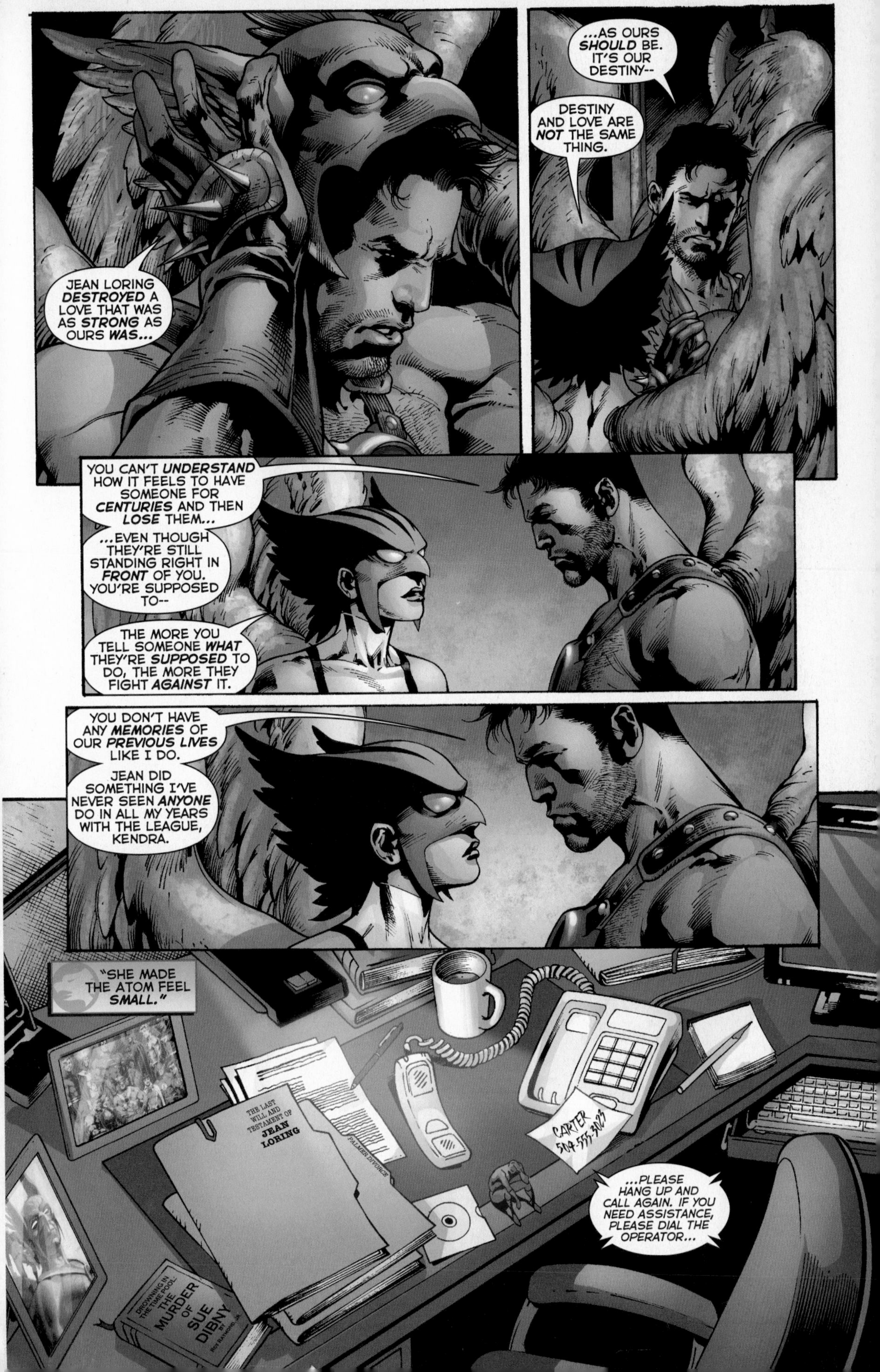
JEAN LORING DESTROYED A LOVE THAT WAS AS STRONG AS OURS WAS...
...AS OURS SHOULD BE. IT'S OUR DESTINY--
DESTINY AND LOVE ARE NOT THE SAME THING.
YOU CAN'T UNDERSTAND HOW IT FEELS TO HAVE SOMEONE FOR CENTURIES AND THEN LOSE THEM...
...EVEN THOUGH THEY'RE STILL STANDING RIGHT IN FRONT OF YOU. YOU'RE SUPPOSED TO--
THE MORE YOU TELL SOMEONE WHAT THEY'RE SUPPOSED TO DO, THE MORE THEY FIGHT AGAINST IT.
YOU DON'T HAVE ANY MEMORIES OF OUR PREVIOUS LIVES LIKE I DO.
JEAN DID SOMETHING I'VE NEVER SEEN ANYONE DO IN ALL MY YEARS WITH THE LEAGUE, KENDRA.
"SHE MADE THE ATOM FEEL SMALL."
THE LAST WILL AND TESTAMENT OF JEAN LORING
PALMER DIVORCE
CARTER 504-555-3023
...PLEASE HANG UP AND CALL AGAIN. IF YOU NEED ASSISTANCE, PLEASE DIAL THE OPERATOR...
THE MURDER OF SUE DIBNY

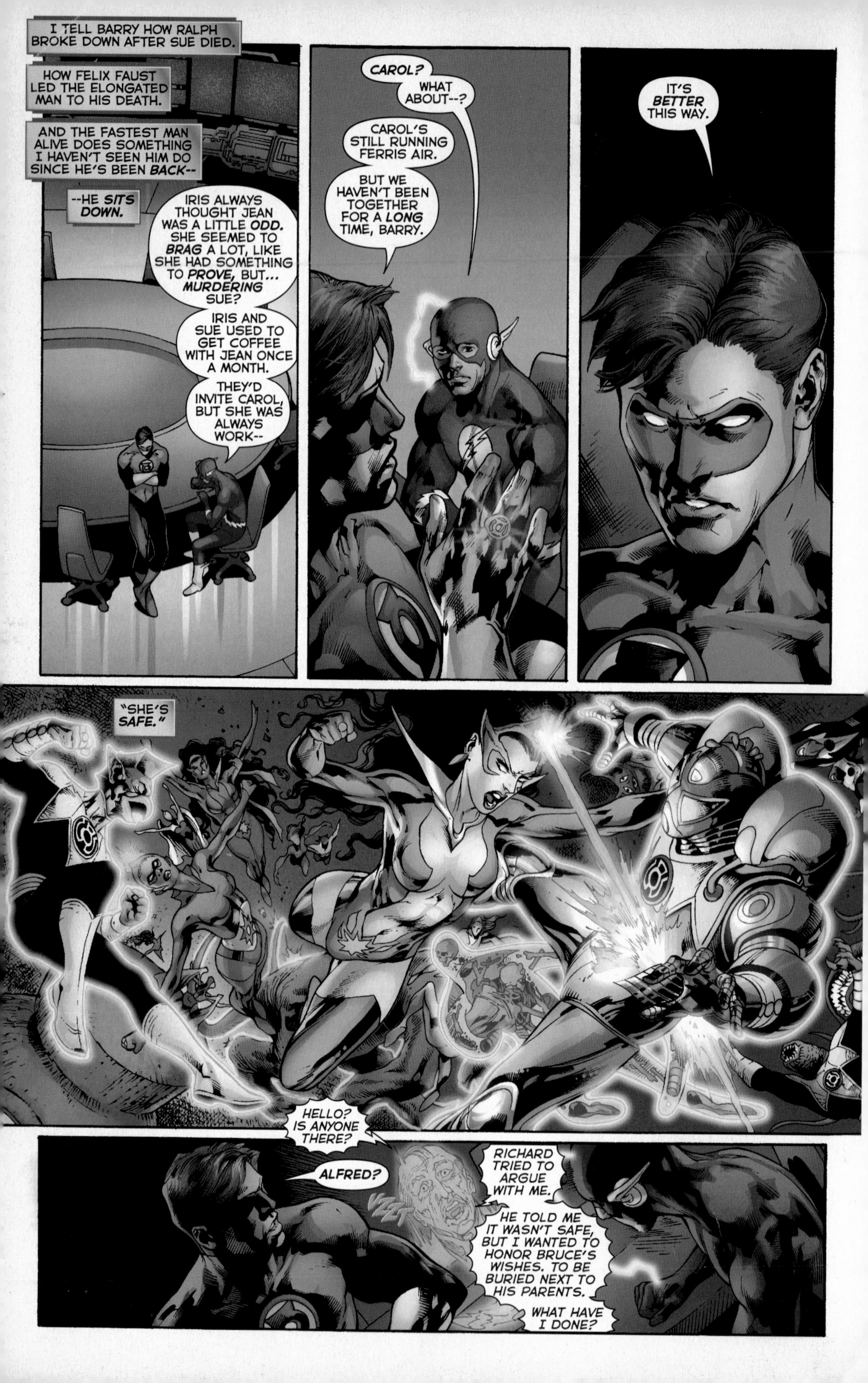
I TELL BARRY HOW RALPH BROKE DOWN AFTER SUE DIED.
HOW FELIX FAUST LED THE ELONGATED MAN TO HIS DEATH.
AND THE FASTEST MAN ALIVE DOES SOMETHING I HAVEN'T SEEN HIM DO SINCE HE'S BEEN *BACK*--
--HE *SITS DOWN.*
IRIS ALWAYS THOUGHT JEAN WAS A LITTLE *ODD.* SHE SEEMED TO *BRAG* A LOT, LIKE SHE HAD SOMETHING TO *PROVE,* BUT... *MURDERING* SUE?
IRIS AND SUE USED TO GET COFFEE WITH JEAN ONCE A MONTH.
THEY'D INVITE CAROL, BUT SHE WAS ALWAYS WORK--
CAROL?
WHAT ABOUT--?
CAROL'S STILL RUNNING FERRIS AIR.
BUT WE HAVEN'T BEEN TOGETHER FOR A *LONG* TIME, BARRY.
IT'S *BETTER* THIS WAY.
"SHE'S *SAFE.*"
HELLO? IS ANYONE THERE?
ALFRED?
VZZT
RICHARD TRIED TO ARGUE WITH ME.
HE TOLD ME IT WASN'T SAFE, BUT I WANTED TO HONOR BRUCE'S WISHES. TO BE BURIED NEXT TO HIS PARENTS.
WHAT HAVE I DONE?

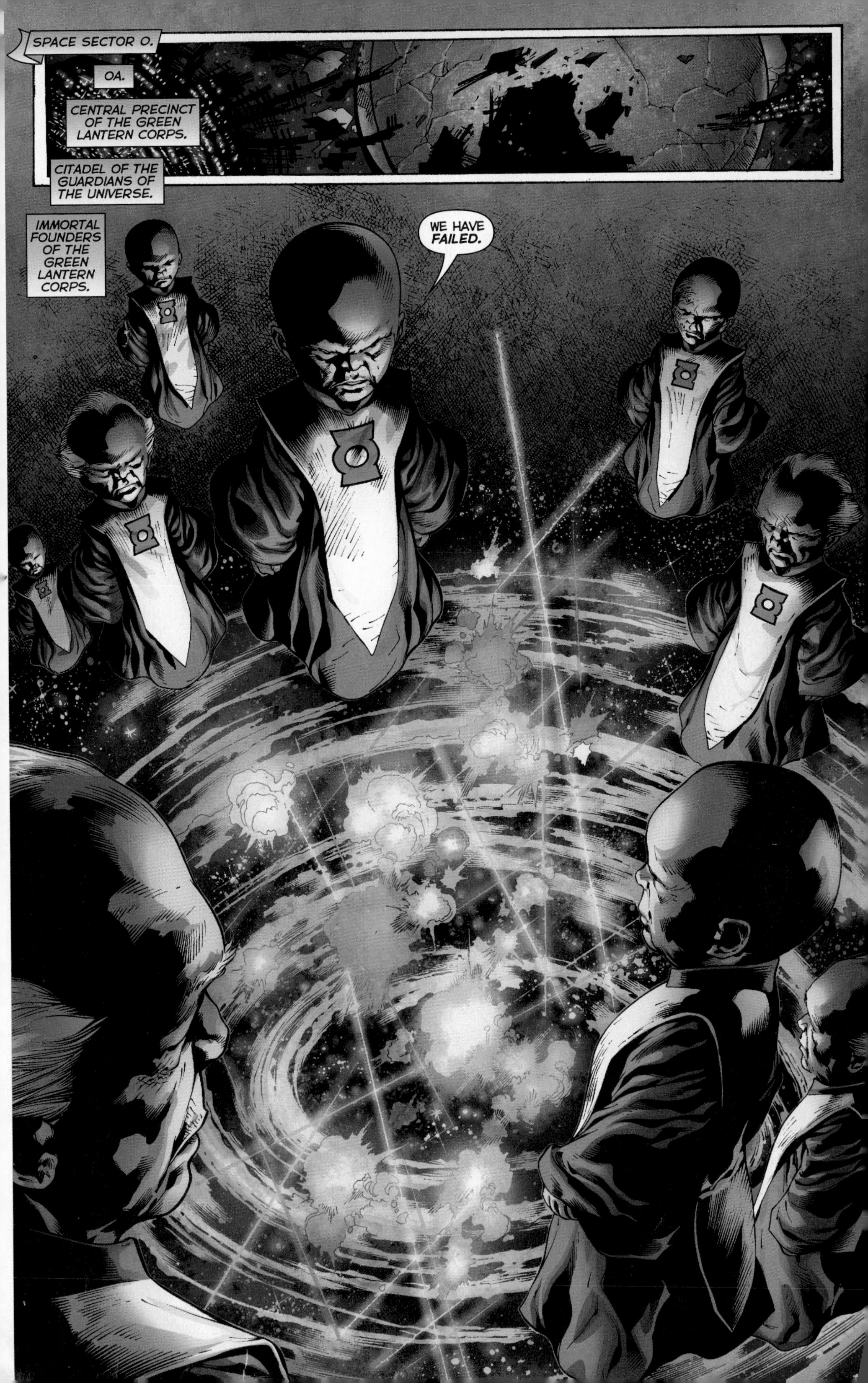
SPACE SECTOR 0.
OA.
CENTRAL PRECINCT OF THE GREEN LANTERN CORPS.
CITADEL OF THE GUARDIANS OF THE UNIVERSE.
IMMORTAL FOUNDERS OF THE GREEN LANTERN CORPS.
WE HAVE FAILED.

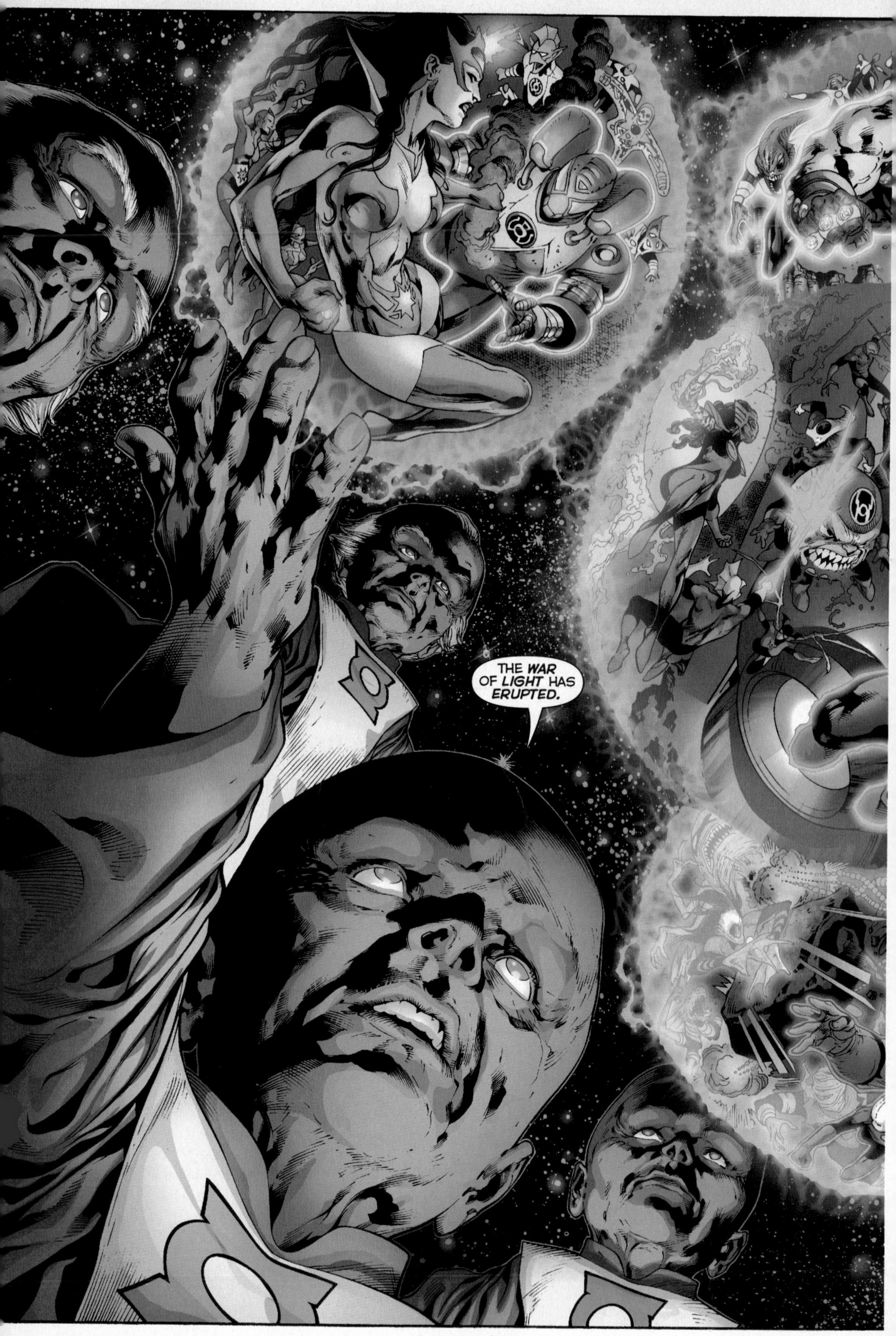
THE *WAR* OF *LIGHT* HAS *ERUPTED.*

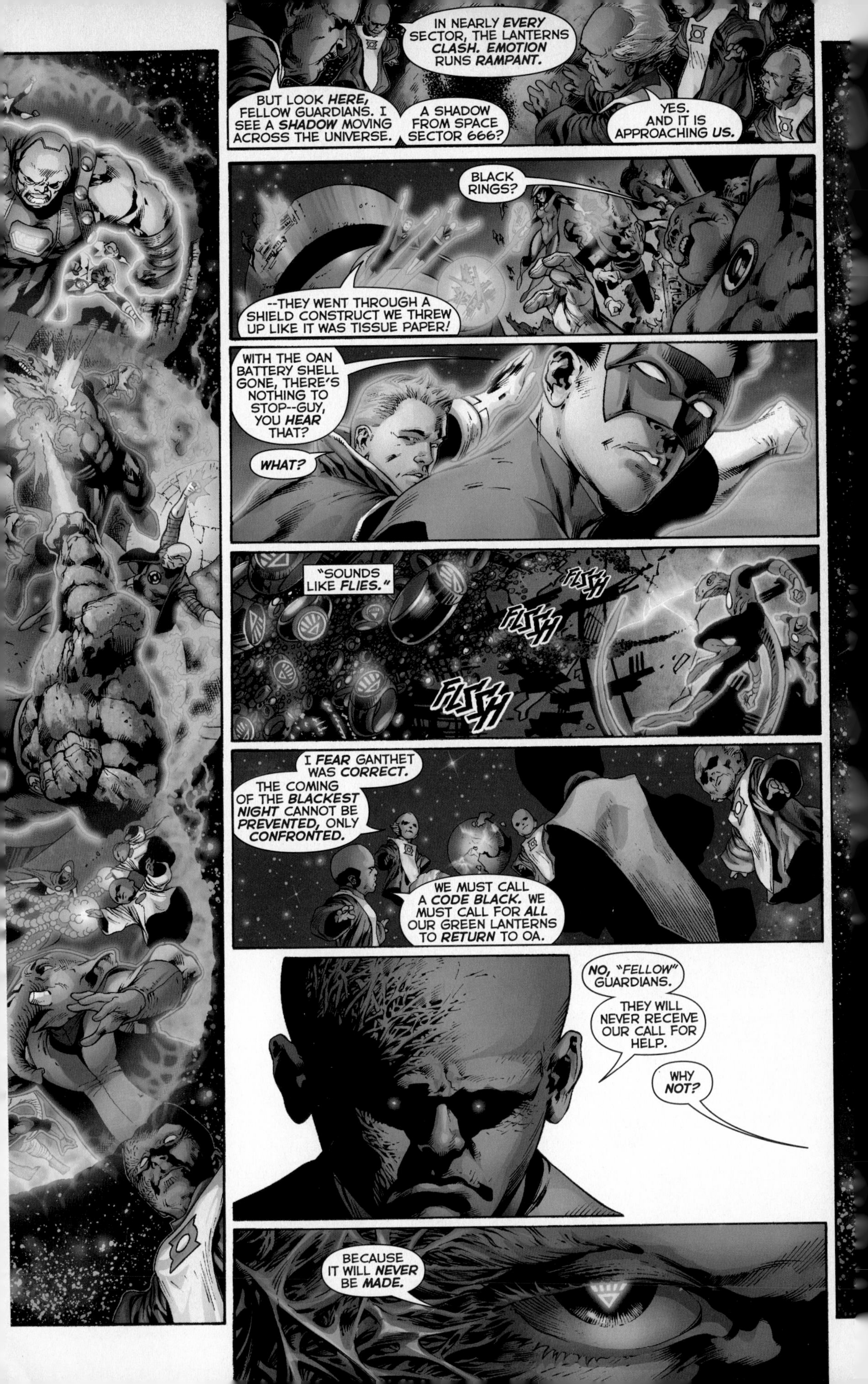
IN NEARLY EVERY SECTOR, THE LANTERNS CLASH. EMOTION RUNS RAMPANT.
BUT LOOK HERE, FELLOW GUARDIANS. I SEE A SHADOW MOVING ACROSS THE UNIVERSE.
A SHADOW FROM SPACE SECTOR 666?
YES. AND IT IS APPROACHING US.
BLACK RINGS?
--THEY WENT THROUGH A SHIELD CONSTRUCT WE THREW UP LIKE IT WAS TISSUE PAPER!
WITH THE OAN BATTERY SHELL GONE, THERE'S NOTHING TO STOP--GUY, YOU HEAR THAT?
WHAT?
"SOUNDS LIKE FLIES."
FLSSH
FLSSH
FLSSH
I FEAR GANTHET WAS CORRECT. THE COMING OF THE BLACKEST NIGHT CANNOT BE PREVENTED, ONLY CONFRONTED.
WE MUST CALL A CODE BLACK. WE MUST CALL FOR ALL OUR GREEN LANTERNS TO RETURN TO OA.
NO, "FELLOW" GUARDIANS.
THEY WILL NEVER RECEIVE OUR CALL FOR HELP.
WHY NOT?
BECAUSE IT WILL NEVER BE MADE.

KRRTCHH

FLESH.

FLESH.

FLESH.

DAMMIT! THEY'RE IN!

EVERYONE-- KEEP SHIELDS AT FULL STRENGTH!

KRAAATCHH

CCHHAKFFFFFFFF

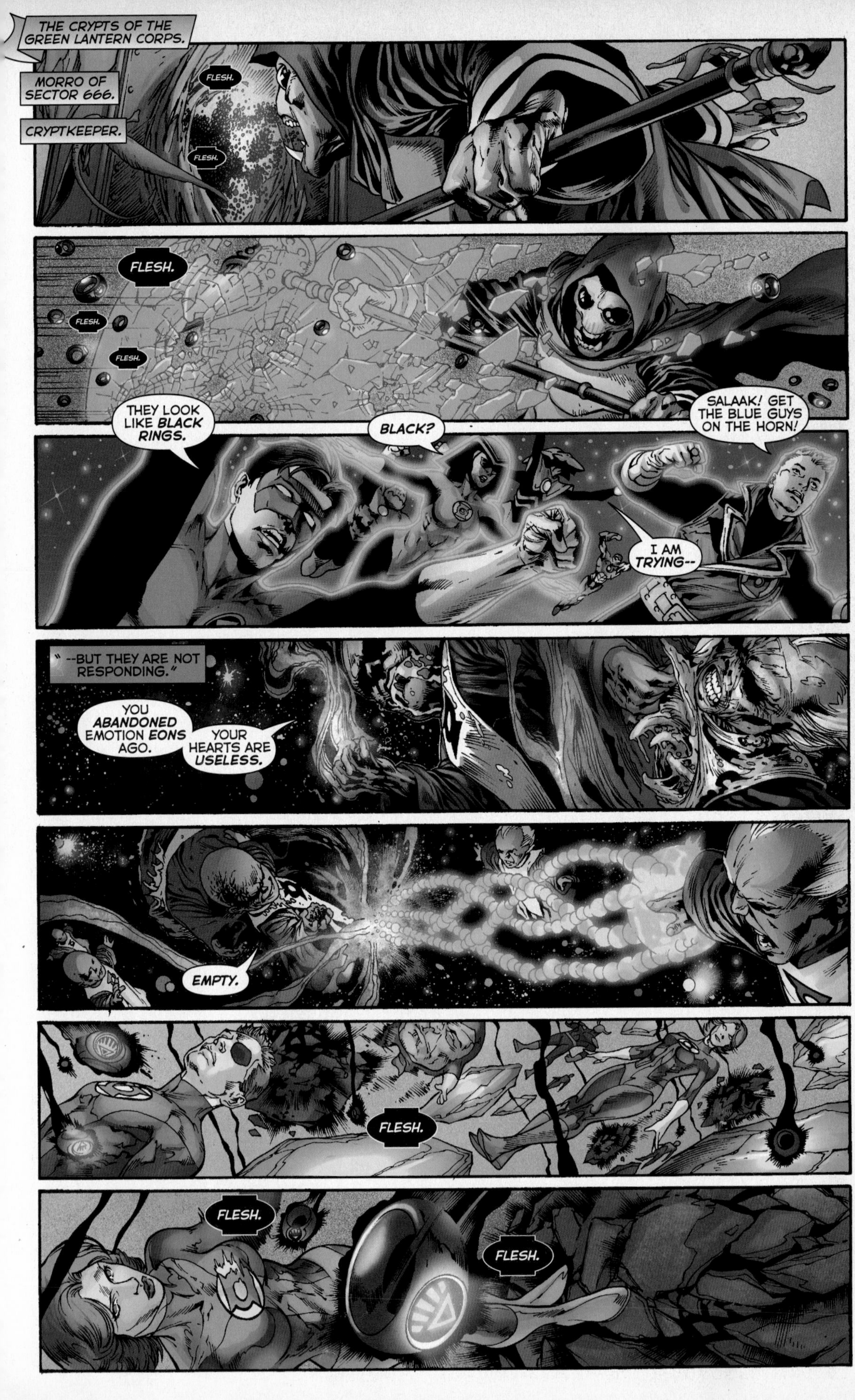
THE CRYPTS OF THE GREEN LANTERN CORPS.
MORRO OF SECTOR 666.
CRYPTKEEPER.
FLESH.
FLESH.
FLESH.
FLESH.
FLESH.
THEY LOOK LIKE BLACK RINGS.
BLACK?
SALAAK! GET THE BLUE GUYS ON THE HORN!
I AM TRYING--
" --BUT THEY ARE NOT RESPONDING."
YOU ABANDONED EMOTION EONS AGO.
YOUR HEARTS ARE USELESS.
EMPTY.
FLESH.
FLESH.
FLESH.

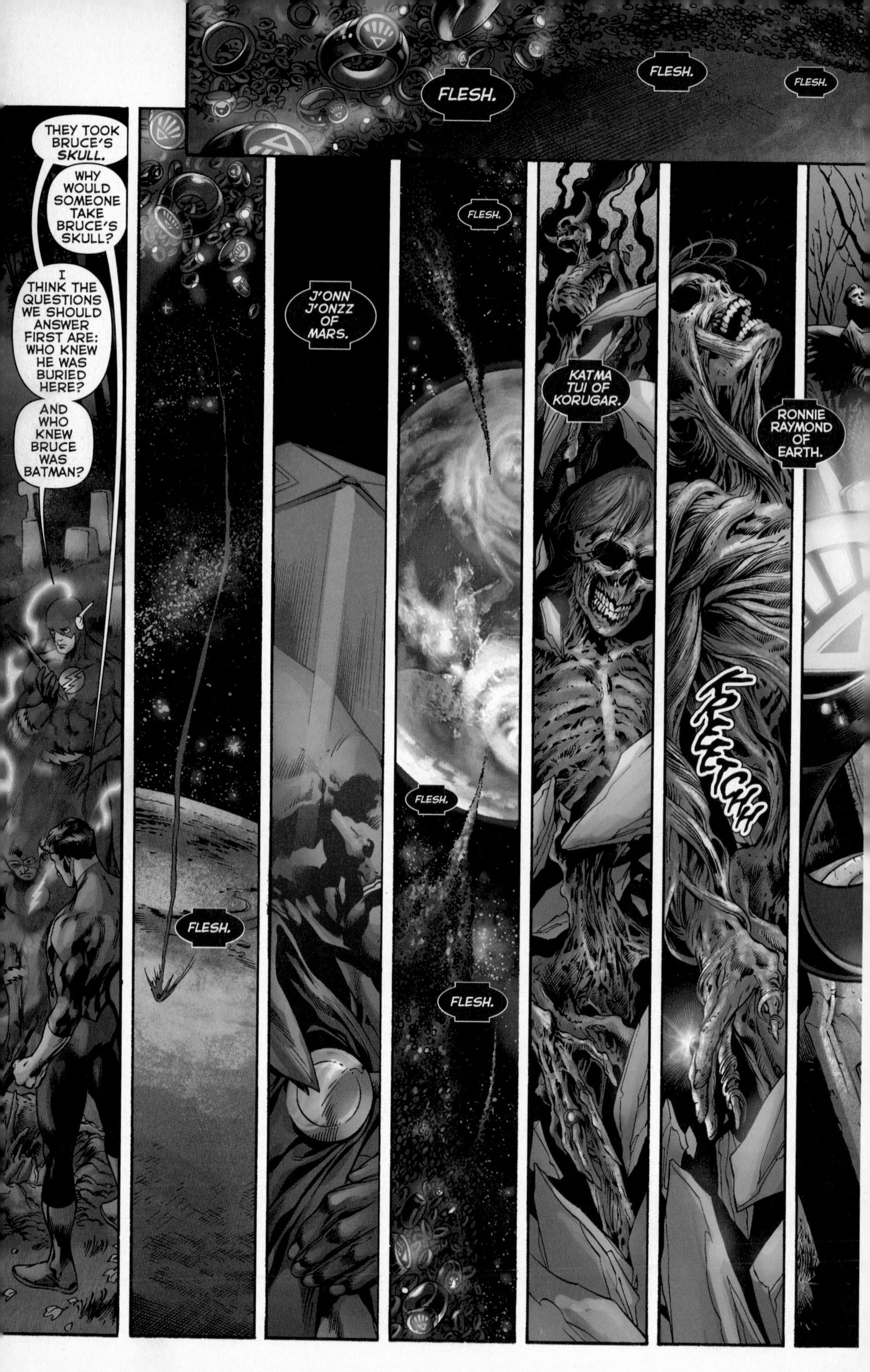
FLESH.
FLESH.
FLESH.
THEY TOOK BRUCE'S SKULL.
WHY WOULD SOMEONE TAKE BRUCE'S SKULL?
I THINK THE QUESTIONS WE SHOULD ANSWER FIRST ARE: WHO KNEW HE WAS BURIED HERE?
AND WHO KNEW BRUCE WAS BATMAN?
FLESH.
J'ONN J'ONZZ OF MARS.
FLESH.
FLESH.
FLESH.
KATMA TUI OF KORUGAR.
RONNIE RAYMOND OF EARTH.
KRUTCH

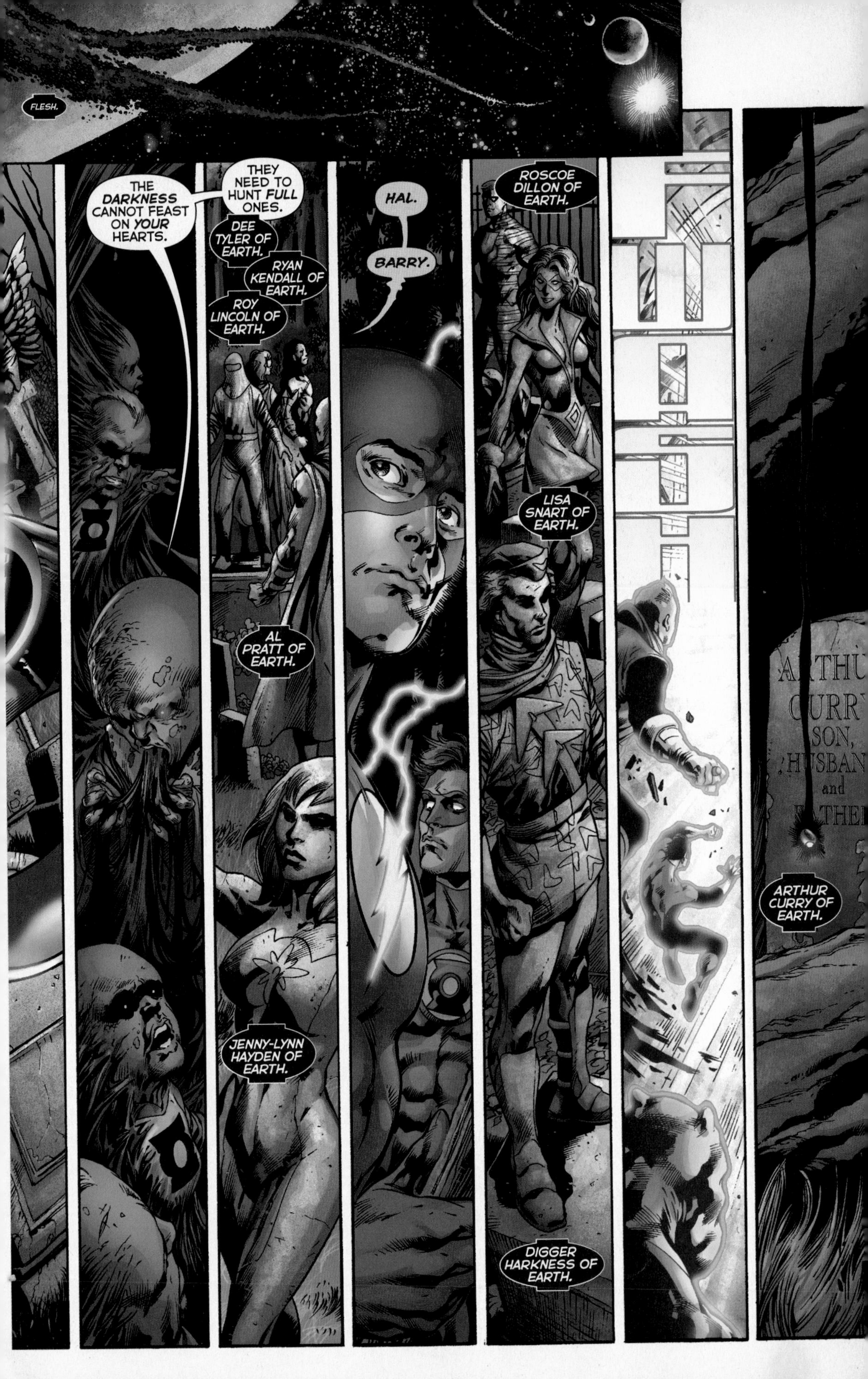
FLESH.
THE DARKNESS CANNOT FEAST ON YOUR HEARTS.
THEY NEED TO HUNT FULL ONES.
DEE TYLER OF EARTH.
RYAN KENDALL OF EARTH.
ROY LINCOLN OF EARTH.
AL PRATT OF EARTH.
JENNY-LYNN HAYDEN OF EARTH.
HAL.
BARRY.
ROSCOE DILLON OF EARTH.
LISA SNART OF EARTH.
DIGGER HARKNESS OF EARTH.
ARTHUR CURRY SON, HUSBAN and FATHE
ARTHUR CURRY OF EARTH.

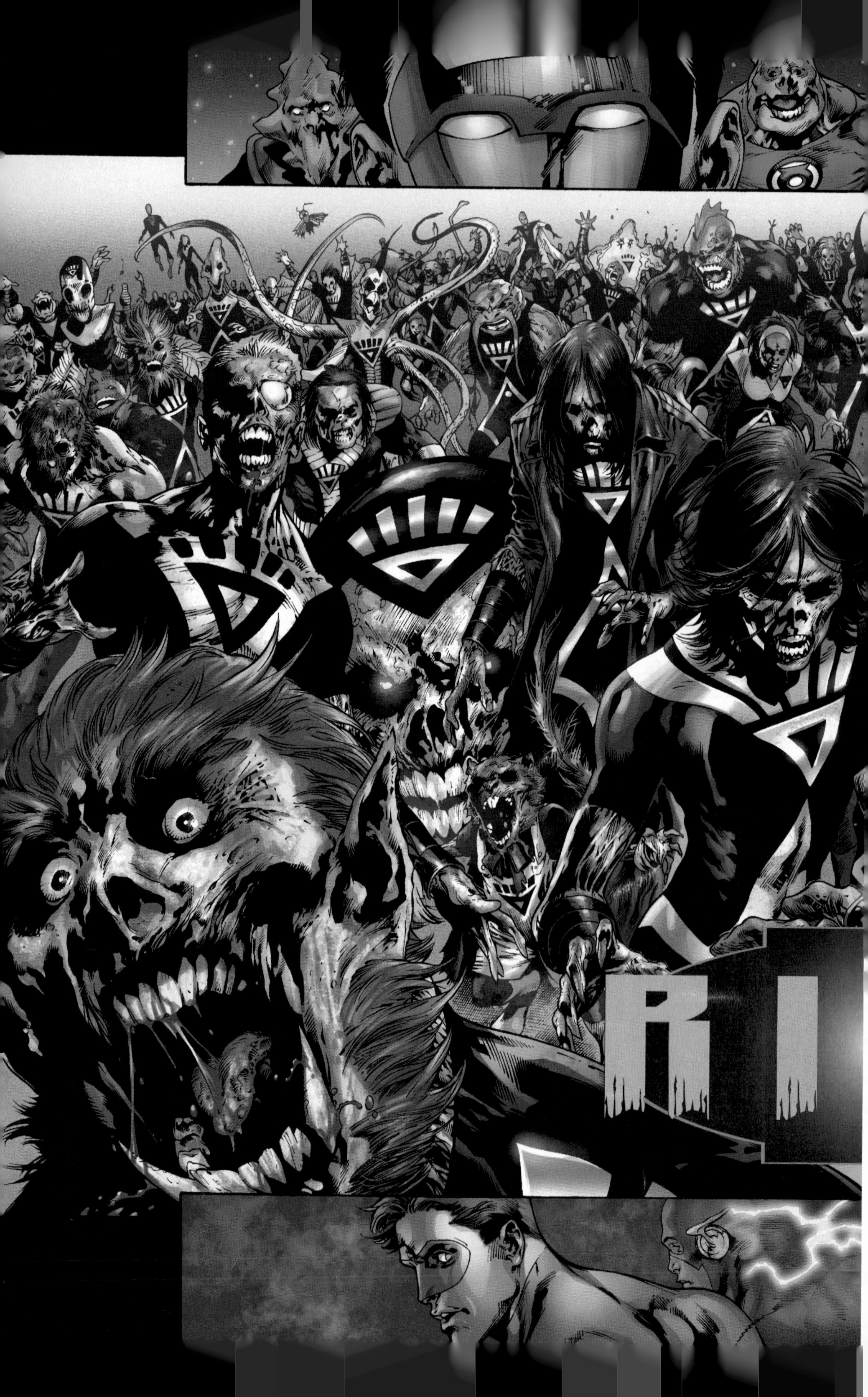

RI

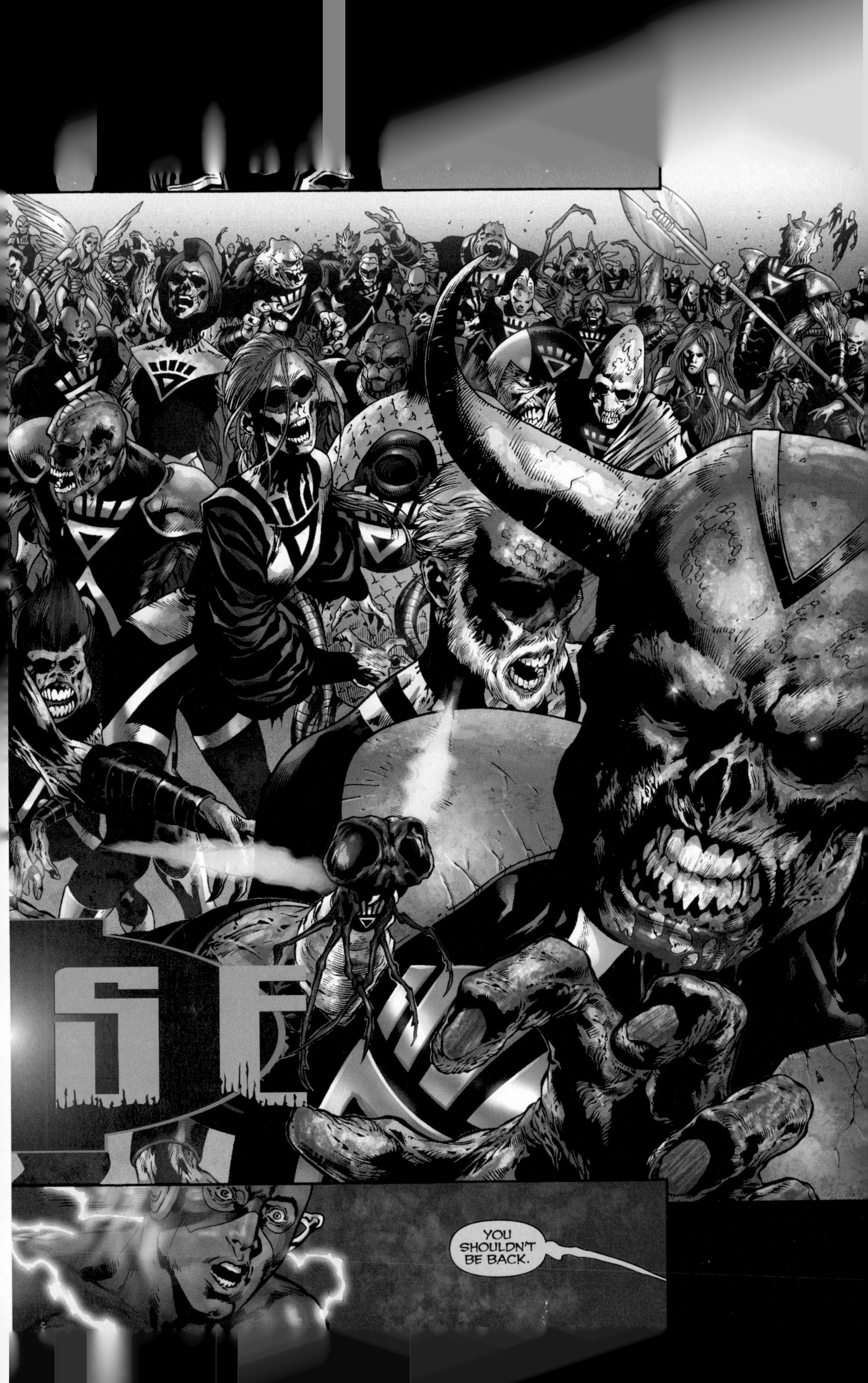
YOU SHOULDN'T BE BACK.

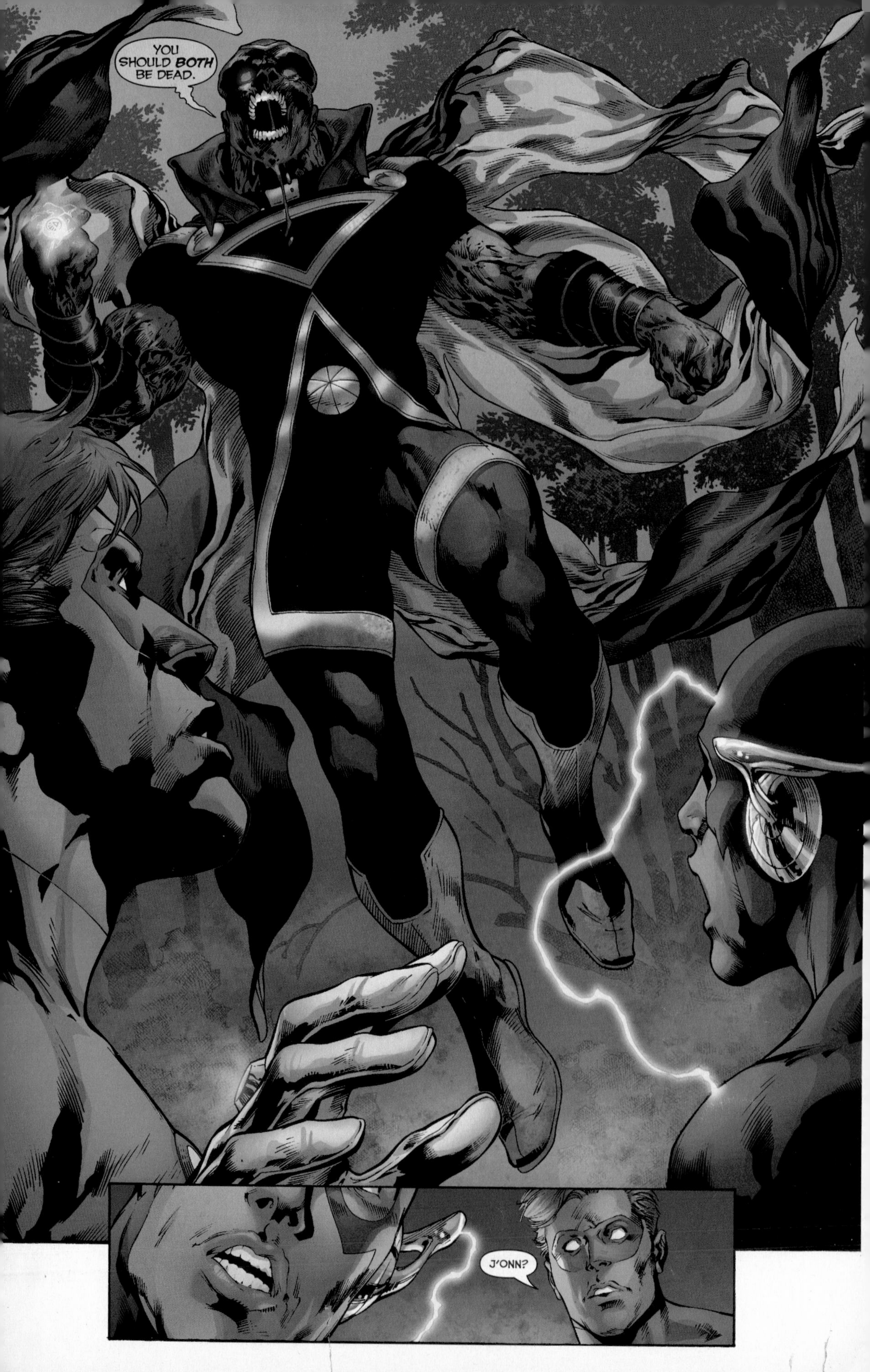
YOU SHOULD BOTH BE DEAD.
J'ONN?

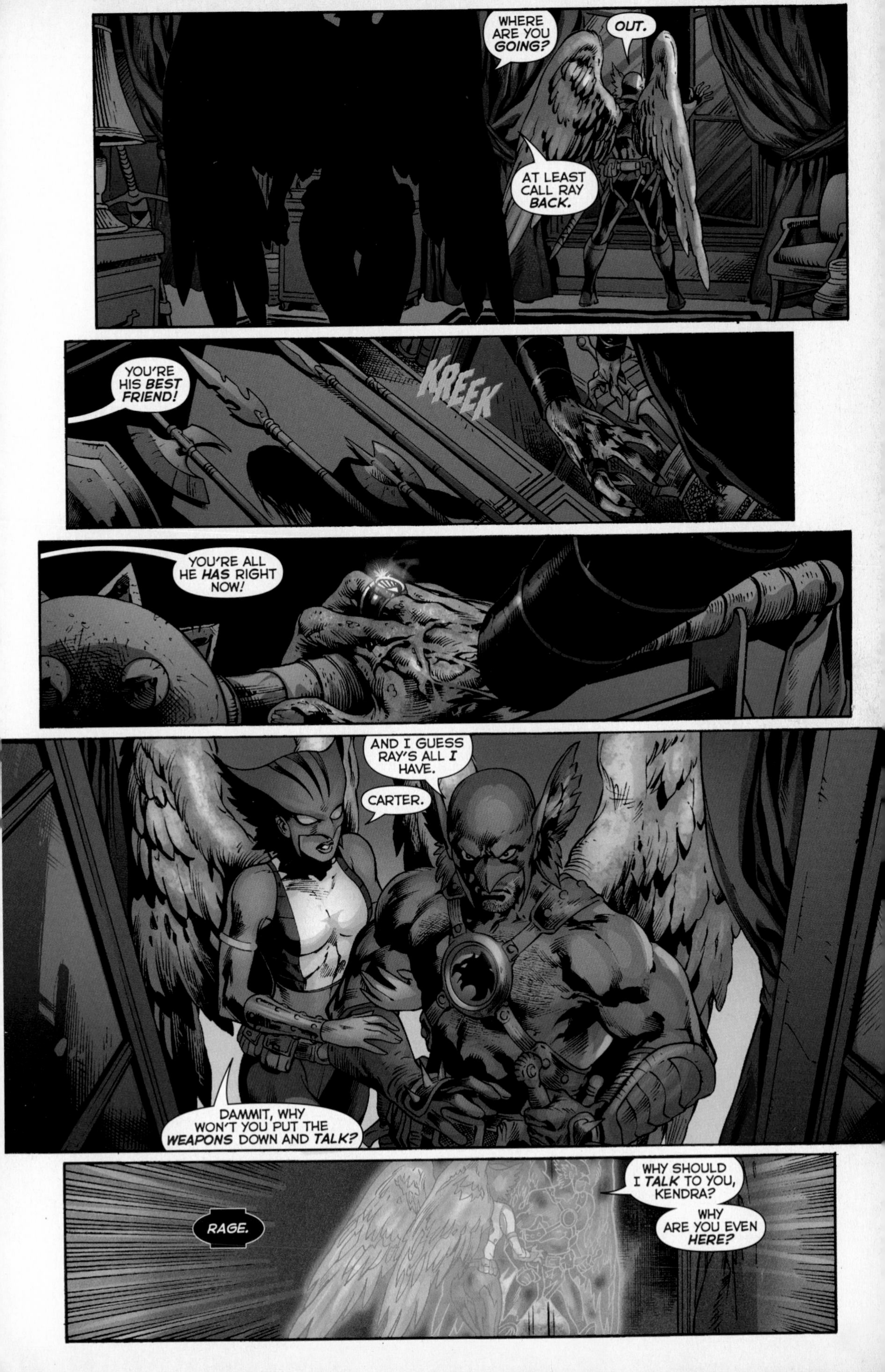
WHERE ARE YOU GOING?
OUT.
AT LEAST CALL RAY BACK.
YOU'RE HIS BEST FRIEND!
KREEK
YOU'RE ALL HE HAS RIGHT NOW!
AND I GUESS RAY'S ALL I HAVE.
CARTER.
DAMMIT, WHY WON'T YOU PUT THE WEAPONS DOWN AND TALK?
RAGE.
WHY SHOULD I TALK TO YOU, KENDRA?
WHY ARE YOU EVEN HERE?

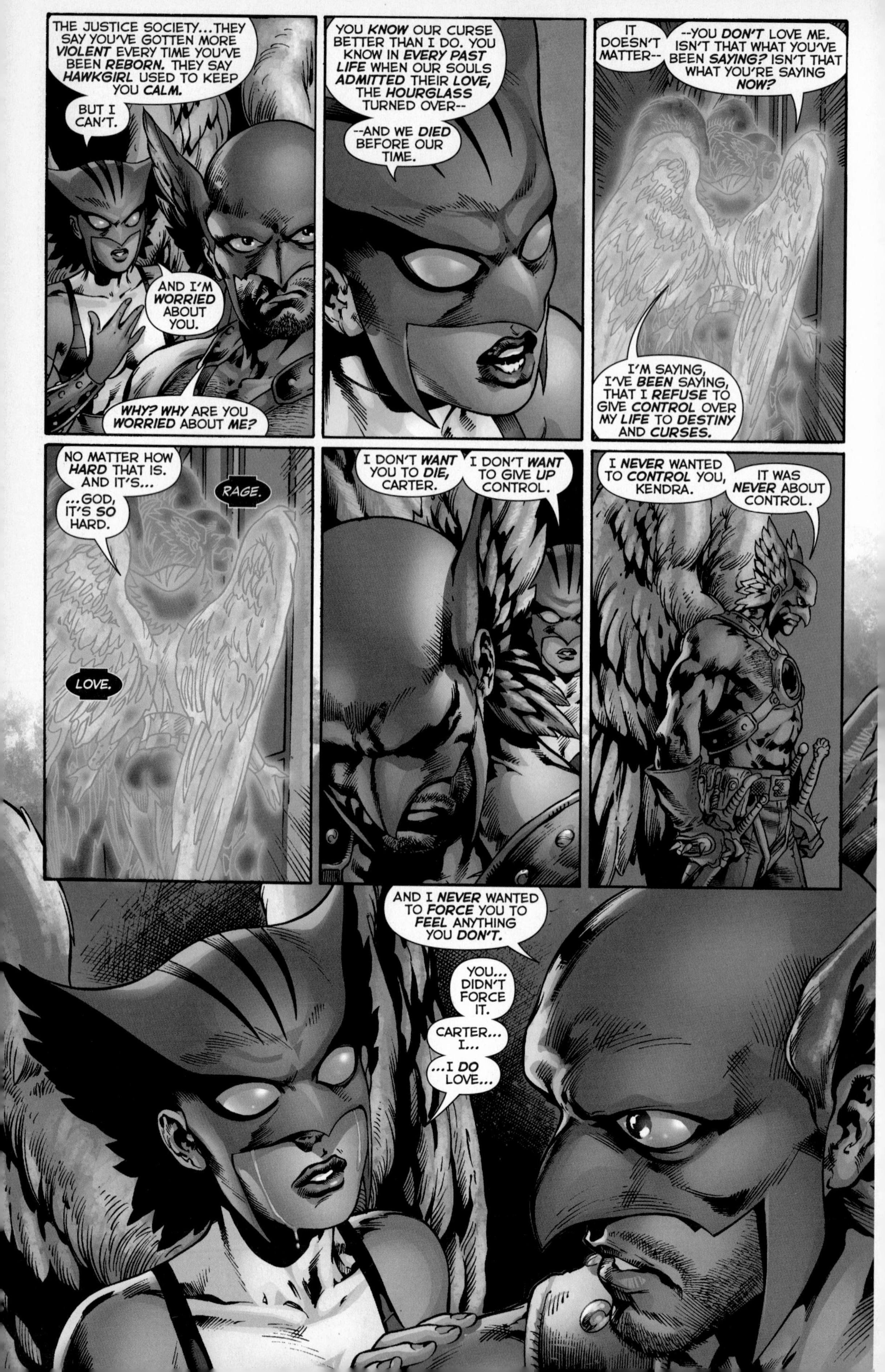
THE JUSTICE SOCIETY...THEY SAY YOU'VE GOTTEN MORE VIOLENT EVERY TIME YOU'VE BEEN REBORN. THEY SAY HAWKGIRL USED TO KEEP YOU CALM.
BUT I CAN'T.
AND I'M WORRIED ABOUT YOU.
WHY? WHY ARE YOU WORRIED ABOUT ME?
YOU KNOW OUR CURSE BETTER THAN I DO. YOU KNOW IN EVERY PAST LIFE WHEN OUR SOULS ADMITTED THEIR LOVE, THE HOURGLASS TURNED OVER--
--AND WE DIED BEFORE OUR TIME.
IT DOESN'T MATTER--
--YOU DON'T LOVE ME. ISN'T THAT WHAT YOU'VE BEEN SAYING? ISN'T THAT WHAT YOU'RE SAYING NOW?
I'M SAYING, I'VE BEEN SAYING, THAT I REFUSE TO GIVE CONTROL OVER MY LIFE TO DESTINY AND CURSES.
NO MATTER HOW HARD THAT IS. AND IT'S...
...GOD, IT'S SO HARD.
RAGE.
LOVE.
I DON'T WANT YOU TO DIE, CARTER.
I DON'T WANT TO GIVE UP CONTROL.
I NEVER WANTED TO CONTROL YOU, KENDRA.
IT WAS NEVER ABOUT CONTROL.
AND I NEVER WANTED TO FORCE YOU TO FEEL ANYTHING YOU DON'T.
YOU... DIDN'T FORCE IT.
CARTER... I...
...I DO LOVE...

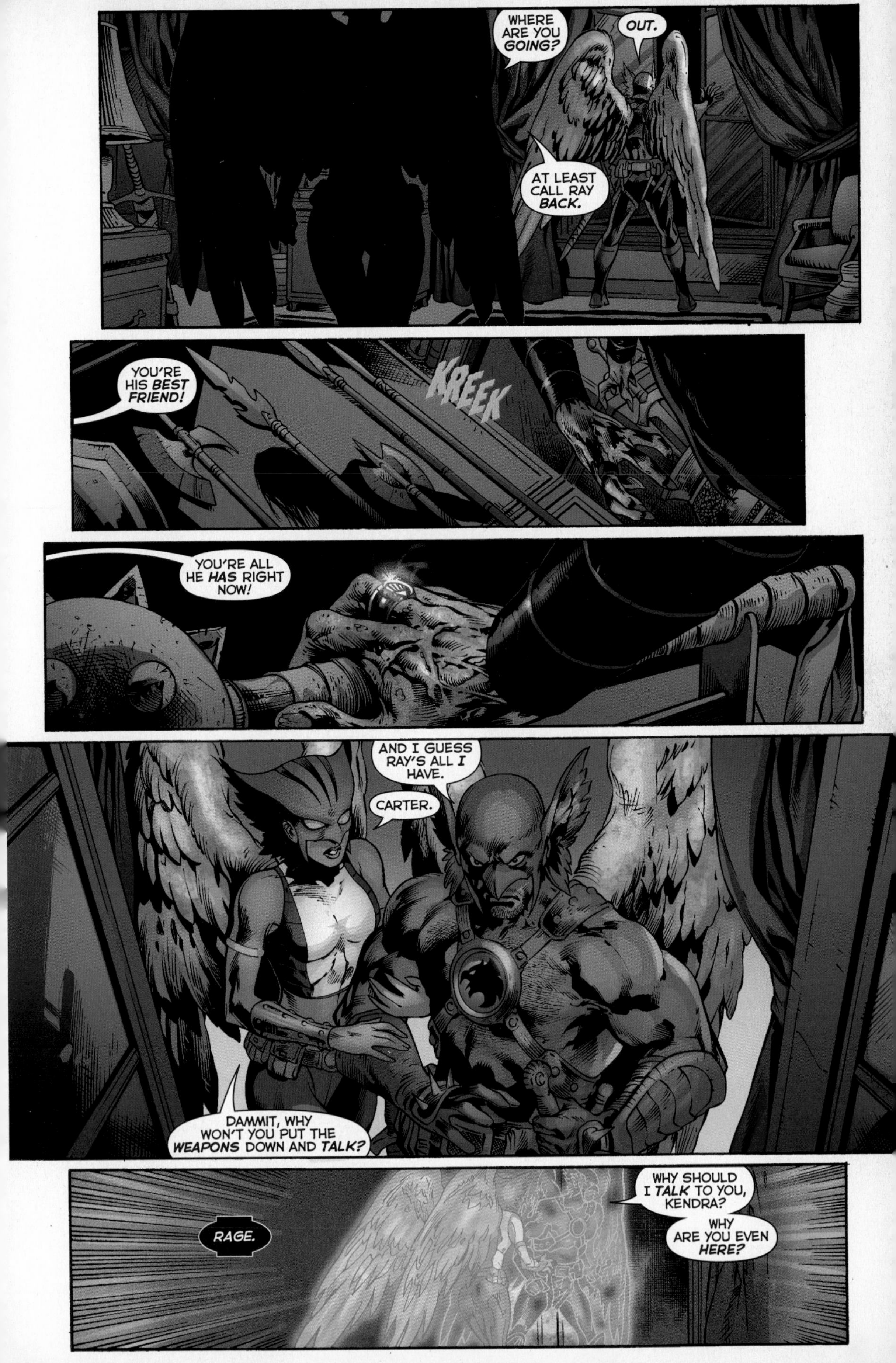
WHERE ARE YOU GOING?
OUT.
AT LEAST CALL RAY BACK.
YOU'RE HIS BEST FRIEND!
KREEK
YOU'RE ALL HE HAS RIGHT NOW!
AND I GUESS RAY'S ALL I HAVE.
CARTER.
DAMMIT, WHY WON'T YOU PUT THE WEAPONS DOWN AND TALK?
RAGE.
WHY SHOULD I TALK TO YOU, KENDRA?
WHY ARE YOU EVEN HERE?

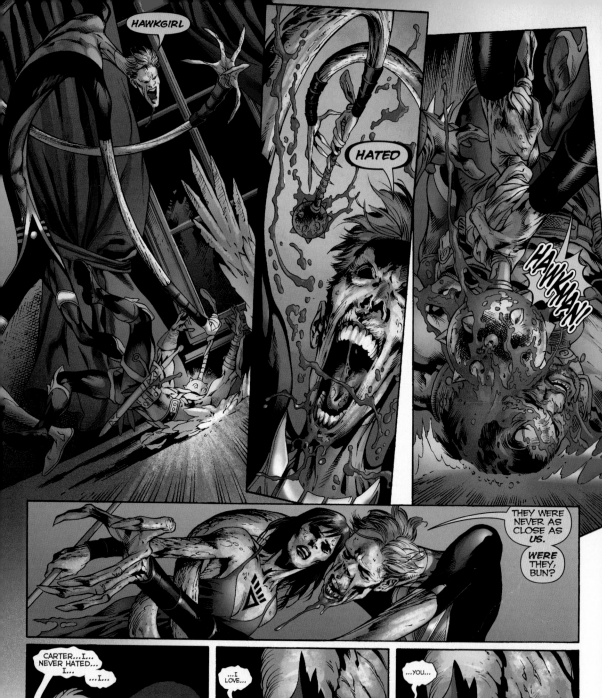

HAWKGIRL

HATED

HAWKMAN!

THEY WERE NEVER AS CLOSE AS *US.*

WERE THEY, BUN?

CARTER...I... NEVER HATED... I.... ...I...

...I LOVE...

...YOU...

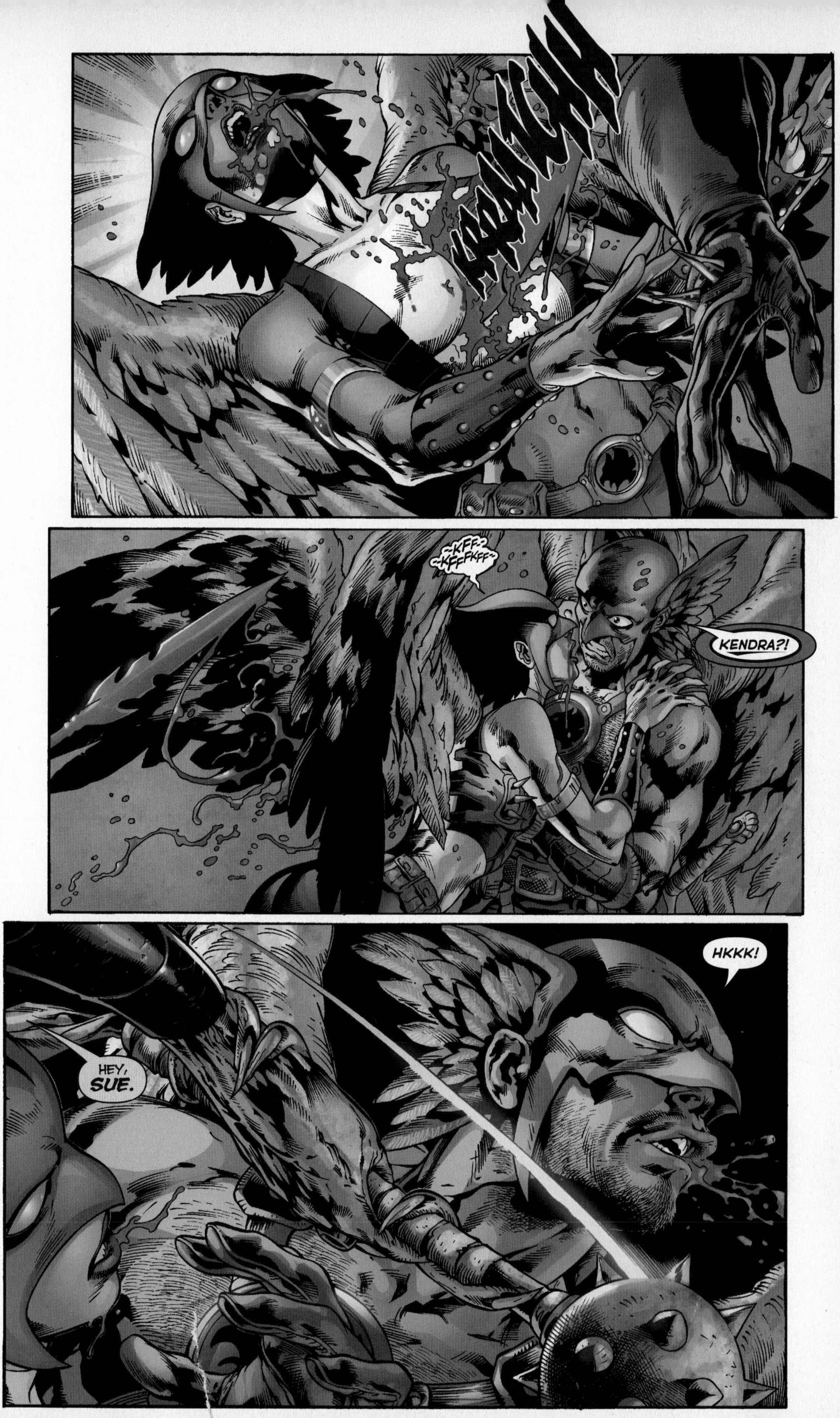
~KFF-
~KFFFKFF~
KENDRA?!
HEY, SUE.
HKKK!

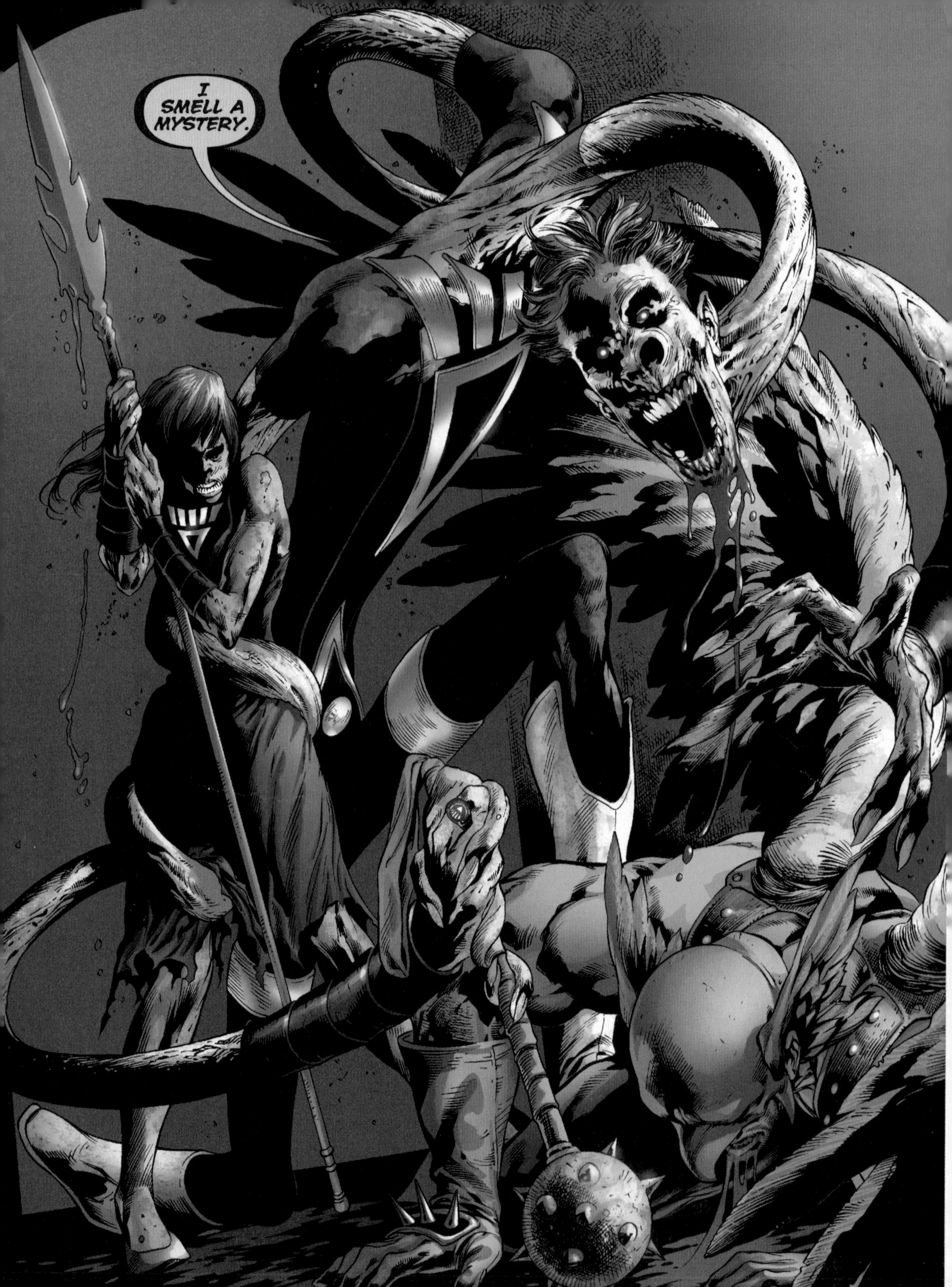
I SMELL A MYSTERY.
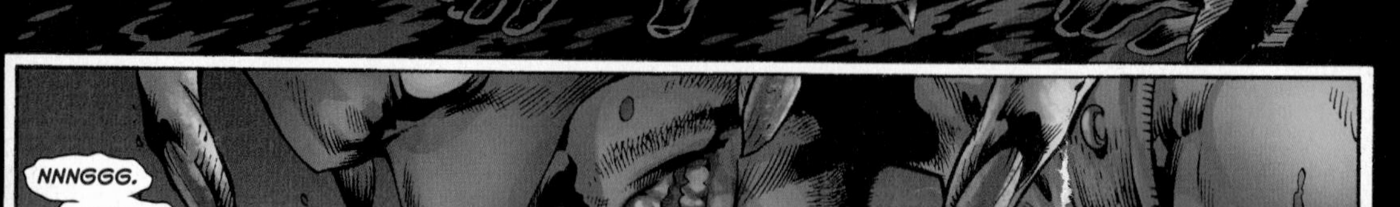
NNNGGG.
R-RALPH?

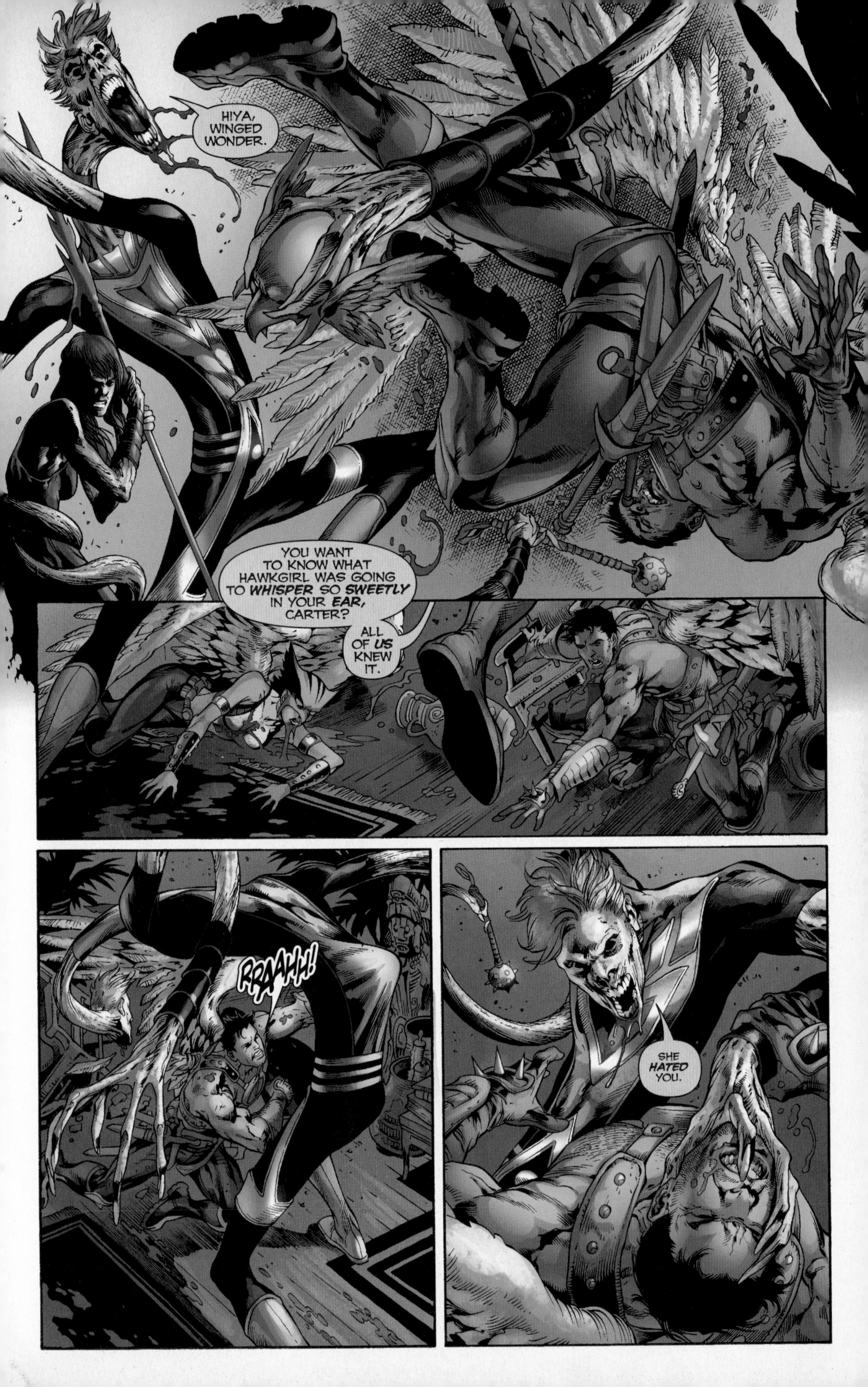
HIYA, WINGED WONDER.
YOU WANT TO KNOW WHAT HAWKGIRL WAS GOING TO *WHISPER* SO *SWEETLY* IN YOUR *EAR*, CARTER?
ALL OF *US* KNEW IT.
RRAAHH!
SHE *HATED* YOU.

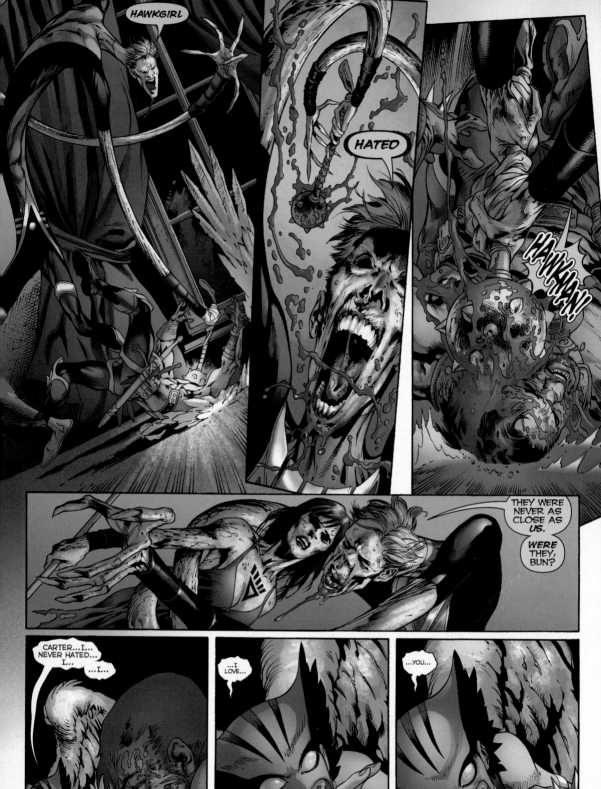

HAWKGIRL

HATED

HAWKMAN!

THEY WERE NEVER AS CLOSE AS US.

WERE THEY, BUN?

CARTER...I... NEVER HATED... I... ...I...

...I LOVE...

...YOU...

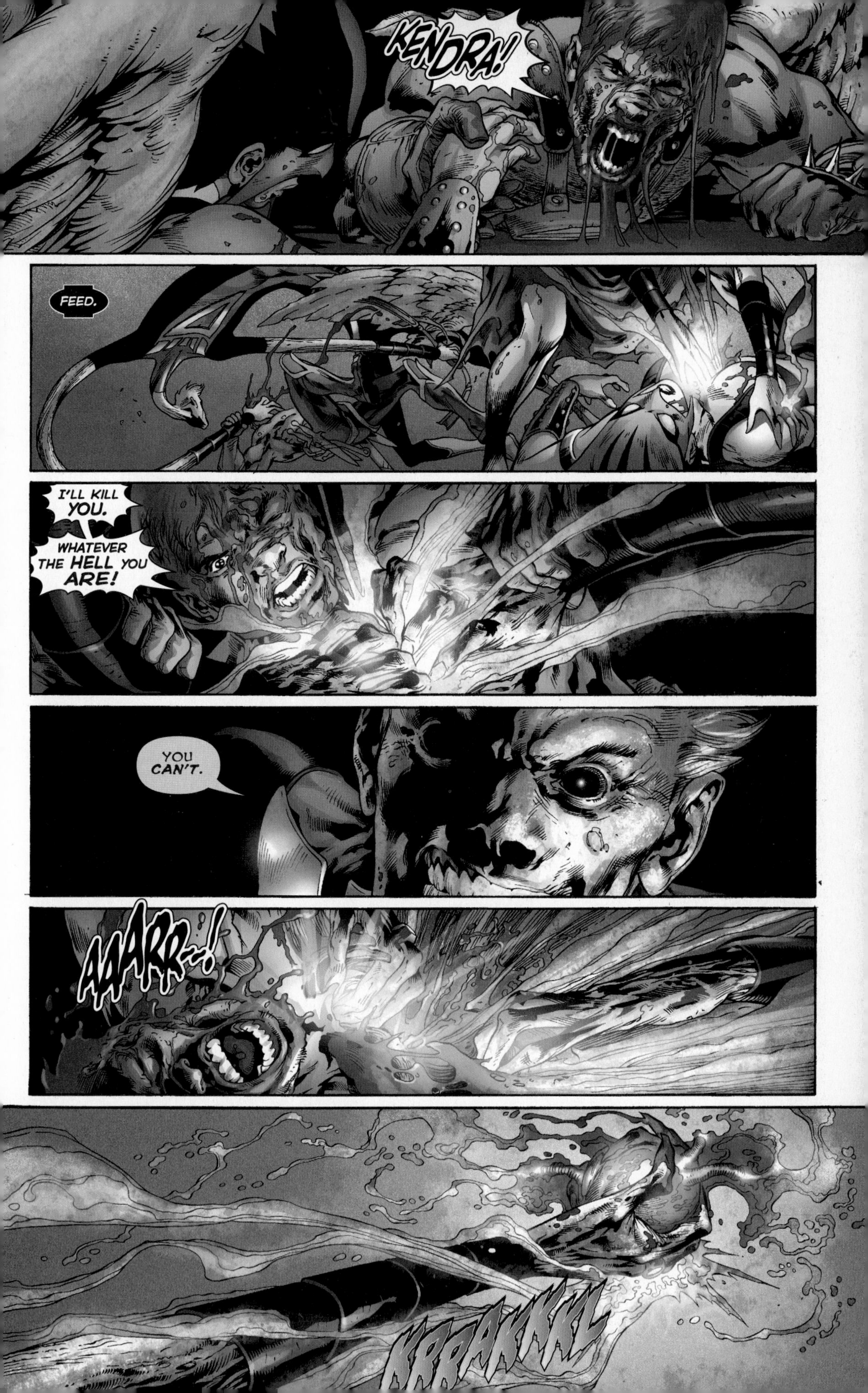
KENDRA!
FEED.
I'LL KILL YOU.
WHATEVER THE HELL YOU ARE!
YOU CAN'T.
AAARR--!
KRRAKKKL

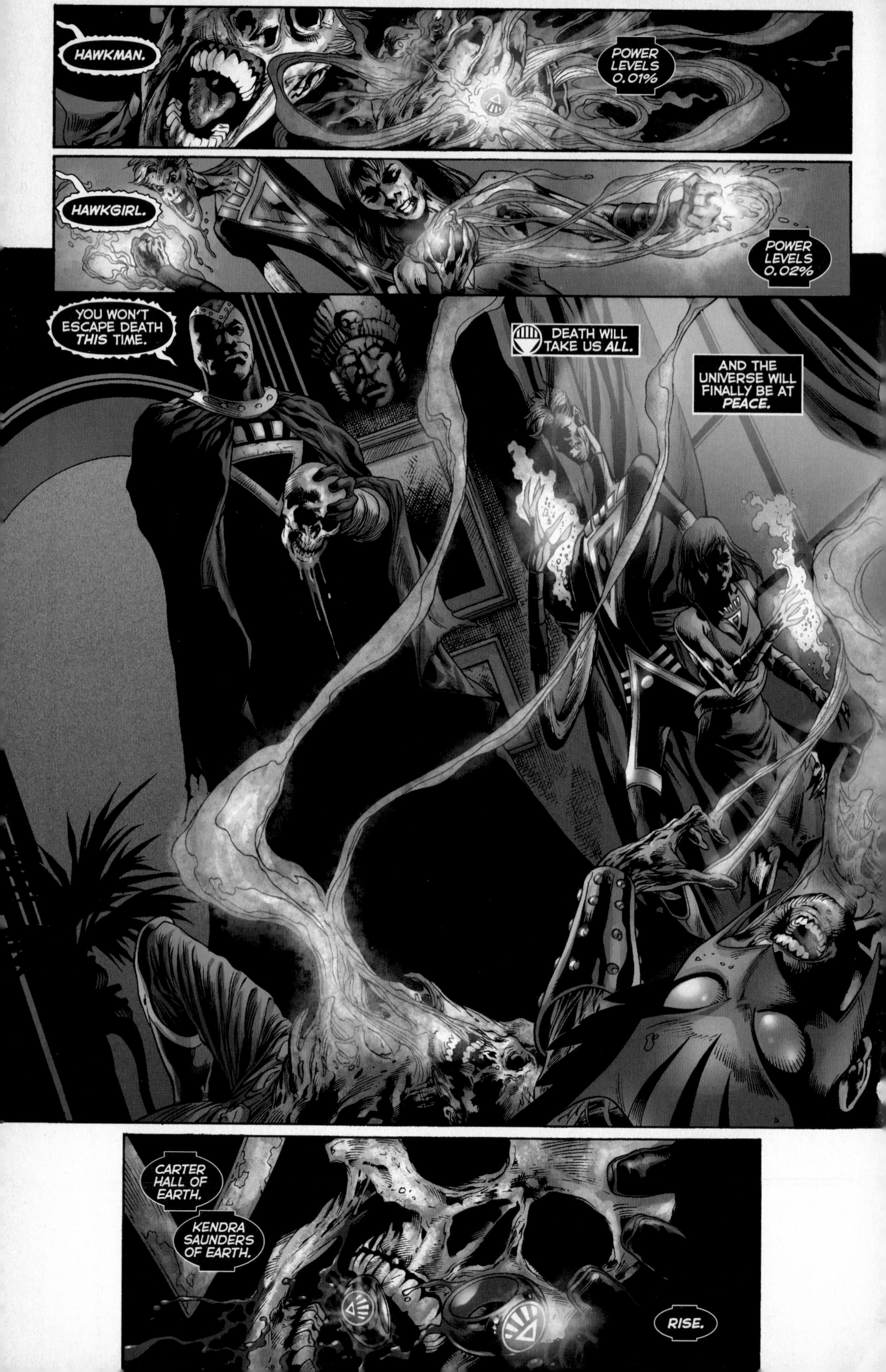
HAWKMAN.
POWER LEVELS 0.01%
HAWKGIRL.
POWER LEVELS 0.02%
YOU WON'T ESCAPE DEATH THIS TIME.
DEATH WILL TAKE US ALL.
AND THE UNIVERSE WILL FINALLY BE AT PEACE.
CARTER HALL OF EARTH.
KENDRA SAUNDERS OF EARTH.
RISE.

PART TWO

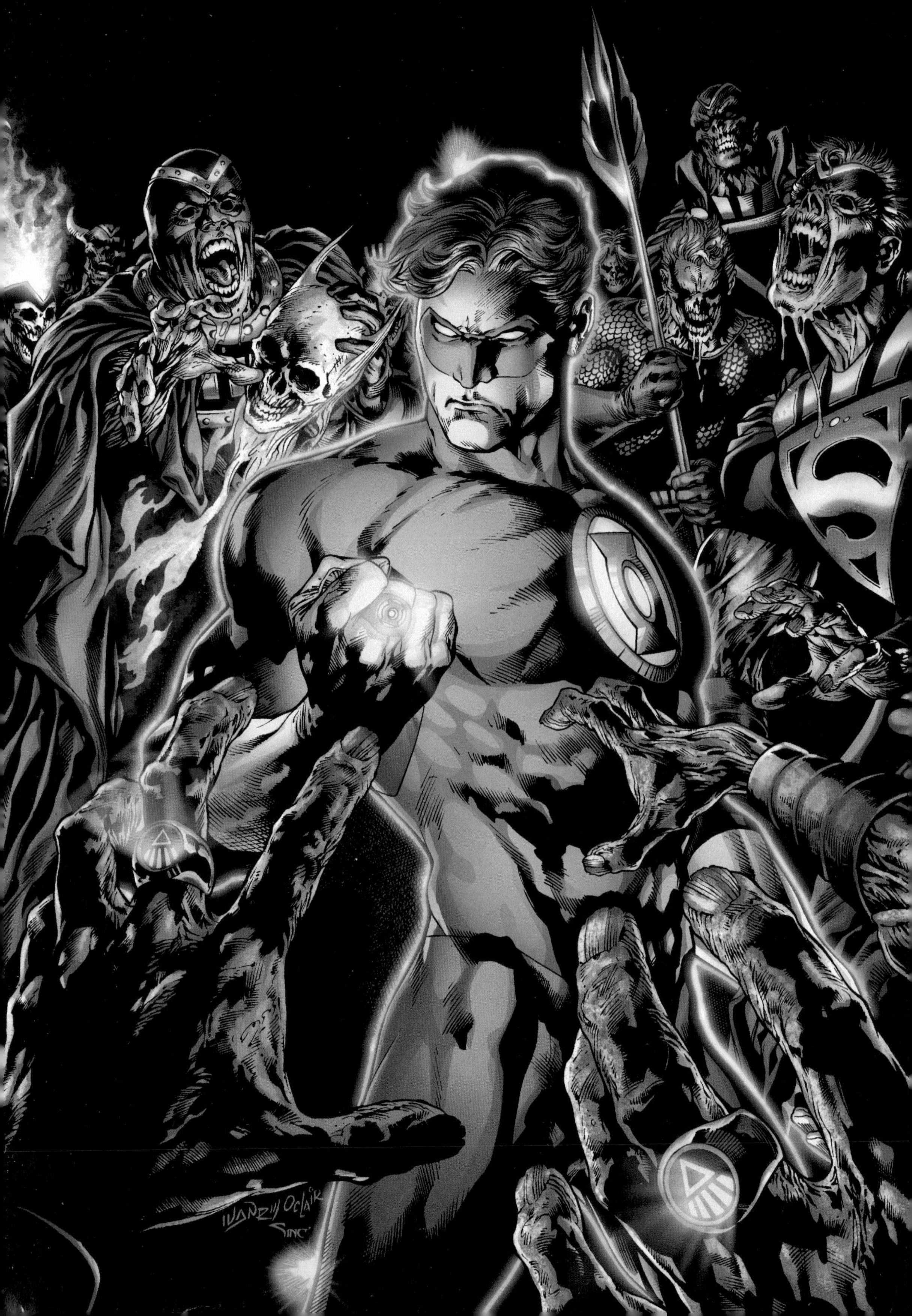

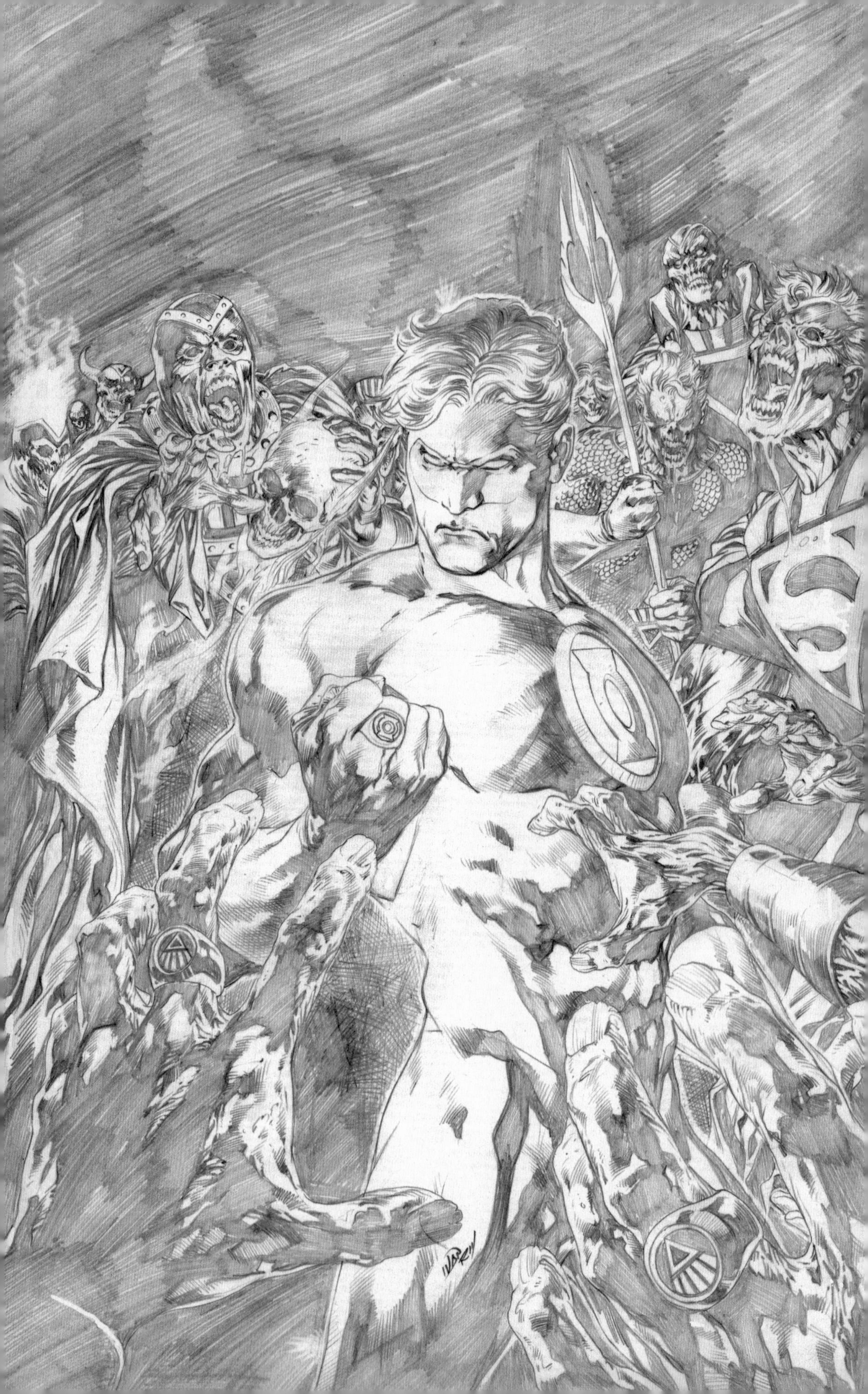

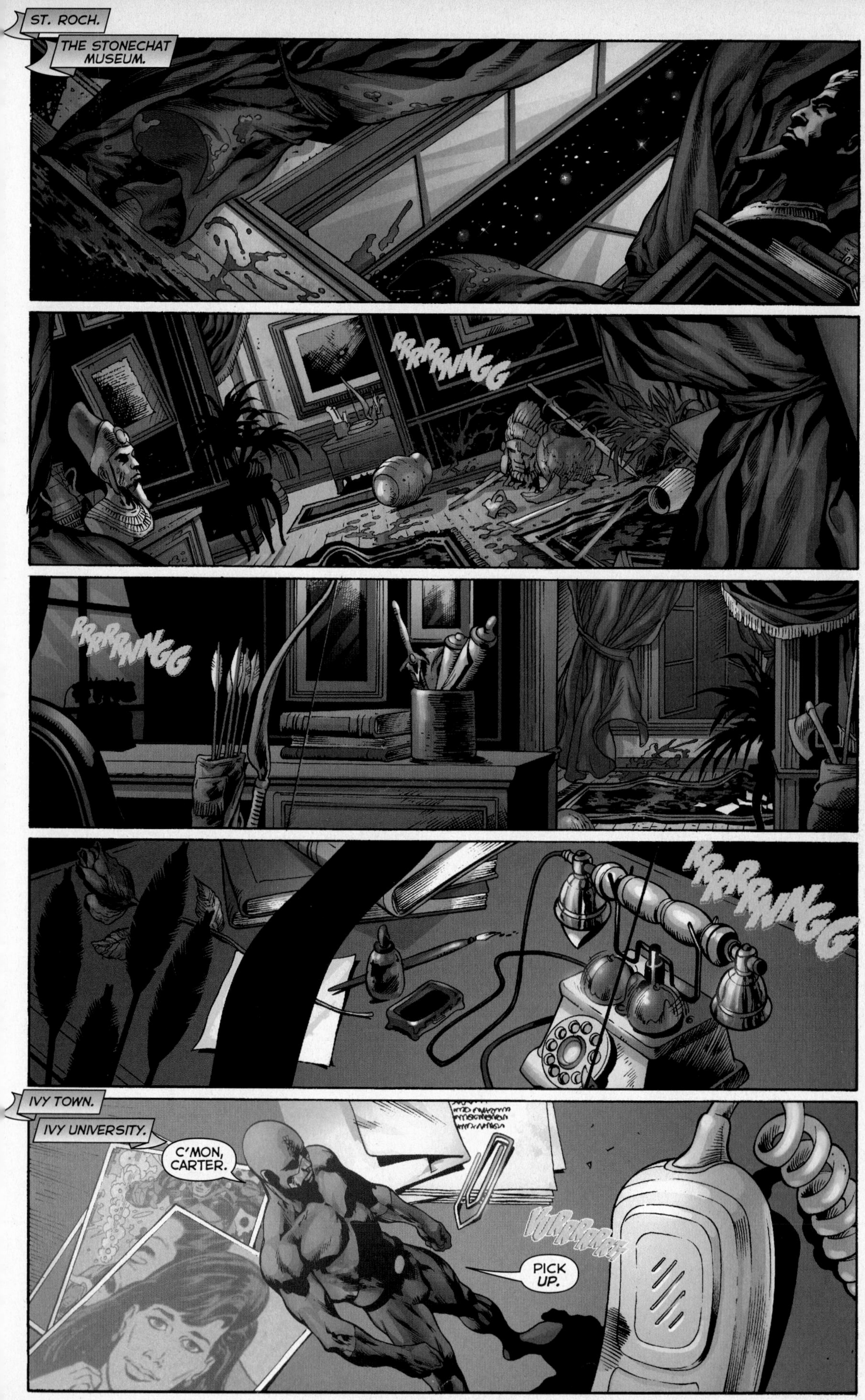
ST. ROCH.
THE STONECHAT MUSEUM.
RRRRRNNGG
RRRRRNNGG
RRRRRNNGG
IVY TOWN.
IVY UNIVERSITY.
C'MON, CARTER.
VURRRRRRR
PICK UP.

KA-KLIK

...HELLO?

HELLO. RAY.

CARTER?

CARTER, PLEASE HEAR ME OUT BEFORE YOU HANG UP AGAIN.

I KNOW IT DOESN'T MAKE ANY SEMBLANCE OF *LOGIC*, BUT EVEN AFTER EVERYTHING JEAN DID I CAN'T STOP THINKING ABOUT HER.

AND WHEN I THINK OF HER, I THINK OF THIS GIRL, THIS BEAUTIFUL, SMART AND WITTY GIRL, THAT WAS *WAY* OUT OF MY LEAGUE SAYING "YES" AS I PROPOSED.

AFTER DEDICATING MY LIFE TO FIGURING OUT HOW THE UNIVERSE WORKS, FOR THAT ONE MOMENT, I THOUGHT I HAD. I THOUGHT I FOUND THE ANSWER TO *WHY* I WAS REALLY HERE.

HOW DID YOU LET KENDRA GO?

...CARTER?

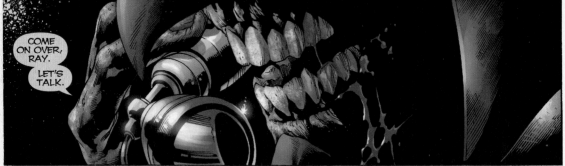

COME ON OVER, RAY.

LET'S TALK.

I'LL BE RIGHT THERE.

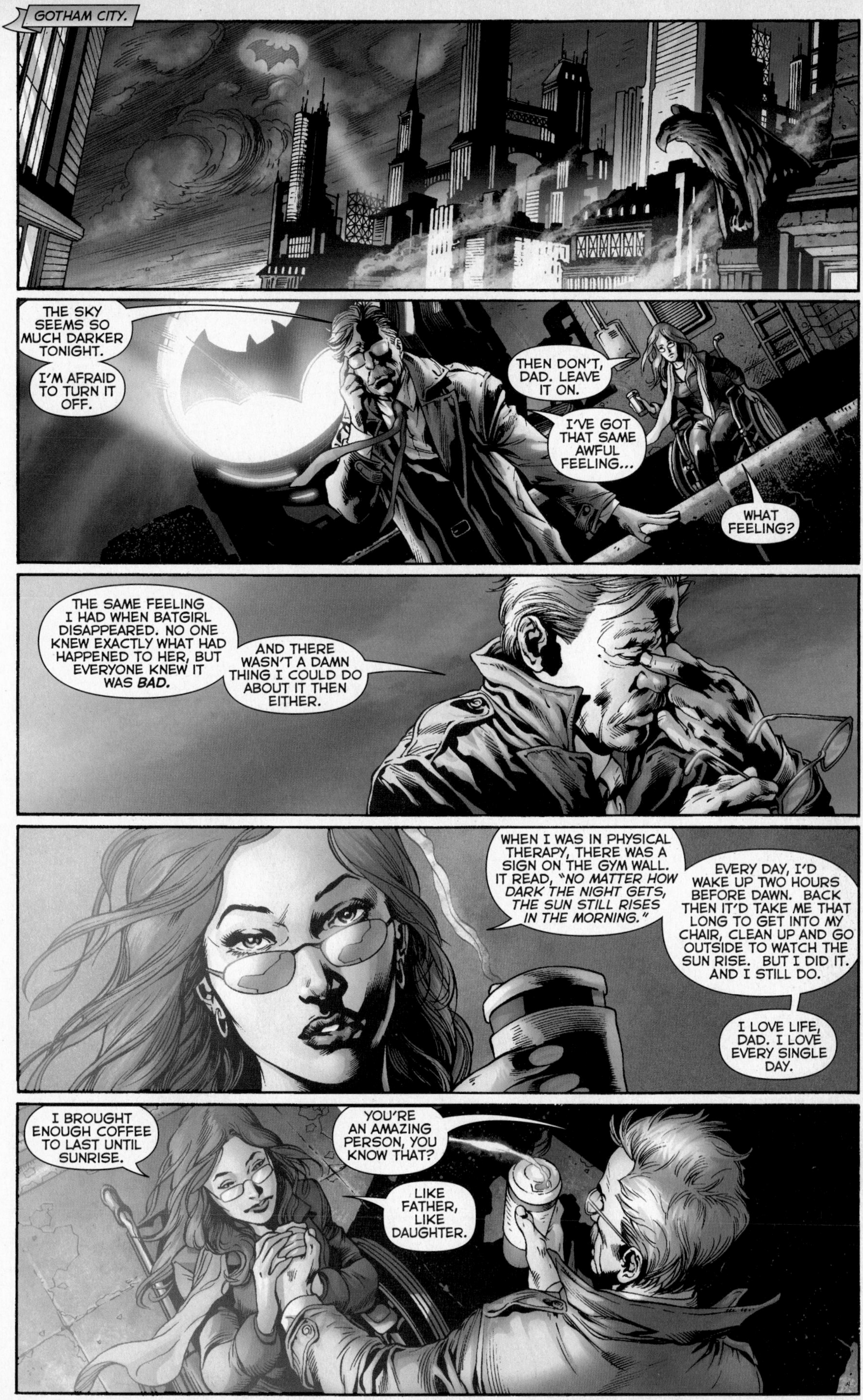
GOTHAM CITY.
THE SKY SEEMS SO MUCH DARKER TONIGHT.
I'M AFRAID TO TURN IT OFF.
THEN DON'T, DAD. LEAVE IT ON.
I'VE GOT THAT SAME AWFUL FEELING...
WHAT FEELING?
THE SAME FEELING I HAD WHEN BATGIRL DISAPPEARED. NO ONE KNEW EXACTLY WHAT HAD HAPPENED TO HER, BUT EVERYONE KNEW IT WAS *BAD.*
AND THERE WASN'T A DAMN THING I COULD DO ABOUT IT THEN EITHER.
WHEN I WAS IN PHYSICAL THERAPY, THERE WAS A SIGN ON THE GYM WALL. IT READ, *"NO MATTER HOW DARK THE NIGHT GETS, THE SUN STILL RISES IN THE MORNING."*
EVERY DAY, I'D WAKE UP TWO HOURS BEFORE DAWN. BACK THEN IT'D TAKE ME THAT LONG TO GET INTO MY CHAIR, CLEAN UP AND GO OUTSIDE TO WATCH THE SUN RISE. BUT I DID IT. AND I STILL DO.
I LOVE LIFE, DAD. I LOVE EVERY SINGLE DAY.
I BROUGHT ENOUGH COFFEE TO LAST UNTIL SUNRISE.
YOU'RE AN AMAZING PERSON, YOU KNOW THAT?
LIKE FATHER, LIKE DAUGHTER.

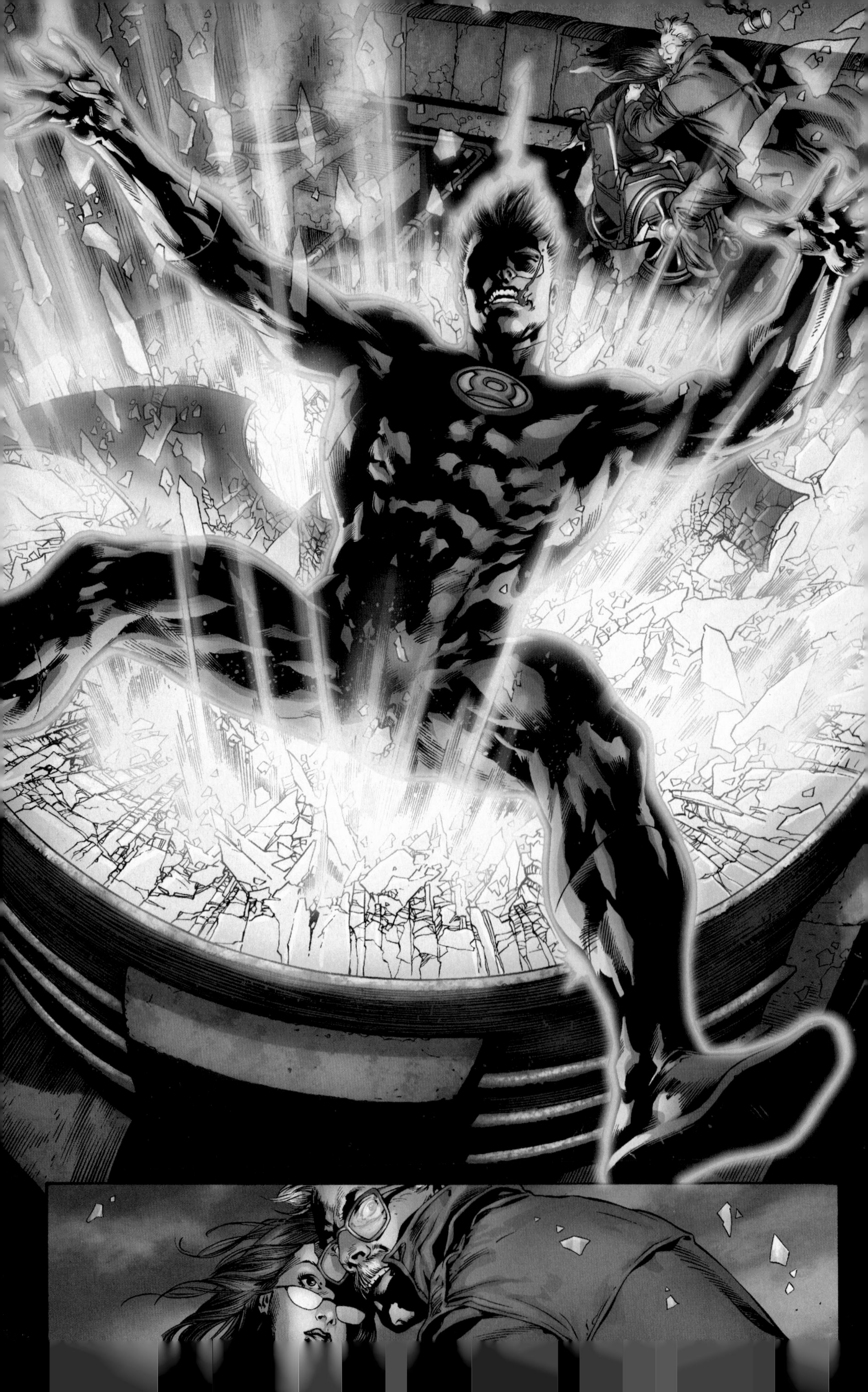

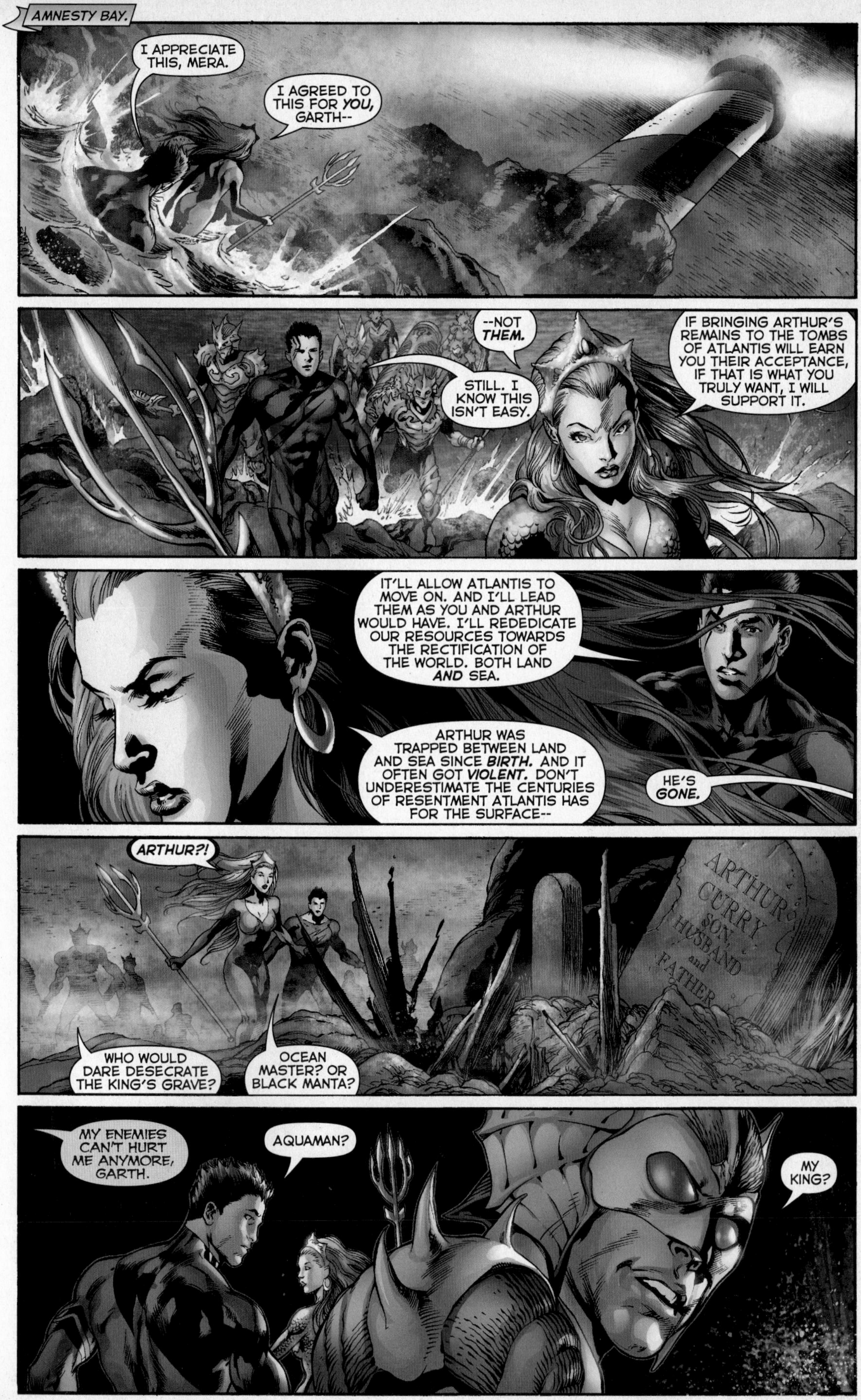
AMNESTY BAY.
I APPRECIATE THIS, MERA.
I AGREED TO THIS FOR YOU, GARTH--
--NOT THEM.
STILL. I KNOW THIS ISN'T EASY.
IF BRINGING ARTHUR'S REMAINS TO THE TOMBS OF ATLANTIS WILL EARN YOU THEIR ACCEPTANCE, IF THAT IS WHAT YOU TRULY WANT, I WILL SUPPORT IT.
IT'LL ALLOW ATLANTIS TO MOVE ON. AND I'LL LEAD THEM AS YOU AND ARTHUR WOULD HAVE. I'LL REDEDICATE OUR RESOURCES TOWARDS THE RECTIFICATION OF THE WORLD. BOTH LAND AND SEA.
ARTHUR WAS TRAPPED BETWEEN LAND AND SEA SINCE BIRTH. AND IT OFTEN GOT VIOLENT. DON'T UNDERESTIMATE THE CENTURIES OF RESENTMENT ATLANTIS HAS FOR THE SURFACE--
HE'S GONE.
ARTHUR?!
ARTHUR CURRY SON, HUSBAND and FATHER
WHO WOULD DARE DESECRATE THE KING'S GRAVE?
OCEAN MASTER? OR BLACK MANTA?
MY ENEMIES CAN'T HURT ME ANYMORE, GARTH.
AQUAMAN?
MY KING?

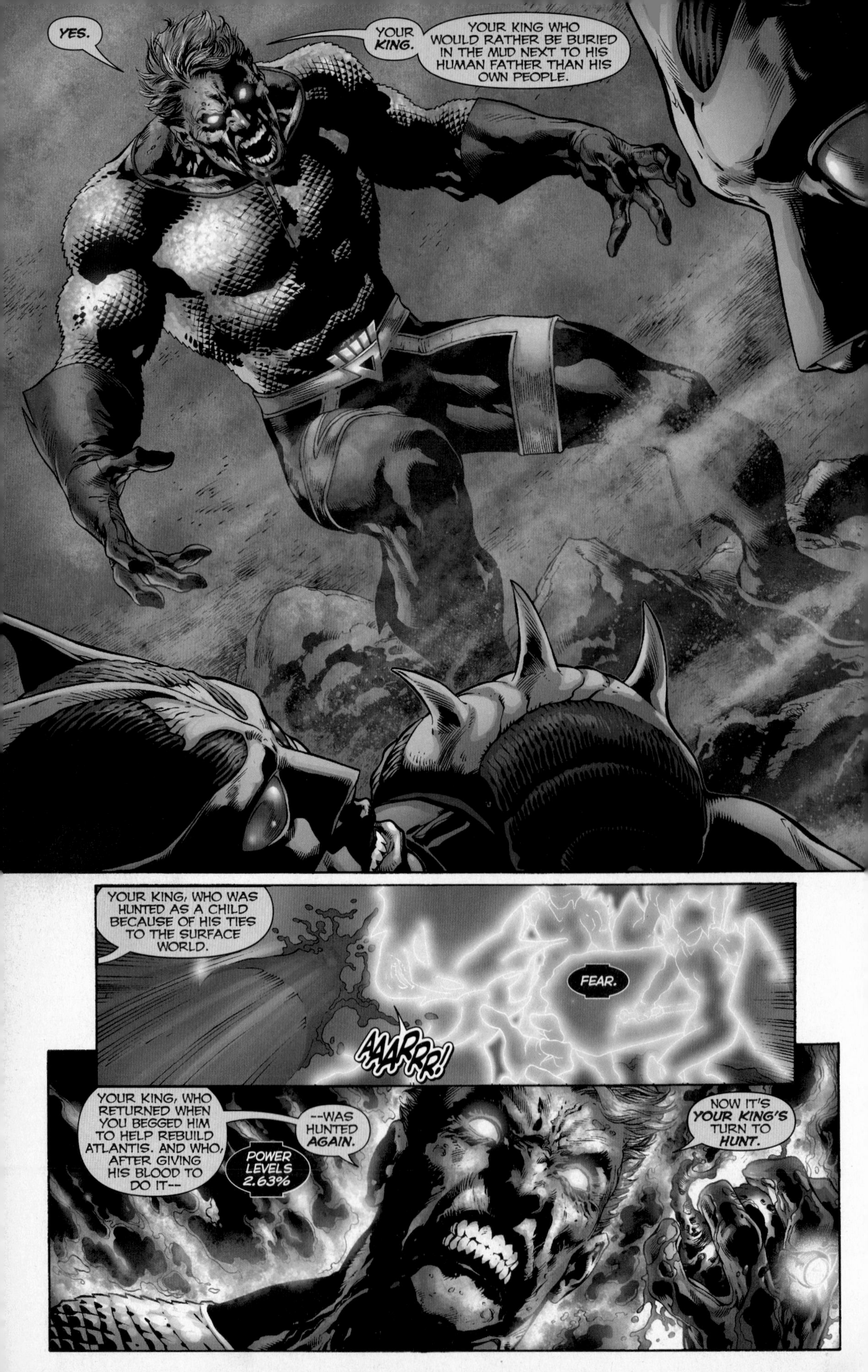
YES.
YOUR KING.
YOUR KING WHO WOULD RATHER BE BURIED IN THE MUD NEXT TO HIS HUMAN FATHER THAN HIS OWN PEOPLE.
YOUR KING, WHO WAS HUNTED AS A CHILD BECAUSE OF HIS TIES TO THE SURFACE WORLD.
FEAR.
AAARRR!
YOUR KING, WHO RETURNED WHEN YOU BEGGED HIM TO HELP REBUILD ATLANTIS. AND WHO, AFTER GIVING HIS BLOOD TO DO IT--
--WAS HUNTED AGAIN.
POWER LEVELS 2.63%
NOW IT'S YOUR KING'S TURN TO HUNT.

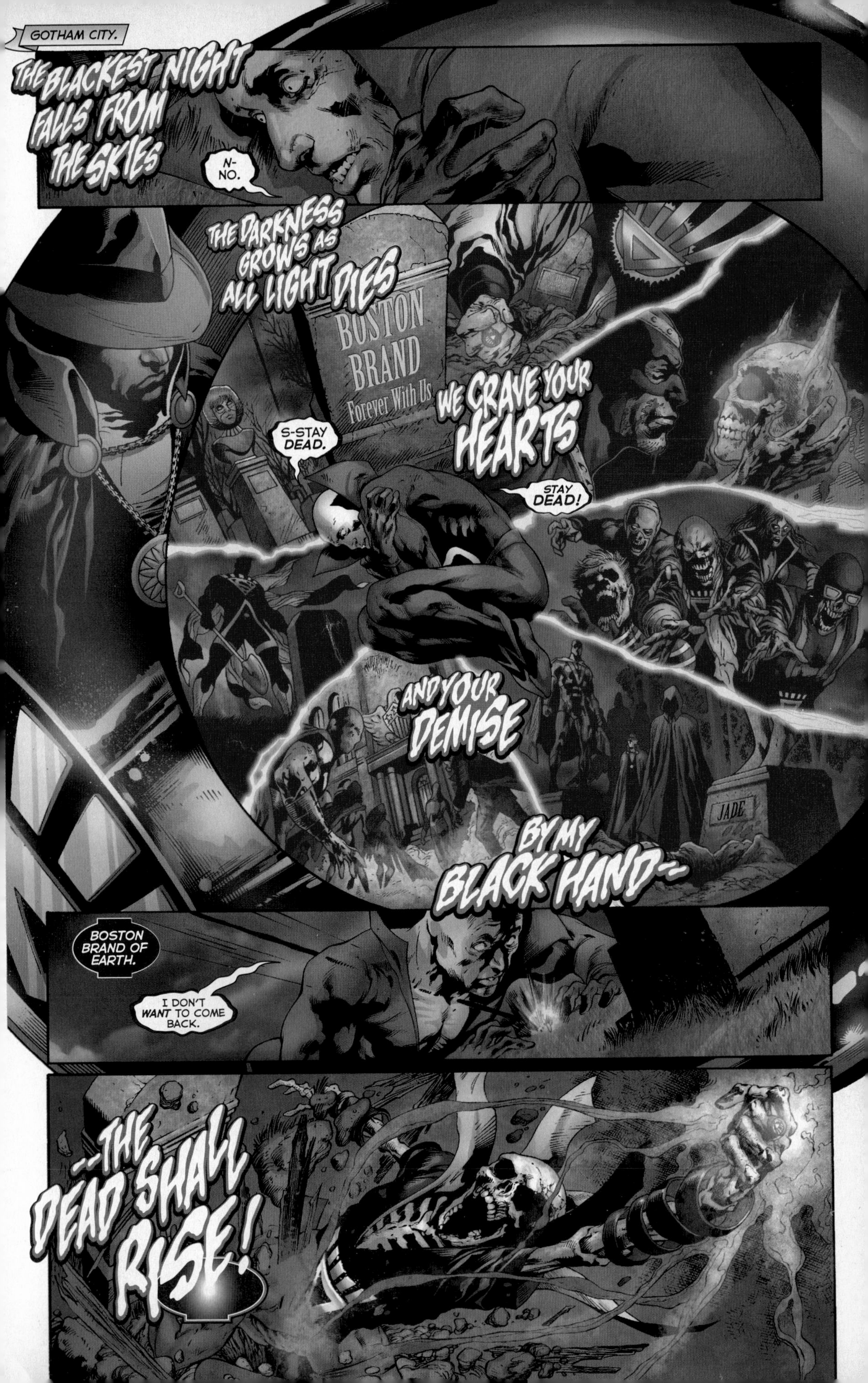
GOTHAM CITY.
THE BLACKEST NIGHT FALLS FROM THE SKIES
N-NO.
THE DARKNESS GROWS AS ALL LIGHT DIES
BOSTON BRAND Forever With Us
WE CRAVE YOUR HEARTS
S-STAY DEAD.
STAY DEAD!
AND YOUR DEMISE
JADE
BY MY BLACK HAND--
BOSTON BRAND OF EARTH.
I DON'T WANT TO COME BACK.
--THE DEAD SHALL RISE!

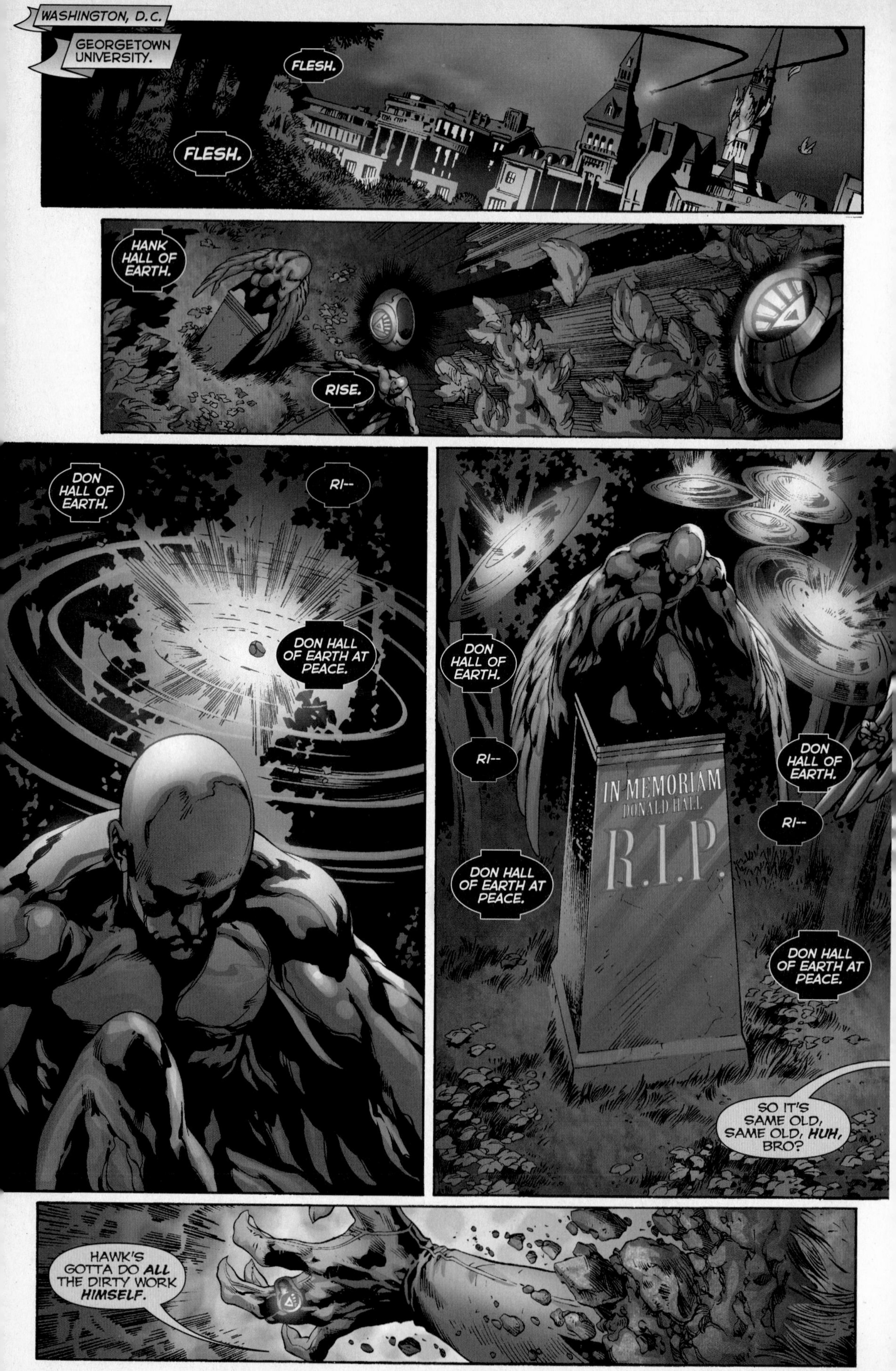
WASHINGTON, D.C.
GEORGETOWN UNIVERSITY.
FLESH.
FLESH.
HANK HALL OF EARTH.
RISE.
DON HALL OF EARTH.
RI--
DON HALL OF EARTH AT PEACE.
DON HALL OF EARTH.
RI--
IN MEMORIAM
DONALD HALL
R.I.P.
DON HALL OF EARTH AT PEACE.
DON HALL OF EARTH.
RI--
DON HALL OF EARTH AT PEACE.
SO IT'S SAME OLD, SAME OLD, *HUH,* BRO?
HAWK'S GOTTA DO **ALL** THE DIRTY WORK ***HIMSELF.***

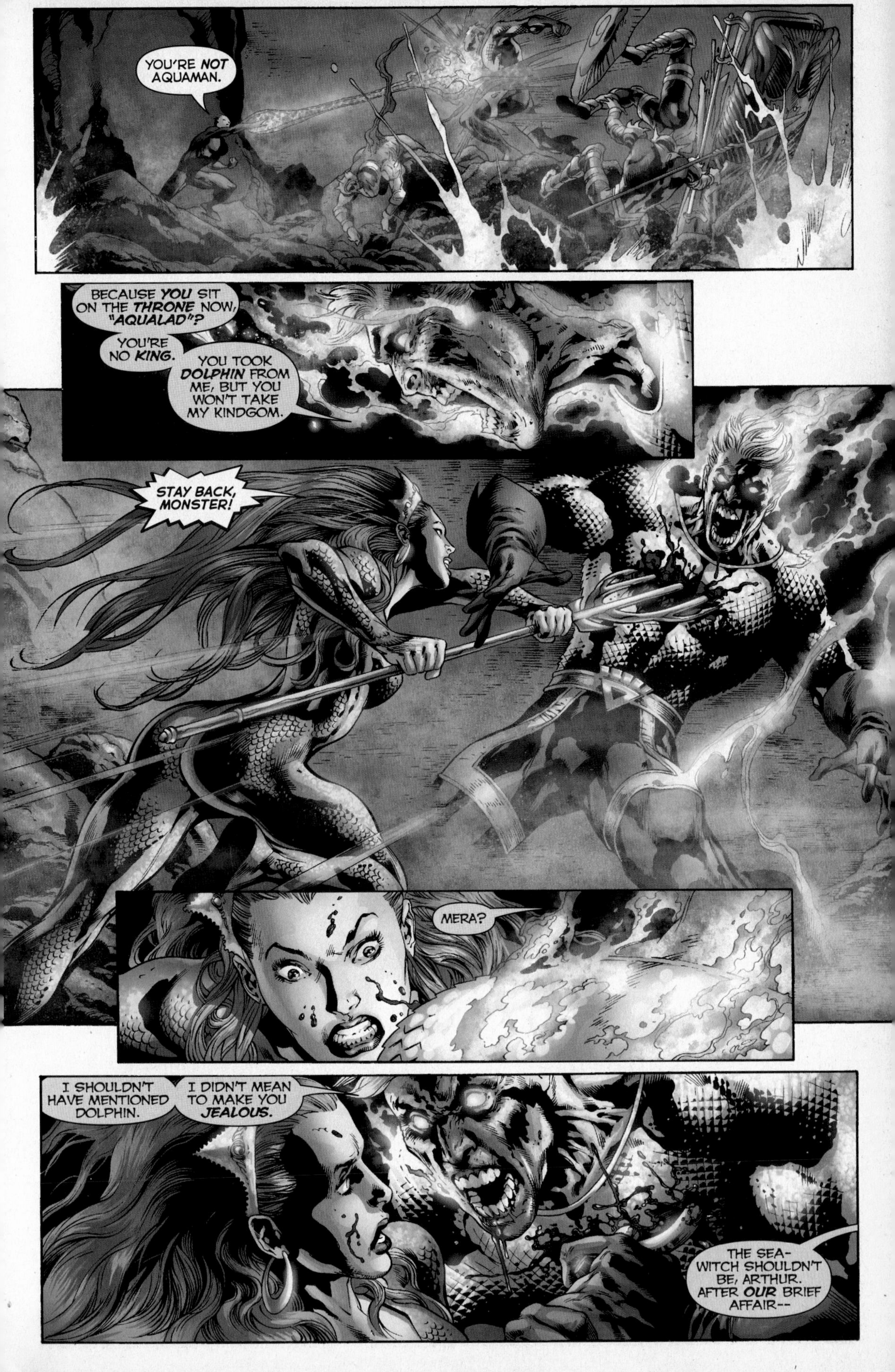
YOU'RE *NOT* AQUAMAN.
BECAUSE *YOU* SIT ON THE *THRONE* NOW, *"AQUALAD"*?
YOU'RE NO *KING*.
YOU TOOK *DOLPHIN* FROM ME, BUT YOU WON'T TAKE MY KINDGOM.
STAY BACK, MONSTER!
MERA?
I SHOULDN'T HAVE MENTIONED DOLPHIN.
I DIDN'T MEAN TO MAKE YOU *JEALOUS*.
THE SEA-WITCH SHOULDN'T BE, ARTHUR. AFTER *OUR* BRIEF AFFAIR--

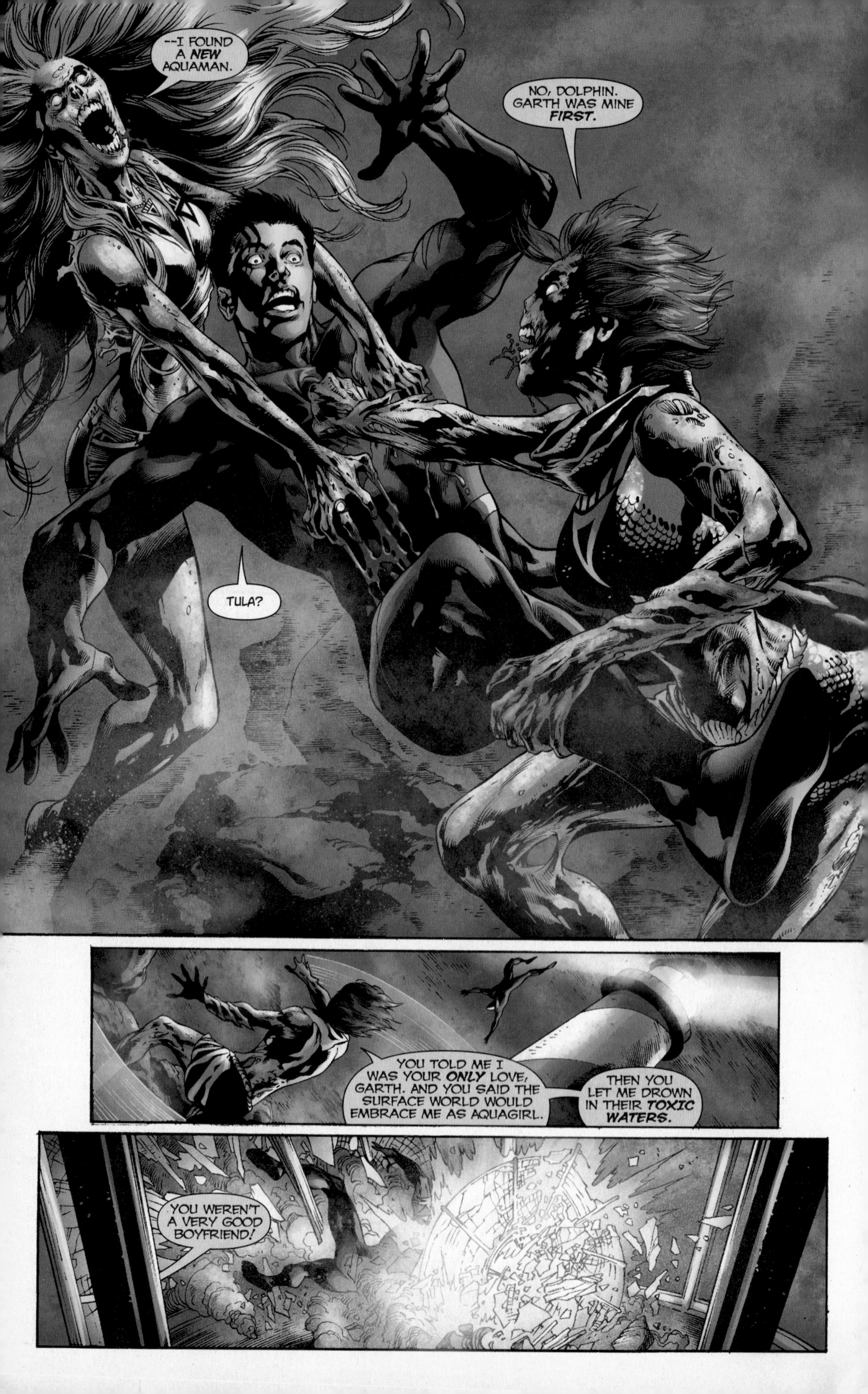
--I FOUND A *NEW* AQUAMAN.
NO, DOLPHIN. GARTH WAS MINE ***FIRST.***
TULA?
YOU TOLD ME I WAS YOUR ***ONLY*** LOVE, GARTH. AND YOU SAID THE SURFACE WORLD WOULD EMBRACE ME AS AQUAGIRL.
THEN YOU LET ME DROWN IN THEIR ***TOXIC WATERS.***
YOU WEREN'T A VERY GOOD BOYFRIEND!

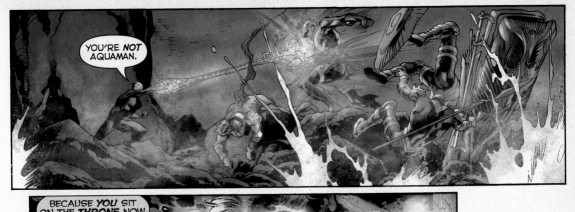

YOU'RE *NOT* AQUAMAN.

BECAUSE *YOU* SIT ON THE *THRONE* NOW, "AQUALAD"?

YOU'RE NO *KING.*

YOU TOOK *DOLPHIN* FROM ME, BUT YOU WON'T TAKE MY KINDGOM.

STAY BACK, MONSTER!

MERA?

I SHOULDN'T HAVE MENTIONED DOLPHIN.

I DIDN'T MEAN TO MAKE YOU *JEALOUS.*

THE SEA-WITCH SHOULDN'T BE, ARTHUR. AFTER *OUR* BRIEF AFFAIR--

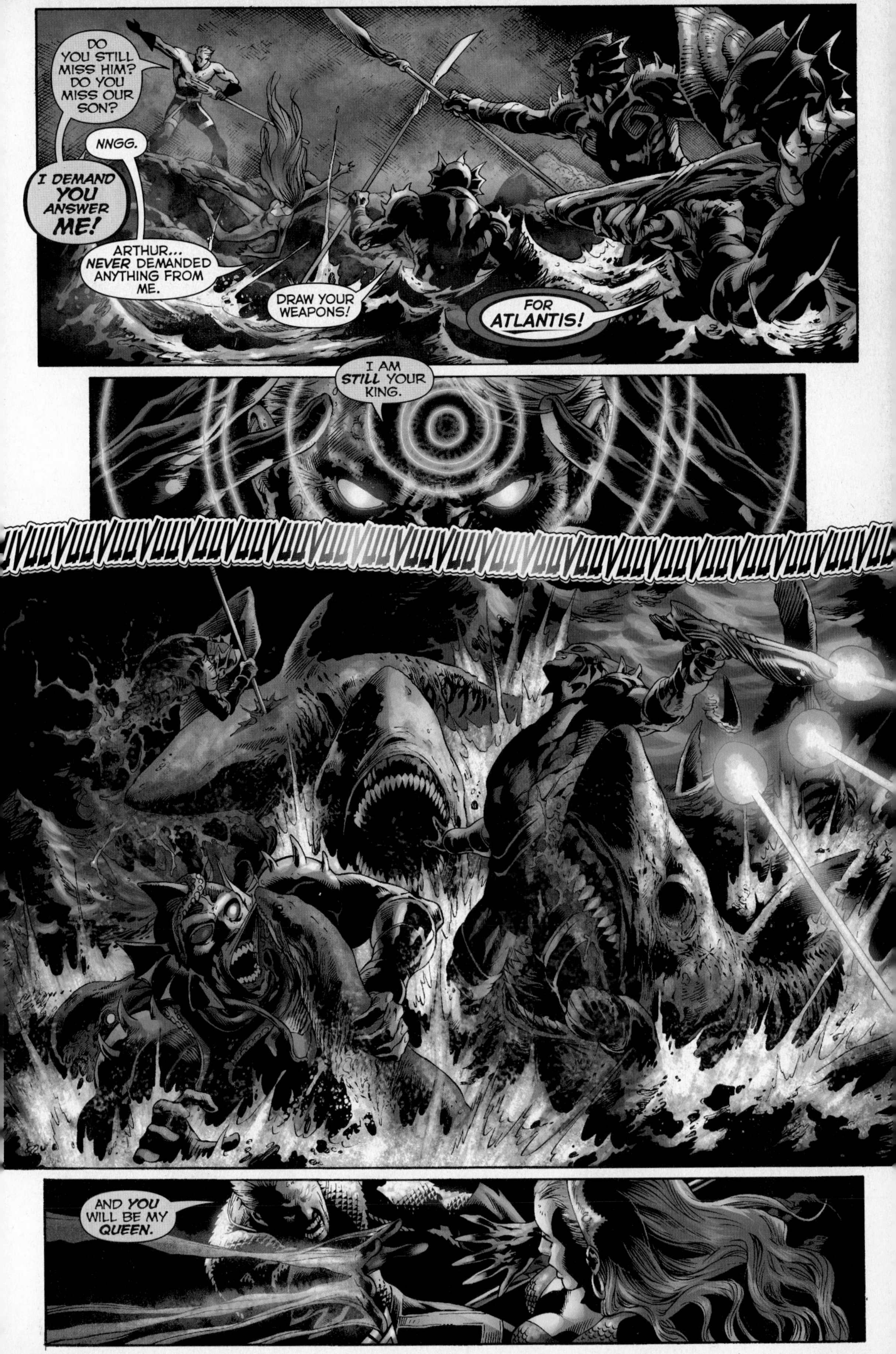
DO YOU STILL MISS HIM? DO YOU MISS OUR SON?
NNGG.
I DEMAND YOU ANSWER ME!
ARTHUR... NEVER DEMANDED ANYTHING FROM ME.
DRAW YOUR WEAPONS!
FOR ATLANTIS!
I AM STILL YOUR KING.
VUUVUUVUUVUUVUUVUUVUUVUUVUUVUUVUUVUUVUUVUUVUUVUUVUUVU
AND YOU WILL BE MY QUEEN.

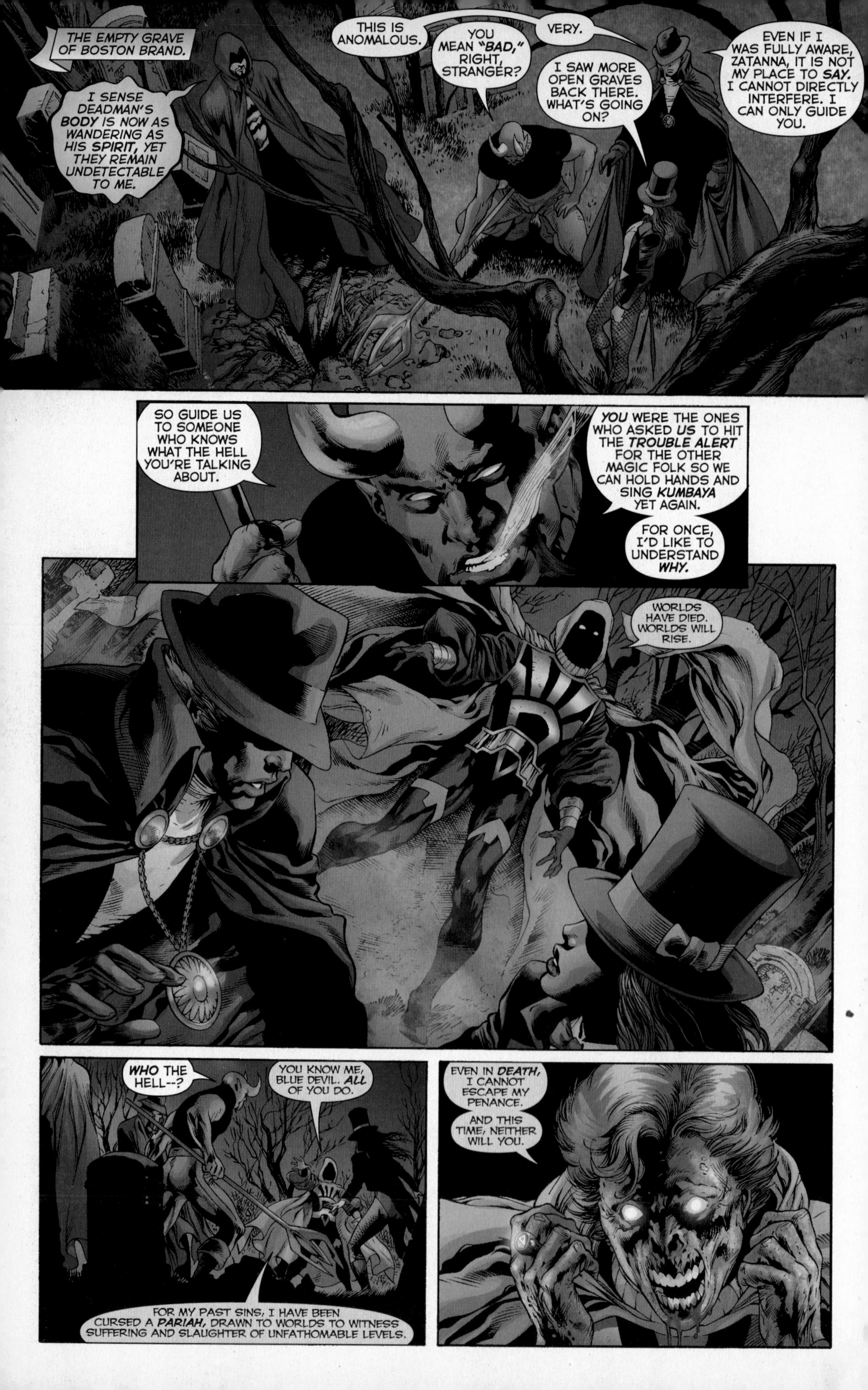
THE EMPTY GRAVE OF BOSTON BRAND.
I SENSE DEADMAN'S BODY IS NOW AS WANDERING AS HIS SPIRIT, YET THEY REMAIN UNDETECTABLE TO ME.
THIS IS ANOMALOUS.
VERY.
YOU MEAN "BAD," RIGHT, STRANGER?
I SAW MORE OPEN GRAVES BACK THERE. WHAT'S GOING ON?
EVEN IF I WAS FULLY AWARE, ZATANNA, IT IS NOT MY PLACE TO SAY. I CANNOT DIRECTLY INTERFERE. I CAN ONLY GUIDE YOU.
SO GUIDE US TO SOMEONE WHO KNOWS WHAT THE HELL YOU'RE TALKING ABOUT.
YOU WERE THE ONES WHO ASKED US TO HIT THE TROUBLE ALERT FOR THE OTHER MAGIC FOLK SO WE CAN HOLD HANDS AND SING KUMBAYA YET AGAIN.
FOR ONCE, I'D LIKE TO UNDERSTAND WHY.
WORLDS HAVE DIED. WORLDS WILL RISE.
WHO THE HELL--?
YOU KNOW ME, BLUE DEVIL. ALL OF YOU DO.
FOR MY PAST SINS, I HAVE BEEN CURSED A PARIAH, DRAWN TO WORLDS TO WITNESS SUFFERING AND SLAUGHTER OF UNFATHOMABLE LEVELS.
EVEN IN DEATH, I CANNOT ESCAPE MY PENANCE.
AND THIS TIME, NEITHER WILL YOU.

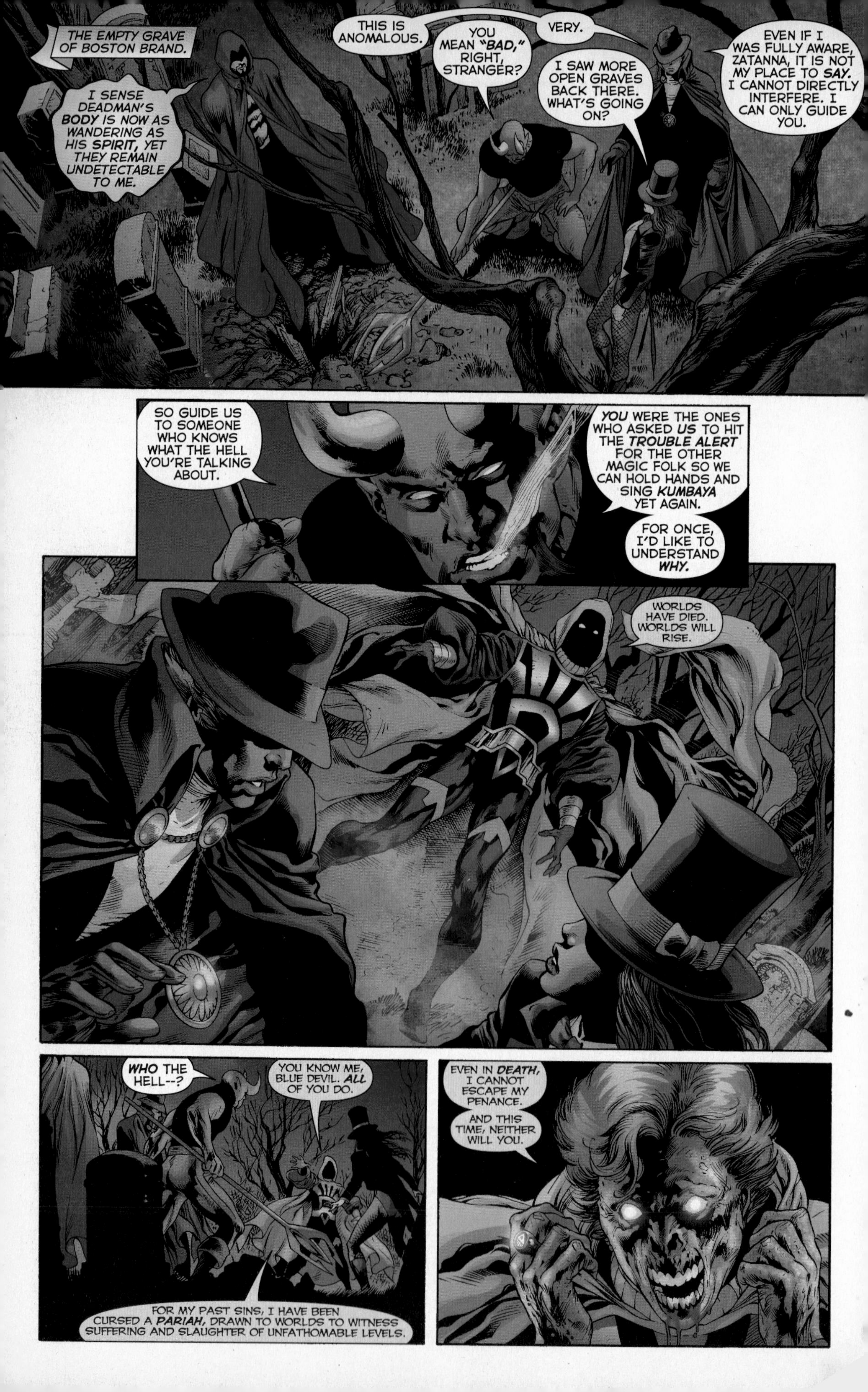

THE EMPTY GRAVE OF BOSTON BRAND.
I SENSE DEADMAN'S BODY IS NOW AS WANDERING AS HIS SPIRIT, YET THEY REMAIN UNDETECTABLE TO ME.
THIS IS ANOMALOUS.
YOU MEAN "BAD," RIGHT, STRANGER?
VERY.
I SAW MORE OPEN GRAVES BACK THERE. WHAT'S GOING ON?
EVEN IF I WAS FULLY AWARE, ZATANNA, IT IS NOT MY PLACE TO SAY. I CANNOT DIRECTLY INTERFERE. I CAN ONLY GUIDE YOU.
SO GUIDE US TO SOMEONE WHO KNOWS WHAT THE HELL YOU'RE TALKING ABOUT.
YOU WERE THE ONES WHO ASKED US TO HIT THE TROUBLE ALERT FOR THE OTHER MAGIC FOLK SO WE CAN HOLD HANDS AND SING KUMBAYA YET AGAIN.
FOR ONCE, I'D LIKE TO UNDERSTAND WHY.
WORLDS HAVE DIED. WORLDS WILL RISE.
WHO THE HELL--?
YOU KNOW ME, BLUE DEVIL. ALL OF YOU DO.
FOR MY PAST SINS, I HAVE BEEN CURSED A PARIAH, DRAWN TO WORLDS TO WITNESS SUFFERING AND SLAUGHTER OF UNFATHOMABLE LEVELS.
EVEN IN DEATH, I CANNOT ESCAPE MY PENANCE.
AND THIS TIME, NEITHER WILL YOU.

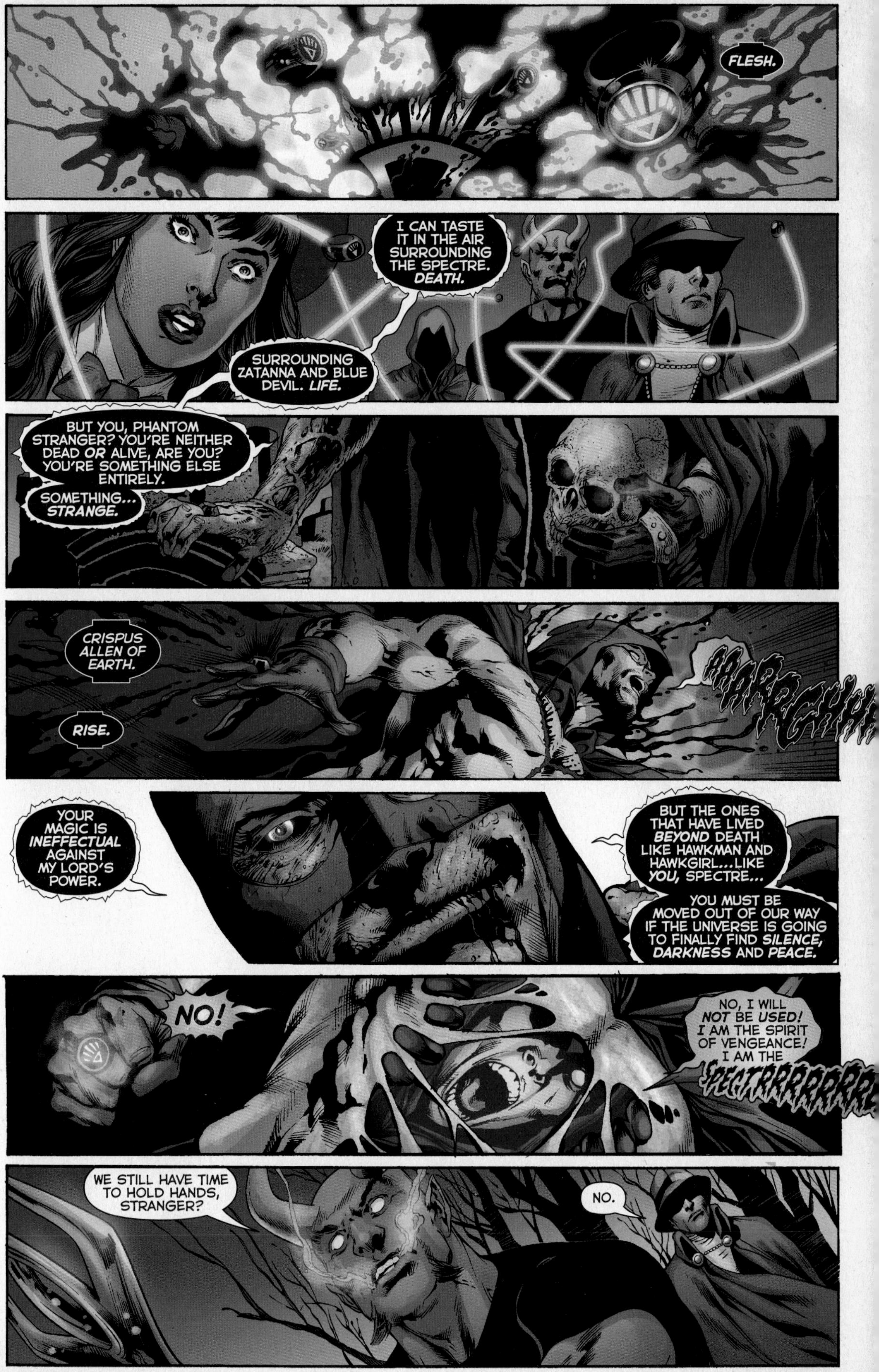
FLESH.
I CAN TASTE IT IN THE AIR SURROUNDING THE SPECTRE. DEATH.
SURROUNDING ZATANNA AND BLUE DEVIL. LIFE.
BUT YOU, PHANTOM STRANGER? YOU'RE NEITHER DEAD OR ALIVE, ARE YOU? YOU'RE SOMETHING ELSE ENTIRELY.
SOMETHING... STRANGE.
CRISPUS ALLEN OF EARTH.
RISE.
AAARRGHHH
YOUR MAGIC IS INEFFECTUAL AGAINST MY LORD'S POWER.
BUT THE ONES THAT HAVE LIVED BEYOND DEATH LIKE HAWKMAN AND HAWKGIRL...LIKE YOU, SPECTRE...
YOU MUST BE MOVED OUT OF OUR WAY IF THE UNIVERSE IS GOING TO FINALLY FIND SILENCE, DARKNESS AND PEACE.
NO!
NO, I WILL NOT BE USED! I AM THE SPIRIT OF VENGEANCE! I AM THE
SPECTRRRRRRRE
WE STILL HAVE TIME TO HOLD HANDS, STRANGER?
NO.

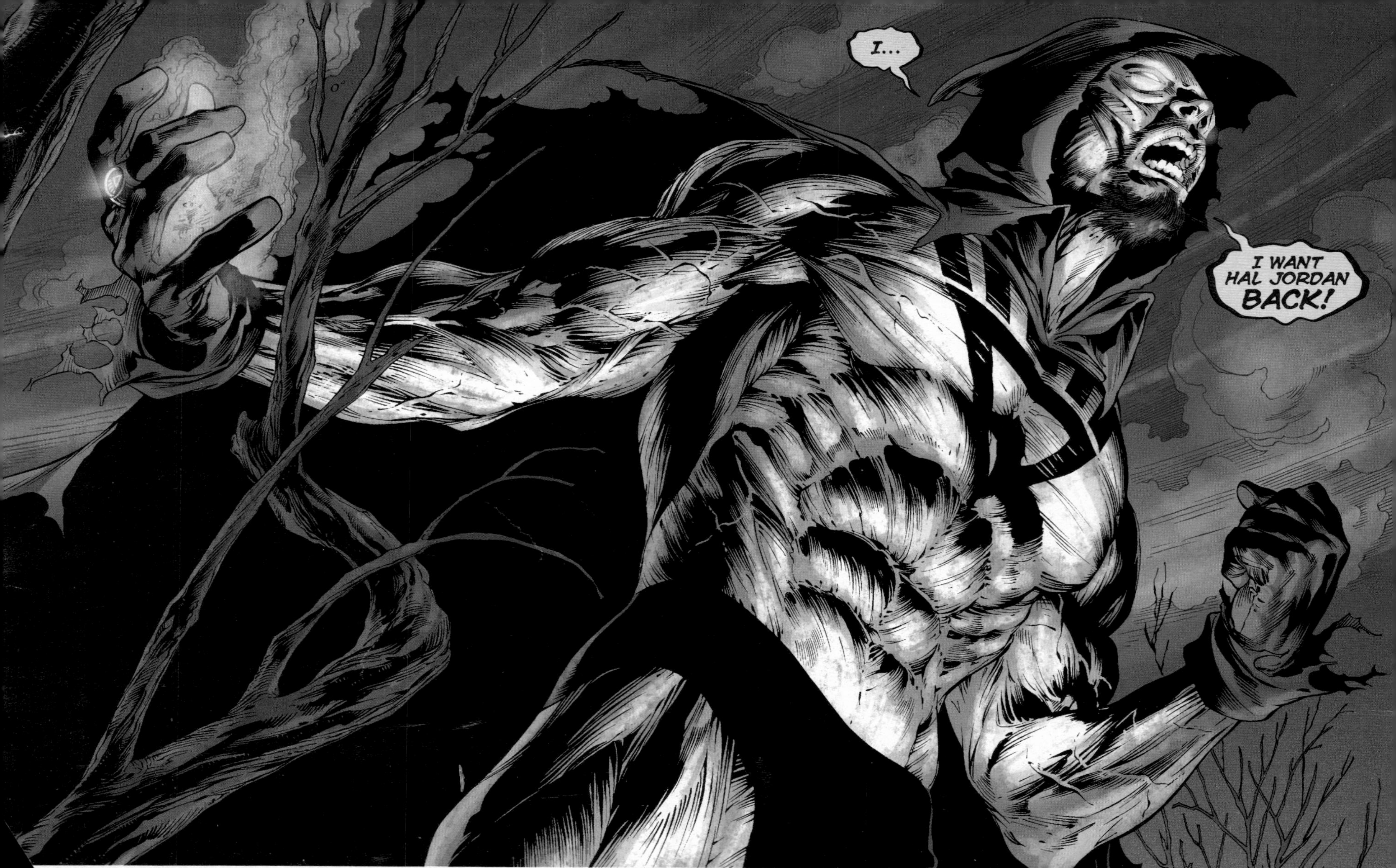
I...
I WANT HAL JORDAN BACK!

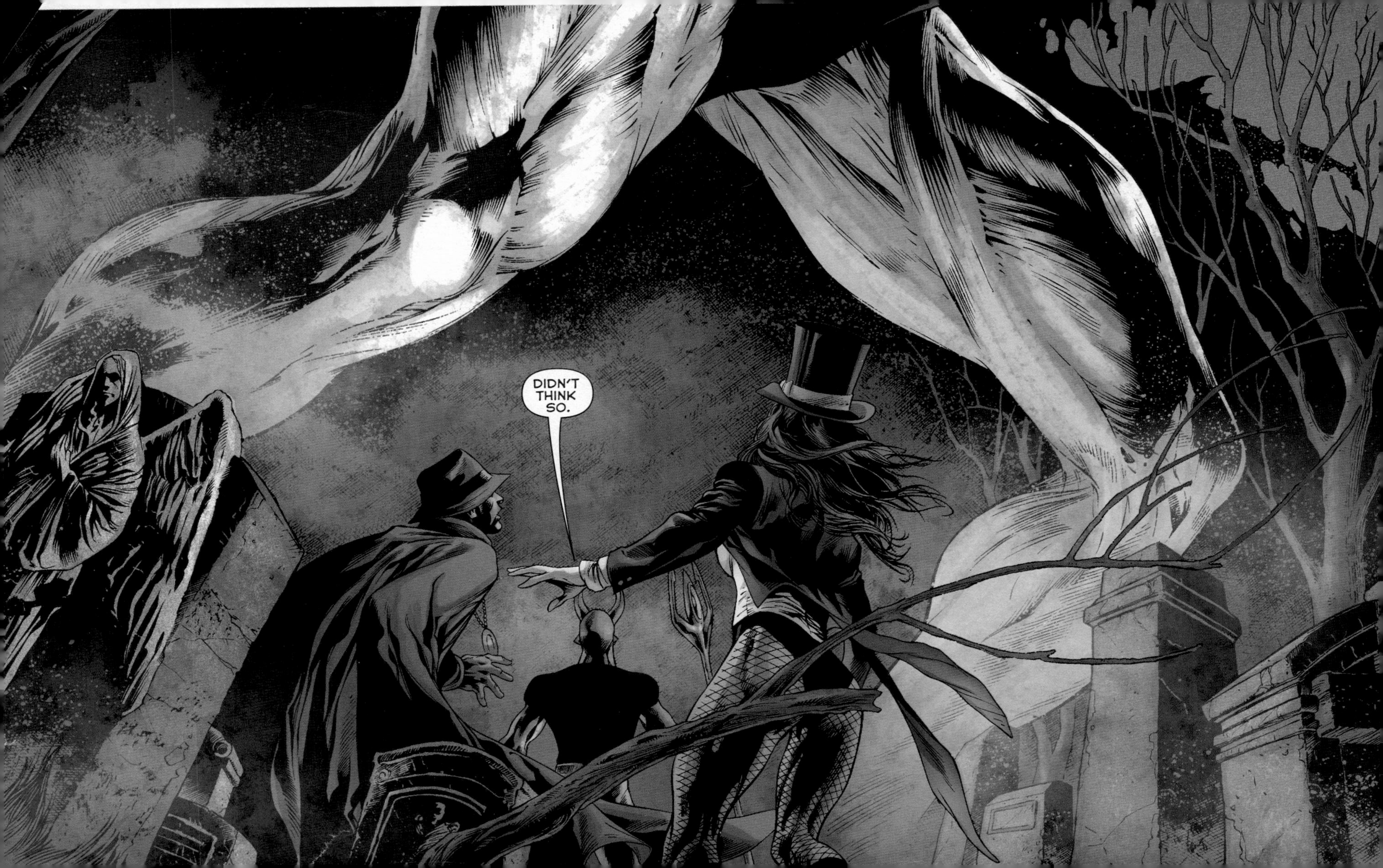
DIDN'T THINK SO.

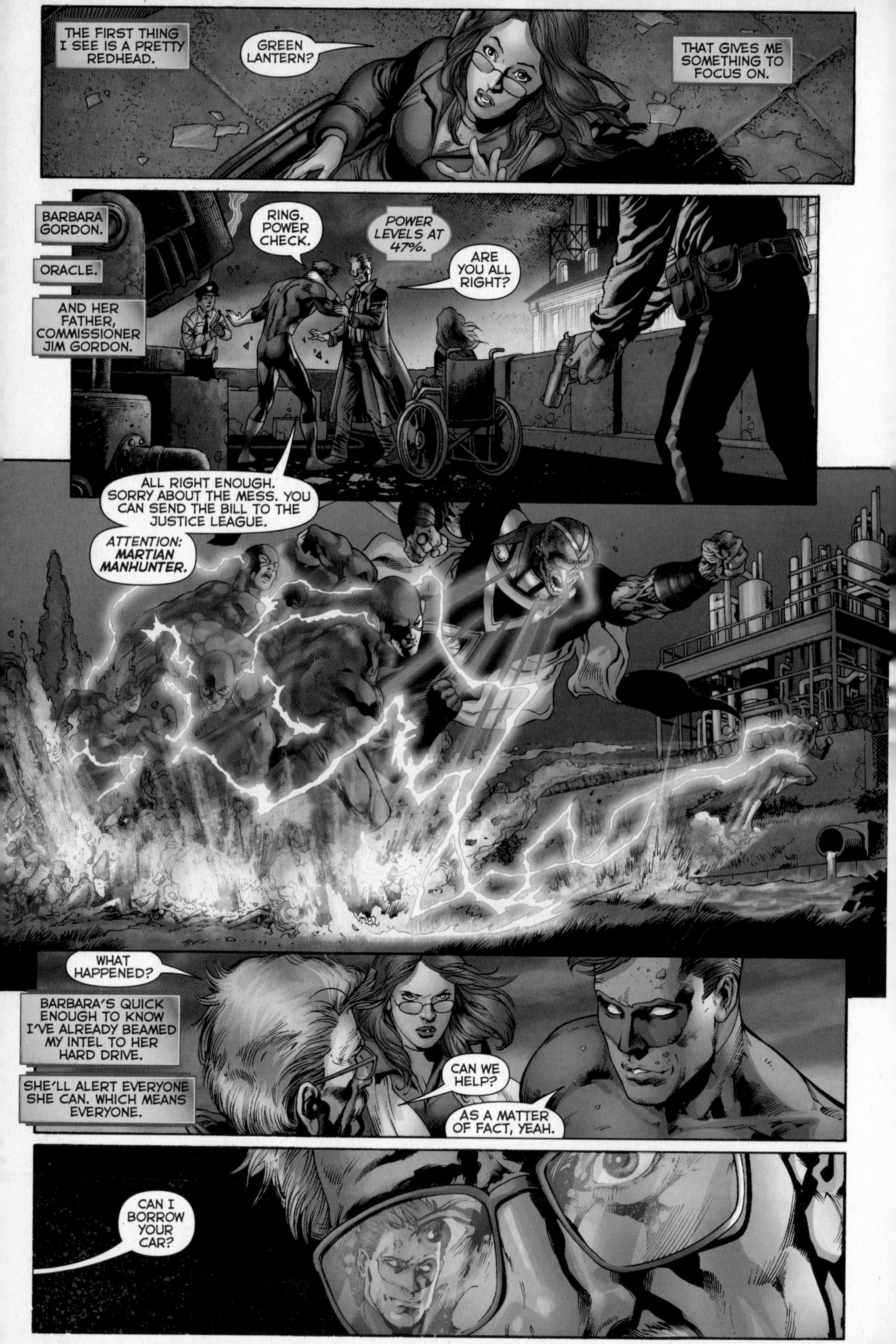

THE FIRST THING I SEE IS A PRETTY REDHEAD.
GREEN LANTERN?
THAT GIVES ME SOMETHING TO FOCUS ON.
BARBARA GORDON.
ORACLE.
AND HER FATHER, COMMISSIONER JIM GORDON.
RING. POWER CHECK.
POWER LEVELS AT 47%.
ARE YOU ALL RIGHT?
ALL RIGHT ENOUGH. SORRY ABOUT THE MESS. YOU CAN SEND THE BILL TO THE JUSTICE LEAGUE.
ATTENTION: MARTIAN MANHUNTER.
WHAT HAPPENED?
BARBARA'S QUICK ENOUGH TO KNOW I'VE ALREADY BEAMED MY INTEL TO HER HARD DRIVE.
SHE'LL ALERT EVERYONE SHE CAN. WHICH MEANS EVERYONE.
CAN WE HELP?
AS A MATTER OF FACT, YEAH.
CAN I BORROW YOUR CAR?

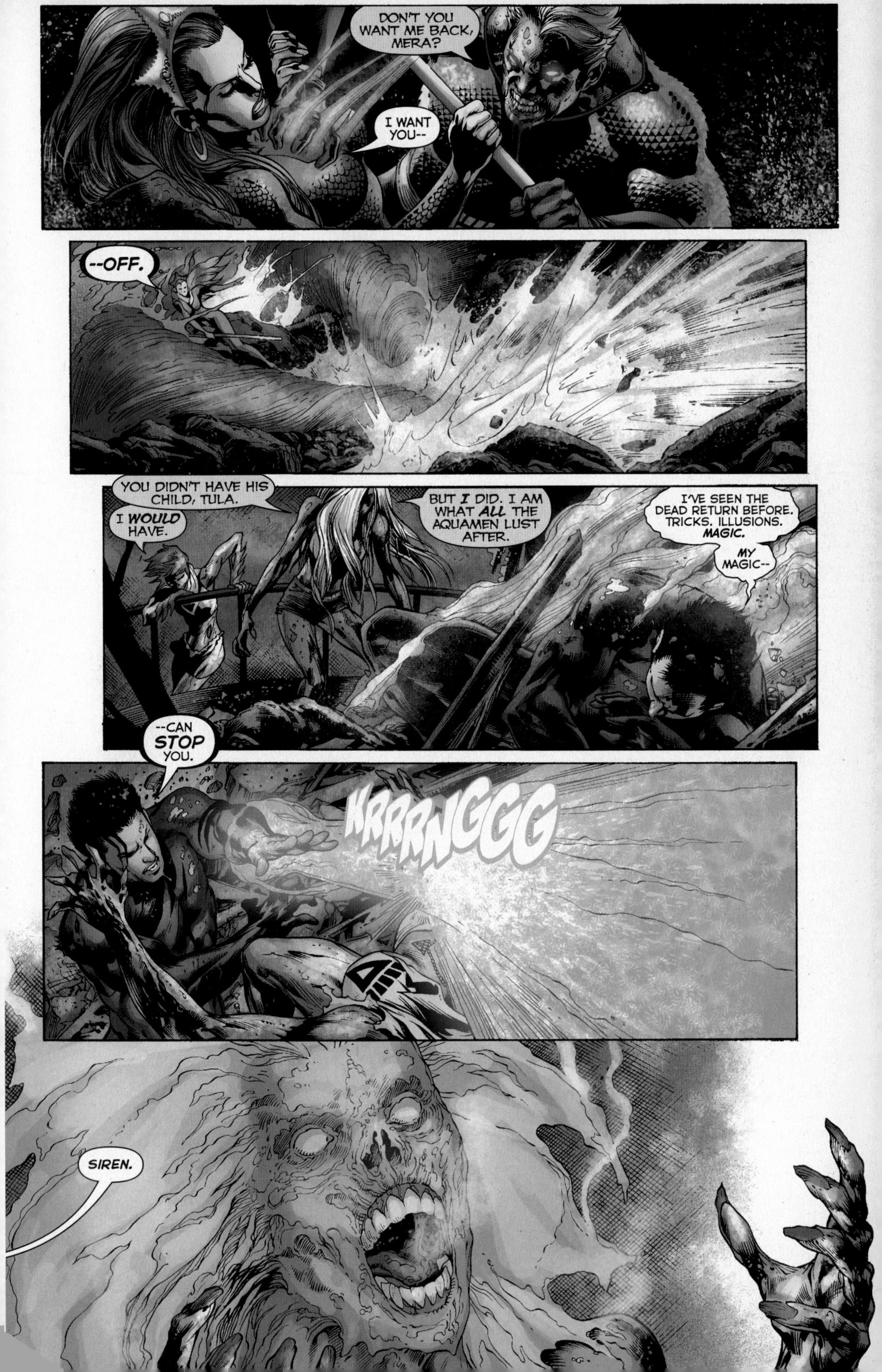
DON'T YOU WANT ME BACK, MERA?
I WANT YOU--
--OFF.
YOU DIDN'T HAVE HIS CHILD, TULA.
I WOULD HAVE.
BUT I DID. I AM WHAT ALL THE AQUAMEN LUST AFTER.
I'VE SEEN THE DEAD RETURN BEFORE. TRICKS. ILLUSIONS. MAGIC.
MY MAGIC--
--CAN STOP YOU.
KRRRNGGG
SIREN.

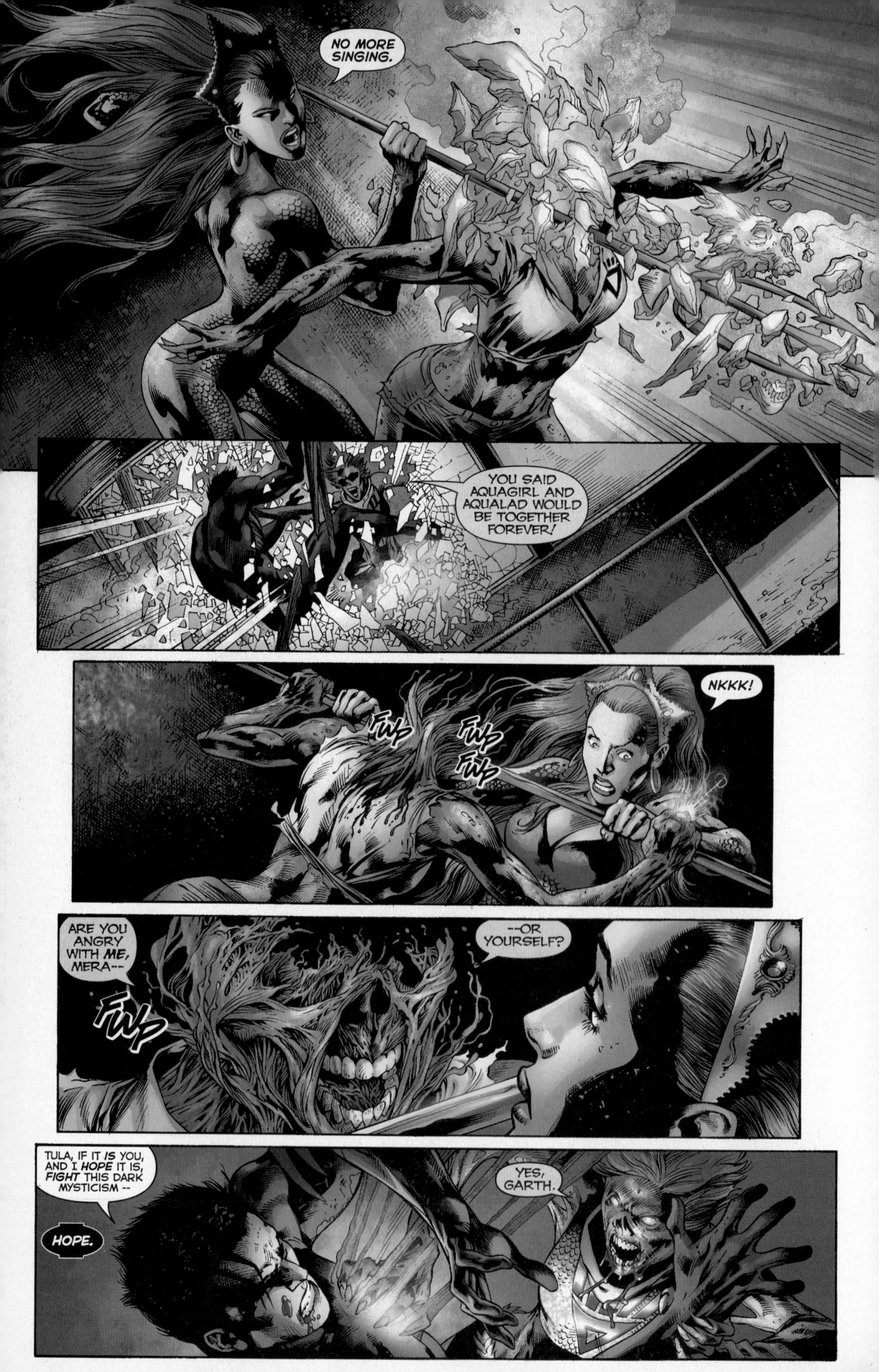
NO MORE SINGING.
YOU SAID AQUAGIRL AND AQUALAD WOULD BE TOGETHER FOREVER!
FWP
FWP
FWP
NKKK!
ARE YOU ANGRY WITH *ME*, MERA--
--OR YOURSELF?
FWP
TULA, IF IT *IS* YOU, AND I *HOPE* IT IS, *FIGHT* THIS DARK MYSTICISM --
HOPE.
YES, GARTH.

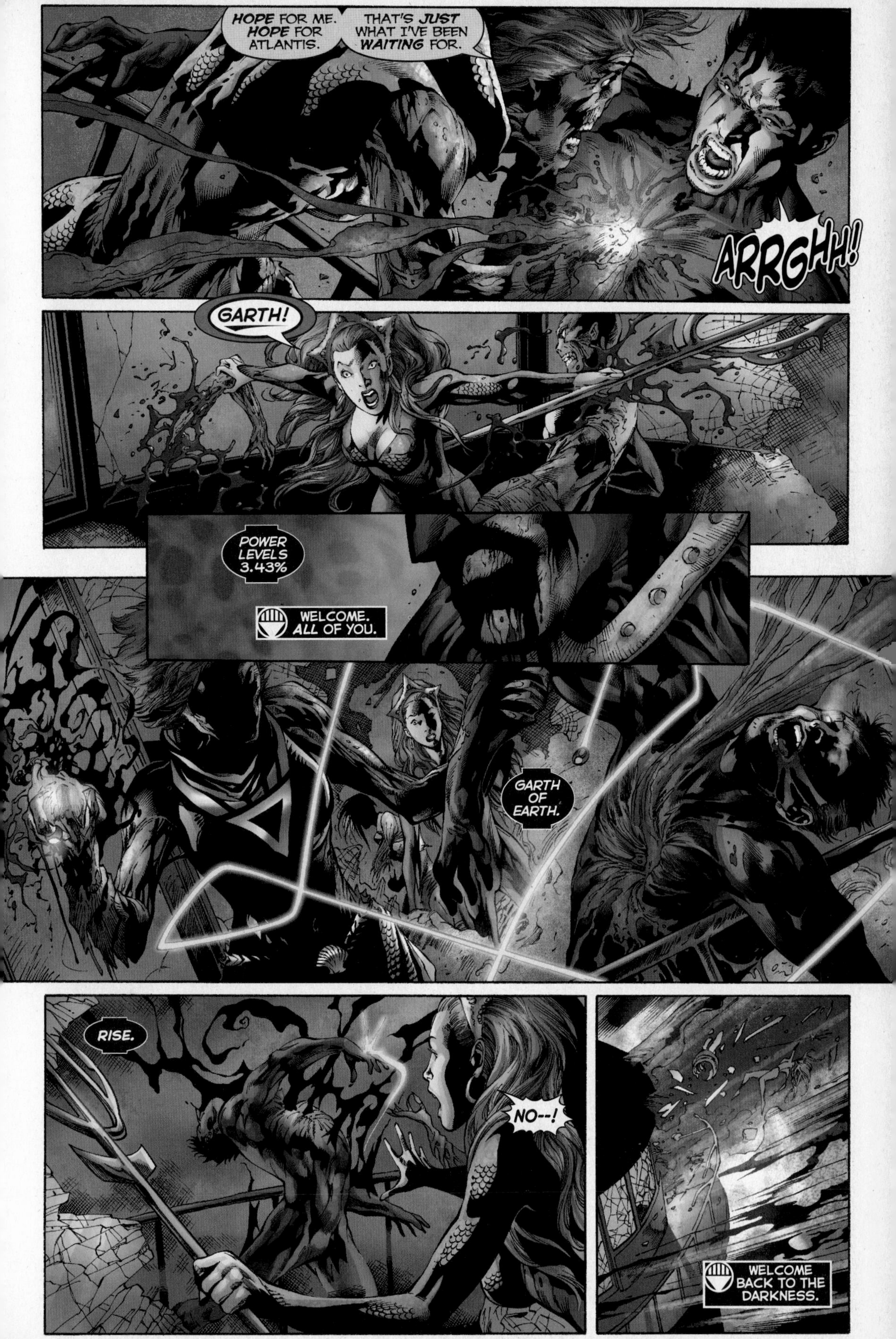

HOPE FOR ME. HOPE FOR ATLANTIS.
THAT'S JUST WHAT I'VE BEEN WAITING FOR.
ARRGHH!
GARTH!
POWER LEVELS 3.43%
WELCOME. ALL OF YOU.
GARTH OF EARTH.
RISE.
NO--!
WELCOME BACK TO THE DARKNESS.

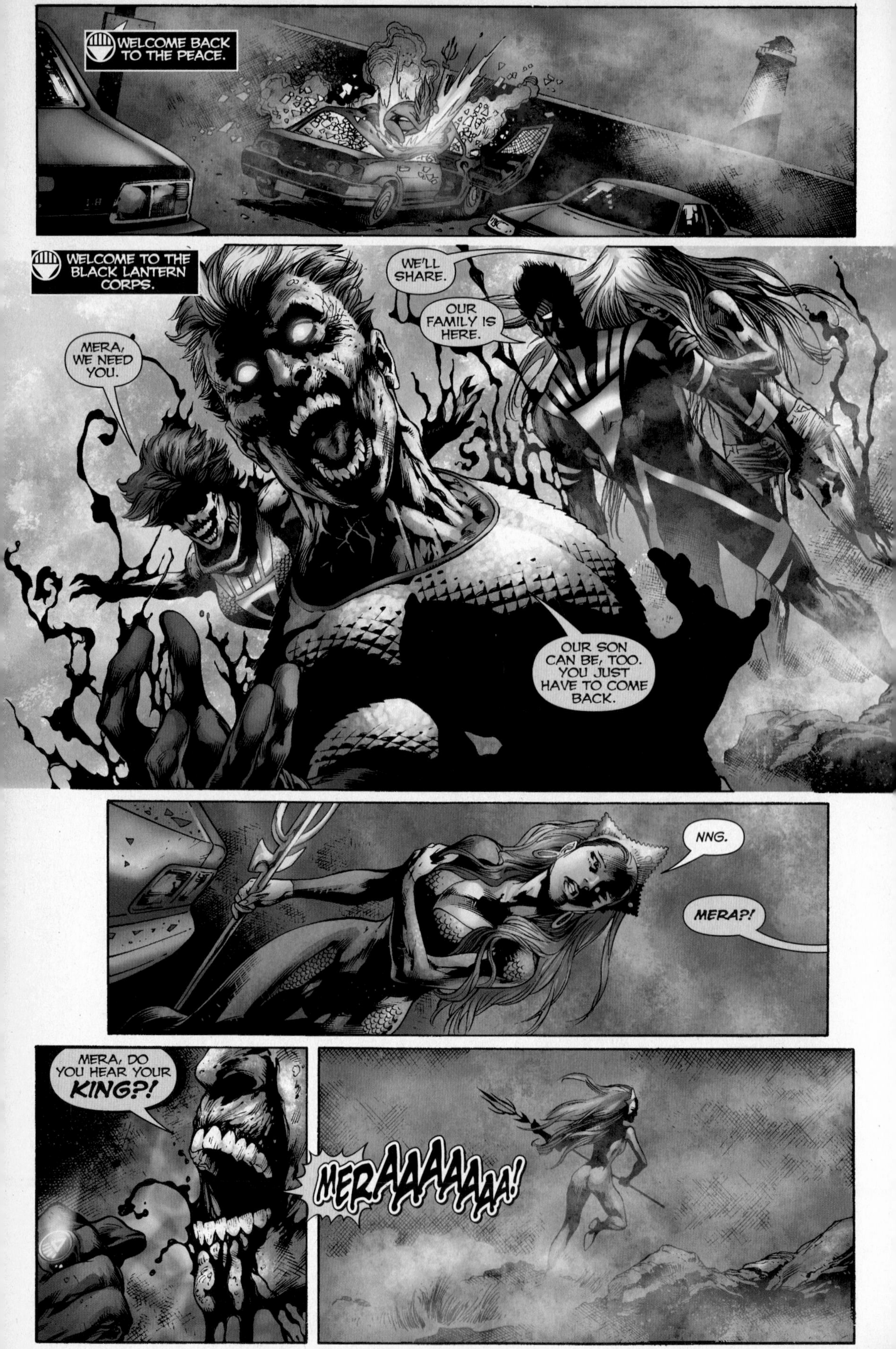
WELCOME BACK TO THE PEACE.
WELCOME TO THE BLACK LANTERN CORPS.
MERA, WE NEED YOU.
WE'LL SHARE.
OUR FAMILY IS HERE.
OUR SON CAN BE, TOO. YOU JUST HAVE TO COME BACK.
NNG.
MERA?!
MERA, DO YOU HEAR YOUR KING?!
MERAAAAAAAA!

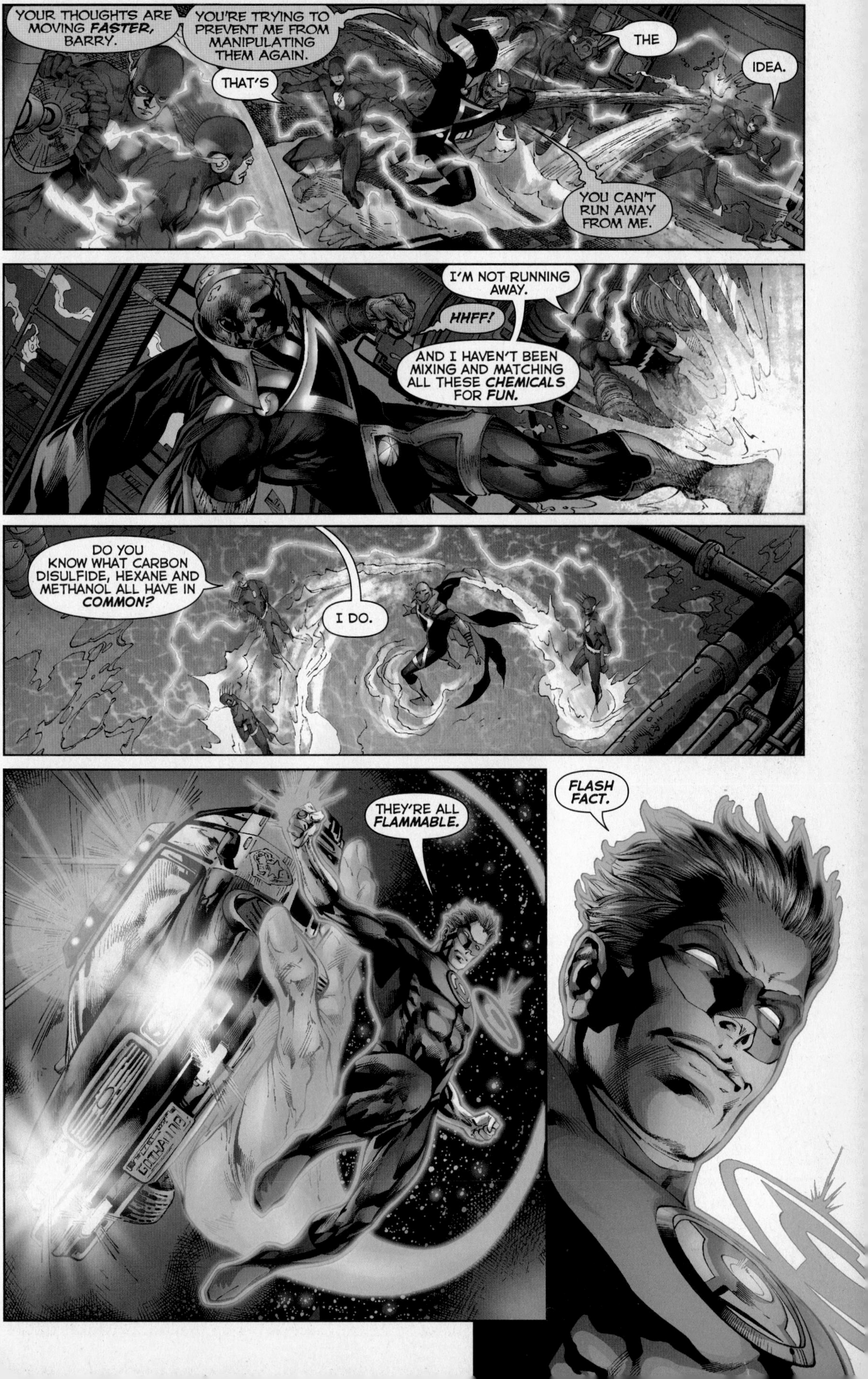
YOUR THOUGHTS ARE MOVING FASTER, BARRY.
YOU'RE TRYING TO PREVENT ME FROM MANIPULATING THEM AGAIN.
THAT'S
THE
IDEA.
YOU CAN'T RUN AWAY FROM ME.
I'M NOT RUNNING AWAY.
HHFF!
AND I HAVEN'T BEEN MIXING AND MATCHING ALL THESE CHEMICALS FOR FUN.
DO YOU KNOW WHAT CARBON DISULFIDE, HEXANE AND METHANOL ALL HAVE IN COMMON?
I DO.
THEY'RE ALL FLAMMABLE.
FLASH FACT.

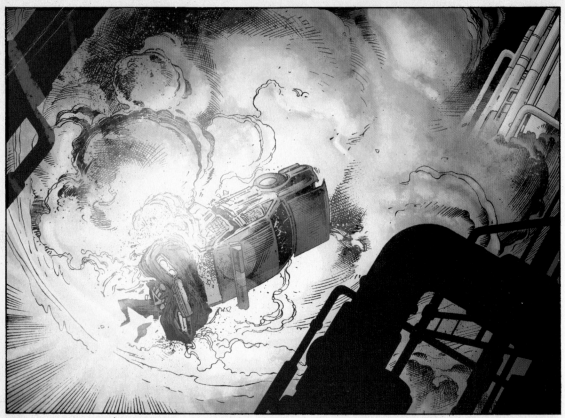

THE FLASH KEEPS THE FLAMES FROM SPREADING.

AND HE CREATES ONE HELL OF A *FURNACE.*

SORRY, J'ONN.

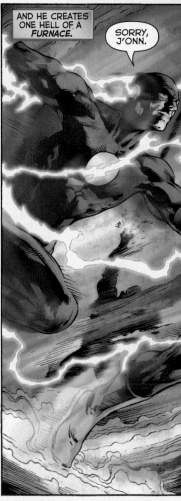

FIRE.

IT WAS J'ONN'S KRYPTONITE.

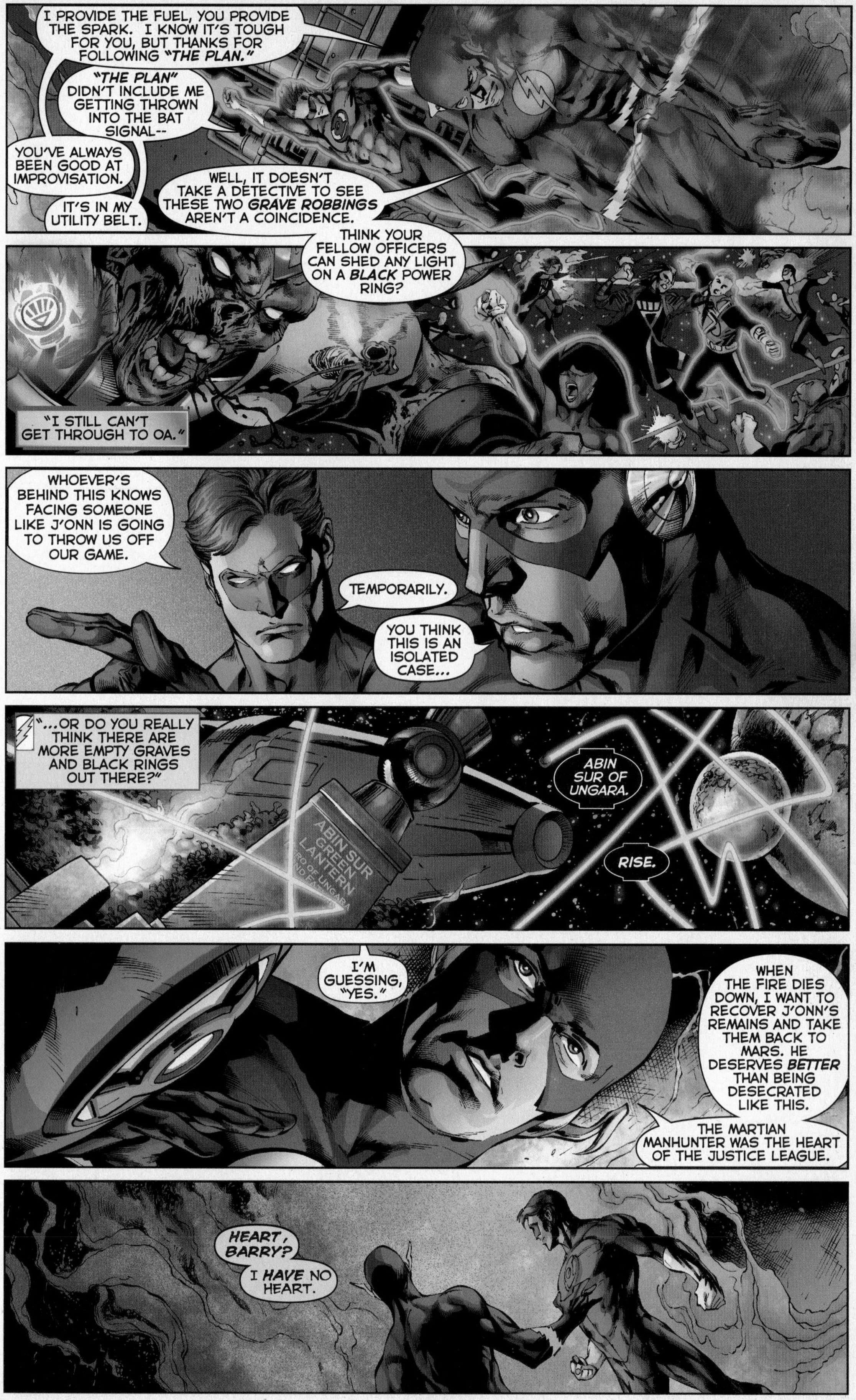
I PROVIDE THE FUEL, YOU PROVIDE THE SPARK. I KNOW IT'S TOUGH FOR YOU, BUT THANKS FOR FOLLOWING "THE PLAN."
"THE PLAN" DIDN'T INCLUDE ME GETTING THROWN INTO THE BAT SIGNAL--
YOU'VE ALWAYS BEEN GOOD AT IMPROVISATION.
IT'S IN MY UTILITY BELT.
WELL, IT DOESN'T TAKE A DETECTIVE TO SEE THESE TWO GRAVE ROBBINGS AREN'T A COINCIDENCE.
THINK YOUR FELLOW OFFICERS CAN SHED ANY LIGHT ON A BLACK POWER RING?
"I STILL CAN'T GET THROUGH TO OA."
WHOEVER'S BEHIND THIS KNOWS FACING SOMEONE LIKE J'ONN IS GOING TO THROW US OFF OUR GAME.
TEMPORARILY.
YOU THINK THIS IS AN ISOLATED CASE...
"...OR DO YOU REALLY THINK THERE ARE MORE EMPTY GRAVES AND BLACK RINGS OUT THERE?"
ABIN SUR GREEN LANTERN
ABIN SUR OF UNGARA.
RISE.
I'M GUESSING, "YES."
WHEN THE FIRE DIES DOWN, I WANT TO RECOVER J'ONN'S REMAINS AND TAKE THEM BACK TO MARS. HE DESERVES BETTER THAN BEING DESECRATED LIKE THIS.
THE MARTIAN MANHUNTER WAS THE HEART OF THE JUSTICE LEAGUE.
HEART, BARRY?
I HAVE NO HEART.

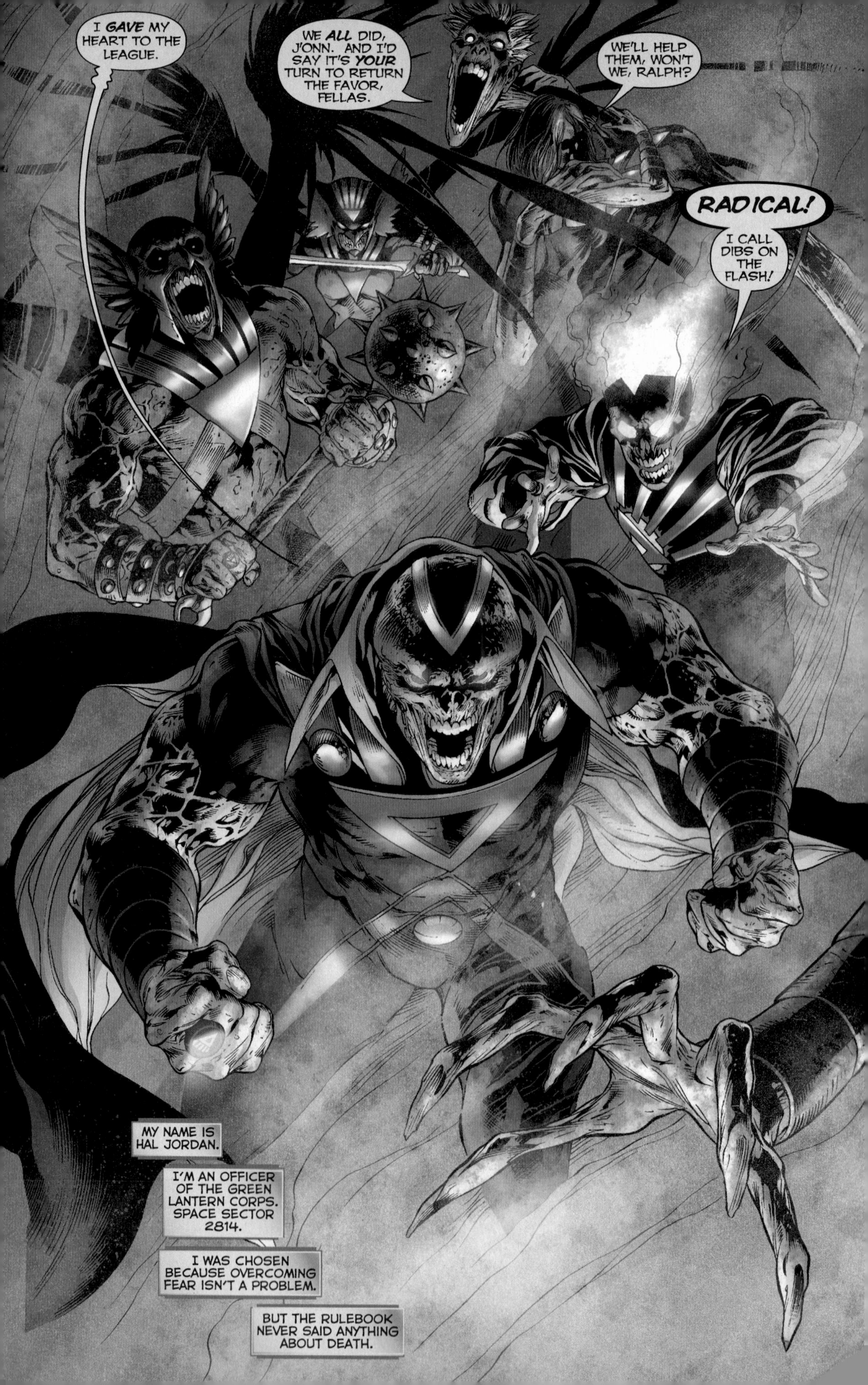
I GAVE MY HEART TO THE LEAGUE.
WE ALL DID, J'ONN. AND I'D SAY IT'S YOUR TURN TO RETURN THE FAVOR, FELLAS.
WE'LL HELP THEM, WON'T WE, RALPH?
RADICAL!
I CALL DIBS ON THE FLASH!
MY NAME IS HAL JORDAN.
I'M AN OFFICER OF THE GREEN LANTERN CORPS. SPACE SECTOR 2814.
I WAS CHOSEN BECAUSE OVERCOMING FEAR ISN'T A PROBLEM.
BUT THE RULEBOOK NEVER SAID ANYTHING ABOUT DEATH.

PART THREE

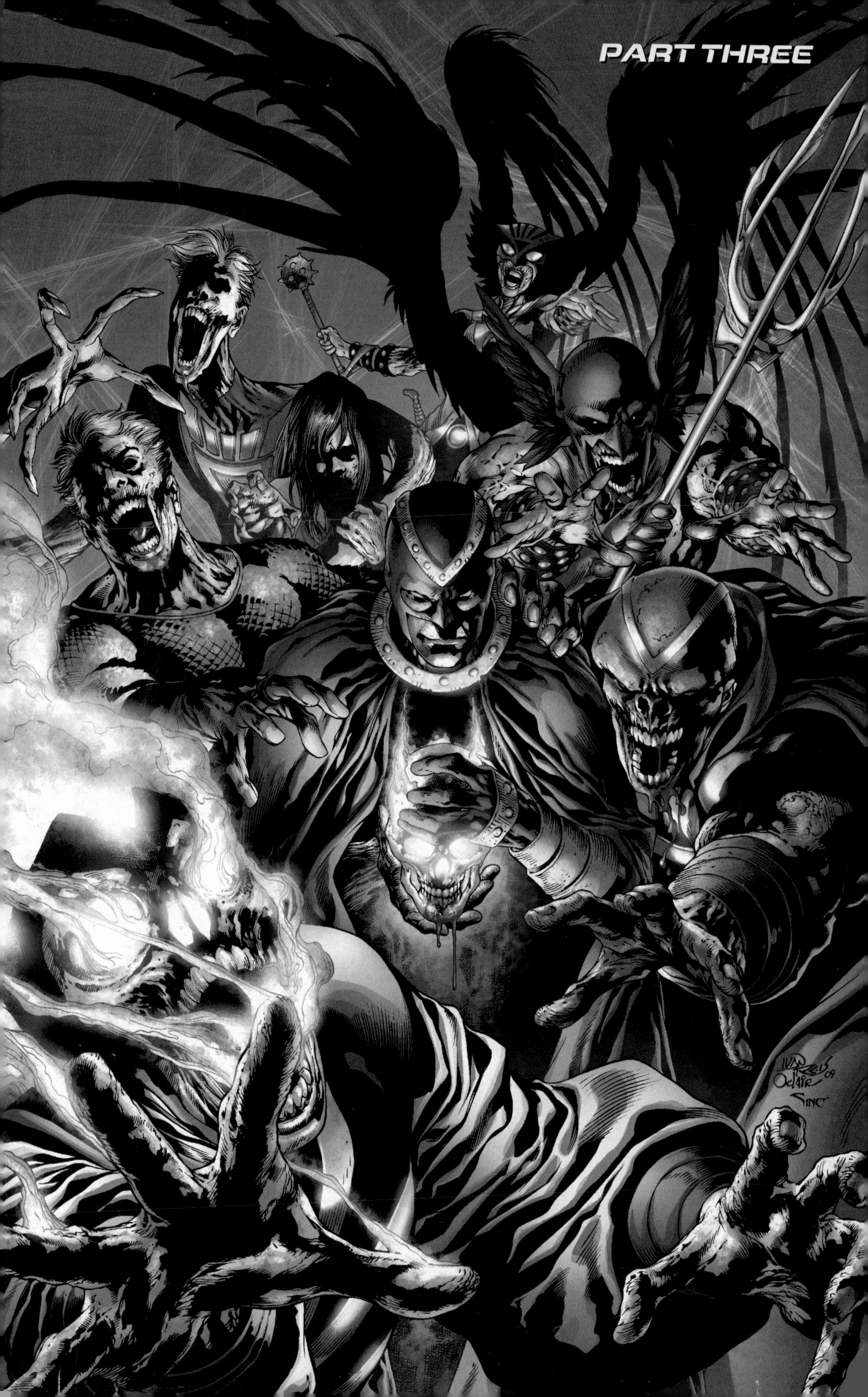

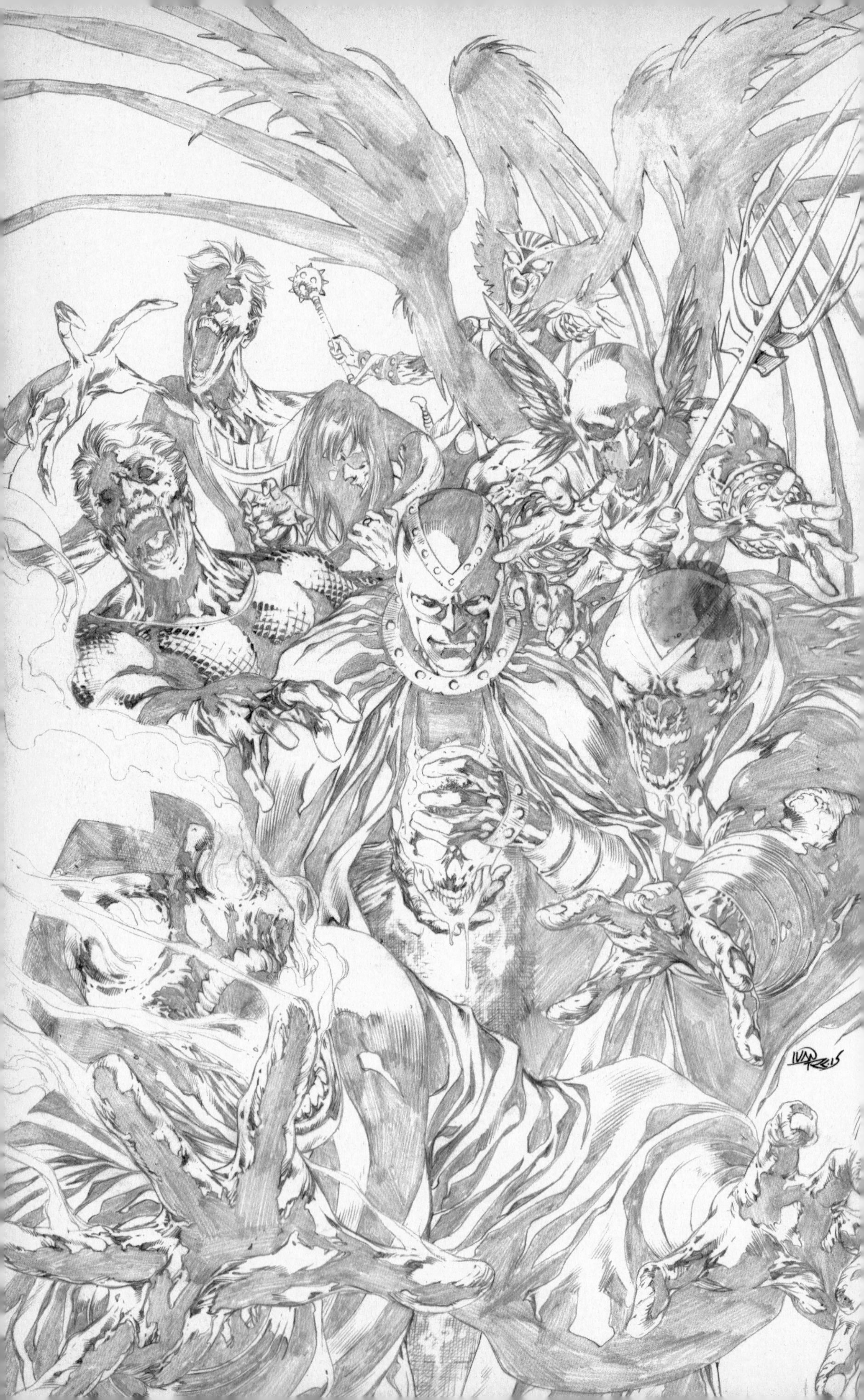

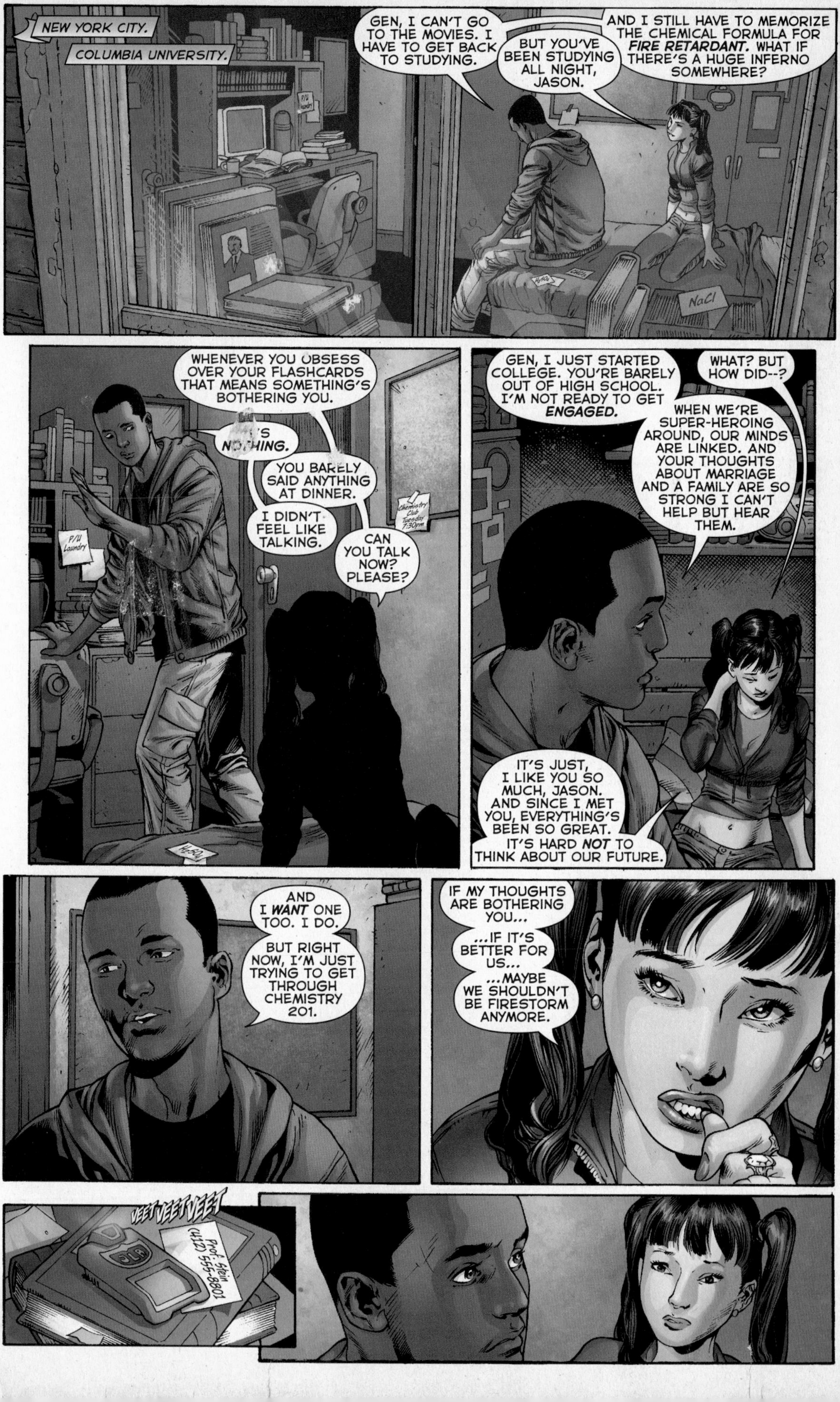
NEW YORK CITY.
COLUMBIA UNIVERSITY.
GEN, I CAN'T GO TO THE MOVIES. I HAVE TO GET BACK TO STUDYING.
BUT YOU'VE BEEN STUDYING ALL NIGHT, JASON.
AND I STILL HAVE TO MEMORIZE THE CHEMICAL FORMULA FOR FIRE RETARDANT. WHAT IF THERE'S A HUGE INFERNO SOMEWHERE?
NaCl
WHENEVER YOU OBSESS OVER YOUR FLASHCARDS THAT MEANS SOMETHING'S BOTHERING YOU.
'S NOTHING.
YOU BARELY SAID ANYTHING AT DINNER.
I DIDN'T FEEL LIKE TALKING.
CAN YOU TALK NOW? PLEASE?
P/U Laundry
Chemistry Club Tuesday 7:30pm
GEN, I JUST STARTED COLLEGE. YOU'RE BARELY OUT OF HIGH SCHOOL. I'M NOT READY TO GET ENGAGED.
WHAT? BUT HOW DID--?
WHEN WE'RE SUPER-HEROING AROUND, OUR MINDS ARE LINKED. AND YOUR THOUGHTS ABOUT MARRIAGE AND A FAMILY ARE SO STRONG I CAN'T HELP BUT HEAR THEM.
IT'S JUST, I LIKE YOU SO MUCH, JASON. AND SINCE I MET YOU, EVERYTHING'S BEEN SO GREAT.
IT'S HARD NOT TO THINK ABOUT OUR FUTURE.
AND I WANT ONE TOO. I DO.
BUT RIGHT NOW, I'M JUST TRYING TO GET THROUGH CHEMISTRY 201.
IF MY THOUGHTS ARE BOTHERING YOU...
...IF IT'S BETTER FOR US...
...MAYBE WE SHOULDN'T BE FIRESTORM ANYMORE.
VEET VEET VEET
JLA
Prof. Stein (412) 555-8801

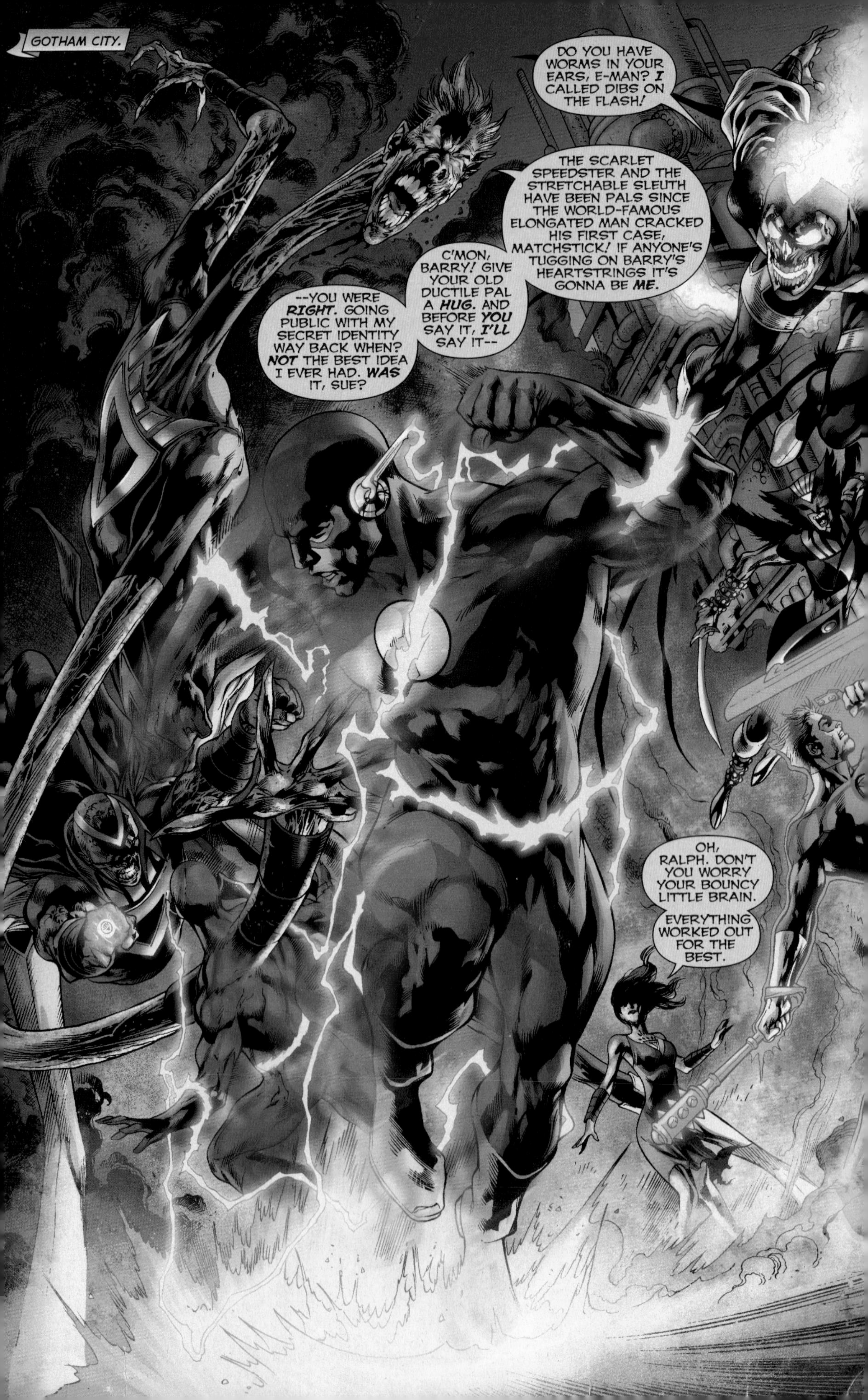
GOTHAM CITY.
DO YOU HAVE WORMS IN YOUR EARS, E-MAN? I CALLED DIBS ON THE FLASH!
THE SCARLET SPEEDSTER AND THE STRETCHABLE SLEUTH HAVE BEEN PALS SINCE THE WORLD-FAMOUS ELONGATED MAN CRACKED HIS FIRST CASE, MATCHSTICK! IF ANYONE'S TUGGING ON BARRY'S HEARTSTRINGS IT'S GONNA BE ME.
C'MON, BARRY! GIVE YOUR OLD DUCTILE PAL A HUG. AND BEFORE YOU SAY IT, I'LL SAY IT--
--YOU WERE RIGHT. GOING PUBLIC WITH MY SECRET IDENTITY WAY BACK WHEN? NOT THE BEST IDEA I EVER HAD. WAS IT, SUE?
OH, RALPH. DON'T YOU WORRY YOUR BOUNCY LITTLE BRAIN.
EVERYTHING WORKED OUT FOR THE BEST.

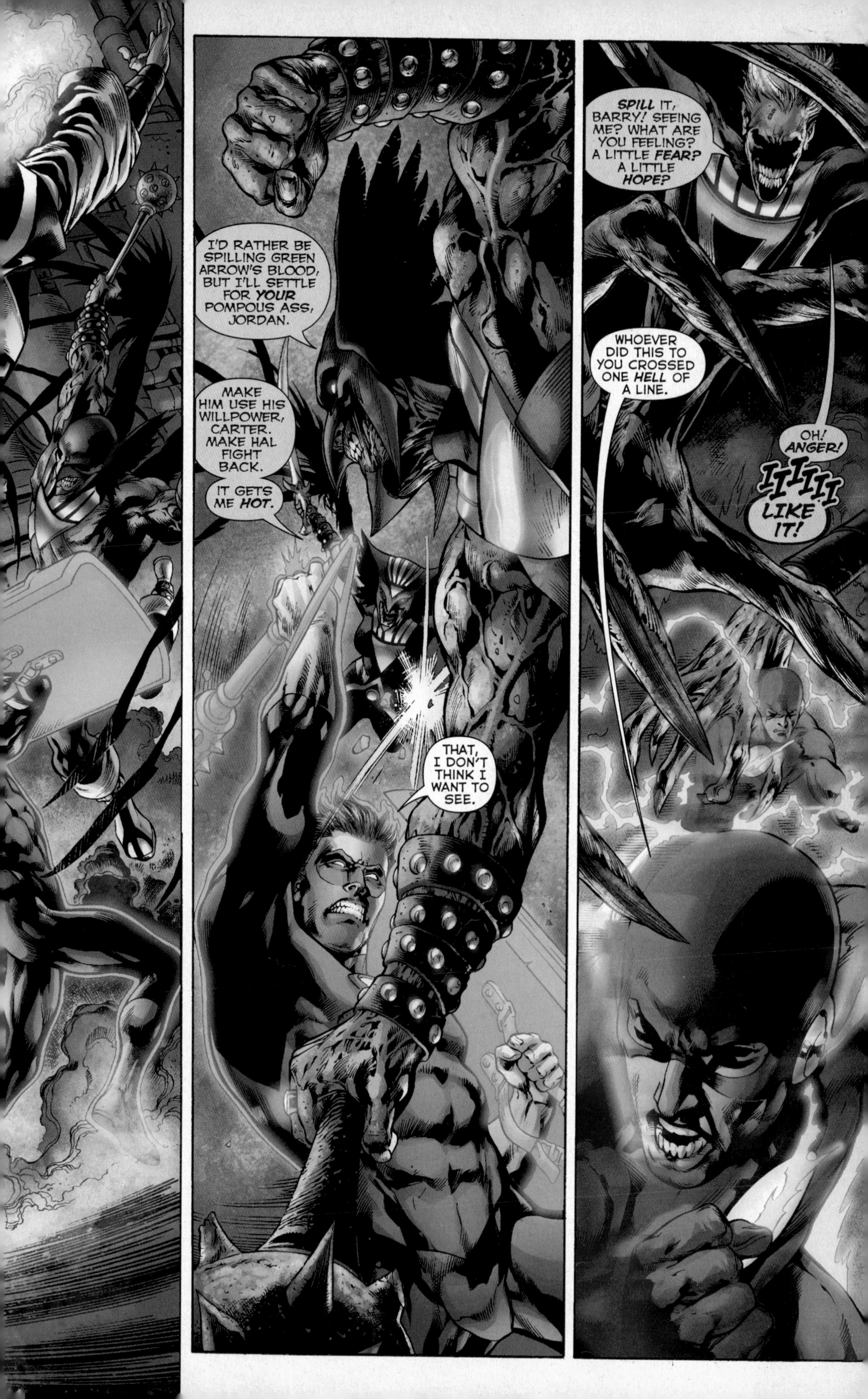
I'D RATHER BE SPILLING GREEN ARROW'S BLOOD, BUT I'LL SETTLE FOR *YOUR* POMPOUS ASS, JORDAN.
MAKE HIM USE HIS WILLPOWER, CARTER. MAKE HAL FIGHT BACK.
IT GETS ME *HOT*.
THAT, I DON'T THINK I WANT TO SEE.
SPILL IT, BARRY! SEEING ME? WHAT ARE YOU FEELING? A LITTLE *FEAR?* A LITTLE *HOPE?*
WHOEVER DID THIS TO YOU CROSSED ONE *HELL* OF A LINE.
OH! *ANGER!*
IIIIII LIKE IT!

I CAN'T BELIEVE I DIDN'T NOTICE THIS BEFORE, FLASH, BUT YOU'RE A *LOT* LIKE PROFESSOR STEIN.

YOU'RE *BOTH* BORING OLD DUDES WHO KNOW ALL ABOUT CHEMICALS AND GIGAWATTS AND JUNK.

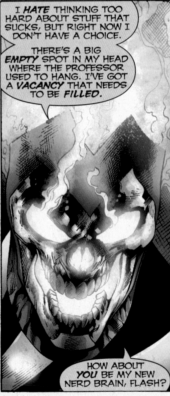

I *HATE* THINKING TOO HARD ABOUT STUFF THAT SUCKS, BUT RIGHT NOW I DON'T HAVE A CHOICE.

THERE'S A BIG *EMPTY* SPOT IN MY HEAD WHERE THE PROFESSOR USED TO HANG. I'VE GOT A *VACANCY* THAT NEEDS TO BE *FILLED.*

HOW ABOUT *YOU* BE MY NEW NERD BRAIN, FLASH?

THE RONNIE RAYMOND *I* KNEW MIGHT'VE MADE *LESS* THAN AVERAGE GRADES, BUT HE NEVER SAW PROFESSOR STEIN AS A *HUMAN DATABASE.*

HEY, I GOT A "*B*" IN P.E.

ONCE.

YOU WANT TO TRY AN EXPERIMENT, "*FIRESTORM*"? LET'S SEE WHAT HAPPENS WHEN I TAKE THIS BLACK RING *OFF.*

RRARRR!!

POWER LEVELS 50.32%

HE WILL RISE, INVADER! AND THERE IS NOTHING YOU CAN DO TO STOP IT!

HAL! THE BLACK RINGS HAVE GROWN *ROOTS* INTO THEIR BODIES LIKE PLANTS.

WE'RE ALL *CONNECTED*, BARRY. INCLUDING YOU.

THEY RE-FORM IF THEY'RE DAMAGED. THEIR POWER LEVELS SOUND LIKE THEY'RE *INCREASING*.

ANY MORE IDEAS ON HOW TO *STOP* THEM?

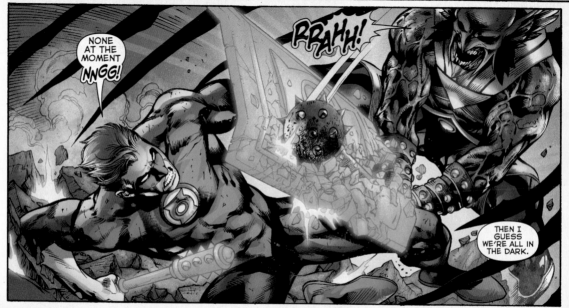

NONE AT THE MOMENT NNGG!

RRAHH!

THEN I GUESS WE'RE ALL IN THE DARK.

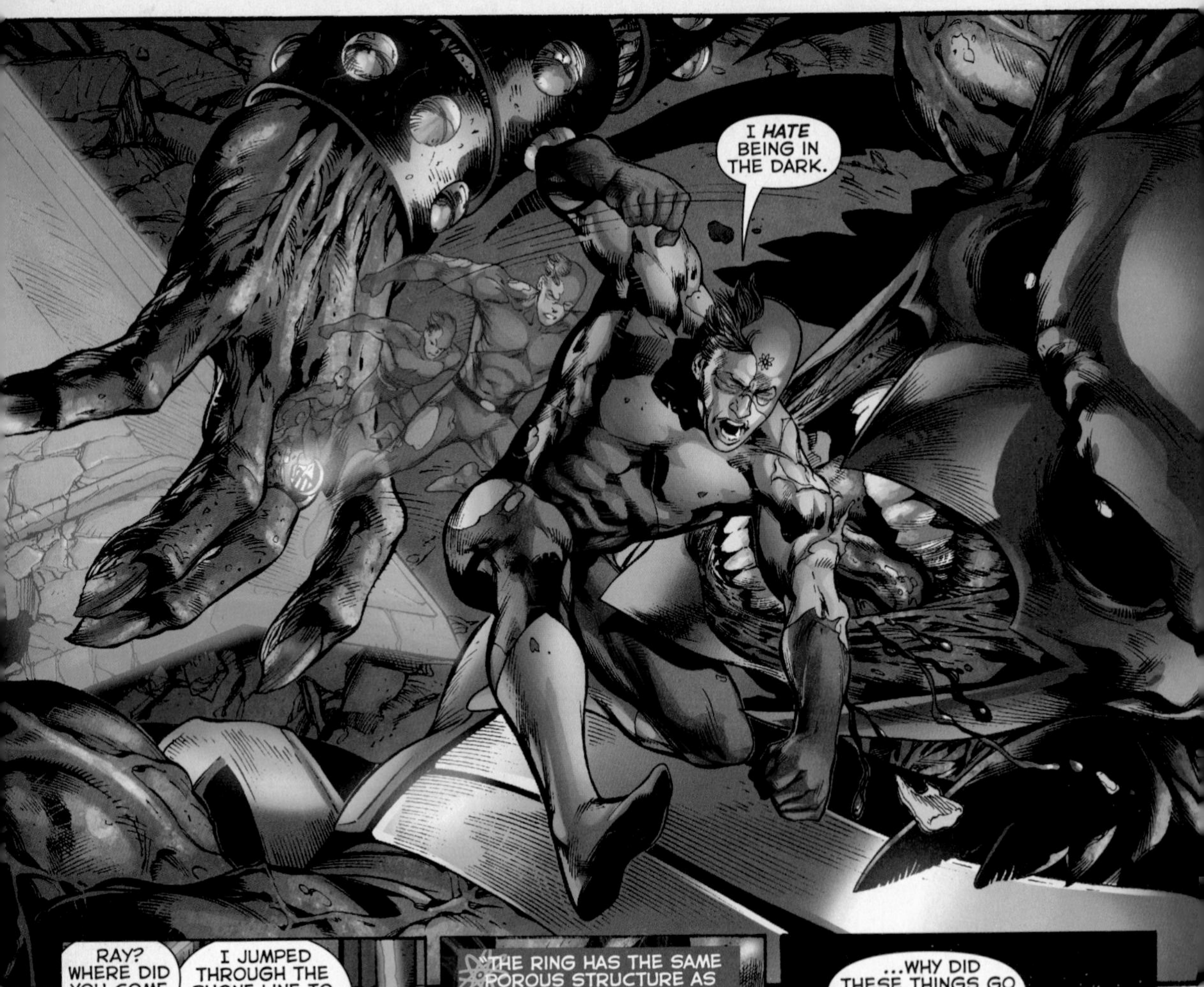
I HATE BEING IN THE DARK.
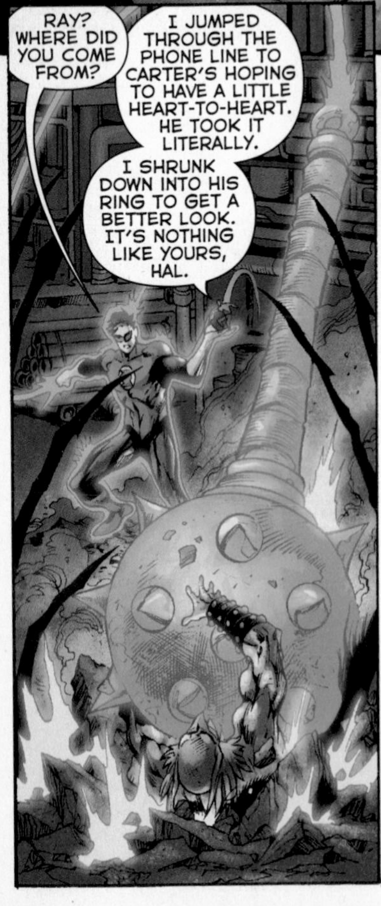
RAY? WHERE DID YOU COME FROM?
I JUMPED THROUGH THE PHONE LINE TO CARTER'S HOPING TO HAVE A LITTLE HEART-TO-HEART. HE TOOK IT LITERALLY.
I SHRUNK DOWN INTO HIS RING TO GET A BETTER LOOK. IT'S NOTHING LIKE YOURS, HAL.
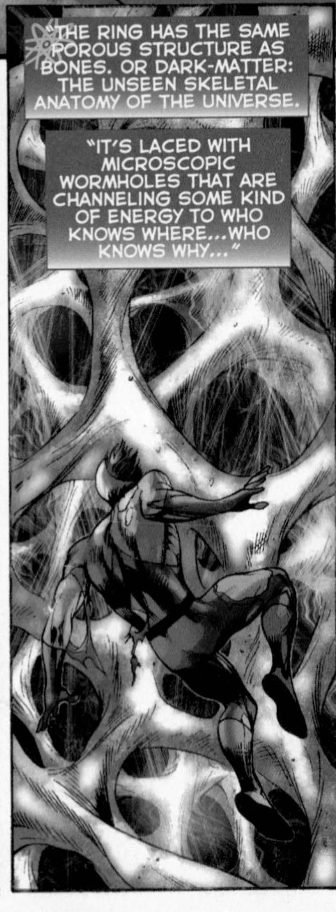
"THE RING HAS THE SAME POROUS STRUCTURE AS BONES. OR DARK-MATTER: THE UNSEEN SKELETAL ANATOMY OF THE UNIVERSE.
"IT'S LACED WITH MICROSCOPIC WORMHOLES THAT ARE CHANNELING SOME KIND OF ENERGY TO WHO KNOWS WHERE...WHO KNOWS WHY..."
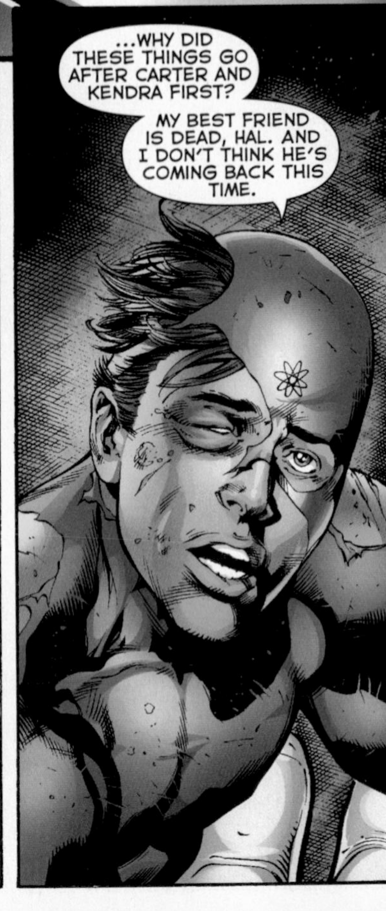
...WHY DID THESE THINGS GO AFTER CARTER AND KENDRA FIRST?
MY BEST FRIEND IS DEAD, HAL. AND I DON'T THINK HE'S COMING BACK THIS TIME.

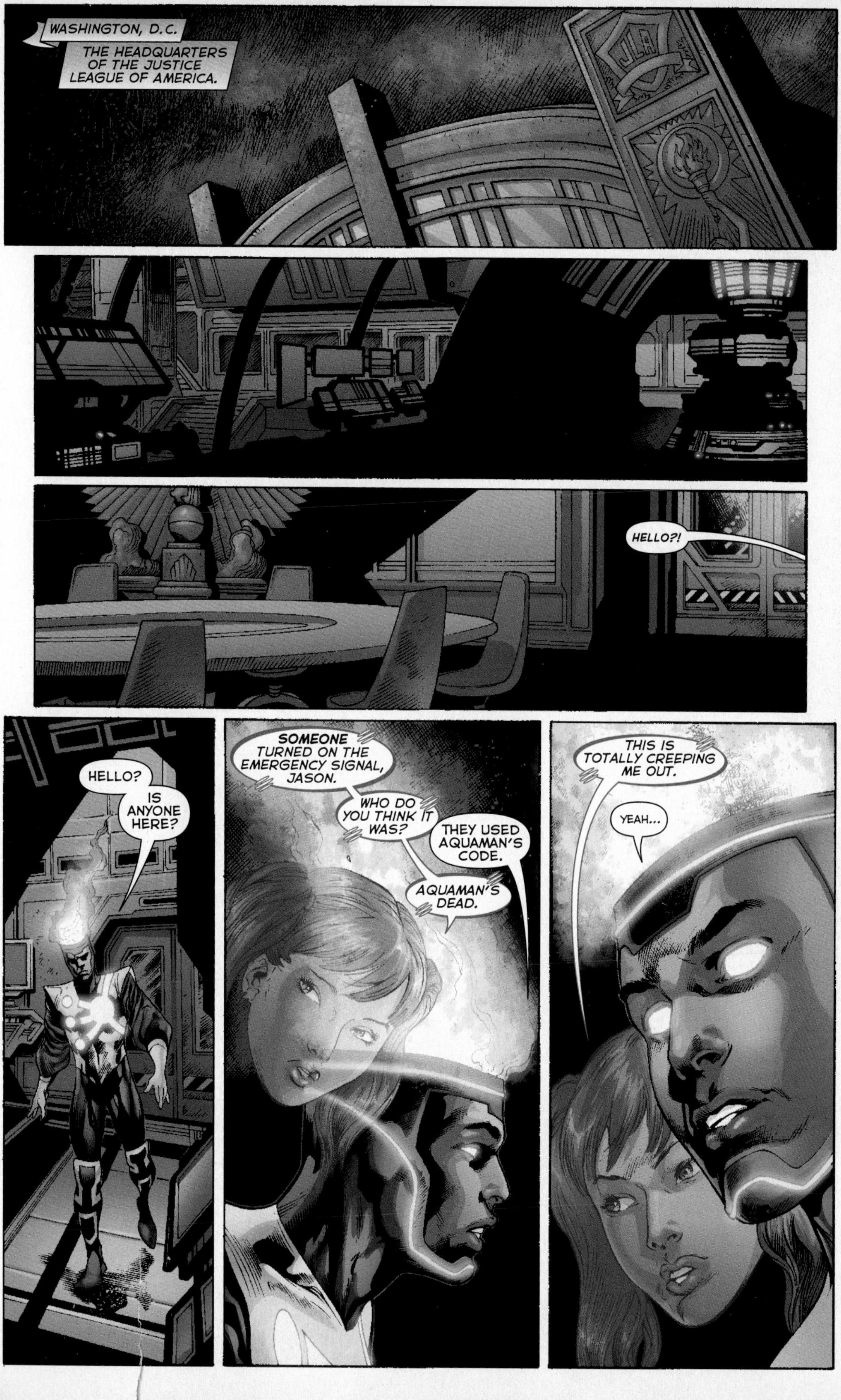
WASHINGTON, D.C.
THE HEADQUARTERS OF THE JUSTICE LEAGUE OF AMERICA.
HELLO?!
HELLO?
IS ANYONE HERE?
SOMEONE TURNED ON THE EMERGENCY SIGNAL, JASON.
WHO DO YOU THINK IT WAS?
THEY USED AQUAMAN'S CODE.
AQUAMAN'S DEAD.
THIS IS TOTALLY CREEPING ME OUT.
YEAH...

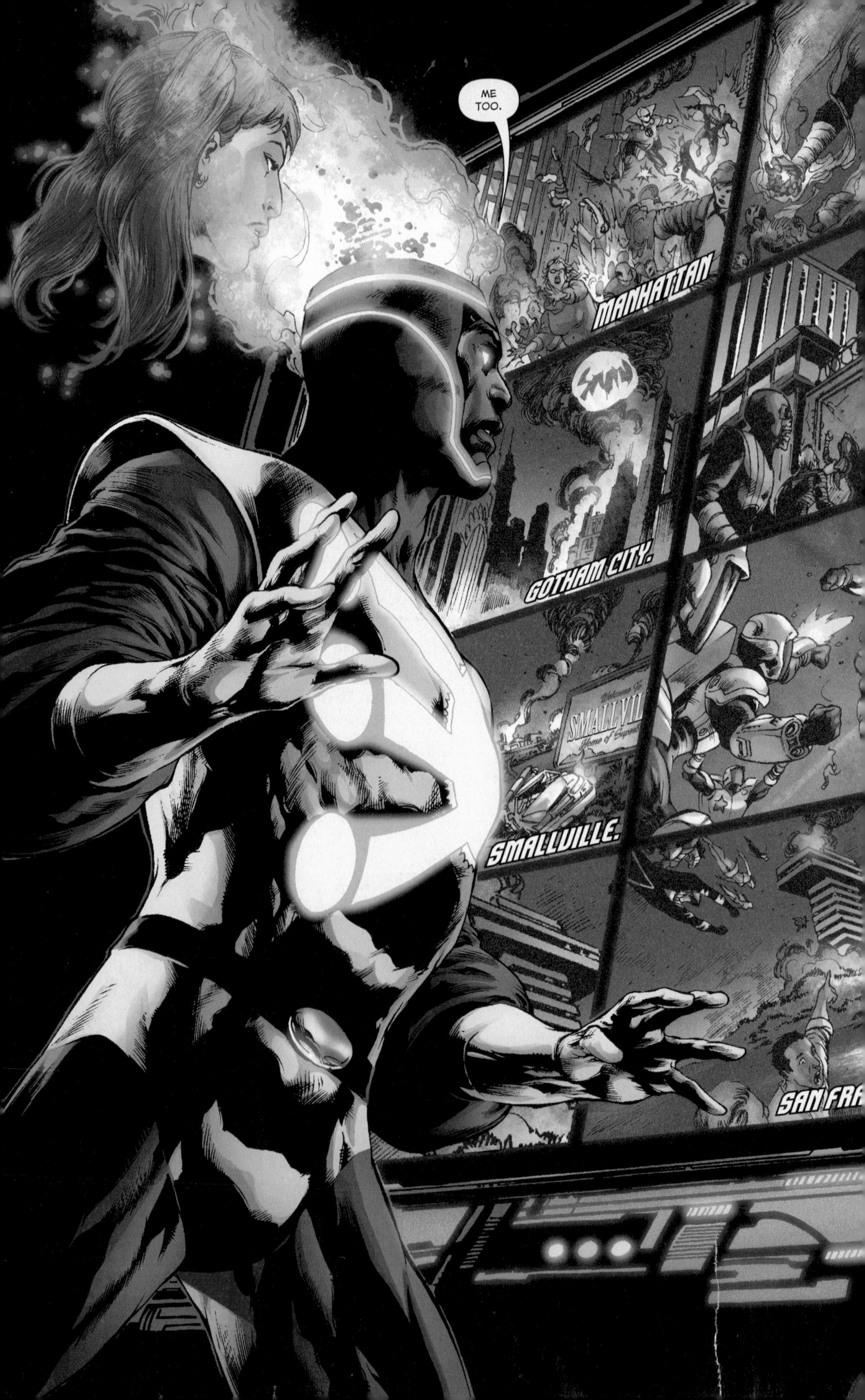
ME TOO.
MANHATTAN
GOTHAM CITY.
SMALLVILLE.
SAN FRA

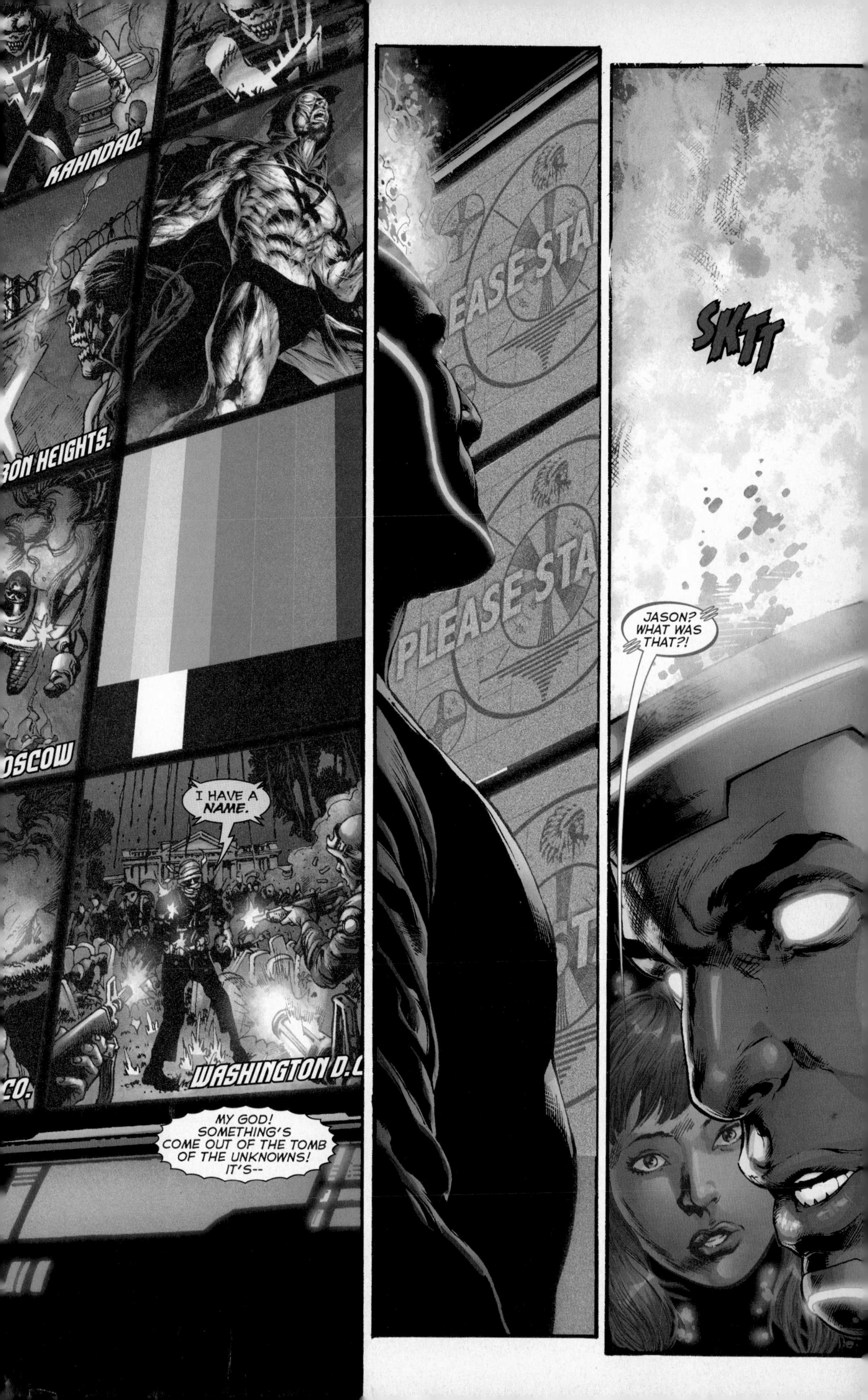
KAHNDAQ.
RON HEIGHTS.
OSCOW
I HAVE A **NAME.**
CO.
WASHINGTON D.C
MY GOD! SOMETHING'S COME OUT OF THE TOMB OF THE UNKNOWNS! IT'S--
PLEASE STA
PLEASE STA
SKTT
JASON? WHAT WAS THAT?!

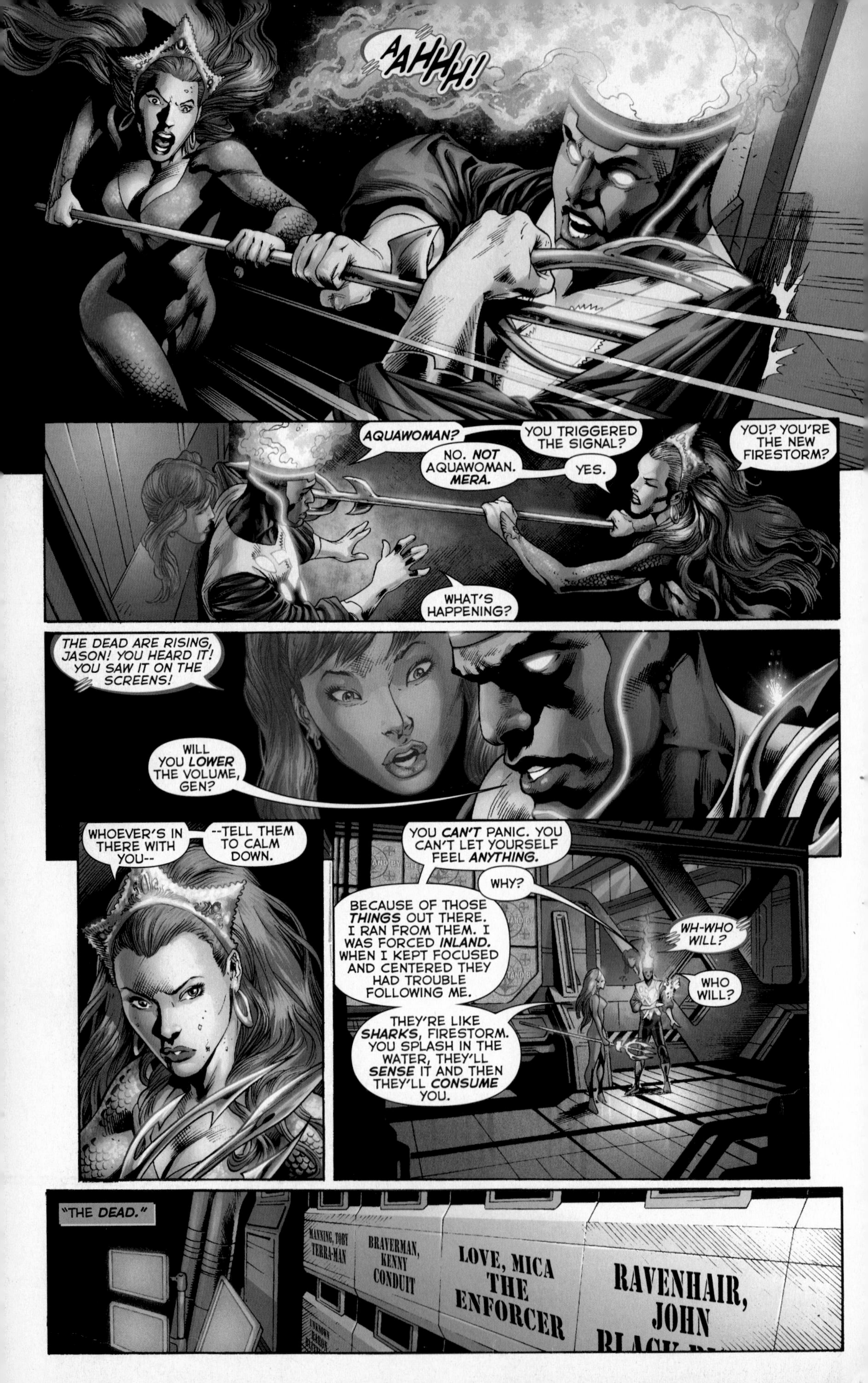
AAHHH!
AQUAWOMAN?
NO. NOT AQUAWOMAN. MERA.
YOU TRIGGERED THE SIGNAL?
YES.
YOU? YOU'RE THE NEW FIRESTORM?
WHAT'S HAPPENING?
THE DEAD ARE RISING, JASON! YOU HEARD IT! YOU SAW IT ON THE SCREENS!
WILL YOU LOWER THE VOLUME, GEN?
WHOEVER'S IN THERE WITH YOU--
--TELL THEM TO CALM DOWN.
YOU CAN'T PANIC. YOU CAN'T LET YOURSELF FEEL ANYTHING.
WHY?
BECAUSE OF THOSE THINGS OUT THERE. I RAN FROM THEM. I WAS FORCED INLAND. WHEN I KEPT FOCUSED AND CENTERED THEY HAD TROUBLE FOLLOWING ME.
WH-WHO WILL?
WHO WILL?
THEY'RE LIKE SHARKS, FIRESTORM. YOU SPLASH IN THE WATER, THEY'LL SENSE IT AND THEN THEY'LL CONSUME YOU.
"THE DEAD."
MANNING, TOBY TERRA-MAN
BRAVERMAN, KENNY CONDUIT
LOVE, MICA THE ENFORCER
RAVENHAIR, JOHN

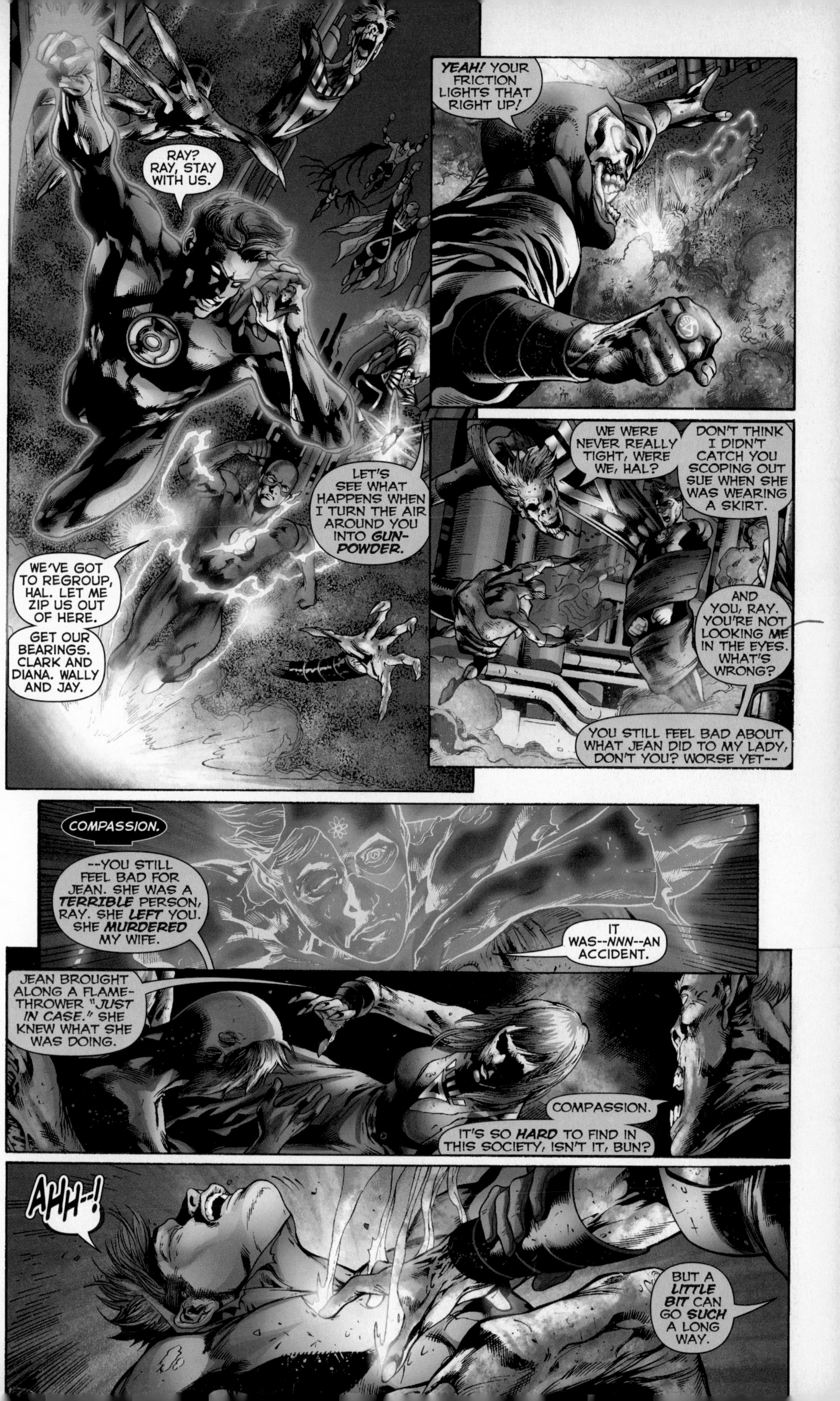
RAY? RAY, STAY WITH US.
LET'S SEE WHAT HAPPENS WHEN I TURN THE AIR AROUND YOU INTO GUN-POWDER.
WE'VE GOT TO REGROUP, HAL. LET ME ZIP US OUT OF HERE.
GET OUR BEARINGS. CLARK AND DIANA. WALLY AND JAY.
YEAH! YOUR FRICTION LIGHTS THAT RIGHT UP!
WE WERE NEVER REALLY TIGHT, WERE WE, HAL?
DON'T THINK I DIDN'T CATCH YOU SCOPING OUT SUE WHEN SHE WAS WEARING A SKIRT.
AND YOU, RAY. YOU'RE NOT LOOKING ME IN THE EYES. WHAT'S WRONG?
YOU STILL FEEL BAD ABOUT WHAT JEAN DID TO MY LADY, DON'T YOU? WORSE YET--
COMPASSION.
--YOU STILL FEEL BAD FOR JEAN. SHE WAS A TERRIBLE PERSON, RAY. SHE LEFT YOU. SHE MURDERED MY WIFE.
IT WAS--NNN--AN ACCIDENT.
JEAN BROUGHT ALONG A FLAME-THROWER "JUST IN CASE." SHE KNEW WHAT SHE WAS DOING.
COMPASSION.
IT'S SO HARD TO FIND IN THIS SOCIETY, ISN'T IT, BUN?
AHH--!
BUT A LITTLE BIT CAN GO SUCH A LONG WAY.

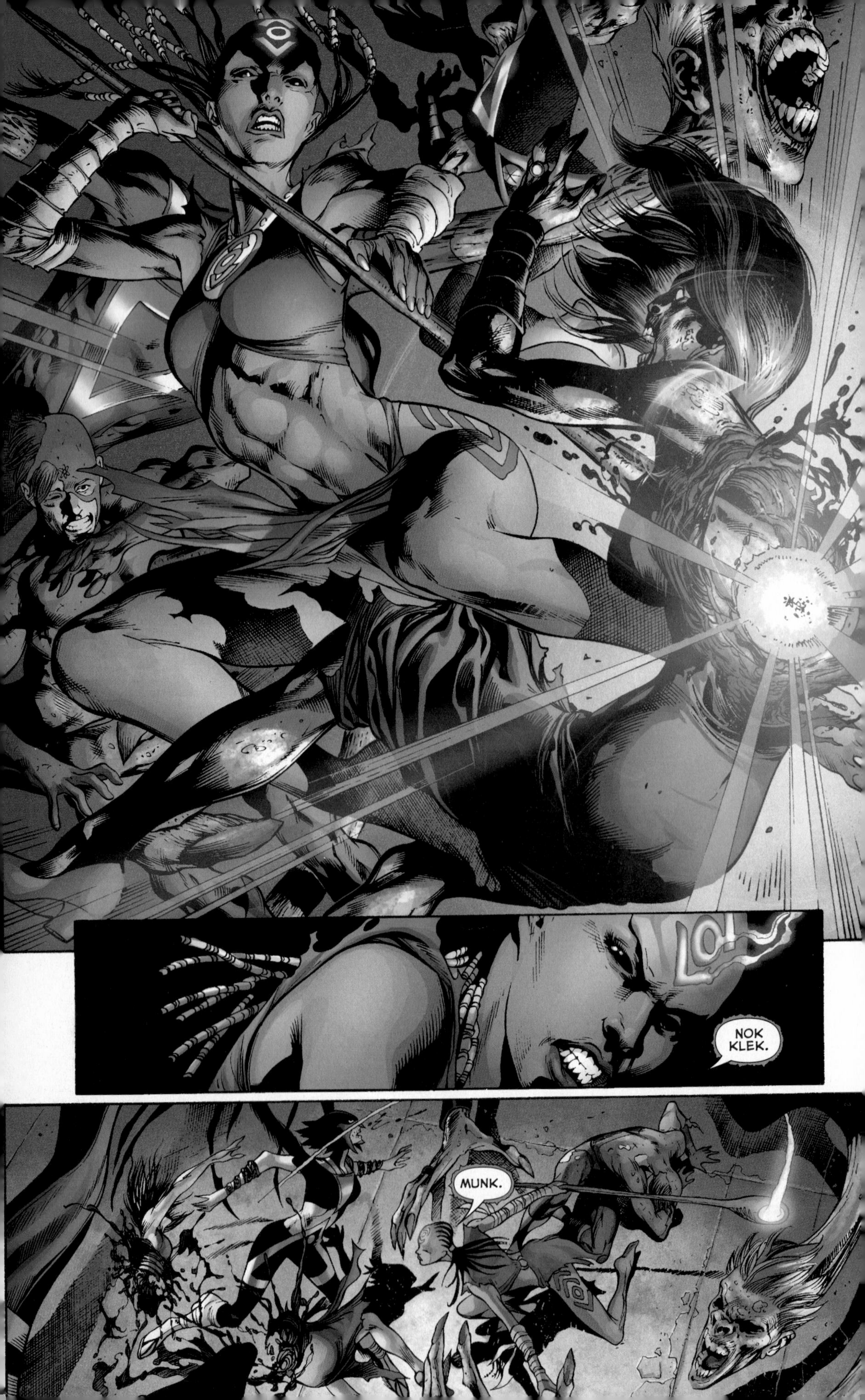
NOK KLEK.
MUNK.

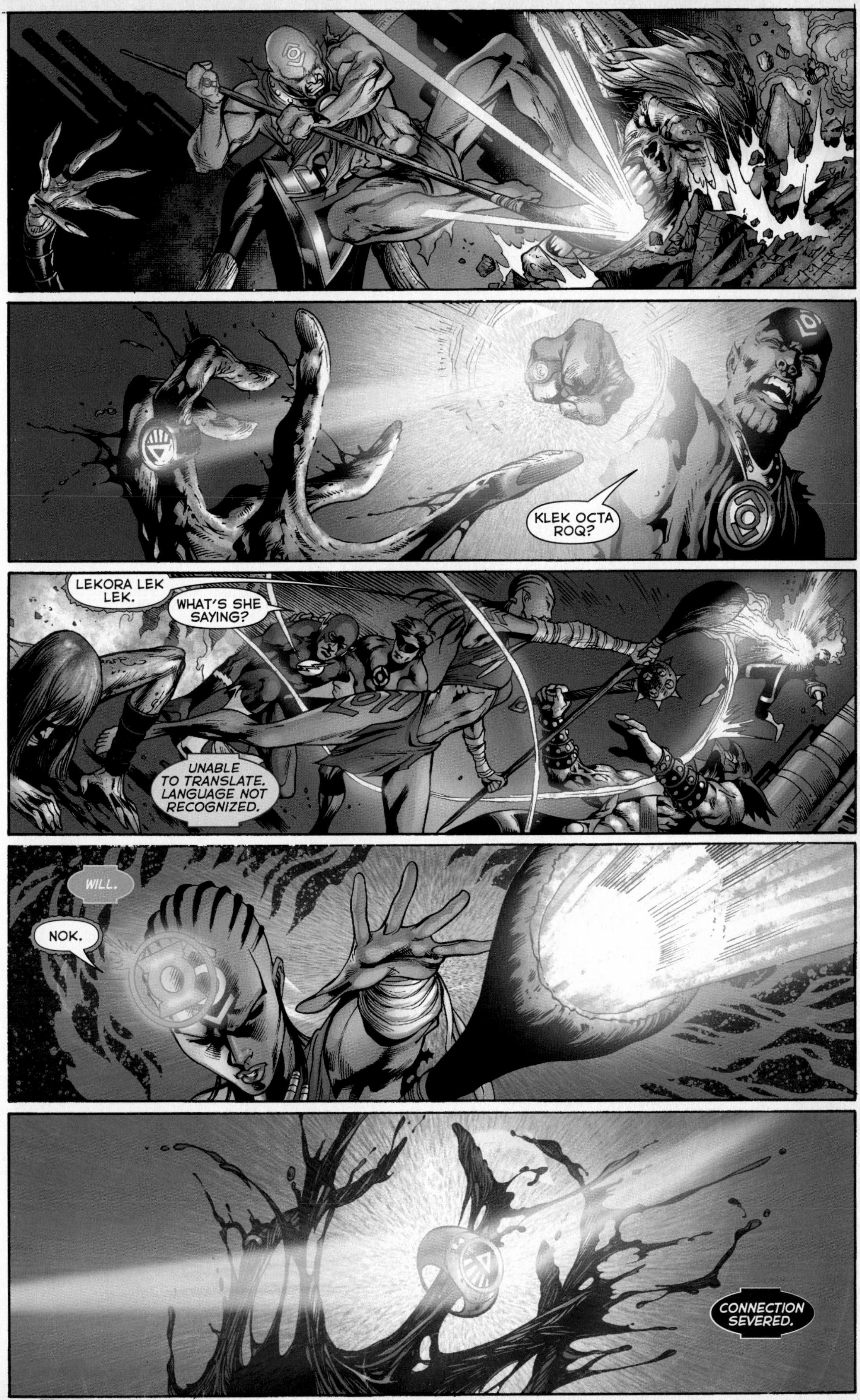
KLEK OCTA ROQ?
LEKORA LEK LEK.
WHAT'S SHE SAYING?
UNABLE TO TRANSLATE. LANGUAGE NOT RECOGNIZED.
WILL.
NOK.
CONNECTION SEVERED.

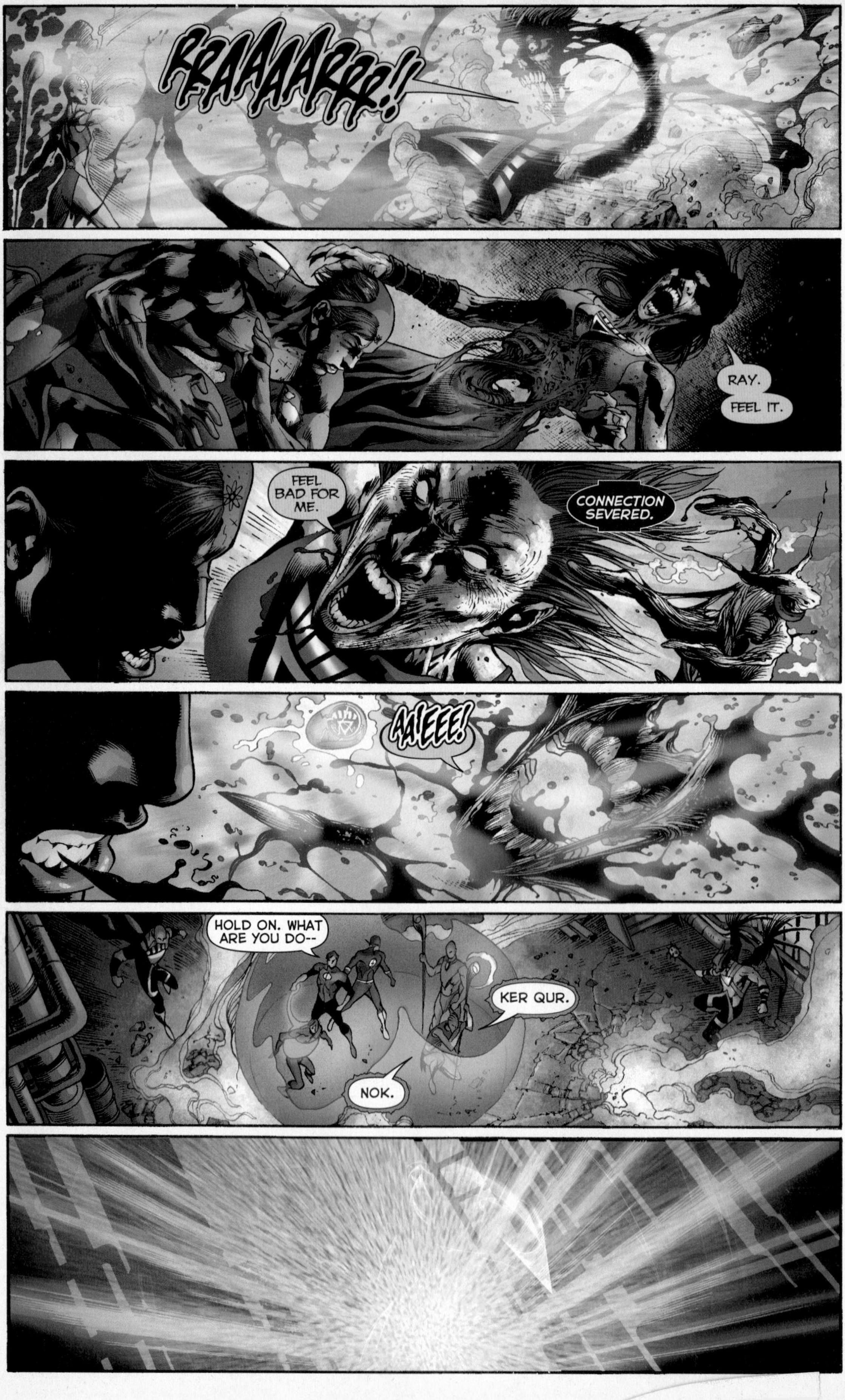
RRAAAAARRR!!
RAY.
FEEL IT.
FEEL BAD FOR ME.
CONNECTION SEVERED.
AAIEEE!
HOLD ON. WHAT ARE YOU DO--
KER QUR.
NOK.

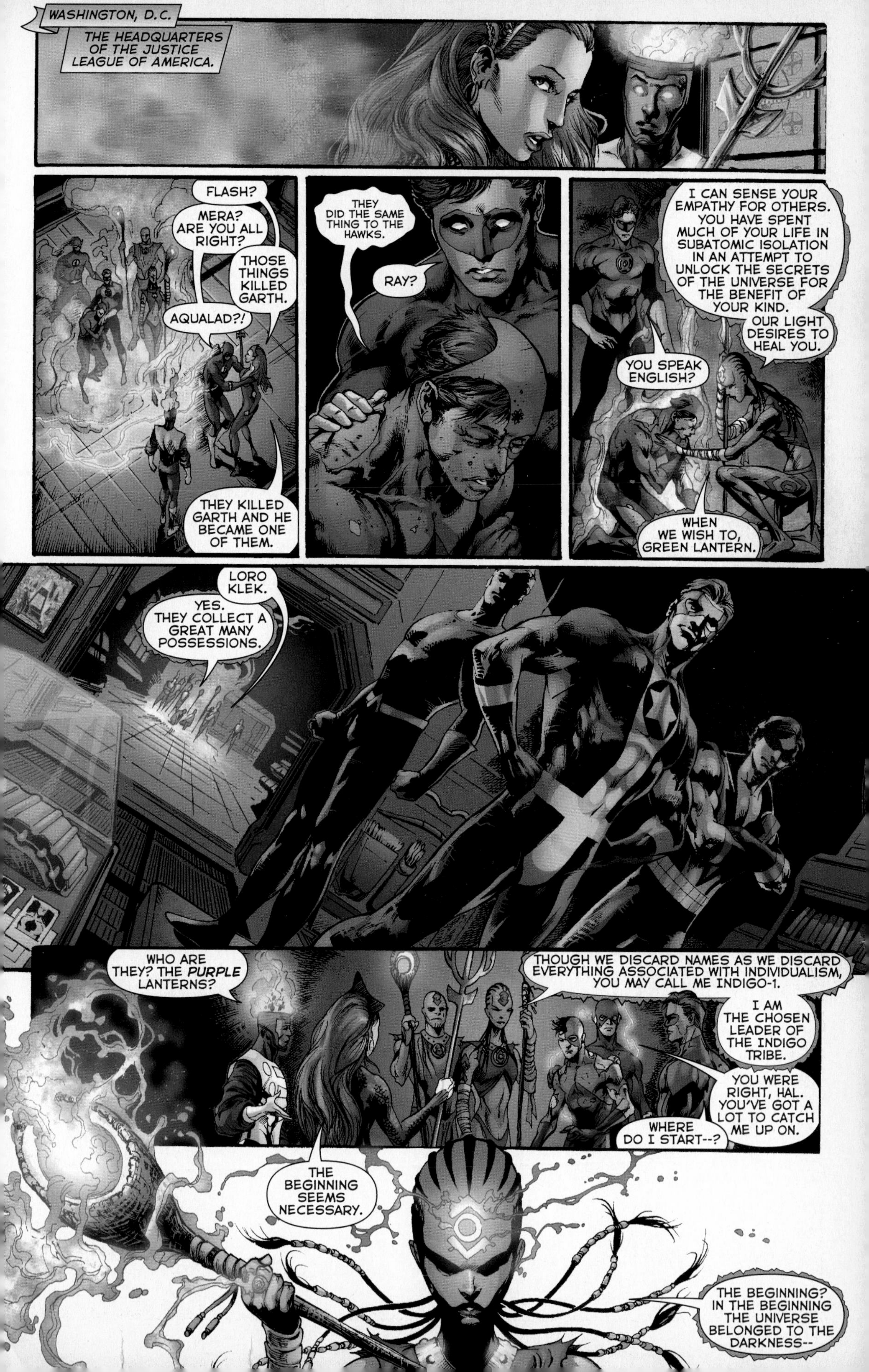
WASHINGTON, D.C.
THE HEADQUARTERS OF THE JUSTICE LEAGUE OF AMERICA.
FLASH?
MERA? ARE YOU ALL RIGHT?
THOSE THINGS KILLED GARTH.
AQUALAD?!
THEY KILLED GARTH AND HE BECAME ONE OF THEM.
THEY DID THE SAME THING TO THE HAWKS.
RAY?
I CAN SENSE YOUR EMPATHY FOR OTHERS. YOU HAVE SPENT MUCH OF YOUR LIFE IN SUBATOMIC ISOLATION IN AN ATTEMPT TO UNLOCK THE SECRETS OF THE UNIVERSE FOR THE BENEFIT OF YOUR KIND.
OUR LIGHT DESIRES TO HEAL YOU.
YOU SPEAK ENGLISH?
WHEN WE WISH TO, GREEN LANTERN.
LORO KLEK.
YES. THEY COLLECT A GREAT MANY POSSESSIONS.
WHO ARE THEY? THE *PURPLE* LANTERNS?
THOUGH WE DISCARD NAMES AS WE DISCARD EVERYTHING ASSOCIATED WITH INDIVIDUALISM, YOU MAY CALL ME INDIGO-1.
I AM THE CHOSEN LEADER OF THE INDIGO TRIBE.
YOU WERE RIGHT, HAL. YOU'VE GOT A LOT TO CATCH ME UP ON.
WHERE DO I START--?
THE BEGINNING SEEMS NECESSARY.
THE BEGINNING? IN THE BEGINNING THE UNIVERSE BELONGED TO THE DARKNESS--

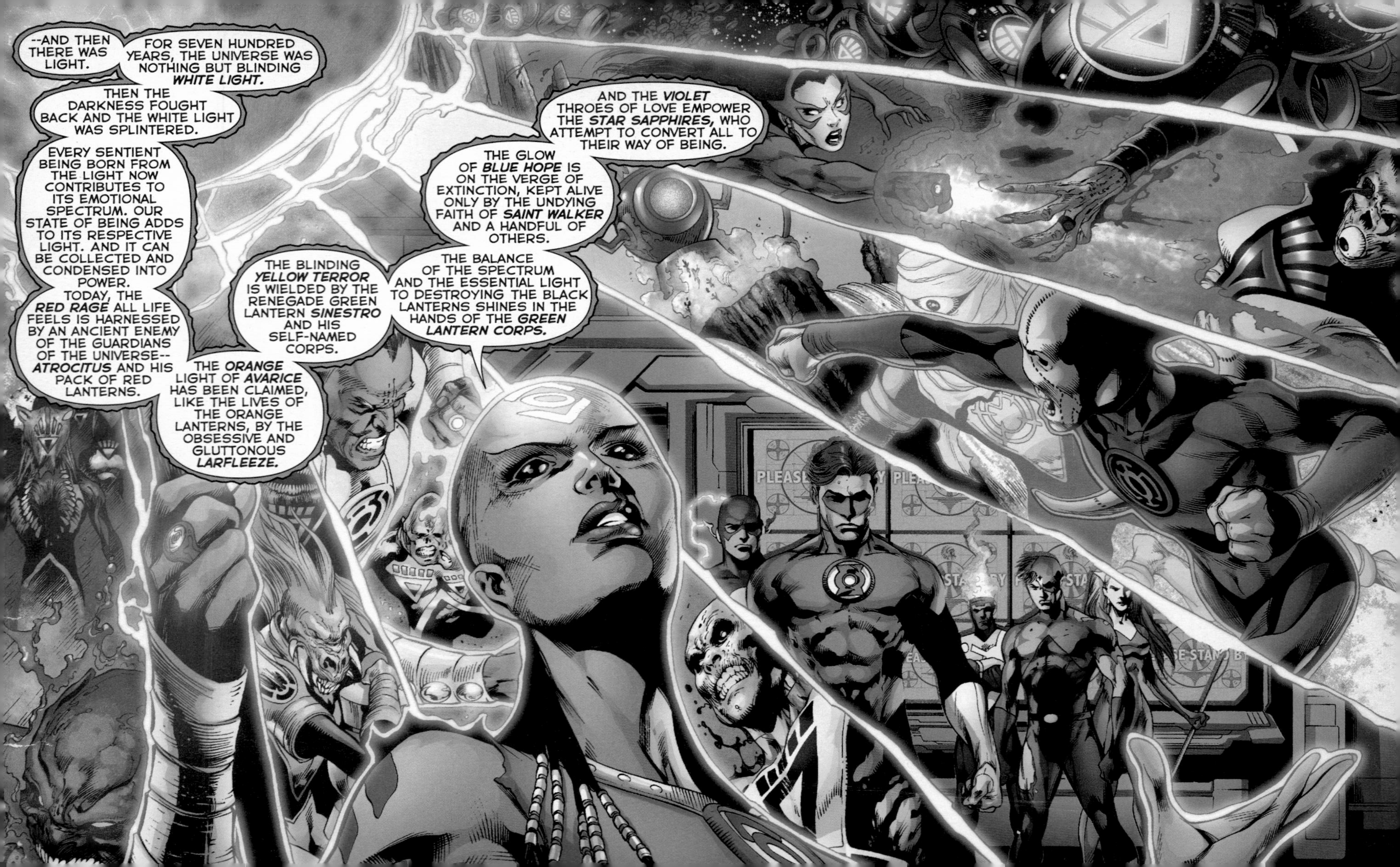
--AND THEN THERE WAS LIGHT.
FOR SEVEN HUNDRED YEARS, THE UNIVERSE WAS NOTHING BUT BLINDING *WHITE LIGHT.*
THEN THE DARKNESS FOUGHT BACK AND THE WHITE LIGHT WAS SPLINTERED.
EVERY SENTIENT BEING BORN FROM THE LIGHT NOW CONTRIBUTES TO ITS EMOTIONAL SPECTRUM. OUR STATE OF BEING ADDS TO ITS RESPECTIVE LIGHT. AND IT CAN BE COLLECTED AND CONDENSED INTO POWER.
TODAY, THE *RED RAGE* ALL LIFE FEELS IS HARNESSED BY AN ANCIENT ENEMY OF THE GUARDIANS OF THE UNIVERSE--*ATROCITUS* AND HIS PACK OF RED LANTERNS.
THE *ORANGE* LIGHT OF *AVARICE* HAS BEEN CLAIMED, LIKE THE LIVES OF THE ORANGE LANTERNS, BY THE OBSESSIVE AND GLUTTONOUS *LARFLEEZE.*
THE BLINDING *YELLOW TERROR* IS WIELDED BY THE RENEGADE GREEN LANTERN *SINESTRO* AND HIS SELF-NAMED CORPS.
THE BALANCE OF THE SPECTRUM AND THE ESSENTIAL LIGHT TO DESTROYING THE BLACK LANTERNS SHINES IN THE HANDS OF THE *GREEN LANTERN CORPS.*
THE GLOW OF *BLUE HOPE* IS ON THE VERGE OF EXTINCTION, KEPT ALIVE ONLY BY THE UNDYING FAITH OF *SAINT WALKER* AND A HANDFUL OF OTHERS.
AND THE *VIOLET* THROES OF LOVE EMPOWER THE *STAR SAPPHIRES,* WHO ATTEMPT TO CONVERT ALL TO THEIR WAY OF BEING.

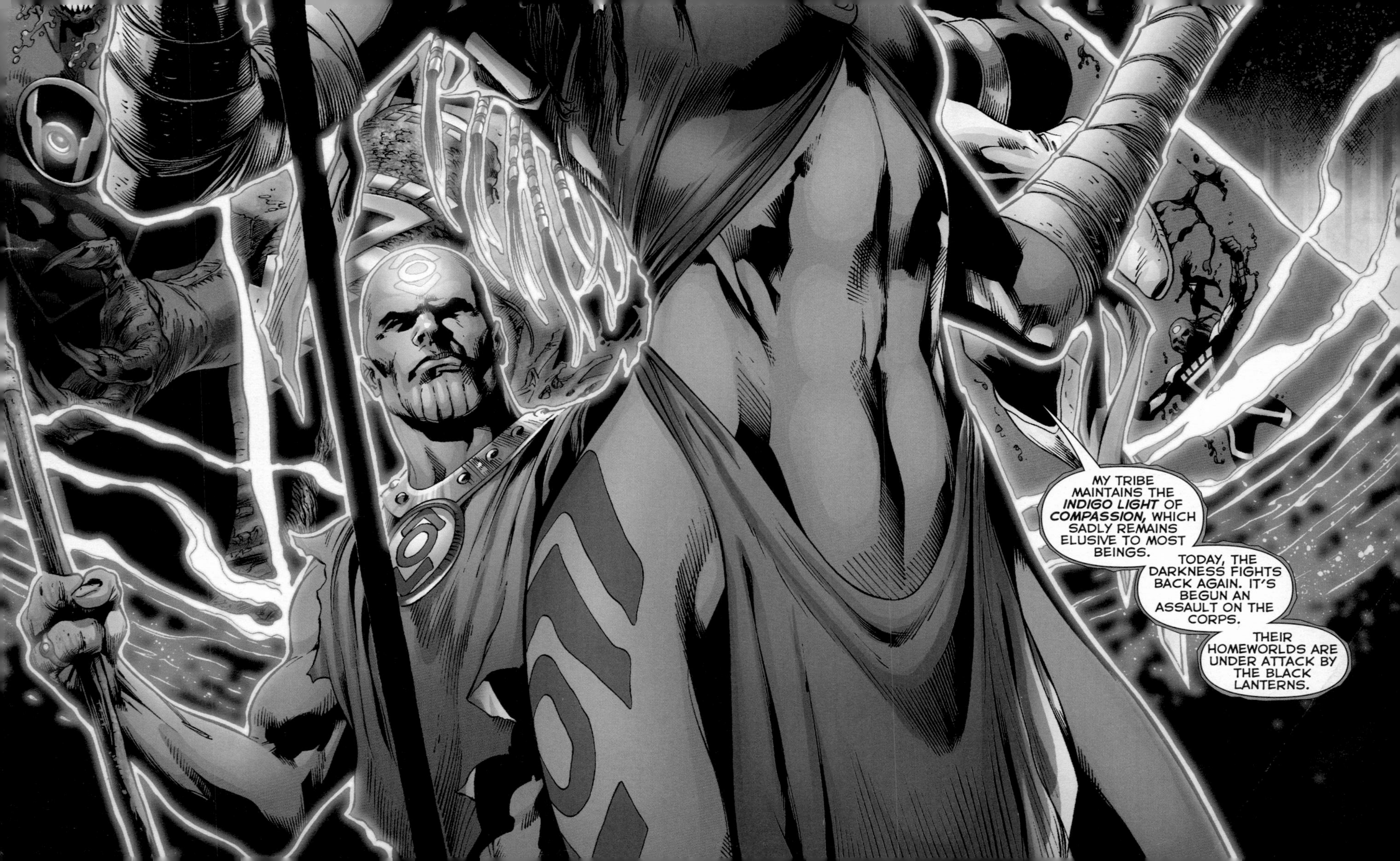
MY TRIBE MAINTAINS THE ***INDIGO LIGHT*** OF ***COMPASSION,*** WHICH SADLY REMAINS ELUSIVE TO MOST BEINGS.
TODAY, THE DARKNESS FIGHTS BACK AGAIN. IT'S BEGUN AN ASSAULT ON THE CORPS.
THEIR HOMEWORLDS ARE UNDER ATTACK BY THE BLACK LANTERNS.

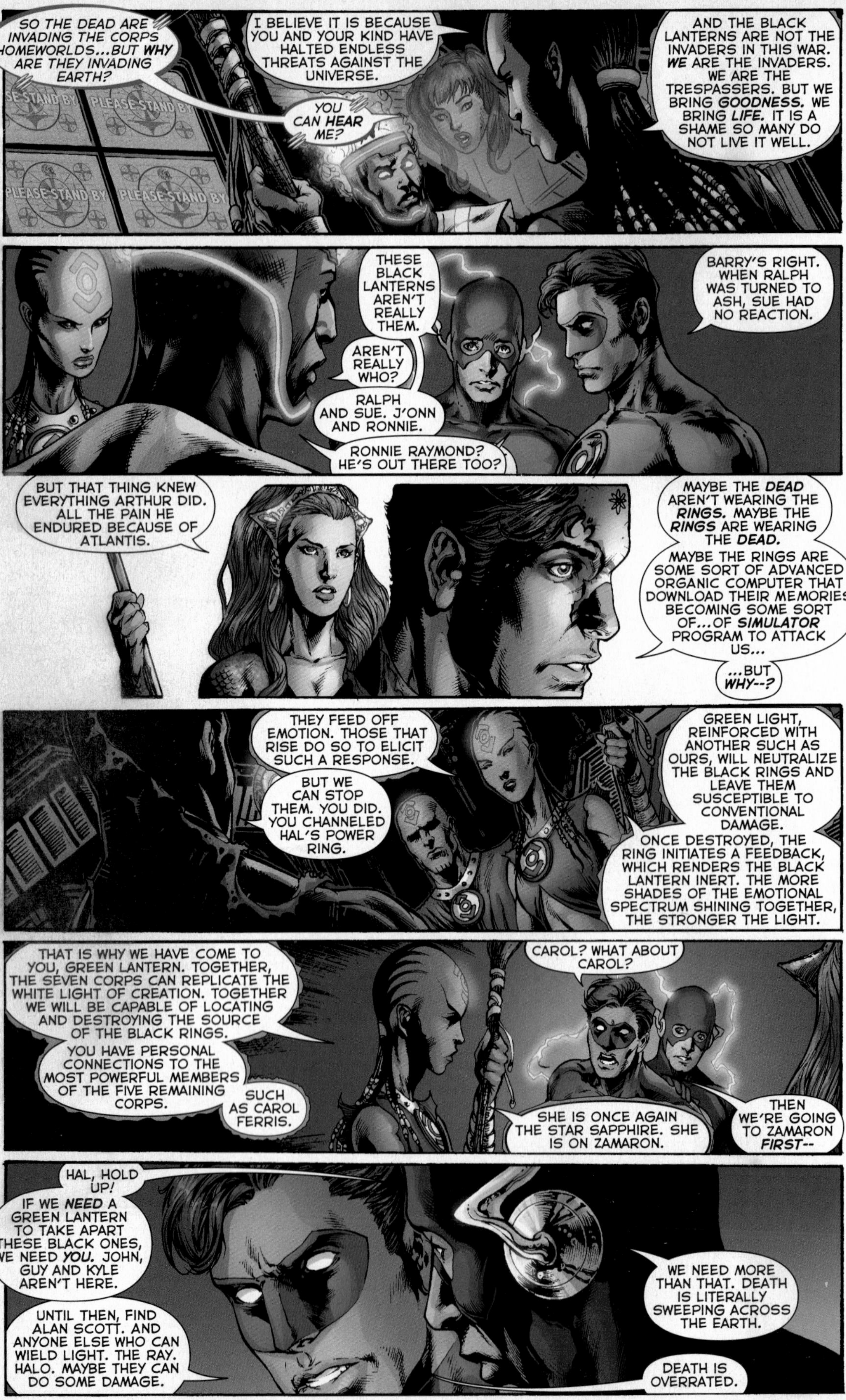

SO THE DEAD ARE INVADING THE CORPS HOMEWORLDS...BUT WHY ARE THEY INVADING EARTH?
I BELIEVE IT IS BECAUSE YOU AND YOUR KIND HAVE HALTED ENDLESS THREATS AGAINST THE UNIVERSE.
PLEASE STAND BY
YOU CAN HEAR ME?
AND THE BLACK LANTERNS ARE NOT THE INVADERS IN THIS WAR. WE ARE THE INVADERS. WE ARE THE TRESPASSERS. BUT WE BRING GOODNESS. WE BRING LIFE. IT IS A SHAME SO MANY DO NOT LIVE IT WELL.
THESE BLACK LANTERNS AREN'T REALLY THEM.
AREN'T REALLY WHO?
RALPH AND SUE. J'ONN AND RONNIE.
RONNIE RAYMOND? HE'S OUT THERE TOO?
BARRY'S RIGHT. WHEN RALPH WAS TURNED TO ASH, SUE HAD NO REACTION.
BUT THAT THING KNEW EVERYTHING ARTHUR DID. ALL THE PAIN HE ENDURED BECAUSE OF ATLANTIS.
MAYBE THE DEAD AREN'T WEARING THE RINGS. MAYBE THE RINGS ARE WEARING THE DEAD.
MAYBE THE RINGS ARE SOME SORT OF ADVANCED ORGANIC COMPUTER THAT DOWNLOAD THEIR MEMORIES BECOMING SOME SORT OF...OF SIMULATOR PROGRAM TO ATTACK US...
...BUT WHY--?
THEY FEED OFF EMOTION. THOSE THAT RISE DO SO TO ELICIT SUCH A RESPONSE.
BUT WE CAN STOP THEM. YOU DID. YOU CHANNELED HAL'S POWER RING.
GREEN LIGHT, REINFORCED WITH ANOTHER SUCH AS OURS, WILL NEUTRALIZE THE BLACK RINGS AND LEAVE THEM SUSCEPTIBLE TO CONVENTIONAL DAMAGE.
ONCE DESTROYED, THE RING INITIATES A FEEDBACK, WHICH RENDERS THE BLACK LANTERN INERT. THE MORE SHADES OF THE EMOTIONAL SPECTRUM SHINING TOGETHER, THE STRONGER THE LIGHT.
THAT IS WHY WE HAVE COME TO YOU, GREEN LANTERN. TOGETHER, THE SEVEN CORPS CAN REPLICATE THE WHITE LIGHT OF CREATION. TOGETHER WE WILL BE CAPABLE OF LOCATING AND DESTROYING THE SOURCE OF THE BLACK RINGS.
YOU HAVE PERSONAL CONNECTIONS TO THE MOST POWERFUL MEMBERS OF THE FIVE REMAINING CORPS.
SUCH AS CAROL FERRIS.
CAROL? WHAT ABOUT CAROL?
SHE IS ONCE AGAIN THE STAR SAPPHIRE. SHE IS ON ZAMARON.
THEN WE'RE GOING TO ZAMARON FIRST--
HAL, HOLD UP!
IF WE NEED A GREEN LANTERN TO TAKE APART THESE BLACK ONES, WE NEED YOU. JOHN, GUY AND KYLE AREN'T HERE.
UNTIL THEN, FIND ALAN SCOTT. AND ANYONE ELSE WHO CAN WIELD LIGHT. THE RAY. HALO. MAYBE THEY CAN DO SOME DAMAGE.
WE NEED MORE THAN THAT. DEATH IS LITERALLY SWEEPING ACROSS THE EARTH.
DEATH IS OVERRATED.

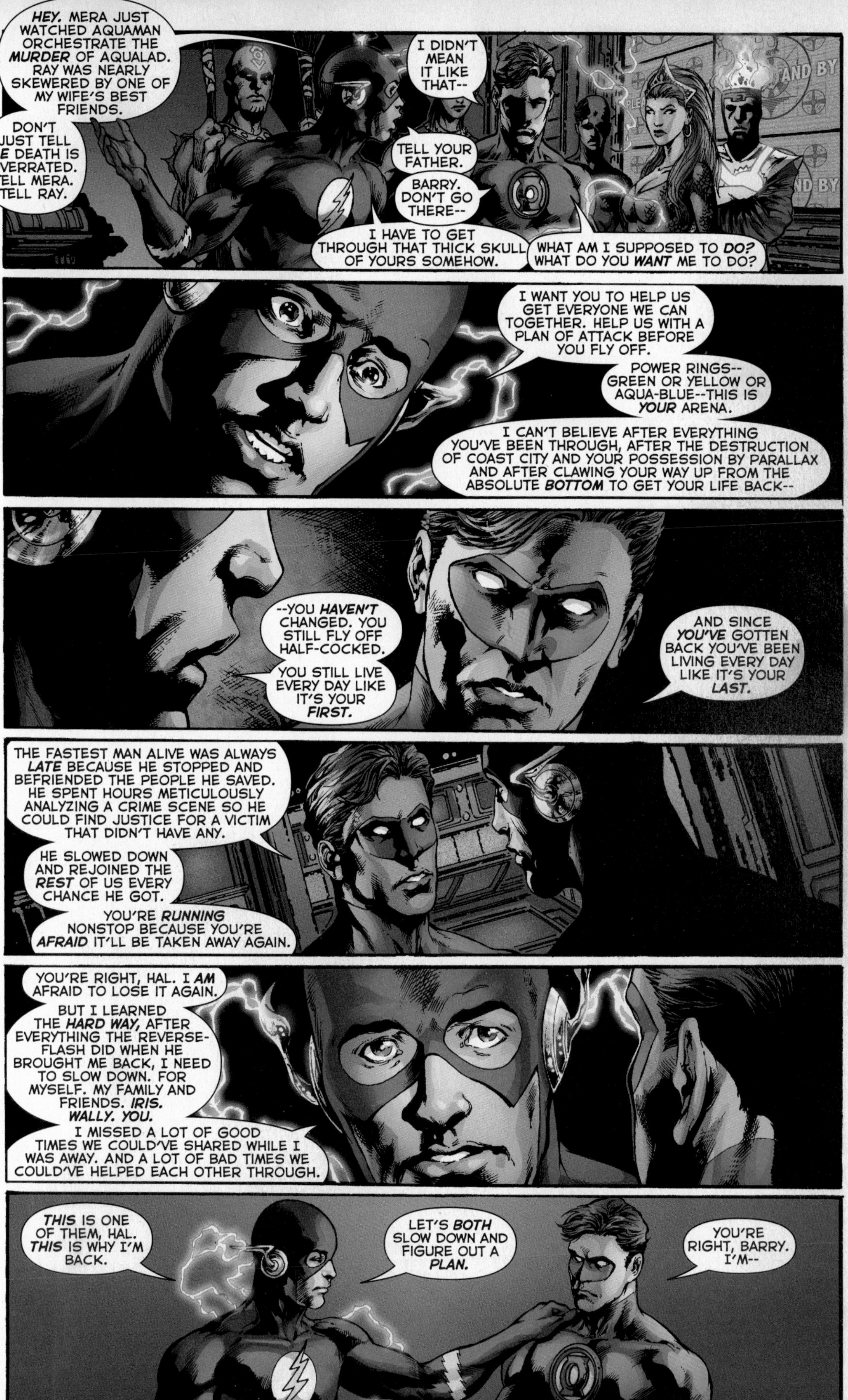
HEY. MERA JUST WATCHED AQUAMAN ORCHESTRATE THE MURDER OF AQUALAD. RAY WAS NEARLY SKEWERED BY ONE OF MY WIFE'S BEST FRIENDS.
DON'T JUST TELL ME DEATH IS OVERRATED. TELL MERA. TELL RAY.
I DIDN'T MEAN IT LIKE THAT--
TELL YOUR FATHER.
BARRY. DON'T GO THERE--
I HAVE TO GET THROUGH THAT THICK SKULL OF YOURS SOMEHOW.
WHAT AM I SUPPOSED TO DO? WHAT DO YOU WANT ME TO DO?
I WANT YOU TO HELP US GET EVERYONE WE CAN TOGETHER. HELP US WITH A PLAN OF ATTACK BEFORE YOU FLY OFF.
POWER RINGS--GREEN OR YELLOW OR AQUA-BLUE--THIS IS YOUR ARENA.
I CAN'T BELIEVE AFTER EVERYTHING YOU'VE BEEN THROUGH, AFTER THE DESTRUCTION OF COAST CITY AND YOUR POSSESSION BY PARALLAX AND AFTER CLAWING YOUR WAY UP FROM THE ABSOLUTE BOTTOM TO GET YOUR LIFE BACK--
--YOU HAVEN'T CHANGED. YOU STILL FLY OFF HALF-COCKED.
YOU STILL LIVE EVERY DAY LIKE IT'S YOUR FIRST.
AND SINCE YOU'VE GOTTEN BACK YOU'VE BEEN LIVING EVERY DAY LIKE IT'S YOUR LAST.
THE FASTEST MAN ALIVE WAS ALWAYS LATE BECAUSE HE STOPPED AND BEFRIENDED THE PEOPLE HE SAVED. HE SPENT HOURS METICULOUSLY ANALYZING A CRIME SCENE SO HE COULD FIND JUSTICE FOR A VICTIM THAT DIDN'T HAVE ANY.
HE SLOWED DOWN AND REJOINED THE REST OF US EVERY CHANCE HE GOT.
YOU'RE RUNNING NONSTOP BECAUSE YOU'RE AFRAID IT'LL BE TAKEN AWAY AGAIN.
YOU'RE RIGHT, HAL. I AM AFRAID TO LOSE IT AGAIN.
BUT I LEARNED THE HARD WAY, AFTER EVERYTHING THE REVERSE-FLASH DID WHEN HE BROUGHT ME BACK, I NEED TO SLOW DOWN. FOR MYSELF. MY FAMILY AND FRIENDS. IRIS. WALLY. YOU.
I MISSED A LOT OF GOOD TIMES WE COULD'VE SHARED WHILE I WAS AWAY. AND A LOT OF BAD TIMES WE COULD'VE HELPED EACH OTHER THROUGH.
THIS IS ONE OF THEM, HAL. THIS IS WHY I'M BACK.
LET'S BOTH SLOW DOWN AND FIGURE OUT A PLAN.
YOU'RE RIGHT, BARRY. I'M--

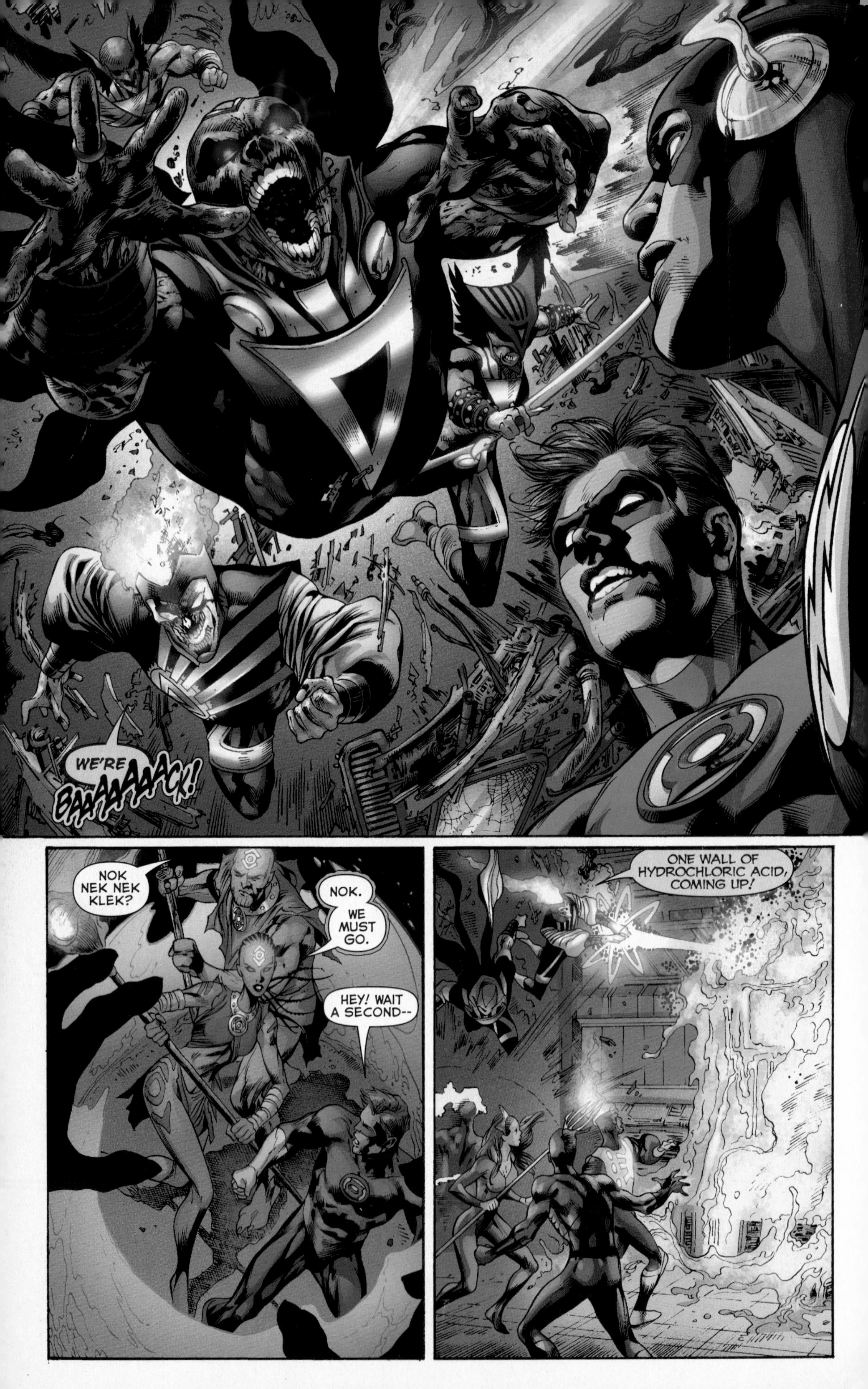
WE'RE BAAAAAAACK!
NOK NEK NEK KLEK?
NOK. WE MUST GO.
HEY! WAIT A SECOND--
ONE WALL OF HYDROCHLORIC ACID, COMING UP!

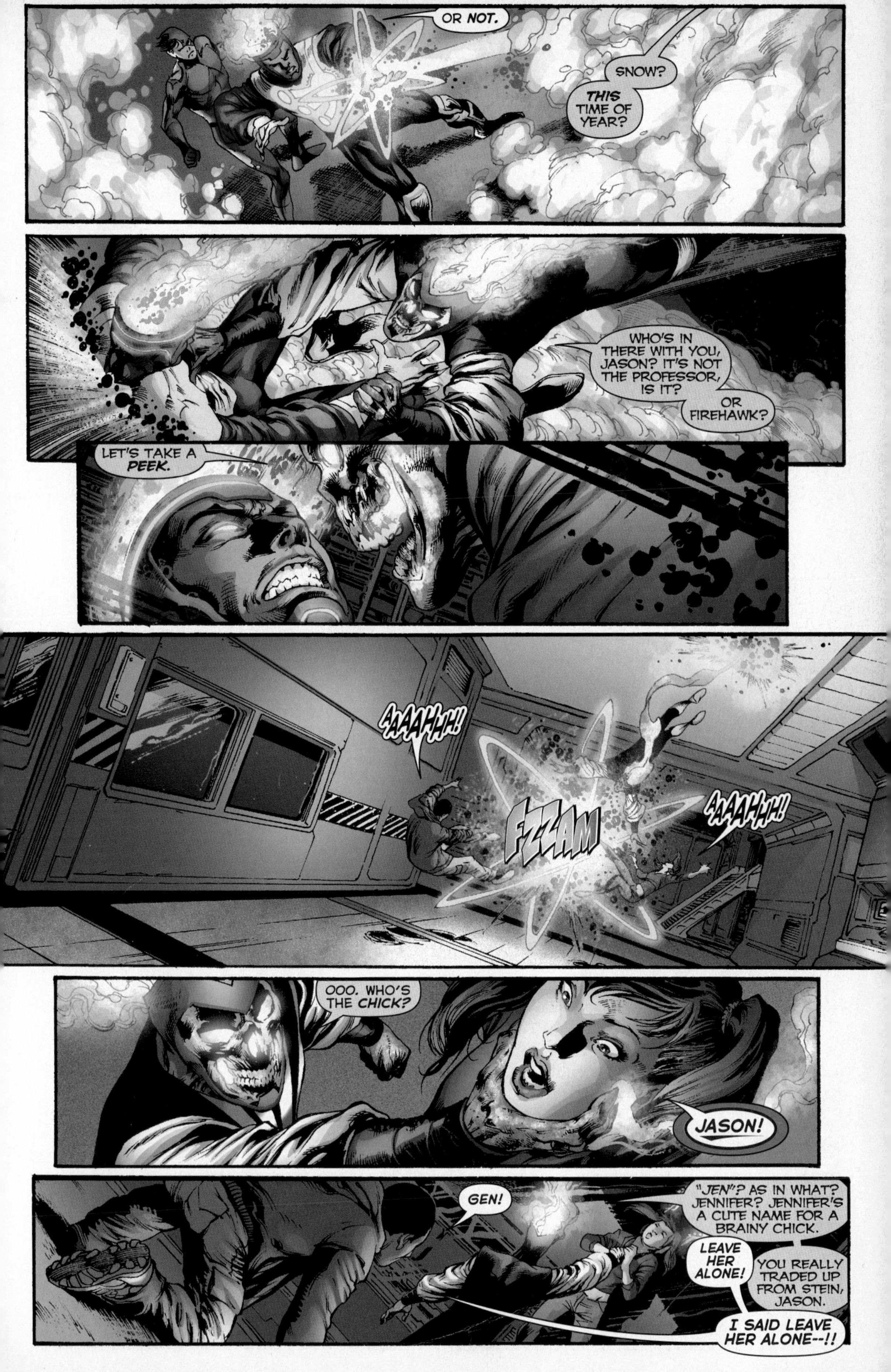
OR NOT.
SNOW? THIS TIME OF YEAR?
WHO'S IN THERE WITH YOU, JASON? IT'S NOT THE PROFESSOR, IS IT?
OR FIREHAWK?
LET'S TAKE A PEEK.
AAAAHHH!
FZZAM
AAAAHHH!
OOO. WHO'S THE CHICK?
JASON!
GEN!
"JEN"? AS IN WHAT? JENNIFER? JENNIFER'S A CUTE NAME FOR A BRAINY CHICK.
LEAVE HER ALONE!
YOU REALLY TRADED UP FROM STEIN, JASON.
I SAID LEAVE HER ALONE--!!

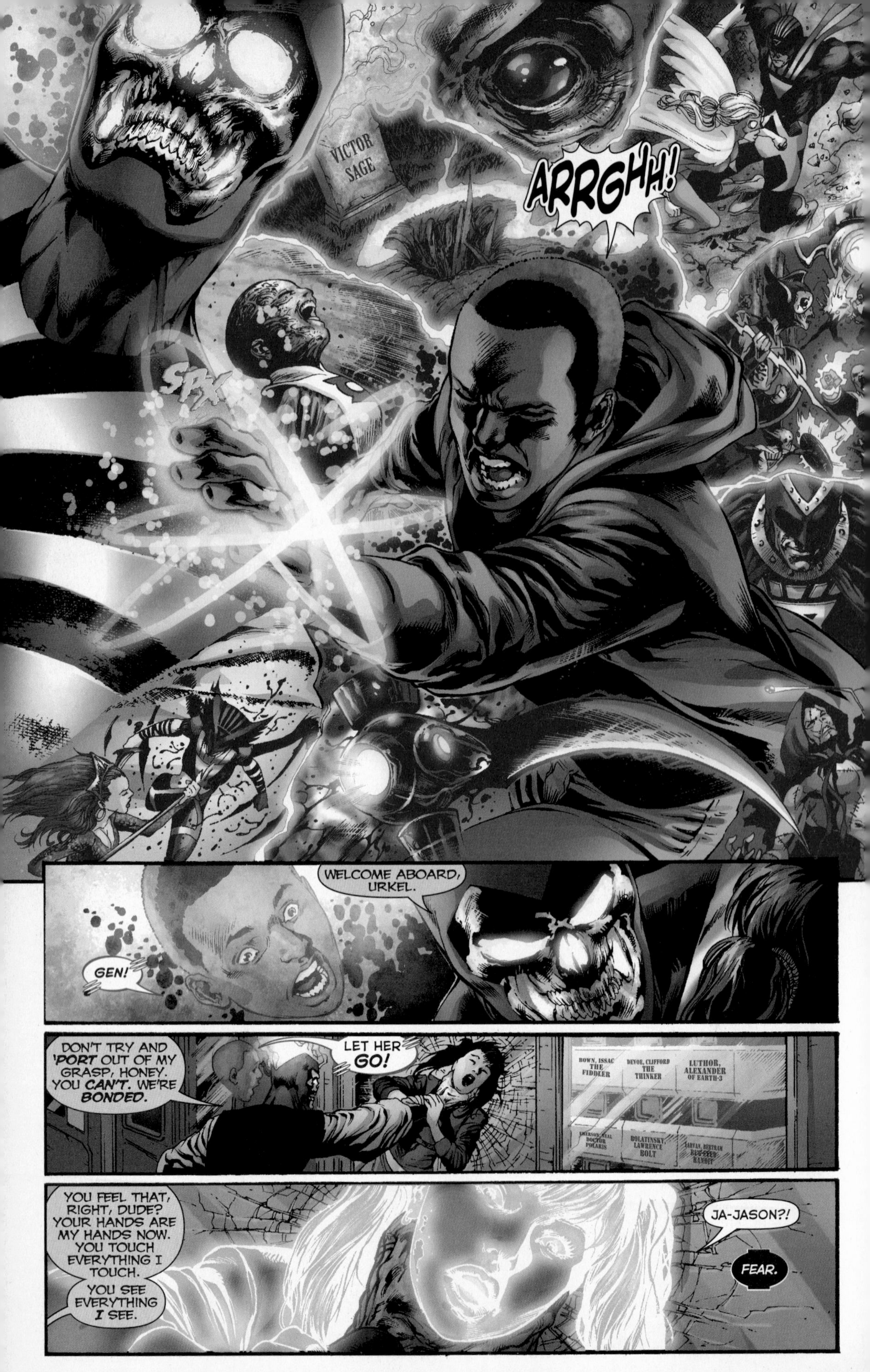
VICTOR SAGE
ARRGHH!
SPX
WELCOME ABOARD, URKEL.
GEN!
DON'T TRY AND 'PORT OUT OF MY GRASP, HONEY. YOU CAN'T. WE'RE BONDED.
LET HER GO!
BOWN, ISSAC THE FIDDLER
DEVOE, CLIFFORD THE THINKER
LUTHOR, ALEXANDER OF EARTH-3
DOCTOR POLARIS
BOLATINSKY, LAWRENCE BOLT
YOU FEEL THAT, RIGHT, DUDE? YOUR HANDS ARE MY HANDS NOW. YOU TOUCH EVERYTHING I TOUCH.
YOU SEE EVERYTHING I SEE.
JA-JASON?!
FEAR.

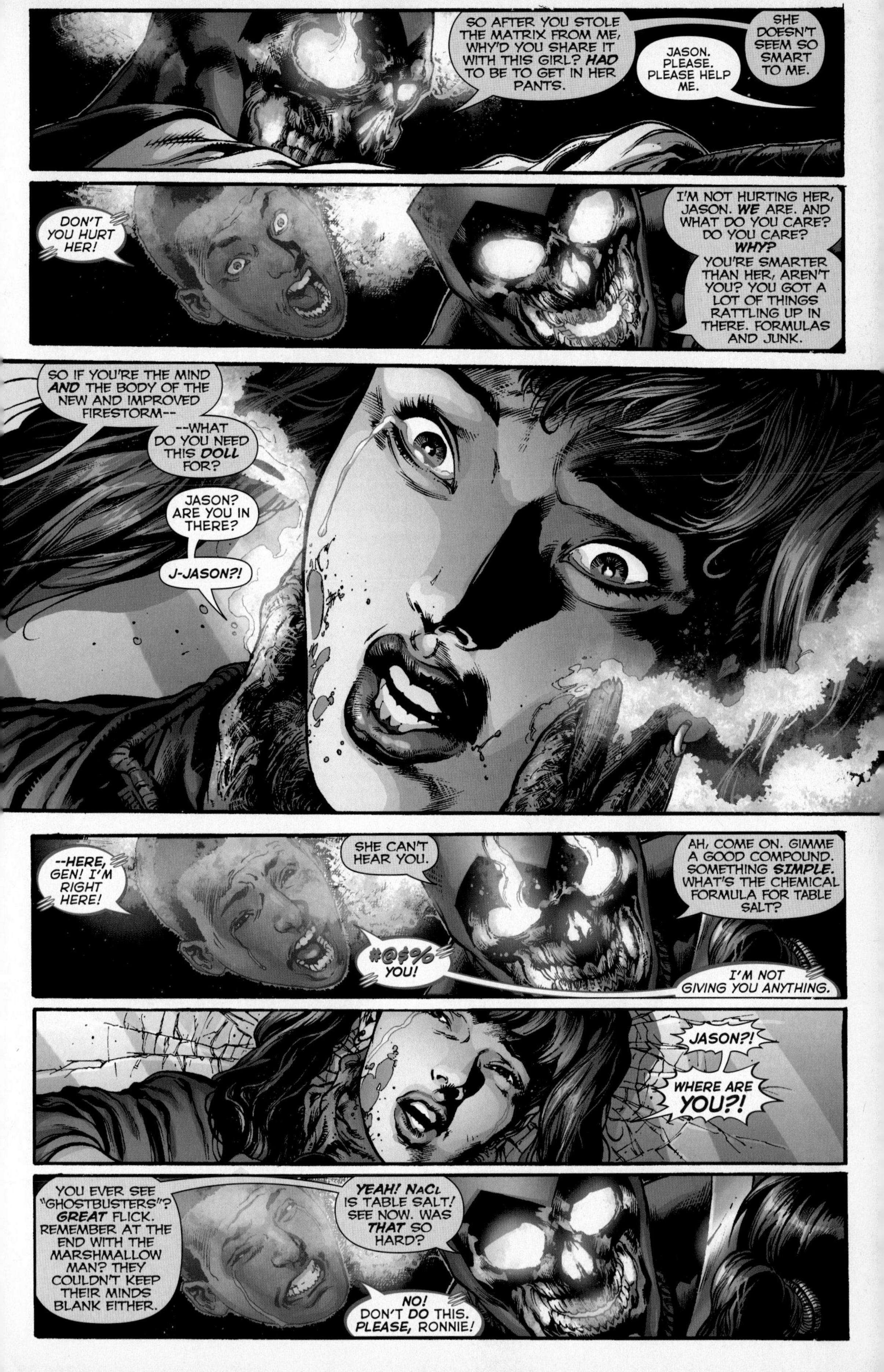
SO AFTER YOU STOLE THE MATRIX FROM ME, WHY'D YOU SHARE IT WITH THIS GIRL? HAD TO BE TO GET IN HER PANTS.
JASON. PLEASE. PLEASE HELP ME.
SHE DOESN'T SEEM SO SMART TO ME.
DON'T YOU HURT HER!
I'M NOT HURTING HER, JASON. WE ARE. AND WHAT DO YOU CARE? DO YOU CARE? WHY?
YOU'RE SMARTER THAN HER, AREN'T YOU? YOU GOT A LOT OF THINGS RATTLING UP IN THERE. FORMULAS AND JUNK.
SO IF YOU'RE THE MIND AND THE BODY OF THE NEW AND IMPROVED FIRESTORM--
--WHAT DO YOU NEED THIS DOLL FOR?
JASON? ARE YOU IN THERE?
J-JASON?!
--HERE, GEN! I'M RIGHT HERE!
SHE CAN'T HEAR YOU.
AH, COME ON. GIMME A GOOD COMPOUND. SOMETHING SIMPLE. WHAT'S THE CHEMICAL FORMULA FOR TABLE SALT?
#@$% YOU!
I'M NOT GIVING YOU ANYTHING.
JASON?!
WHERE ARE YOU?!
YOU EVER SEE "GHOSTBUSTERS"? GREAT FLICK. REMEMBER AT THE END WITH THE MARSHMALLOW MAN? THEY COULDN'T KEEP THEIR MINDS BLANK EITHER.
YEAH! NaCl IS TABLE SALT! SEE NOW. WAS THAT SO HARD?
NO! DON'T DO THIS. PLEASE, RONNIE!

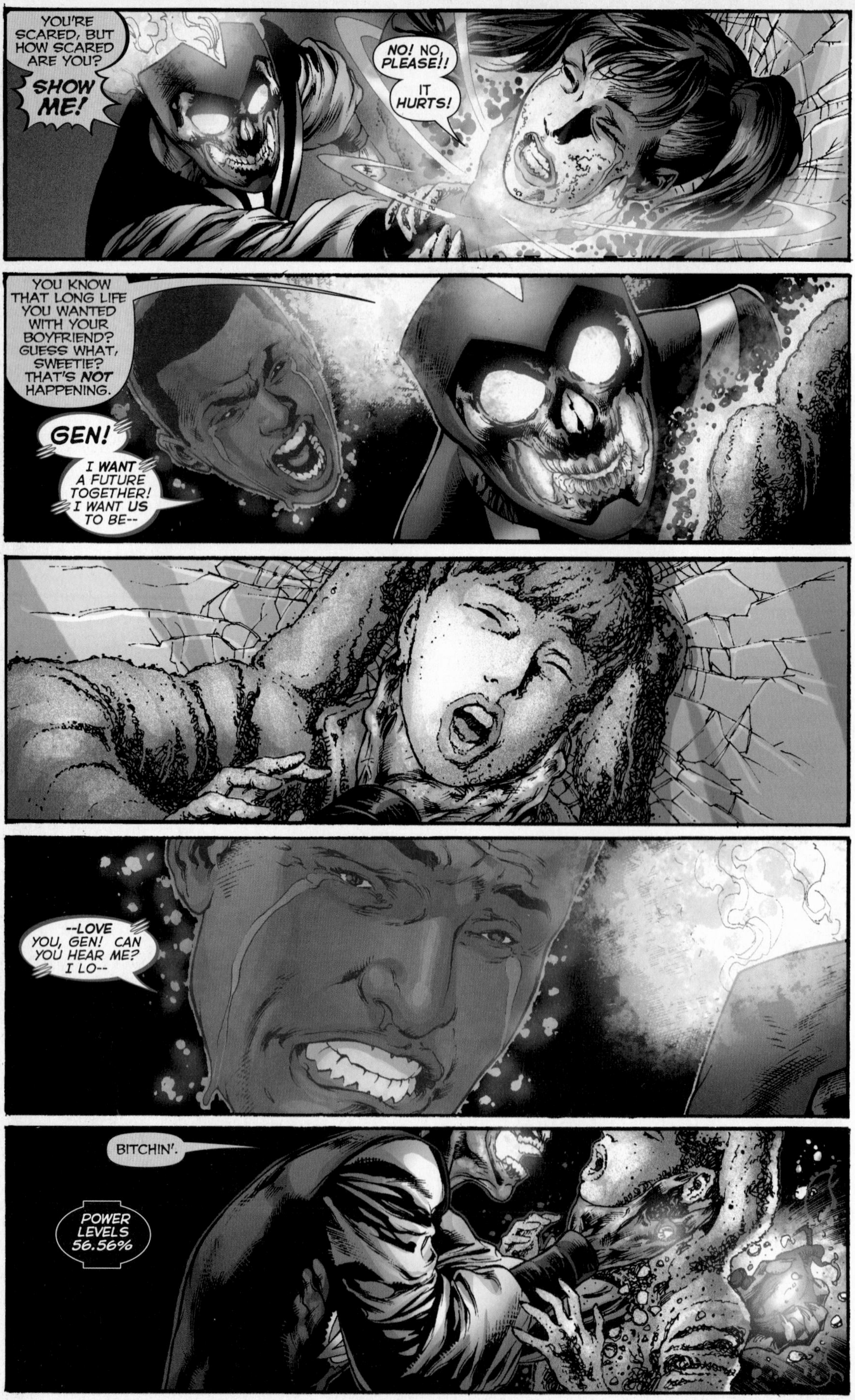
YOU'RE SCARED, BUT HOW SCARED ARE YOU? SHOW ME!
NO! NO, PLEASE!!
IT HURTS!
YOU KNOW THAT LONG LIFE YOU WANTED WITH YOUR BOYFRIEND? GUESS WHAT, SWEETIE? THAT'S NOT HAPPENING.
GEN!
I WANT A FUTURE TOGETHER! I WANT US TO BE--
--LOVE YOU, GEN! CAN YOU HEAR ME? I LO--
BITCHIN'.
POWER LEVELS 56.56%

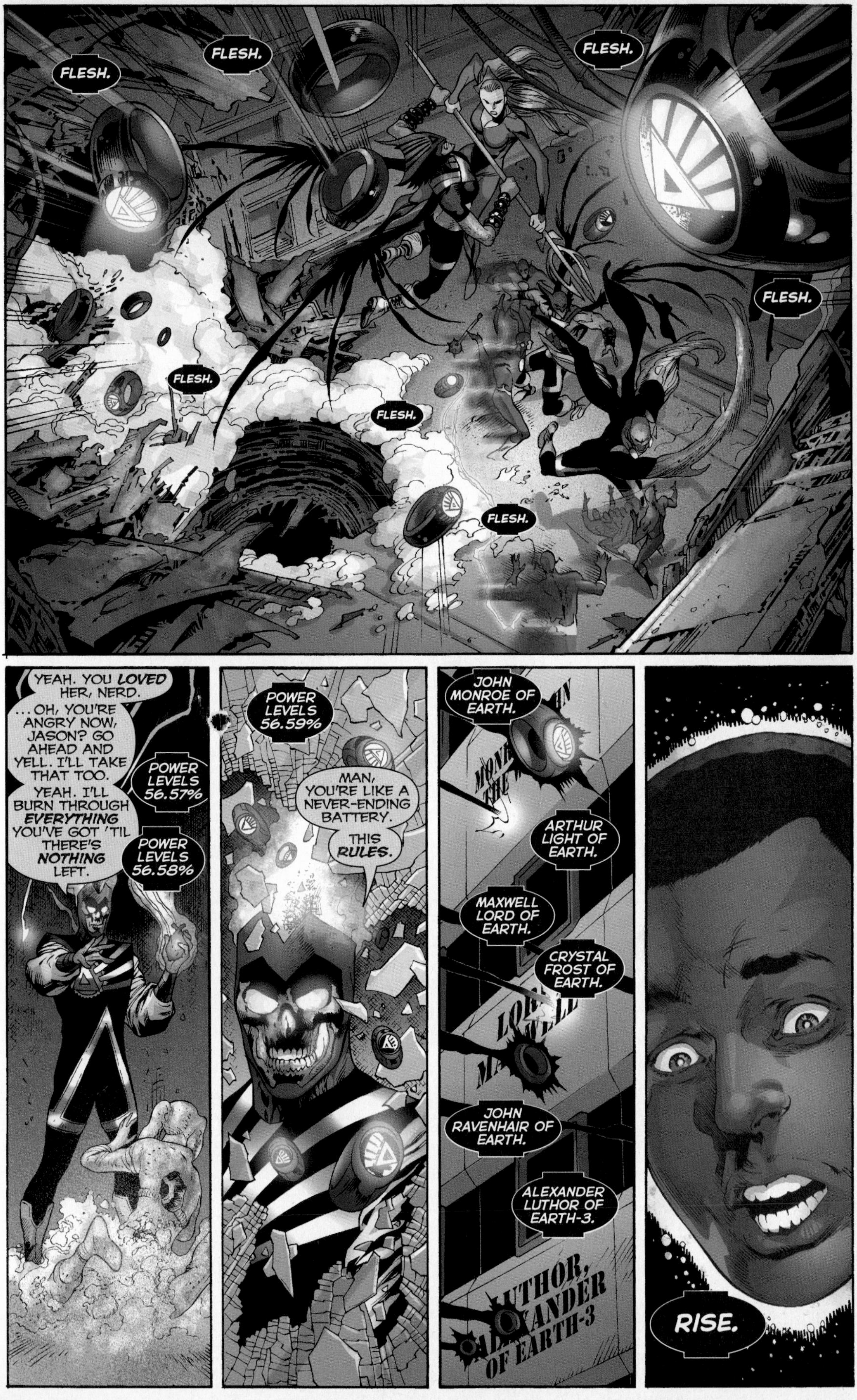
FLESH.
FLESH.
FLESH.
FLESH.
FLESH.
FLESH.
FLESH.
YEAH. YOU LOVED HER, NERD.
...OH, YOU'RE ANGRY NOW, JASON? GO AHEAD AND YELL. I'LL TAKE THAT TOO.
POWER LEVELS 56.57%
YEAH. I'LL BURN THROUGH EVERYTHING YOU'VE GOT 'TIL THERE'S NOTHING LEFT.
POWER LEVELS 56.58%
POWER LEVELS 56.59%
MAN, YOU'RE LIKE A NEVER-ENDING BATTERY.
THIS RULES.
JOHN MONROE OF EARTH.
ARTHUR LIGHT OF EARTH.
MAXWELL LORD OF EARTH.
CRYSTAL FROST OF EARTH.
JOHN RAVENHAIR OF EARTH.
ALEXANDER LUTHOR OF EARTH-3.
RISE.

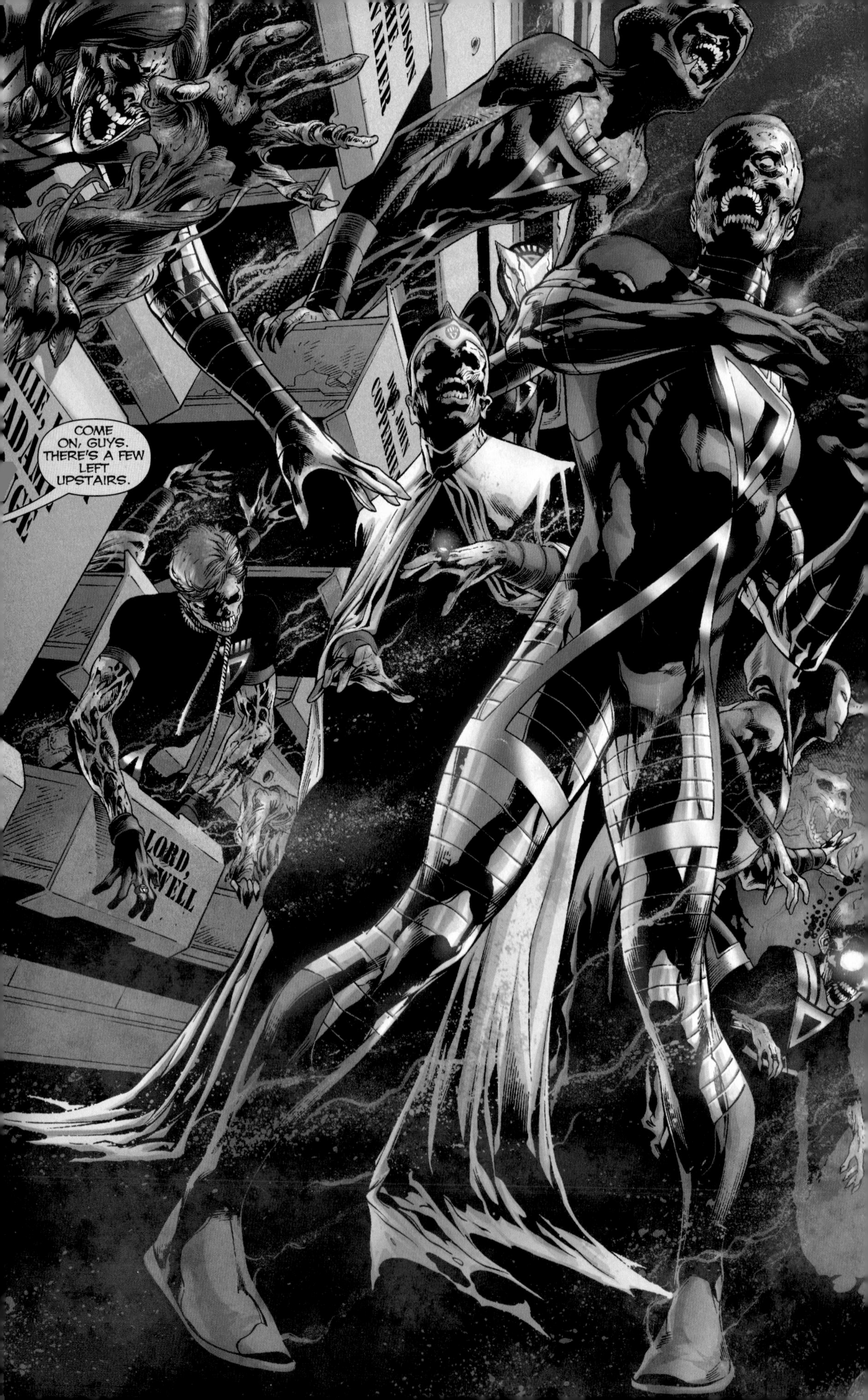
COME ON, GUYS. THERE'S A FEW LEFT UPSTAIRS.
LORD,

PART FOUR

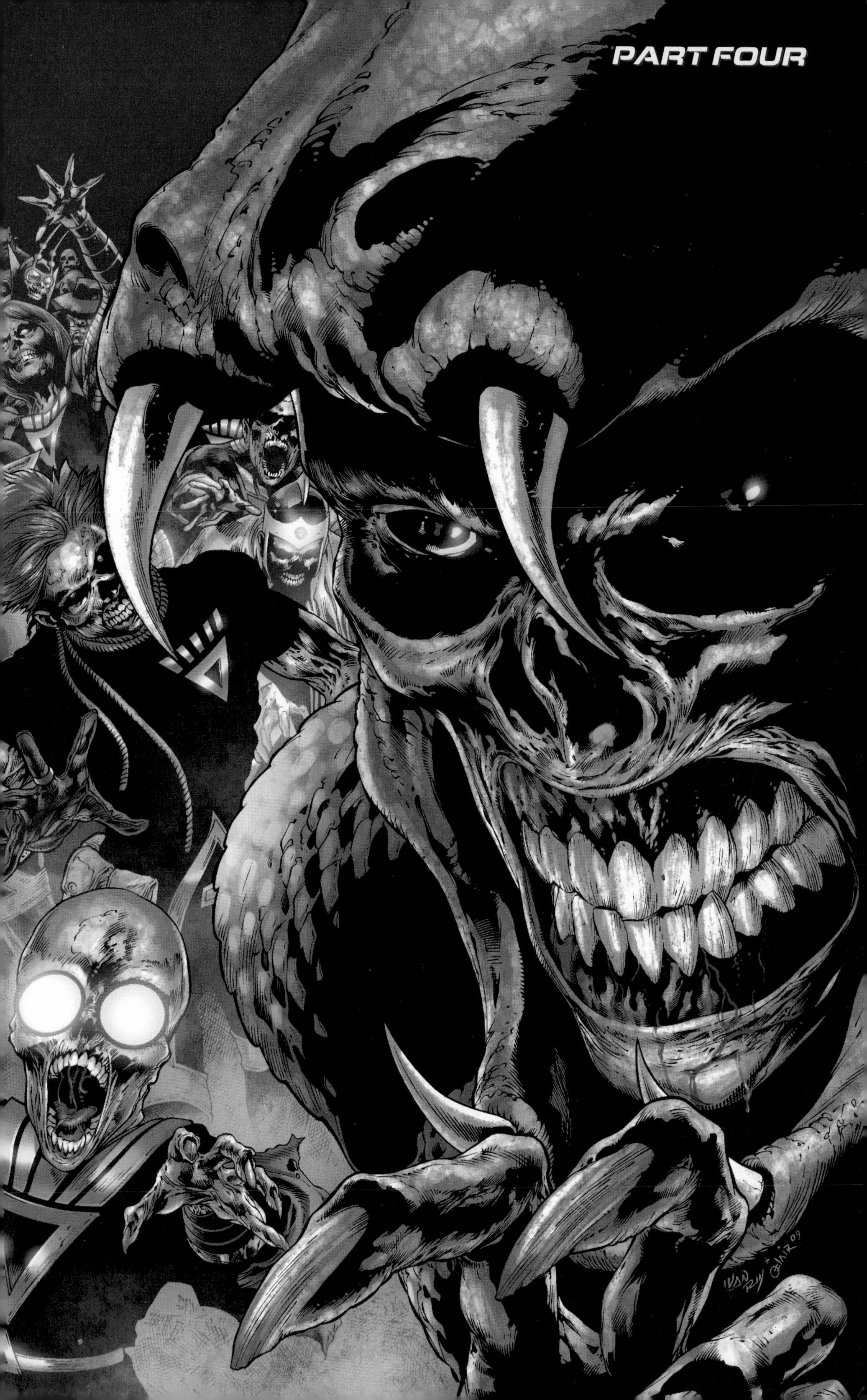

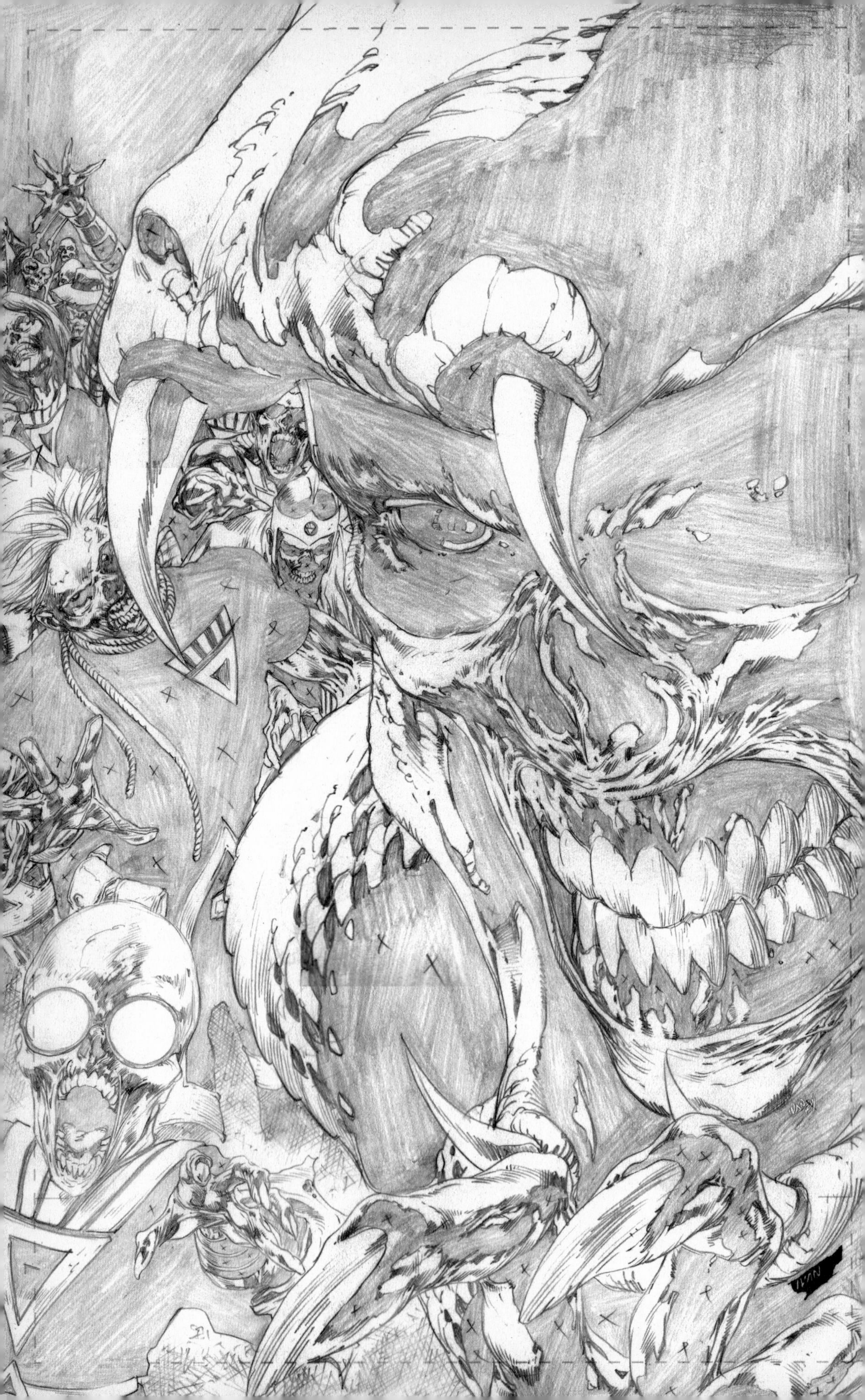
IVAN

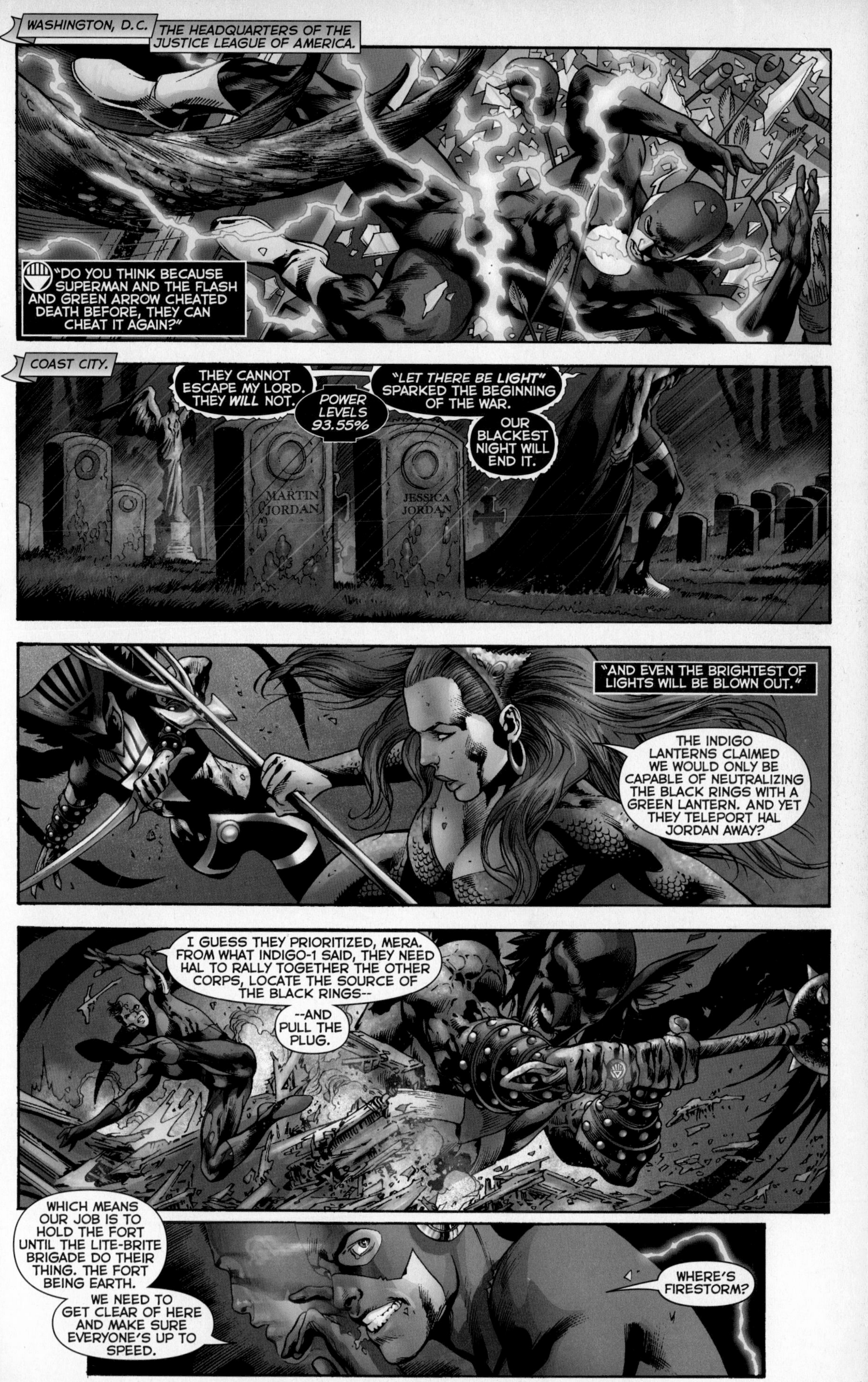
WASHINGTON, D.C.
THE HEADQUARTERS OF THE JUSTICE LEAGUE OF AMERICA.
"DO YOU THINK BECAUSE SUPERMAN AND THE FLASH AND GREEN ARROW CHEATED DEATH BEFORE, THEY CAN CHEAT IT AGAIN?"
COAST CITY.
THEY CANNOT ESCAPE MY LORD. THEY WILL NOT.
POWER LEVELS 93.55%
"LET THERE BE LIGHT" SPARKED THE BEGINNING OF THE WAR.
OUR BLACKEST NIGHT WILL END IT.
MARTIN JORDAN
JESSICA JORDAN
"AND EVEN THE BRIGHTEST OF LIGHTS WILL BE BLOWN OUT."
THE INDIGO LANTERNS CLAIMED WE WOULD ONLY BE CAPABLE OF NEUTRALIZING THE BLACK RINGS WITH A GREEN LANTERN. AND YET THEY TELEPORT HAL JORDAN AWAY?
I GUESS THEY PRIORITIZED, MERA. FROM WHAT INDIGO-1 SAID, THEY NEED HAL TO RALLY TOGETHER THE OTHER CORPS, LOCATE THE SOURCE OF THE BLACK RINGS--
--AND PULL THE PLUG.
WHICH MEANS OUR JOB IS TO HOLD THE FORT UNTIL THE LITE-BRITE BRIGADE DO THEIR THING. THE FORT BEING EARTH.
WE NEED TO GET CLEAR OF HERE AND MAKE SURE EVERYONE'S UP TO SPEED.
WHERE'S FIRESTORM?

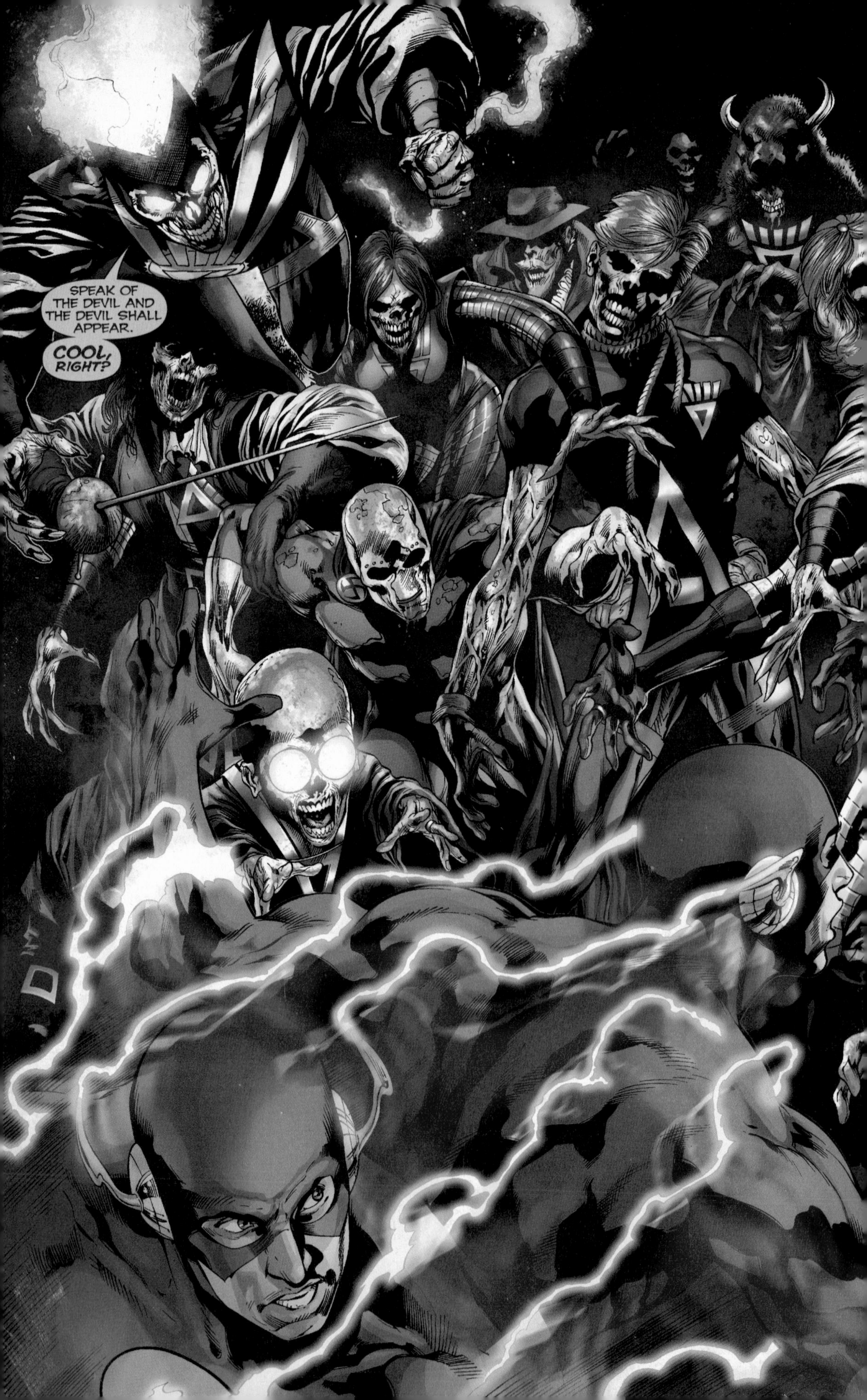
SPEAK OF THE DEVIL AND THE DEVIL SHALL APPEAR.
COOL, RIGHT?

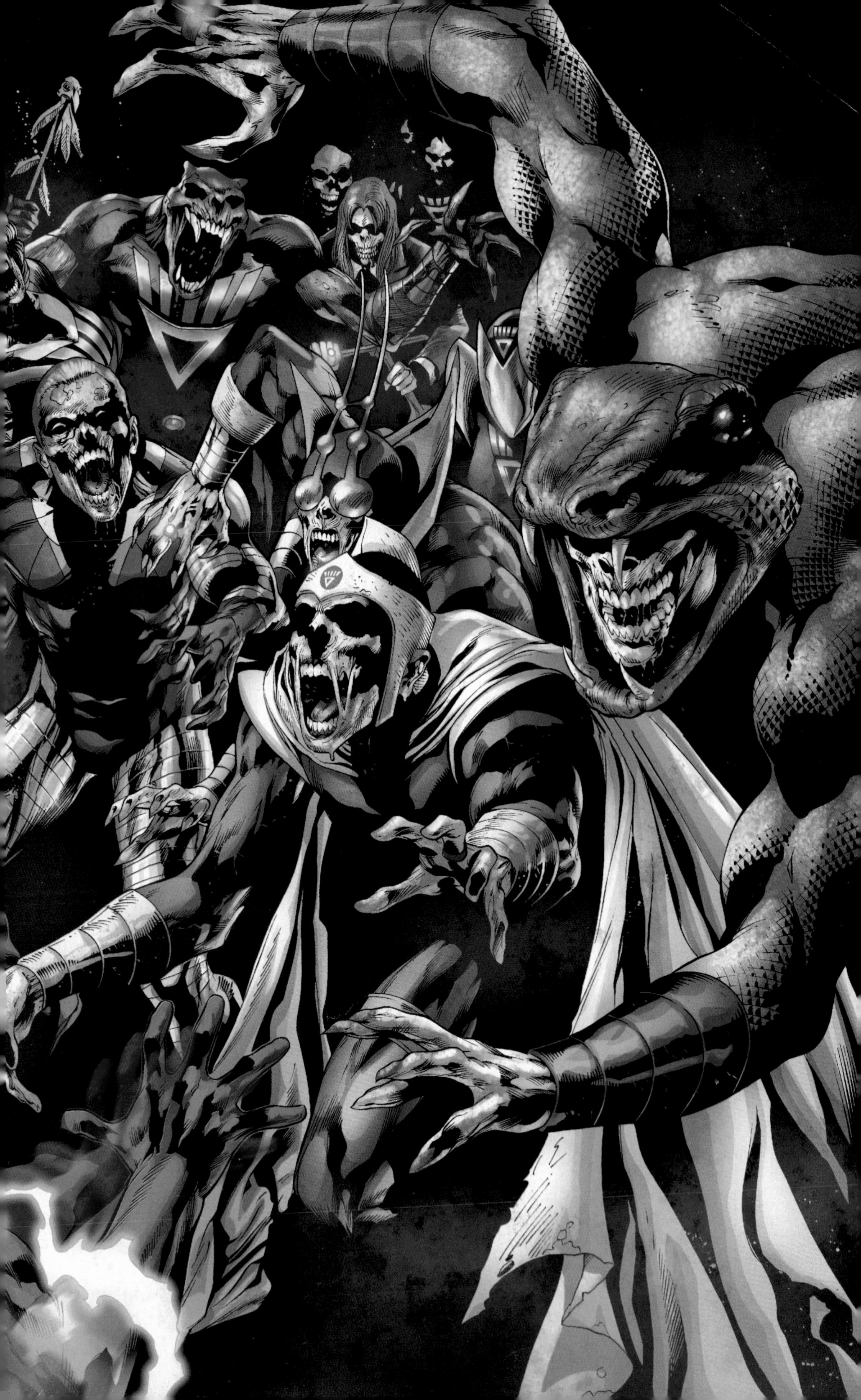

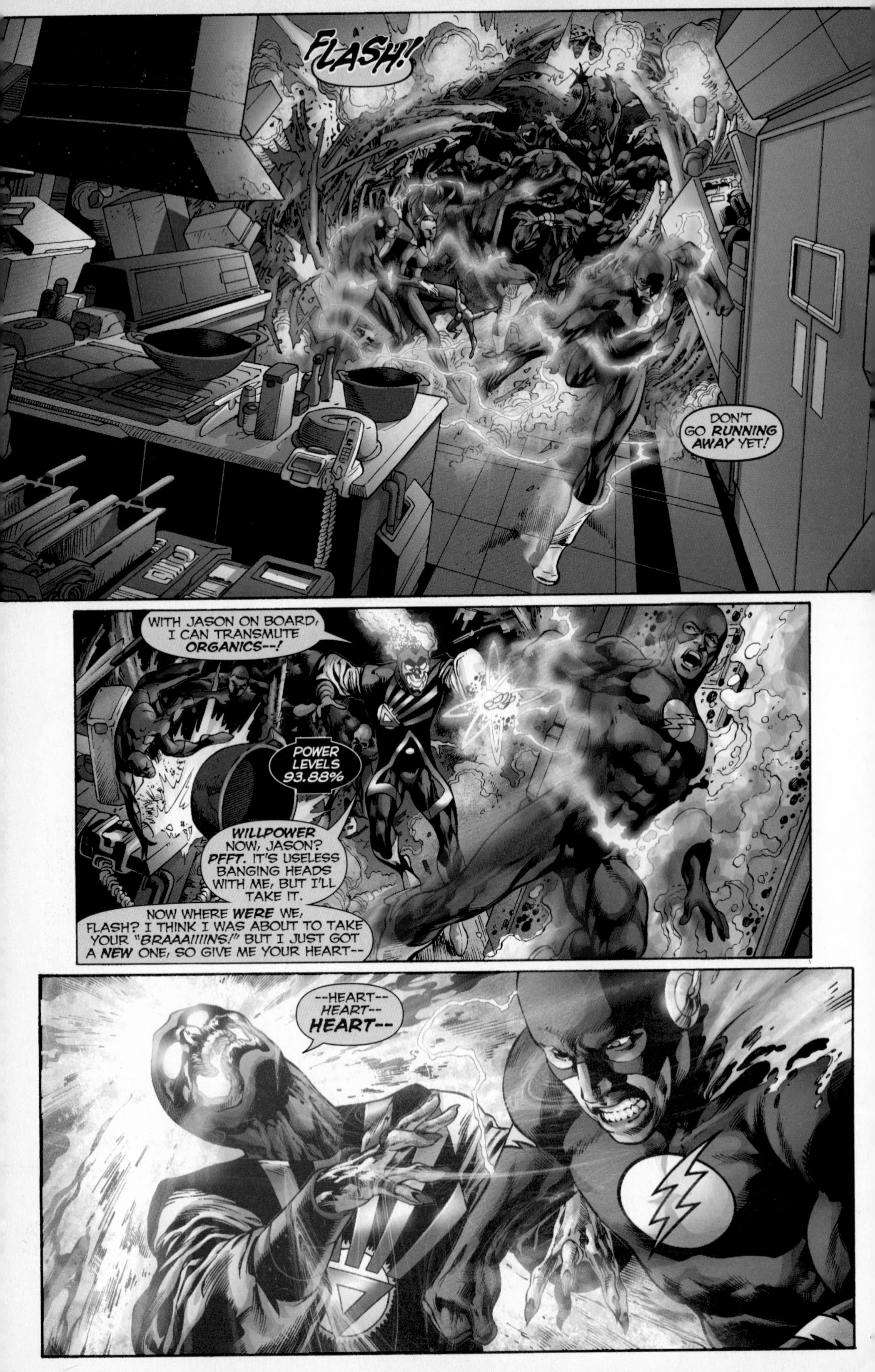
FLASH!
DON'T GO RUNNING AWAY YET!
WITH JASON ON BOARD, I CAN TRANSMUTE ORGANICS--!
POWER LEVELS 93.88%
WILLPOWER NOW, JASON? PFFT. IT'S USELESS BANGING HEADS WITH ME, BUT I'LL TAKE IT.
NOW WHERE WERE WE, FLASH? I THINK I WAS ABOUT TO TAKE YOUR "BRAAAIIIINS!" BUT I JUST GOT A NEW ONE, SO GIVE ME YOUR HEART--
--HEART-- HEART-- HEART--

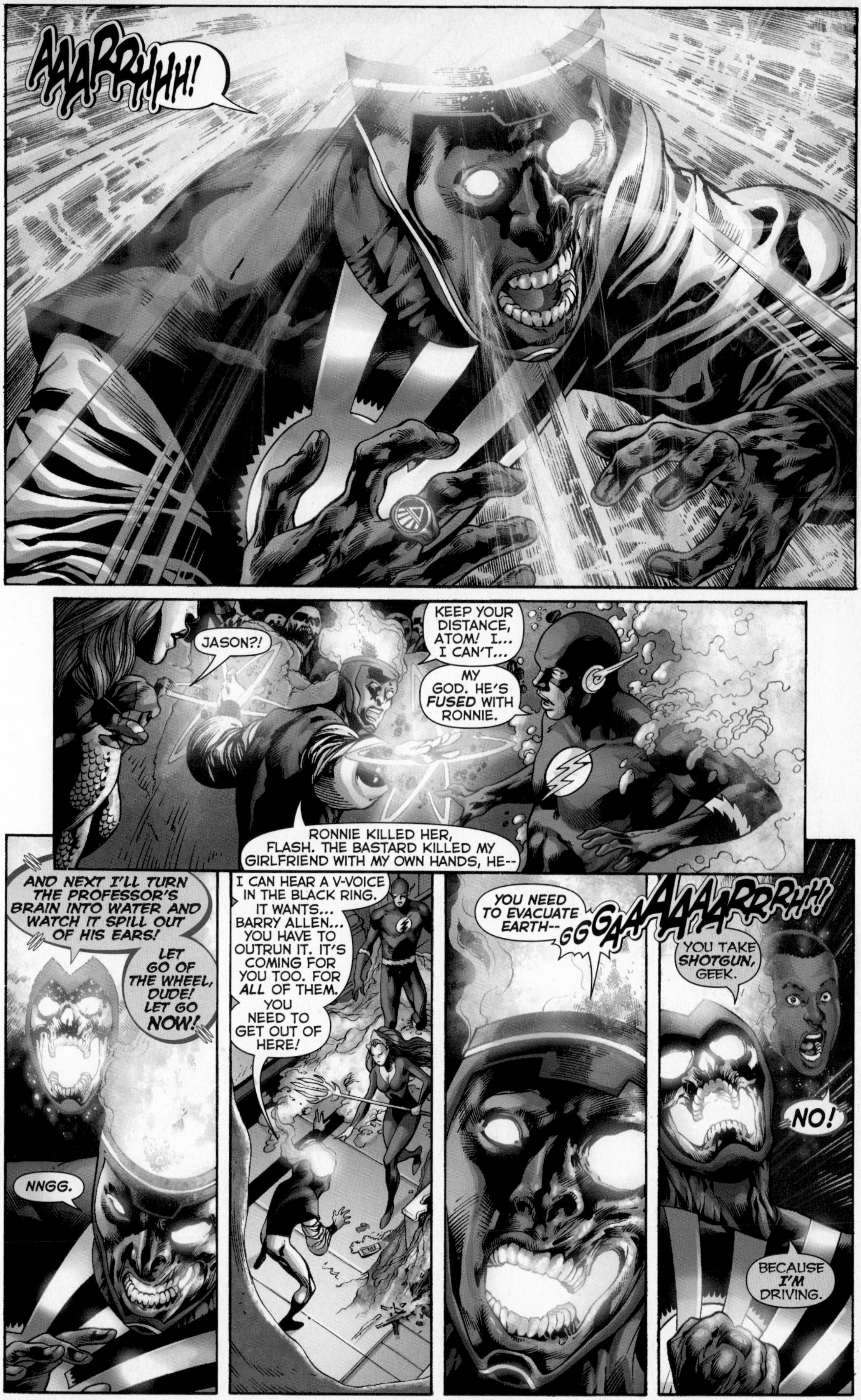
AAARRHHH!
JASON?!
KEEP YOUR DISTANCE, ATOM! I... I CAN'T...
MY GOD. HE'S *FUSED* WITH RONNIE.
RONNIE KILLED HER, FLASH. THE BASTARD KILLED MY GIRLFRIEND WITH MY OWN HANDS, HE--
AND NEXT I'LL TURN THE PROFESSOR'S BRAIN INTO WATER AND WATCH IT SPILL OUT OF HIS EARS!
LET GO OF THE WHEEL, DUDE! LET GO *NOW!*
NNGG.
I CAN HEAR A V-VOICE IN THE BLACK RING. IT WANTS... BARRY ALLEN... YOU HAVE TO OUTRUN IT. IT'S COMING FOR YOU TOO. FOR *ALL* OF THEM.
YOU NEED TO GET OUT OF HERE!
YOU NEED TO EVACUATE EARTH--
GGGAAAAAARRRHH!
YOU TAKE *SHOTGUN*, GEEK.
NO!
BECAUSE *I'M* DRIVING.

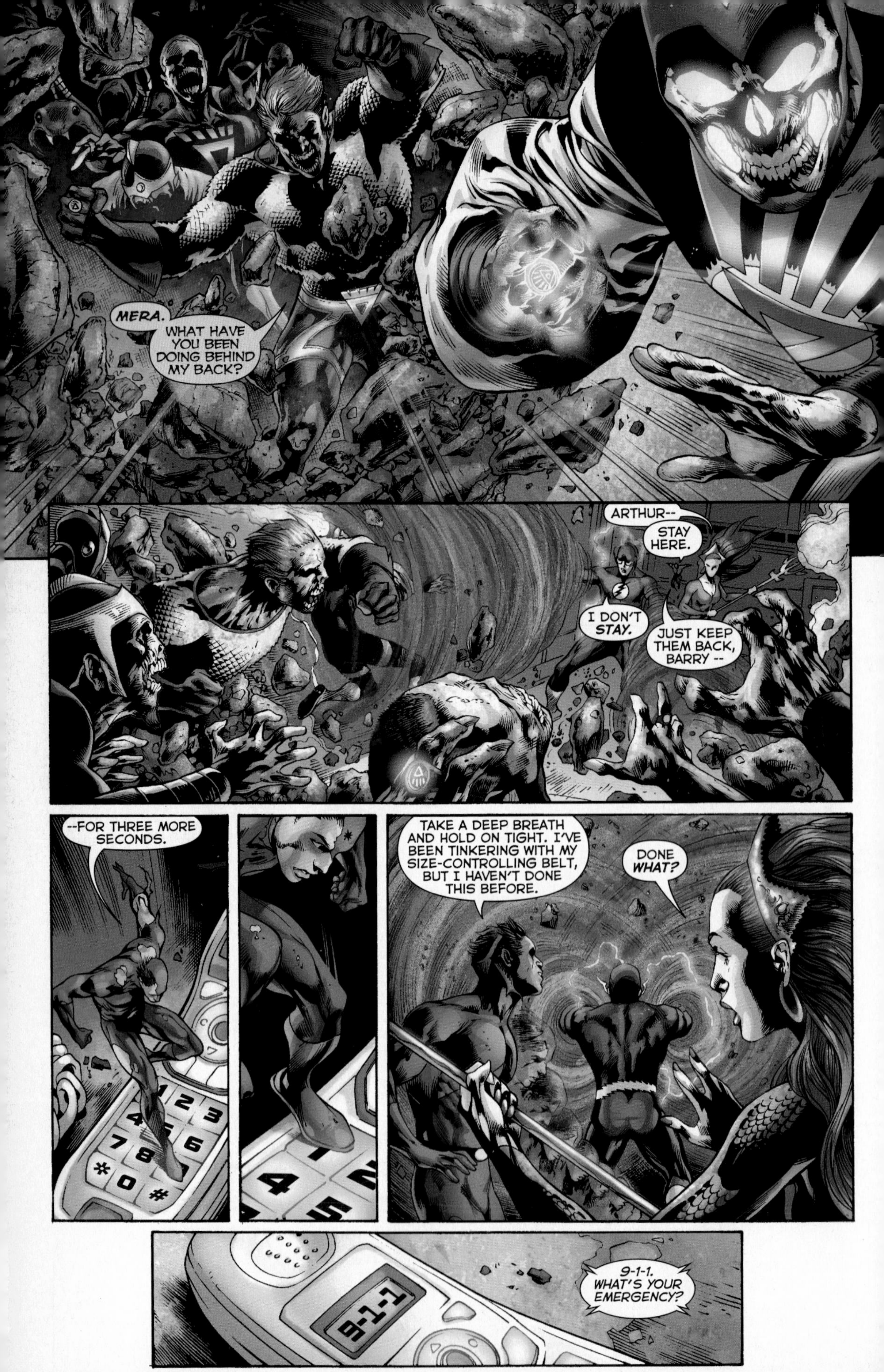
MERA.
WHAT HAVE YOU BEEN DOING BEHIND MY BACK?
ARTHUR--
STAY HERE.
I DON'T STAY.
JUST KEEP THEM BACK, BARRY --
--FOR THREE MORE SECONDS.
TAKE A DEEP BREATH AND HOLD ON TIGHT. I'VE BEEN TINKERING WITH MY SIZE-CONTROLLING BELT, BUT I HAVEN'T DONE THIS BEFORE.
DONE WHAT?
9-1-1
9-1-1. WHAT'S YOUR EMERGENCY?

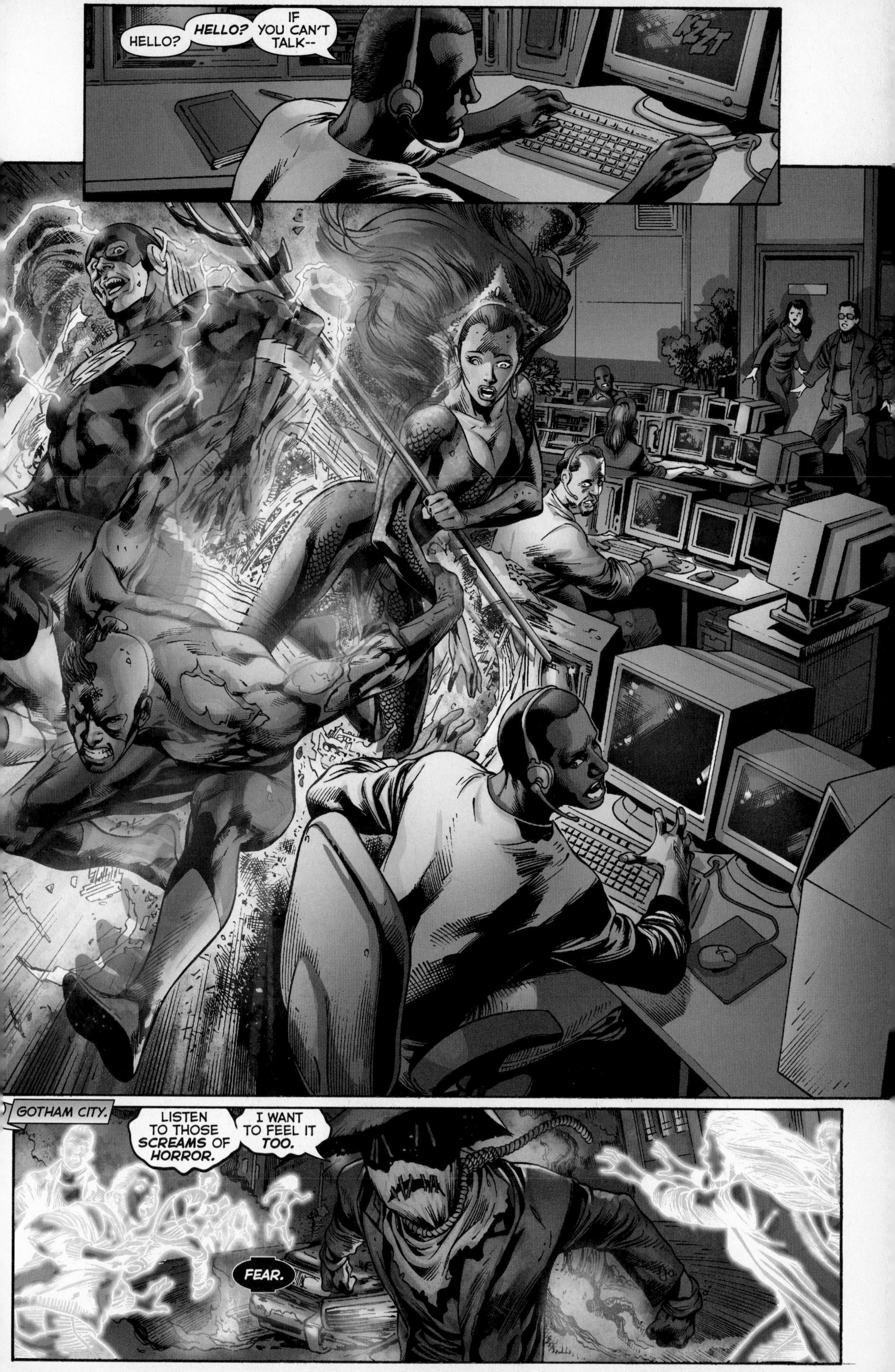
HELLO?
HELLO?
IF YOU CAN'T TALK--
KZZT
GOTHAM CITY.
LISTEN TO THOSE SCREAMS OF HORROR.
I WANT TO FEEL IT TOO.
FEAR.

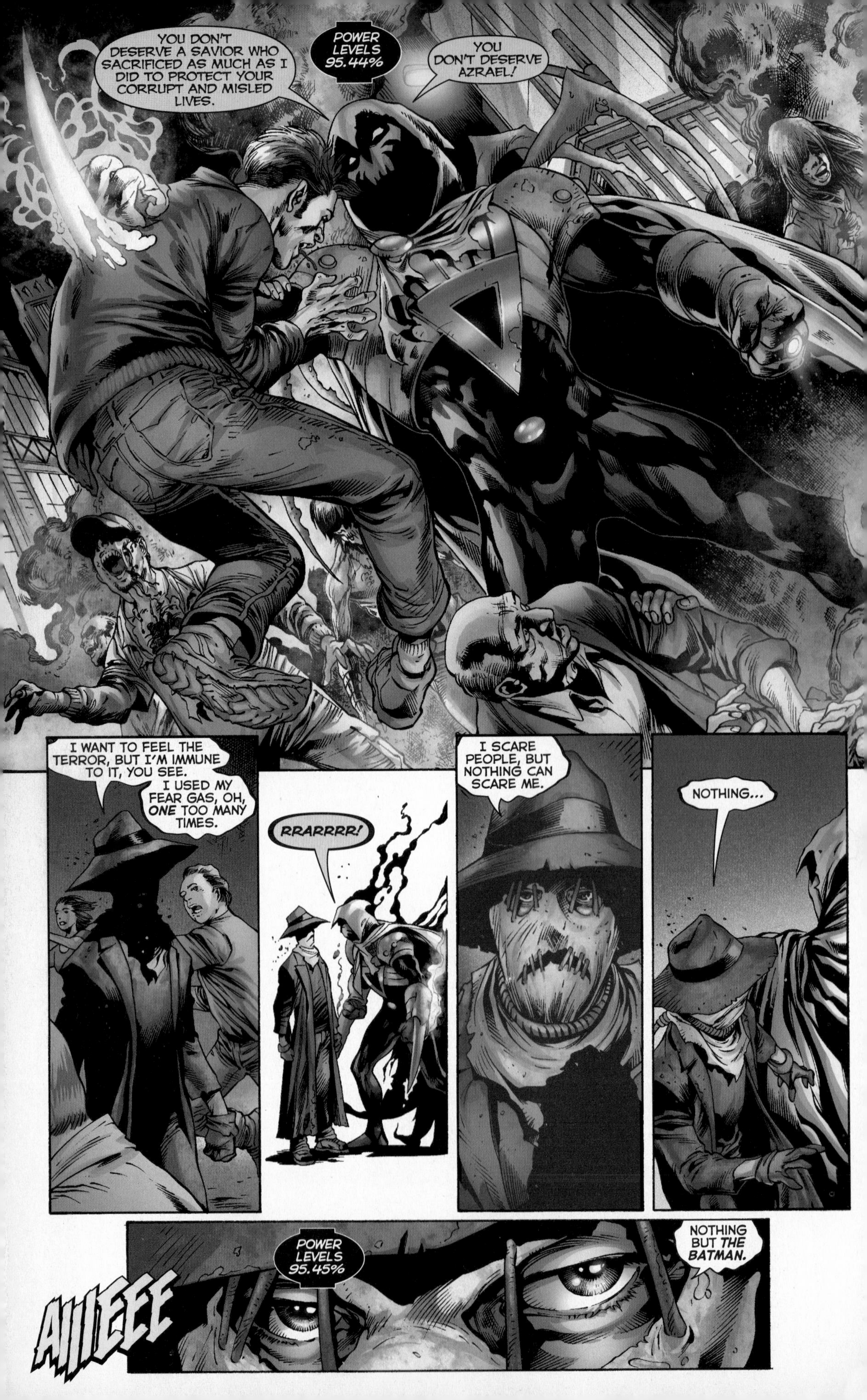
YOU DON'T DESERVE A SAVIOR WHO SACRIFICED AS MUCH AS I DID TO PROTECT YOUR CORRUPT AND MISLED LIVES.
POWER LEVELS 95.44%
YOU DON'T DESERVE AZRAEL!
I WANT TO FEEL THE TERROR, BUT I'M IMMUNE TO IT, YOU SEE.
I USED MY FEAR GAS, OH, *ONE* TOO MANY TIMES.
RRARRRR!
I SCARE PEOPLE, BUT NOTHING CAN SCARE ME.
NOTHING...
AIIIEEE
POWER LEVELS 95.45%
NOTHING BUT *THE BATMAN.*

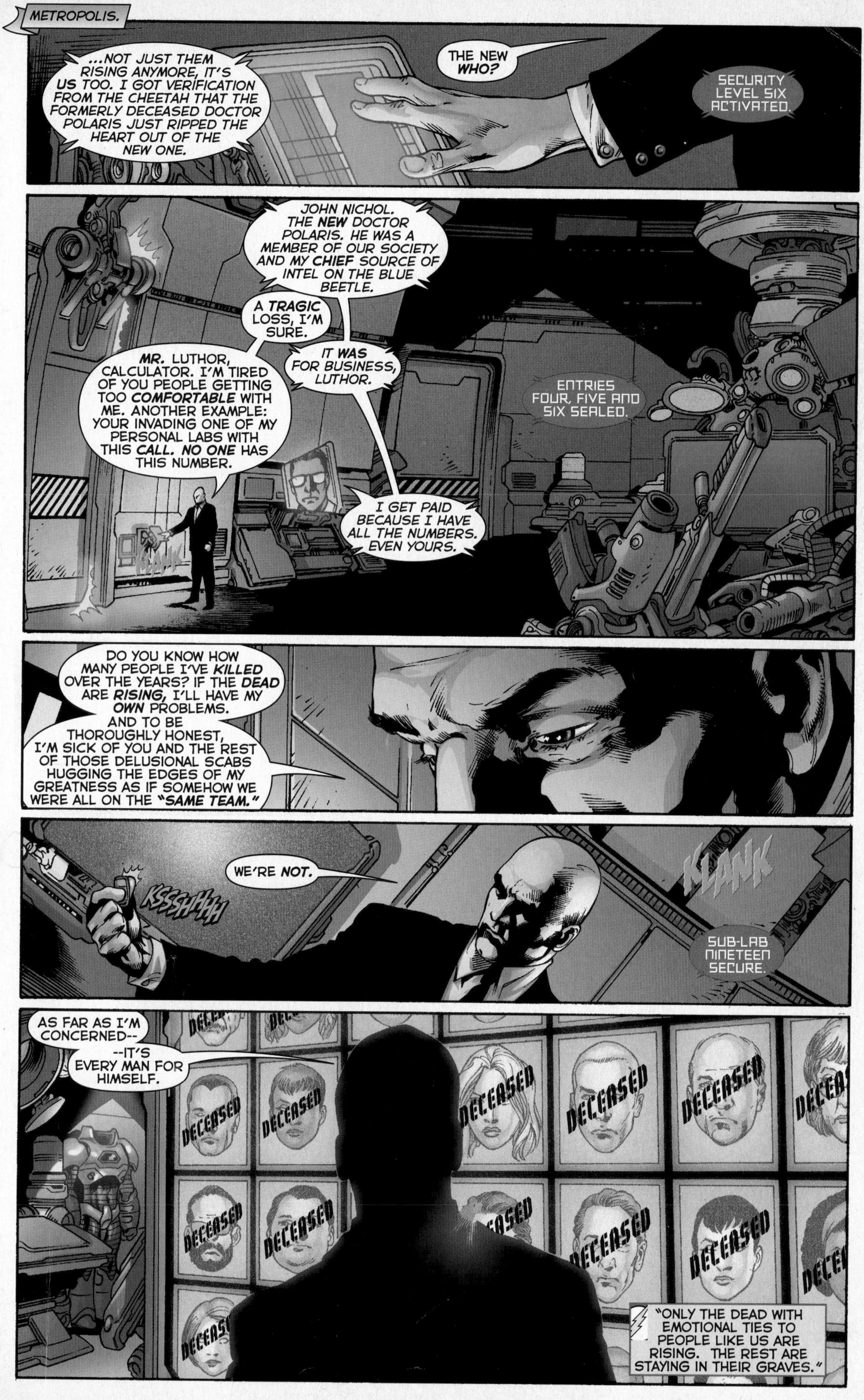
METROPOLIS.
...NOT JUST THEM RISING ANYMORE, IT'S US TOO. I GOT VERIFICATION FROM THE CHEETAH THAT THE FORMERLY DECEASED DOCTOR POLARIS JUST RIPPED THE HEART OUT OF THE NEW ONE.
THE NEW WHO?
SECURITY LEVEL SIX ACTIVATED.
JOHN NICHOL. THE NEW DOCTOR POLARIS. HE WAS A MEMBER OF OUR SOCIETY AND MY CHIEF SOURCE OF INTEL ON THE BLUE BEETLE.
A TRAGIC LOSS, I'M SURE.
IT WAS FOR BUSINESS, LUTHOR.
MR. LUTHOR, CALCULATOR. I'M TIRED OF YOU PEOPLE GETTING TOO COMFORTABLE WITH ME. ANOTHER EXAMPLE: YOUR INVADING ONE OF MY PERSONAL LABS WITH THIS CALL. NO ONE HAS THIS NUMBER.
KLANK
ENTRIES FOUR, FIVE AND SIX SEALED.
I GET PAID BECAUSE I HAVE ALL THE NUMBERS. EVEN YOURS.
DO YOU KNOW HOW MANY PEOPLE I'VE KILLED OVER THE YEARS? IF THE DEAD ARE RISING, I'LL HAVE MY OWN PROBLEMS. AND TO BE THOROUGHLY HONEST, I'M SICK OF YOU AND THE REST OF THOSE DELUSIONAL SCABS HUGGING THE EDGES OF MY GREATNESS AS IF SOMEHOW WE WERE ALL ON THE "SAME TEAM."
WE'RE NOT.
KSSSHHH
KLANK
SUB-LAB NINETEEN SECURE.
AS FAR AS I'M CONCERNED--
--IT'S EVERY MAN FOR HIMSELF.
DECEASED
"ONLY THE DEAD WITH EMOTIONAL TIES TO PEOPLE LIKE US ARE RISING. THE REST ARE STAYING IN THEIR GRAVES."

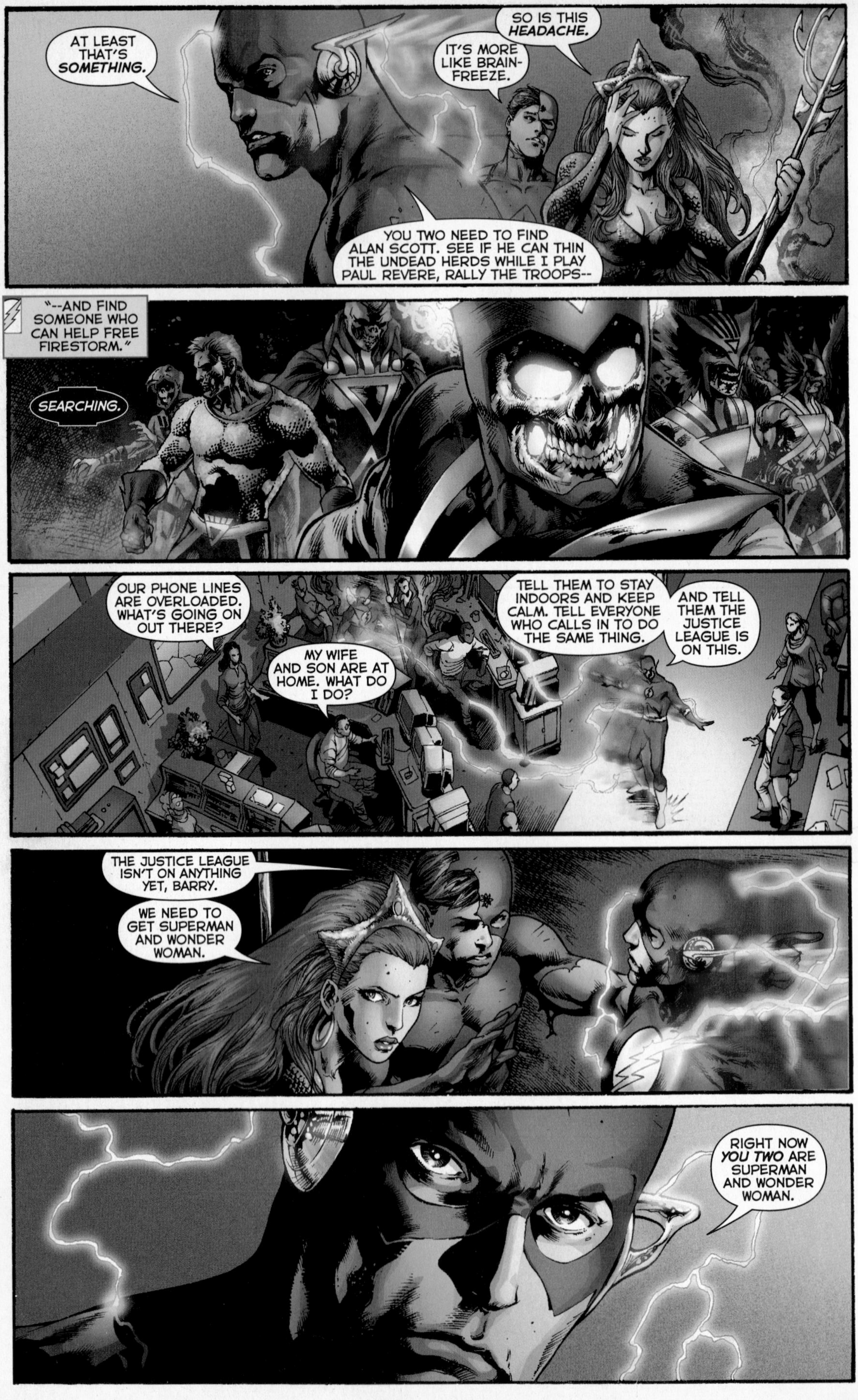
AT LEAST THAT'S SOMETHING.
SO IS THIS HEADACHE.
IT'S MORE LIKE BRAIN-FREEZE.
YOU TWO NEED TO FIND ALAN SCOTT. SEE IF HE CAN THIN THE UNDEAD HERDS WHILE I PLAY PAUL REVERE, RALLY THE TROOPS--
"--AND FIND SOMEONE WHO CAN HELP FREE FIRESTORM."
SEARCHING.
OUR PHONE LINES ARE OVERLOADED. WHAT'S GOING ON OUT THERE?
MY WIFE AND SON ARE AT HOME. WHAT DO I DO?
TELL THEM TO STAY INDOORS AND KEEP CALM. TELL EVERYONE WHO CALLS IN TO DO THE SAME THING.
AND TELL THEM THE JUSTICE LEAGUE IS ON THIS.
THE JUSTICE LEAGUE ISN'T ON ANYTHING YET, BARRY.
WE NEED TO GET SUPERMAN AND WONDER WOMAN.
RIGHT NOW YOU TWO ARE SUPERMAN AND WONDER WOMAN.

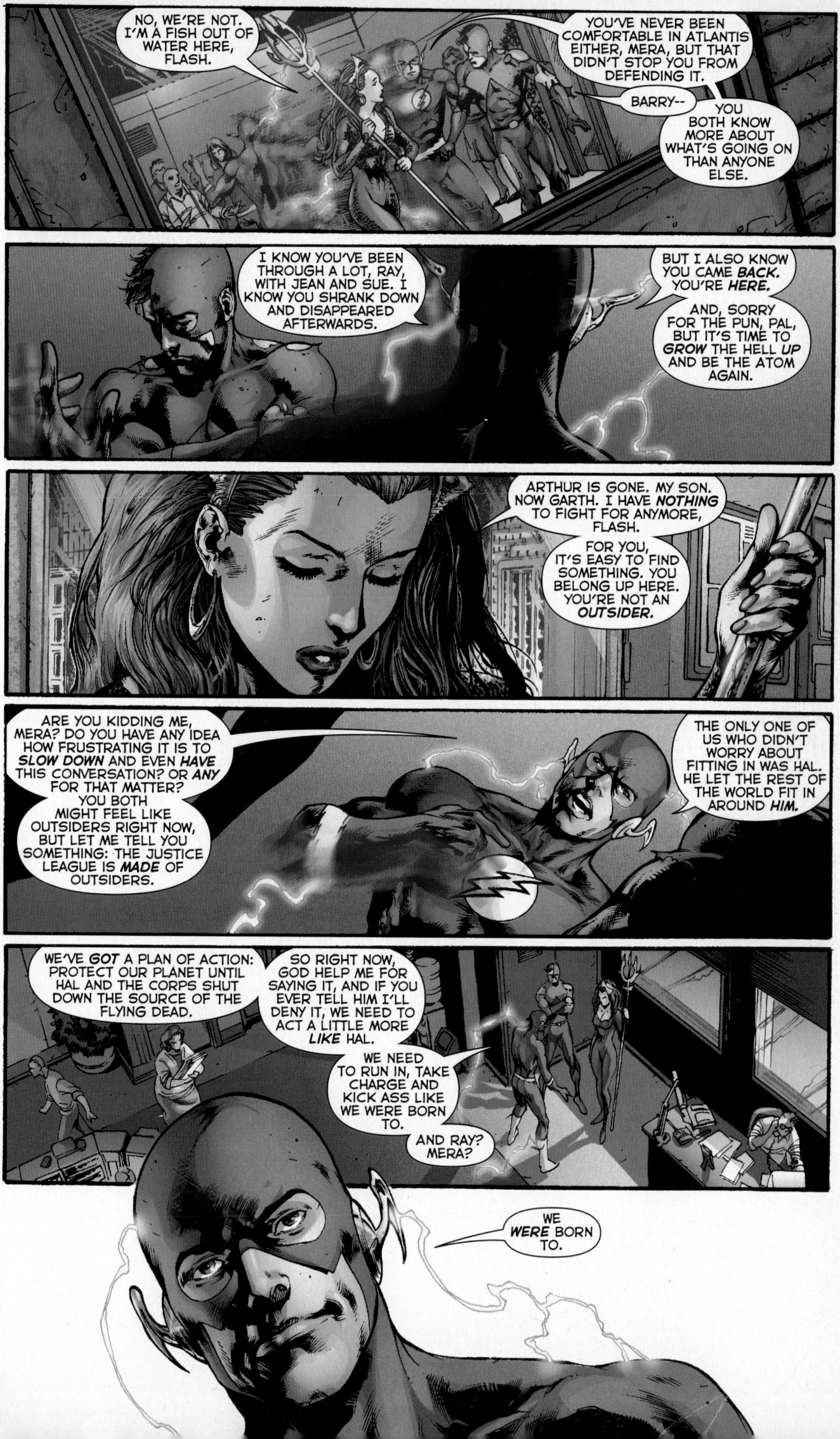

NO, WE'RE NOT. I'M A FISH OUT OF WATER HERE, FLASH.
YOU'VE NEVER BEEN COMFORTABLE IN ATLANTIS EITHER, MERA, BUT THAT DIDN'T STOP YOU FROM DEFENDING IT.
BARRY--
YOU BOTH KNOW MORE ABOUT WHAT'S GOING ON THAN ANYONE ELSE.
I KNOW YOU'VE BEEN THROUGH A LOT, RAY, WITH JEAN AND SUE. I KNOW YOU SHRANK DOWN AND DISAPPEARED AFTERWARDS.
BUT I ALSO KNOW YOU CAME BACK. YOU'RE HERE.
AND, SORRY FOR THE PUN, PAL, BUT IT'S TIME TO GROW THE HELL UP AND BE THE ATOM AGAIN.
ARTHUR IS GONE. MY SON. NOW GARTH. I HAVE NOTHING TO FIGHT FOR ANYMORE, FLASH.
FOR YOU, IT'S EASY TO FIND SOMETHING. YOU BELONG UP HERE. YOU'RE NOT AN OUTSIDER.
ARE YOU KIDDING ME, MERA? DO YOU HAVE ANY IDEA HOW FRUSTRATING IT IS TO SLOW DOWN AND EVEN HAVE THIS CONVERSATION? OR ANY FOR THAT MATTER?
YOU BOTH MIGHT FEEL LIKE OUTSIDERS RIGHT NOW, BUT LET ME TELL YOU SOMETHING: THE JUSTICE LEAGUE IS MADE OF OUTSIDERS.
THE ONLY ONE OF US WHO DIDN'T WORRY ABOUT FITTING IN WAS HAL. HE LET THE REST OF THE WORLD FIT IN AROUND HIM.
WE'VE GOT A PLAN OF ACTION: PROTECT OUR PLANET UNTIL HAL AND THE CORPS SHUT DOWN THE SOURCE OF THE FLYING DEAD.
SO RIGHT NOW, GOD HELP ME FOR SAYING IT, AND IF YOU EVER TELL HIM I'LL DENY IT, WE NEED TO ACT A LITTLE MORE LIKE HAL.
WE NEED TO RUN IN, TAKE CHARGE AND KICK ASS LIKE WE WERE BORN TO.
AND RAY? MERA?
WE WERE BORN TO.

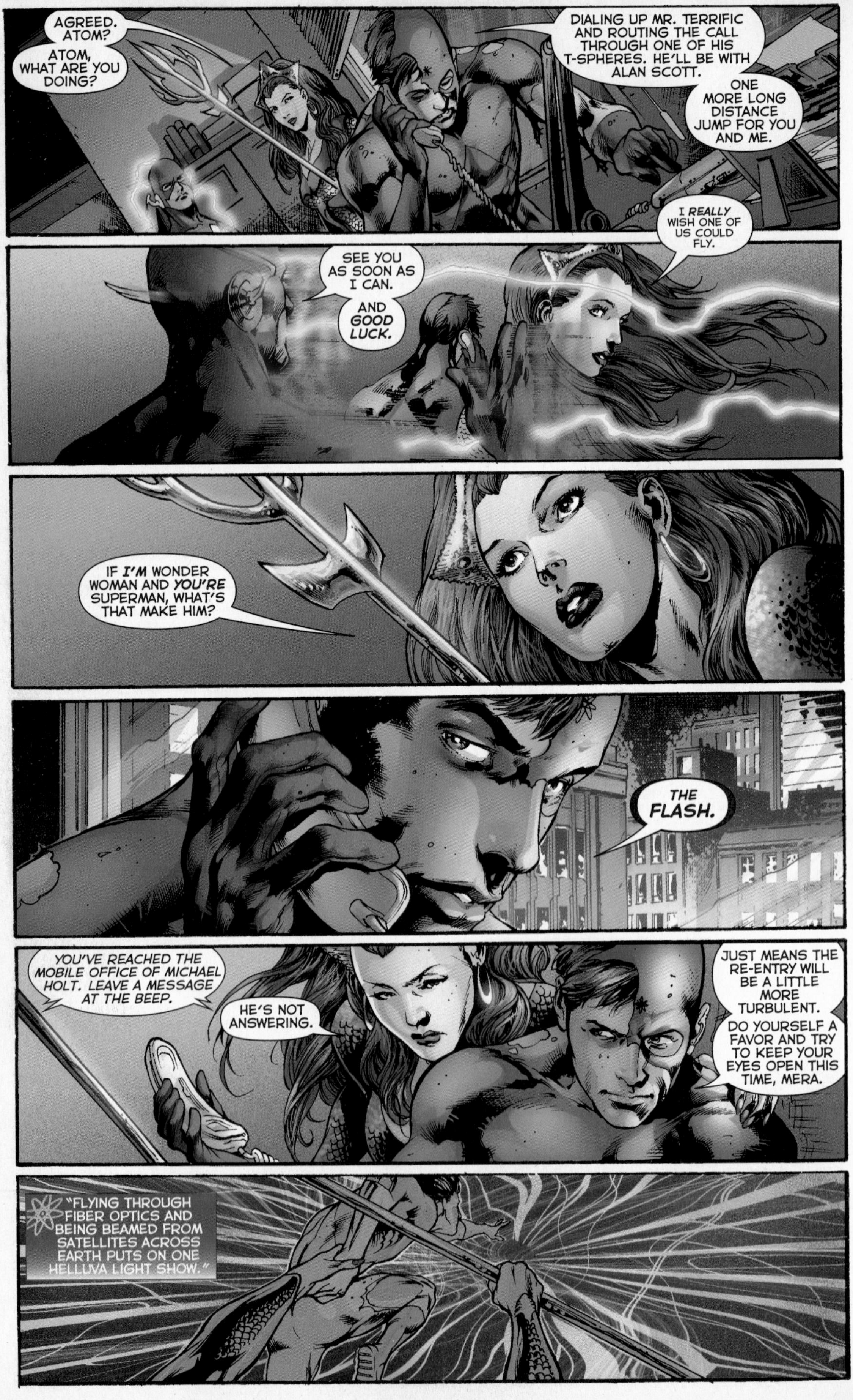
AGREED. ATOM?
ATOM, WHAT ARE YOU DOING?
DIALING UP MR. TERRIFIC AND ROUTING THE CALL THROUGH ONE OF HIS T-SPHERES. HE'LL BE WITH ALAN SCOTT.
ONE MORE LONG DISTANCE JUMP FOR YOU AND ME.
I *REALLY* WISH ONE OF US COULD FLY.
SEE YOU AS SOON AS I CAN.
AND *GOOD LUCK.*
IF *I'M* WONDER WOMAN AND *YOU'RE* SUPERMAN, WHAT'S THAT MAKE HIM?
THE FLASH.
YOU'VE REACHED THE MOBILE OFFICE OF MICHAEL HOLT. LEAVE A MESSAGE AT THE BEEP.
HE'S NOT ANSWERING.
JUST MEANS THE RE-ENTRY WILL BE A LITTLE MORE TURBULENT.
DO YOURSELF A FAVOR AND TRY TO KEEP YOUR EYES OPEN THIS TIME, MERA.
"FLYING THROUGH FIBER OPTICS AND BEING BEAMED FROM SATELLITES ACROSS EARTH PUTS ON ONE HELLUVA LIGHT SHOW."

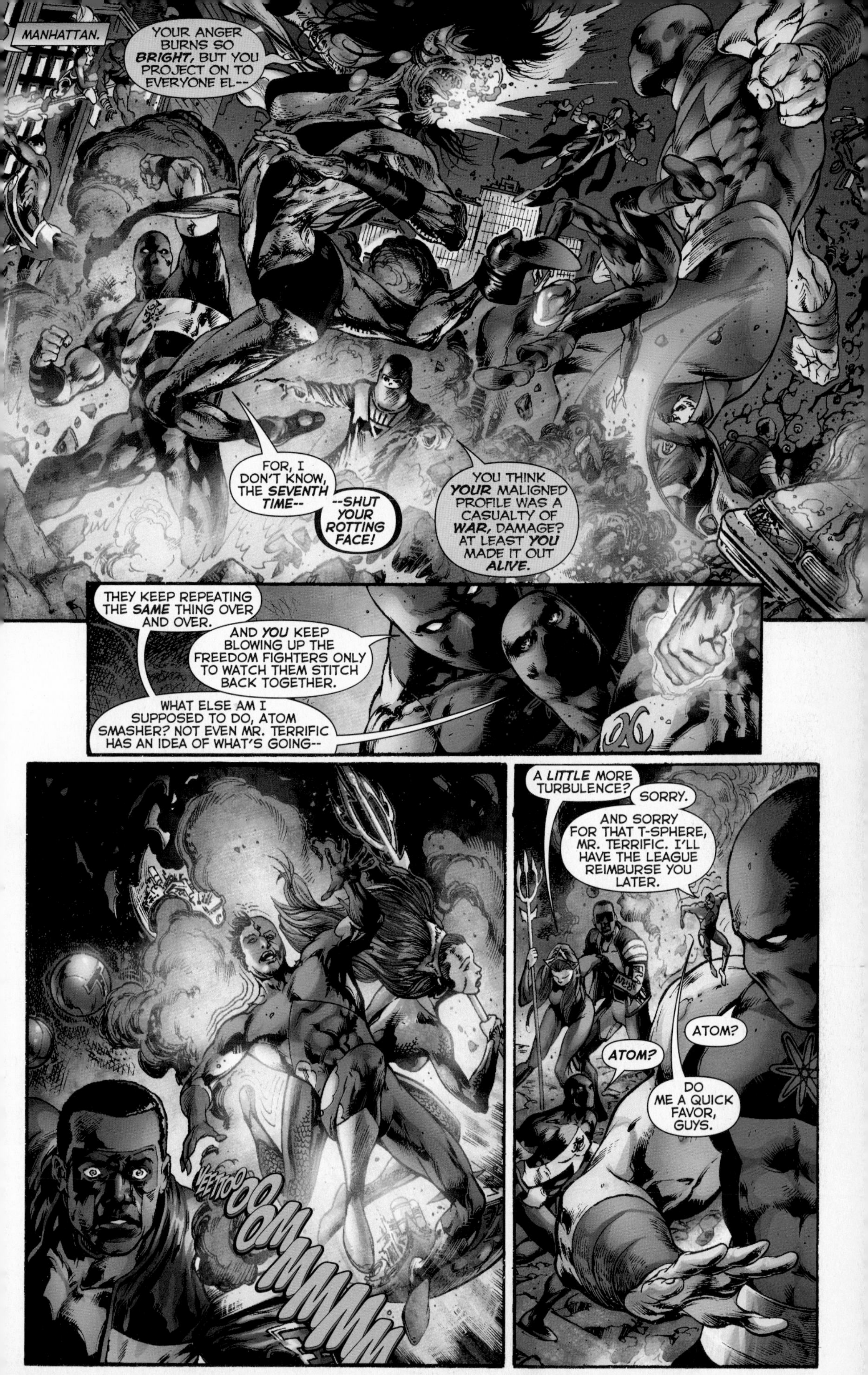
MANHATTAN.
YOUR ANGER BURNS SO BRIGHT, BUT YOU PROJECT ON TO EVERYONE EL--
FOR, I DON'T KNOW, THE SEVENTH TIME--
--SHUT YOUR ROTTING FACE!
YOU THINK YOUR MALIGNED PROFILE WAS A CASUALTY OF WAR, DAMAGE? AT LEAST YOU MADE IT OUT ALIVE.
THEY KEEP REPEATING THE SAME THING OVER AND OVER.
AND YOU KEEP BLOWING UP THE FREEDOM FIGHTERS ONLY TO WATCH THEM STITCH BACK TOGETHER.
WHAT ELSE AM I SUPPOSED TO DO, ATOM SMASHER? NOT EVEN MR. TERRIFIC HAS AN IDEA OF WHAT'S GOING--
VEETOOOOOMMMMMM
A LITTLE MORE TURBULENCE?
SORRY.
AND SORRY FOR THAT T-SPHERE, MR. TERRIFIC. I'LL HAVE THE LEAGUE REIMBURSE YOU LATER.
ATOM?
ATOM?
DO ME A QUICK FAVOR, GUYS.

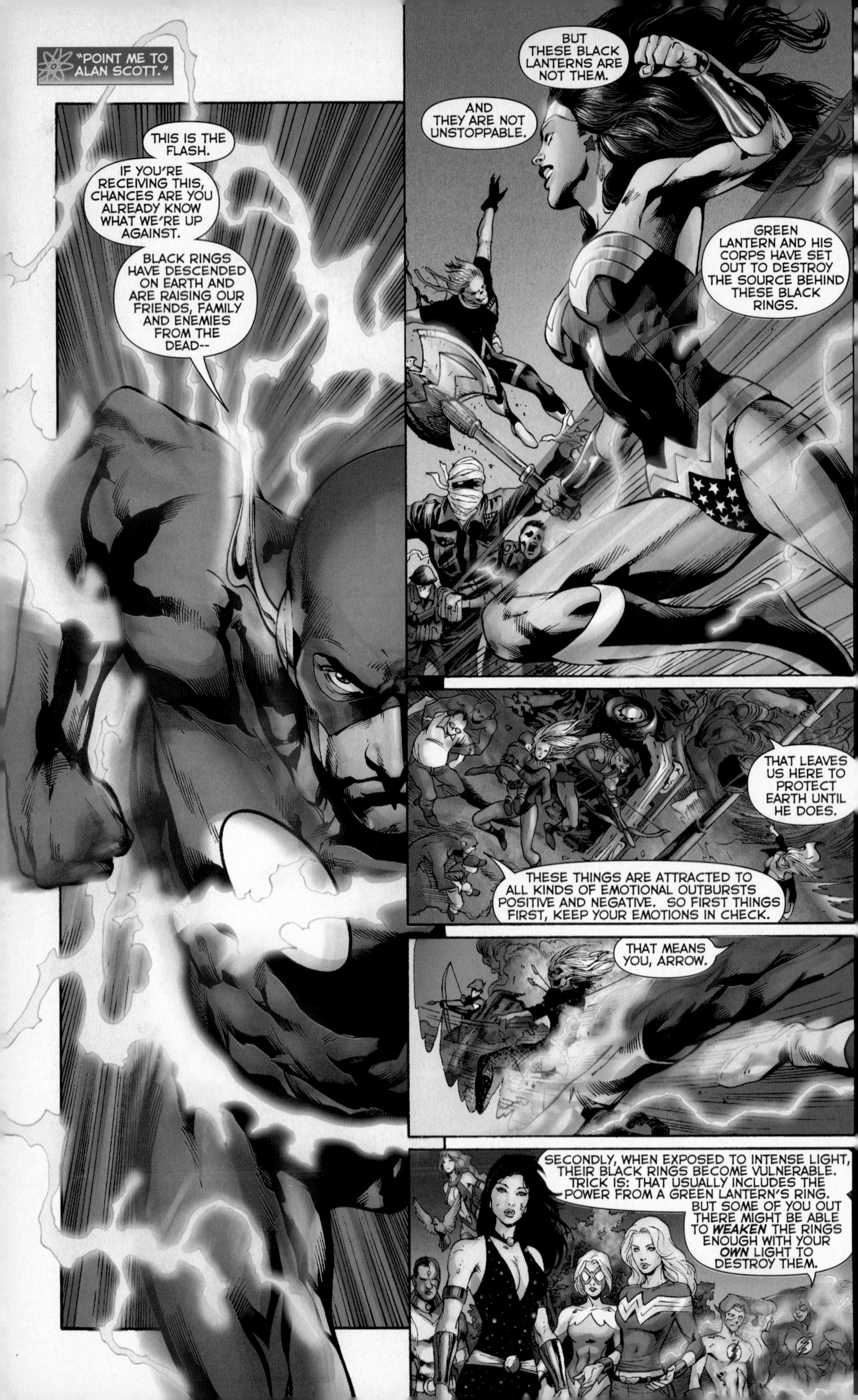

"POINT ME TO ALAN SCOTT."
THIS IS THE FLASH.
IF YOU'RE RECEIVING THIS, CHANCES ARE YOU ALREADY KNOW WHAT WE'RE UP AGAINST.
BLACK RINGS HAVE DESCENDED ON EARTH AND ARE RAISING OUR FRIENDS, FAMILY AND ENEMIES FROM THE DEAD--
BUT THESE BLACK LANTERNS ARE NOT THEM.
AND THEY ARE NOT UNSTOPPABLE.
GREEN LANTERN AND HIS CORPS HAVE SET OUT TO DESTROY THE SOURCE BEHIND THESE BLACK RINGS.
THAT LEAVES US HERE TO PROTECT EARTH UNTIL HE DOES.
THESE THINGS ARE ATTRACTED TO ALL KINDS OF EMOTIONAL OUTBURSTS POSITIVE AND NEGATIVE. SO FIRST THINGS FIRST, KEEP YOUR EMOTIONS IN CHECK.
THAT MEANS YOU, ARROW.
SECONDLY, WHEN EXPOSED TO INTENSE LIGHT, THEIR BLACK RINGS BECOME VULNERABLE. TRICK IS: THAT USUALLY INCLUDES THE POWER FROM A GREEN LANTERN'S RING.
BUT SOME OF YOU OUT THERE MIGHT BE ABLE TO *WEAKEN* THE RINGS ENOUGH WITH YOUR *OWN* LIGHT TO DESTROY THEM.

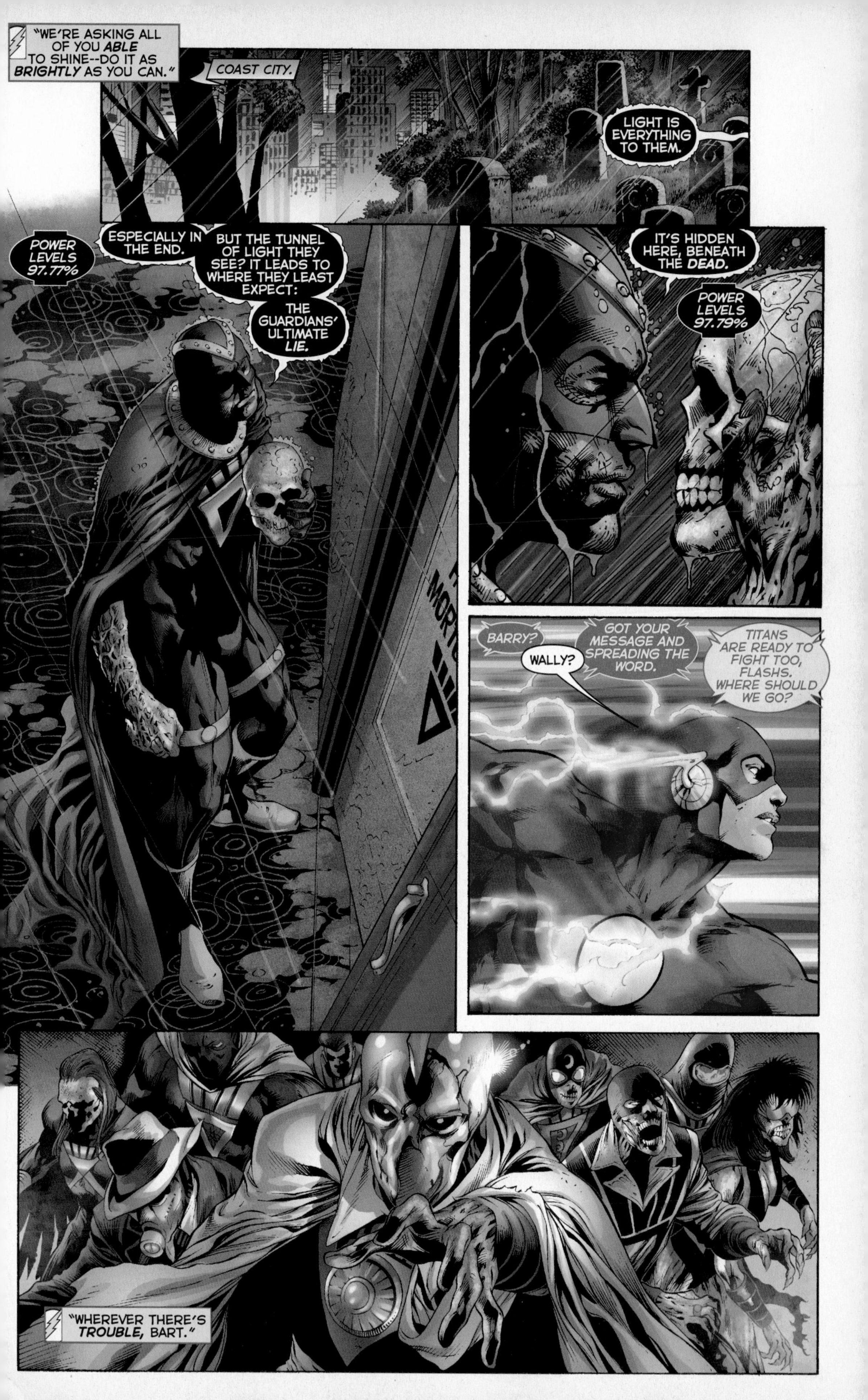
"WE'RE ASKING ALL OF YOU ABLE TO SHINE--DO IT AS BRIGHTLY AS YOU CAN."
COAST CITY.
LIGHT IS EVERYTHING TO THEM.
POWER LEVELS 97.77%
ESPECIALLY IN THE END.
BUT THE TUNNEL OF LIGHT THEY SEE? IT LEADS TO WHERE THEY LEAST EXPECT:
THE GUARDIANS' ULTIMATE LIE.
IT'S HIDDEN HERE, BENEATH THE DEAD.
POWER LEVELS 97.79%
BARRY?
WALLY?
GOT YOUR MESSAGE AND SPREADING THE WORD.
TITANS ARE READY TO FIGHT TOO, FLASHS. WHERE SHOULD WE GO?
"WHEREVER THERE'S TROUBLE, BART."

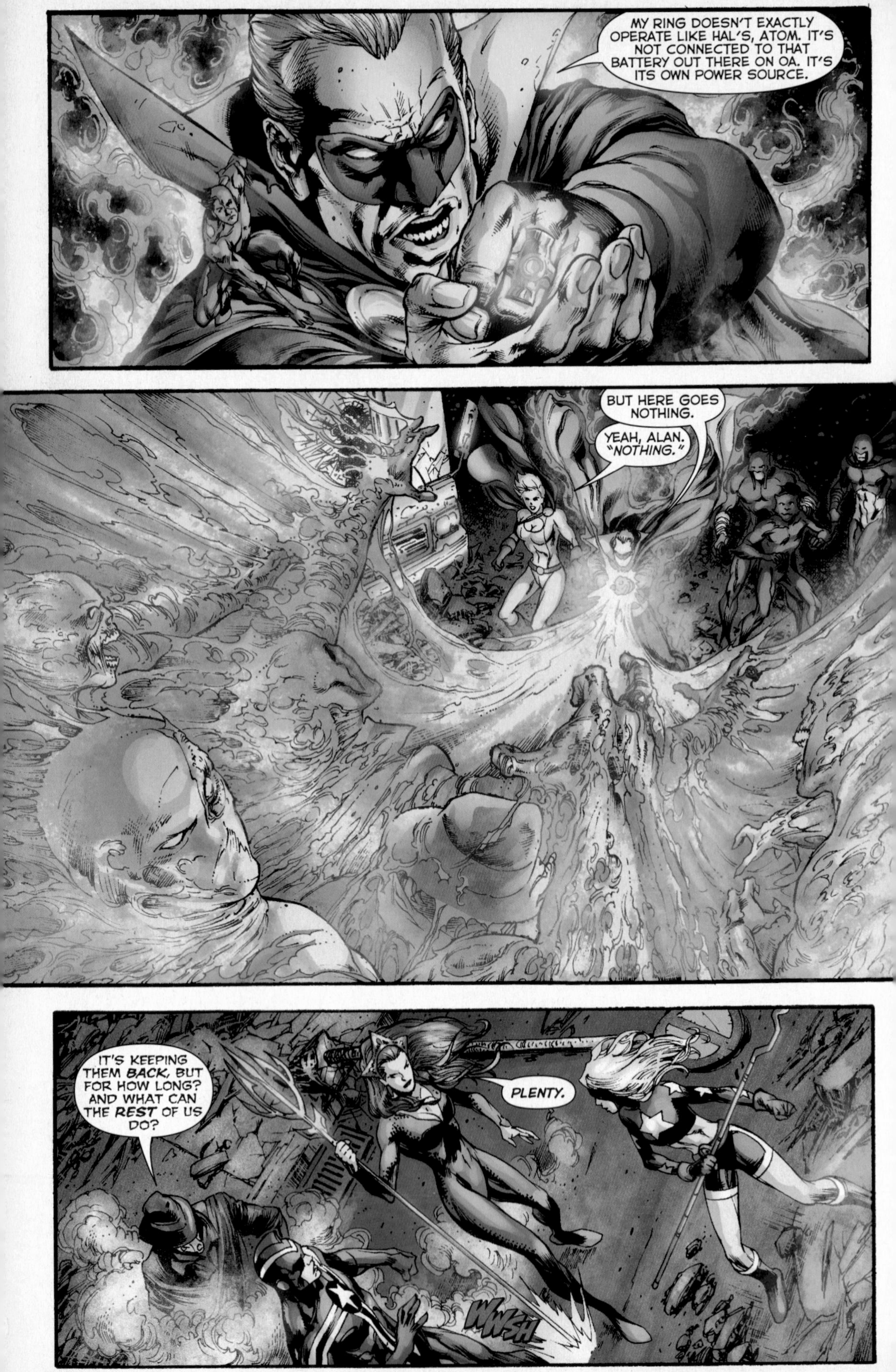
MY RING DOESN'T EXACTLY OPERATE LIKE HAL'S, ATOM. IT'S NOT CONNECTED TO THAT BATTERY OUT THERE ON OA. IT'S ITS OWN POWER SOURCE.
BUT HERE GOES NOTHING.
YEAH, ALAN. *"NOTHING."*
IT'S KEEPING THEM *BACK*, BUT FOR HOW LONG? AND WHAT CAN THE *REST* OF US DO?
PLENTY.
WWSH

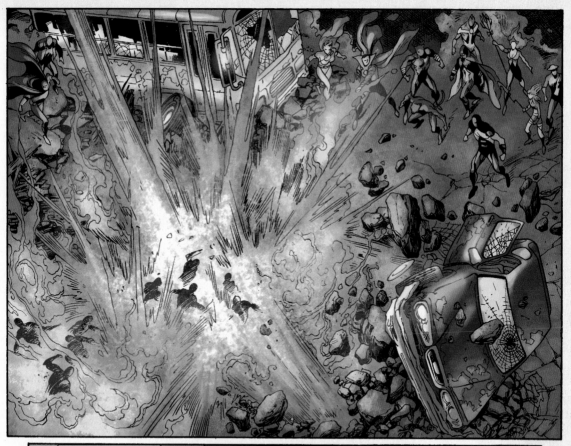

WATER? WHAT'S SHE GONNA DO? **DROWN** THEM?

YOU CAN'T FEEL FEAR, DAMAGE. THAT'S JUST WHAT THEY WANT.

I'M **NOT** AFRAID, ATOM. I WAS POINTING OUT THE **ABSURDITY** OF TRYING TO SUFFOCATE THE DEAD.

MEANING YOU'RE COVERING UP FEAR WITH ATTITUDE.

WHY ARE YOU HANGING ON MY SHOULDER?

YOU'RE **AL PRATT'S** BOY.

THOUGH TO TELL YOU THE TRUTH, I WASN'T THAT AWARE OF YOUR FATHER UNTIL **AFTER** I TOOK THE NAME.

I DON'T WEAR THIS MASK FOR THE ATOM. I WEAR IT SO I **REMEMBER** NOT TO PULL MY PUNCHES LIKE THE REST OF YOU.

BECAUSE YOU'RE SCARED.

WELL, AFTER ALL OF **THIS**, WHO THE HELL **WOULDN'T** BE?!

AL?

DON'T LISTEN TO THE LITTLE MAN, SON.

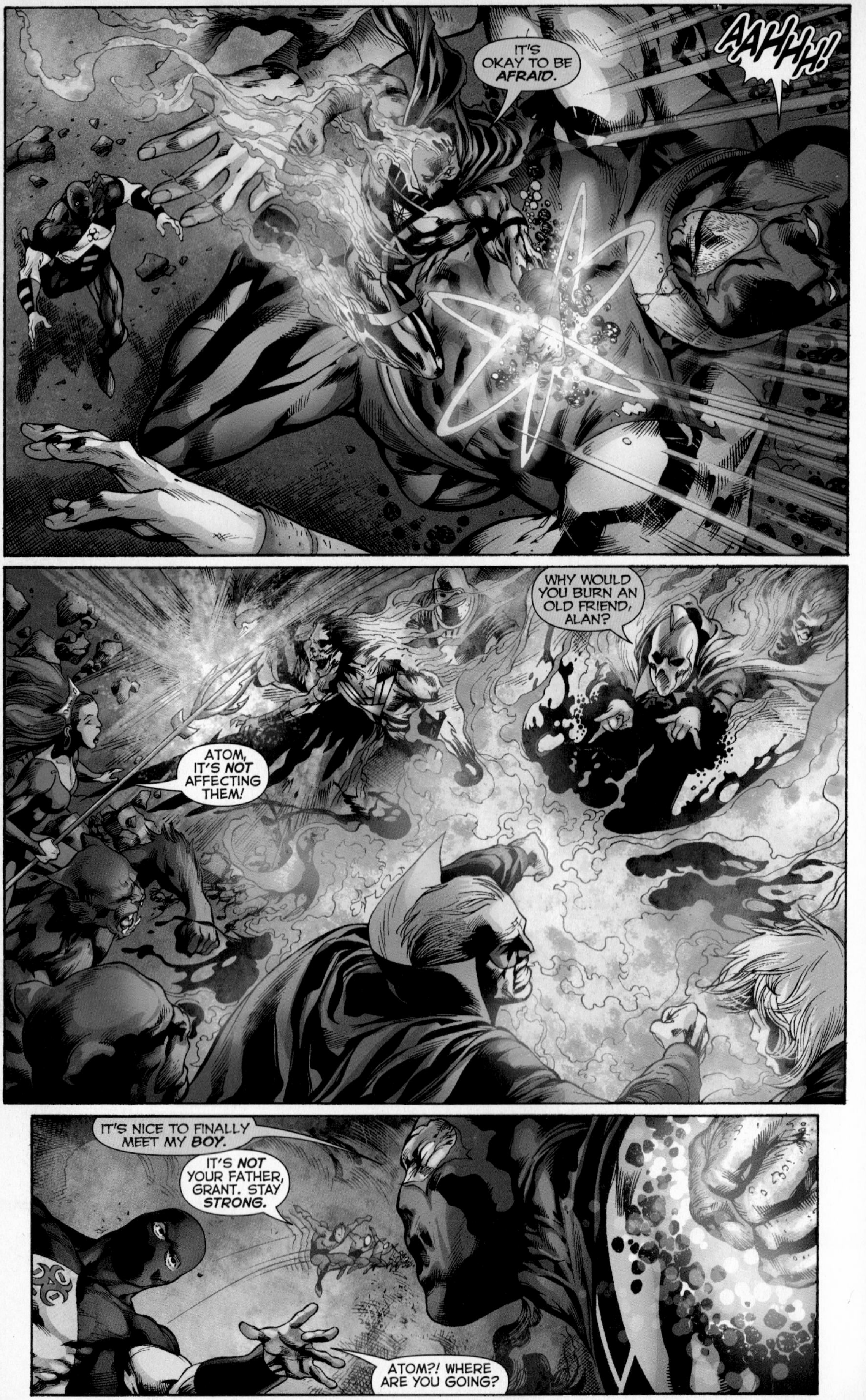
IT'S OKAY TO BE AFRAID.
AAHHH!
WHY WOULD YOU BURN AN OLD FRIEND, ALAN?
ATOM, IT'S NOT AFFECTING THEM!
IT'S NICE TO FINALLY MEET MY BOY.
IT'S NOT YOUR FATHER, GRANT. STAY STRONG.
ATOM?! WHERE ARE YOU GOING?

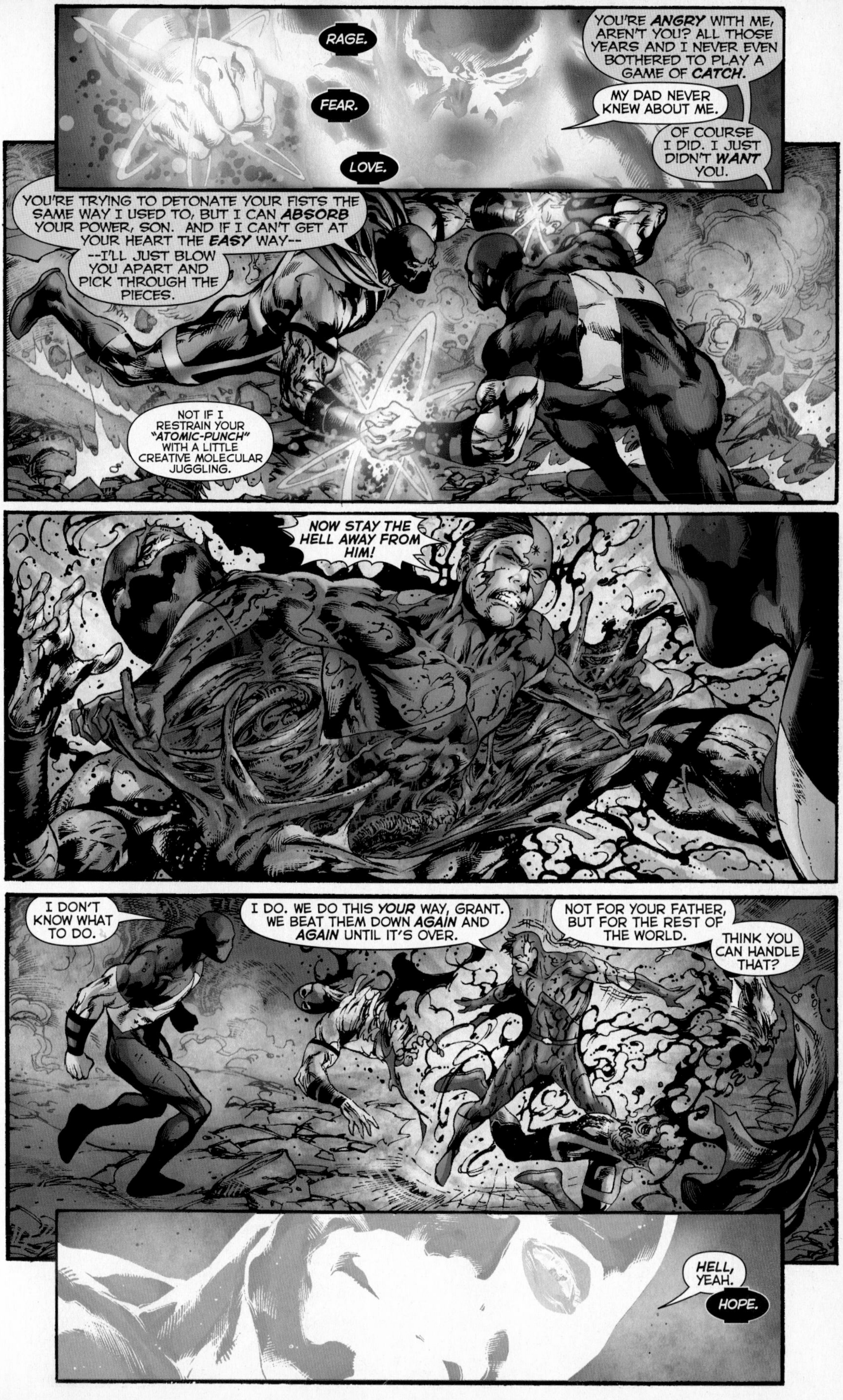
RAGE.
FEAR.
LOVE.
YOU'RE ANGRY WITH ME, AREN'T YOU? ALL THOSE YEARS AND I NEVER EVEN BOTHERED TO PLAY A GAME OF CATCH.
MY DAD NEVER KNEW ABOUT ME.
OF COURSE I DID. I JUST DIDN'T WANT YOU.
YOU'RE TRYING TO DETONATE YOUR FISTS THE SAME WAY I USED TO, BUT I CAN ABSORB YOUR POWER, SON. AND IF I CAN'T GET AT YOUR HEART THE EASY WAY--
--I'LL JUST BLOW YOU APART AND PICK THROUGH THE PIECES.
NOT IF I RESTRAIN YOUR "ATOMIC-PUNCH" WITH A LITTLE CREATIVE MOLECULAR JUGGLING.
NOW STAY THE HELL AWAY FROM HIM!
I DON'T KNOW WHAT TO DO.
I DO. WE DO THIS YOUR WAY, GRANT. WE BEAT THEM DOWN AGAIN AND AGAIN UNTIL IT'S OVER.
NOT FOR YOUR FATHER, BUT FOR THE REST OF THE WORLD.
THINK YOU CAN HANDLE THAT?
HELL, YEAH.
HOPE.

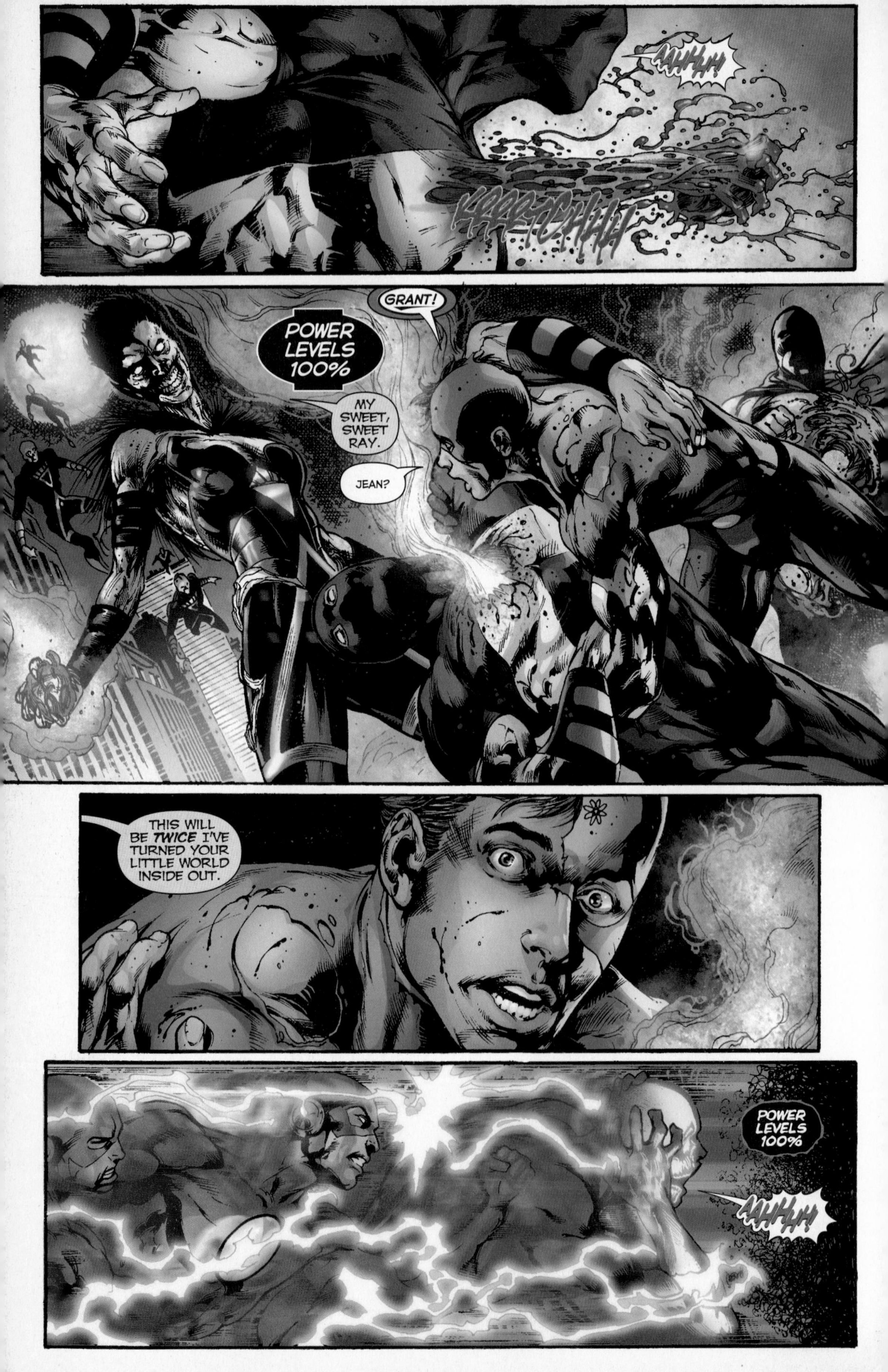
AAHHH!
KRRRSCHHH
GRANT!
POWER LEVELS 100%
MY SWEET, SWEET RAY.
JEAN?
THIS WILL BE *TWICE* I'VE TURNED YOUR LITTLE WORLD INSIDE OUT.
POWER LEVELS 100%
AAHHHH!

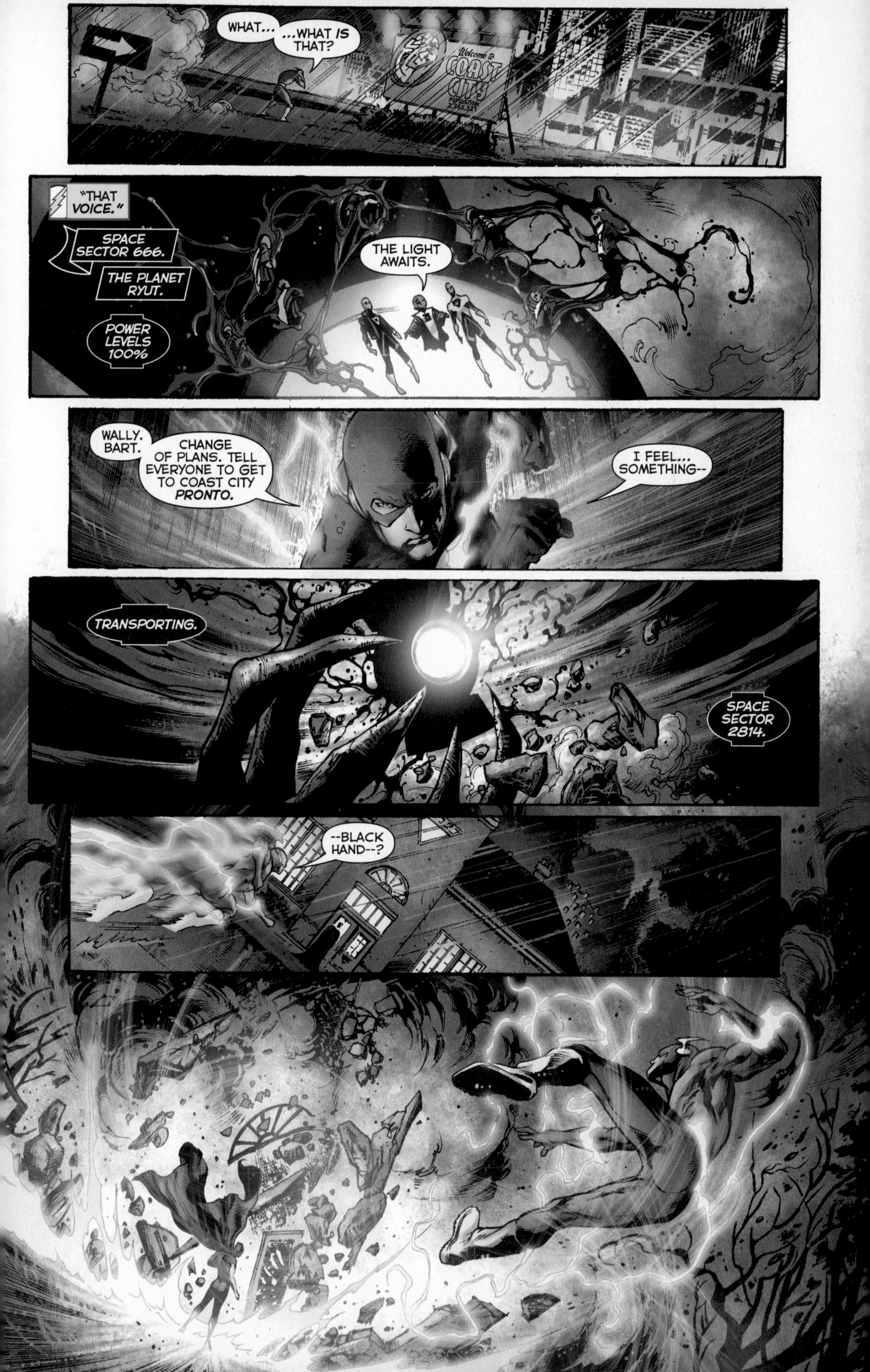
WHAT...
...WHAT IS THAT?
Welcome to COAST CITY
"THAT VOICE."
SPACE SECTOR 666.
THE PLANET RYUT.
THE LIGHT AWAITS.
POWER LEVELS 100%
WALLY. BART.
CHANGE OF PLANS. TELL EVERYONE TO GET TO COAST CITY PRONTO.
I FEEL... SOMETHING--
TRANSPORTING.
SPACE SECTOR 2814.
--BLACK HAND--?

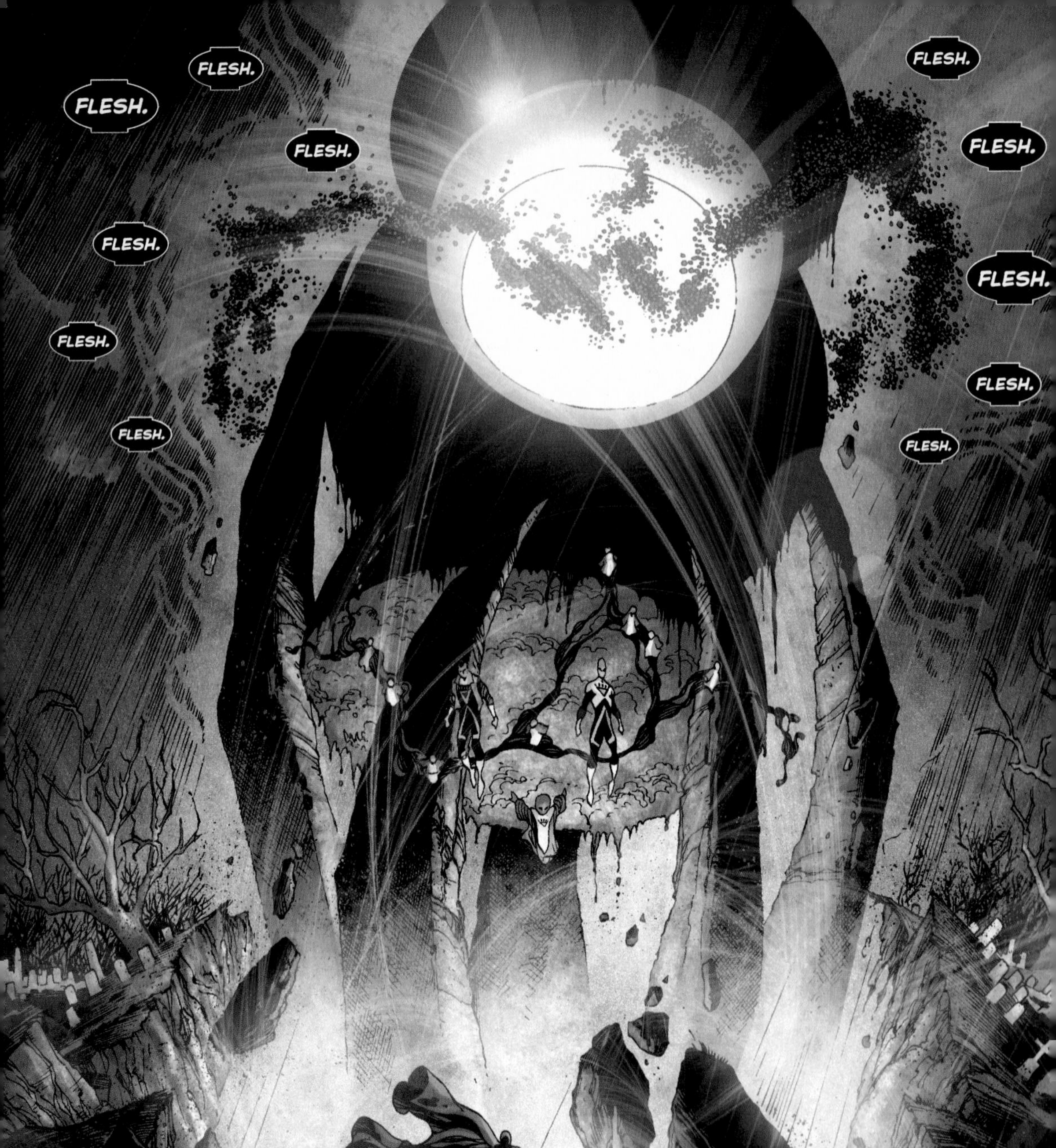
FLESH.
FLESH.
FLESH.
FLESH.
FLESH.
FLESH.
FLESH.
FLESH.
FLESH.
FLESH.
FLESH.

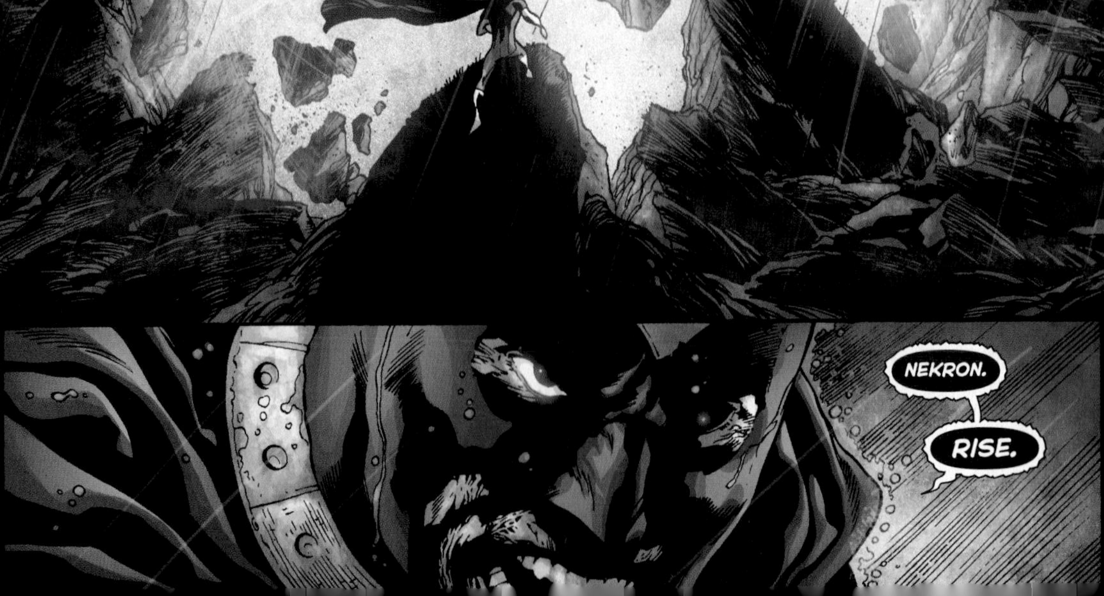
NEKRON.
RISE.

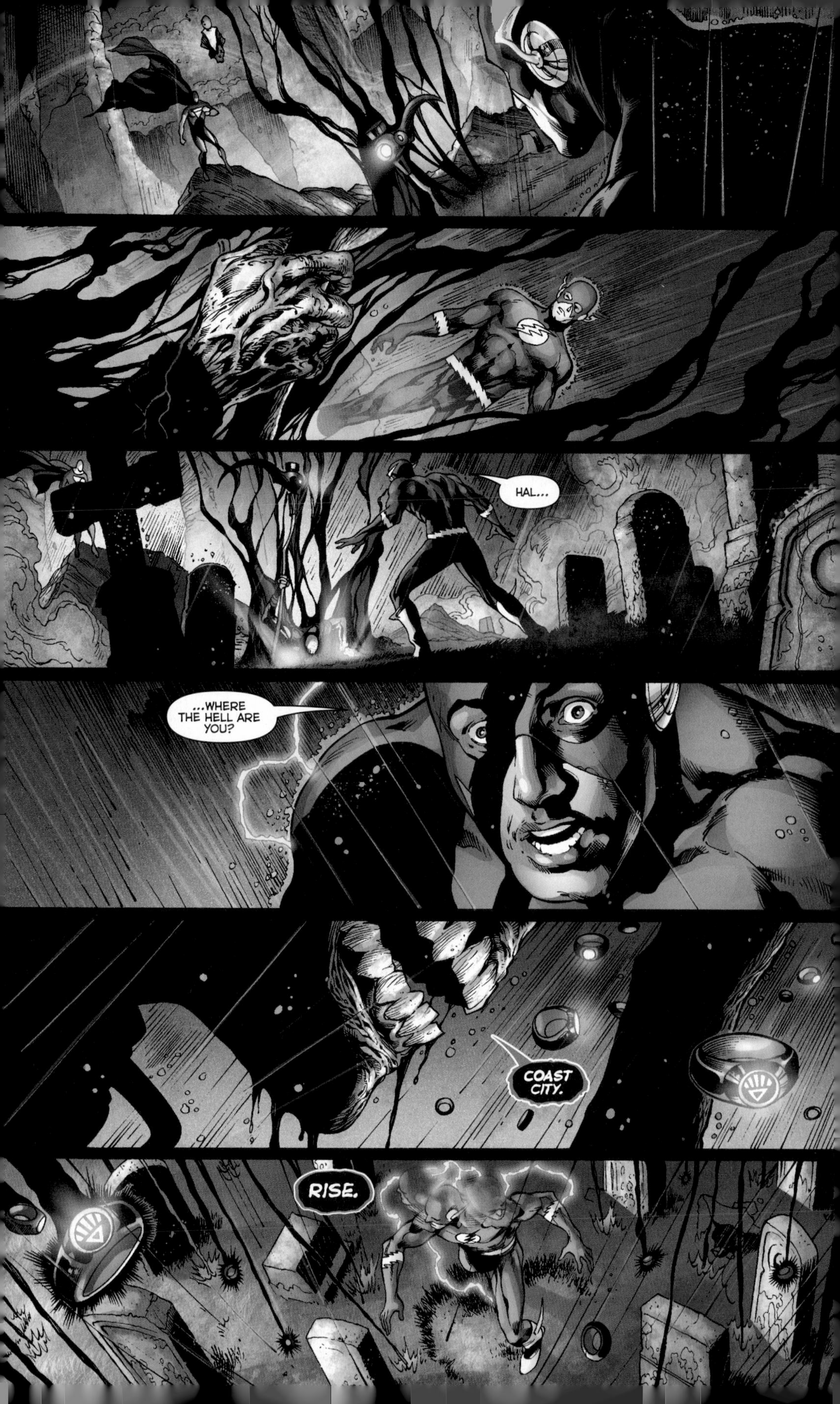
HAL...
...WHERE THE HELL ARE YOU?
COAST CITY.
RISE.

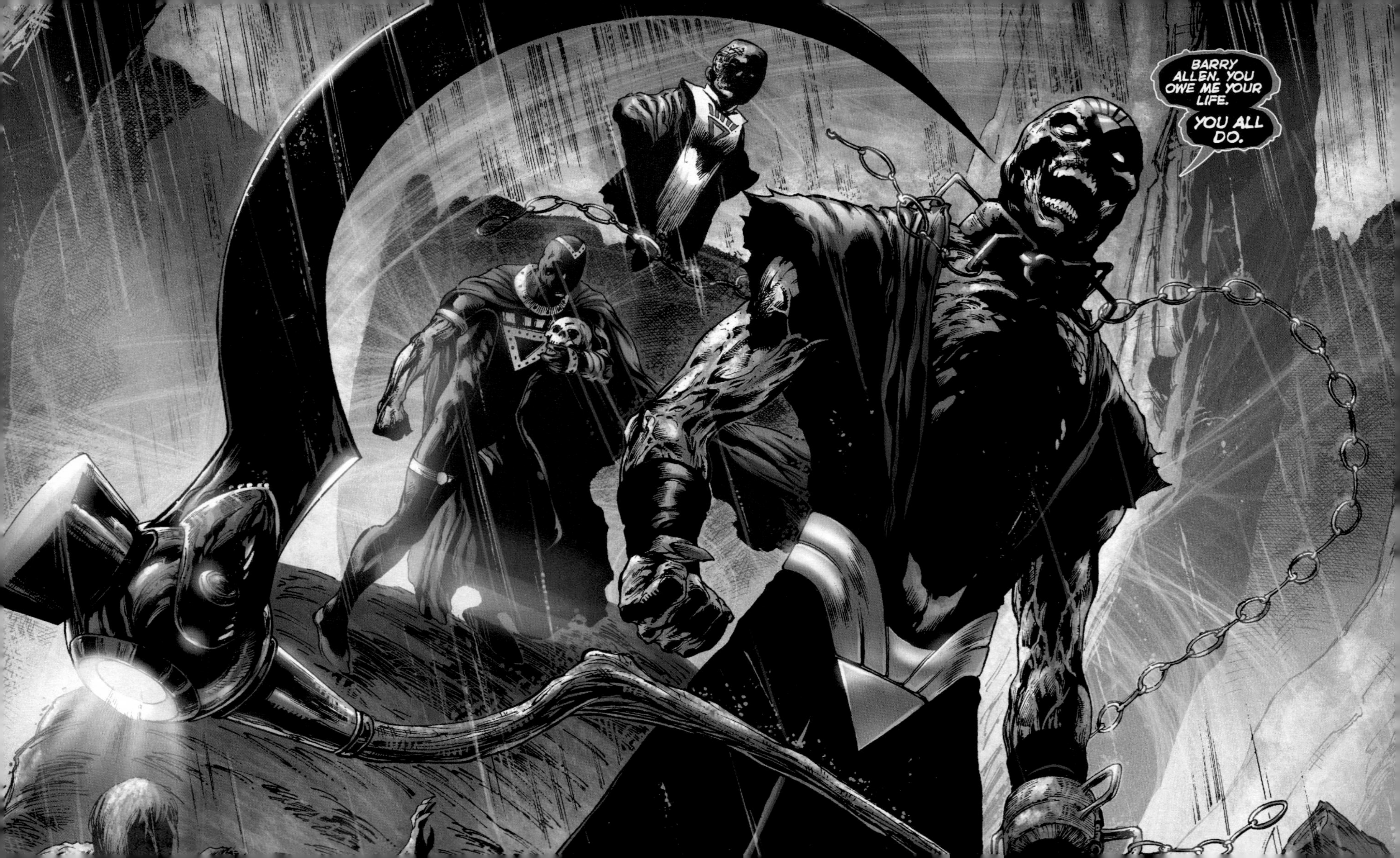
BARRY ALLEN. YOU OWE ME YOUR LIFE.
YOU ALL DO.

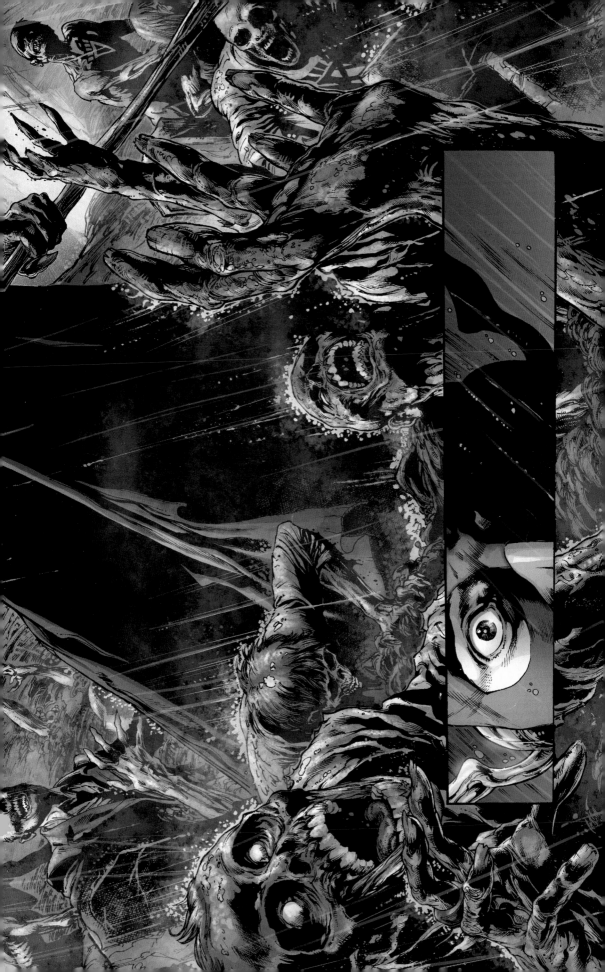

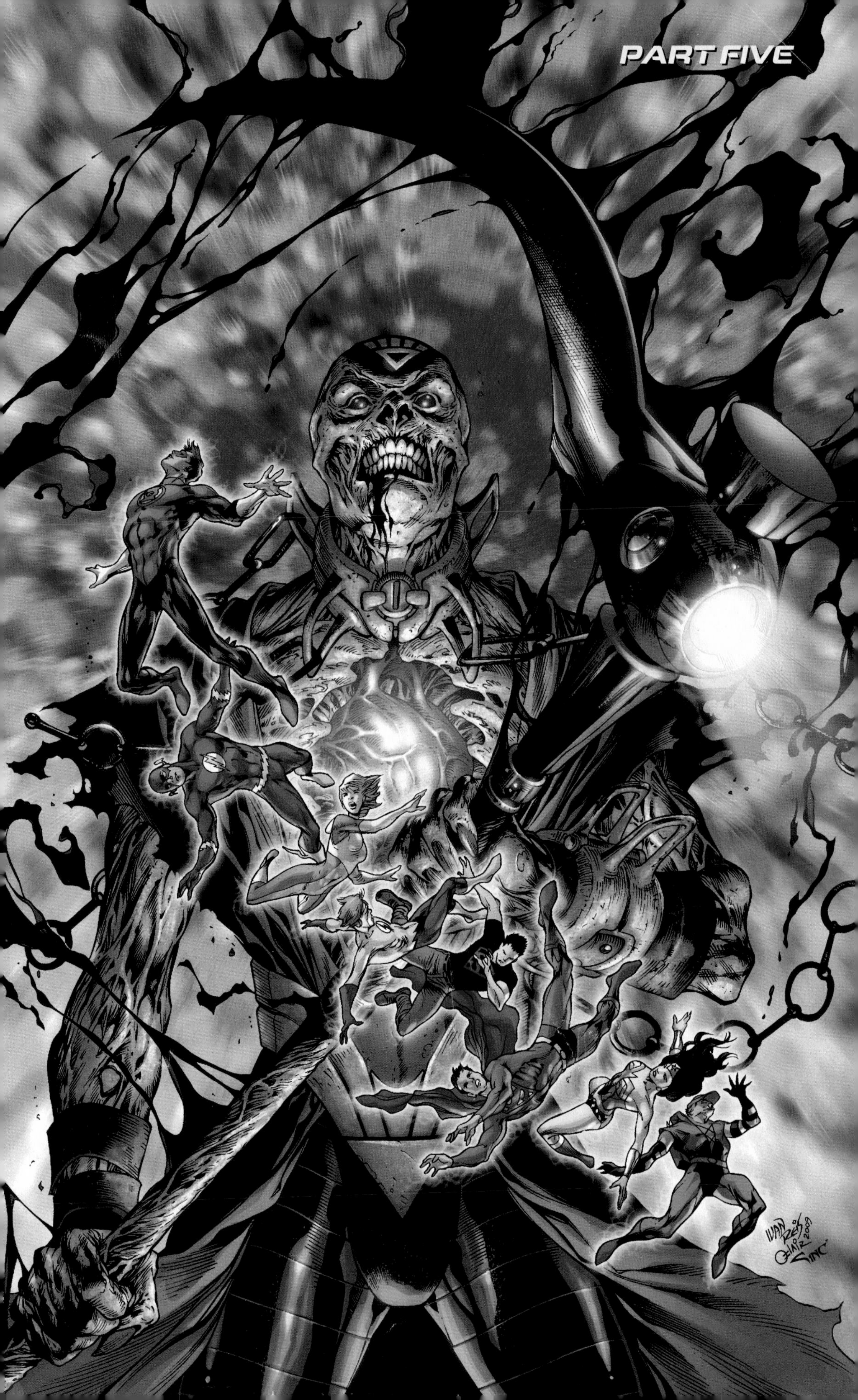
PART FIVE

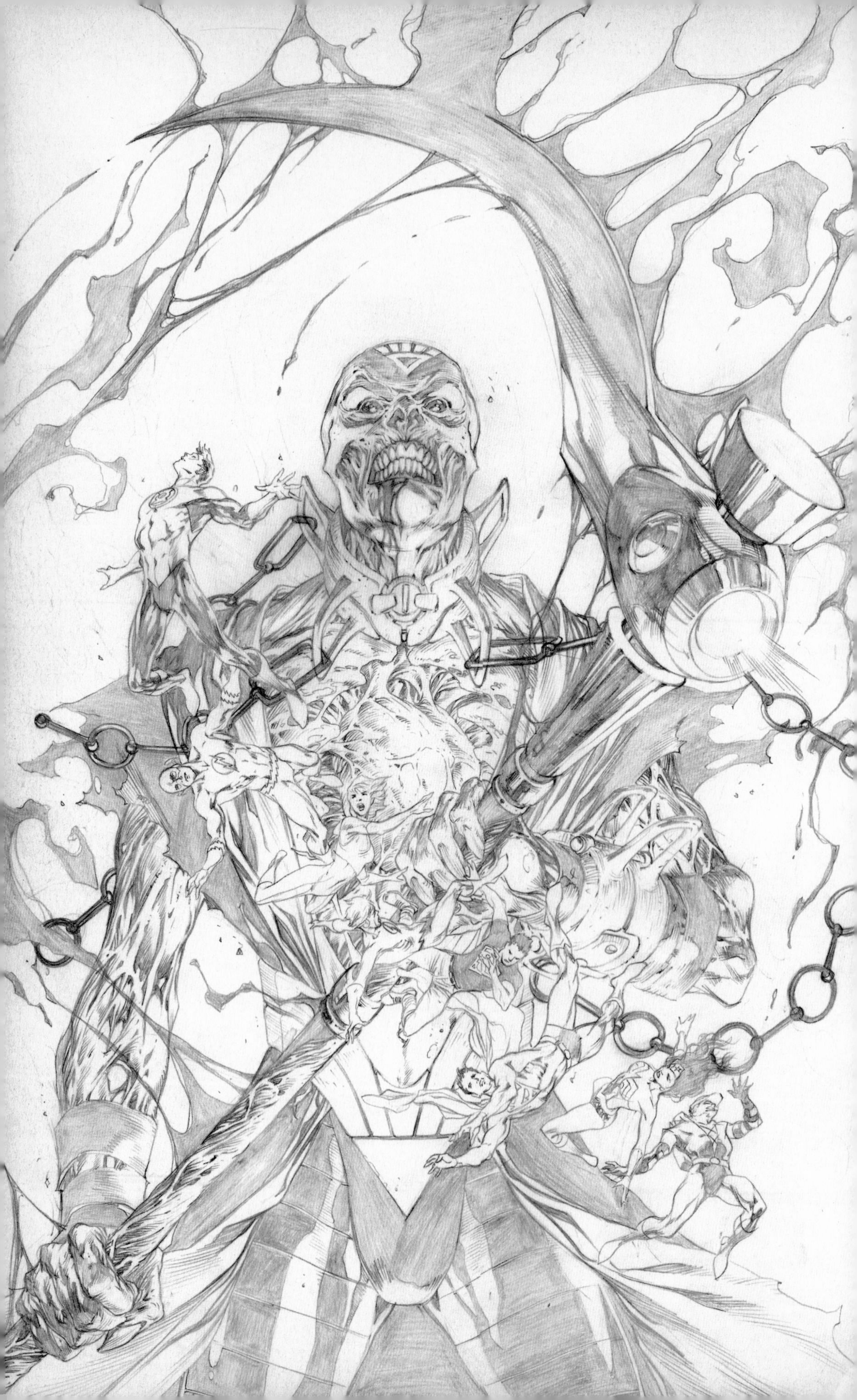

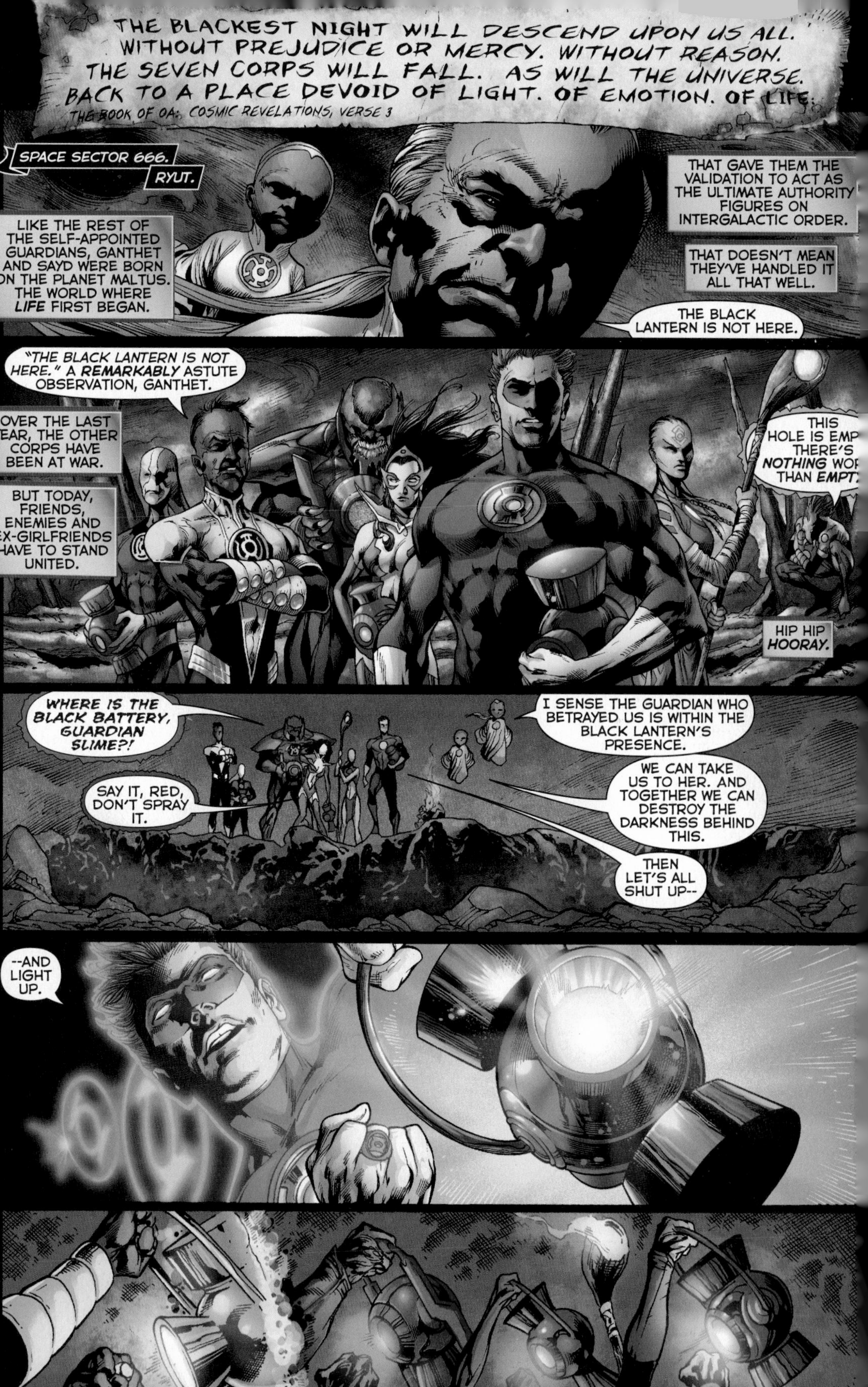
THE BLACKEST NIGHT WILL DESCEND UPON US ALL. WITHOUT PREJUDICE OR MERCY. WITHOUT REASON. THE SEVEN CORPS WILL FALL. AS WILL THE UNIVERSE. BACK TO A PLACE DEVOID OF LIGHT. OF EMOTION. OF LIFE.
THE BOOK OF OA: COSMIC REVELATIONS, VERSE 3
SPACE SECTOR 666.
RYUT.
LIKE THE REST OF THE SELF-APPOINTED GUARDIANS, GANTHET AND SAYD WERE BORN ON THE PLANET MALTUS. THE WORLD WHERE LIFE FIRST BEGAN.
THAT GAVE THEM THE VALIDATION TO ACT AS THE ULTIMATE AUTHORITY FIGURES ON INTERGALACTIC ORDER.
THAT DOESN'T MEAN THEY'VE HANDLED IT ALL THAT WELL.
THE BLACK LANTERN IS NOT HERE.
"THE BLACK LANTERN IS NOT HERE." A REMARKABLY ASTUTE OBSERVATION, GANTHET.
OVER THE LAST YEAR, THE OTHER CORPS HAVE BEEN AT WAR.
BUT TODAY, FRIENDS, ENEMIES AND EX-GIRLFRIENDS HAVE TO STAND UNITED.
THIS HOLE IS EMP THERE'S NOTHING WOR THAN EMPT
HIP HIP HOORAY.
WHERE IS THE BLACK BATTERY, GUARDIAN SLIME?!
SAY IT, RED, DON'T SPRAY IT.
I SENSE THE GUARDIAN WHO BETRAYED US IS WITHIN THE BLACK LANTERN'S PRESENCE.
WE CAN TAKE US TO HER. AND TOGETHER WE CAN DESTROY THE DARKNESS BEHIND THIS.
THEN LET'S ALL SHUT UP--
--AND LIGHT UP.

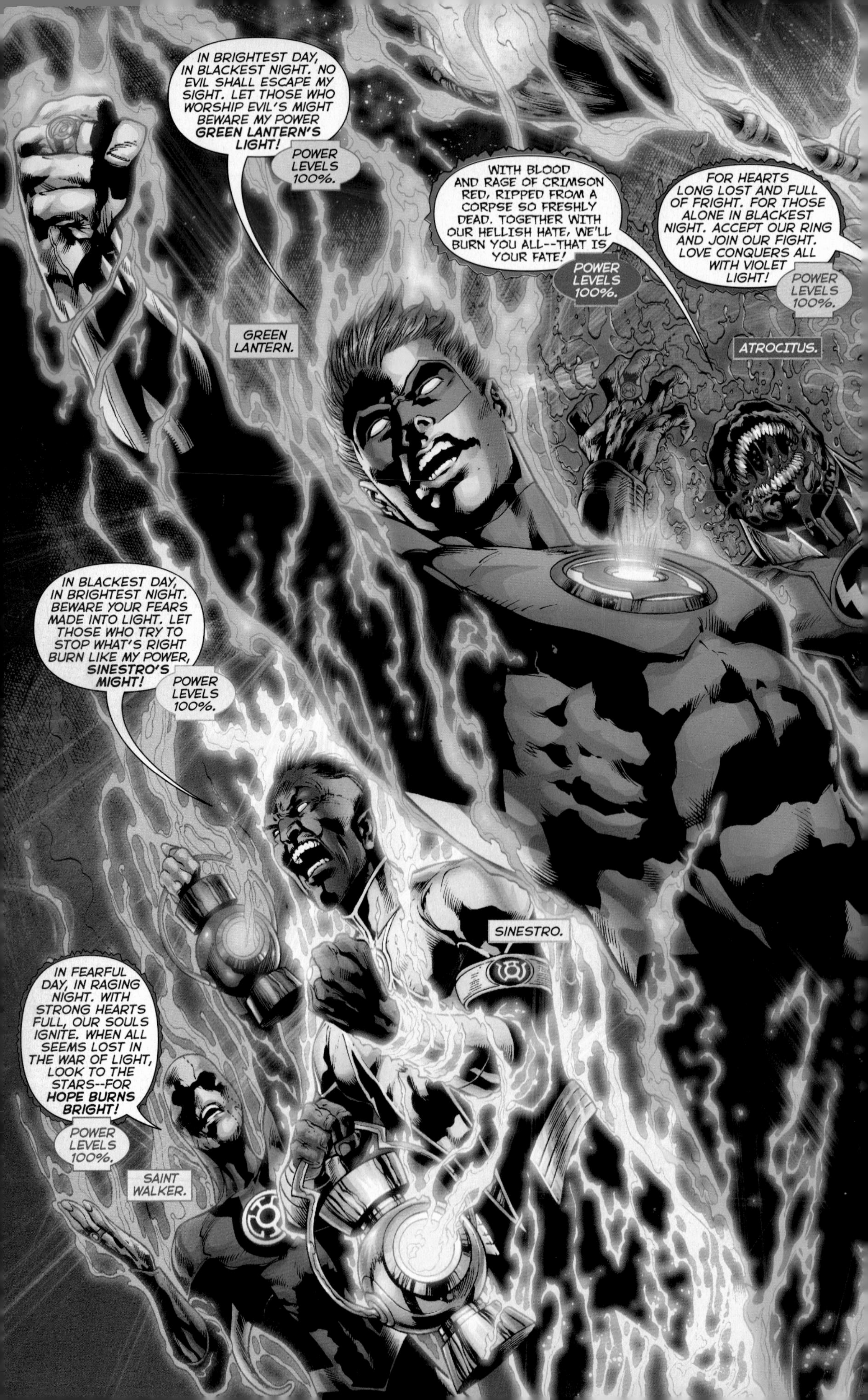
IN BRIGHTEST DAY, IN BLACKEST NIGHT. NO EVIL SHALL ESCAPE MY SIGHT. LET THOSE WHO WORSHIP EVIL'S MIGHT BEWARE MY POWER **GREEN LANTERN'S LIGHT!**
POWER LEVELS 100%.
GREEN LANTERN.
WITH BLOOD AND RAGE OF CRIMSON RED, RIPPED FROM A CORPSE SO FRESHLY DEAD. TOGETHER WITH OUR HELLISH HATE, WE'LL BURN YOU ALL--THAT IS YOUR FATE!
POWER LEVELS 100%.
FOR HEARTS LONG LOST AND FULL OF FRIGHT. FOR THOSE ALONE IN BLACKEST NIGHT. ACCEPT OUR RING AND JOIN OUR FIGHT. LOVE CONQUERS ALL WITH VIOLET LIGHT!
POWER LEVELS 100%.
ATROCITUS.
IN BLACKEST DAY, IN BRIGHTEST NIGHT. BEWARE YOUR FEARS MADE INTO LIGHT. LET THOSE WHO TRY TO STOP WHAT'S RIGHT BURN LIKE MY POWER, **SINESTRO'S MIGHT!**
POWER LEVELS 100%.
SINESTRO.
IN FEARFUL DAY, IN RAGING NIGHT. WITH STRONG HEARTS FULL, OUR SOULS IGNITE. WHEN ALL SEEMS LOST IN THE WAR OF LIGHT, LOOK TO THE STARS--FOR **HOPE BURNS BRIGHT!**
POWER LEVELS 100%.
SAINT WALKER.

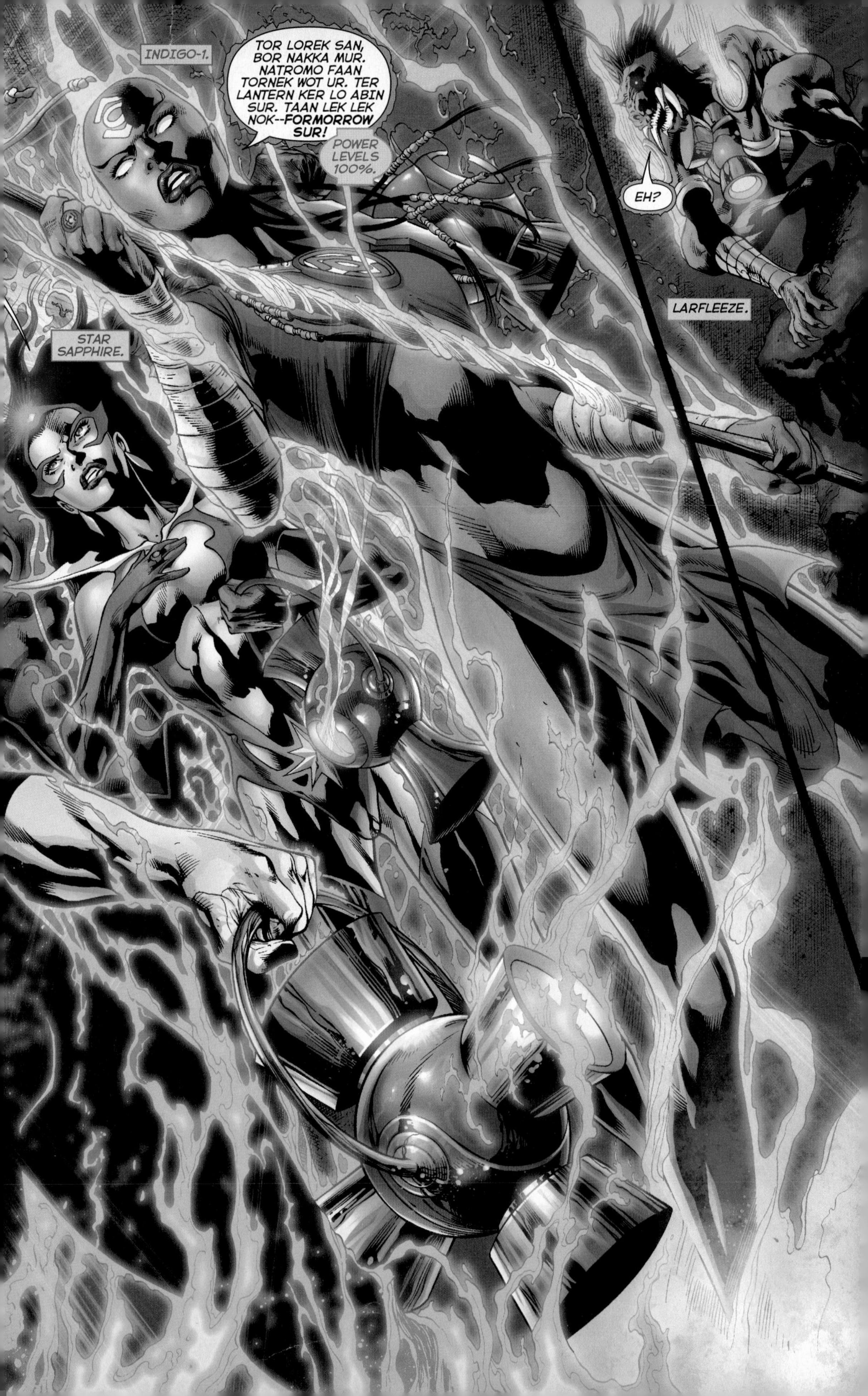
INDIGO-1.
TOR LOREK SAN, BOR NAKKA MUR. NATROMO FAAN TORNEK WOT UR. TER LANTERN KER LO ABIN SUR. TAAN LEK LEK NOK--**FORMORROW SUR!**
POWER LEVELS 100%.
STAR SAPPHIRE.
EH?
LARFLEEZE.

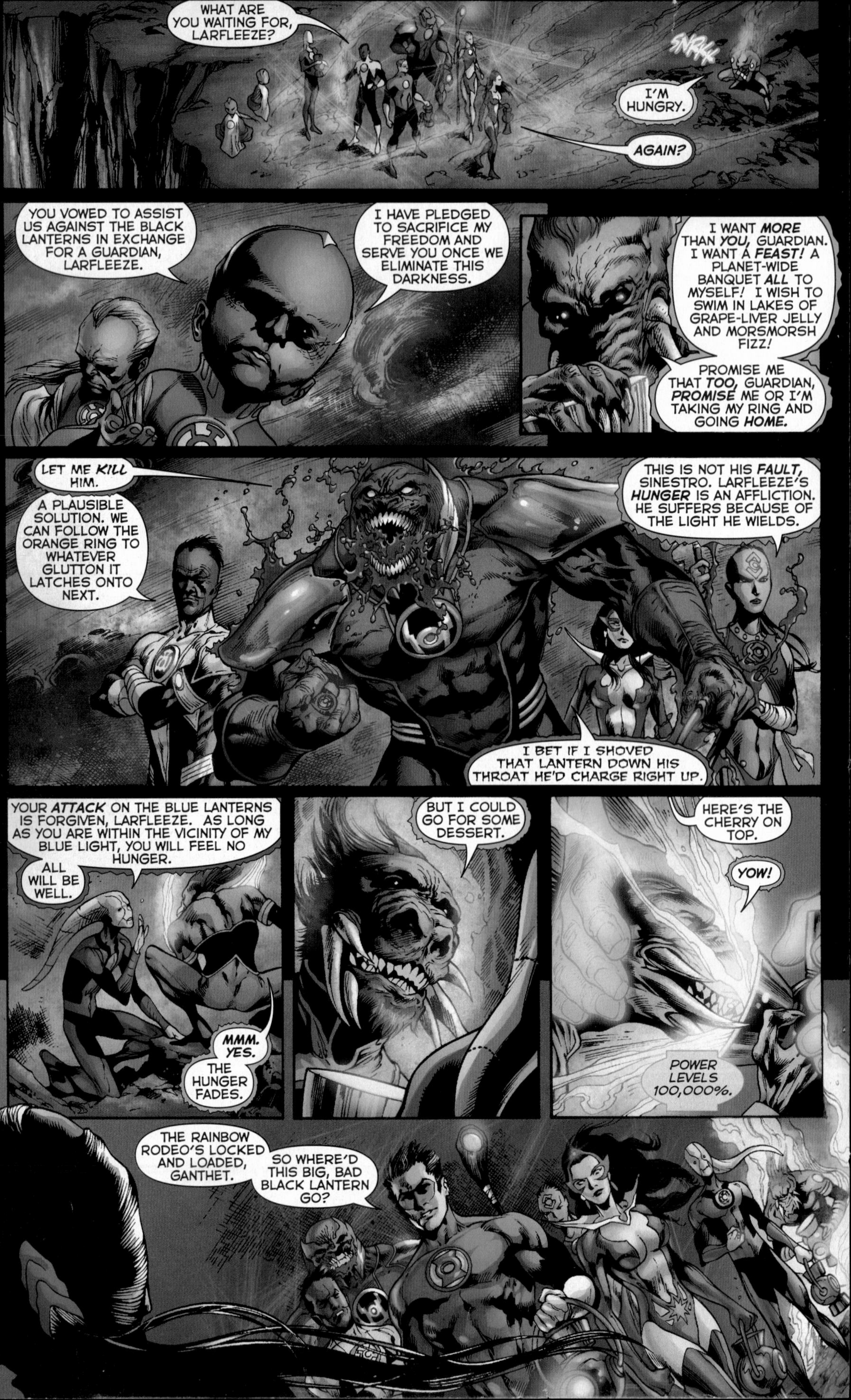

WHAT ARE YOU WAITING FOR, LARFLEEZE?
SNRKK
I'M HUNGRY.
AGAIN?
YOU VOWED TO ASSIST US AGAINST THE BLACK LANTERNS IN EXCHANGE FOR A GUARDIAN, LARFLEEZE.
I HAVE PLEDGED TO SACRIFICE MY FREEDOM AND SERVE YOU ONCE WE ELIMINATE THIS DARKNESS.
I WANT MORE THAN YOU, GUARDIAN. I WANT A FEAST! A PLANET-WIDE BANQUET ALL TO MYSELF! I WISH TO SWIM IN LAKES OF GRAPE-LIVER JELLY AND MORSMORSH FIZZ!
PROMISE ME THAT TOO, GUARDIAN, PROMISE ME OR I'M TAKING MY RING AND GOING HOME.
LET ME KILL HIM.
A PLAUSIBLE SOLUTION. WE CAN FOLLOW THE ORANGE RING TO WHATEVER GLUTTON IT LATCHES ONTO NEXT.
THIS IS NOT HIS FAULT, SINESTRO. LARFLEEZE'S HUNGER IS AN AFFLICTION. HE SUFFERS BECAUSE OF THE LIGHT HE WIELDS.
I BET IF I SHOVED THAT LANTERN DOWN HIS THROAT HE'D CHARGE RIGHT UP.
YOUR ATTACK ON THE BLUE LANTERNS IS FORGIVEN, LARFLEEZE. AS LONG AS YOU ARE WITHIN THE VICINITY OF MY BLUE LIGHT, YOU WILL FEEL NO HUNGER.
ALL WILL BE WELL.
MMM. YES. THE HUNGER FADES.
BUT I COULD GO FOR SOME DESSERT.
HERE'S THE CHERRY ON TOP.
YOW!
POWER LEVELS 100,000%.
THE RAINBOW RODEO'S LOCKED AND LOADED, GANTHET.
SO WHERE'D THIS BIG, BAD BLACK LANTERN GO?

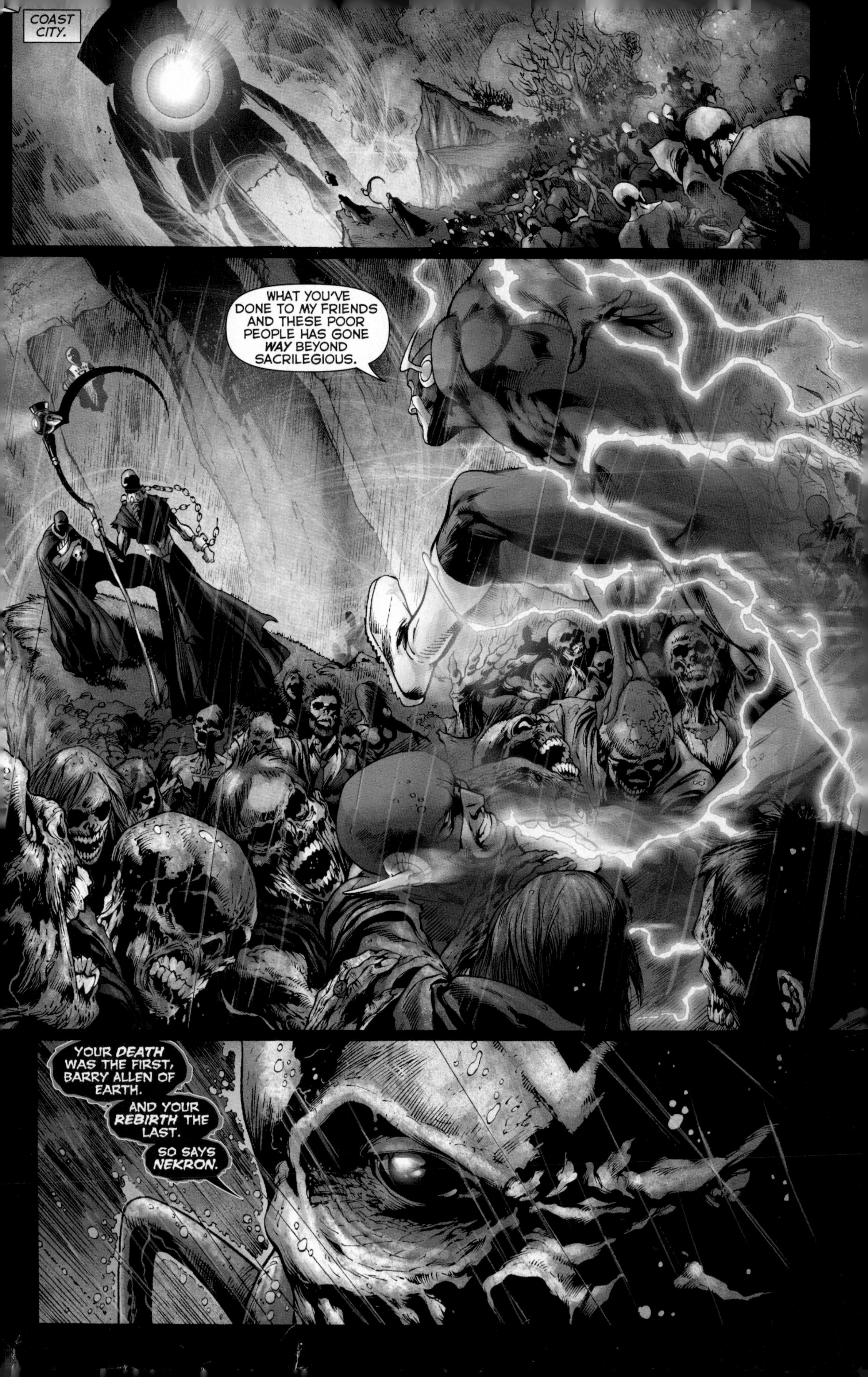
COAST CITY.
WHAT YOU'VE DONE TO MY FRIENDS AND THESE POOR PEOPLE HAS GONE WAY BEYOND SACRILEGIOUS.
YOUR DEATH WAS THE FIRST, BARRY ALLEN OF EARTH.
AND YOUR REBIRTH THE LAST.
SO SAYS NEKRON.

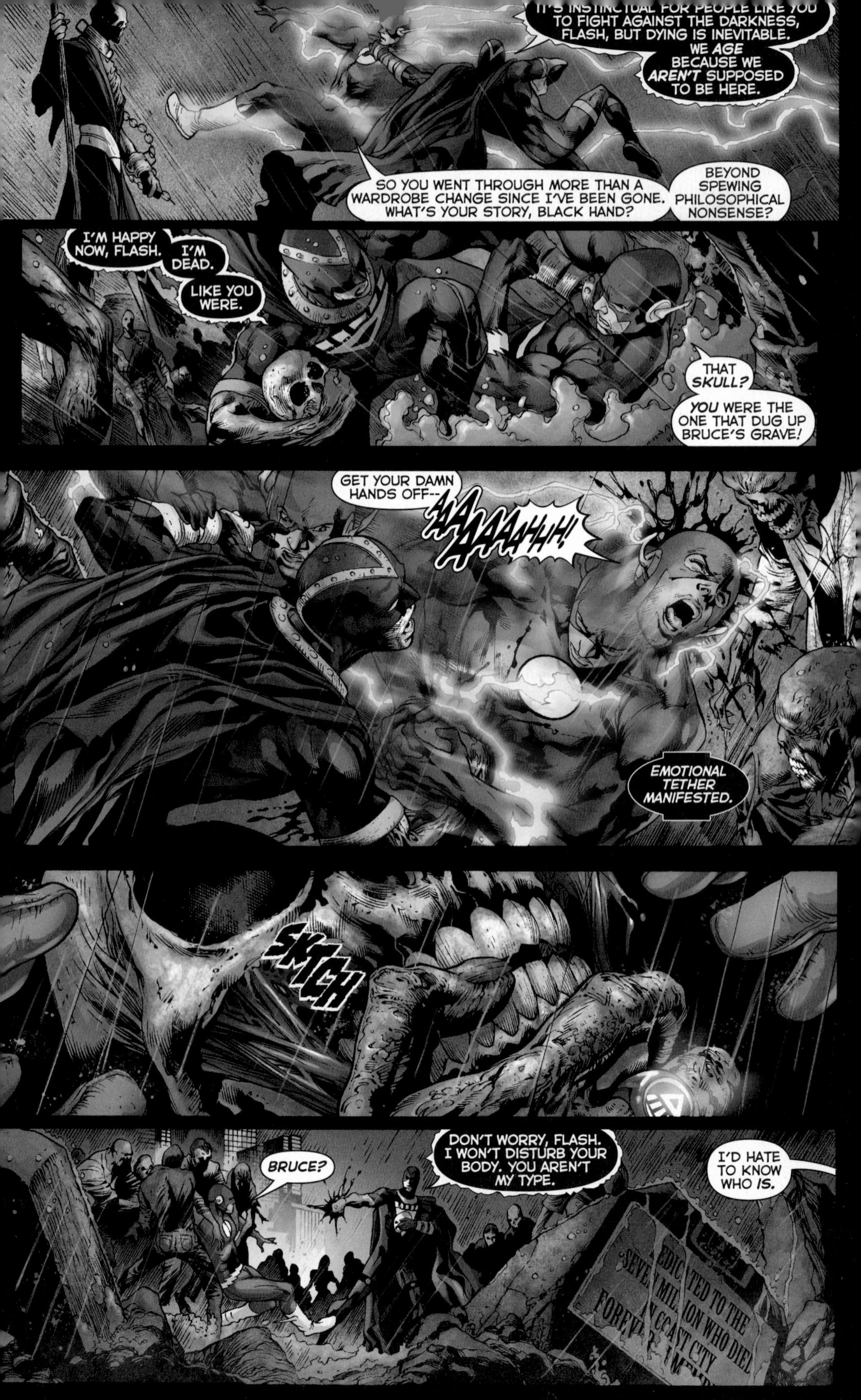
IT'S INSTINCTUAL FOR PEOPLE LIKE YOU TO FIGHT AGAINST THE DARKNESS, FLASH, BUT DYING IS INEVITABLE.
WE AGE BECAUSE WE AREN'T SUPPOSED TO BE HERE.
SO YOU WENT THROUGH MORE THAN A WARDROBE CHANGE SINCE I'VE BEEN GONE. WHAT'S YOUR STORY, BLACK HAND?
BEYOND SPEWING PHILOSOPHICAL NONSENSE?
I'M HAPPY NOW, FLASH.
I'M DEAD.
LIKE YOU WERE.
THAT SKULL?
YOU WERE THE ONE THAT DUG UP BRUCE'S GRAVE!
GET YOUR DAMN HANDS OFF--
AAAAAAAAHHH!
EMOTIONAL TETHER MANIFESTED.
SKTCH
BRUCE?
DON'T WORRY, FLASH. I WON'T DISTURB YOUR BODY. YOU AREN'T MY TYPE.
I'D HATE TO KNOW WHO IS.

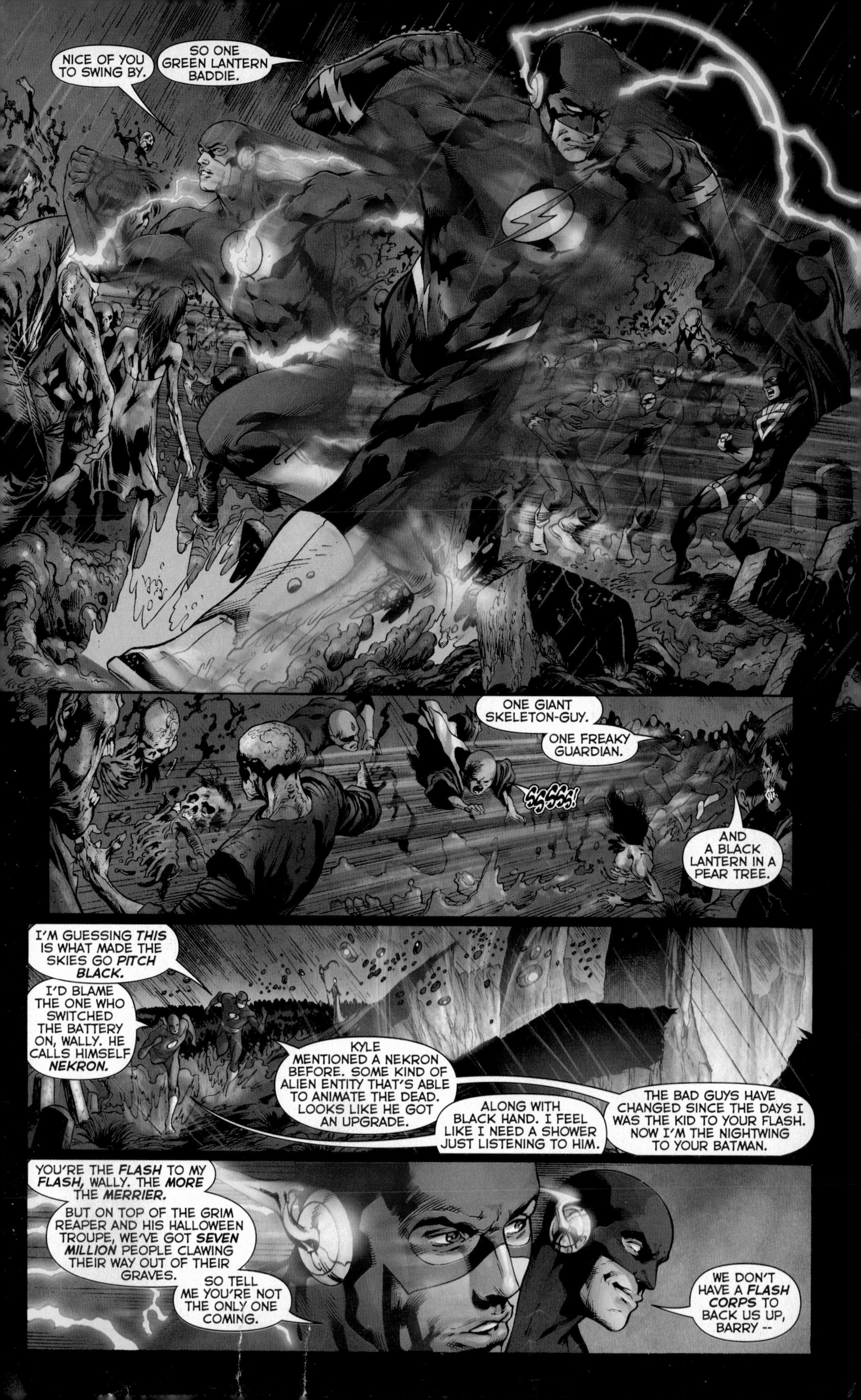
NICE OF YOU TO SWING BY.
SO ONE GREEN LANTERN BADDIE.
ONE GIANT SKELETON-GUY.
ONE FREAKY GUARDIAN.
SSSSS!
AND A BLACK LANTERN IN A PEAR TREE.
I'M GUESSING THIS IS WHAT MADE THE SKIES GO PITCH BLACK.
I'D BLAME THE ONE WHO SWITCHED THE BATTERY ON, WALLY. HE CALLS HIMSELF NEKRON.
KYLE MENTIONED A NEKRON BEFORE. SOME KIND OF ALIEN ENTITY THAT'S ABLE TO ANIMATE THE DEAD. LOOKS LIKE HE GOT AN UPGRADE.
ALONG WITH BLACK HAND. I FEEL LIKE I NEED A SHOWER JUST LISTENING TO HIM.
THE BAD GUYS HAVE CHANGED SINCE THE DAYS I WAS THE KID TO YOUR FLASH. NOW I'M THE NIGHTWING TO YOUR BATMAN.
YOU'RE THE FLASH TO MY FLASH, WALLY. THE MORE THE MERRIER.
BUT ON TOP OF THE GRIM REAPER AND HIS HALLOWEEN TROUPE, WE'VE GOT SEVEN MILLION PEOPLE CLAWING THEIR WAY OUT OF THEIR GRAVES.
SO TELL ME YOU'RE NOT THE ONLY ONE COMING.
WE DON'T HAVE A FLASH CORPS TO BACK US UP, BARRY --

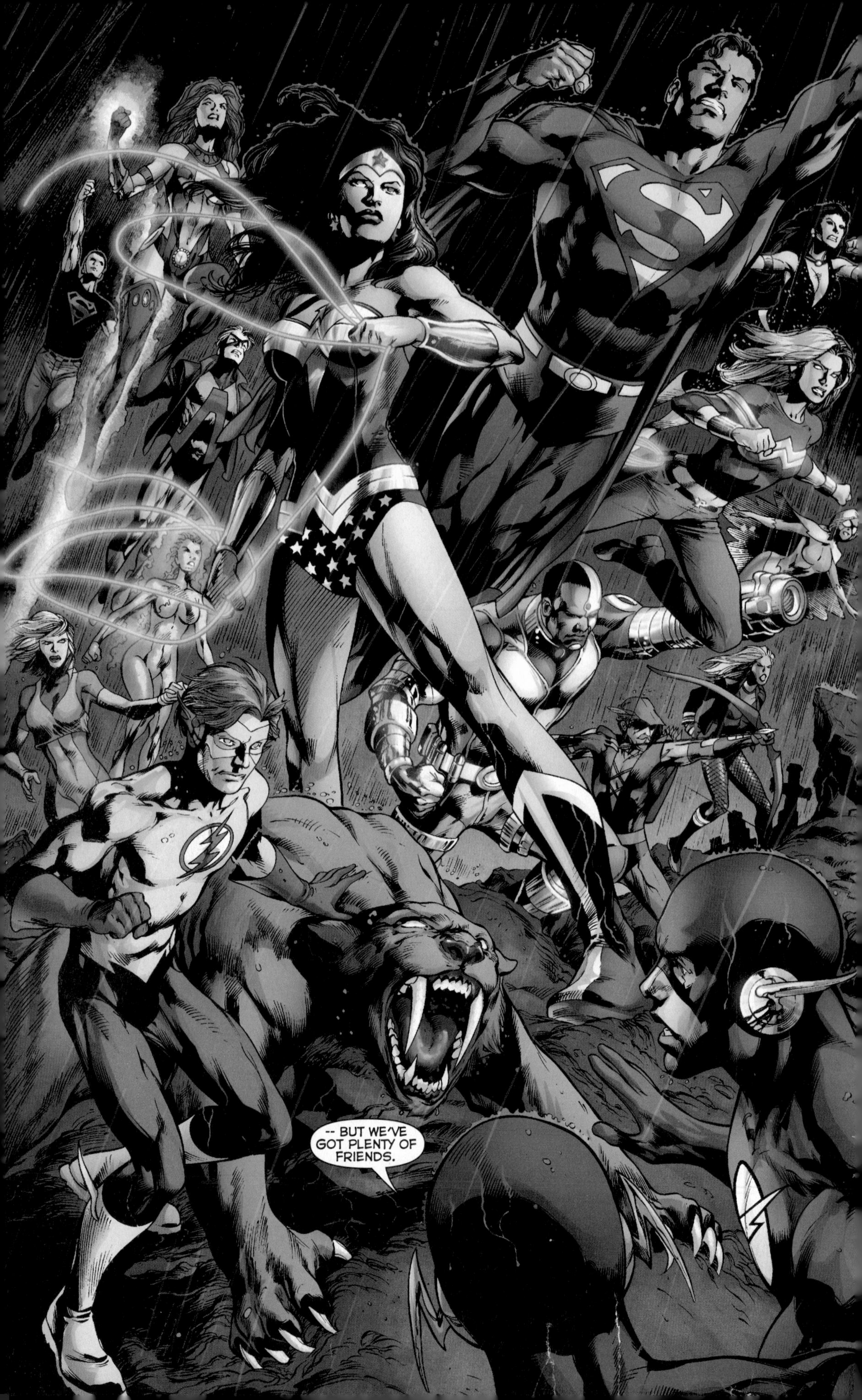
-- BUT WE'VE GOT PLENTY OF FRIENDS.

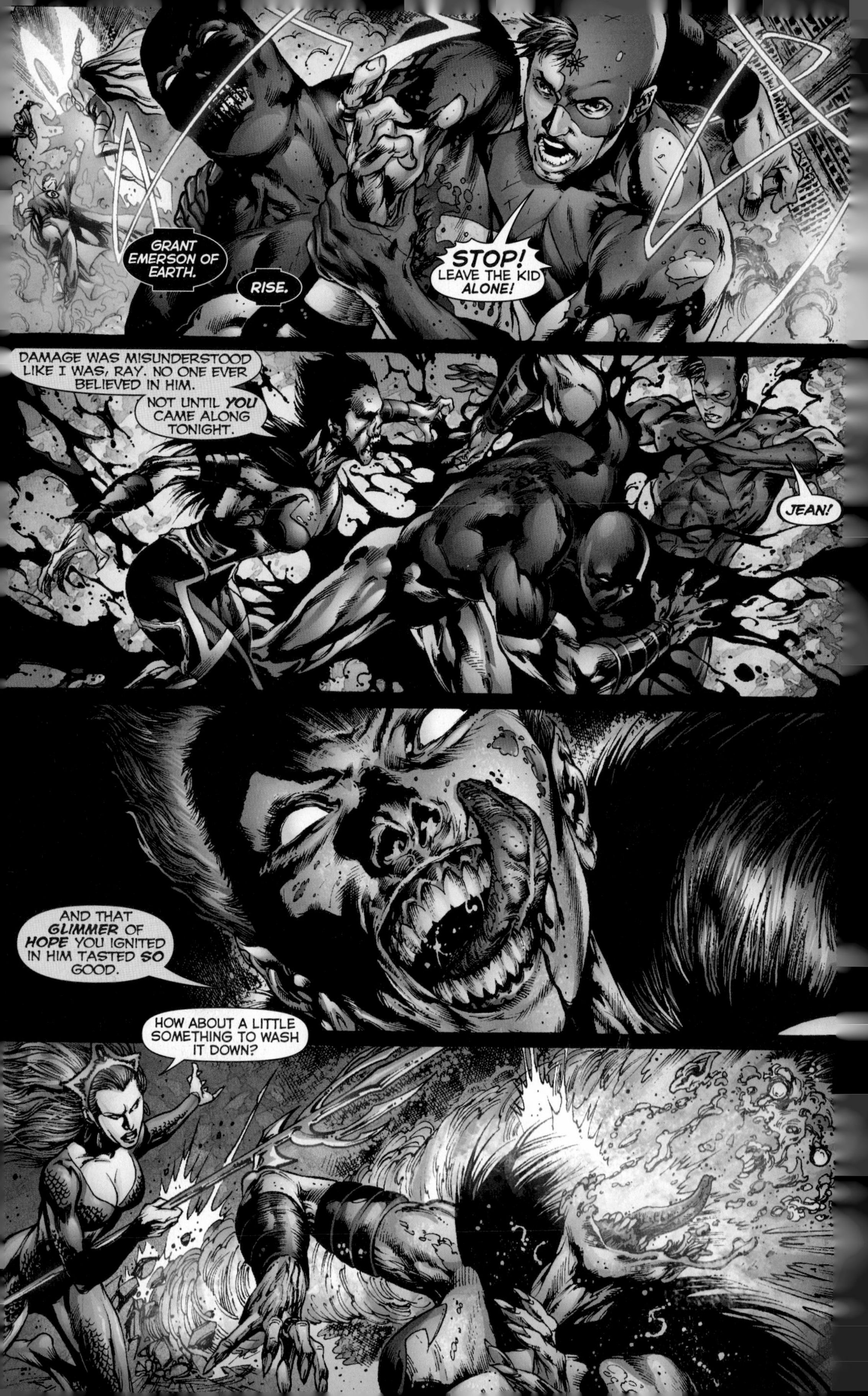
GRANT EMERSON OF EARTH.
RISE.
STOP! LEAVE THE KID ALONE!
DAMAGE WAS MISUNDERSTOOD LIKE I WAS, RAY. NO ONE EVER BELIEVED IN HIM.
NOT UNTIL YOU CAME ALONG TONIGHT.
JEAN!
AND THAT GLIMMER OF HOPE YOU IGNITED IN HIM TASTED SO GOOD.
HOW ABOUT A LITTLE SOMETHING TO WASH IT DOWN?

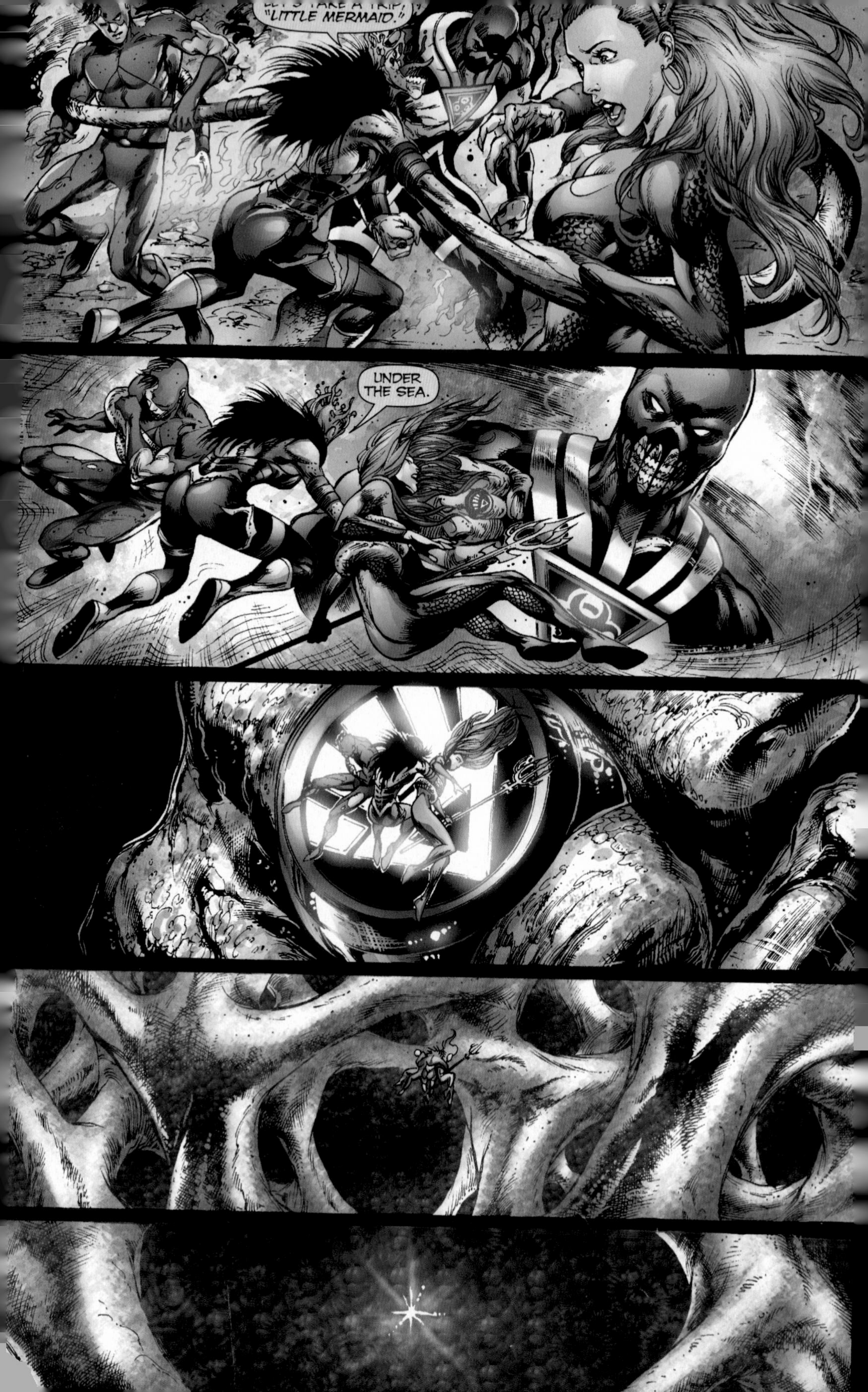
LET'S TAKE A TRIP, "LITTLE MERMAID."
UNDER THE SEA.

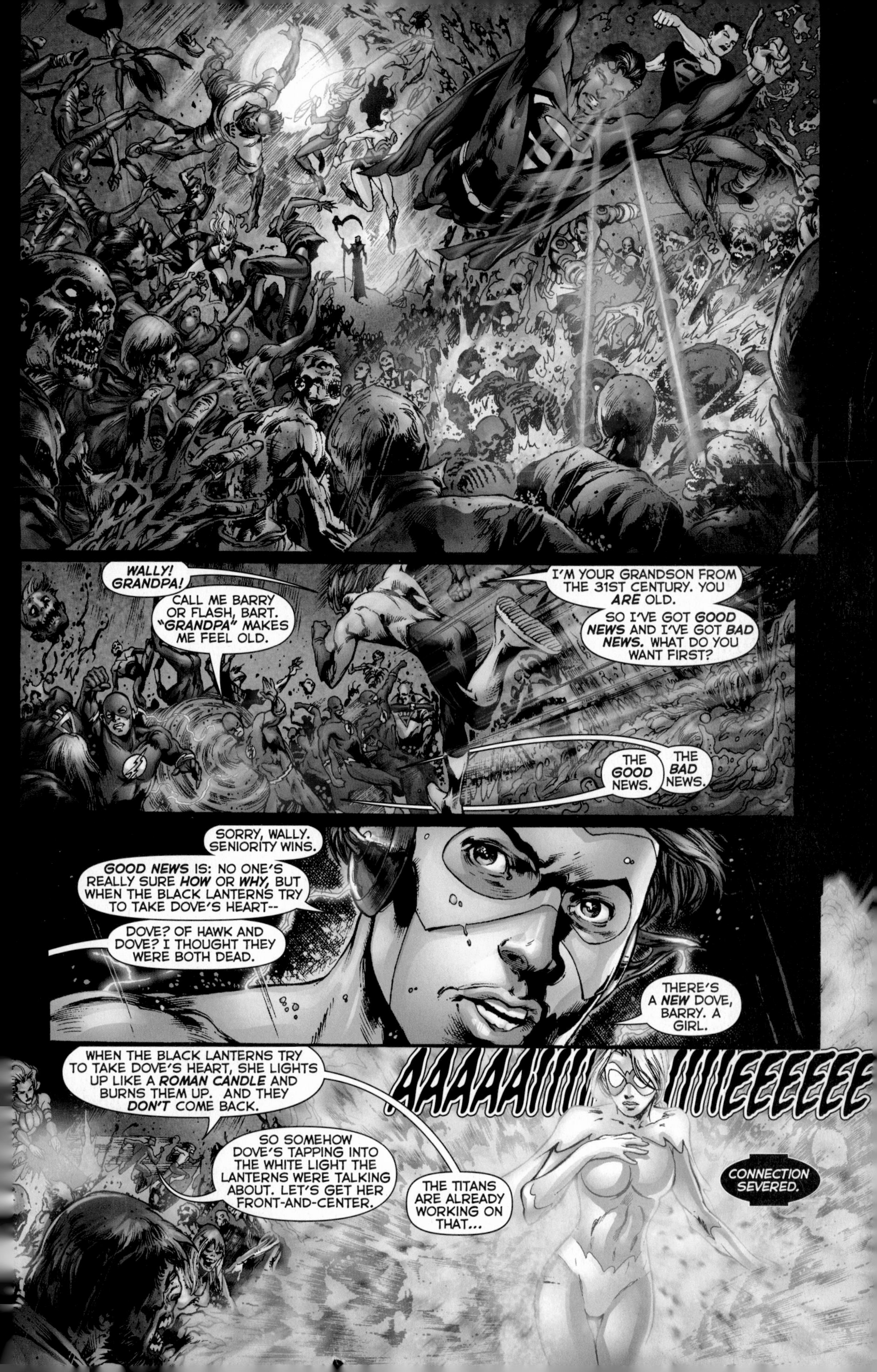
WALLY! GRANDPA!
CALL ME BARRY OR FLASH, BART. "GRANDPA" MAKES ME FEEL OLD.
I'M YOUR GRANDSON FROM THE 31ST CENTURY. YOU ARE OLD.
SO I'VE GOT GOOD NEWS AND I'VE GOT BAD NEWS. WHAT DO YOU WANT FIRST?
THE GOOD NEWS.
THE BAD NEWS.
SORRY, WALLY. SENIORITY WINS.
GOOD NEWS IS: NO ONE'S REALLY SURE HOW OR WHY, BUT WHEN THE BLACK LANTERNS TRY TO TAKE DOVE'S HEART--
DOVE? OF HAWK AND DOVE? I THOUGHT THEY WERE BOTH DEAD.
THERE'S A NEW DOVE, BARRY. A GIRL.
WHEN THE BLACK LANTERNS TRY TO TAKE DOVE'S HEART, SHE LIGHTS UP LIKE A ROMAN CANDLE AND BURNS THEM UP. AND THEY DON'T COME BACK.
AAAAAIIII IIIIEEEEEEE
SO SOMEHOW DOVE'S TAPPING INTO THE WHITE LIGHT THE LANTERNS WERE TALKING ABOUT. LET'S GET HER FRONT-AND-CENTER.
THE TITANS ARE ALREADY WORKING ON THAT...
CONNECTION SEVERED.

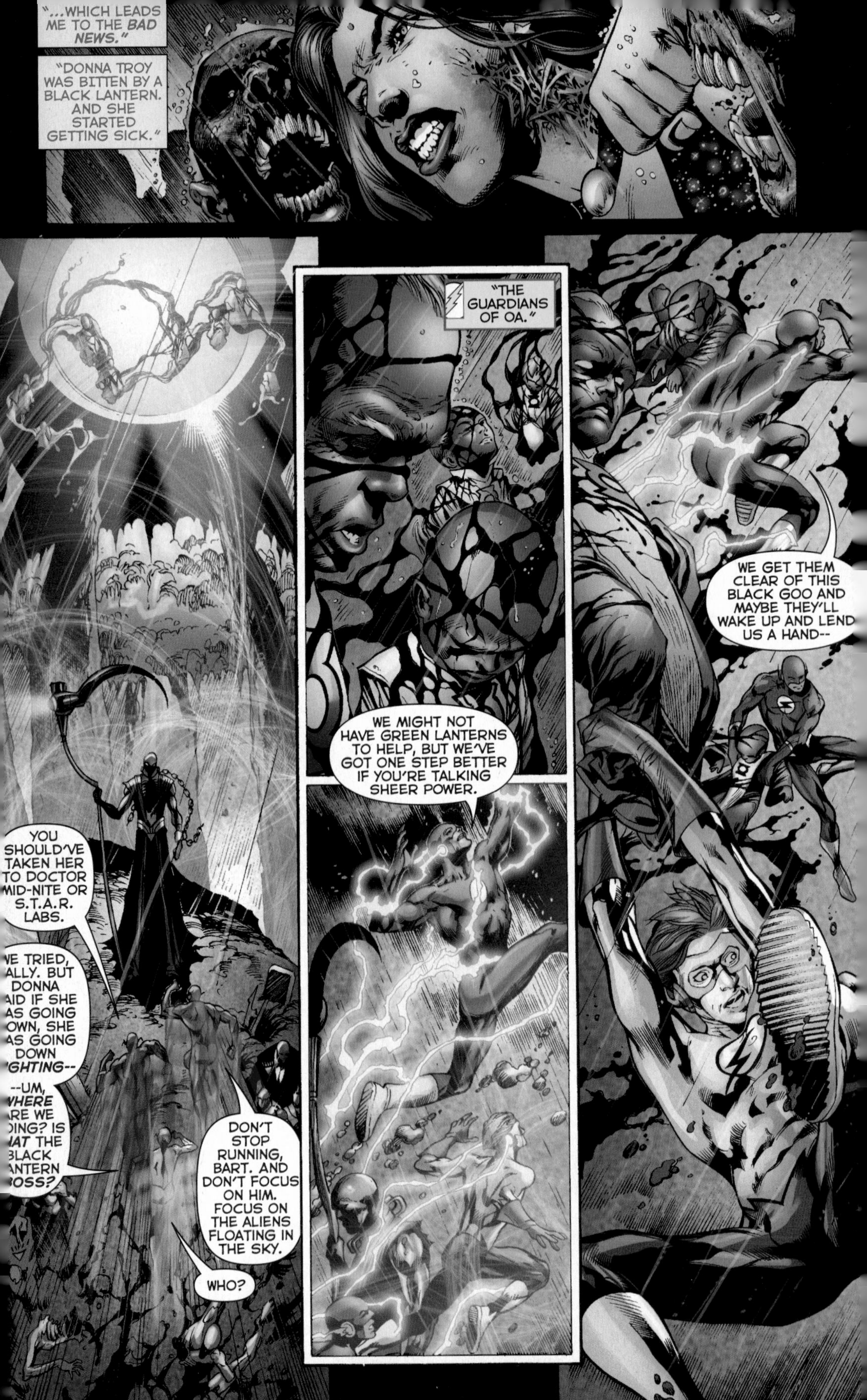
"...WHICH LEADS ME TO THE *BAD NEWS.*"
"DONNA TROY WAS BITTEN BY A BLACK LANTERN. AND SHE STARTED GETTING SICK."
YOU SHOULD'VE TAKEN HER TO DOCTOR MID-NITE OR S.T.A.R. LABS.
E TRIED, ALLY. BUT DONNA AID IF SHE AS GOING OWN, SHE AS GOING DOWN *IGHTING*--
--UM, *WHERE* RE WE OING? IS *HAT* THE BLACK ANTERN BOSS?
DON'T STOP RUNNING, BART. AND DON'T FOCUS ON HIM. FOCUS ON THE ALIENS FLOATING IN THE SKY.
WHO?
"THE GUARDIANS OF OA."
WE MIGHT NOT HAVE GREEN LANTERNS TO HELP, BUT WE'VE GOT ONE STEP BETTER IF YOU'RE TALKING SHEER POWER.
WE GET THEM CLEAR OF THIS BLACK GOO AND MAYBE THEY'LL WAKE UP AND LEND US A HAND--

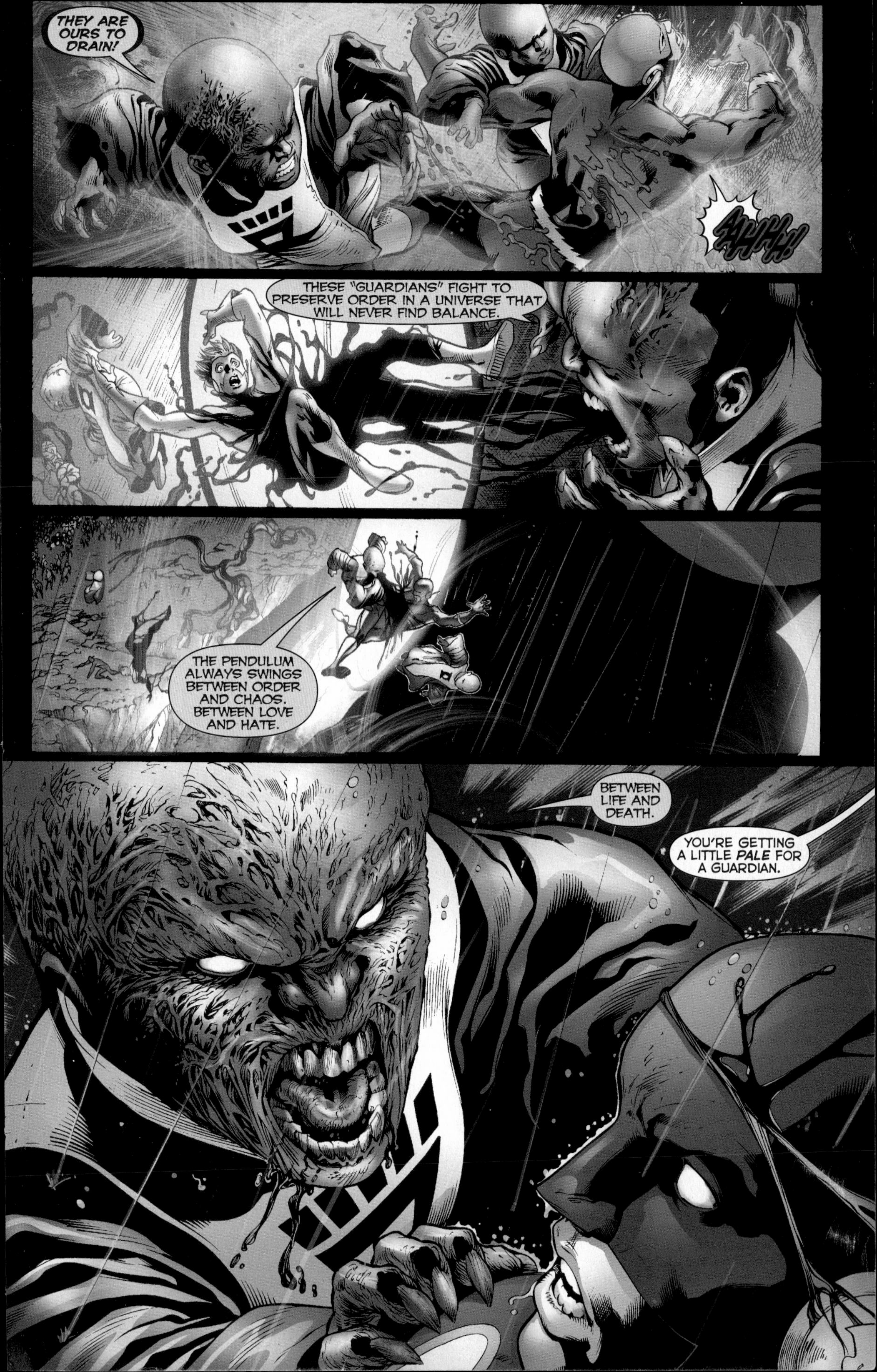
THEY ARE OURS TO DRAIN!
AAHHH!!
THESE "GUARDIANS" FIGHT TO PRESERVE ORDER IN A UNIVERSE THAT WILL NEVER FIND BALANCE.
THE PENDULUM ALWAYS SWINGS BETWEEN ORDER AND CHAOS. BETWEEN LOVE AND HATE.
BETWEEN LIFE AND DEATH.
YOU'RE GETTING A LITTLE *PALE* FOR A GUARDIAN.

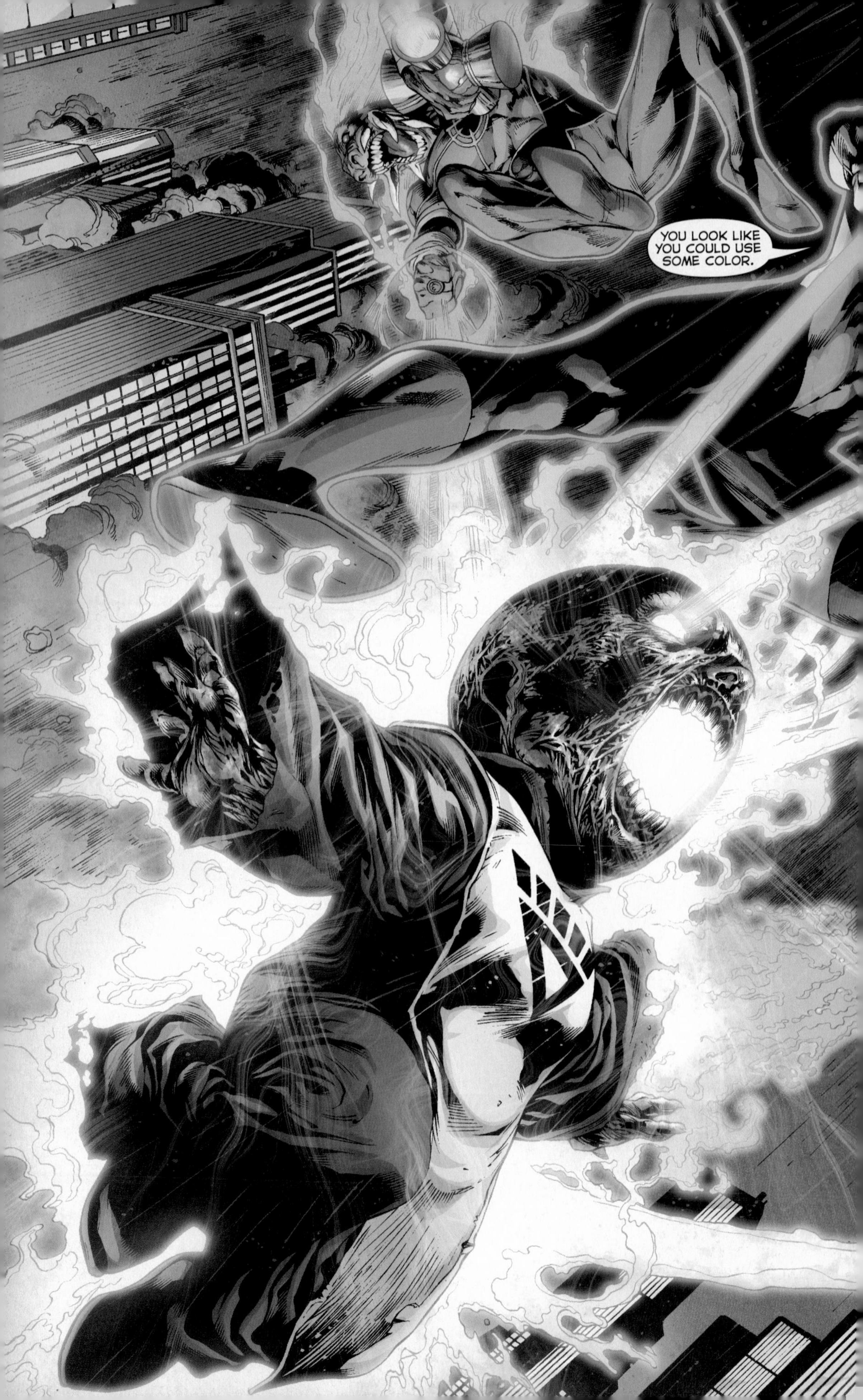
YOU LOOK LIKE YOU COULD USE SOME COLOR.

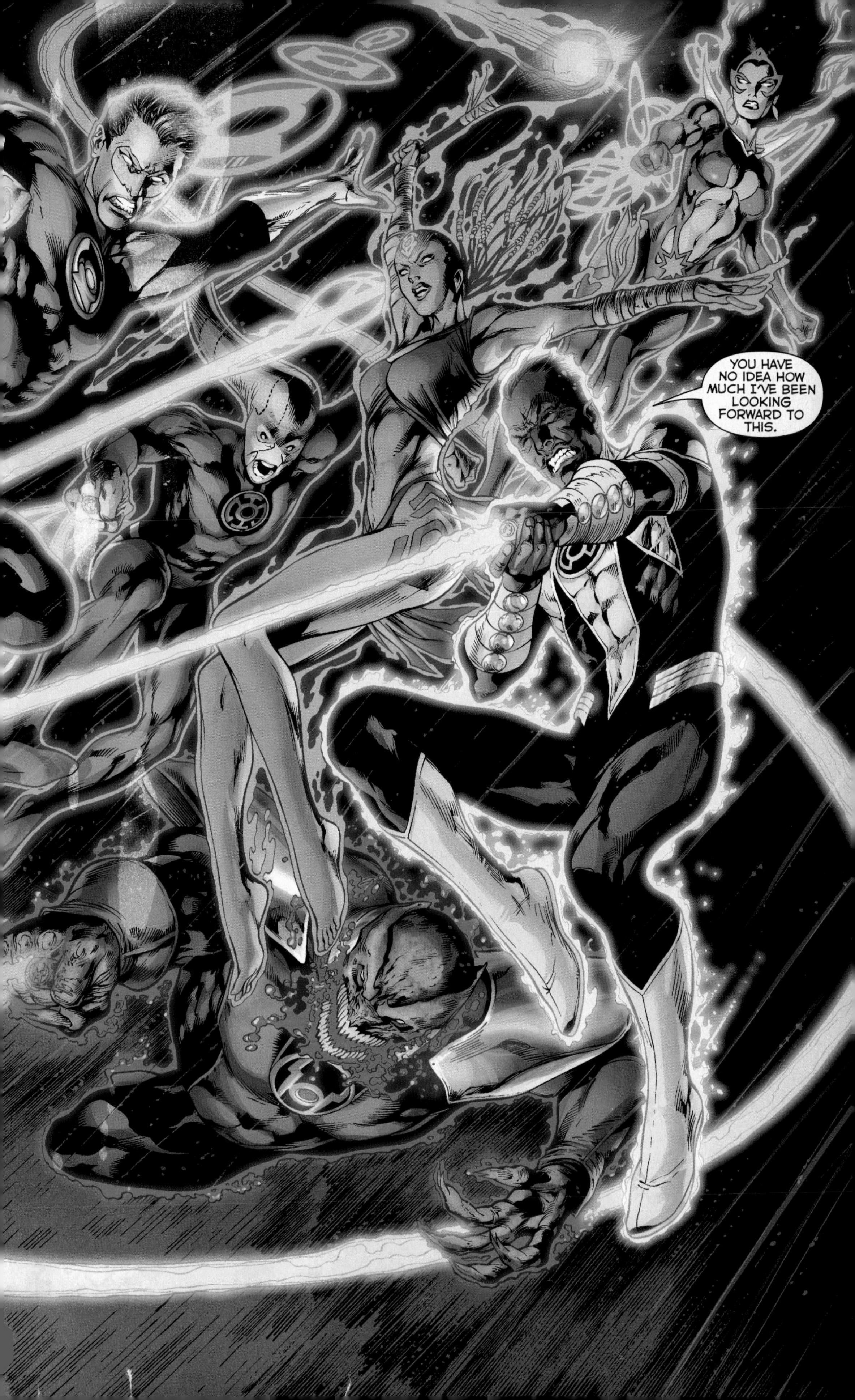
YOU HAVE NO IDEA HOW MUCH I'VE BEEN LOOKING FORWARD TO THIS.

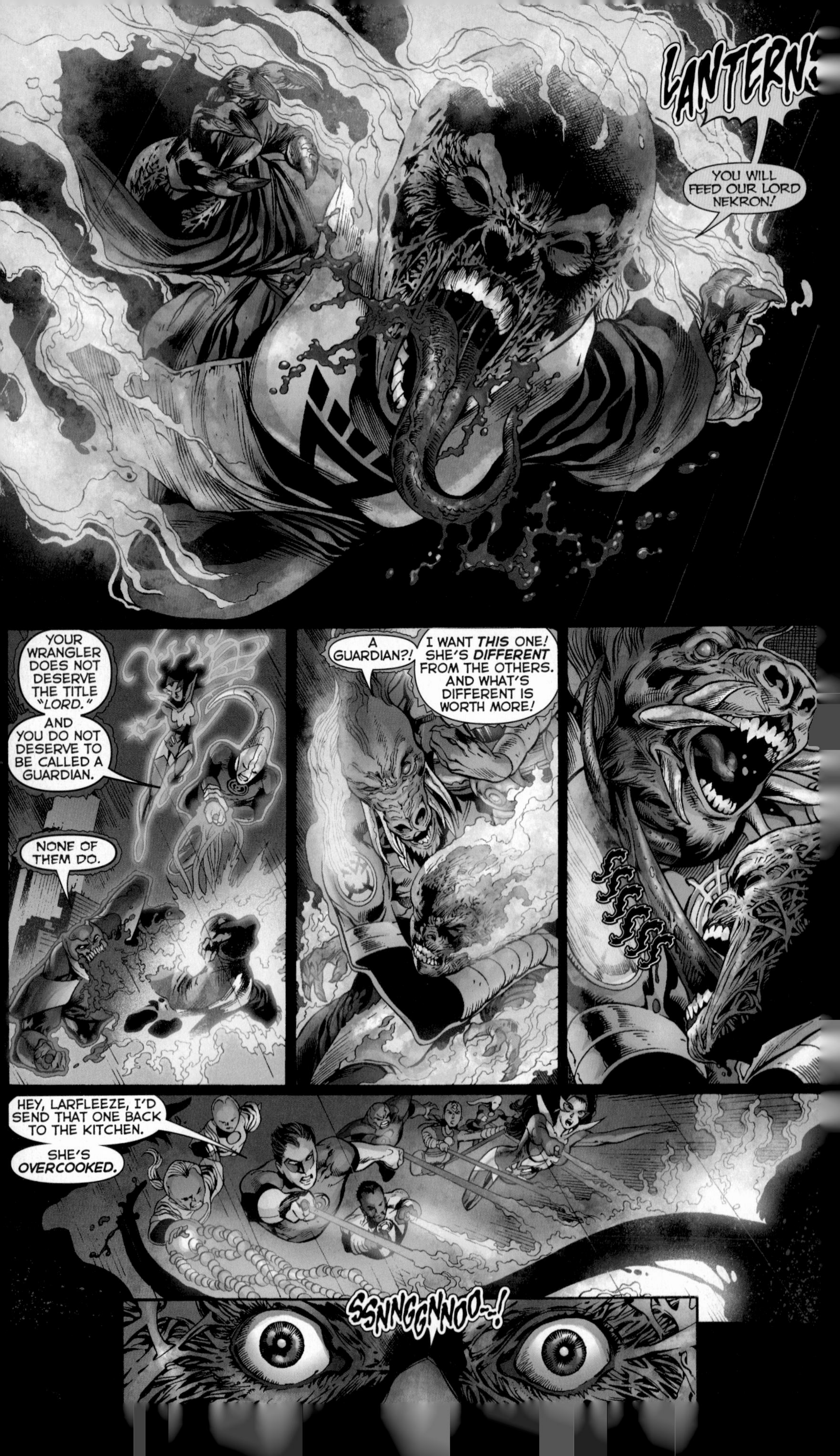
LANTERNS
YOU WILL FEED OUR LORD NEKRON!
YOUR WRANGLER DOES NOT DESERVE THE TITLE "LORD."
AND YOU DO NOT DESERVE TO BE CALLED A GUARDIAN.
NONE OF THEM DO.
A GUARDIAN?!
I WANT THIS ONE! SHE'S DIFFERENT FROM THE OTHERS. AND WHAT'S DIFFERENT IS WORTH MORE!
HEY, LARFLEEZE, I'D SEND THAT ONE BACK TO THE KITCHEN.
SHE'S OVERCOOKED.
SSNNGGNNOO--!

AAAAAAAII!!IEEE!

HAL! YOU'RE LATE!

THAT'S MY LINE.

YOU KNOW ANYTHING ABOUT THIS NEKRON?

THE CORPS HAS FACED HIM BEFORE. SOME KIND OF UNDEAD CREATURE WHO USES THE DECEASED AS PUPPETS. BUT THE BLACK RINGS ARE NEW.

NO WORRIES THOUGH. I BROUGHT THE COLOR-CODED CAVALRY.

THERE IT IS. THE CENTRAL BLACK LANTERN.

WE DESTROY THE LANTERN AND WE DESTROY EVERYTHING CONNECTED TO IT.

WHAT DO WE NEED TO DO?

WE MUST RECREATE THE WHITE LIGHT THAT GAVE BIRTH TO LIFE, SINESTRO.

IT IS THE ANTITHESIS OF THE DEATH POWERING THE BLACK LANTERN.

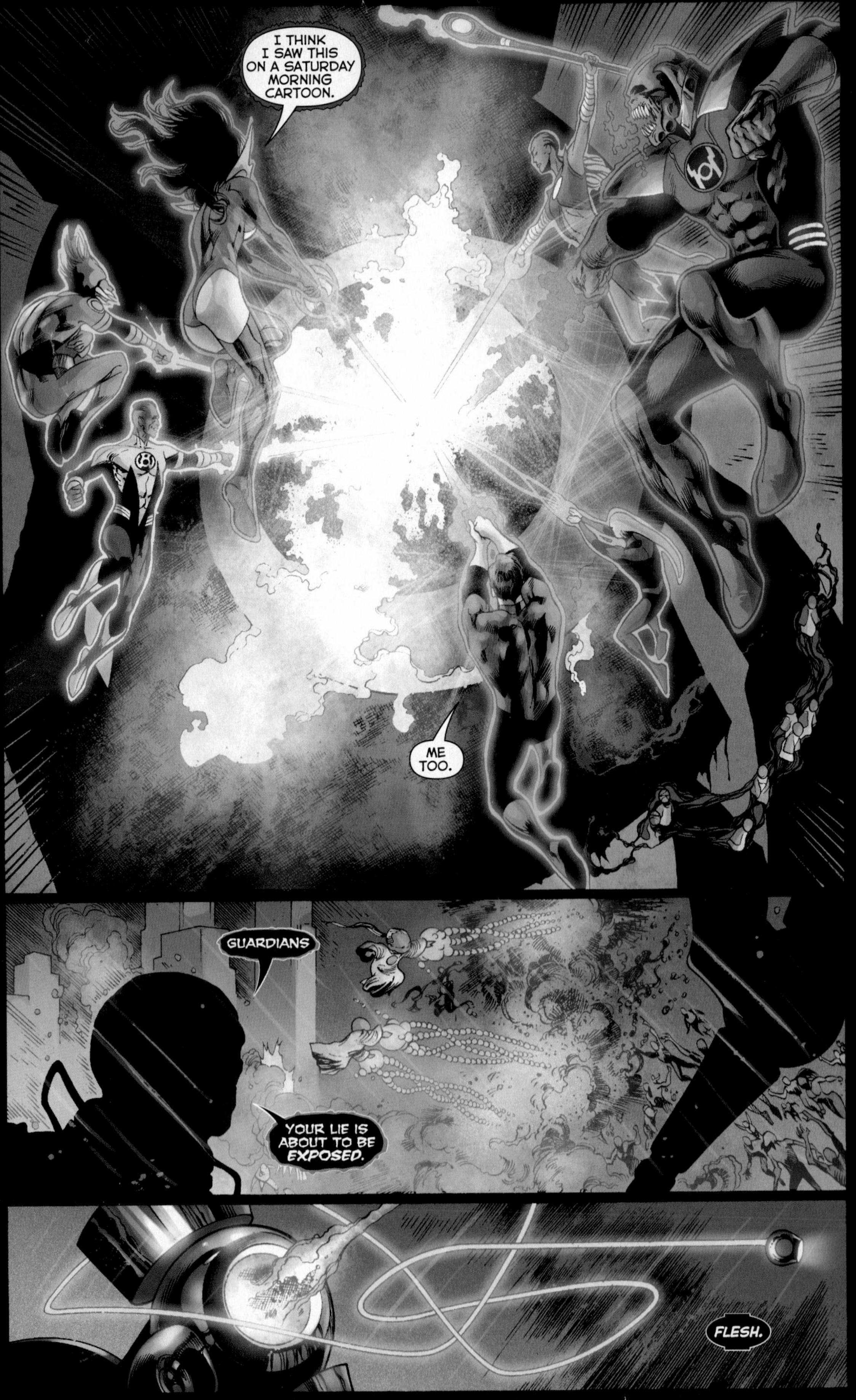
I THINK I SAW THIS ON A SATURDAY MORNING CARTOON.
ME TOO.
GUARDIANS
YOUR LIE IS ABOUT TO BE *EXPOSED.*
FLESH.

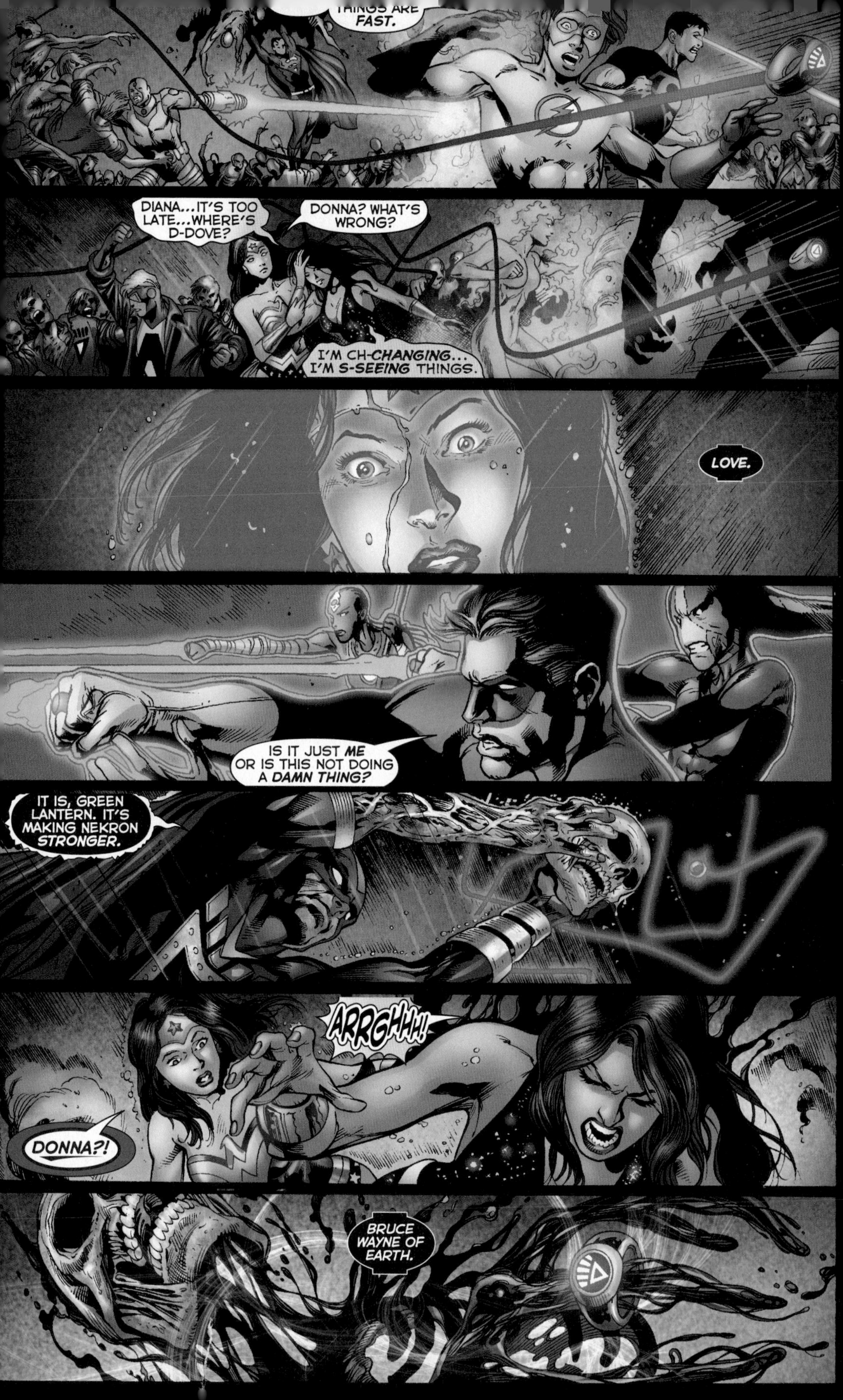
THINGS ARE FAST.
DIANA...IT'S TOO LATE...WHERE'S D-DOVE?
DONNA? WHAT'S WRONG?
I'M CH-CHANGING... I'M S-SEEING THINGS.
LOVE.
IS IT JUST ME OR IS THIS NOT DOING A DAMN THING?
IT IS, GREEN LANTERN. IT'S MAKING NEKRON STRONGER.
ARRGHHH!
DONNA?!
BRUCE WAYNE OF EARTH.

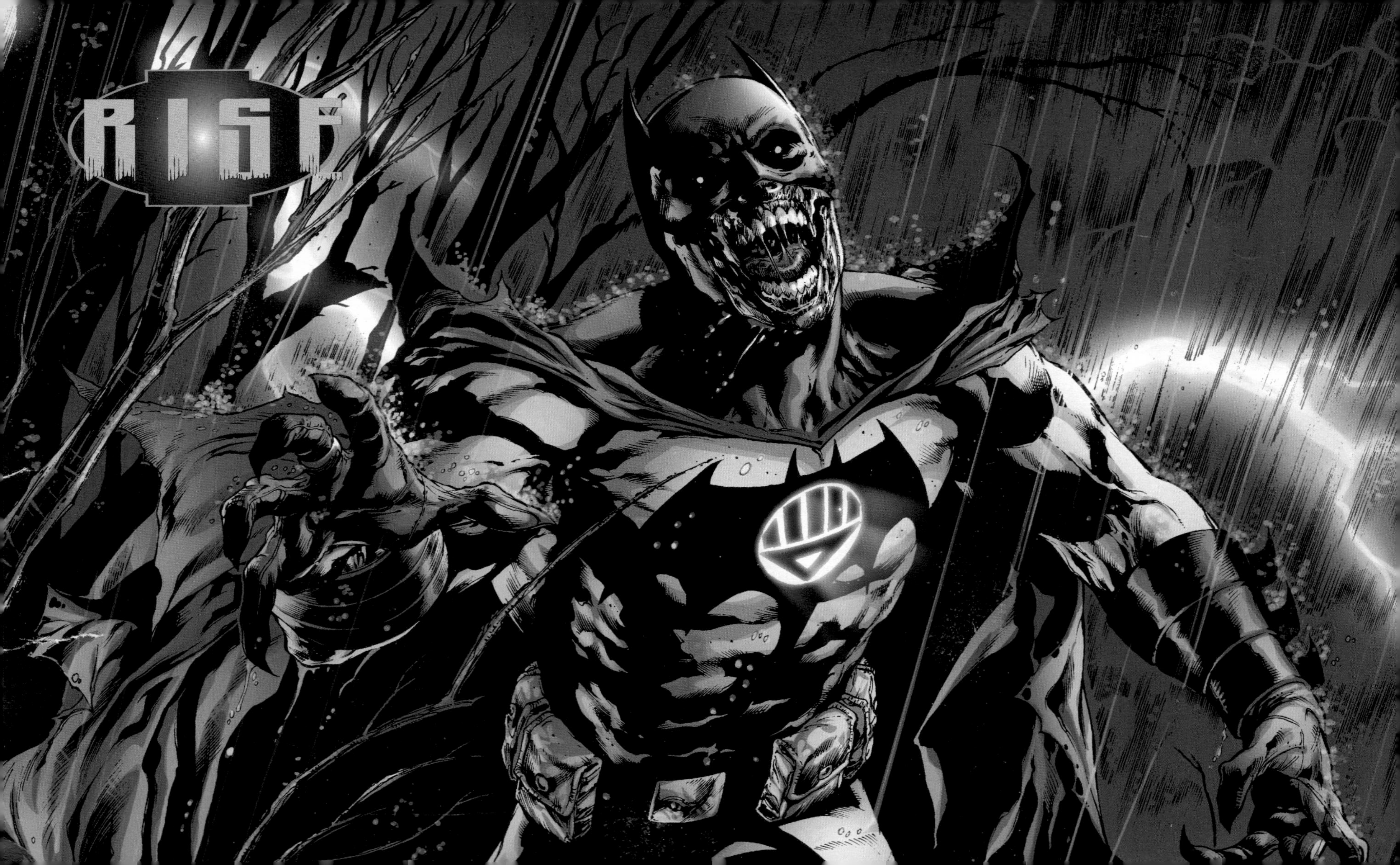
RISE

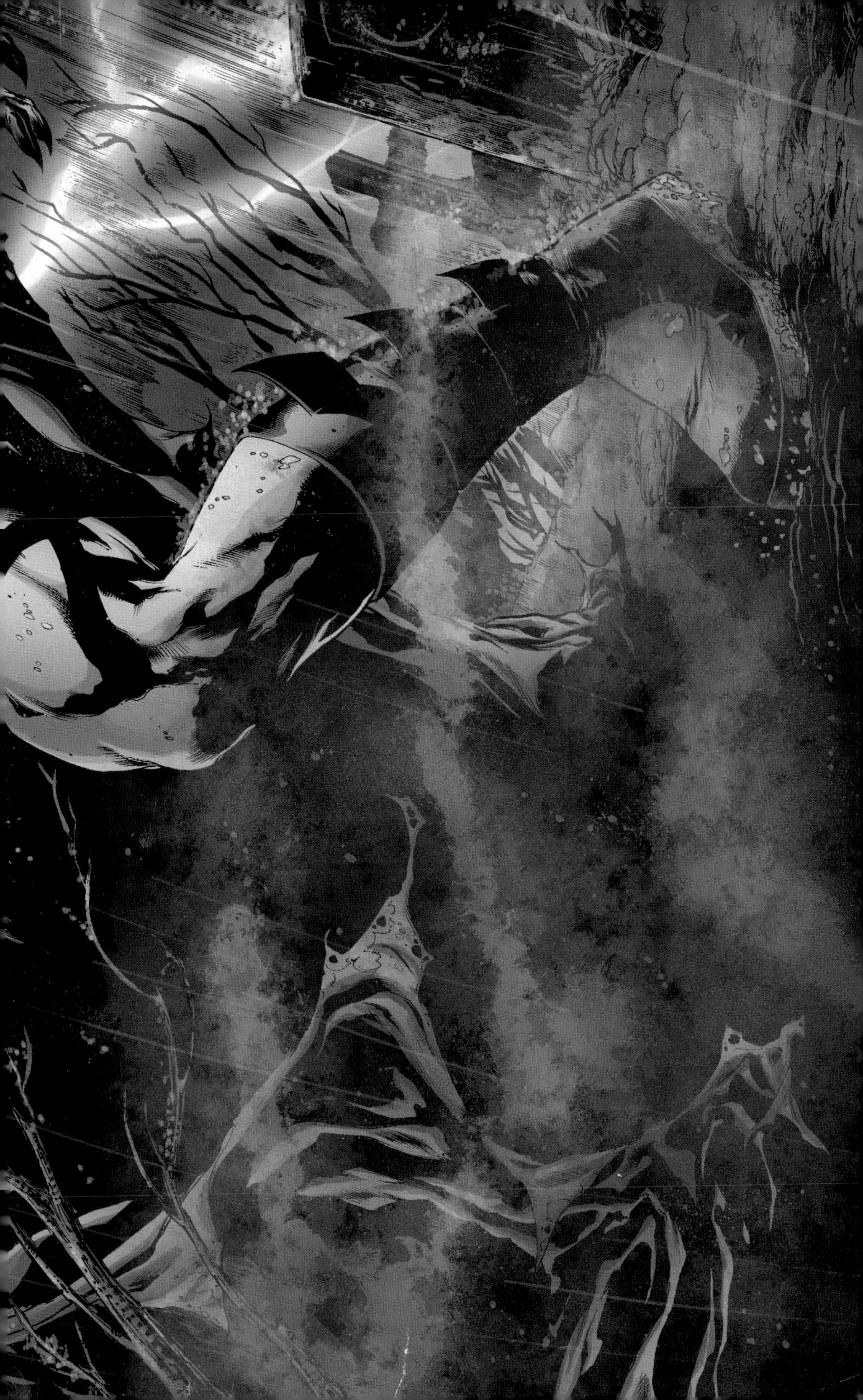

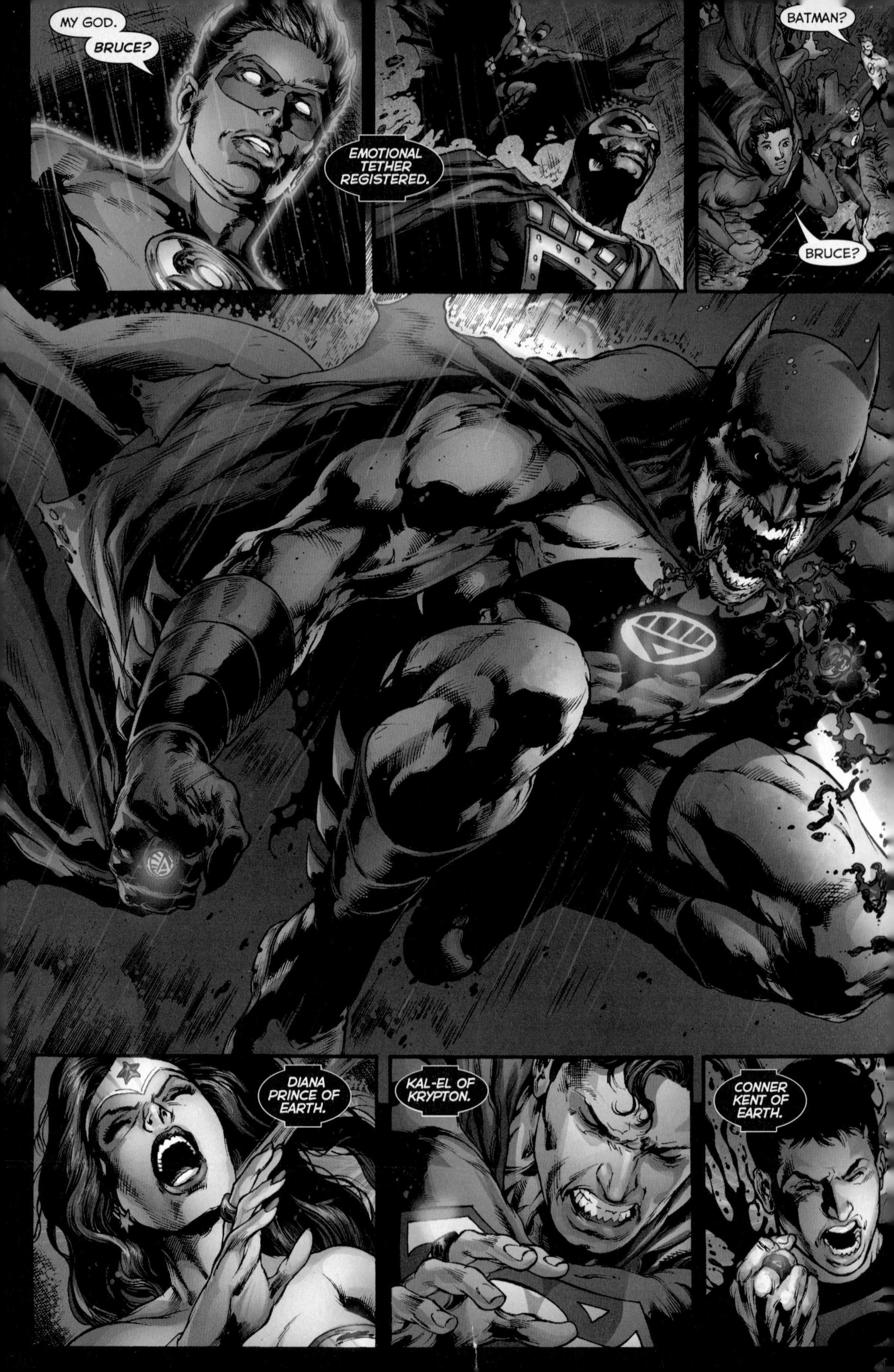
MY GOD.
BRUCE?
EMOTIONAL TETHER REGISTERED.
BATMAN?
BRUCE?
DIANA PRINCE OF EARTH.
KAL-EL OF KRYPTON.
CONNER KENT OF EARTH.

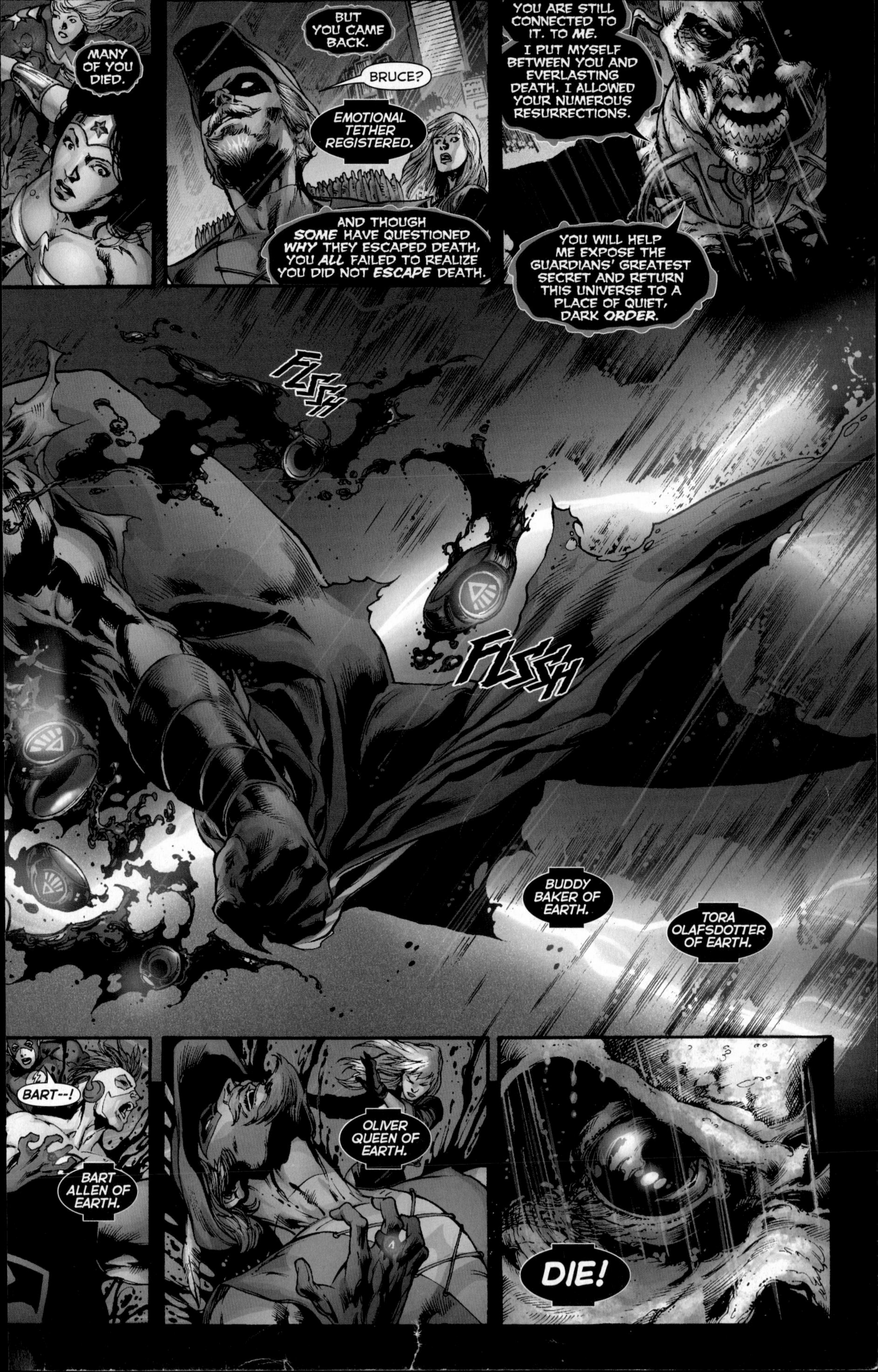
MANY OF YOU DIED.
BUT YOU CAME BACK.
BRUCE?
EMOTIONAL TETHER REGISTERED.
AND THOUGH SOME HAVE QUESTIONED WHY THEY ESCAPED DEATH, YOU ALL FAILED TO REALIZE YOU DID NOT ESCAPE DEATH.
YOU ARE STILL CONNECTED TO IT. TO ME.
I PUT MYSELF BETWEEN YOU AND EVERLASTING DEATH. I ALLOWED YOUR NUMEROUS RESURRECTIONS.
YOU WILL HELP ME EXPOSE THE GUARDIANS' GREATEST SECRET AND RETURN THIS UNIVERSE TO A PLACE OF QUIET, DARK ORDER.
FLSSH
FLSSH
BUDDY BAKER OF EARTH.
TORA OLAFSDOTTER OF EARTH.
BART--!
BART ALLEN OF EARTH.
OLIVER QUEEN OF EARTH.
DIE!

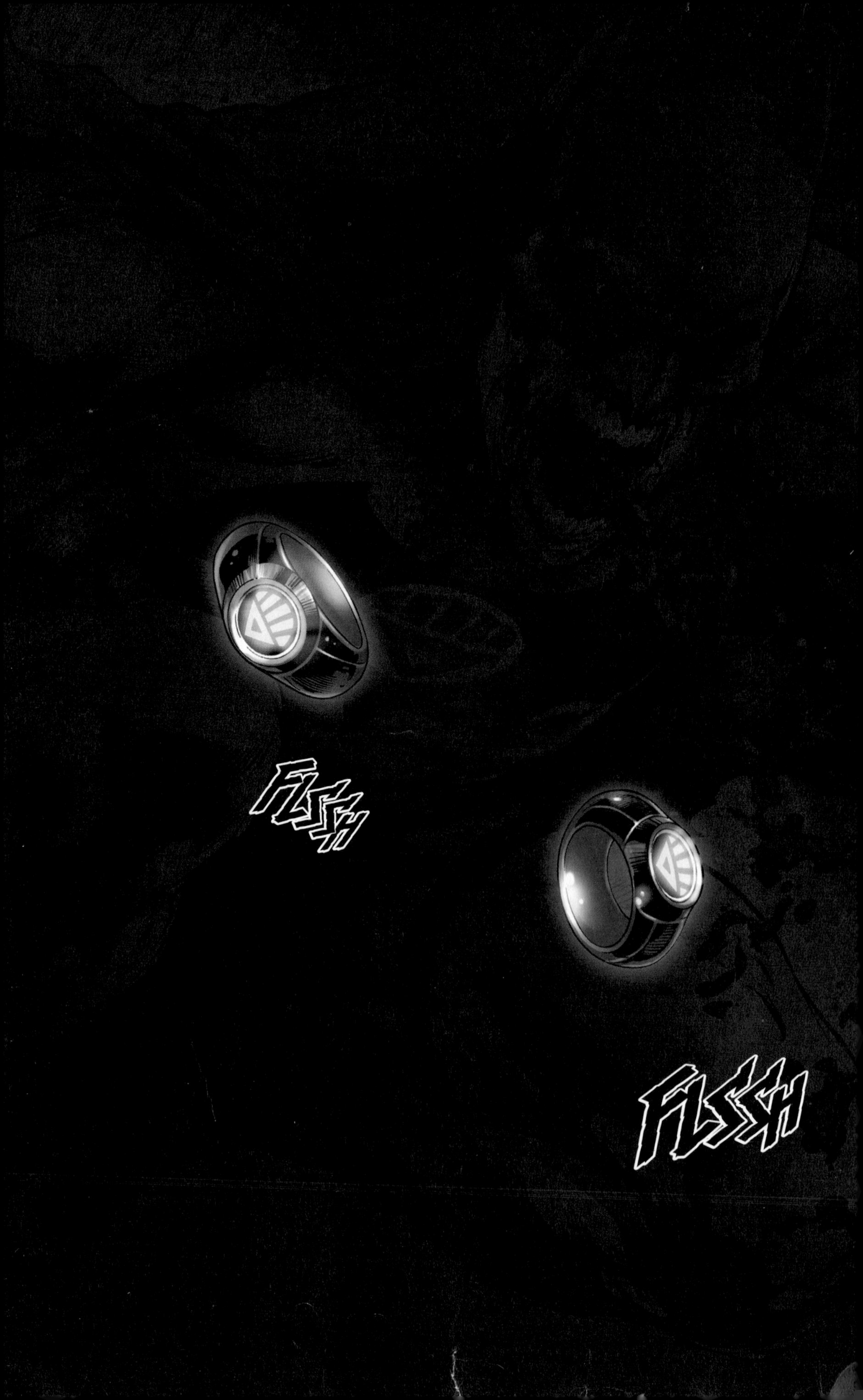
FLSSH
FLSSH

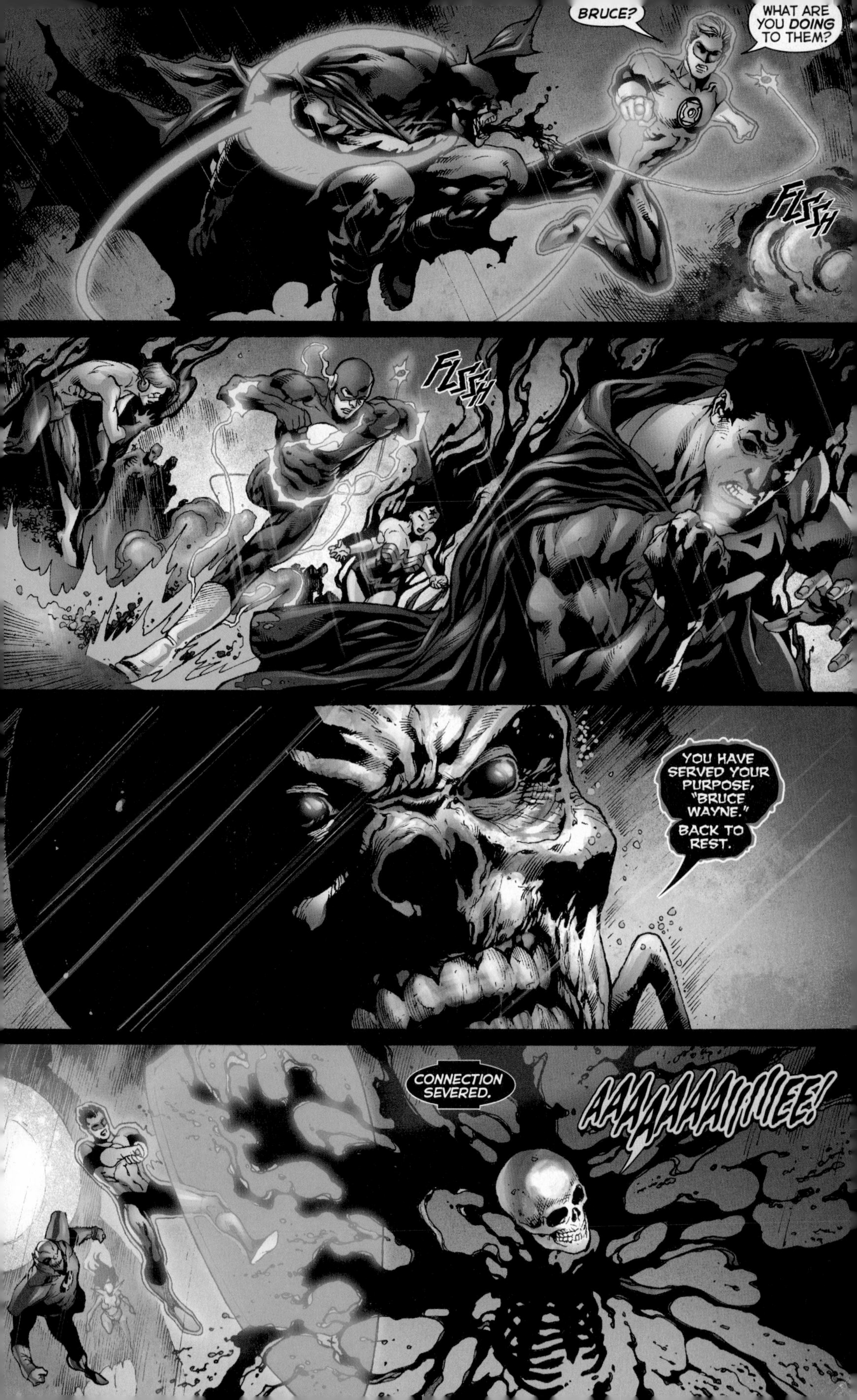
BRUCE?
WHAT ARE YOU DOING TO THEM?
FLSSH
FLSSH
YOU HAVE SERVED YOUR PURPOSE, "BRUCE WAYNE."
BACK TO REST.
CONNECTION SEVERED.
AAAAAAAIIIIEE!

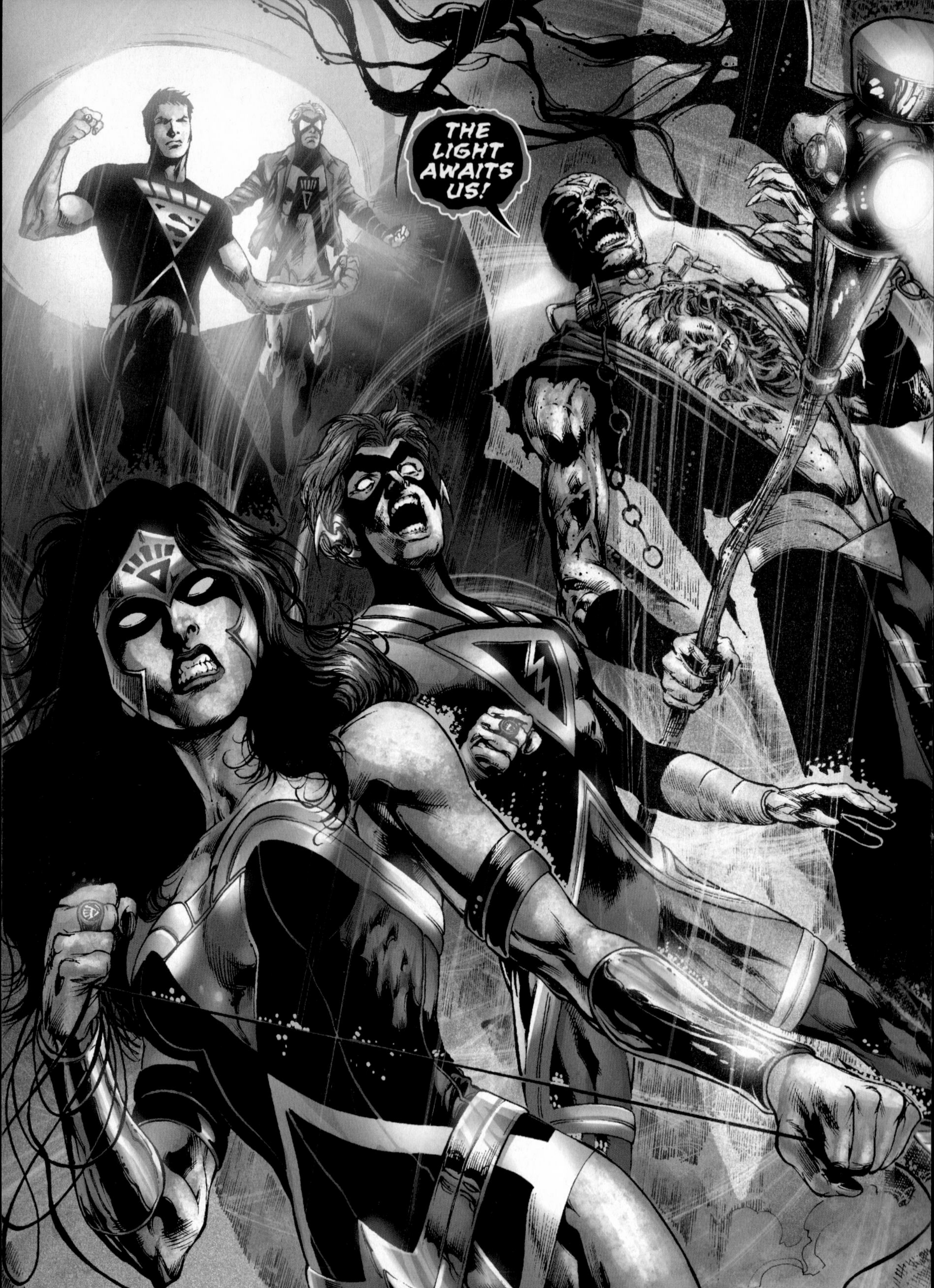
THE LIGHT AWAITS US!
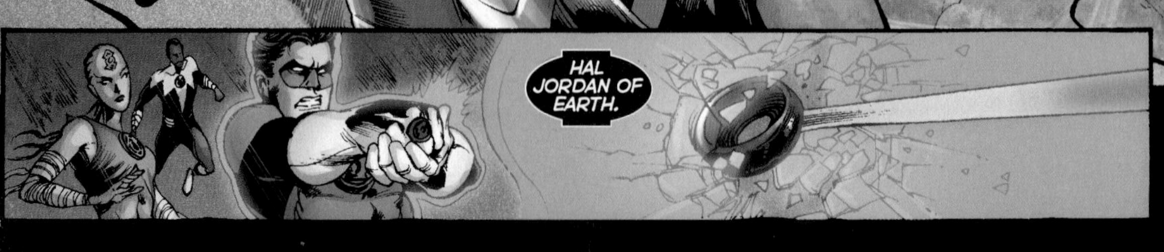
HAL JORDAN OF EARTH.

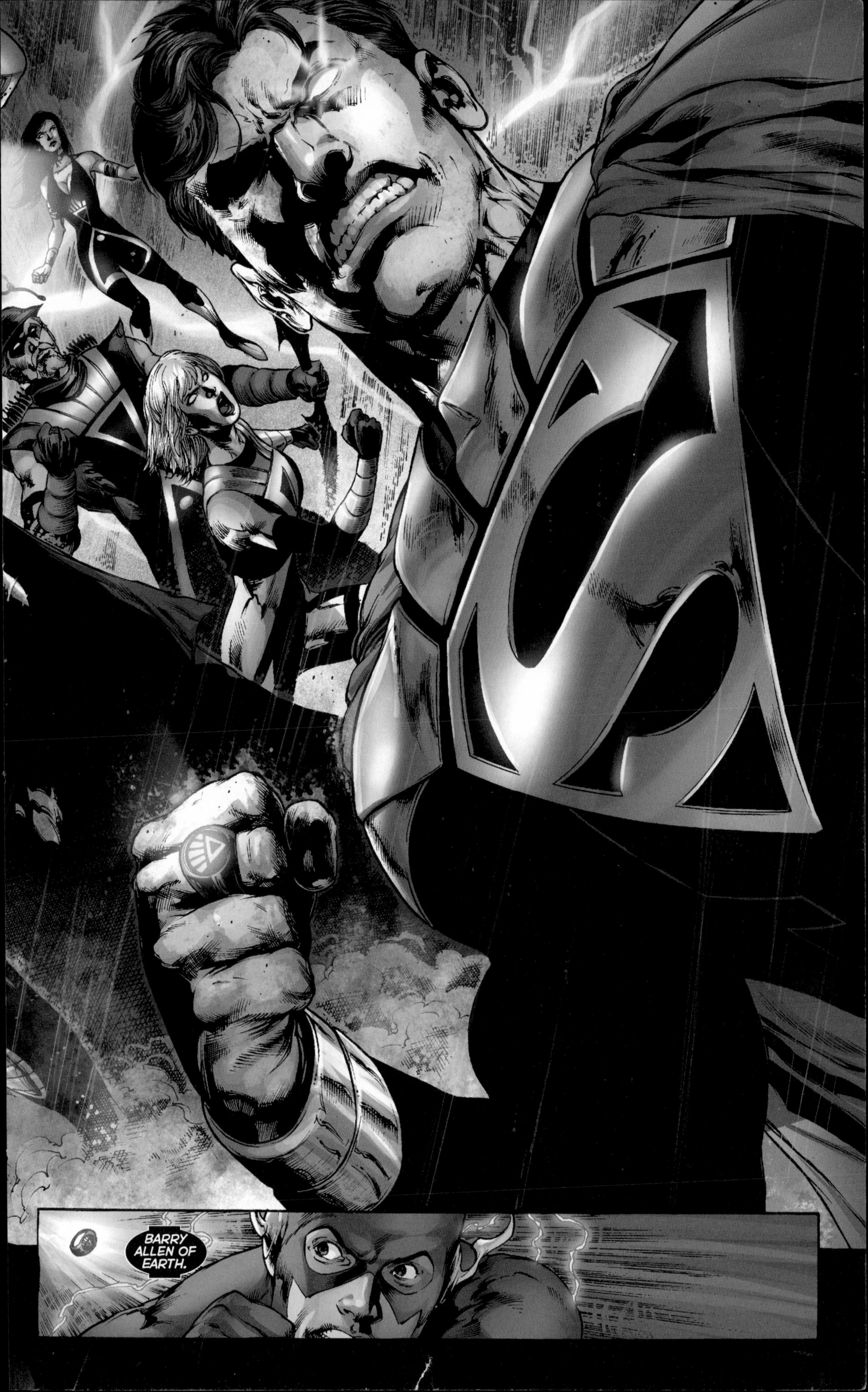
BARRY ALLEN OF EARTH.

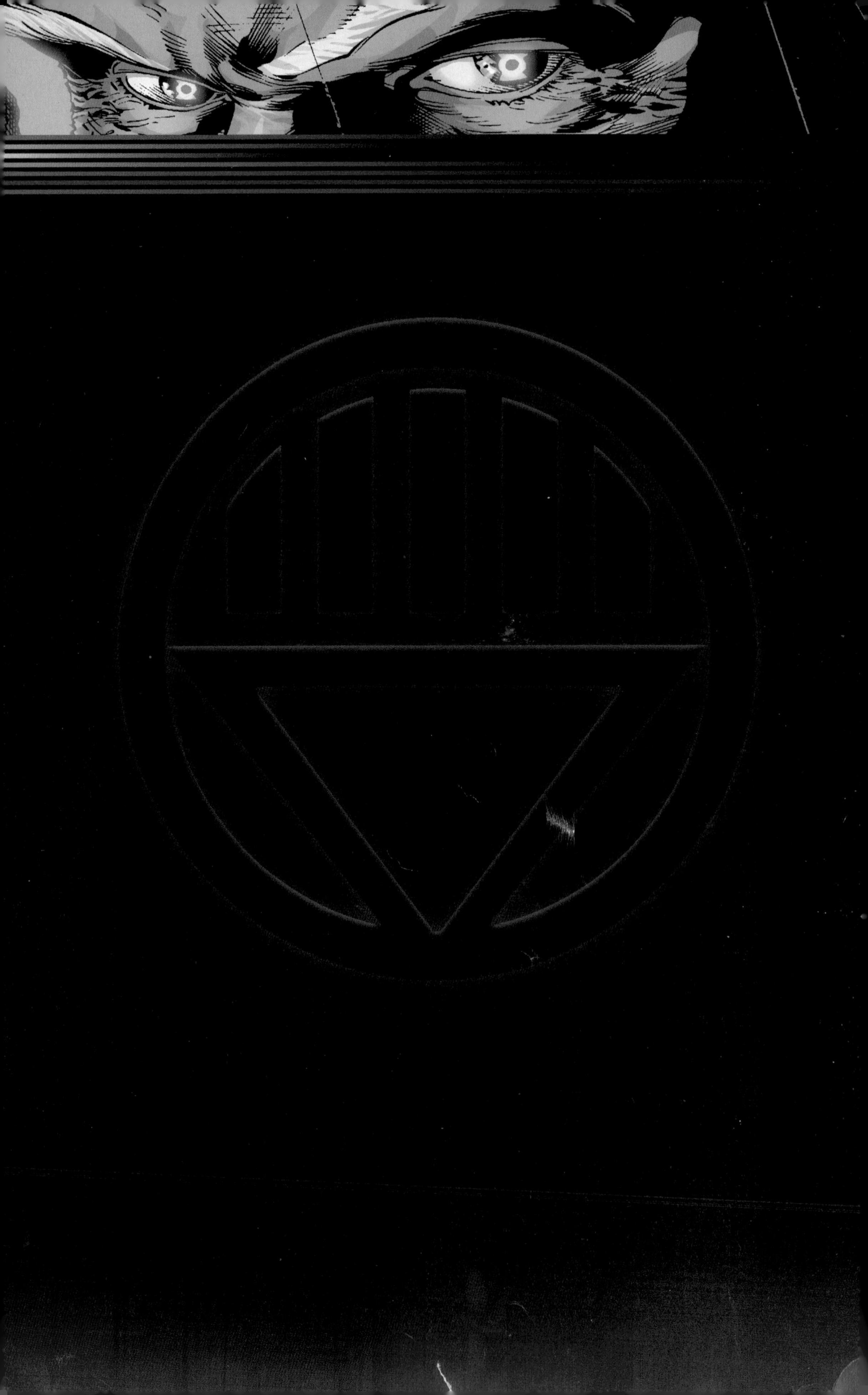

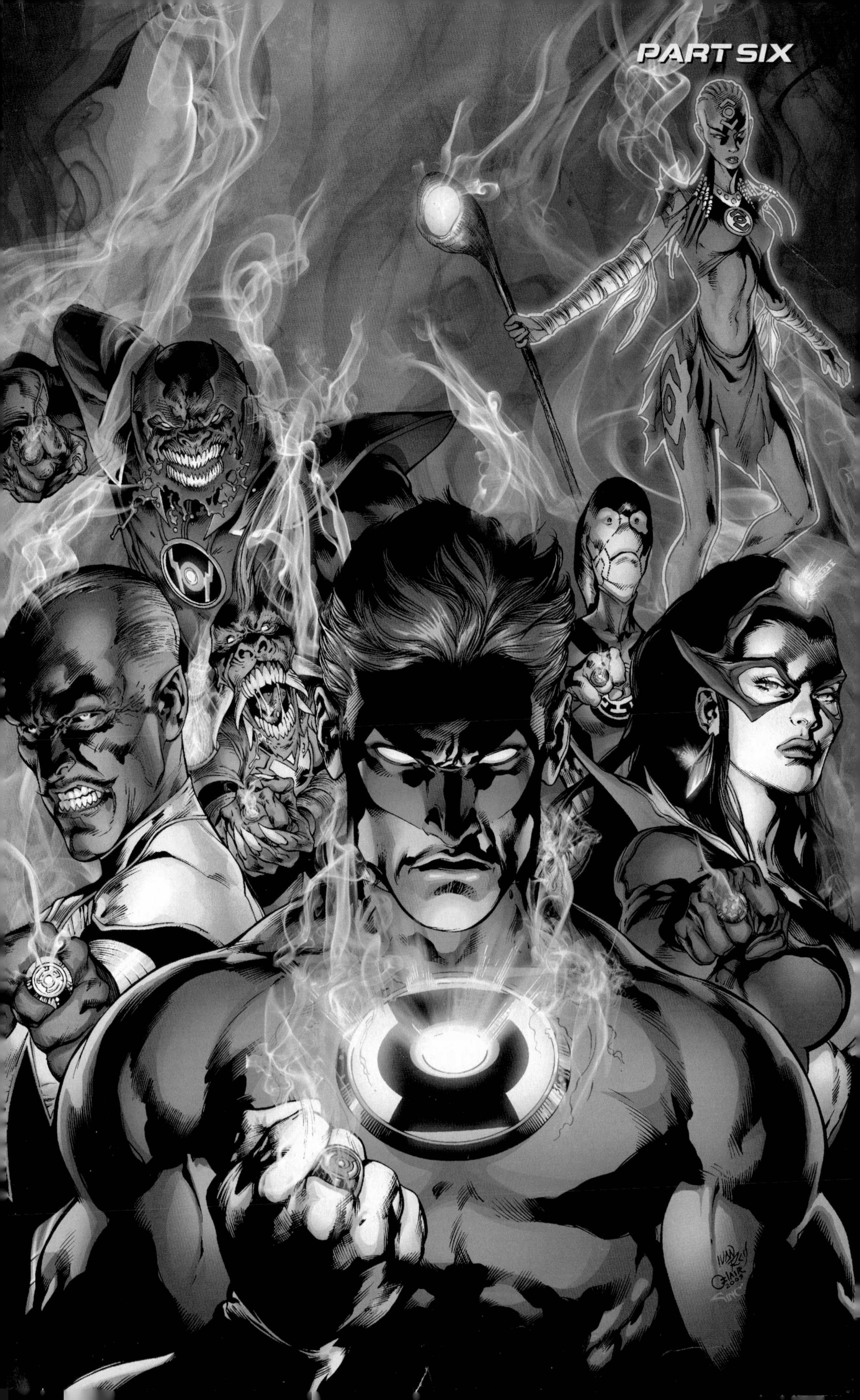
PART SIX

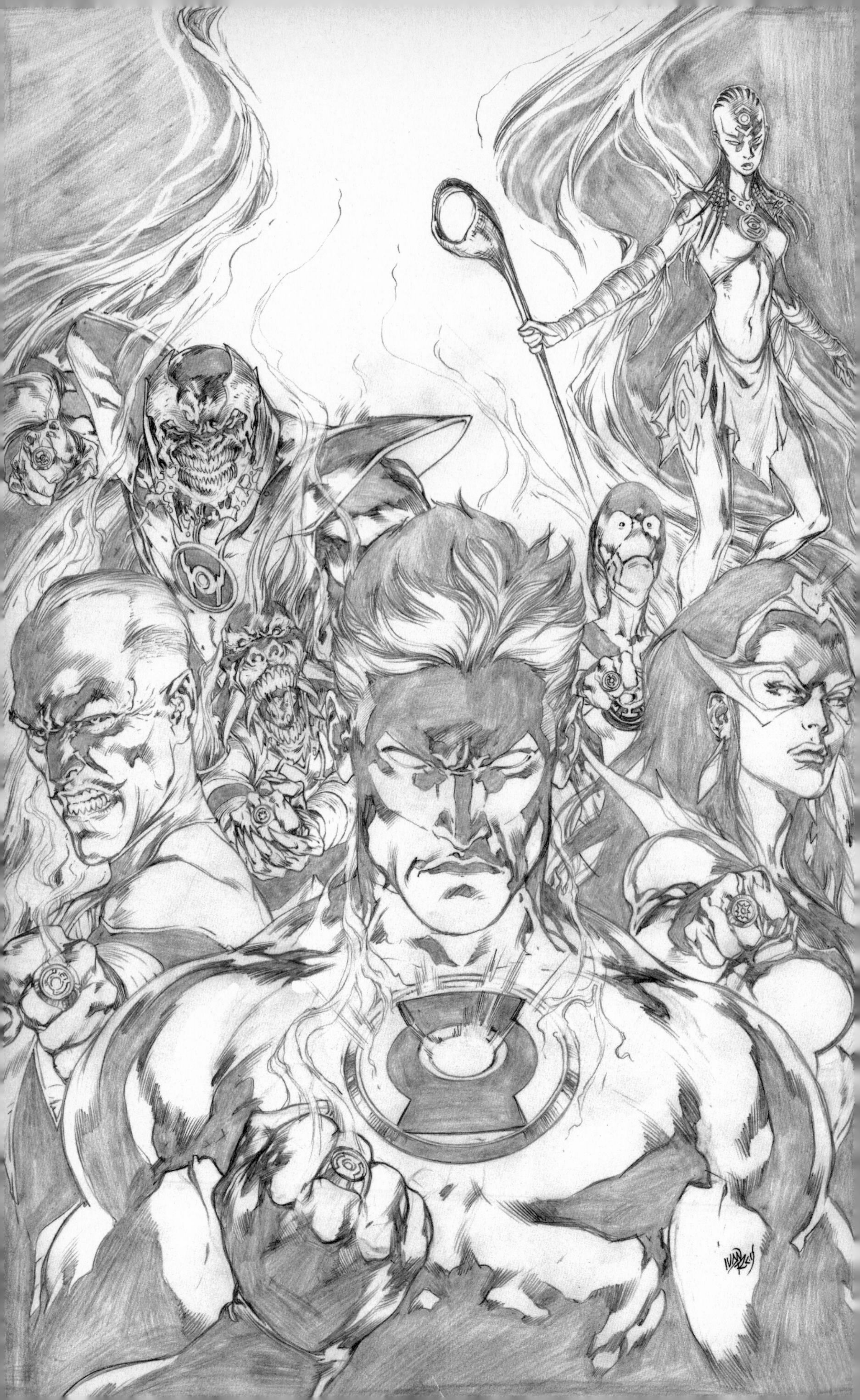

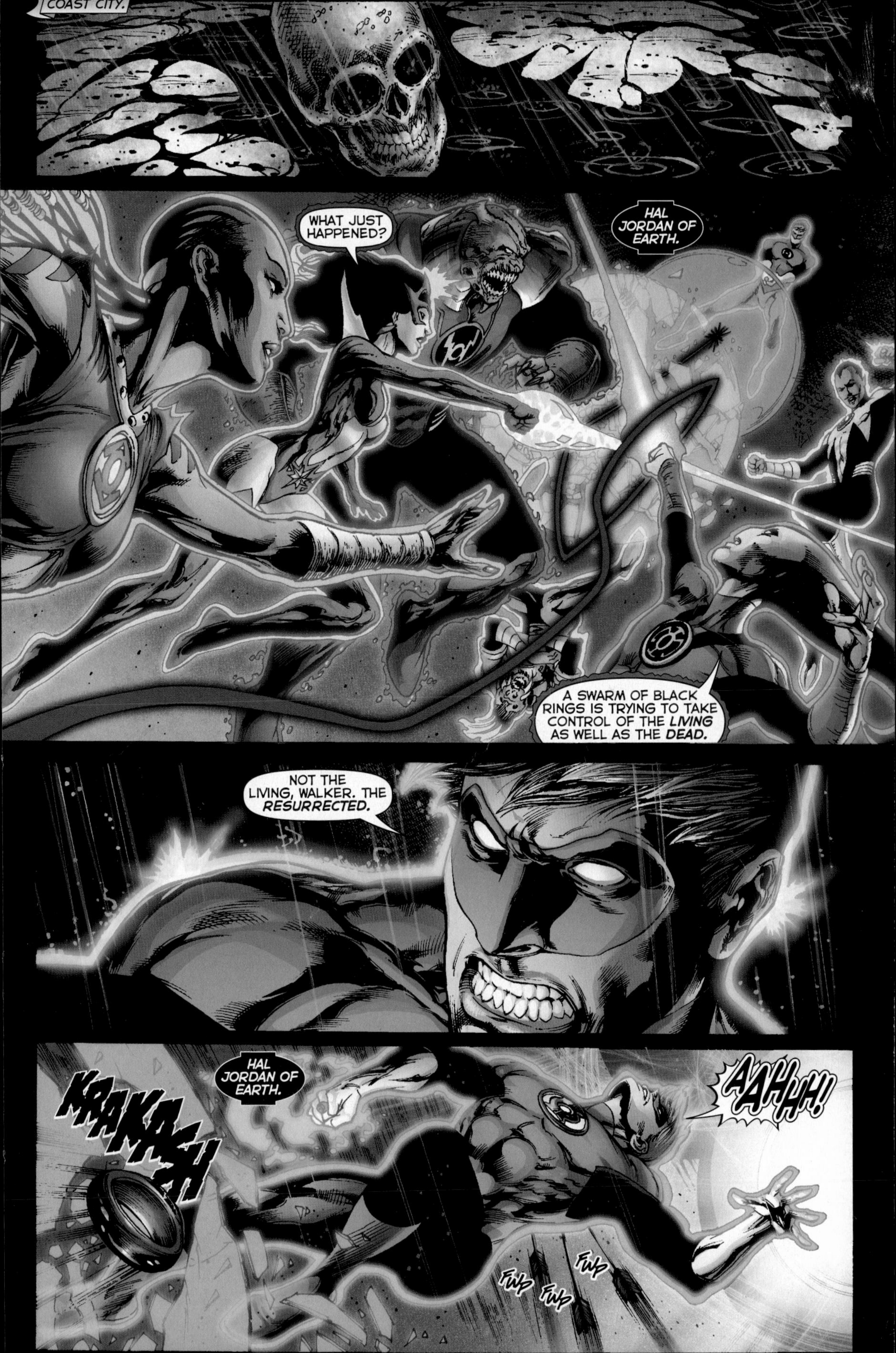
COAST CITY.
WHAT JUST HAPPENED?
HAL JORDAN OF EARTH.
A SWARM OF BLACK RINGS IS TRYING TO TAKE CONTROL OF THE LIVING AS WELL AS THE DEAD.
NOT THE LIVING, WALKER. THE RESURRECTED.
HAL JORDAN OF EARTH.
KRAKASH
AAHHH!
FWP FWP FWP FWP

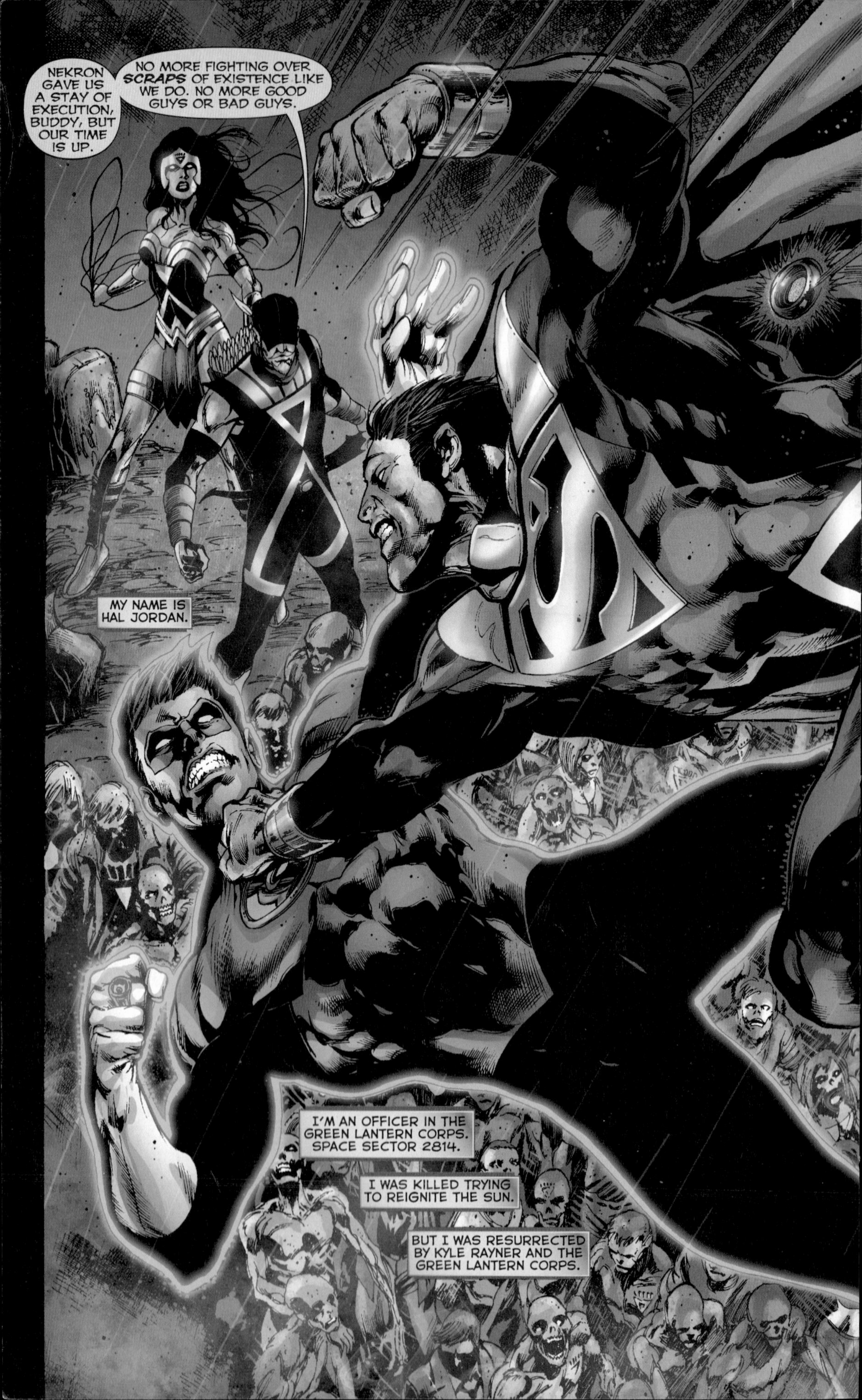
NEKRON GAVE US A STAY OF EXECUTION, BUDDY, BUT OUR TIME IS UP.
NO MORE FIGHTING OVER SCRAPS OF EXISTENCE LIKE WE DO. NO MORE GOOD GUYS OR BAD GUYS.
MY NAME IS HAL JORDAN.
I'M AN OFFICER IN THE GREEN LANTERN CORPS. SPACE SECTOR 2814.
I WAS KILLED TRYING TO REIGNITE THE SUN.
BUT I WAS RESURRECTED BY KYLE RAYNER AND THE GREEN LANTERN CORPS.

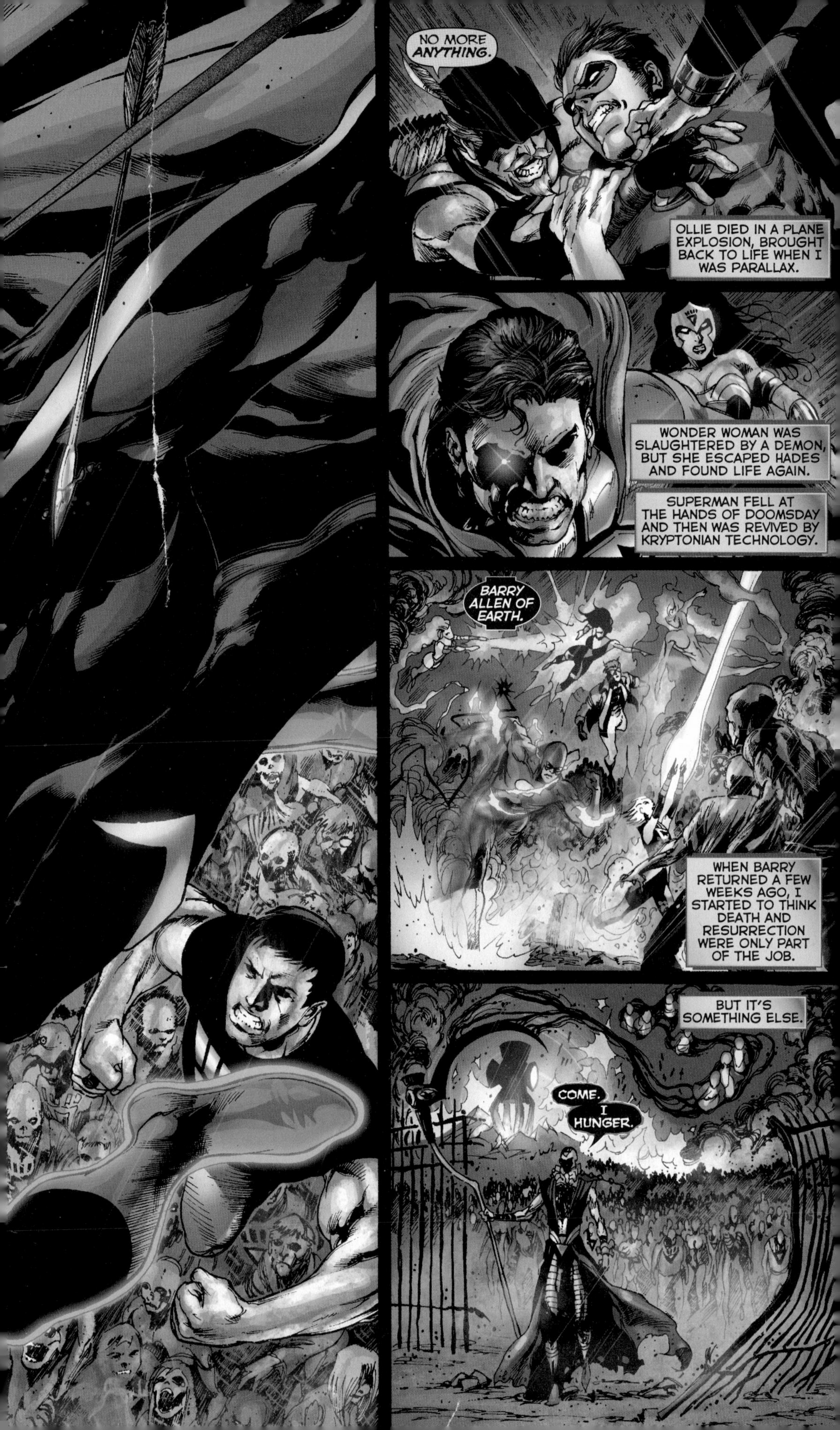
NO MORE ANYTHING.
OLLIE DIED IN A PLANE EXPLOSION, BROUGHT BACK TO LIFE WHEN I WAS PARALLAX.
WONDER WOMAN WAS SLAUGHTERED BY A DEMON, BUT SHE ESCAPED HADES AND FOUND LIFE AGAIN.
SUPERMAN FELL AT THE HANDS OF DOOMSDAY AND THEN WAS REVIVED BY KRYPTONIAN TECHNOLOGY.
BARRY ALLEN OF EARTH.
WHEN BARRY RETURNED A FEW WEEKS AGO, I STARTED TO THINK DEATH AND RESURRECTION WERE ONLY PART OF THE JOB.
BUT IT'S SOMETHING ELSE.
COME. I HUNGER.

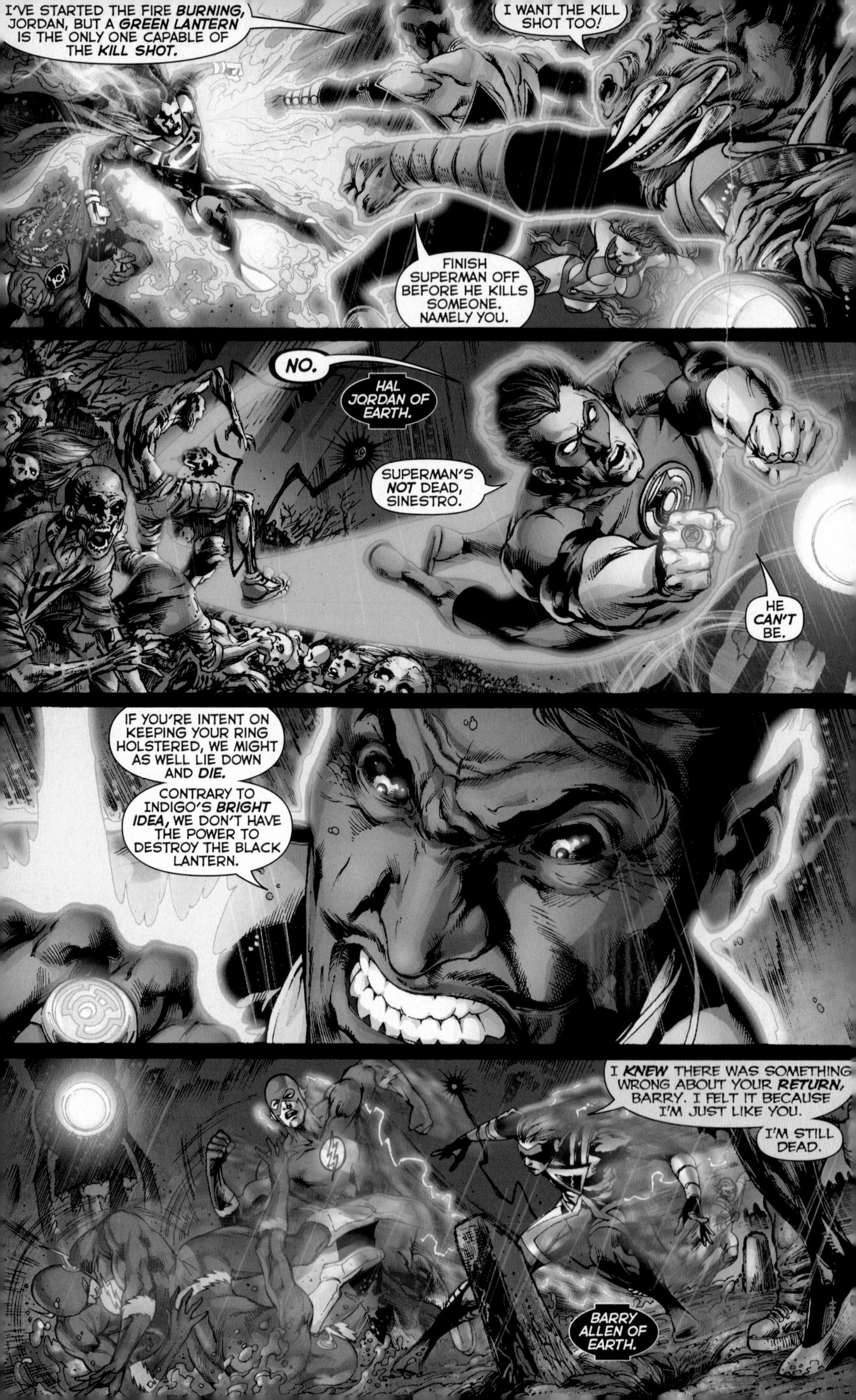
I'VE STARTED THE FIRE BURNING, JORDAN, BUT A GREEN LANTERN IS THE ONLY ONE CAPABLE OF THE KILL SHOT.
I WANT THE KILL SHOT TOO!
FINISH SUPERMAN OFF BEFORE HE KILLS SOMEONE. NAMELY YOU.
NO.
HAL JORDAN OF EARTH.
SUPERMAN'S NOT DEAD, SINESTRO.
HE CAN'T BE.
IF YOU'RE INTENT ON KEEPING YOUR RING HOLSTERED, WE MIGHT AS WELL LIE DOWN AND DIE.
CONTRARY TO INDIGO'S BRIGHT IDEA, WE DON'T HAVE THE POWER TO DESTROY THE BLACK LANTERN.
I KNEW THERE WAS SOMETHING WRONG ABOUT YOUR RETURN, BARRY. I FELT IT BECAUSE I'M JUST LIKE YOU.
I'M STILL DEAD.
BARRY ALLEN OF EARTH.

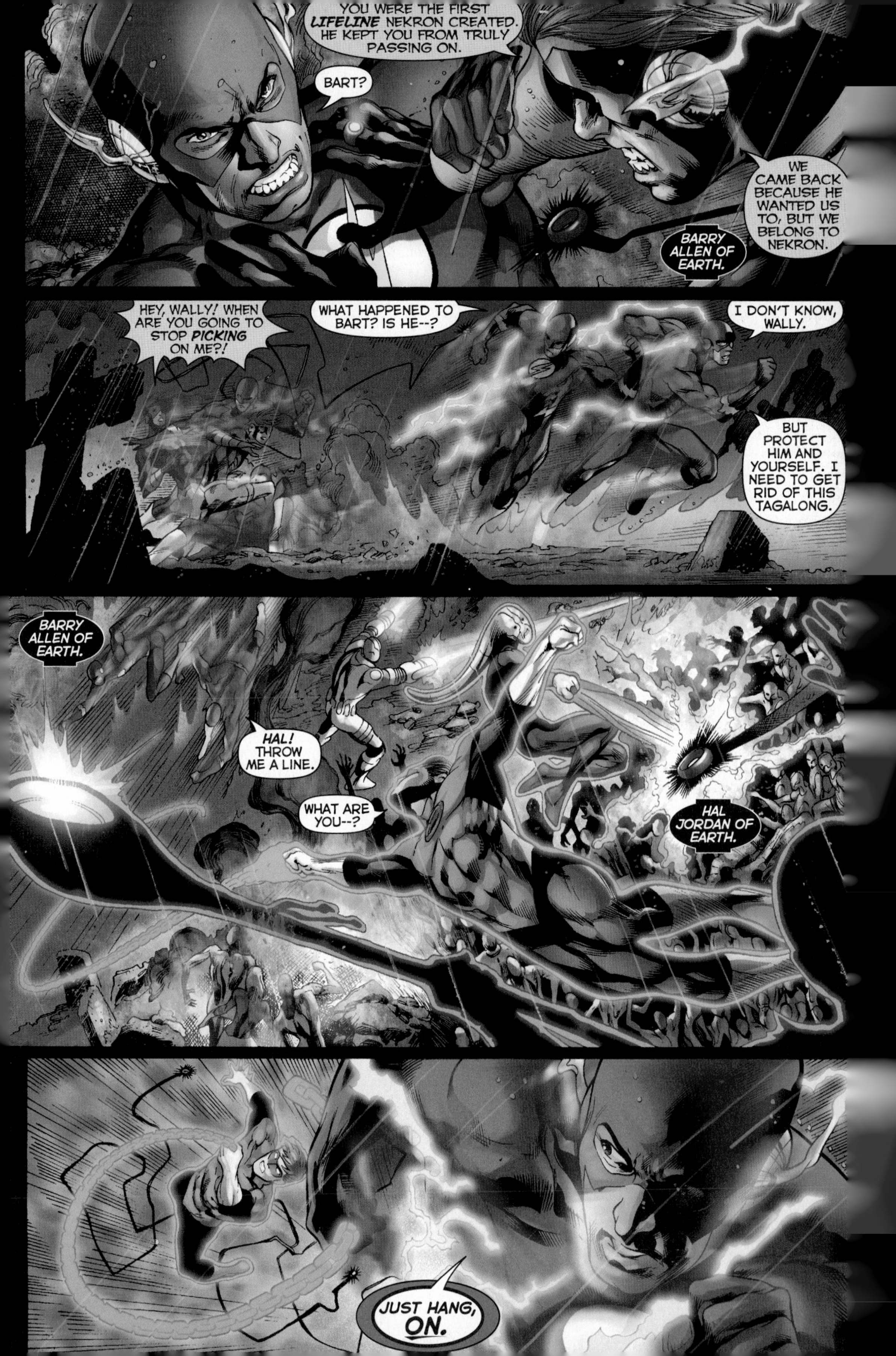
YOU WERE THE FIRST *LIFELINE* NEKRON CREATED. HE KEPT YOU FROM TRULY PASSING ON.
BART?
WE CAME BACK BECAUSE HE WANTED US TO, BUT WE BELONG TO NEKRON.
BARRY ALLEN OF EARTH.
HEY, WALLY! WHEN ARE YOU GOING TO STOP *PICKING* ON ME?!
WHAT HAPPENED TO BART? IS HE--?
I DON'T KNOW, WALLY.
BUT PROTECT HIM AND YOURSELF. I NEED TO GET RID OF THIS TAGALONG.
BARRY ALLEN OF EARTH.
HAL! THROW ME A LINE.
WHAT ARE YOU--?
HAL JORDAN OF EARTH.
JUST HANG, ON.

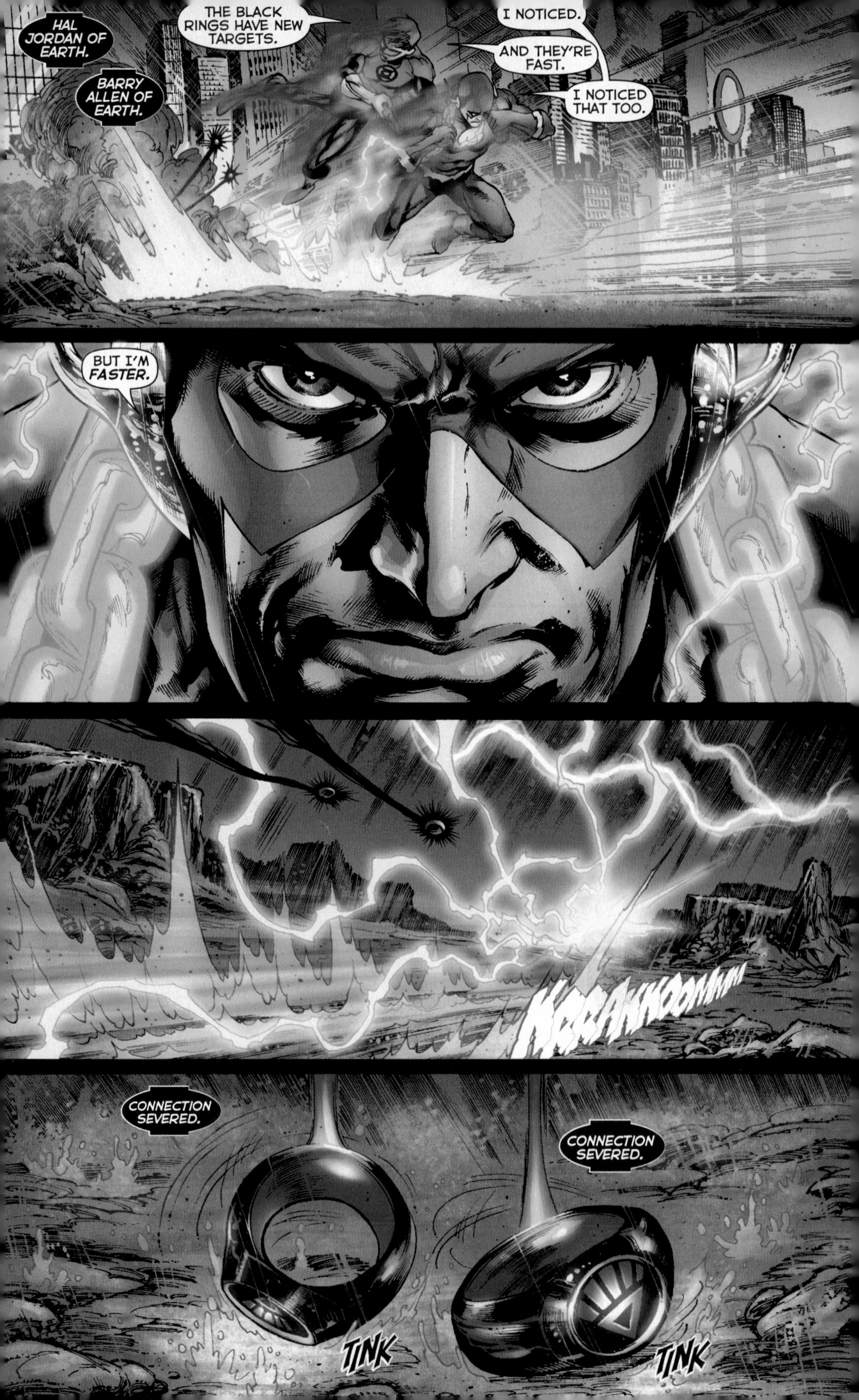
HAL JORDAN OF EARTH.
BARRY ALLEN OF EARTH.
THE BLACK RINGS HAVE NEW TARGETS.
I NOTICED.
AND THEY'RE FAST.
I NOTICED THAT TOO.
BUT I'M FASTER.
CONNECTION SEVERED.
CONNECTION SEVERED.
TINK
TINK

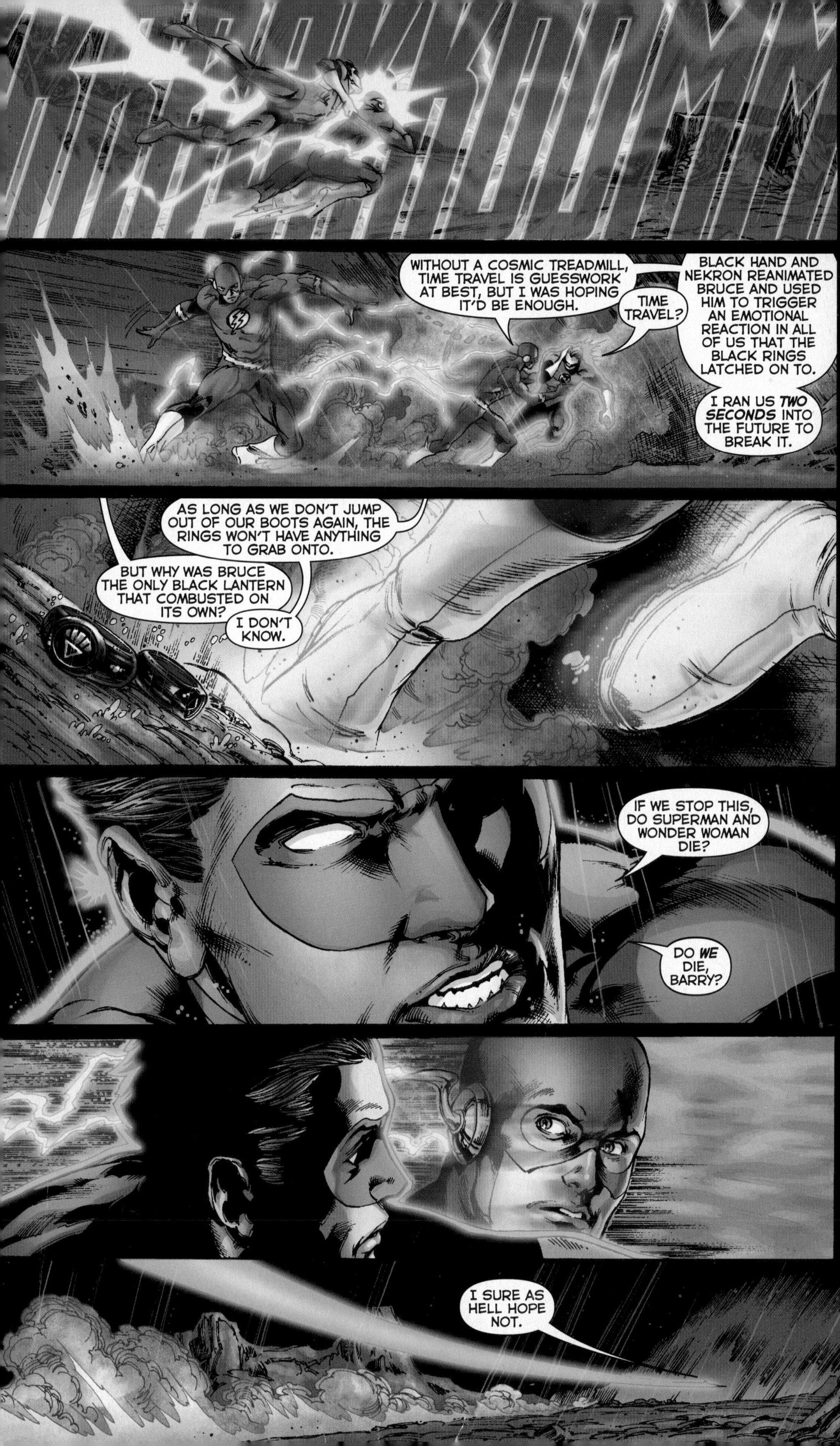
WITHOUT A COSMIC TREADMILL, TIME TRAVEL IS GUESSWORK AT BEST, BUT I WAS HOPING IT'D BE ENOUGH.
TIME TRAVEL?
BLACK HAND AND NEKRON REANIMATED BRUCE AND USED HIM TO TRIGGER AN EMOTIONAL REACTION IN ALL OF US THAT THE BLACK RINGS LATCHED ON TO.
I RAN US TWO SECONDS INTO THE FUTURE TO BREAK IT.
AS LONG AS WE DON'T JUMP OUT OF OUR BOOTS AGAIN, THE RINGS WON'T HAVE ANYTHING TO GRAB ONTO.
BUT WHY WAS BRUCE THE ONLY BLACK LANTERN THAT COMBUSTED ON ITS OWN?
I DON'T KNOW.
IF WE STOP THIS, DO SUPERMAN AND WONDER WOMAN DIE?
DO WE DIE, BARRY?
I SURE AS HELL HOPE NOT.

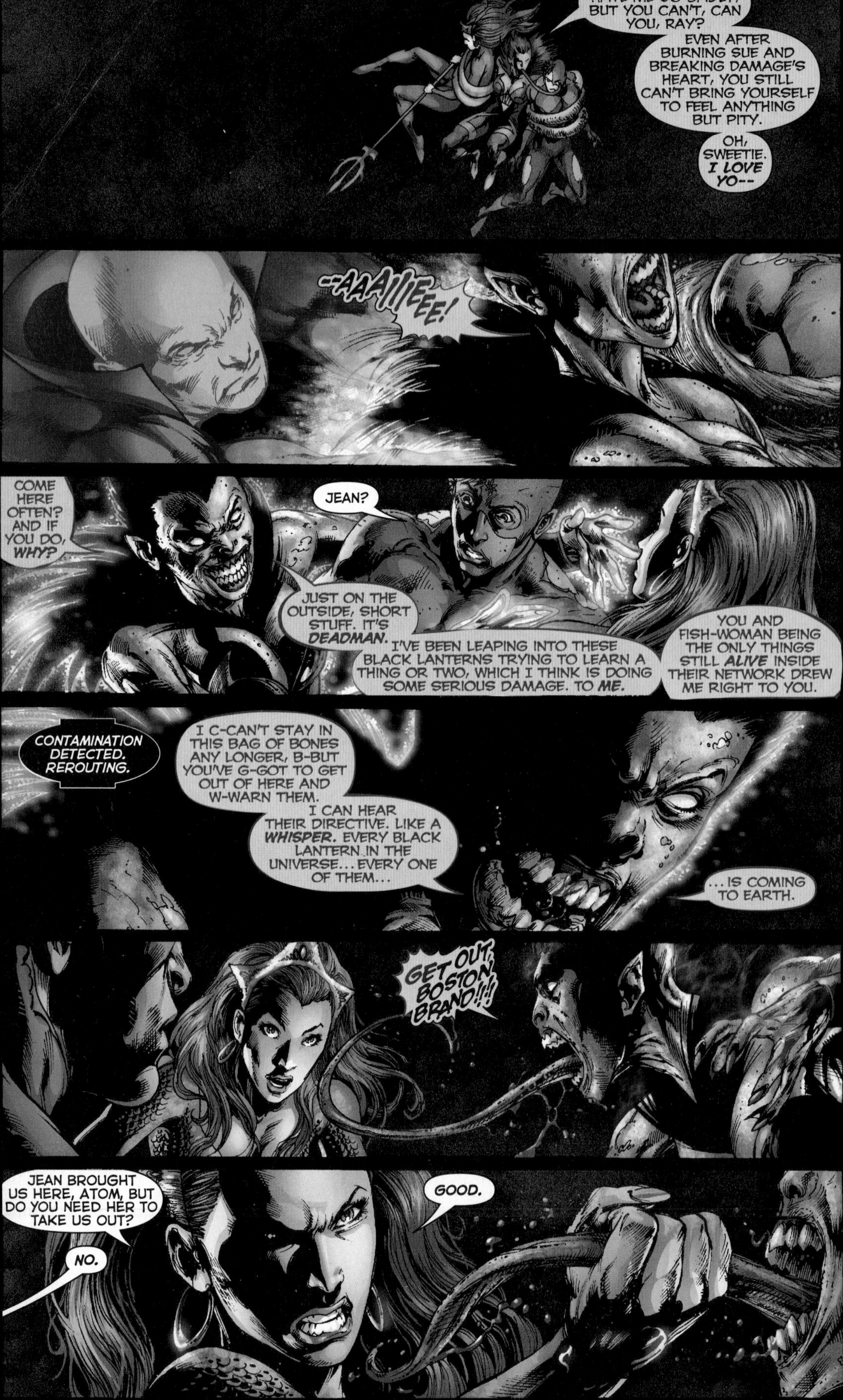

BUT YOU CAN'T, CAN YOU, RAY?
EVEN AFTER BURNING SUE AND BREAKING DAMAGE'S HEART, YOU STILL CAN'T BRING YOURSELF TO FEEL ANYTHING BUT PITY.
OH, SWEETIE. I LOVE YO--
--AAAIIIEEE!
COME HERE OFTEN? AND IF YOU DO, WHY?
JEAN?
JUST ON THE OUTSIDE, SHORT STUFF. IT'S DEADMAN.
I'VE BEEN LEAPING INTO THESE BLACK LANTERNS TRYING TO LEARN A THING OR TWO, WHICH I THINK IS DOING SOME SERIOUS DAMAGE. TO ME.
YOU AND FISH-WOMAN BEING THE ONLY THINGS STILL ALIVE INSIDE THEIR NETWORK DREW ME RIGHT TO YOU.
CONTAMINATION DETECTED. REROUTING.
I C-CAN'T STAY IN THIS BAG OF BONES ANY LONGER, B-BUT YOU'VE G-GOT TO GET OUT OF HERE AND W-WARN THEM.
I CAN HEAR THEIR DIRECTIVE. LIKE A WHISPER. EVERY BLACK LANTERN IN THE UNIVERSE... EVERY ONE OF THEM...
...IS COMING TO EARTH.
GET OUT, BOSTON BRAND!!!
JEAN BROUGHT US HERE, ATOM, BUT DO YOU NEED HER TO TAKE US OUT?
NO.
GOOD.

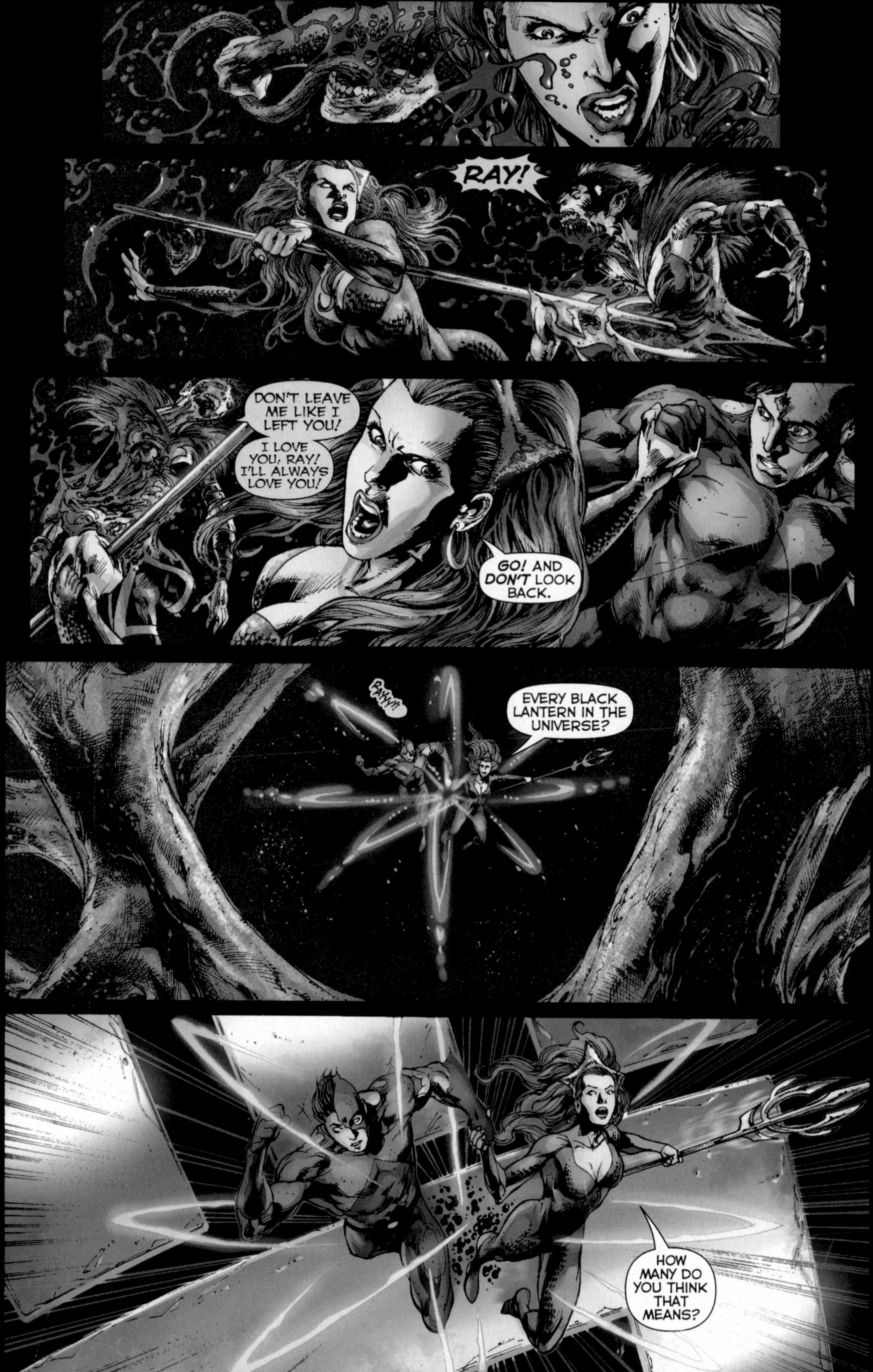
RAY!
DON'T LEAVE ME LIKE I LEFT YOU!
I LOVE YOU, RAY! I'LL ALWAYS LOVE YOU!
GO! AND DON'T LOOK BACK.
RAYYY!!
EVERY BLACK LANTERN IN THE UNIVERSE?
HOW MANY DO YOU THINK THAT MEANS?

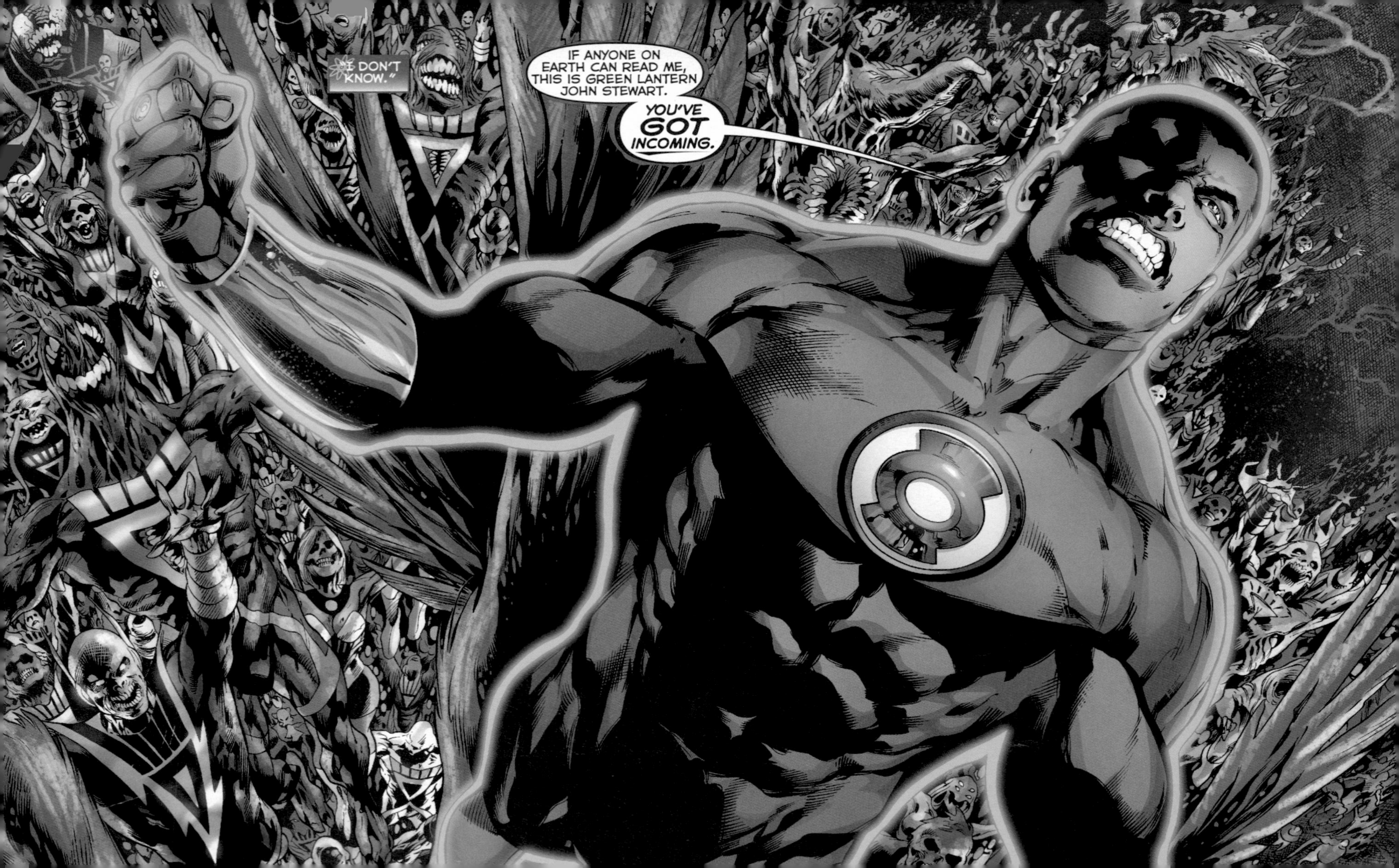

"I DON'T KNOW."
IF ANYONE ON EARTH CAN READ ME, THIS IS GREEN LANTERN JOHN STEWART.
YOU'VE GOT INCOMING.

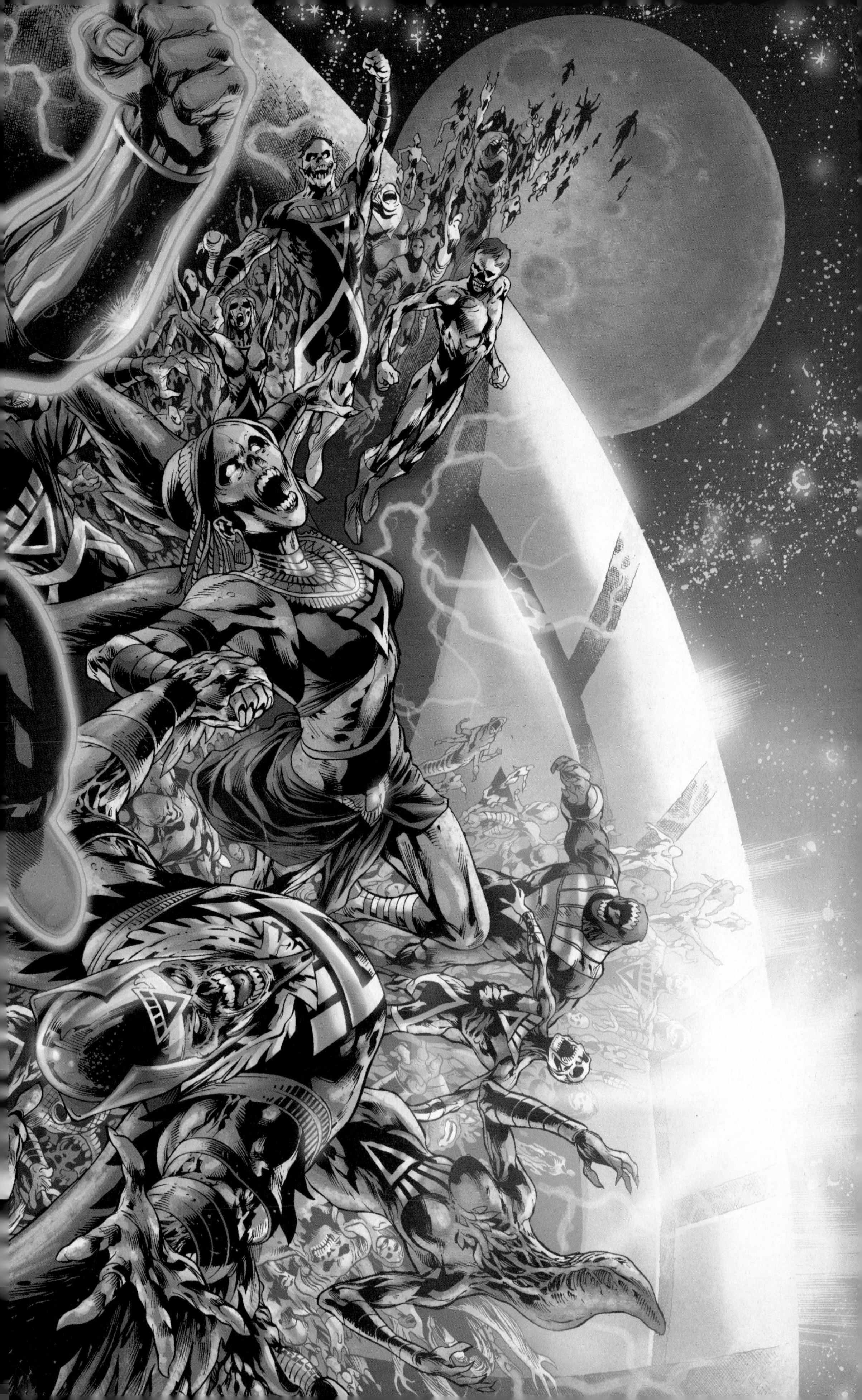

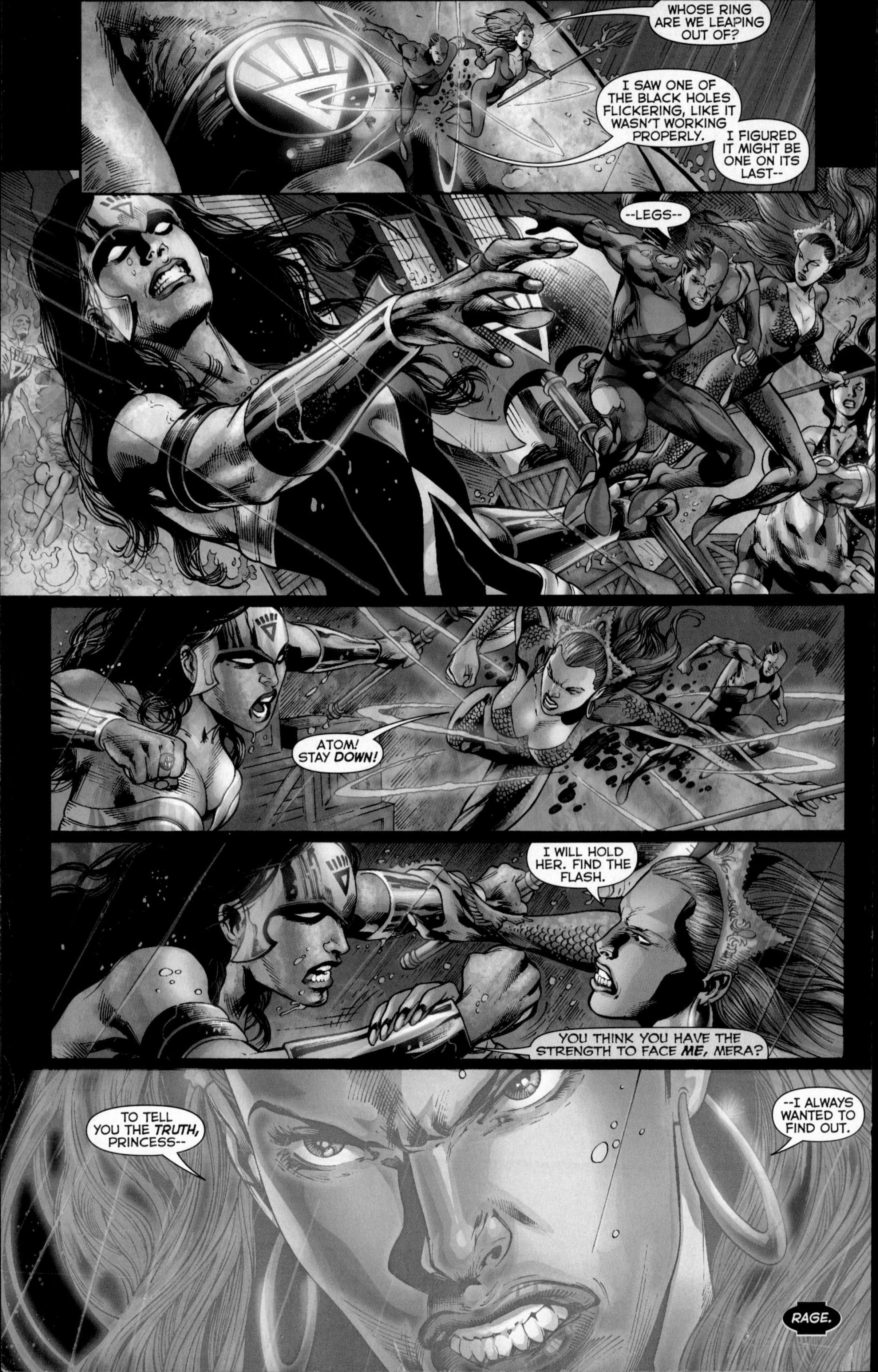
WHOSE RING ARE WE LEAPING OUT OF?
I SAW ONE OF THE BLACK HOLES FLICKERING, LIKE IT WASN'T WORKING PROPERLY.
I FIGURED IT MIGHT BE ONE ON ITS LAST--
--LEGS--
ATOM! STAY *DOWN!*
I WILL HOLD HER. FIND THE FLASH.
YOU THINK YOU HAVE THE STRENGTH TO FACE *ME,* MERA?
TO TELL YOU THE *TRUTH,* PRINCESS--
--I ALWAYS WANTED TO FIND OUT.
RAGE.

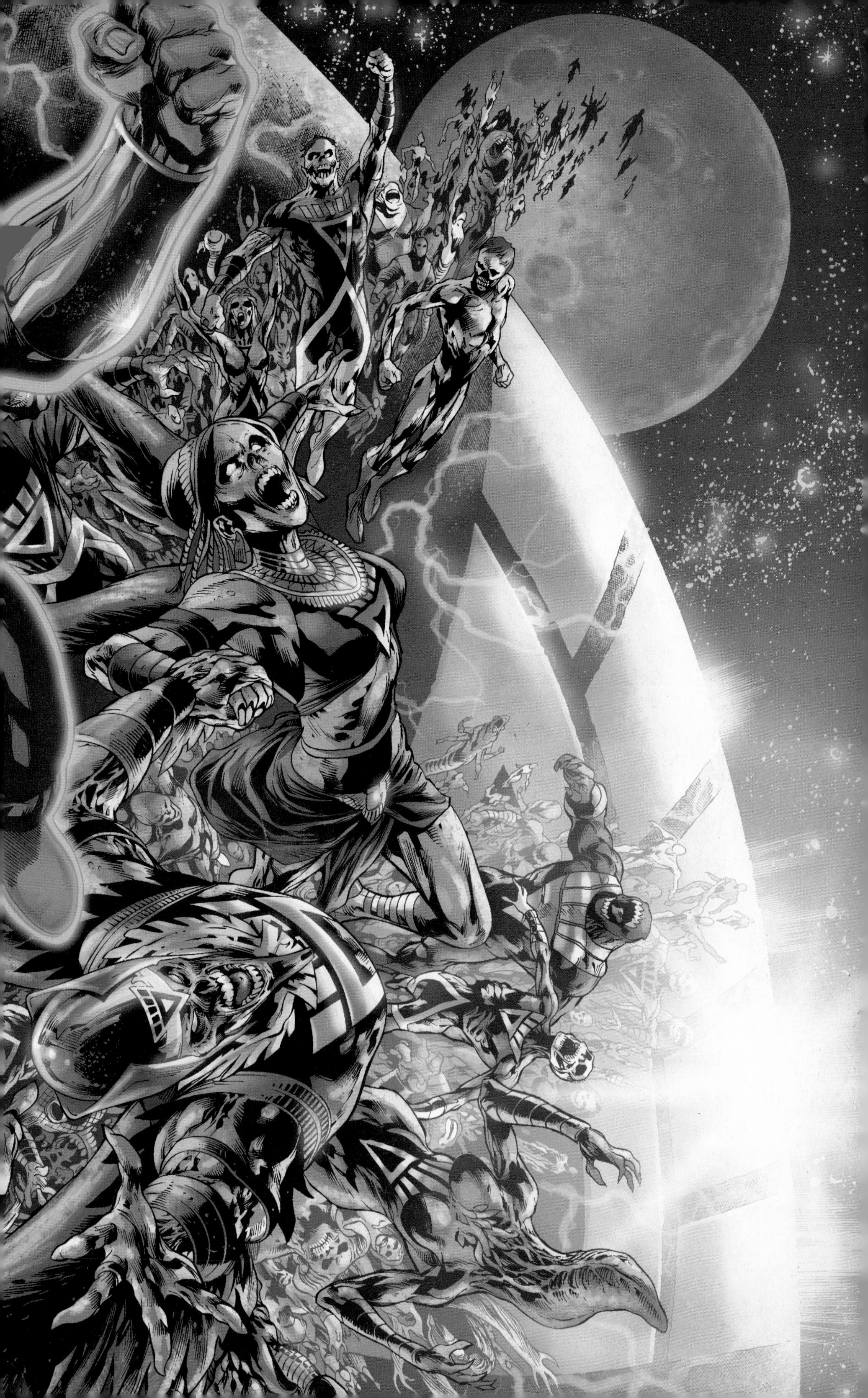

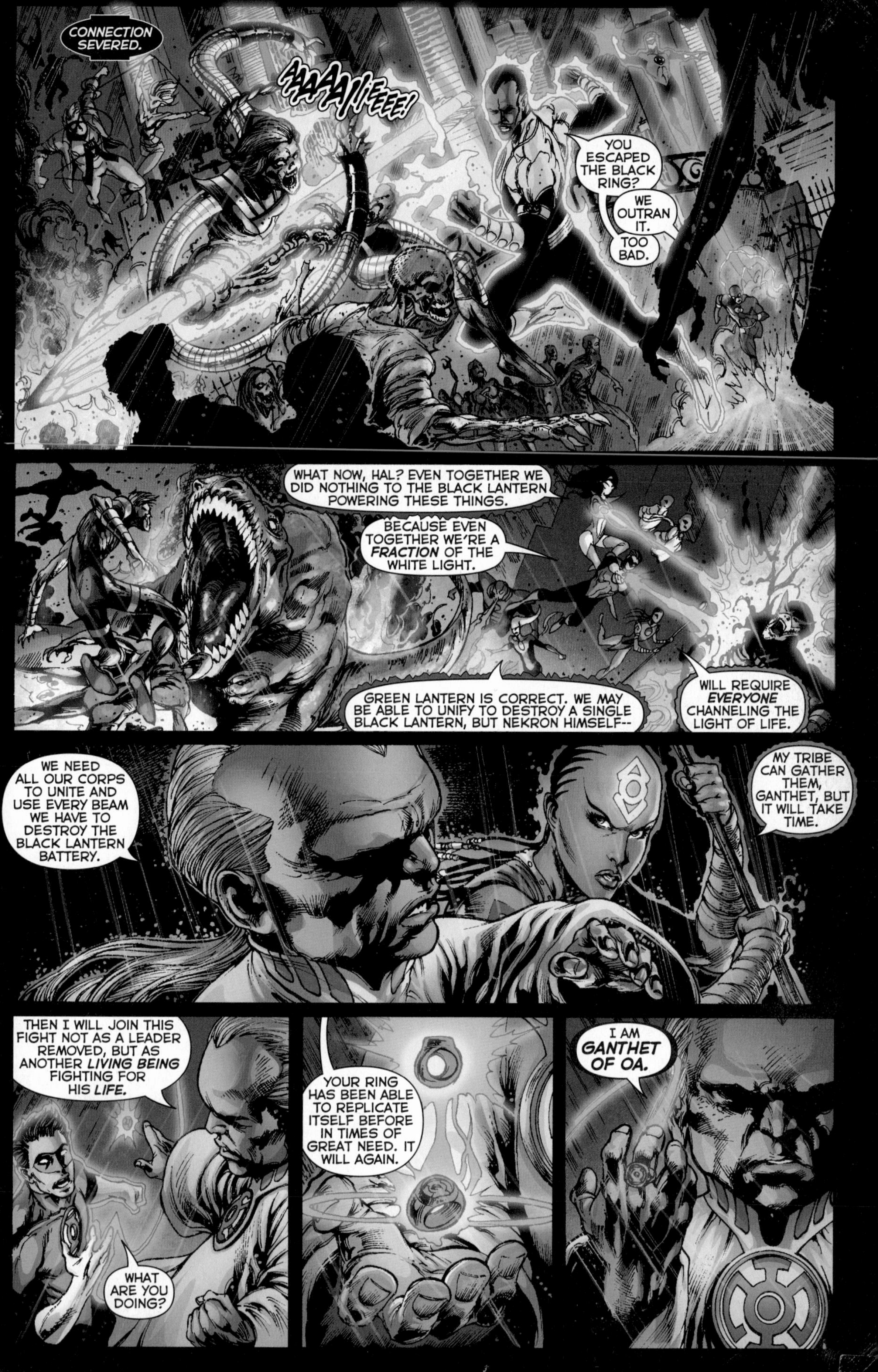
CONNECTION SEVERED.
AAAAAIIEEEE!
YOU ESCAPED THE BLACK RING?
WE OUTRAN IT.
TOO BAD.
WHAT NOW, HAL? EVEN TOGETHER WE DID NOTHING TO THE BLACK LANTERN POWERING THESE THINGS.
BECAUSE EVEN TOGETHER WE'RE A FRACTION OF THE WHITE LIGHT.
GREEN LANTERN IS CORRECT. WE MAY BE ABLE TO UNIFY TO DESTROY A SINGLE BLACK LANTERN, BUT NEKRON HIMSELF--
WILL REQUIRE EVERYONE CHANNELING THE LIGHT OF LIFE.
WE NEED ALL OUR CORPS TO UNITE AND USE EVERY BEAM WE HAVE TO DESTROY THE BLACK LANTERN BATTERY.
MY TRIBE CAN GATHER THEM, GANTHET, BUT IT WILL TAKE TIME.
THEN I WILL JOIN THIS FIGHT NOT AS A LEADER REMOVED, BUT AS ANOTHER LIVING BEING FIGHTING FOR HIS LIFE.
WHAT ARE YOU DOING?
YOUR RING HAS BEEN ABLE TO REPLICATE ITSELF BEFORE IN TIMES OF GREAT NEED. IT WILL AGAIN.
I AM GANTHET OF OA.

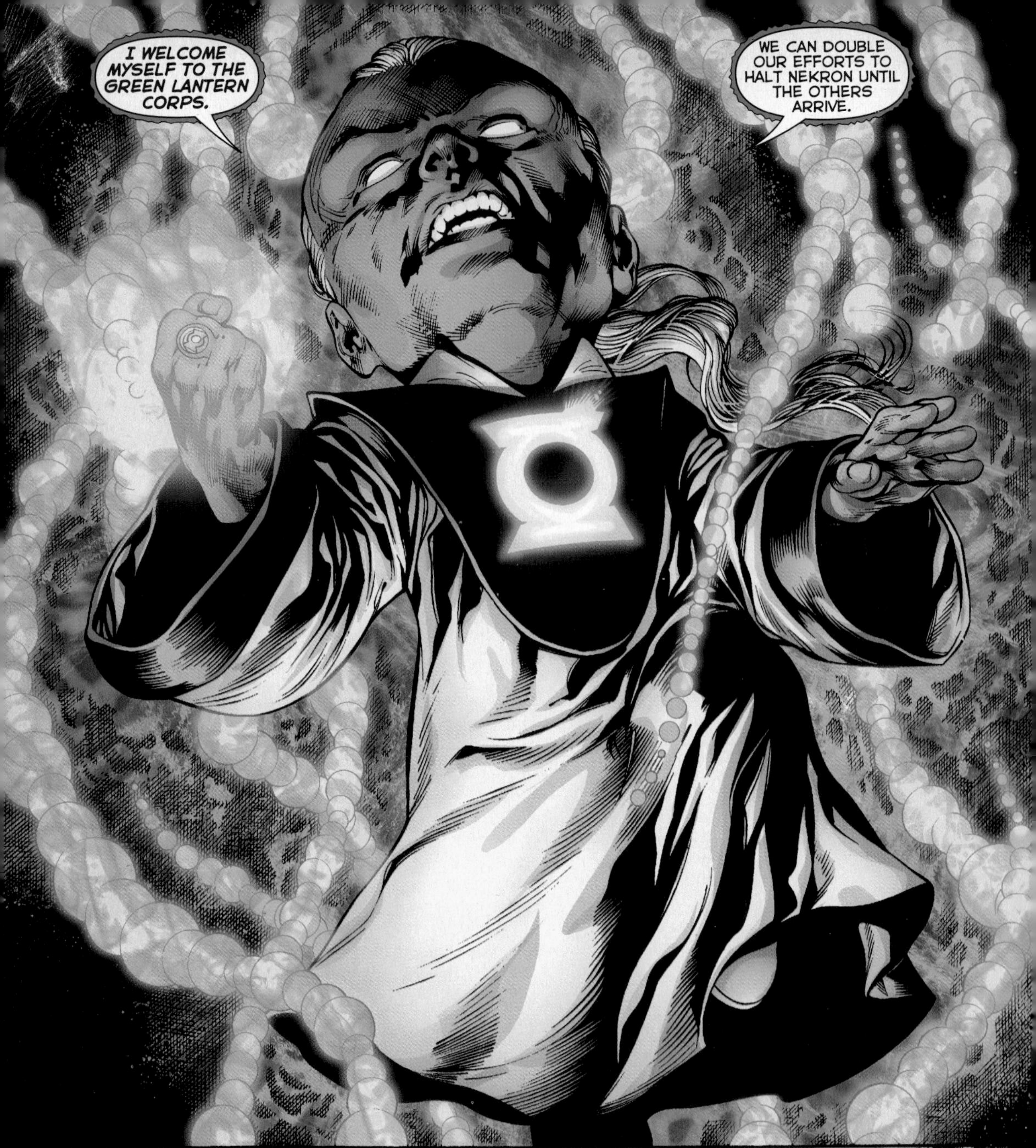
I WELCOME MYSELF TO THE GREEN LANTERN CORPS.
WE CAN DOUBLE OUR EFFORTS TO HALT NEKRON UNTIL THE OTHERS ARRIVE.

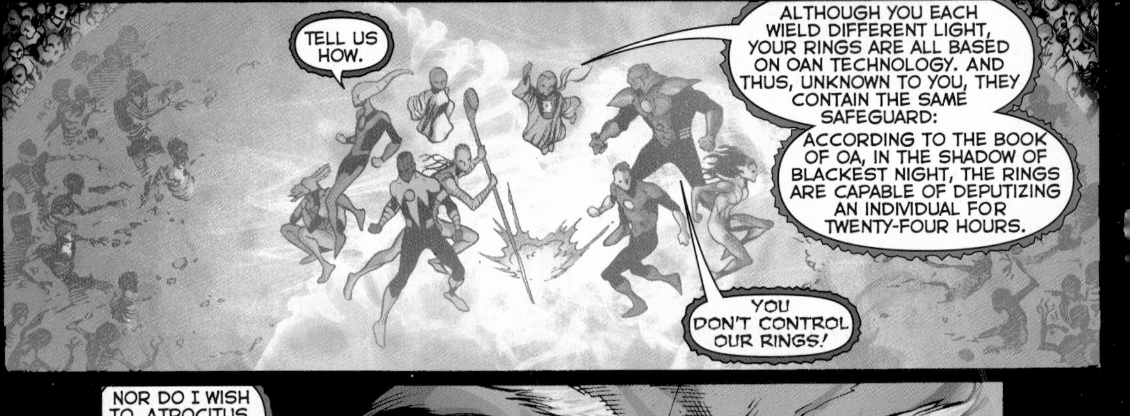
TELL US HOW.
ALTHOUGH YOU EACH WIELD DIFFERENT LIGHT, YOUR RINGS ARE ALL BASED ON OAN TECHNOLOGY. AND THUS, UNKNOWN TO YOU, THEY CONTAIN THE SAME SAFEGUARD:
ACCORDING TO THE BOOK OF OA, IN THE SHADOW OF BLACKEST NIGHT, THE RINGS ARE CAPABLE OF DEPUTIZING AN INDIVIDUAL FOR TWENTY-FOUR HOURS.
YOU DON'T CONTROL OUR RINGS!

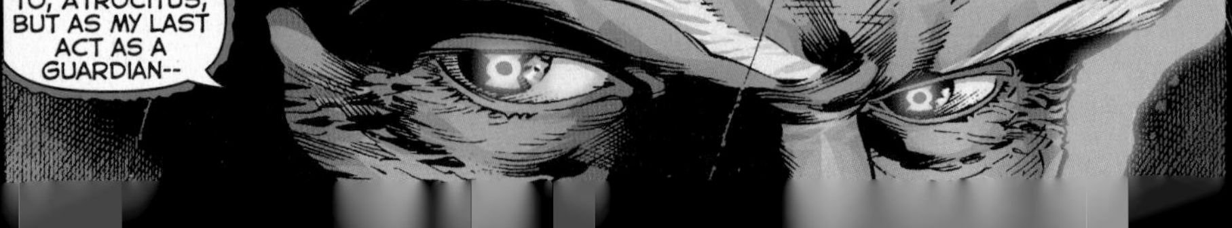
NOR DO I WISH TO, ATROCITUS, BUT AS MY LAST ACT AS A GUARDIAN--

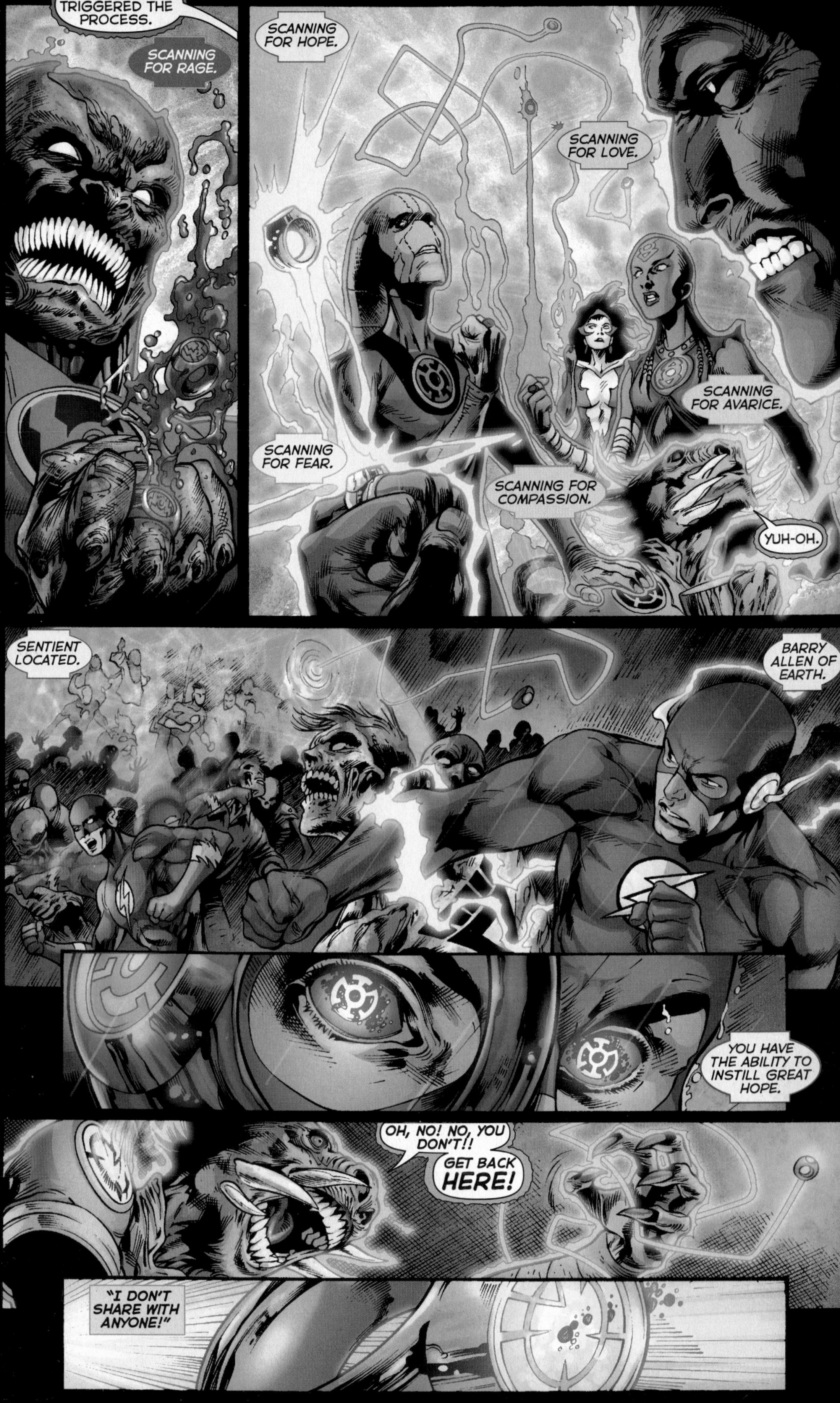
--I'VE ALREADY TRIGGERED THE PROCESS.
SCANNING FOR RAGE.
SCANNING FOR HOPE.
SCANNING FOR LOVE.
SCANNING FOR AVARICE.
SCANNING FOR FEAR.
SCANNING FOR COMPASSION.
YUH-OH.
SENTIENT LOCATED.
BARRY ALLEN OF EARTH.
YOU HAVE THE ABILITY TO INSTILL GREAT HOPE.
OH, NO! NO, YOU DON'T!!
GET BACK HERE!
"I DON'T SHARE WITH ANYONE!"

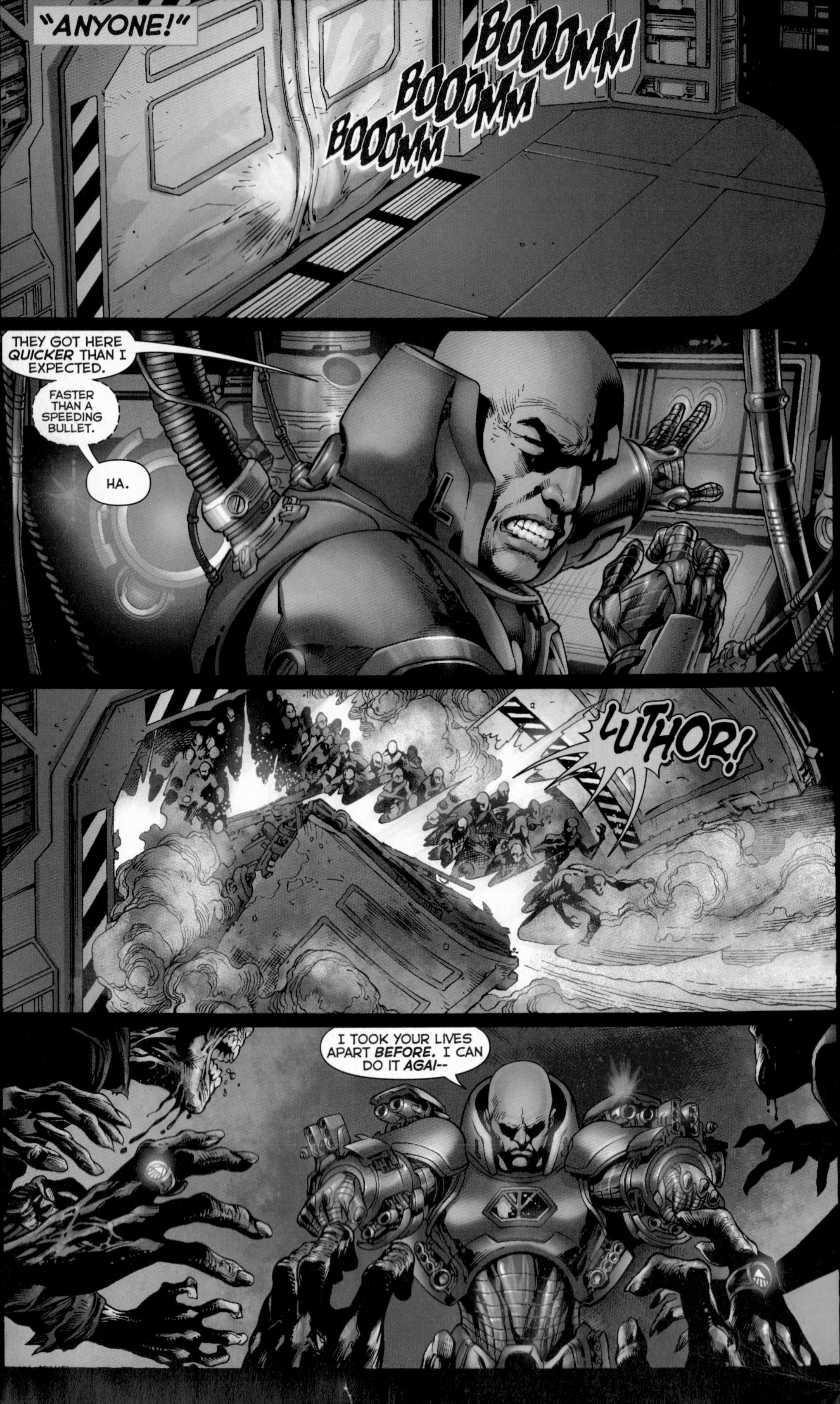
"ANYONE!"
BOOOMM BOOOMM BOOOMM
THEY GOT HERE QUICKER THAN I EXPECTED.
FASTER THAN A SPEEDING BULLET.
HA.
LUTHOR!
I TOOK YOUR LIVES APART BEFORE. I CAN DO IT AGAI--

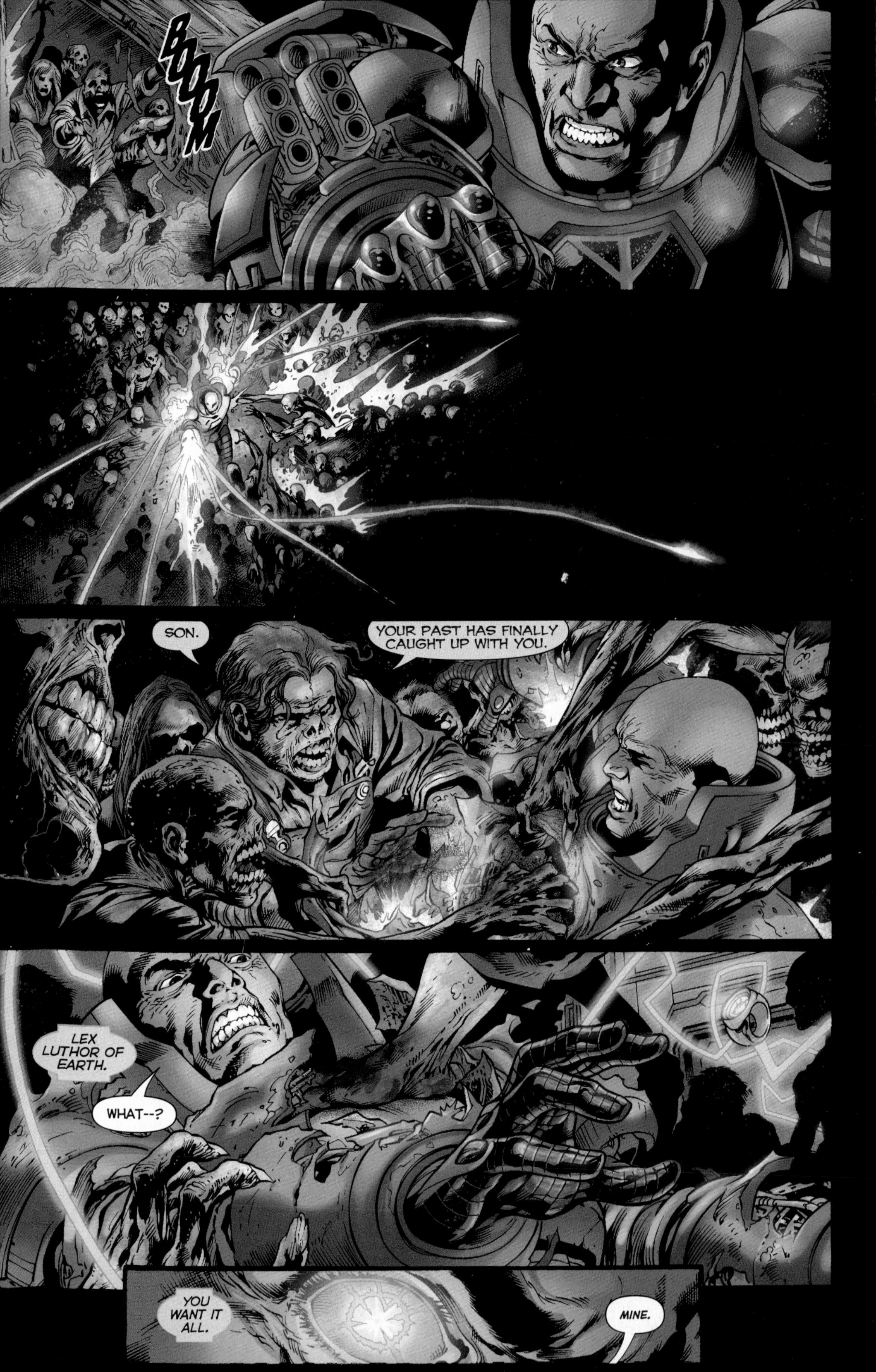

BOOOM
SON.
YOUR PAST HAS FINALLY CAUGHT UP WITH YOU.
LEX LUTHOR OF EARTH.
WHAT--?
YOU WANT IT ALL.
MINE.

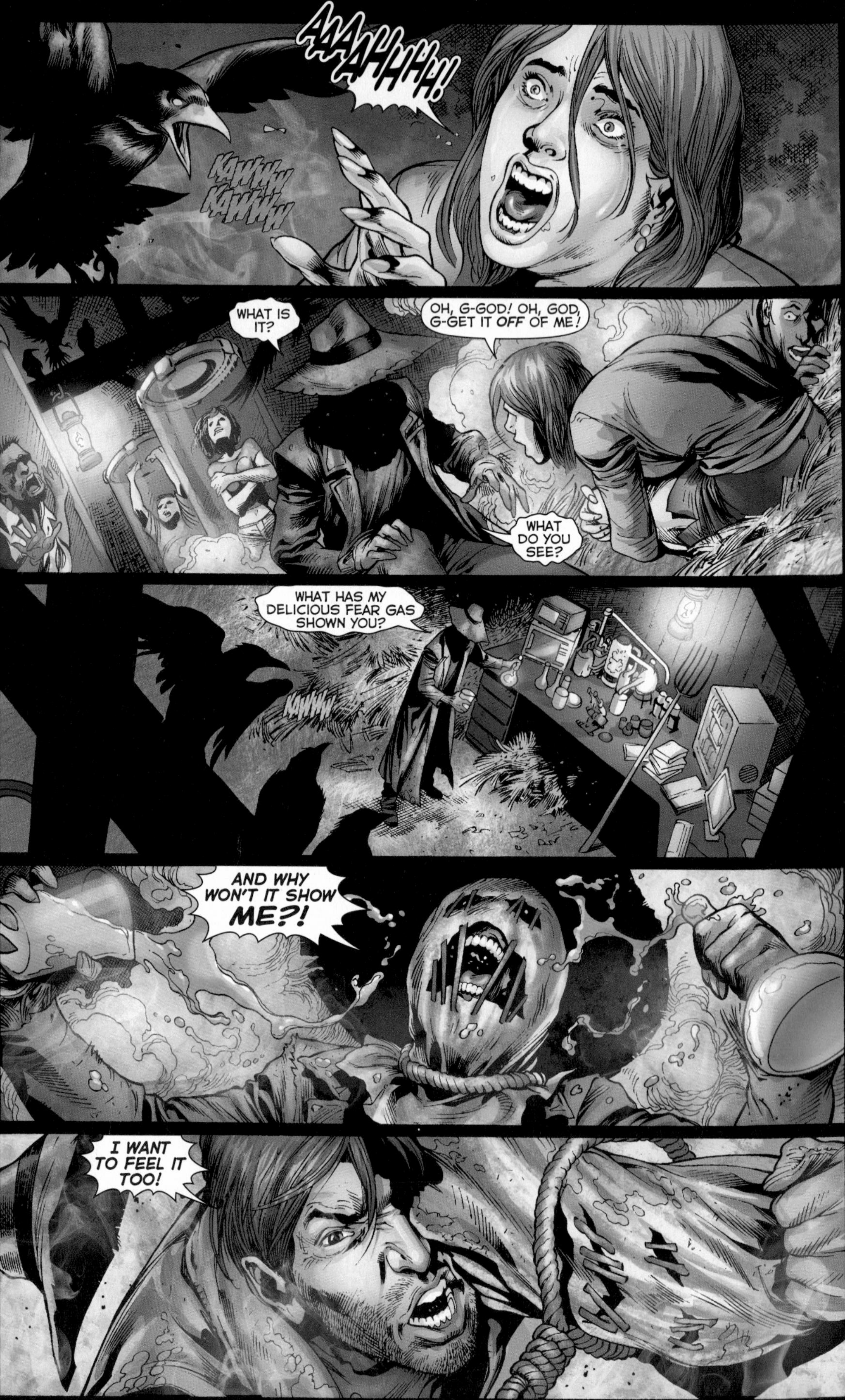
AAAAHHHH!
KAWWW KAWWW
WHAT IS IT?
OH, G-GOD! OH, GOD, G-GET IT OFF OF ME!
WHAT DO YOU SEE?
WHAT HAS MY DELICIOUS FEAR GAS SHOWN YOU?
KAWW
AND WHY WON'T IT SHOW ME?!
I WANT TO FEEL IT TOO!

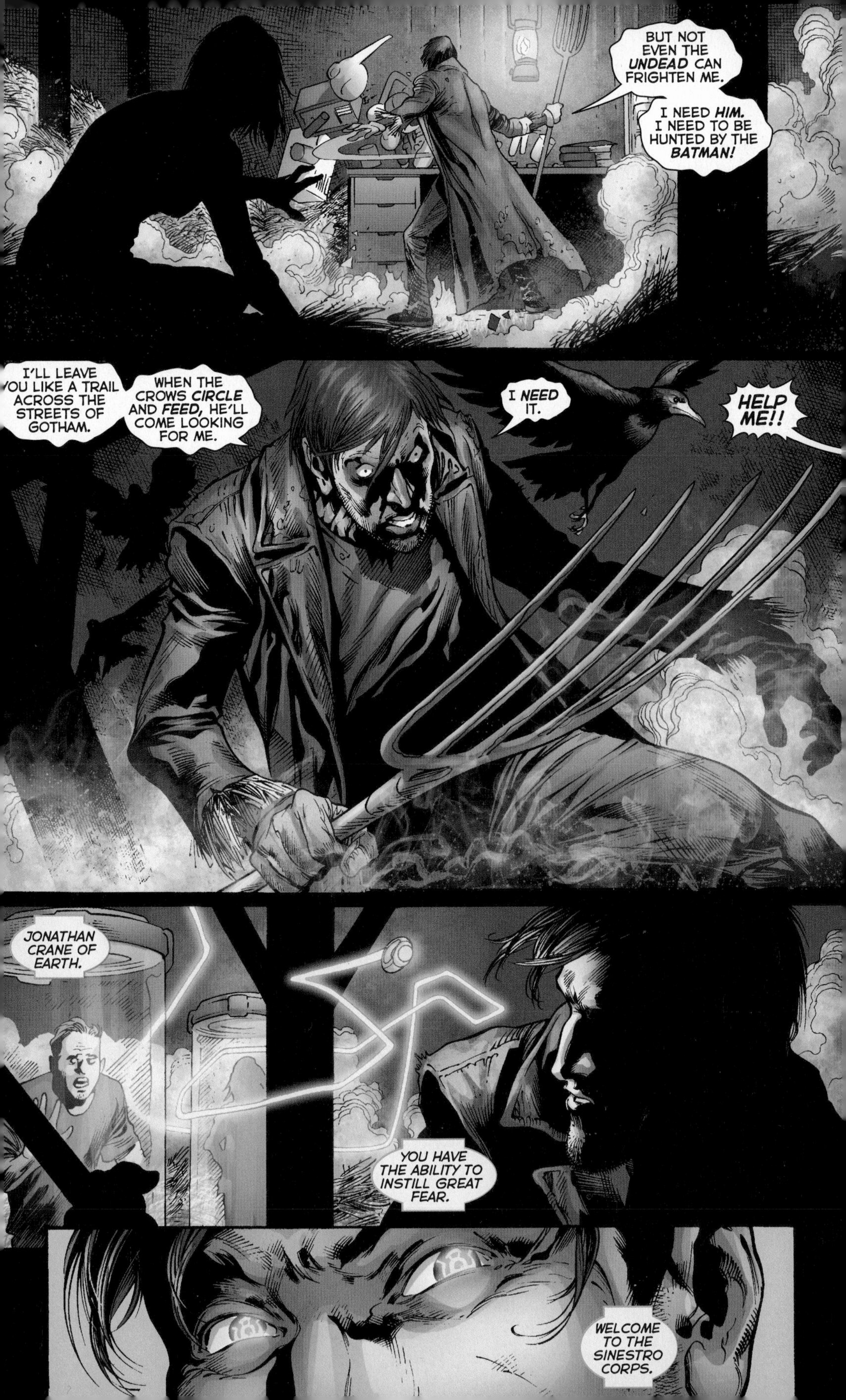
BUT NOT EVEN THE UNDEAD CAN FRIGHTEN ME.
I NEED HIM. I NEED TO BE HUNTED BY THE BATMAN!
I'LL LEAVE YOU LIKE A TRAIL ACROSS THE STREETS OF GOTHAM.
WHEN THE CROWS CIRCLE AND FEED, HE'LL COME LOOKING FOR ME.
I NEED IT.
HELP ME!!
JONATHAN CRANE OF EARTH.
YOU HAVE THE ABILITY TO INSTILL GREAT FEAR.
WELCOME TO THE SINESTRO CORPS.

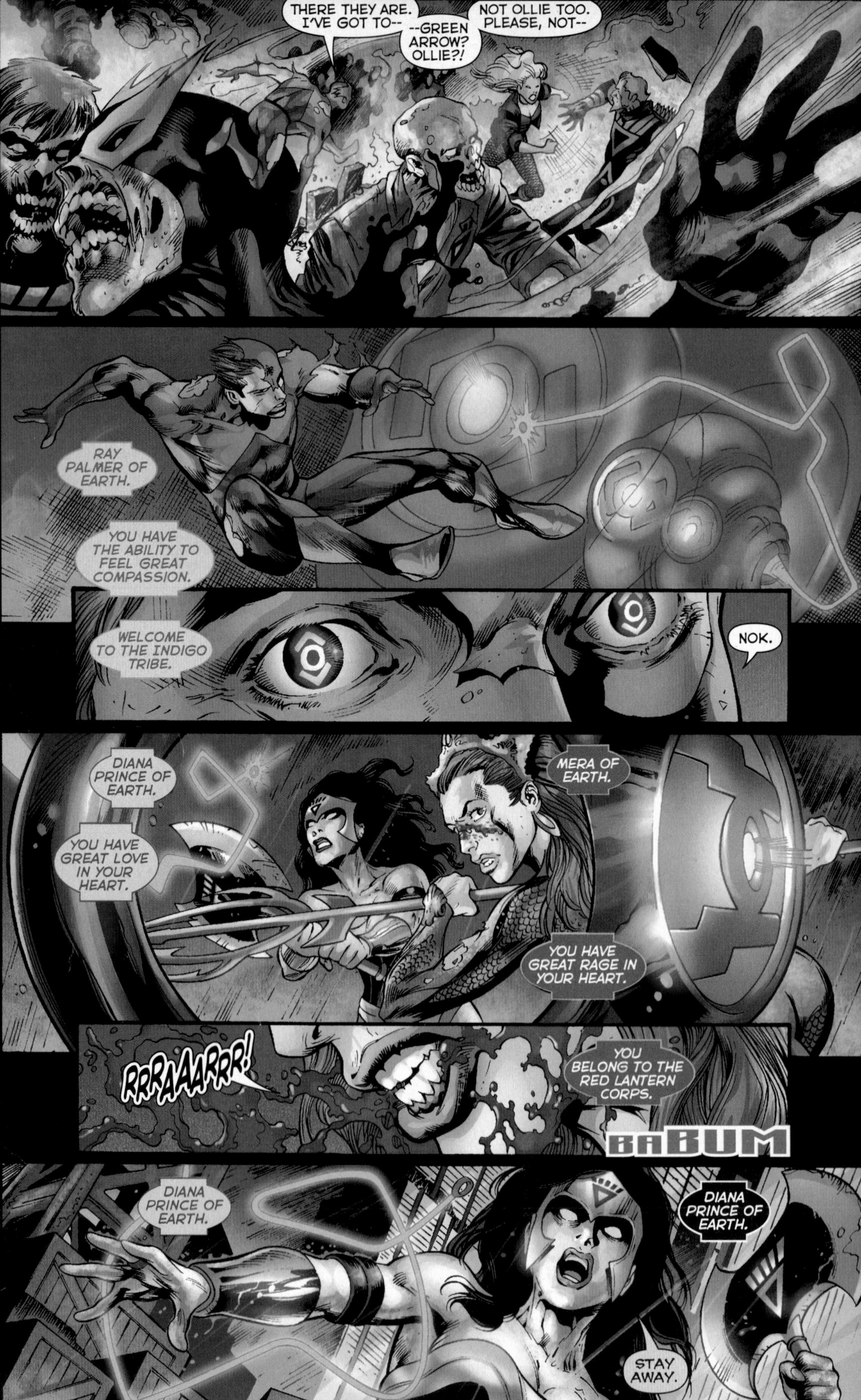
THERE THEY ARE. I'VE GOT TO--
--GREEN ARROW? OLLIE?!
NOT OLLIE TOO. PLEASE, NOT--
RAY PALMER OF EARTH.
YOU HAVE THE ABILITY TO FEEL GREAT COMPASSION.
WELCOME TO THE INDIGO TRIBE.
NOK.
DIANA PRINCE OF EARTH.
YOU HAVE GREAT LOVE IN YOUR HEART.
MERA OF EARTH.
YOU HAVE GREAT RAGE IN YOUR HEART.
RRRAAARRR!
YOU BELONG TO THE RED LANTERN CORPS.
BABUM
DIANA PRINCE OF EARTH.
DIANA PRINCE OF EARTH.
STAY AWAY.

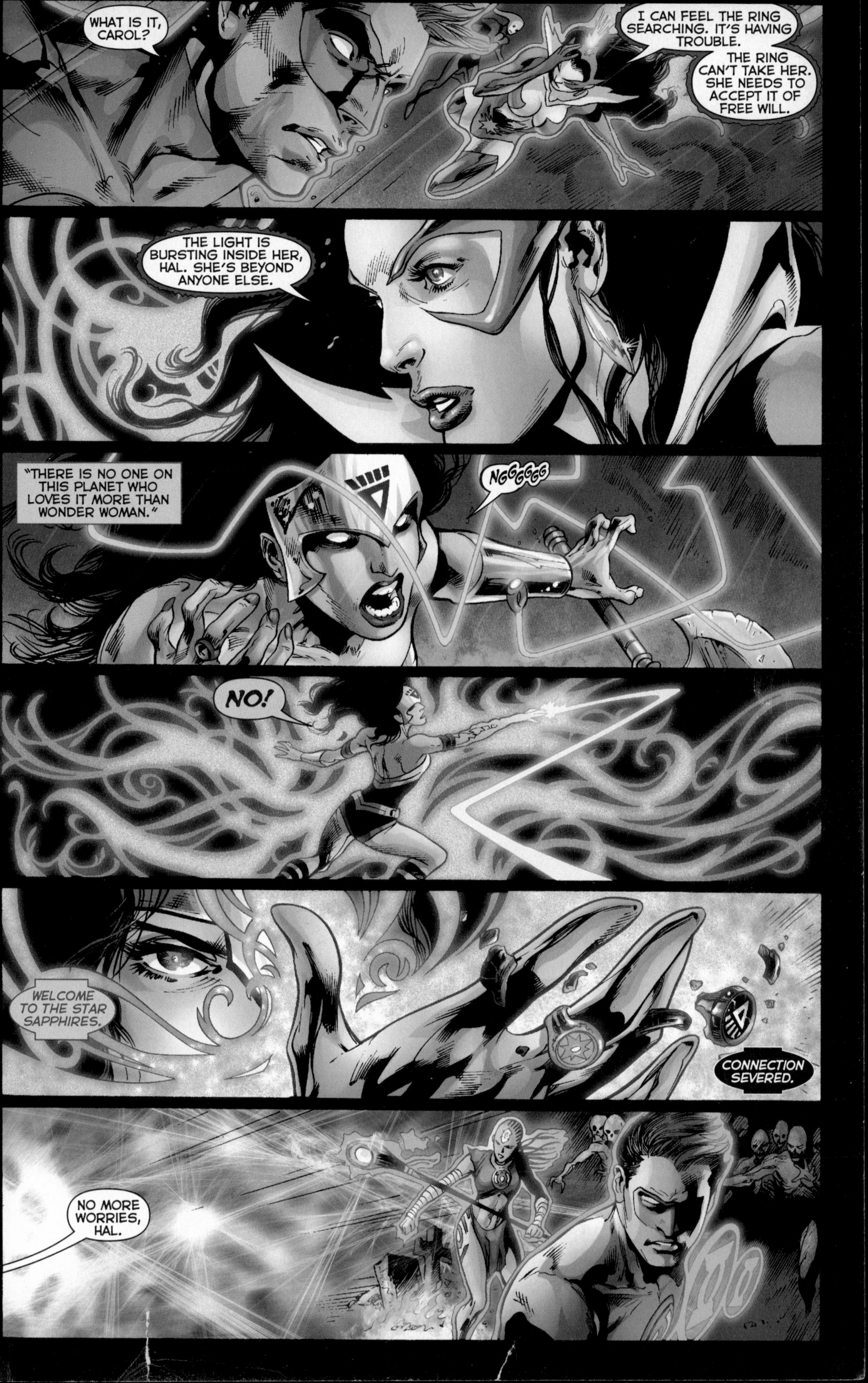
WHAT IS IT, CAROL?
I CAN FEEL THE RING SEARCHING. IT'S HAVING TROUBLE.
THE RING CAN'T TAKE HER. SHE NEEDS TO ACCEPT IT OF FREE WILL.
THE LIGHT IS BURSTING INSIDE HER, HAL. SHE'S BEYOND ANYONE ELSE.
"THERE IS NO ONE ON THIS PLANET WHO LOVES IT MORE THAN WONDER WOMAN."
NGGGGGG
NO!
WELCOME TO THE STAR SAPPHIRES.
CONNECTION SEVERED.
NO MORE WORRIES, HAL.

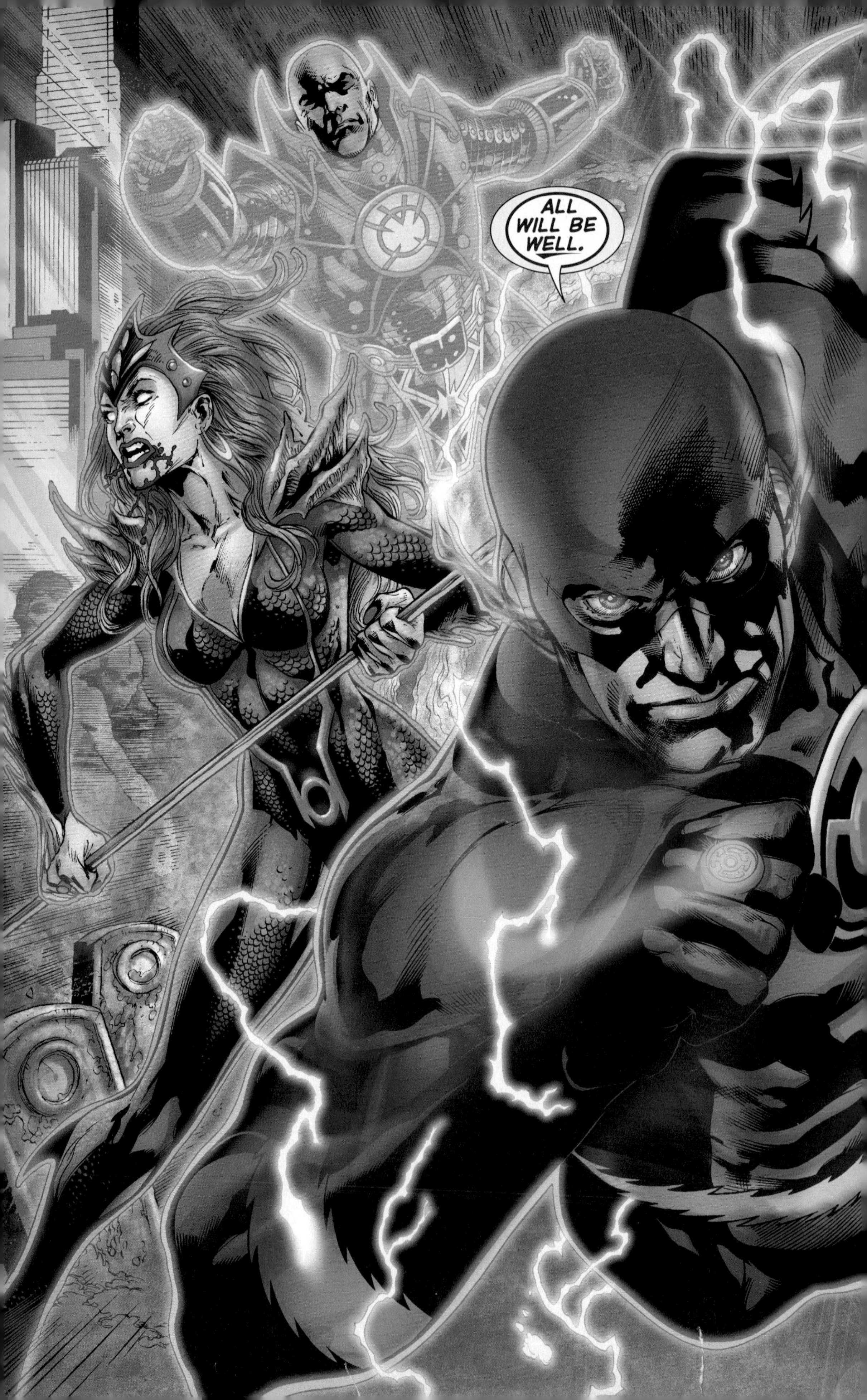
ALL WILL BE WELL.

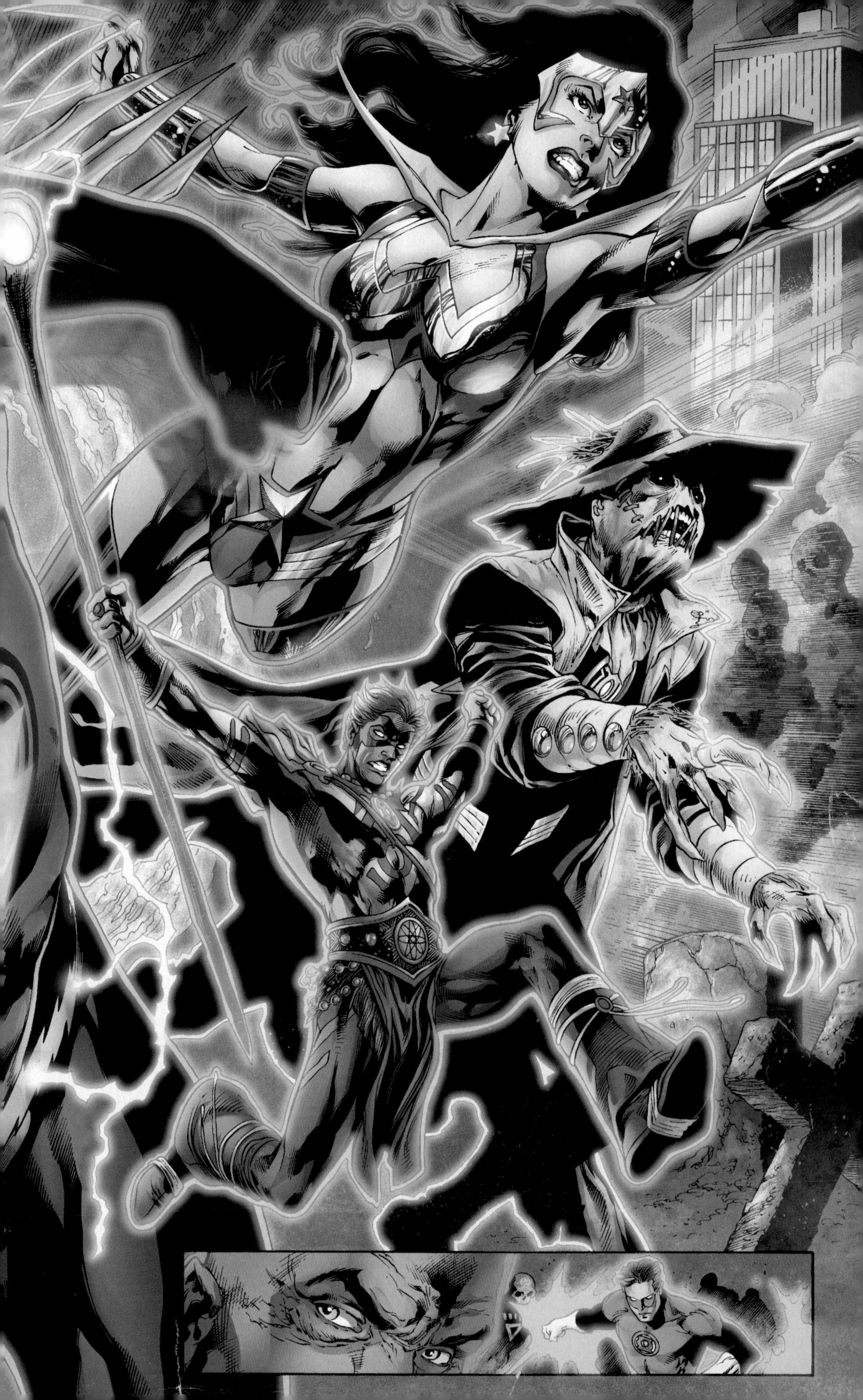

PART SEVEN

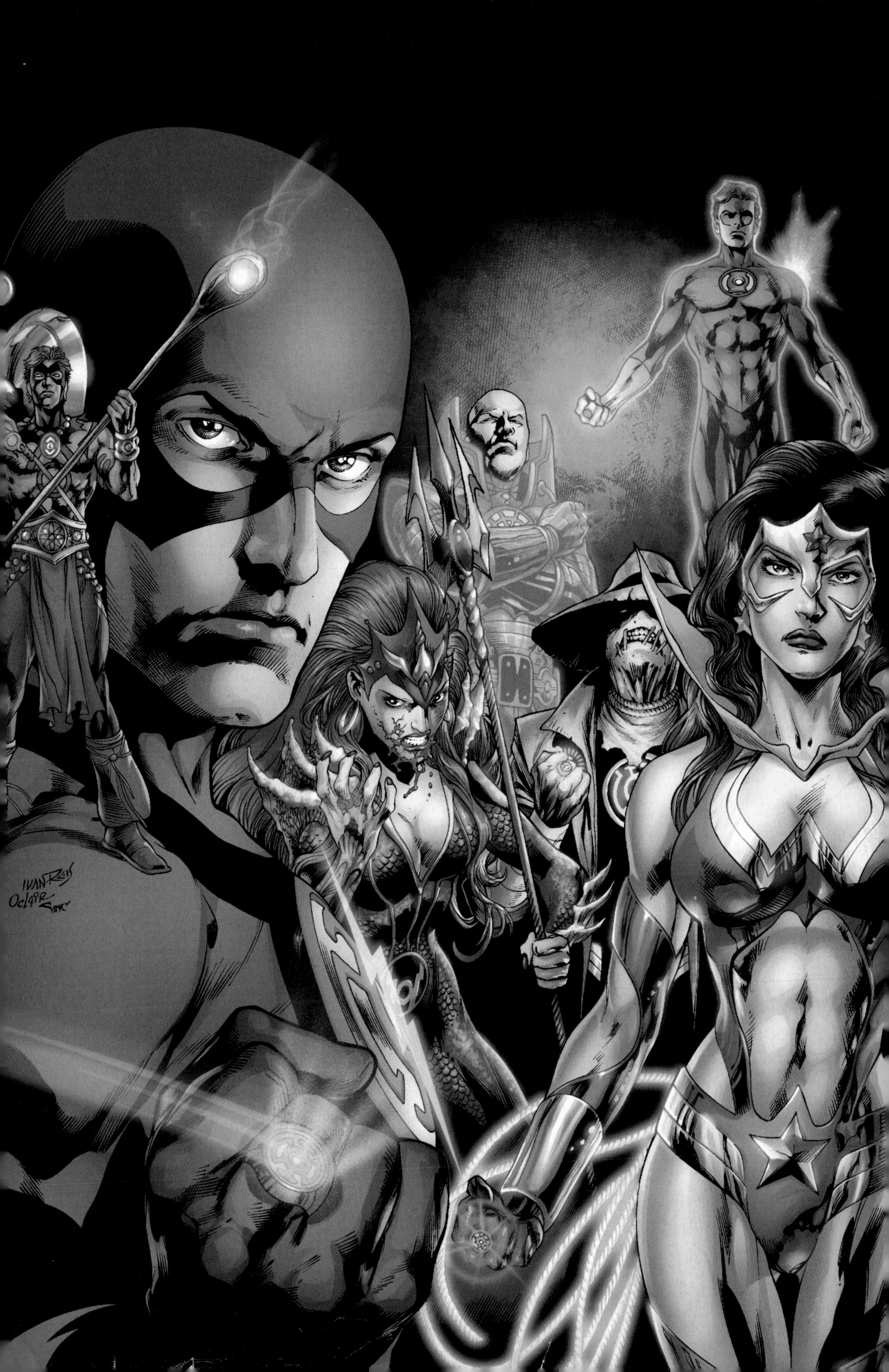

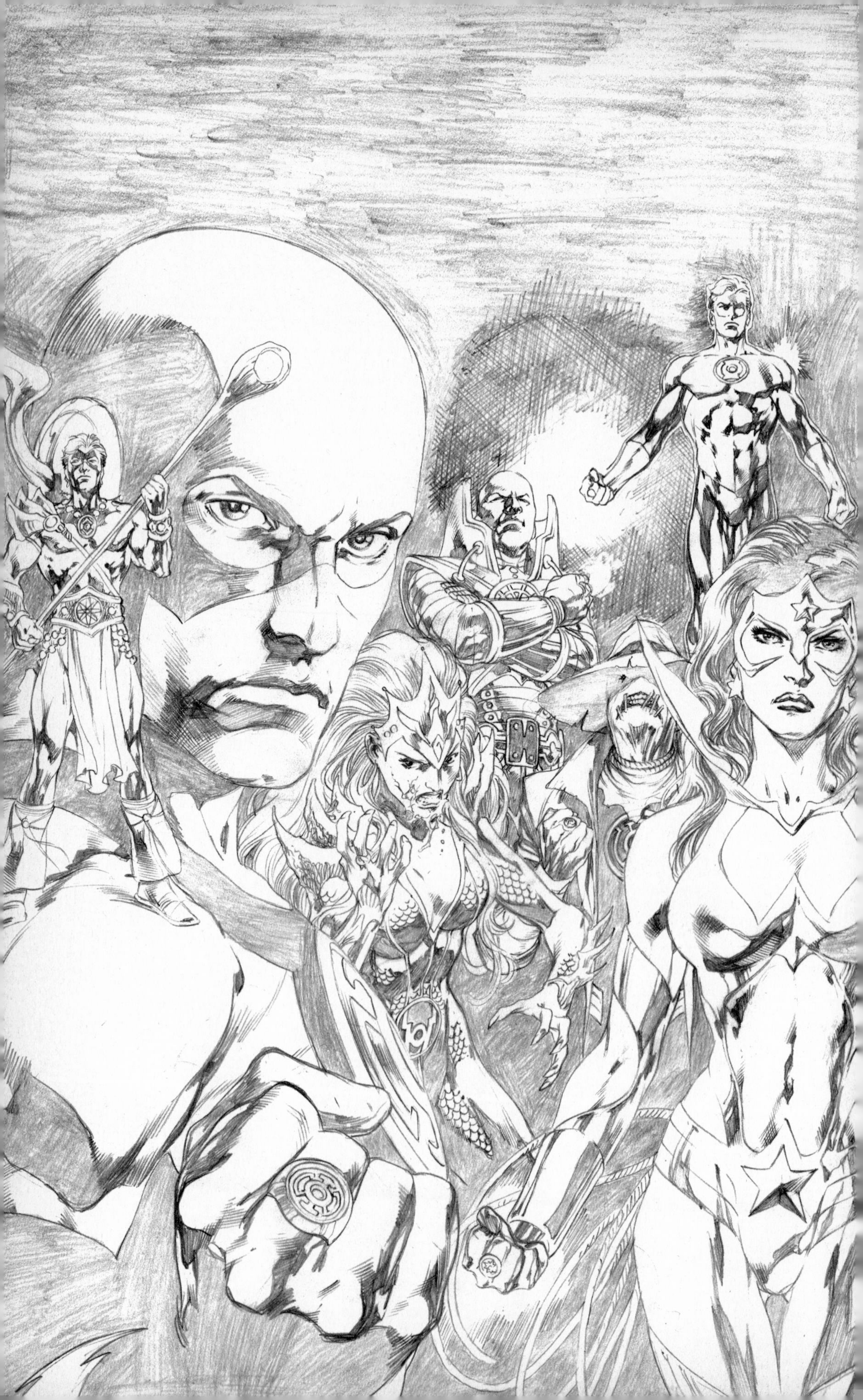

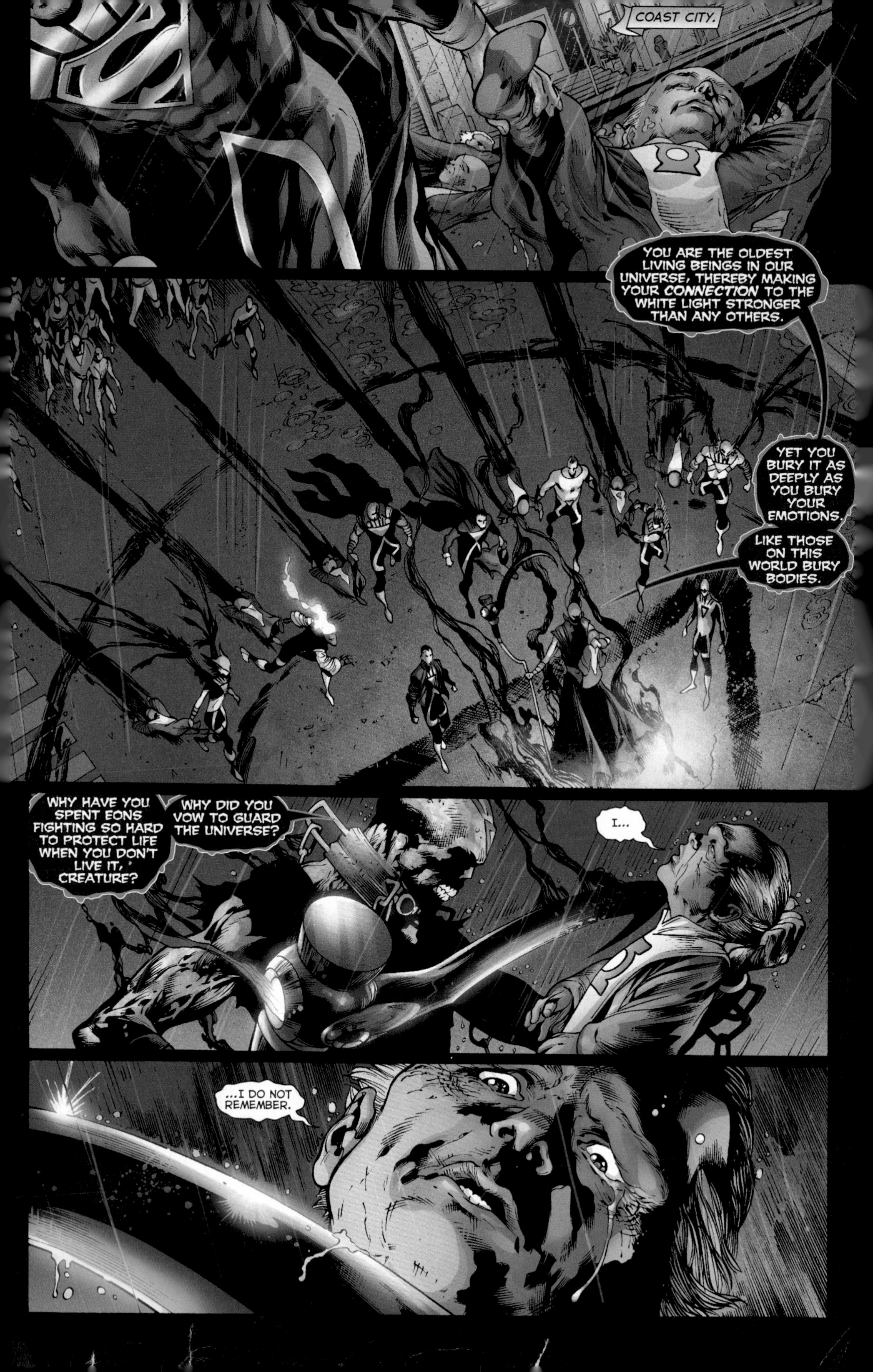
COAST CITY.
YOU ARE THE OLDEST LIVING BEINGS IN OUR UNIVERSE, THEREBY MAKING YOUR CONNECTION TO THE WHITE LIGHT STRONGER THAN ANY OTHERS.
YET YOU BURY IT AS DEEPLY AS YOU BURY YOUR EMOTIONS.
LIKE THOSE ON THIS WORLD BURY BODIES.
WHY HAVE YOU SPENT EONS FIGHTING SO HARD TO PROTECT LIFE WHEN YOU DON'T LIVE IT, CREATURE?
WHY DID YOU VOW TO GUARD THE UNIVERSE?
I...
...I DO NOT REMEMBER.

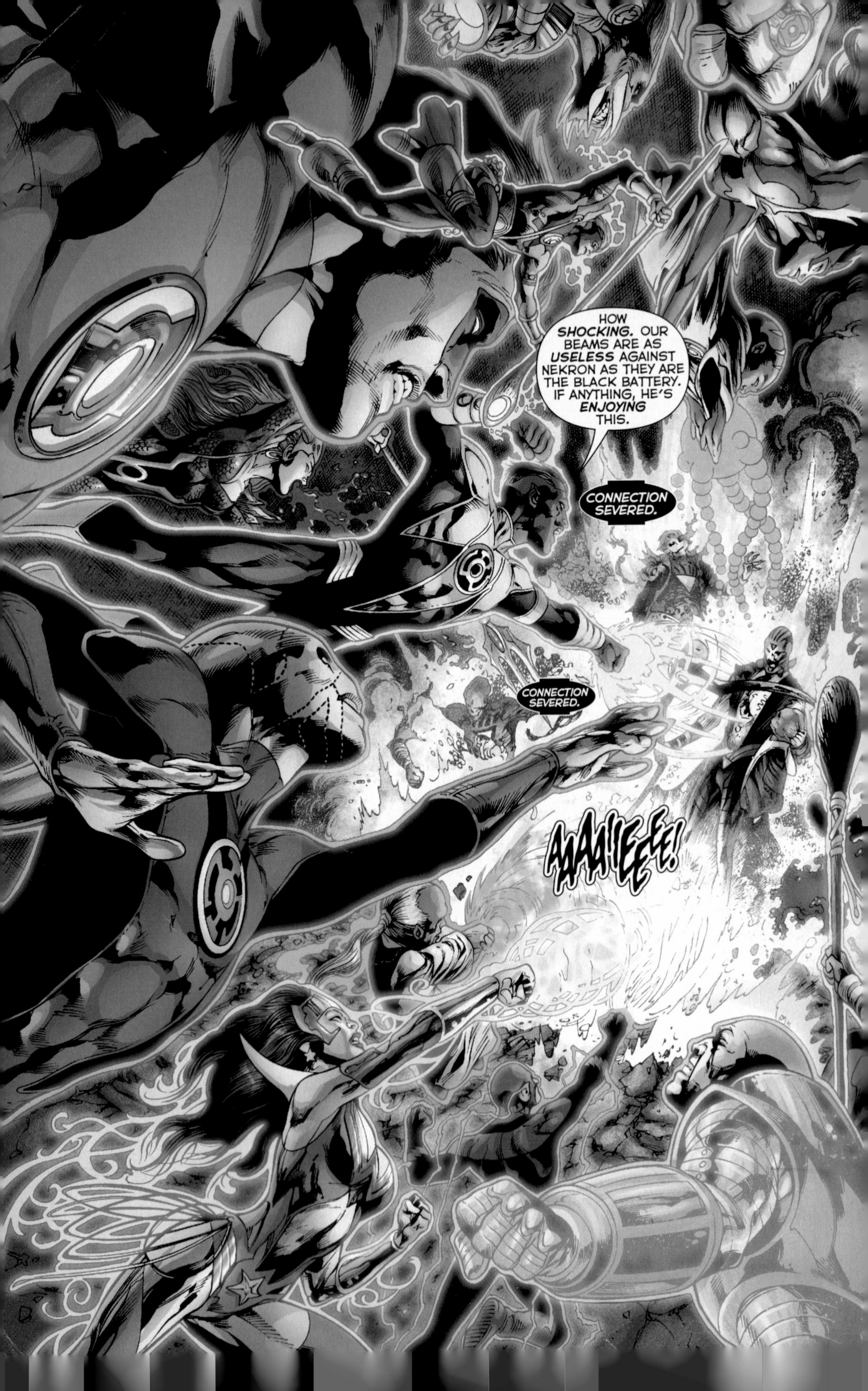
HOW SHOCKING. OUR BEAMS ARE AS USELESS AGAINST NEKRON AS THEY ARE THE BLACK BATTERY. IF ANYTHING, HE'S ENJOYING THIS.
CONNECTION SEVERED.
CONNECTION SEVERED.
AAAAIIEEEE!

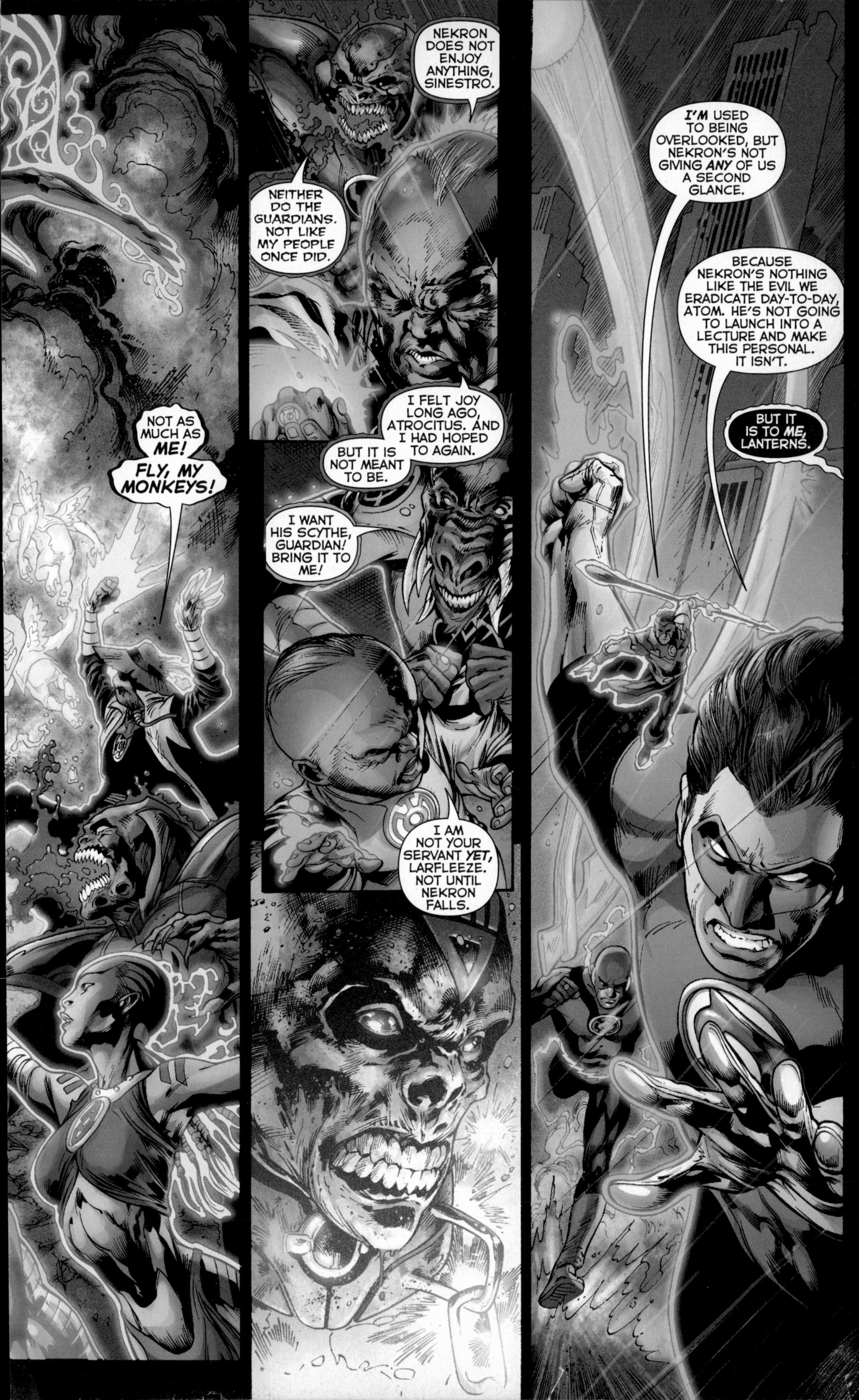

NOT AS MUCH AS *ME!*
FLY, MY MONKEYS!
NEKRON DOES NOT ENJOY ANYTHING, SINESTRO.
NEITHER DO THE GUARDIANS. NOT LIKE MY PEOPLE ONCE DID.
I FELT JOY LONG AGO, ATROCITUS. AND I HAD HOPED TO AGAIN.
BUT IT IS NOT MEANT TO BE.
I WANT HIS SCYTHE, GUARDIAN! BRING IT TO ME!
I AM NOT YOUR SERVANT *YET,* LARFLEEZE. NOT UNTIL NEKRON FALLS.
I'M USED TO BEING OVERLOOKED, BUT NEKRON'S NOT GIVING *ANY* OF US A SECOND GLANCE.
BECAUSE NEKRON'S NOTHING LIKE THE EVIL WE ERADICATE DAY-TO-DAY, ATOM. HE'S NOT GOING TO LAUNCH INTO A LECTURE AND MAKE THIS PERSONAL. IT ISN'T.
BUT IT IS TO *ME,* LANTERNS.

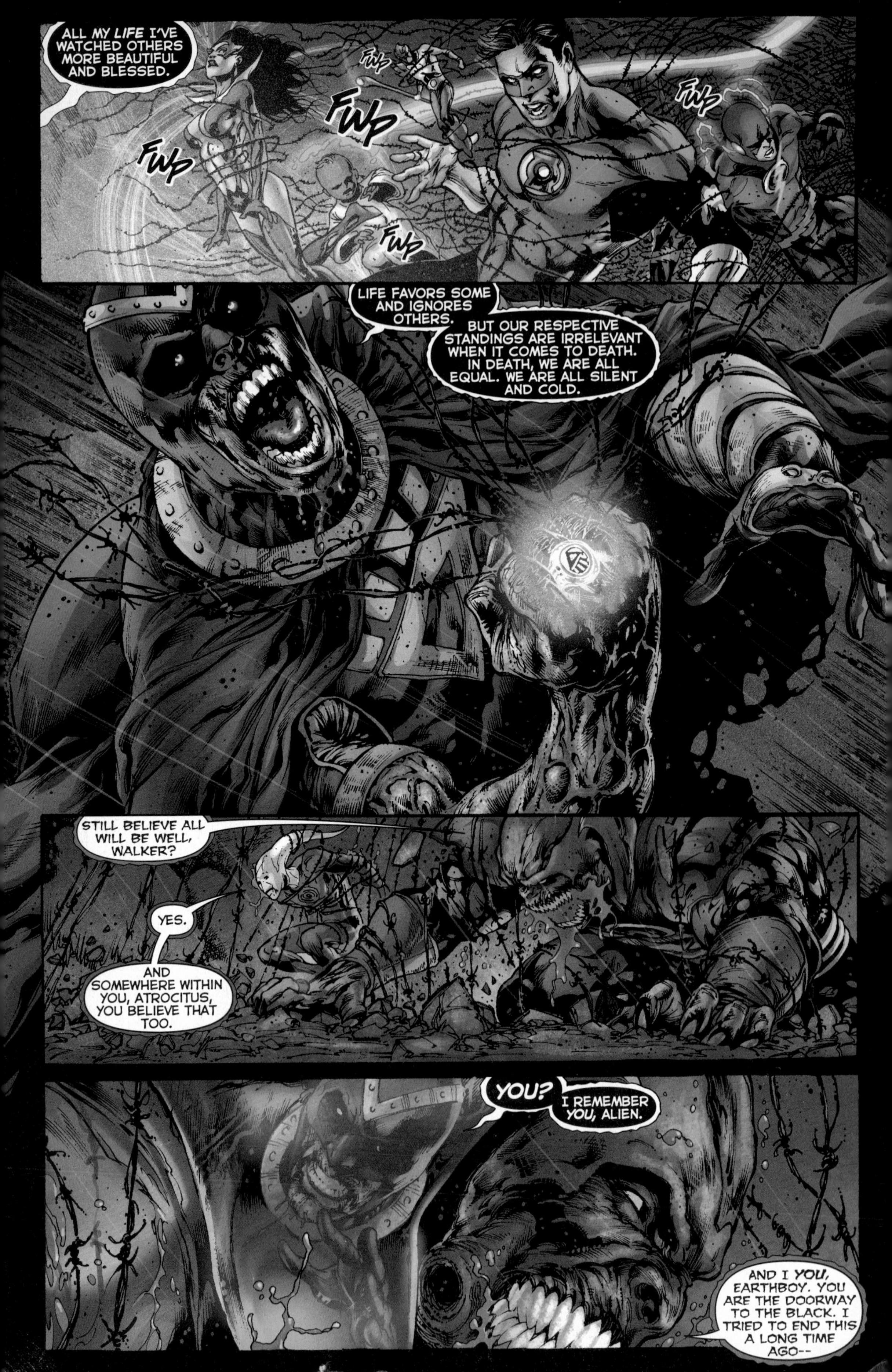
ALL MY LIFE I'VE WATCHED OTHERS MORE BEAUTIFUL AND BLESSED.
FWP
FWP
FWP
FWP
FWP
LIFE FAVORS SOME AND IGNORES OTHERS.
BUT OUR RESPECTIVE STANDINGS ARE IRRELEVANT WHEN IT COMES TO DEATH. IN DEATH, WE ARE ALL EQUAL. WE ARE ALL SILENT AND COLD.
STILL BELIEVE ALL WILL BE WELL, WALKER?
YES.
AND SOMEWHERE WITHIN YOU, ATROCITUS, YOU BELIEVE THAT TOO.
YOU?
I REMEMBER YOU, ALIEN.
AND I YOU, EARTHBOY. YOU ARE THE DOORWAY TO THE BLACK. I TRIED TO END THIS A LONG TIME AGO--

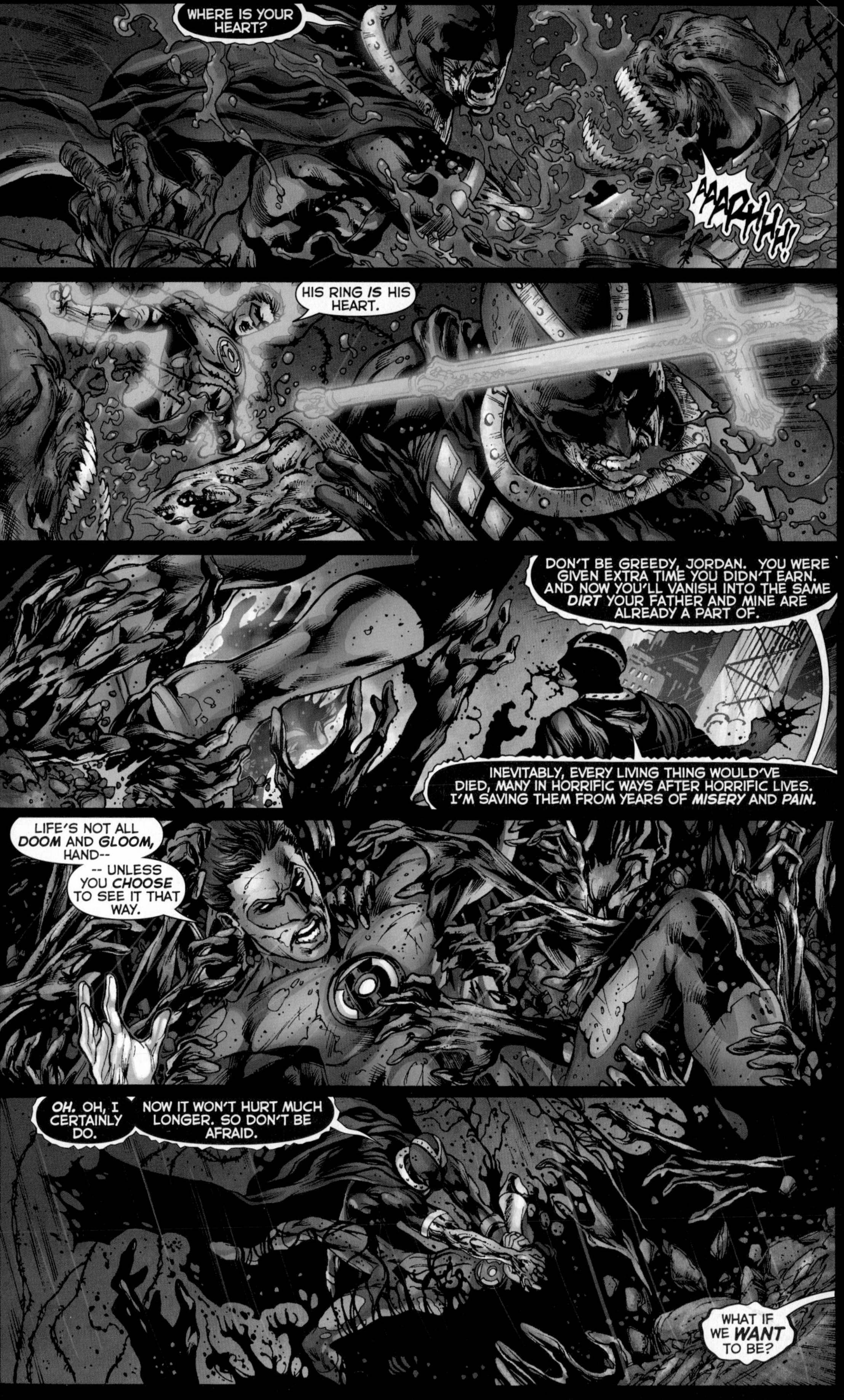
WHERE IS YOUR HEART?
AAARHHH!
HIS RING IS HIS HEART.
DON'T BE GREEDY, JORDAN. YOU WERE GIVEN EXTRA TIME YOU DIDN'T EARN. AND NOW YOU'LL VANISH INTO THE SAME DIRT YOUR FATHER AND MINE ARE ALREADY A PART OF.
INEVITABLY, EVERY LIVING THING WOULD'VE DIED, MANY IN HORRIFIC WAYS AFTER HORRIFIC LIVES. I'M SAVING THEM FROM YEARS OF MISERY AND PAIN.
LIFE'S NOT ALL DOOM AND GLOOM, HAND--
-- UNLESS YOU CHOOSE TO SEE IT THAT WAY.
OH. OH, I CERTAINLY DO.
NOW IT WON'T HURT MUCH LONGER. SO DON'T BE AFRAID.
WHAT IF WE WANT TO BE?

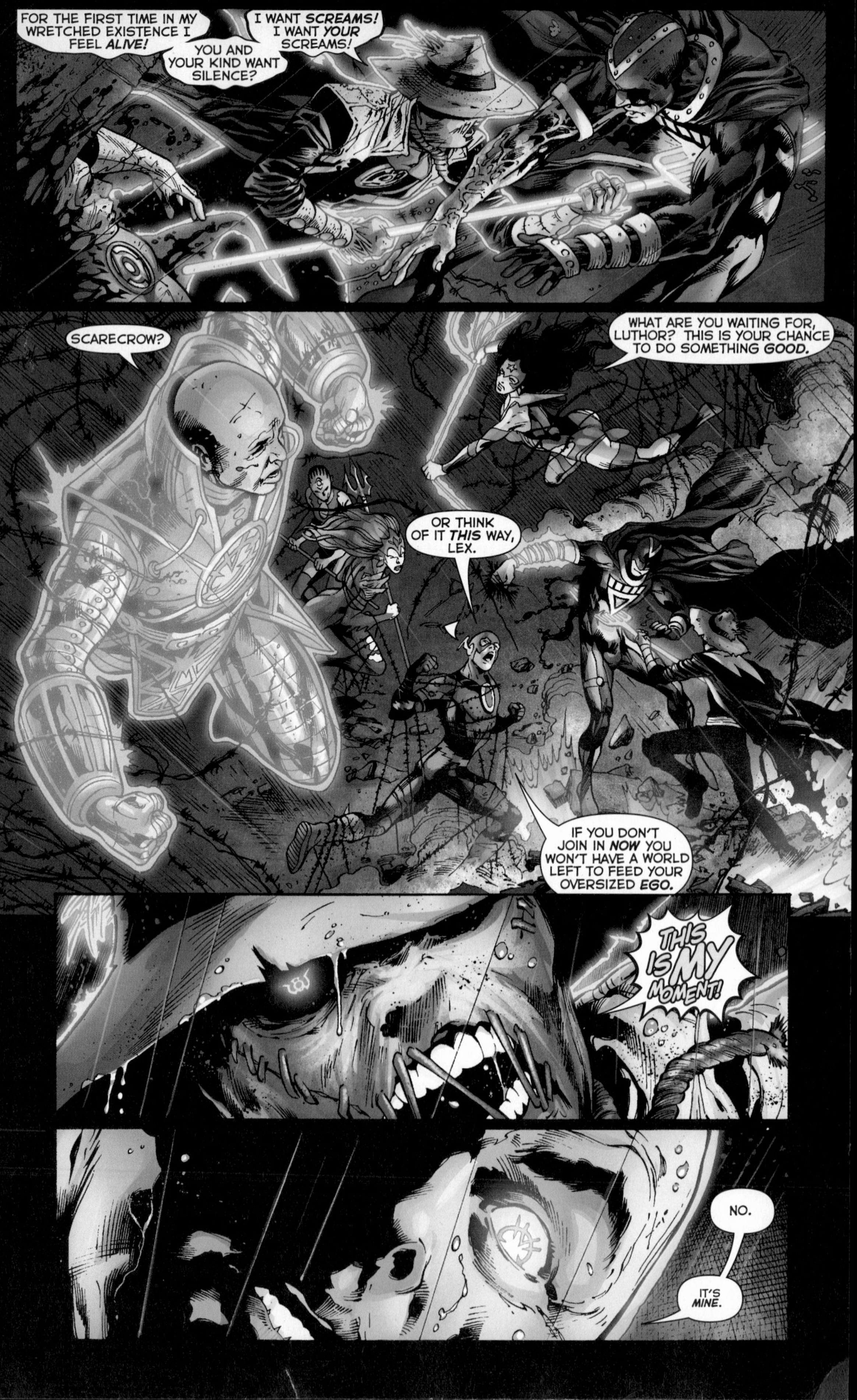
FOR THE FIRST TIME IN MY WRETCHED EXISTENCE I FEEL ALIVE!
YOU AND YOUR KIND WANT SILENCE?
I WANT SCREAMS! I WANT YOUR SCREAMS!
SCARECROW?
WHAT ARE YOU WAITING FOR, LUTHOR? THIS IS YOUR CHANCE TO DO SOMETHING GOOD.
OR THINK OF IT THIS WAY, LEX.
IF YOU DON'T JOIN IN NOW YOU WON'T HAVE A WORLD LEFT TO FEED YOUR OVERSIZED EGO.
THIS IS MY MOMENT!
NO.
IT'S MINE.

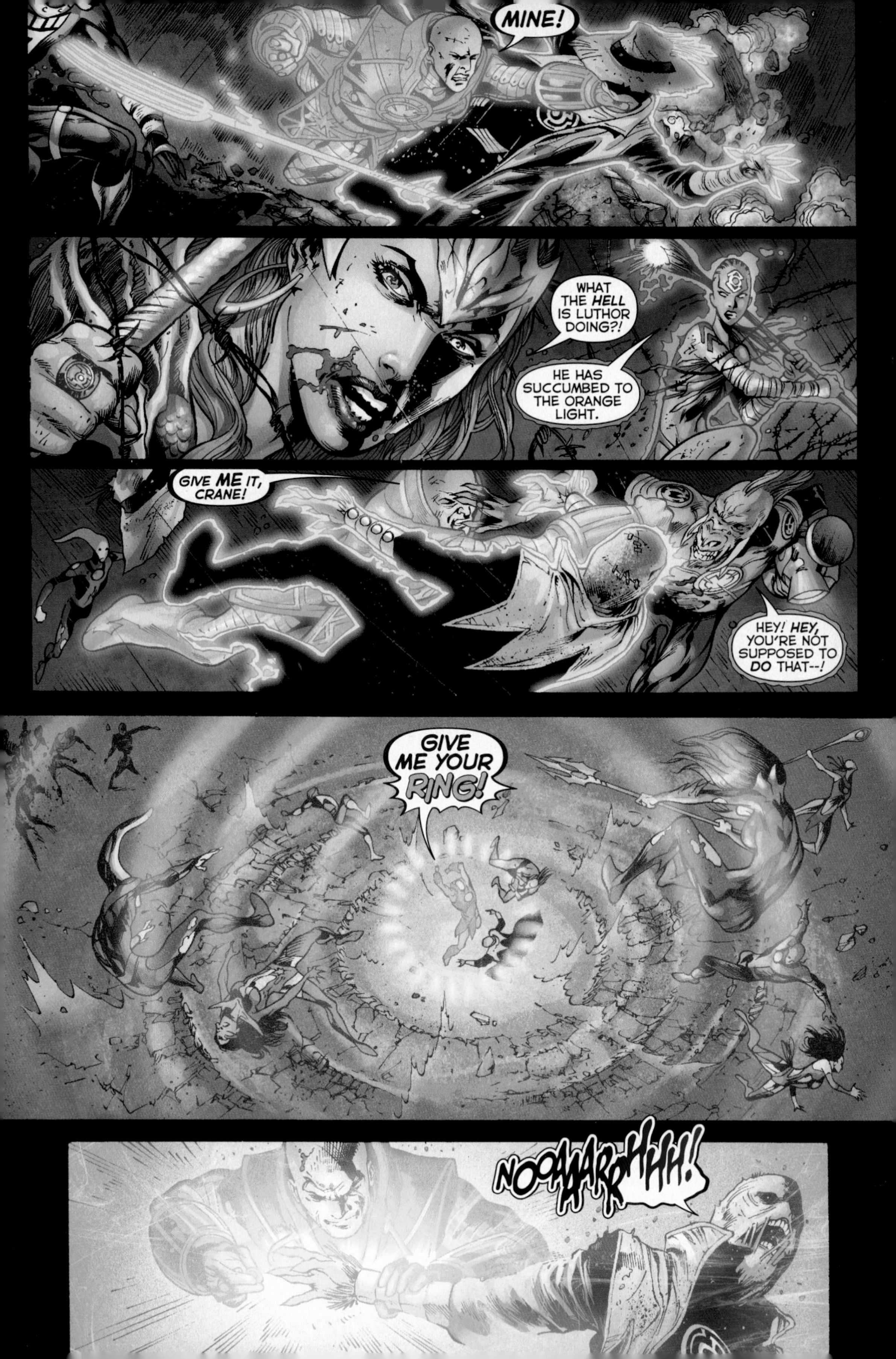
MINE!
WHAT THE HELL IS LUTHOR DOING?!
HE HAS SUCCUMBED TO THE ORANGE LIGHT.
GIVE ME IT, CRANE!
HEY! HEY, YOU'RE NOT SUPPOSED TO DO THAT--!
GIVE ME YOUR RING!
NOOAAARRHHH!

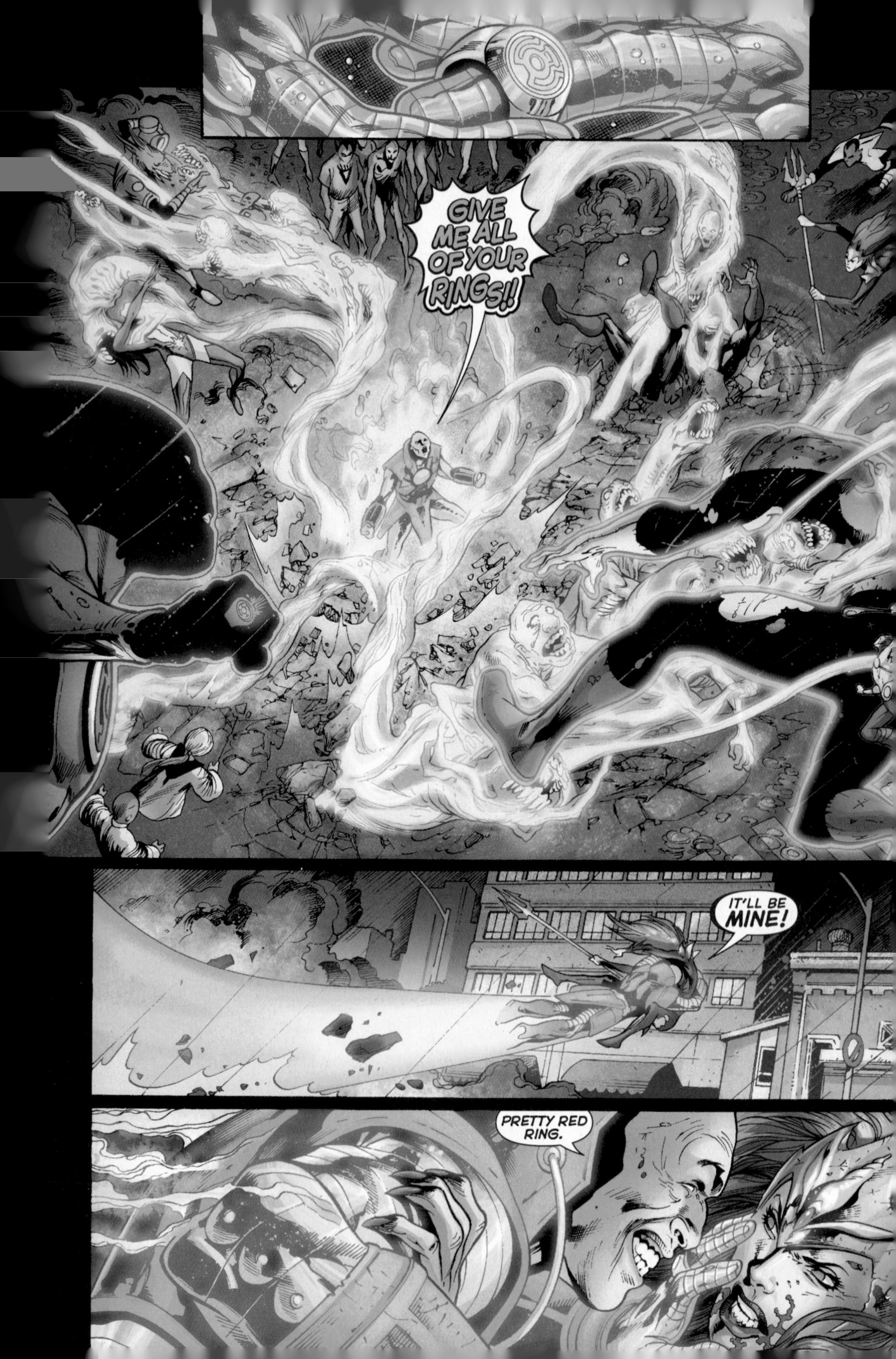
GIVE ME ALL OF YOUR RINGS!!
IT'LL BE MINE!
PRETTY RED RING.

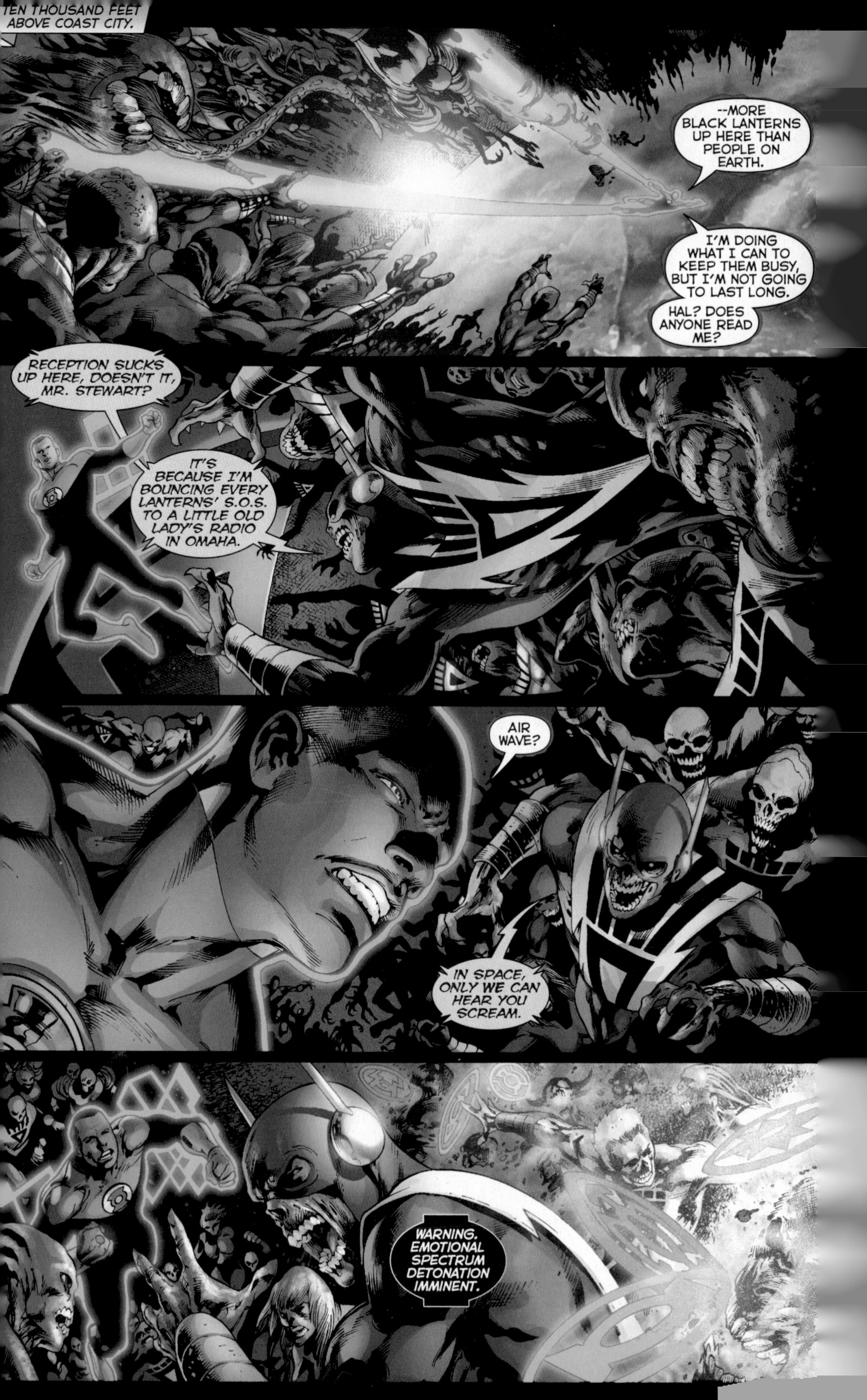
TEN THOUSAND FEET ABOVE COAST CITY.
--MORE BLACK LANTERNS UP HERE THAN PEOPLE ON EARTH.
I'M DOING WHAT I CAN TO KEEP THEM BUSY, BUT I'M NOT GOING TO LAST LONG.
HAL? DOES ANYONE READ ME?
RECEPTION SUCKS UP HERE, DOESN'T IT, MR. STEWART?
IT'S BECAUSE I'M BOUNCING EVERY LANTERNS' S.O.S. TO A LITTLE OLD LADY'S RADIO IN OMAHA.
AIR WAVE?
IN SPACE, ONLY WE CAN HEAR YOU SCREAM.
WARNING. EMOTIONAL SPECTRUM DETONATION IMMINENT.

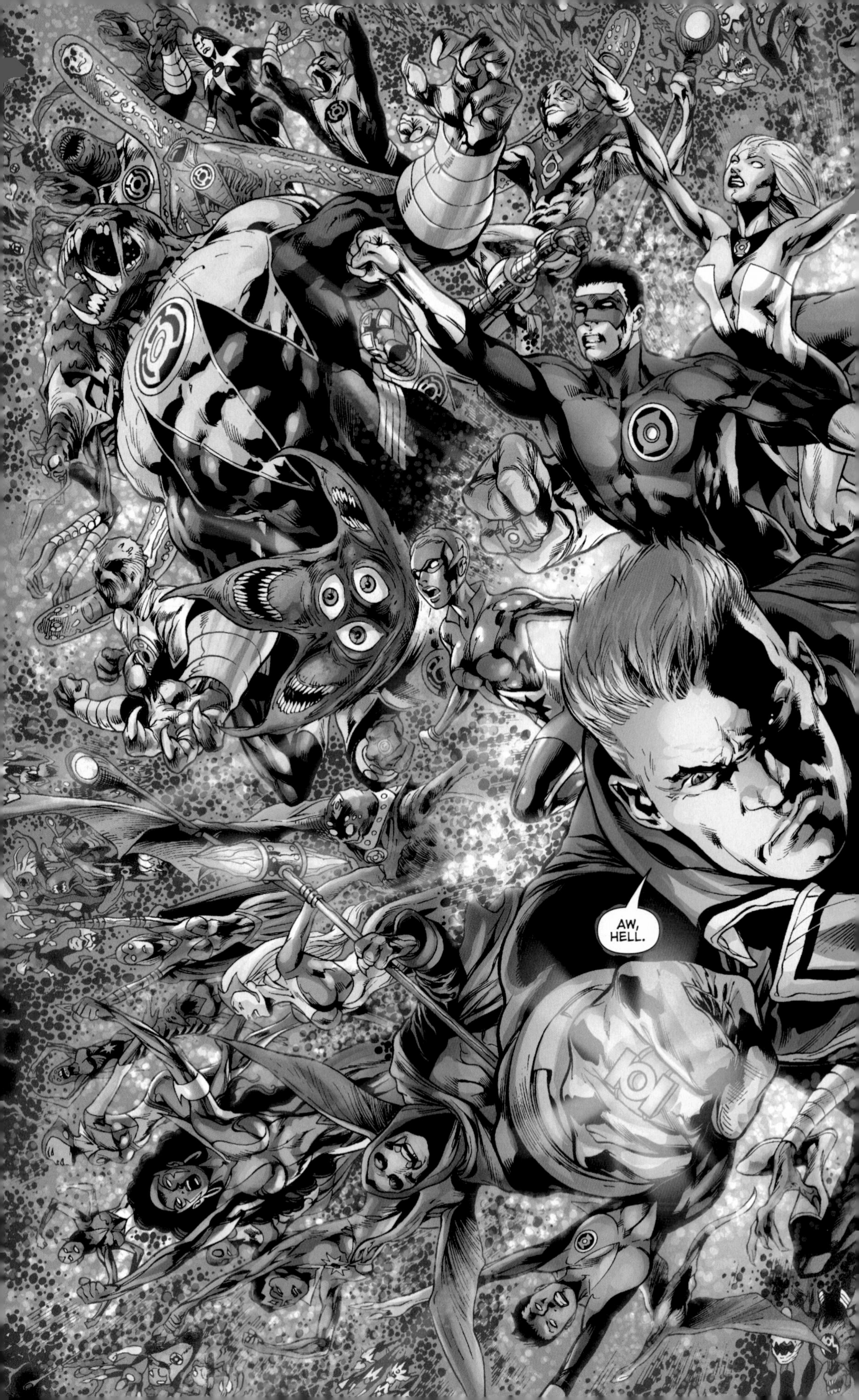
AW, HELL.

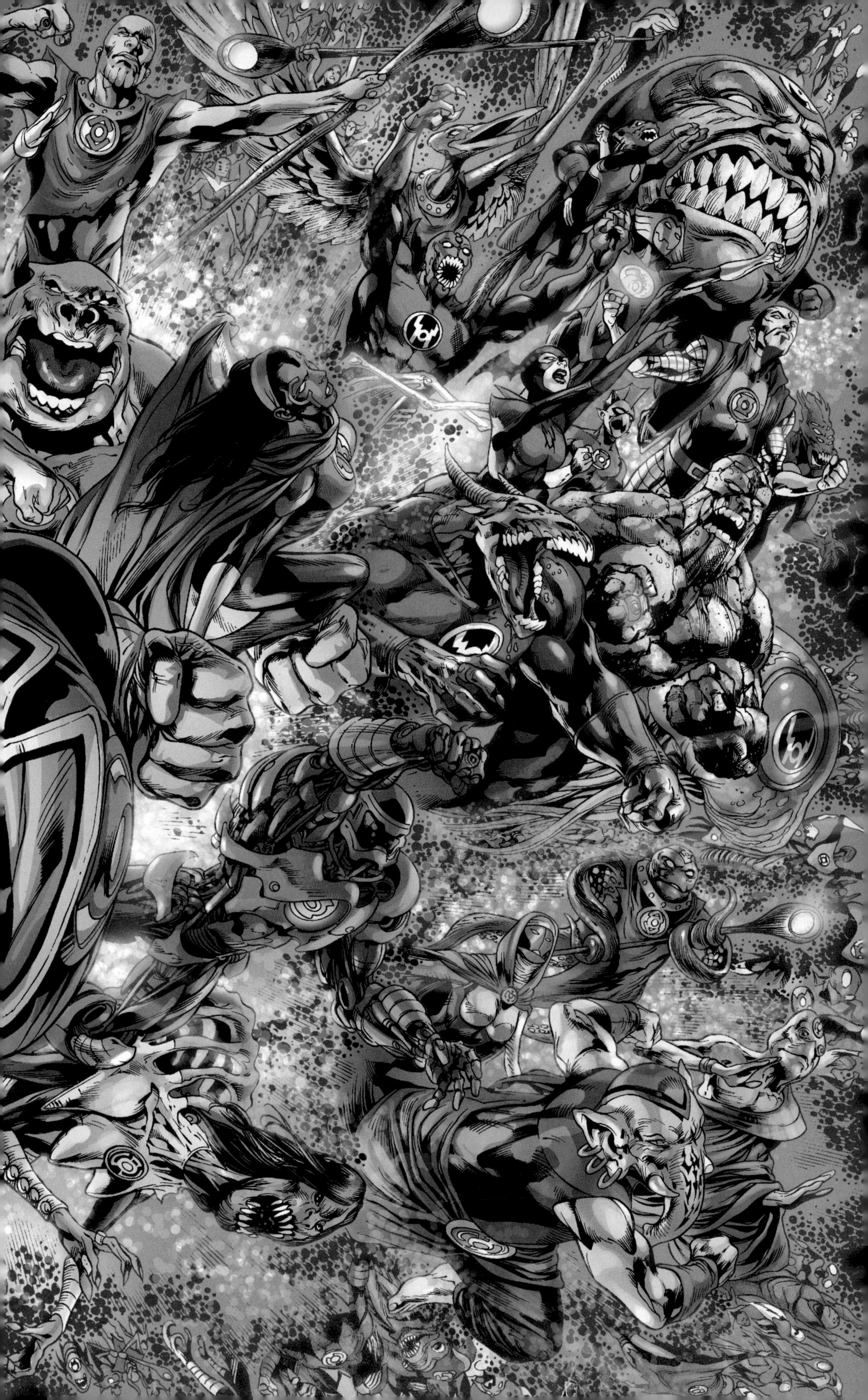

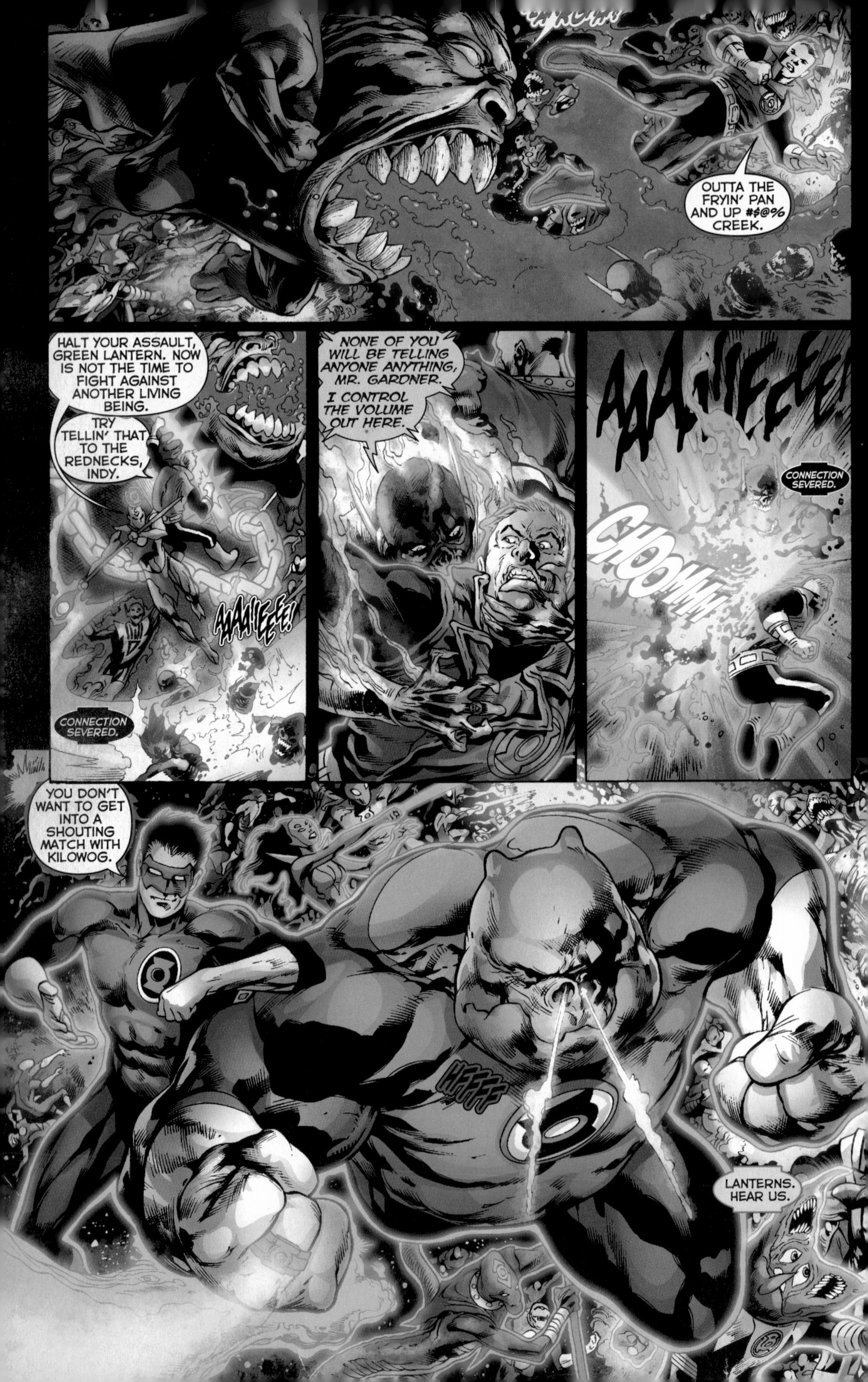
OUTTA THE FRYIN' PAN AND UP #$@% CREEK.
HALT YOUR ASSAULT, GREEN LANTERN. NOW IS NOT THE TIME TO FIGHT AGAINST ANOTHER LIVING BEING.
TRY TELLIN' THAT TO THE REDNECKS, INDY.
CONNECTION SEVERED.
NONE OF YOU WILL BE TELLING ANYONE ANYTHING, MR. GARDNER.
I CONTROL THE VOLUME OUT HERE.
CONNECTION SEVERED.
CHOOMM
YOU DON'T WANT TO GET INTO A SHOUTING MATCH WITH KILOWOG.
LANTERNS. HEAR US.

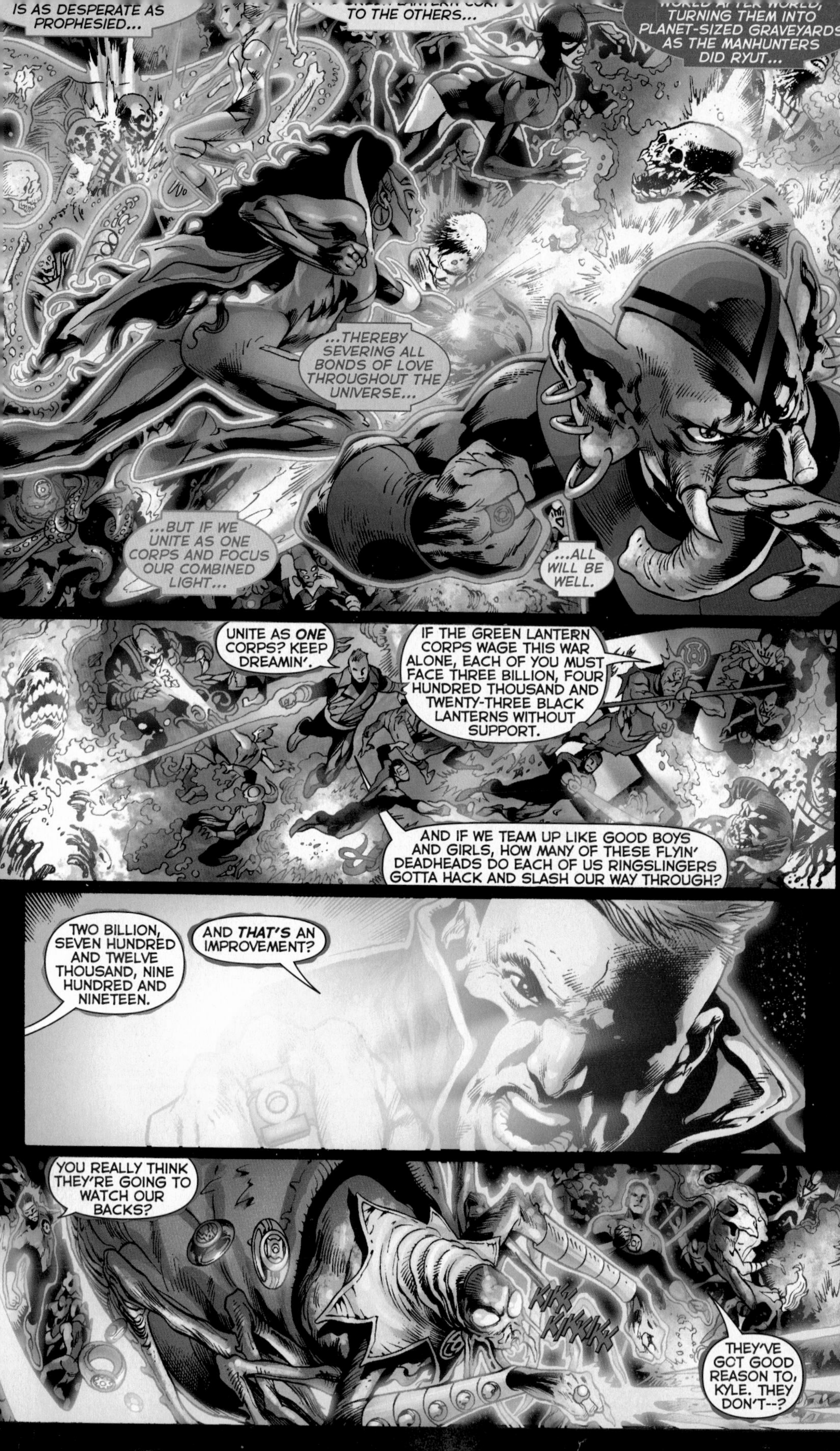
IS AS DESPERATE AS PROPHESIED...
TO THE OTHERS...
TURNING THEM INTO PLANET-SIZED GRAVEYARDS AS THE MANHUNTERS DID RYUT...
...THEREBY SEVERING ALL BONDS OF LOVE THROUGHOUT THE UNIVERSE...
...BUT IF WE UNITE AS ONE CORPS AND FOCUS OUR COMBINED LIGHT...
...ALL WILL BE WELL.
UNITE AS *ONE* CORPS? KEEP DREAMIN'.
IF THE GREEN LANTERN CORPS WAGE THIS WAR ALONE, EACH OF YOU MUST FACE THREE BILLION, FOUR HUNDRED THOUSAND AND TWENTY-THREE BLACK LANTERNS WITHOUT SUPPORT.
AND IF WE TEAM UP LIKE GOOD BOYS AND GIRLS, HOW MANY OF THESE FLYIN' DEADHEADS DO EACH OF US RINGSLINGERS GOTTA HACK AND SLASH OUR WAY THROUGH?
TWO BILLION, SEVEN HUNDRED AND TWELVE THOUSAND, NINE HUNDRED AND NINETEEN.
AND *THAT'S* AN IMPROVEMENT?
YOU REALLY THINK THEY'RE GOING TO WATCH OUR BACKS?
KIKK KIKKKKK
THEY'VE GOT GOOD REASON TO, KYLE. THEY DON'T--?

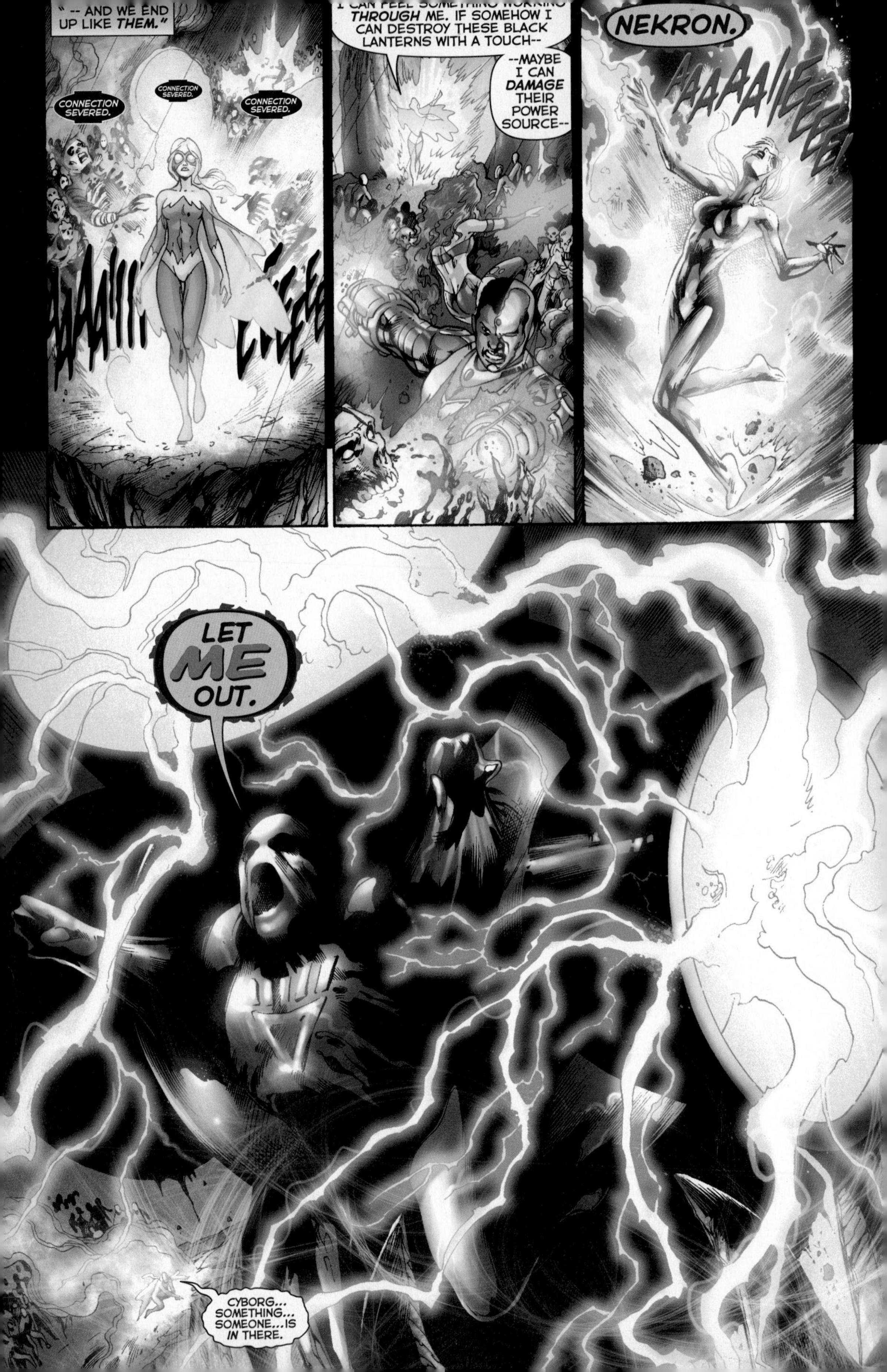
" -- AND WE END UP LIKE THEM."
CONNECTION SEVERED.
CONNECTION SEVERED.
CONNECTION SEVERED.
THROUGH ME. IF SOMEHOW I CAN DESTROY THESE BLACK LANTERNS WITH A TOUCH--
--MAYBE I CAN DAMAGE THEIR POWER SOURCE--
NEKRON.
AAAAAIIEEEEE!
LET ME OUT.
CYBORG... SOMETHING... SOMEONE...IS IN THERE.

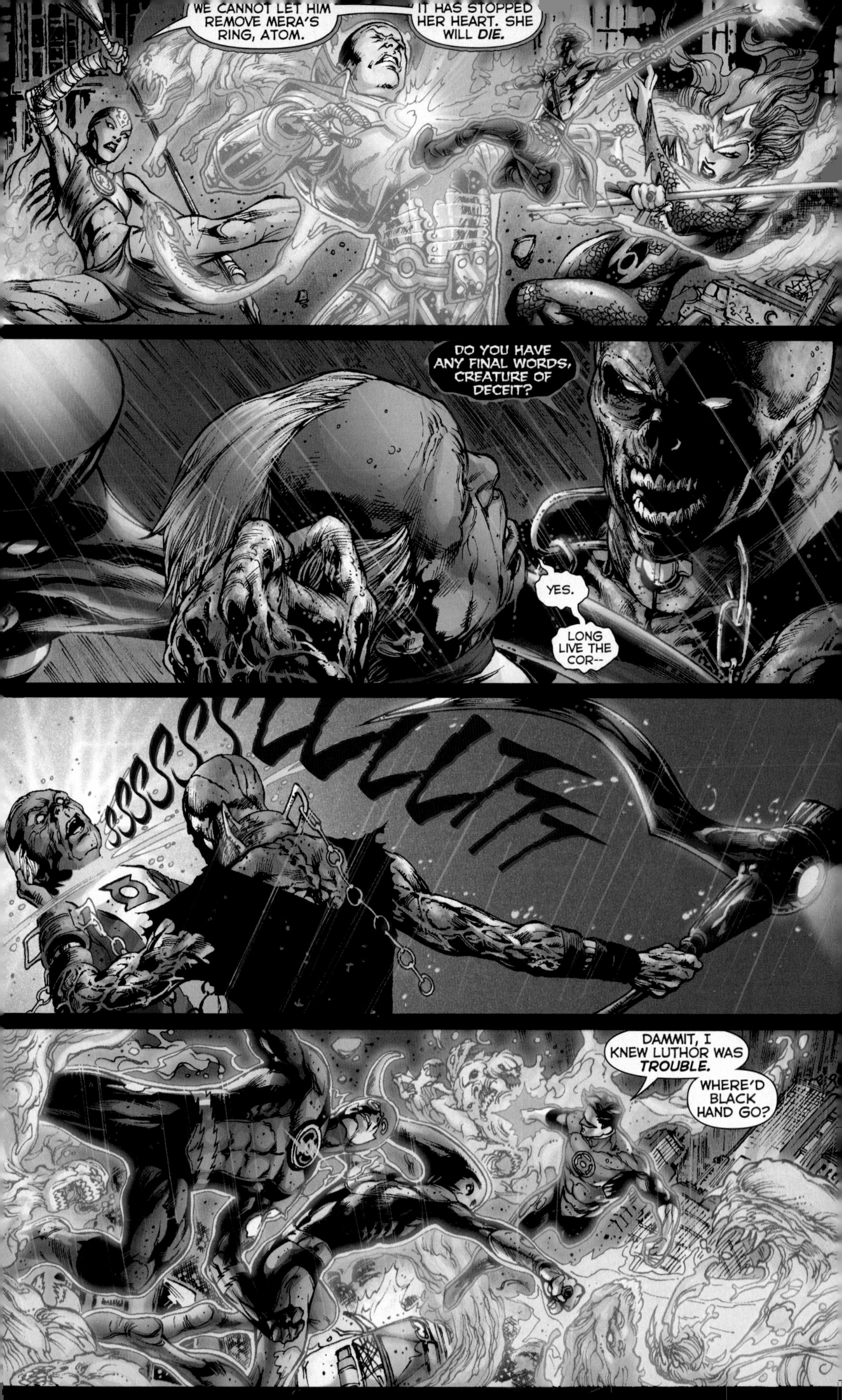
WE CANNOT LET HIM REMOVE MERA'S RING, ATOM.
IT HAS STOPPED HER HEART. SHE WILL *DIE.*
DO YOU HAVE ANY FINAL WORDS, CREATURE OF DECEIT?
YES.
LONG LIVE THE COR--
SSSSSSCHLLLLITT
DAMMIT, I KNEW LUTHOR WAS *TROUBLE.*
WHERE'D BLACK HAND GO?

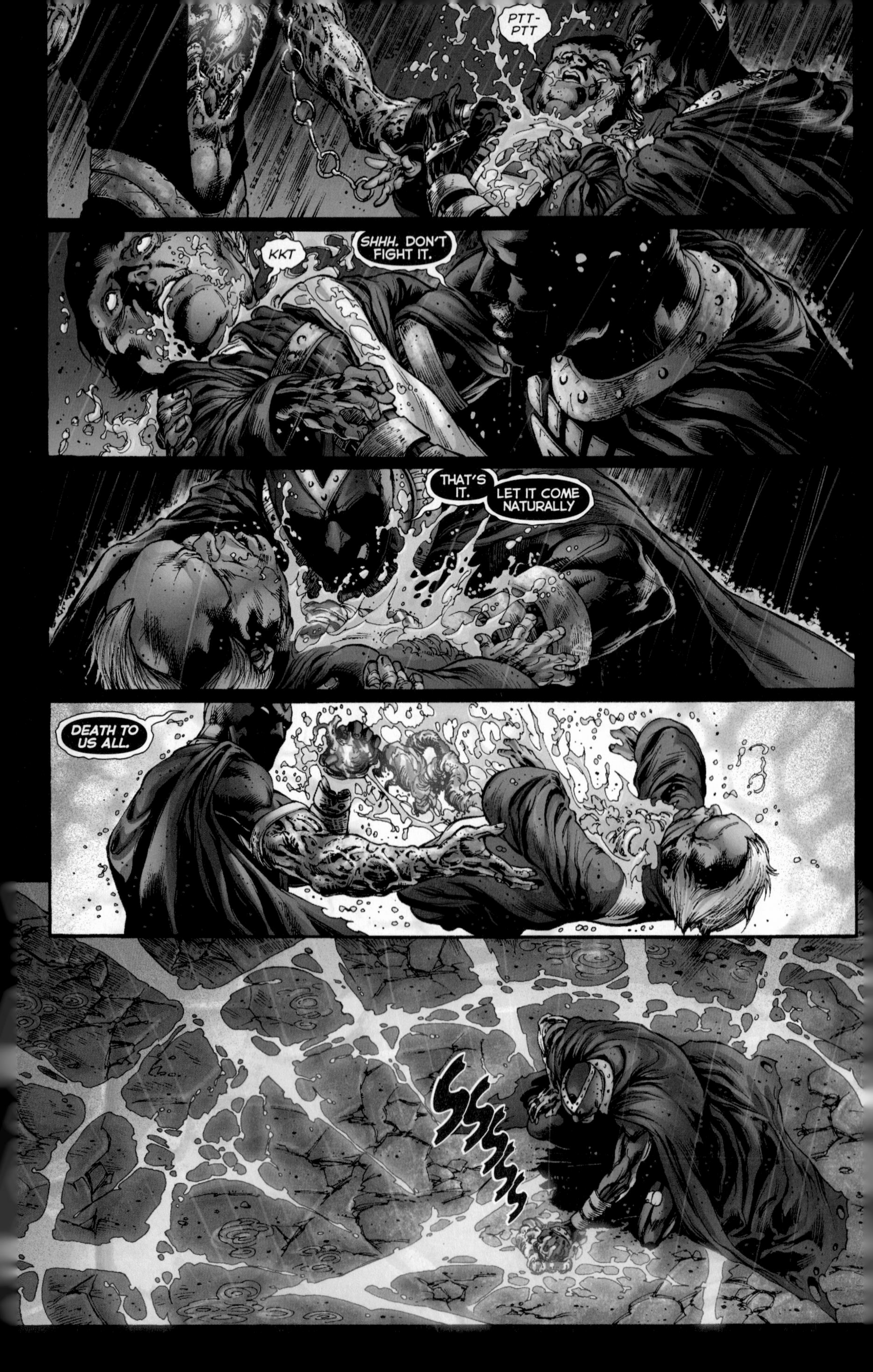
PTT-PTT
KKT
SHHH. DON'T FIGHT IT.
THAT'S IT.
LET IT COME NATURALLY
DEATH TO US ALL.
SSSSSS

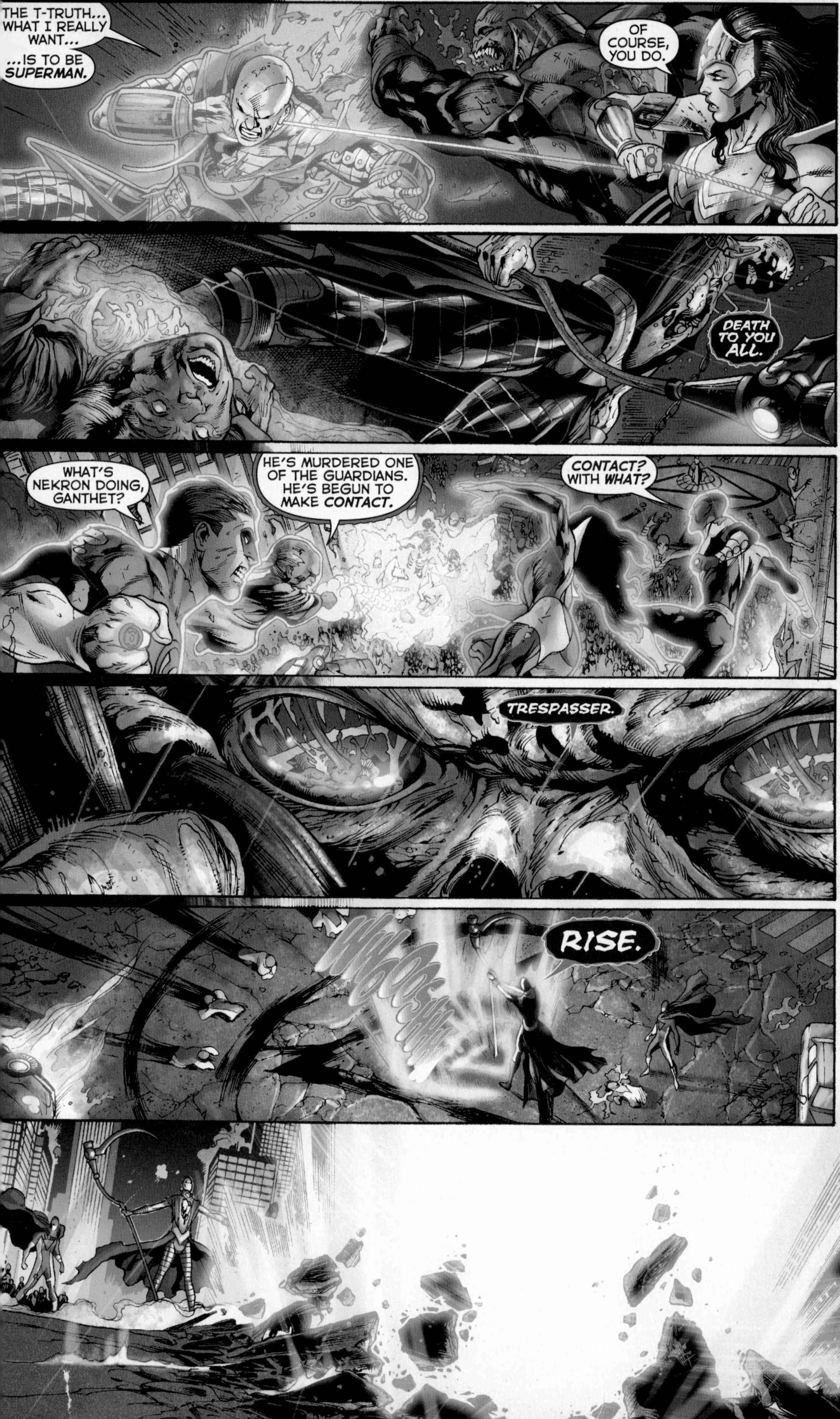
THE T-TRUTH... WHAT I REALLY WANT... ...IS TO BE SUPERMAN.
OF COURSE, YOU DO.
DEATH TO YOU ALL.
WHAT'S NEKRON DOING, GANTHET?
HE'S MURDERED ONE OF THE GUARDIANS. HE'S BEGUN TO MAKE CONTACT.
CONTACT? WITH WHAT?
TRESPASSER.
WHOOSHH
RISE.

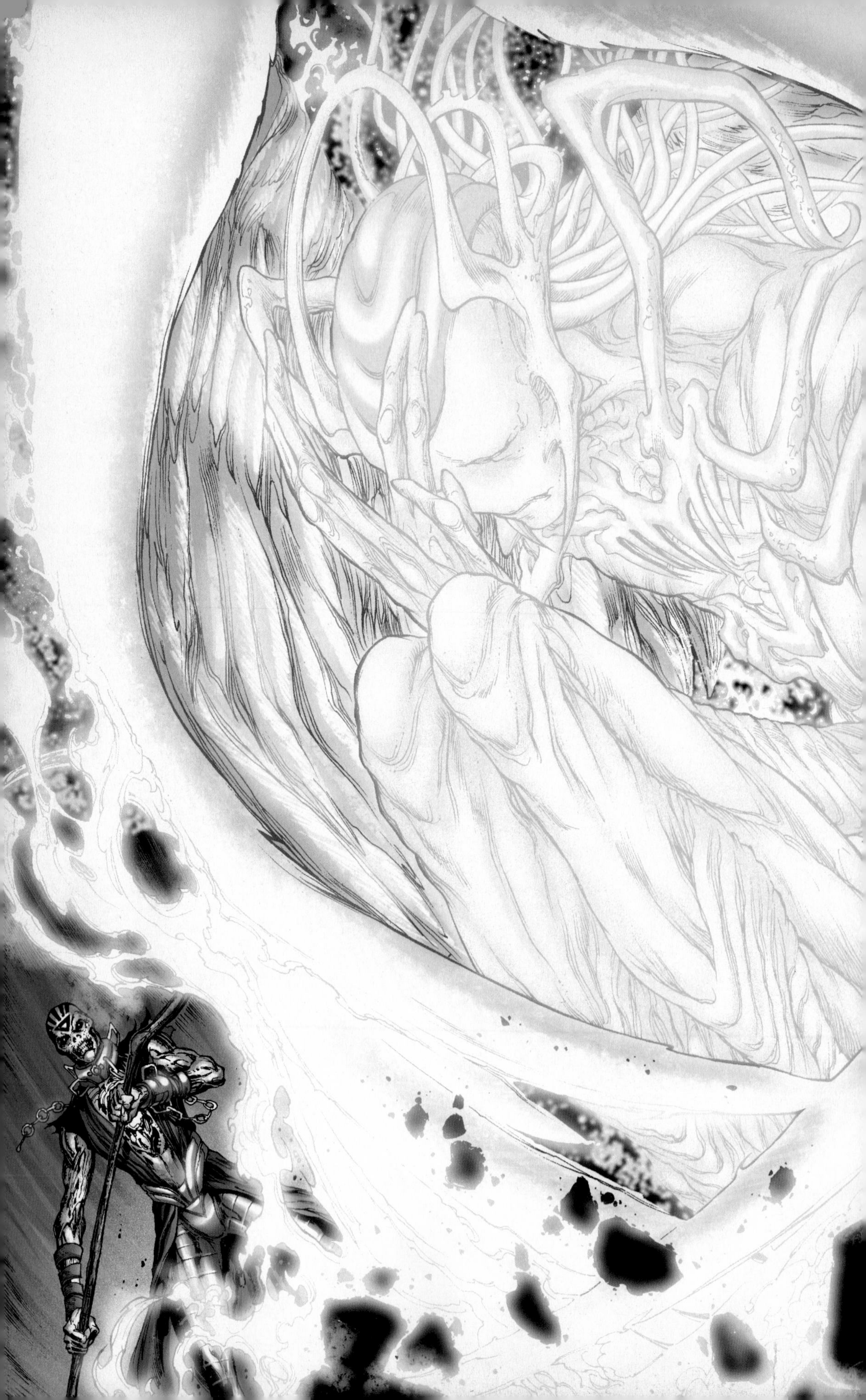

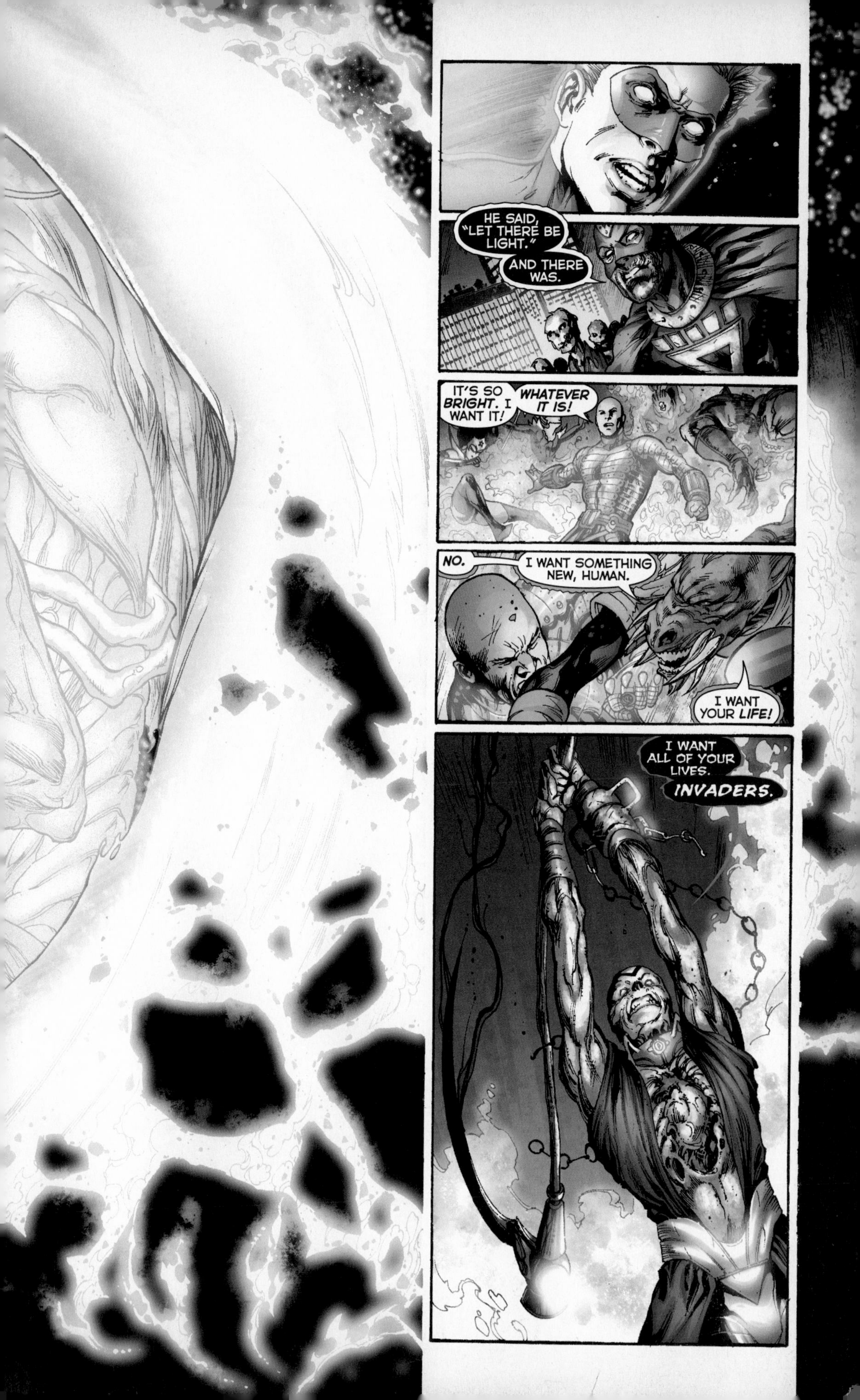
HE SAID, "LET THERE BE LIGHT."
AND THERE WAS.
IT'S SO BRIGHT. I WANT IT!
WHATEVER IT IS!
NO.
I WANT SOMETHING NEW, HUMAN.
I WANT YOUR LIFE!
I WANT ALL OF YOUR LIVES.
INVADERS.

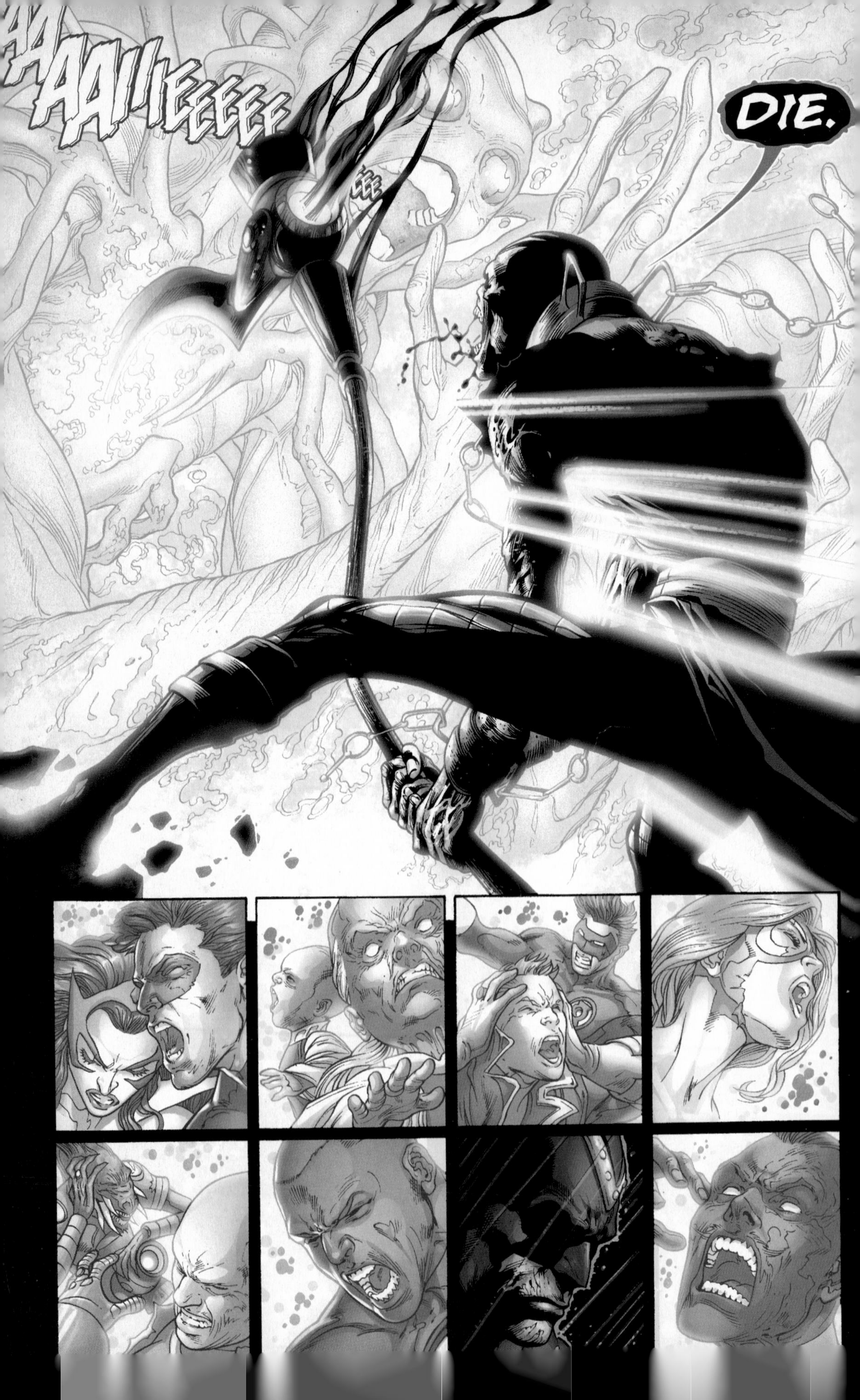
AAAAIIEEEEE
EEE
DIE.

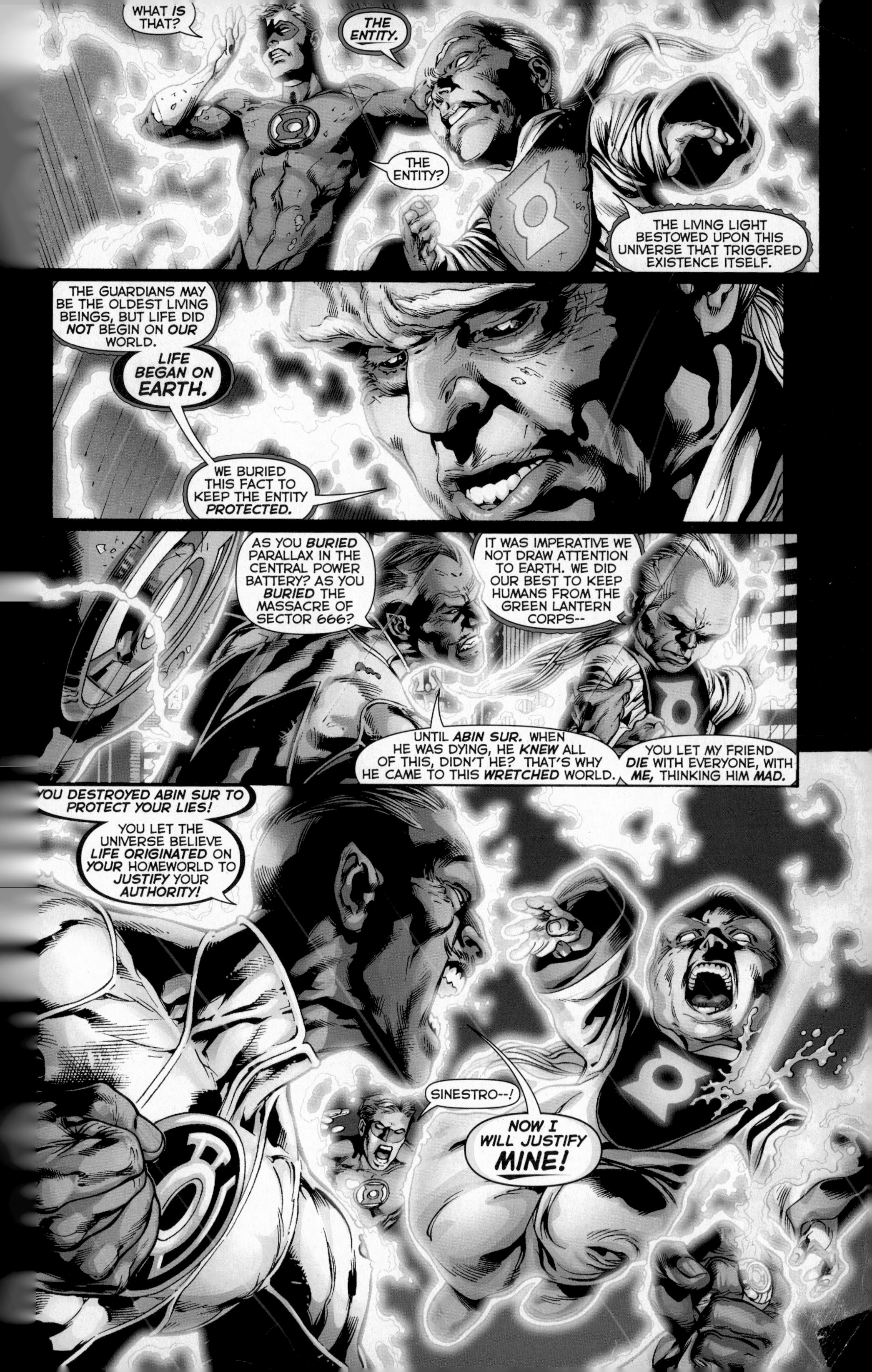
WHAT IS THAT?
THE ENTITY.
THE ENTITY?
THE LIVING LIGHT BESTOWED UPON THIS UNIVERSE THAT TRIGGERED EXISTENCE ITSELF.
THE GUARDIANS MAY BE THE OLDEST LIVING BEINGS, BUT LIFE DID NOT BEGIN ON OUR WORLD.
LIFE BEGAN ON EARTH.
WE BURIED THIS FACT TO KEEP THE ENTITY PROTECTED.
AS YOU BURIED PARALLAX IN THE CENTRAL POWER BATTERY? AS YOU BURIED THE MASSACRE OF SECTOR 666?
IT WAS IMPERATIVE WE NOT DRAW ATTENTION TO EARTH. WE DID OUR BEST TO KEEP HUMANS FROM THE GREEN LANTERN CORPS--
UNTIL ABIN SUR. WHEN HE WAS DYING, HE KNEW ALL OF THIS, DIDN'T HE? THAT'S WHY HE CAME TO THIS WRETCHED WORLD.
YOU LET MY FRIEND DIE WITH EVERYONE, WITH ME, THINKING HIM MAD.
YOU DESTROYED ABIN SUR TO PROTECT YOUR LIES!
YOU LET THE UNIVERSE BELIEVE LIFE ORIGINATED ON YOUR HOMEWORLD TO JUSTIFY YOUR AUTHORITY!
SINESTRO--!
NOW I WILL JUSTIFY MINE!

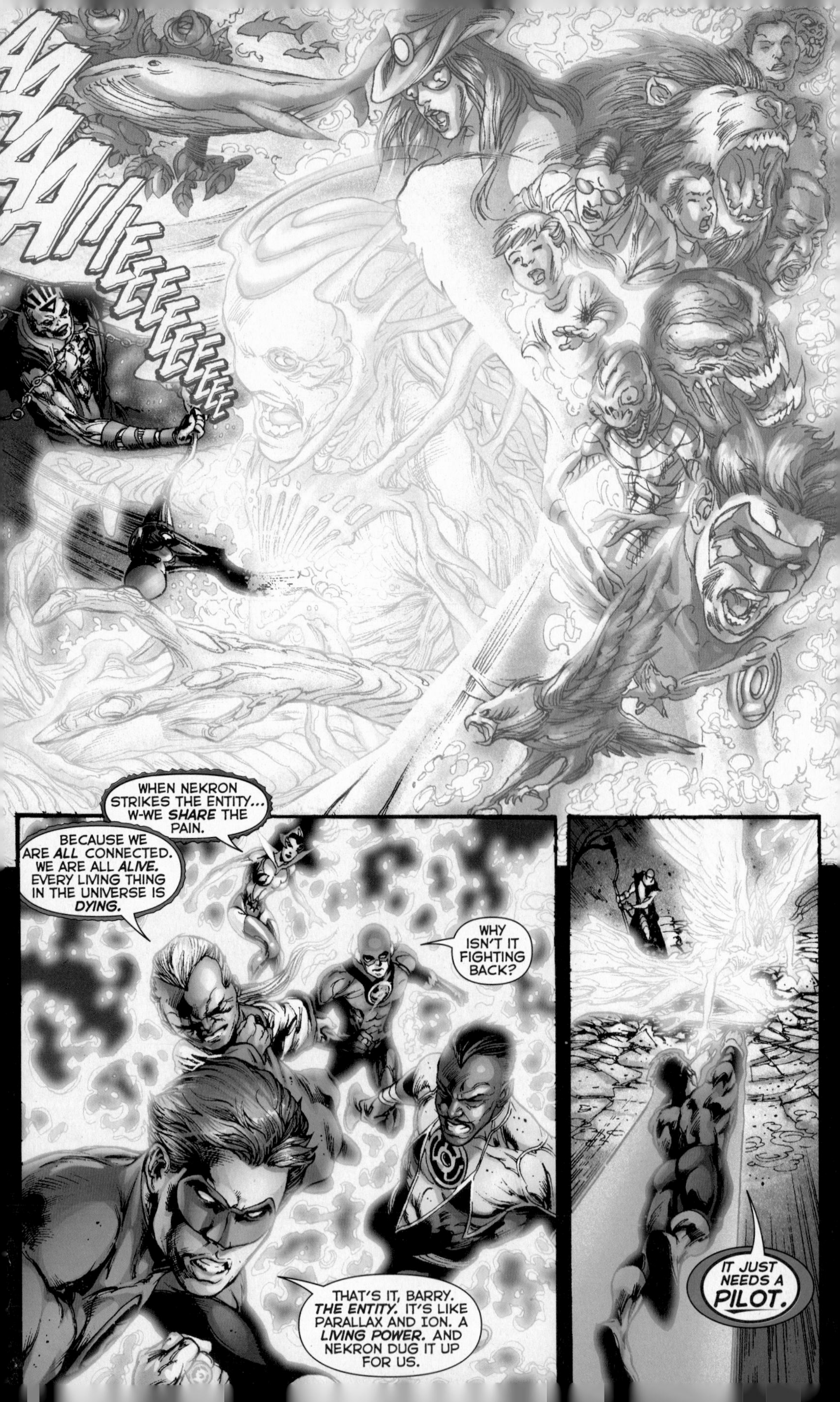
AAAAIIEEEEEEEEE
WHEN NEKRON STRIKES THE ENTITY... W-WE SHARE THE PAIN.
BECAUSE WE ARE ALL CONNECTED. WE ARE ALL ALIVE. EVERY LIVING THING IN THE UNIVERSE IS DYING.
WHY ISN'T IT FIGHTING BACK?
THAT'S IT, BARRY. THE ENTITY. IT'S LIKE PARALLAX AND ION. A LIVING POWER. AND NEKRON DUG IT UP FOR US.
IT JUST NEEDS A PILOT.

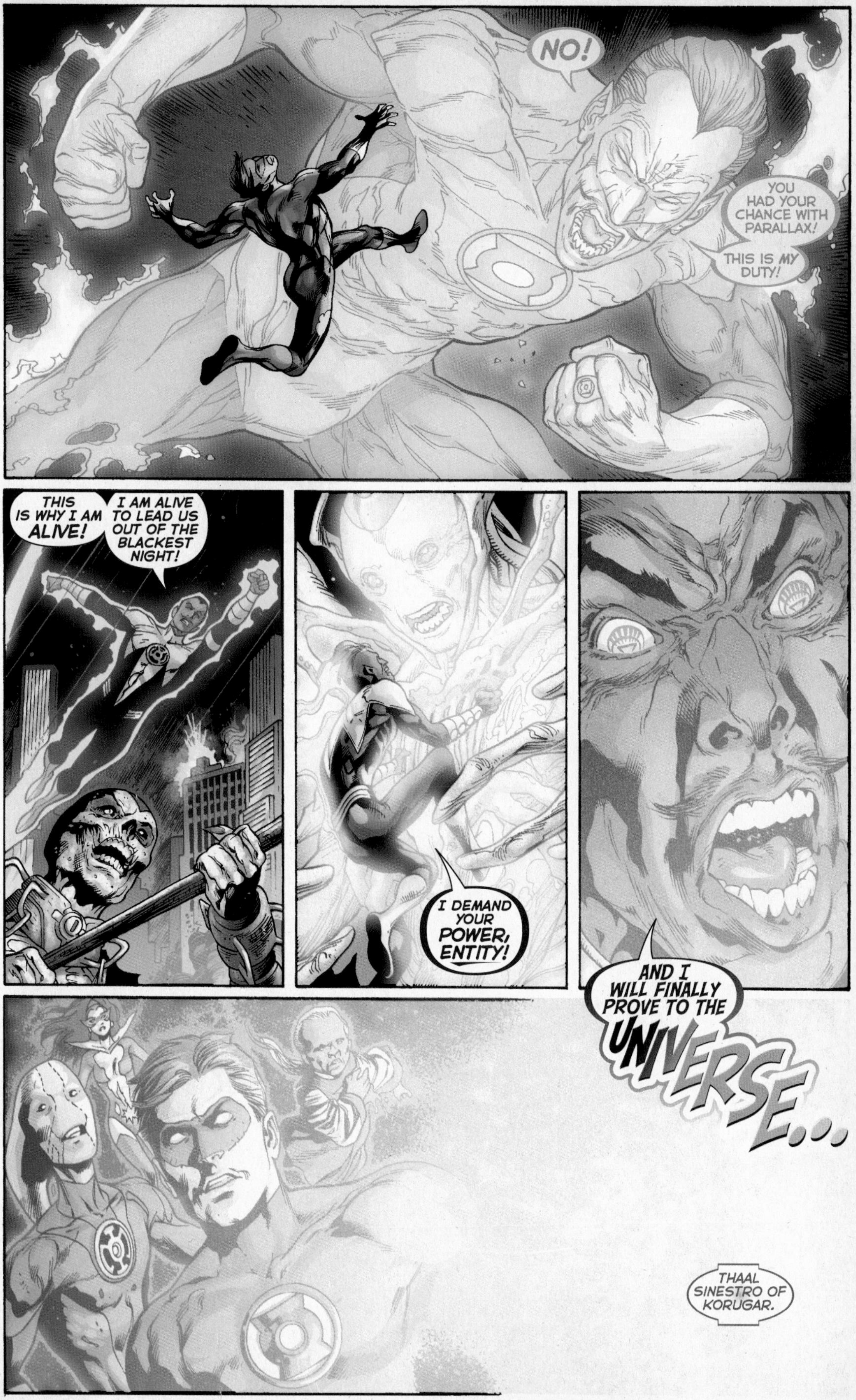
NO!
YOU HAD YOUR CHANCE WITH PARALLAX!
THIS IS MY DUTY!
THIS IS WHY I AM ALIVE!
I AM ALIVE TO LEAD US OUT OF THE BLACKEST NIGHT!
I DEMAND YOUR POWER, ENTITY!
AND I WILL FINALLY PROVE TO THE
UNIVERSE...
THAAL SINESTRO OF KORUGAR.

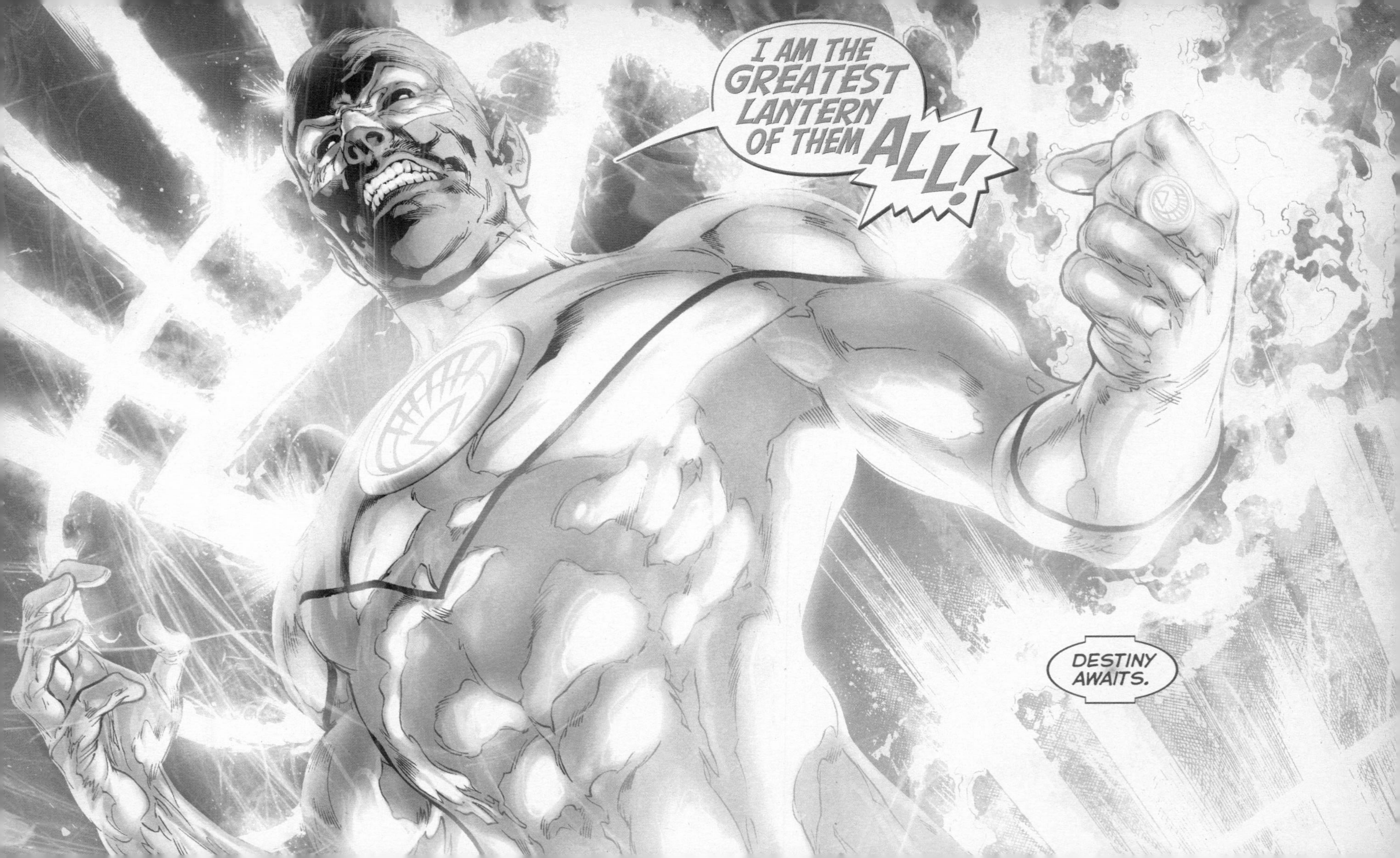
I AM THE GREATEST LANTERN OF THEM ALL!
DESTINY AWAITS.

PART EIGHT

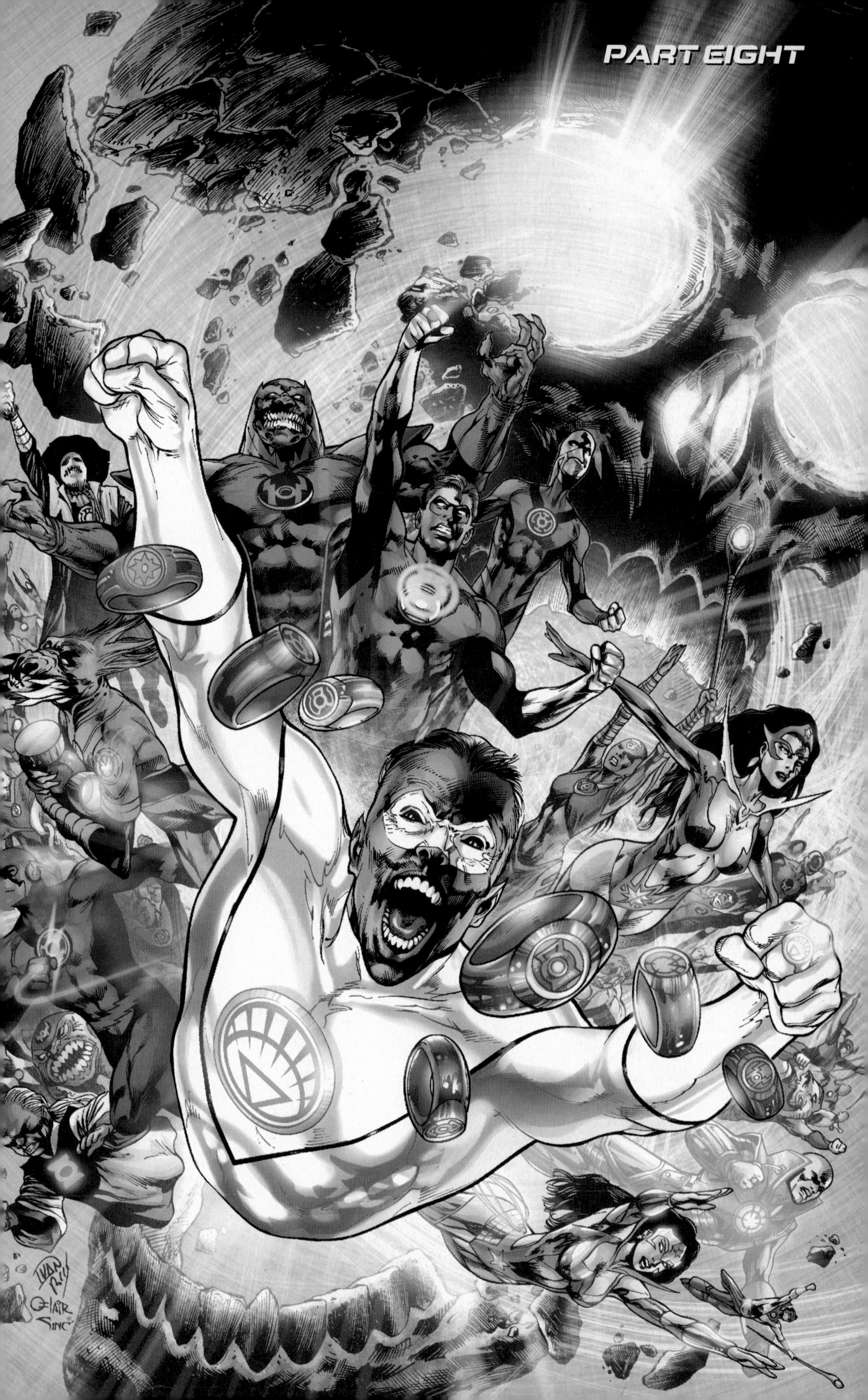

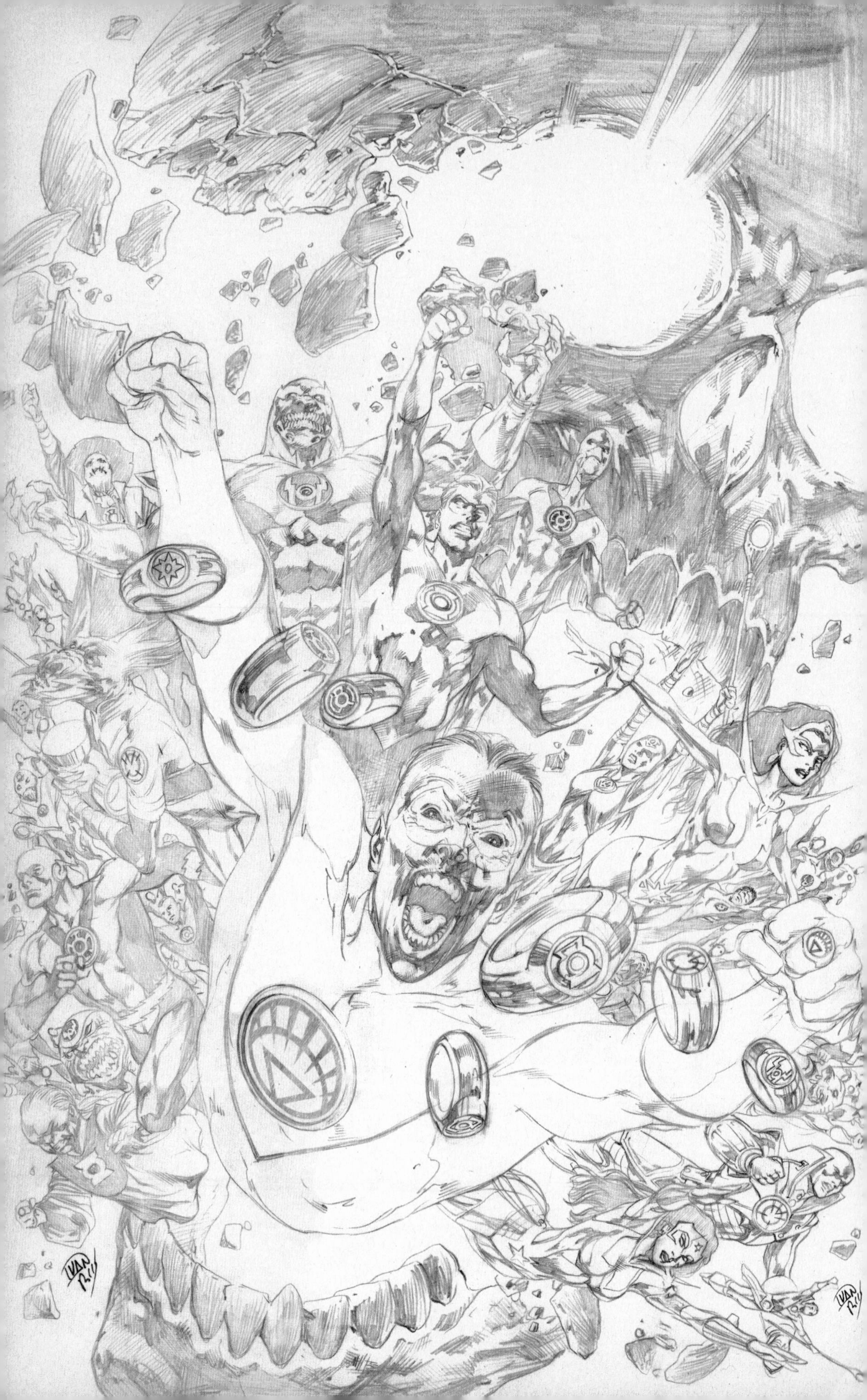

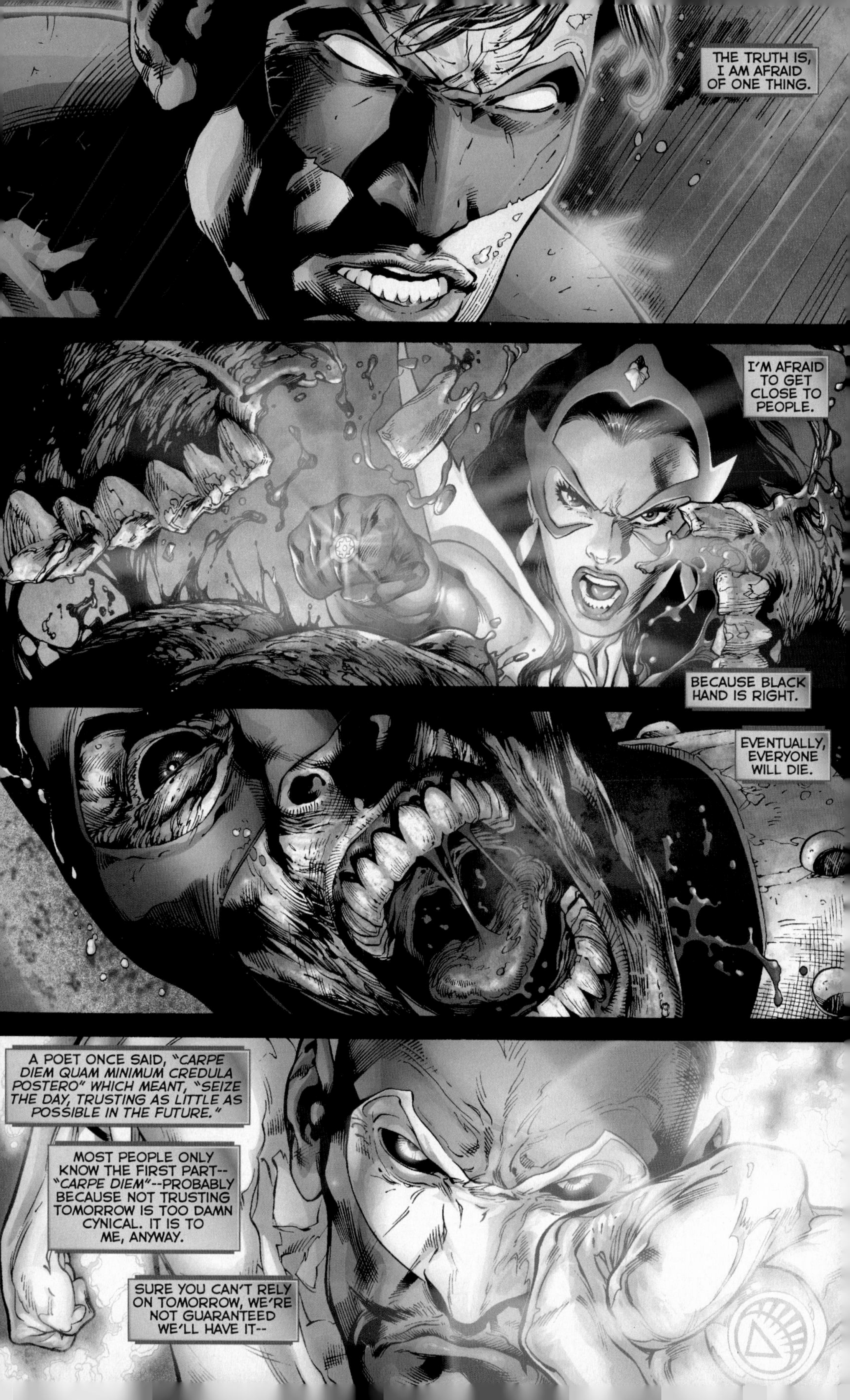

THE TRUTH IS, I AM AFRAID OF ONE THING.
I'M AFRAID TO GET CLOSE TO PEOPLE.
BECAUSE BLACK HAND IS RIGHT.
EVENTUALLY, EVERYONE WILL DIE.
A POET ONCE SAID, "CARPE DIEM QUAM MINIMUM CREDULA POSTERO" WHICH MEANT, "SEIZE THE DAY, TRUSTING AS LITTLE AS POSSIBLE IN THE FUTURE."
MOST PEOPLE ONLY KNOW THE FIRST PART--"CARPE DIEM"--PROBABLY BECAUSE NOT TRUSTING TOMORROW IS TOO DAMN CYNICAL. IT IS TO ME, ANYWAY.
SURE YOU CAN'T RELY ON TOMORROW, WE'RE NOT GUARANTEED WE'LL HAVE IT--

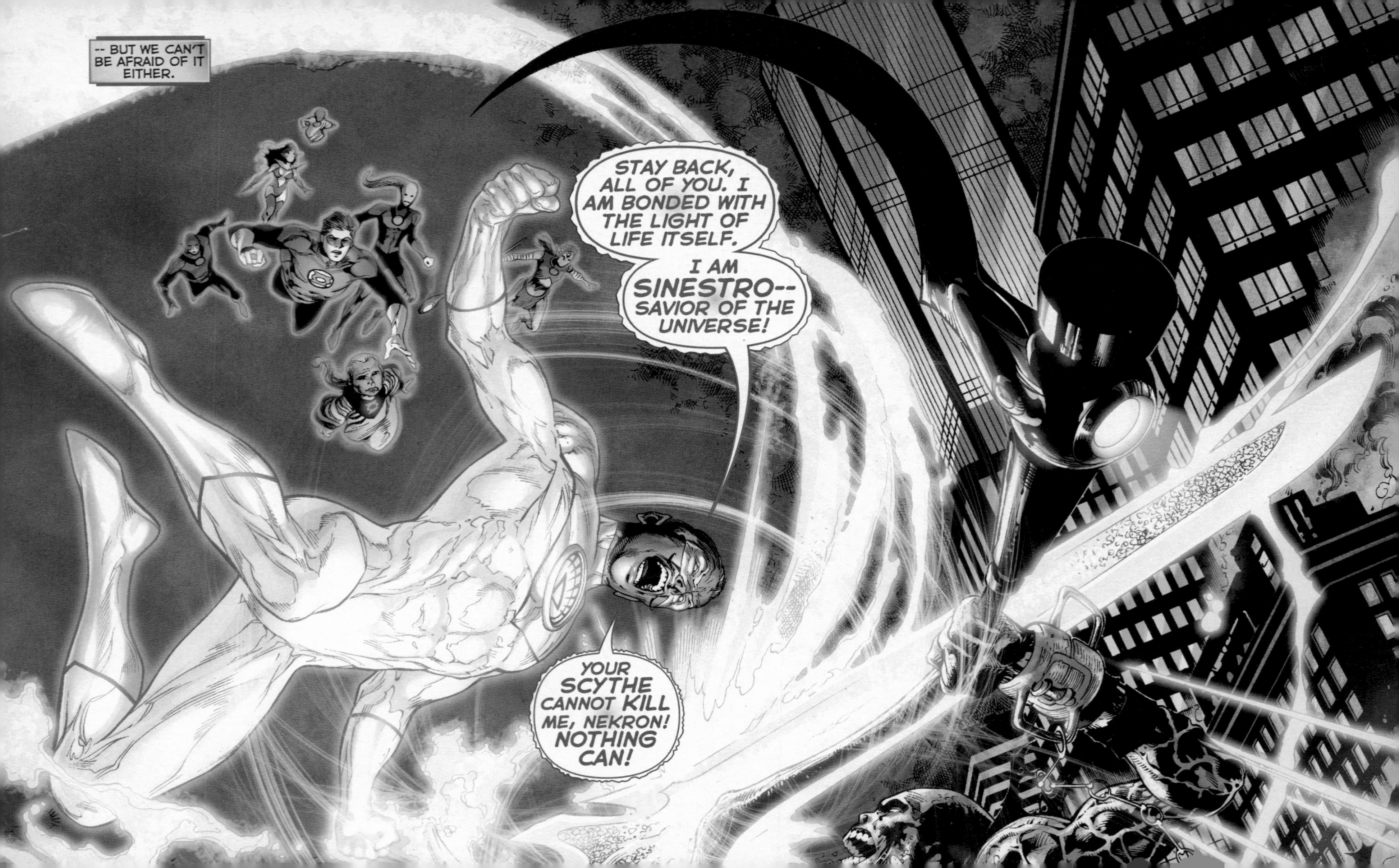
-- BUT WE CAN'T BE AFRAID OF IT EITHER.
STAY BACK, ALL OF YOU. I AM BONDED WITH THE LIGHT OF LIFE ITSELF.
I AM SINESTRO-- SAVIOR OF THE UNIVERSE!
YOUR SCYTHE CANNOT KILL ME, NEKRON! NOTHING CAN!

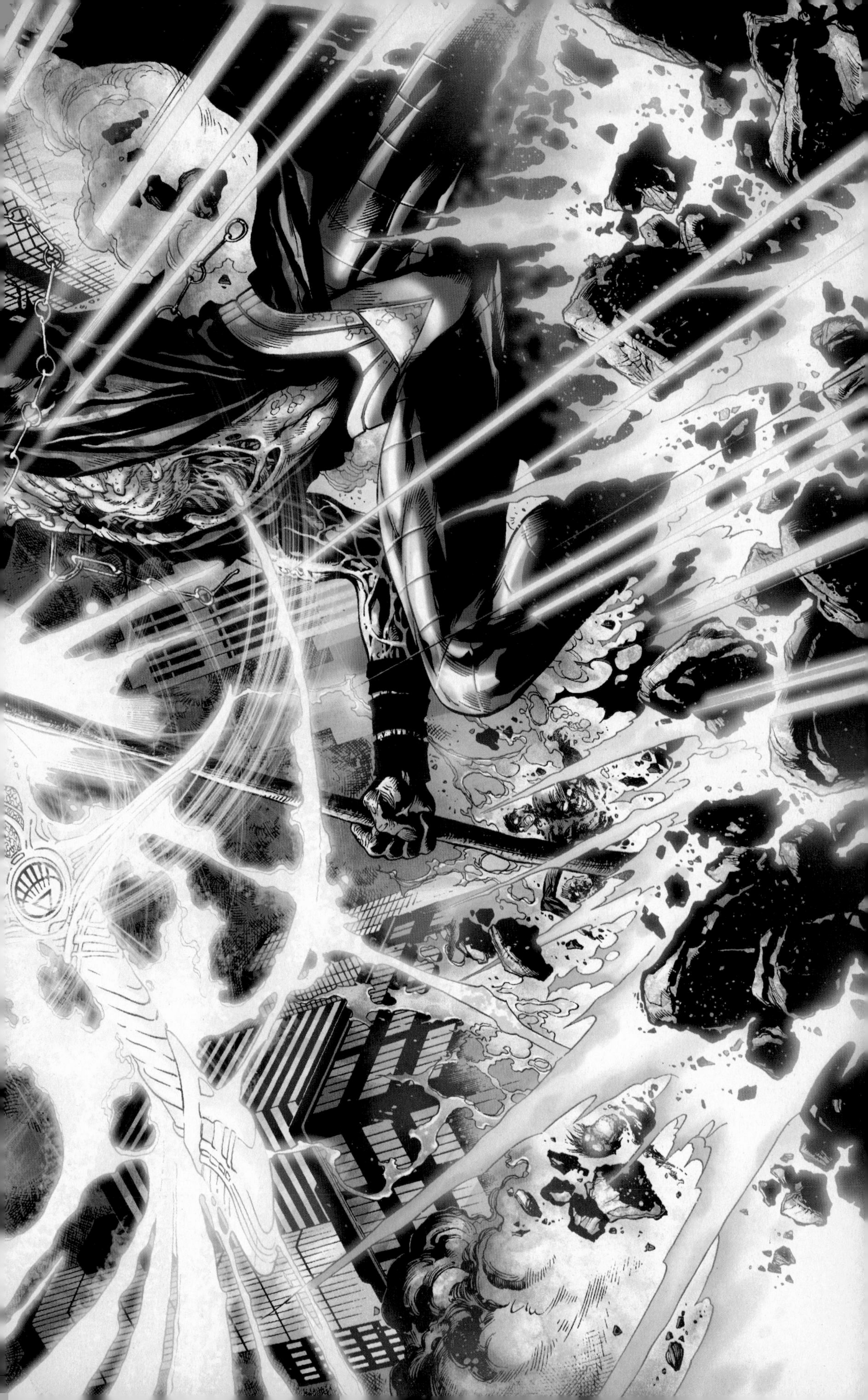

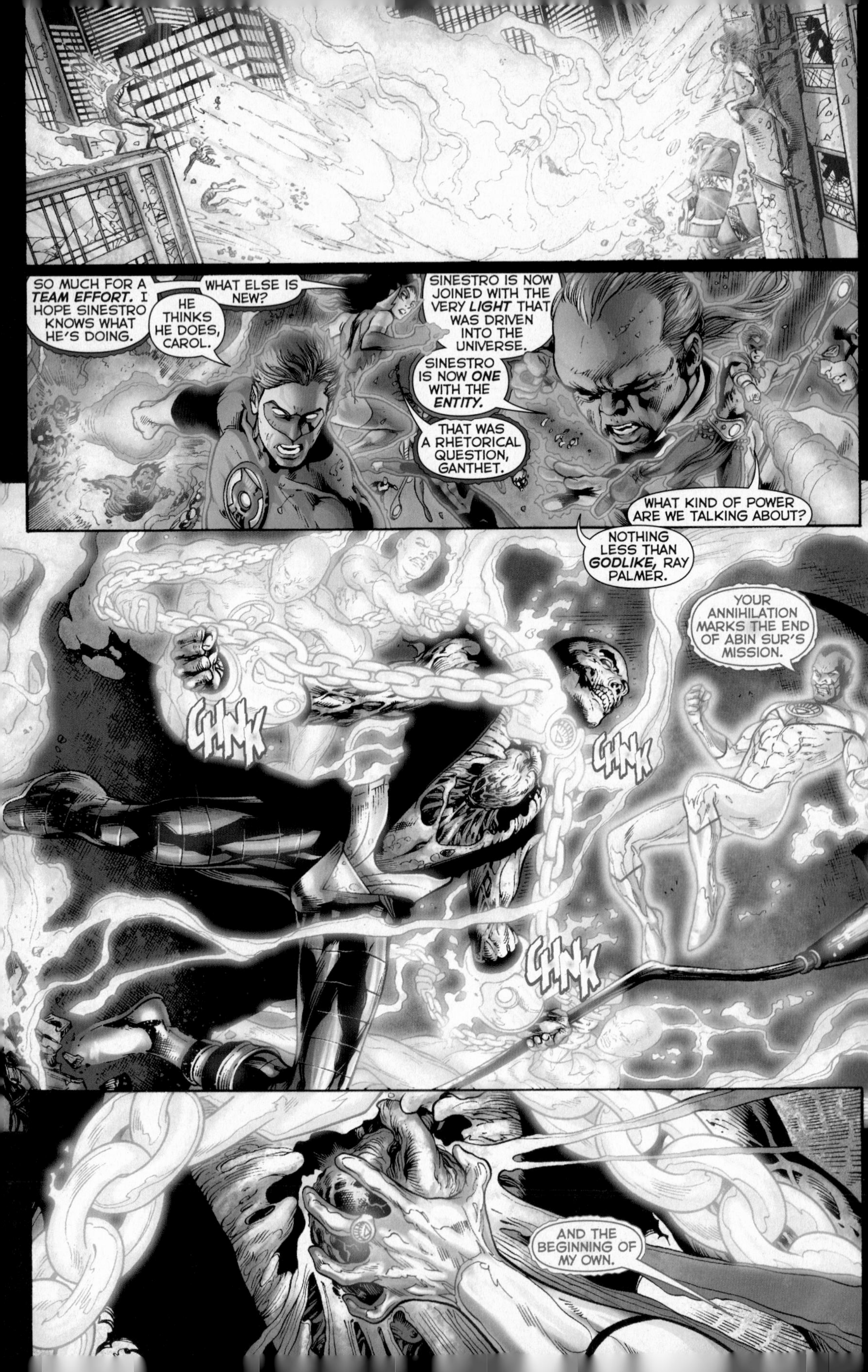
SO MUCH FOR A TEAM EFFORT. I HOPE SINESTRO KNOWS WHAT HE'S DOING.
WHAT ELSE IS NEW?
HE THINKS HE DOES, CAROL.
SINESTRO IS NOW JOINED WITH THE VERY LIGHT THAT WAS DRIVEN INTO THE UNIVERSE.
SINESTRO IS NOW ONE WITH THE ENTITY.
THAT WAS A RHETORICAL QUESTION, GANTHET.
WHAT KIND OF POWER ARE WE TALKING ABOUT?
NOTHING LESS THAN GODLIKE, RAY PALMER.
YOUR ANNIHILATION MARKS THE END OF ABIN SUR'S MISSION.
CHNK
CHNK
CHNK
AND THE BEGINNING OF MY OWN.

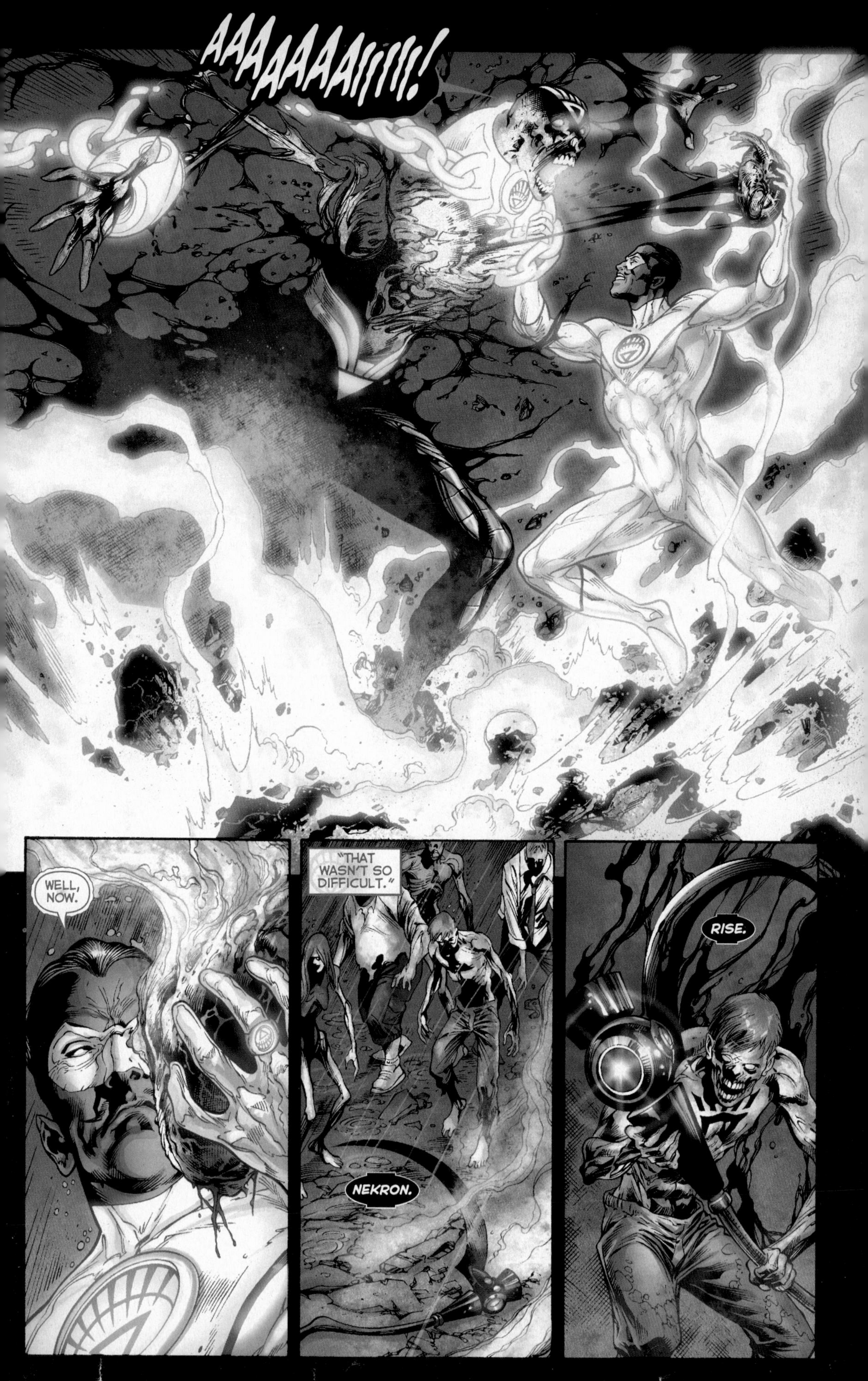
AAAAAAAIIIII!
WELL, NOW.
"THAT WASN'T SO DIFFICULT."
NEKRON.
RISE.

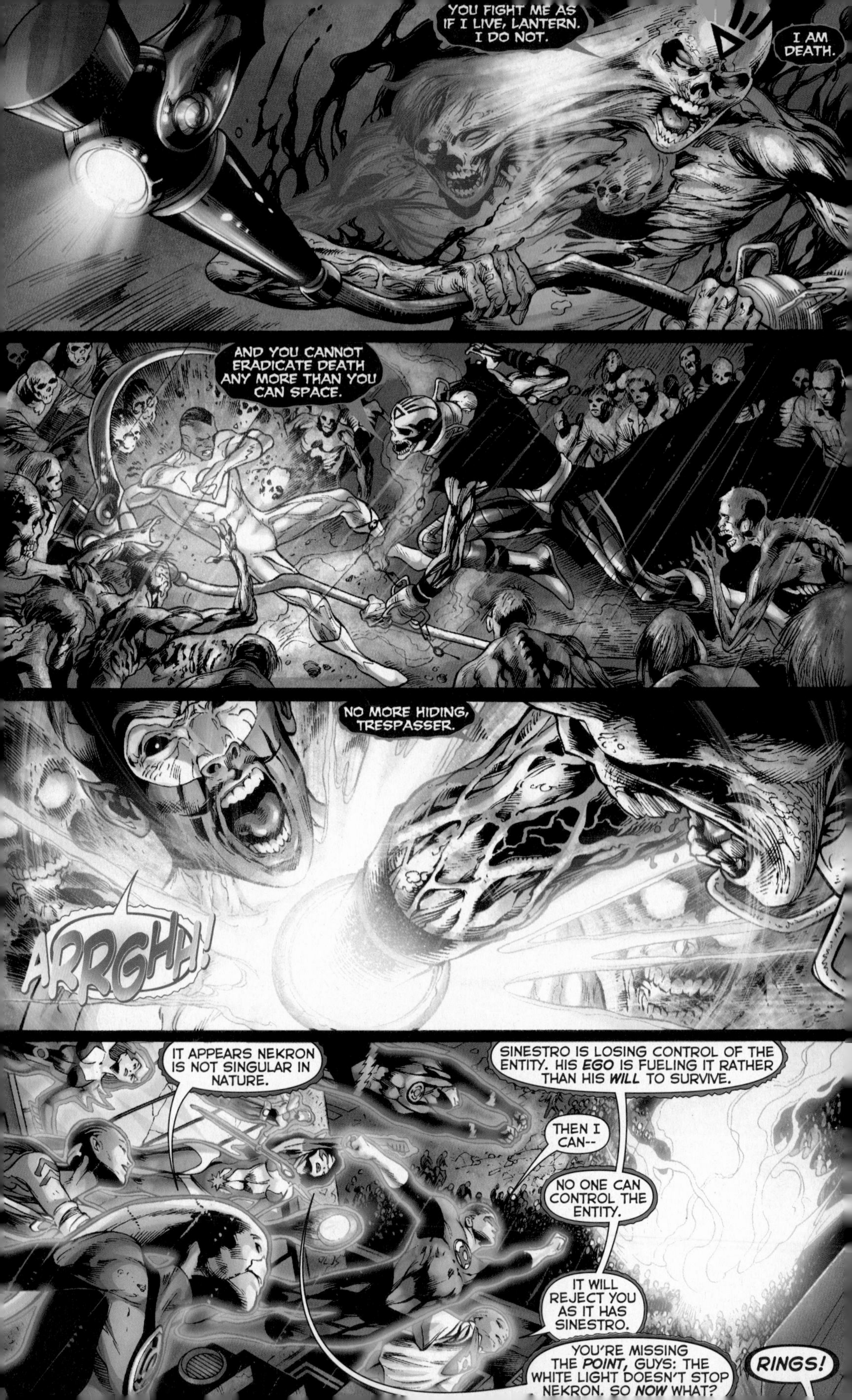
YOU FIGHT ME AS IF I LIVE, LANTERN. I DO NOT.
I AM DEATH.
AND YOU CANNOT ERADICATE DEATH ANY MORE THAN YOU CAN SPACE.
NO MORE HIDING, TRESPASSER.
ARRGHH!
IT APPEARS NEKRON IS NOT SINGULAR IN NATURE.
SINESTRO IS LOSING CONTROL OF THE ENTITY. HIS EGO IS FUELING IT RATHER THAN HIS WILL TO SURVIVE.
THEN I CAN--
NO ONE CAN CONTROL THE ENTITY.
IT WILL REJECT YOU AS IT HAS SINESTRO.
YOU'RE MISSING THE POINT, GUYS: THE WHITE LIGHT DOESN'T STOP NEKRON. SO NOW WHAT?
RINGS!

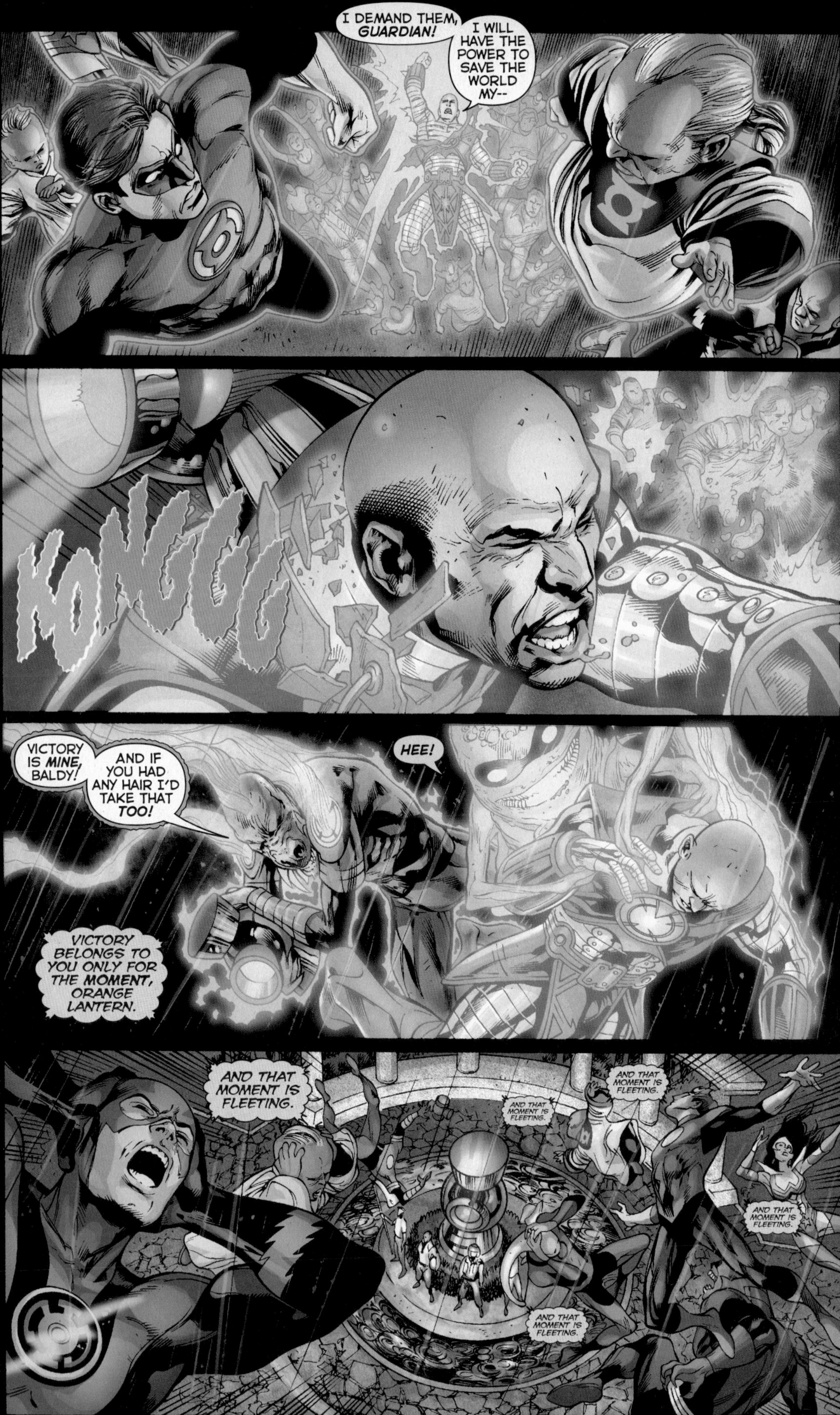
I DEMAND THEM, GUARDIAN!
I WILL HAVE THE POWER TO SAVE THE WORLD MY--
KONGGG
VICTORY IS MINE, BALDY!
AND IF YOU HAD ANY HAIR I'D TAKE THAT TOO!
HEE!
VICTORY BELONGS TO YOU ONLY FOR THE MOMENT, ORANGE LANTERN.
AND THAT MOMENT IS FLEETING.
AND THAT MOMENT IS FLEETING.
AND THAT MOMENT IS FLEETING.
AND THAT MOMENT IS FLEETING.
AND THAT MOMENT IS FLEETING.

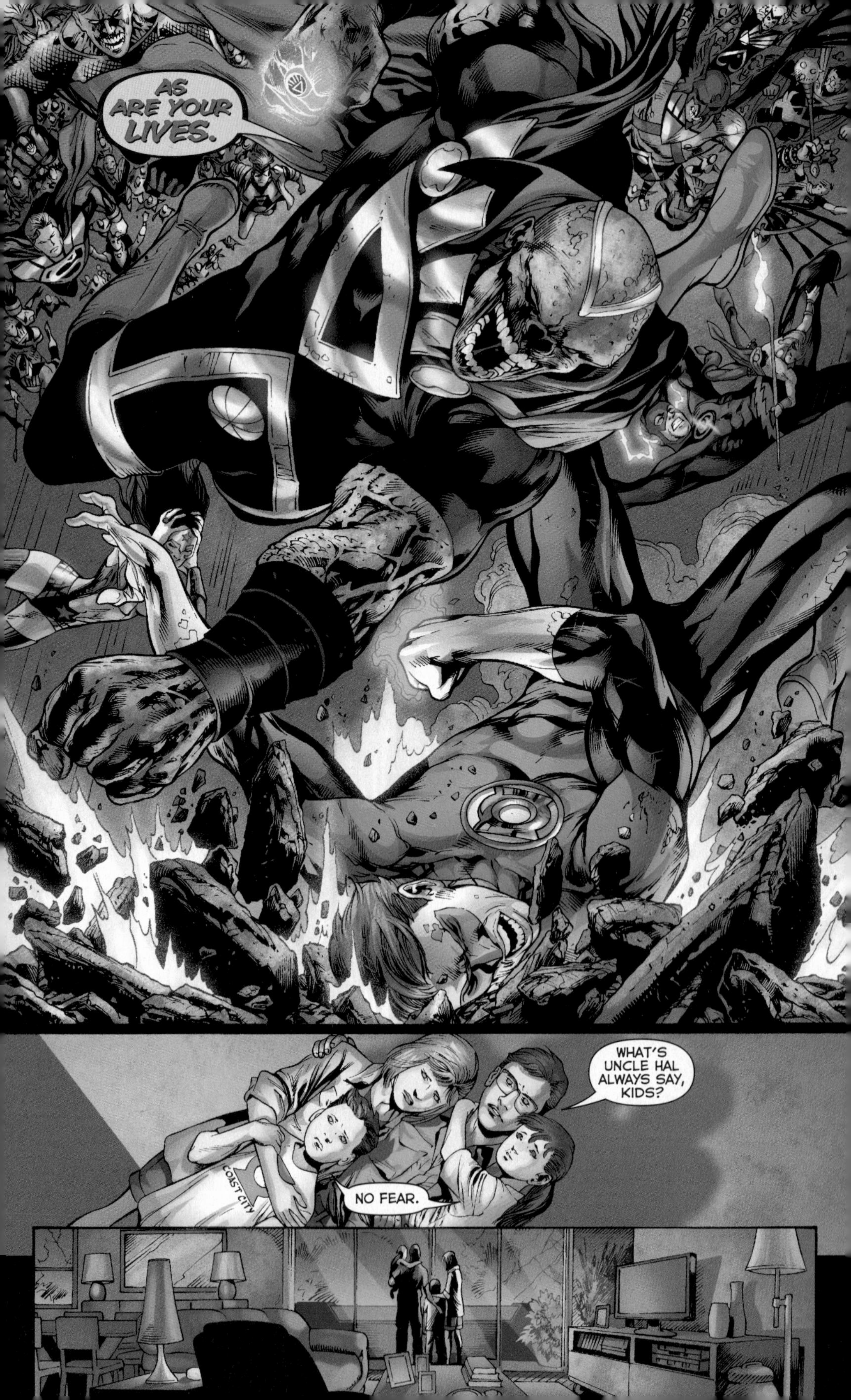
AS ARE YOUR LIVES.
WHAT'S UNCLE HAL ALWAYS SAY, KIDS?
NO FEAR.
COAST CITY

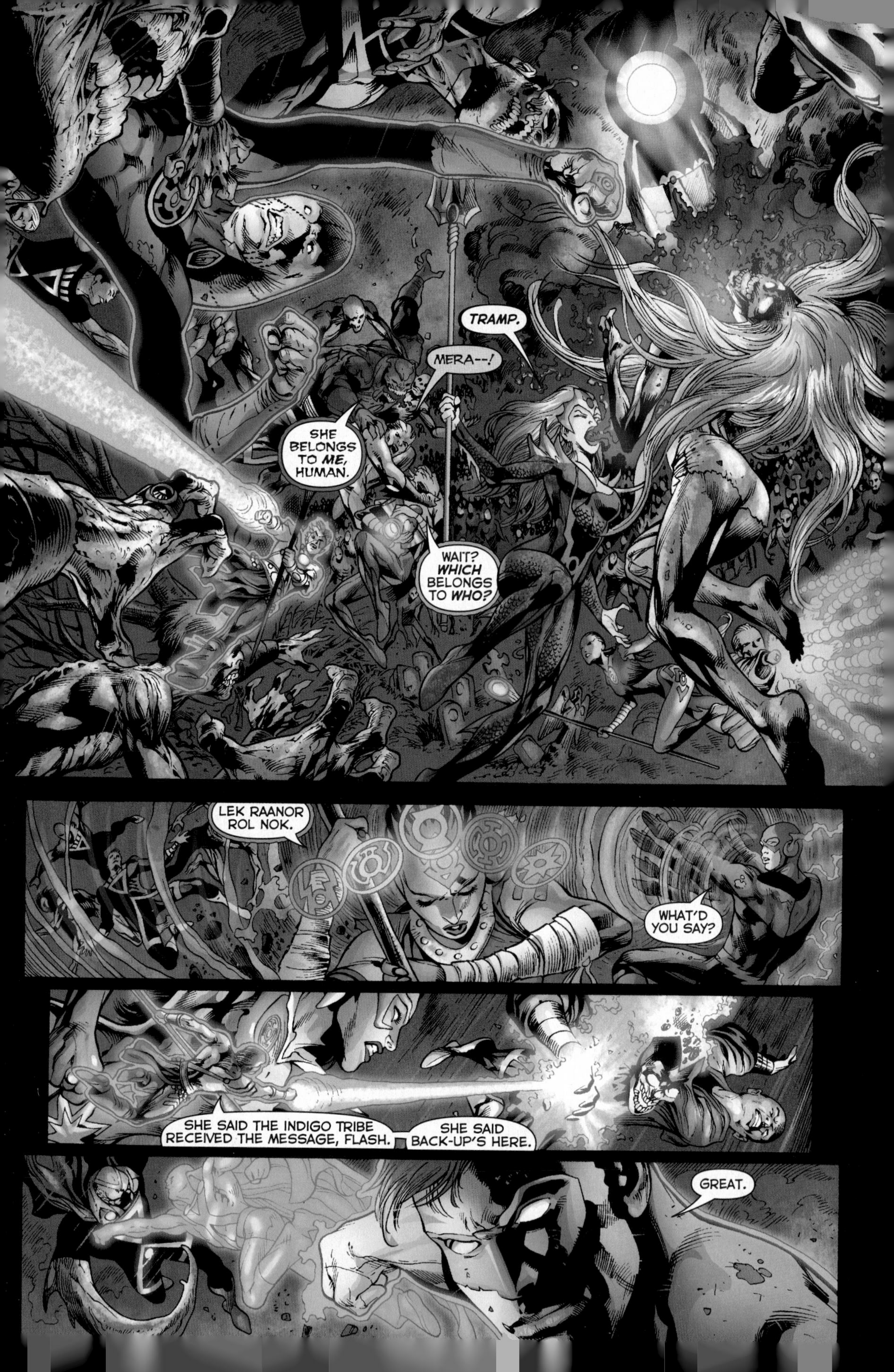
TRAMP.
MERA--!
SHE BELONGS TO ME, HUMAN.
WAIT? WHICH BELONGS TO WHO?
LEK RAANOR ROL NOK.
WHAT'D YOU SAY?
SHE SAID THE INDIGO TRIBE RECEIVED THE MESSAGE, FLASH.
SHE SAID BACK-UP'S HERE.
GREAT.

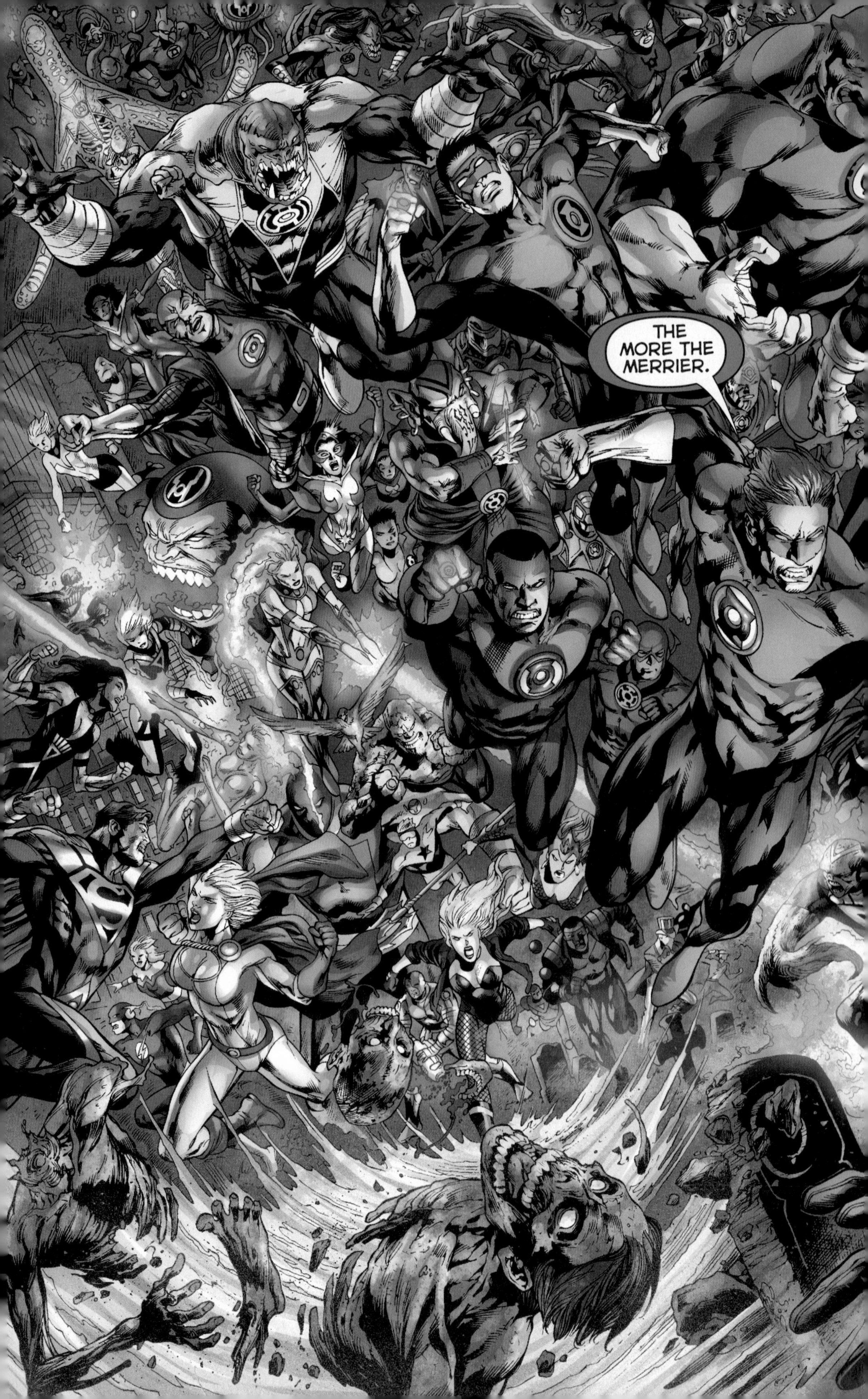
THE MORE THE MERRIER.

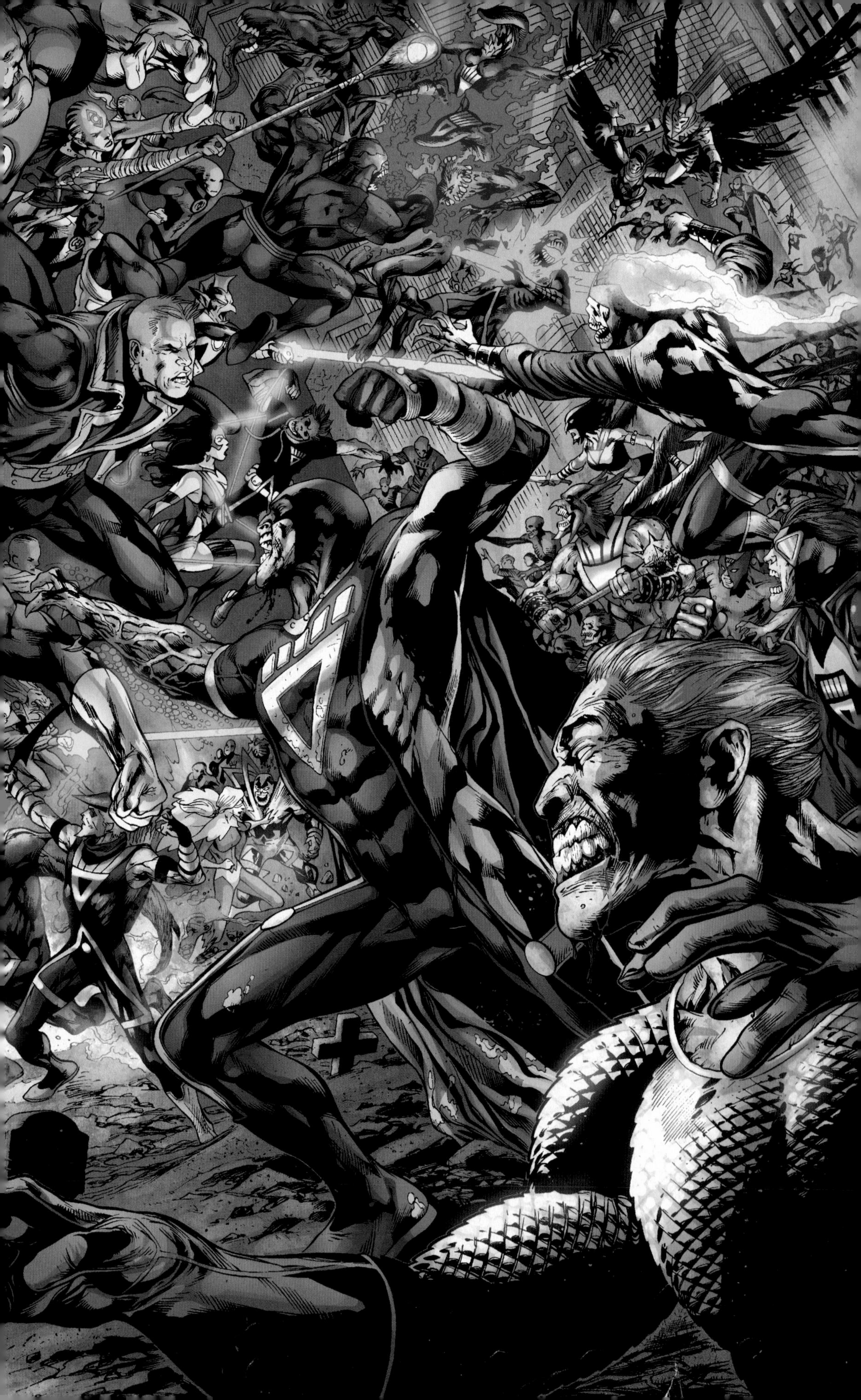

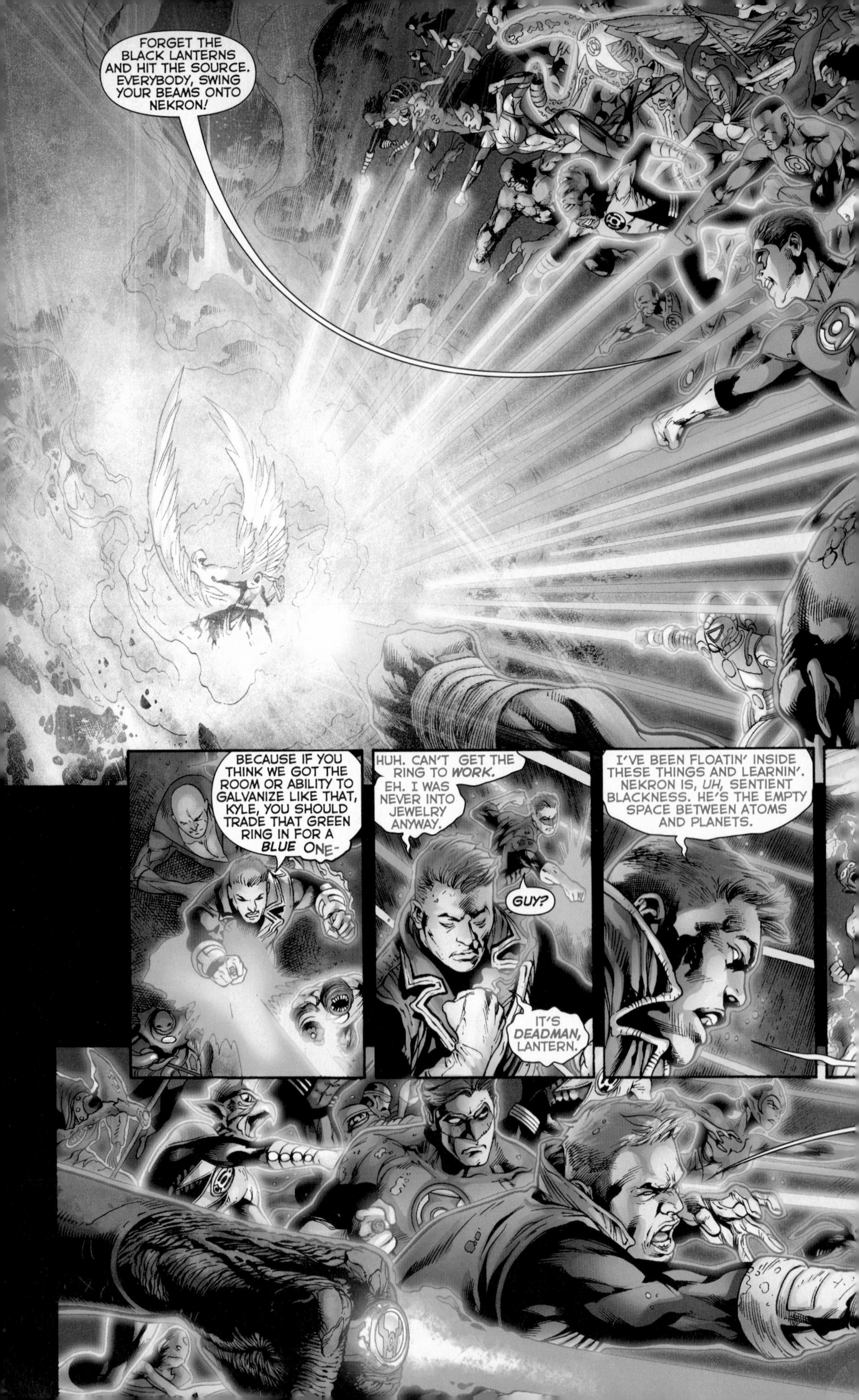
FORGET THE BLACK LANTERNS AND HIT THE SOURCE. EVERYBODY, SWING YOUR BEAMS ONTO NEKRON!
BECAUSE IF YOU THINK WE GOT THE ROOM OR ABILITY TO GALVANIZE LIKE THAT, KYLE, YOU SHOULD TRADE THAT GREEN RING IN FOR A BLUE ONE-
HUH. CAN'T GET THE RING TO WORK.
EH. I WAS NEVER INTO JEWELRY ANYWAY.
GUY?
IT'S DEADMAN, LANTERN.
I'VE BEEN FLOATIN' INSIDE THESE THINGS AND LEARNIN'. NEKRON IS, UH, SENTIENT BLACKNESS. HE'S THE EMPTY SPACE BETWEEN ATOMS AND PLANETS.

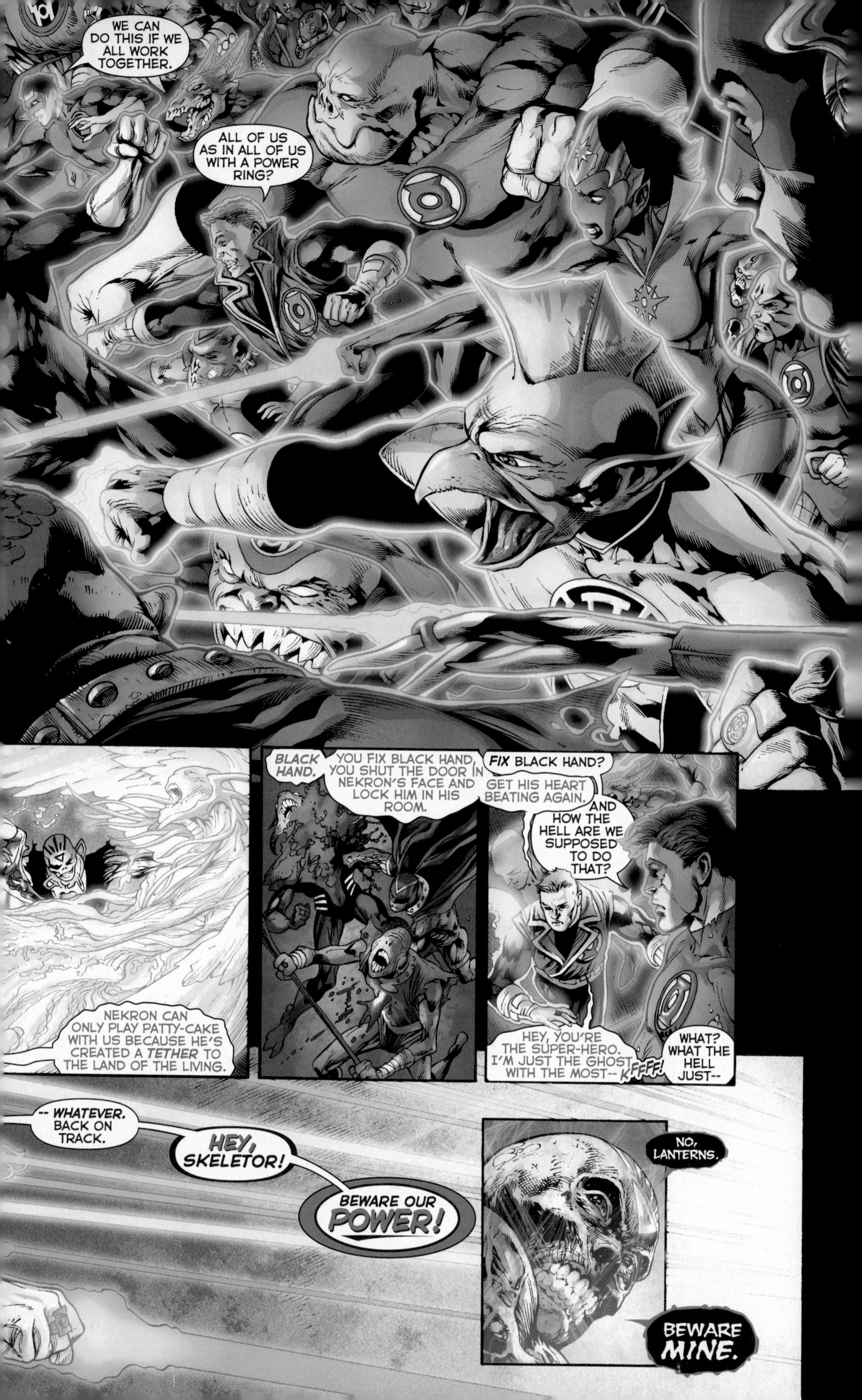
WE CAN DO THIS IF WE ALL WORK TOGETHER.
ALL OF US AS IN ALL OF US WITH A POWER RING?
NEKRON CAN ONLY PLAY PATTY-CAKE WITH US BECAUSE HE'S CREATED A TETHER TO THE LAND OF THE LIVING.
BLACK HAND.
YOU FIX BLACK HAND, YOU SHUT THE DOOR IN NEKRON'S FACE AND LOCK HIM IN HIS ROOM.
FIX BLACK HAND?
GET HIS HEART BEATING AGAIN.
AND HOW THE HELL ARE WE SUPPOSED TO DO THAT?
HEY, YOU'RE THE SUPER-HERO. I'M JUST THE GHOST WITH THE MOST--
KFFFF!
WHAT? WHAT THE HELL JUST--
-- WHATEVER. BACK ON TRACK.
HEY, SKELETOR!
BEWARE OUR POWER!
NO, LANTERNS.
BEWARE MINE.

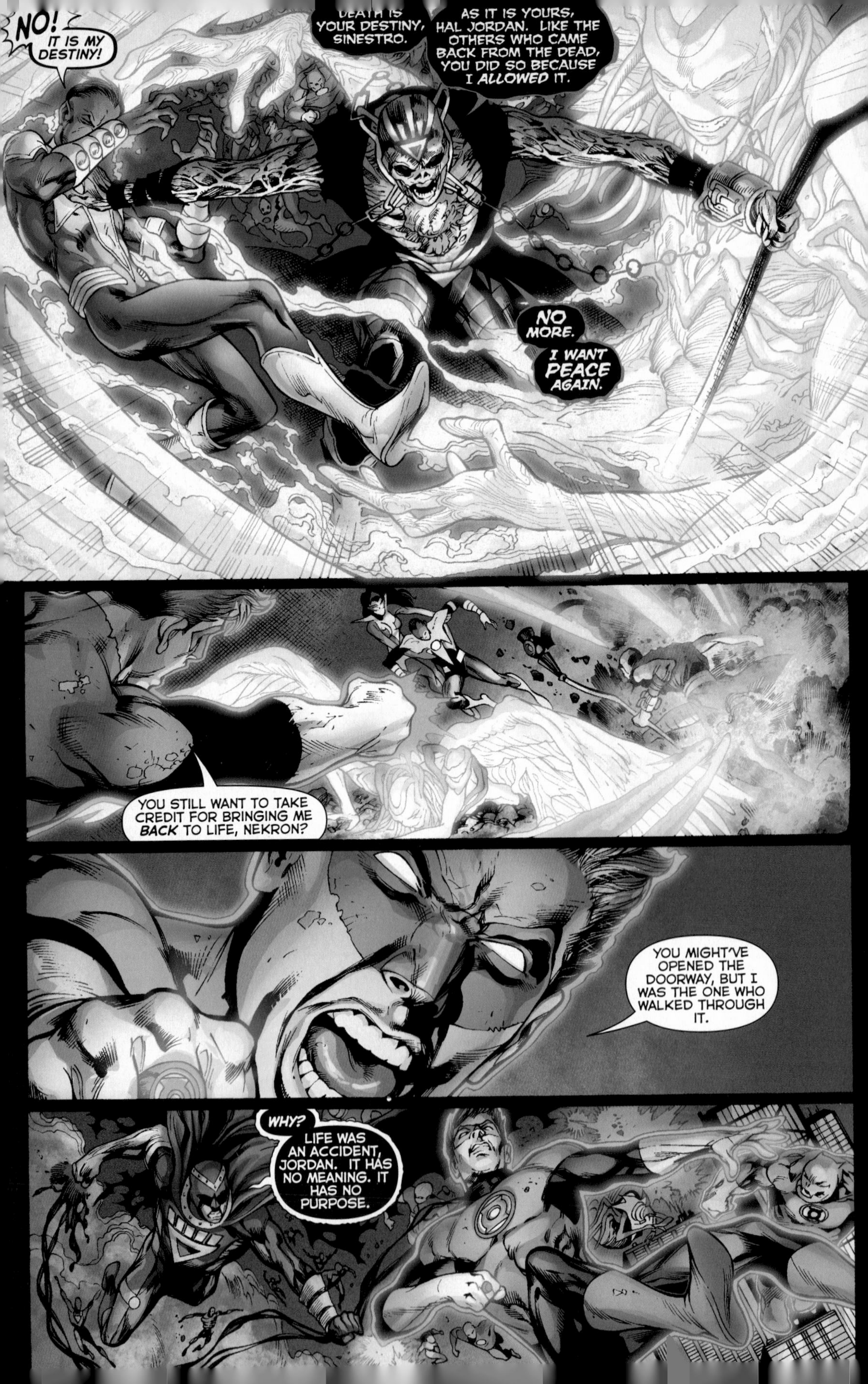
NO! IT IS MY DESTINY!
DEATH IS YOUR DESTINY, SINESTRO.
AS IT IS YOURS, HAL JORDAN. LIKE THE OTHERS WHO CAME BACK FROM THE DEAD, YOU DID SO BECAUSE I ALLOWED IT.
NO MORE.
I WANT PEACE AGAIN.
YOU STILL WANT TO TAKE CREDIT FOR BRINGING ME BACK TO LIFE, NEKRON?
YOU MIGHT'VE OPENED THE DOORWAY, BUT I WAS THE ONE WHO WALKED THROUGH IT.
WHY?
LIFE WAS AN ACCIDENT, JORDAN. IT HAS NO MEANING. IT HAS NO PURPOSE.

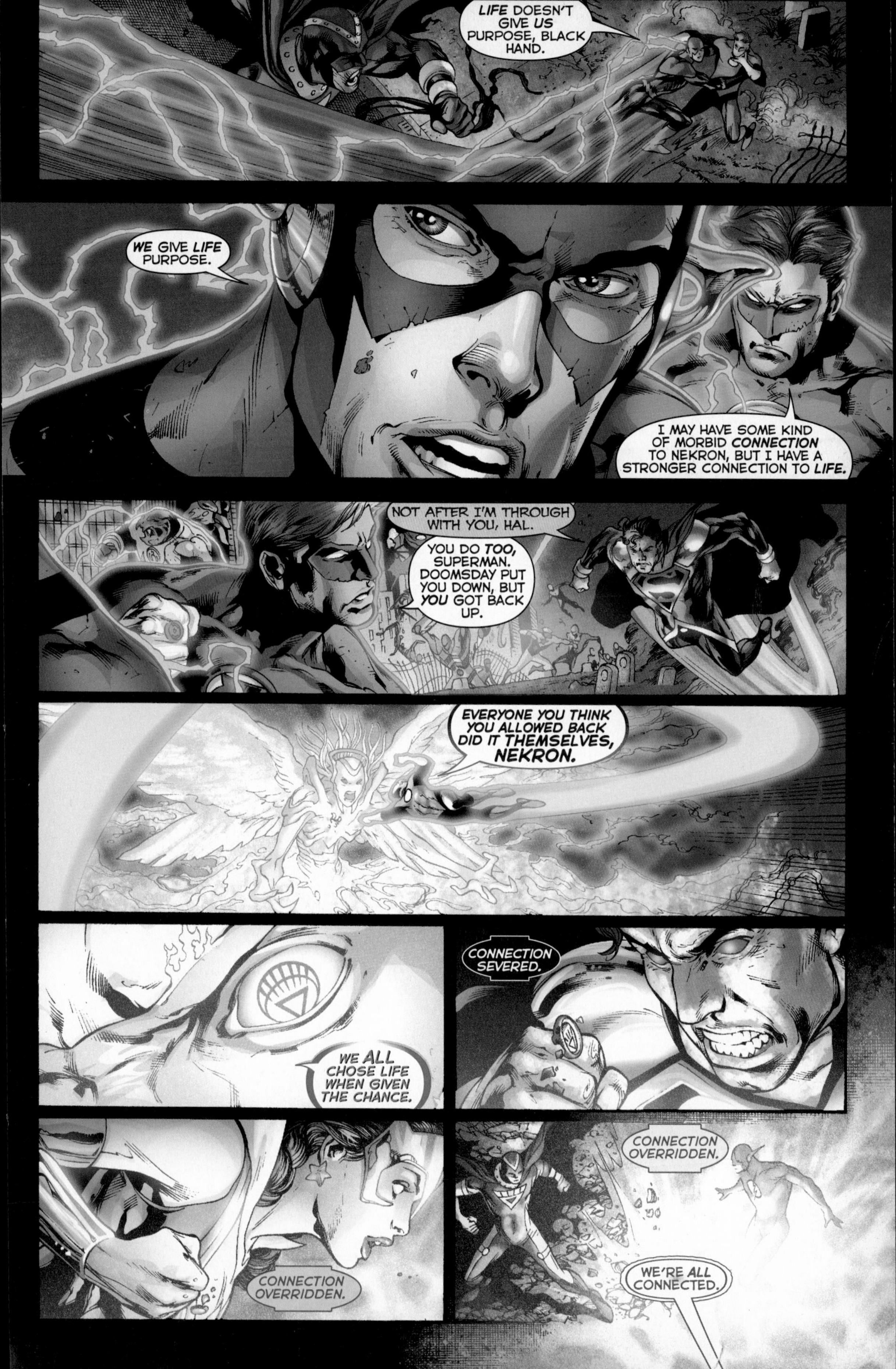
LIFE DOESN'T GIVE US PURPOSE, BLACK HAND.
WE GIVE LIFE PURPOSE.
I MAY HAVE SOME KIND OF MORBID CONNECTION TO NEKRON, BUT I HAVE A STRONGER CONNECTION TO LIFE.
NOT AFTER I'M THROUGH WITH YOU, HAL.
YOU DO TOO, SUPERMAN. DOOMSDAY PUT YOU DOWN, BUT YOU GOT BACK UP.
EVERYONE YOU THINK YOU ALLOWED BACK DID IT THEMSELVES, NEKRON.
WE ALL CHOSE LIFE WHEN GIVEN THE CHANCE.
CONNECTION SEVERED.
CONNECTION OVERRIDDEN.
CONNECTION OVERRIDDEN.
WE'RE ALL CONNECTED.

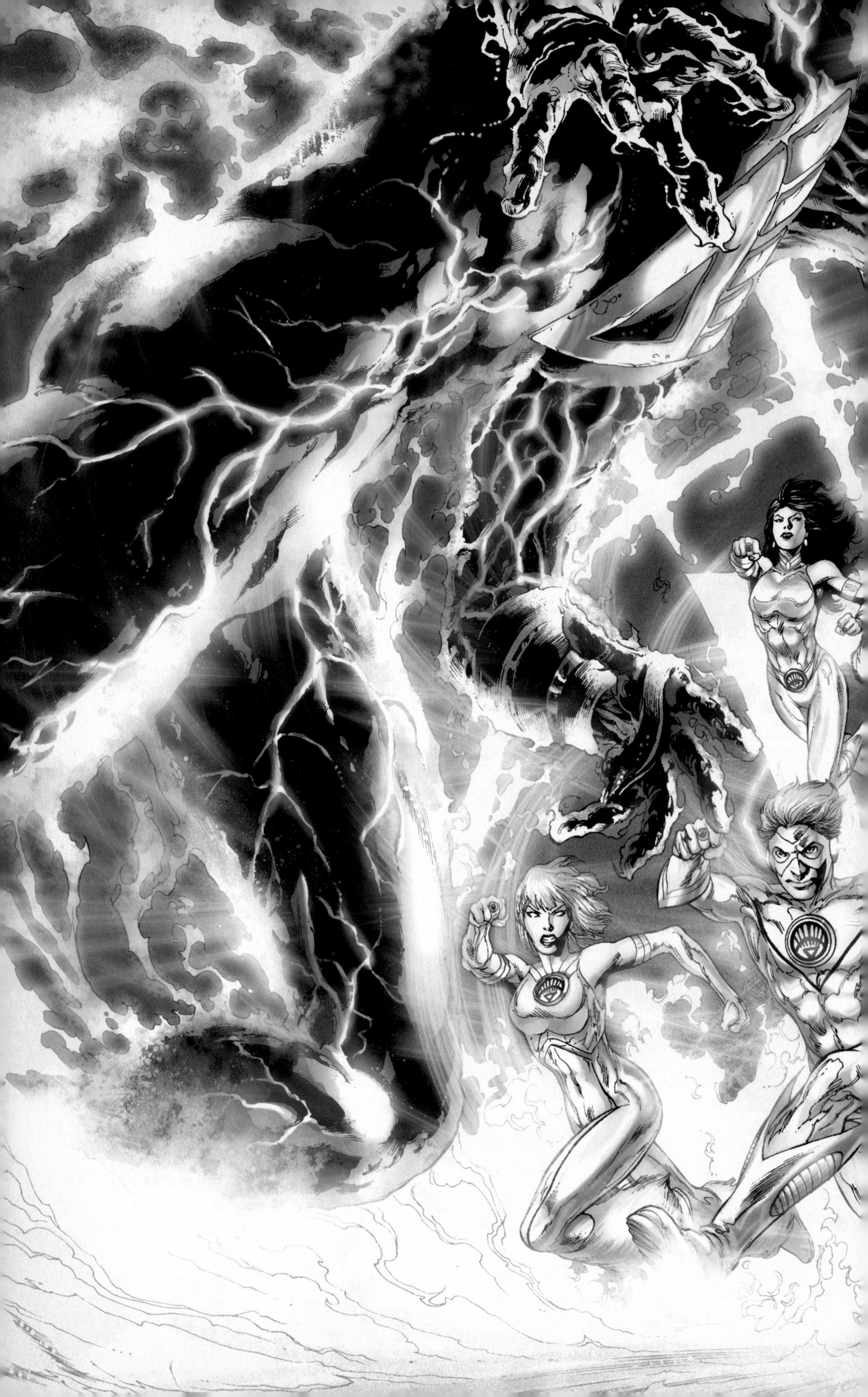

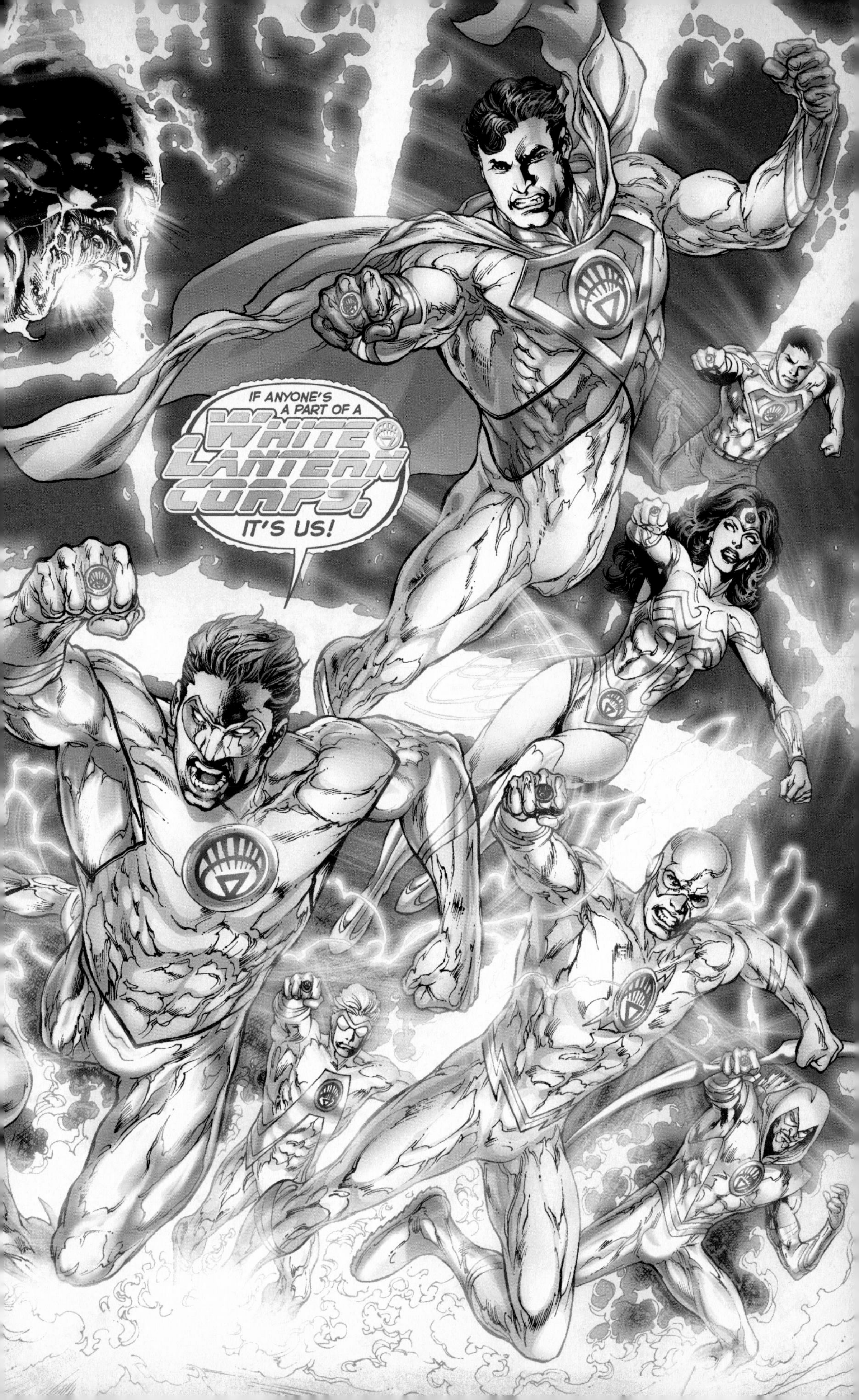
IF ANYONE'S A PART OF A WHITE LANTERN CORPS, IT'S US!

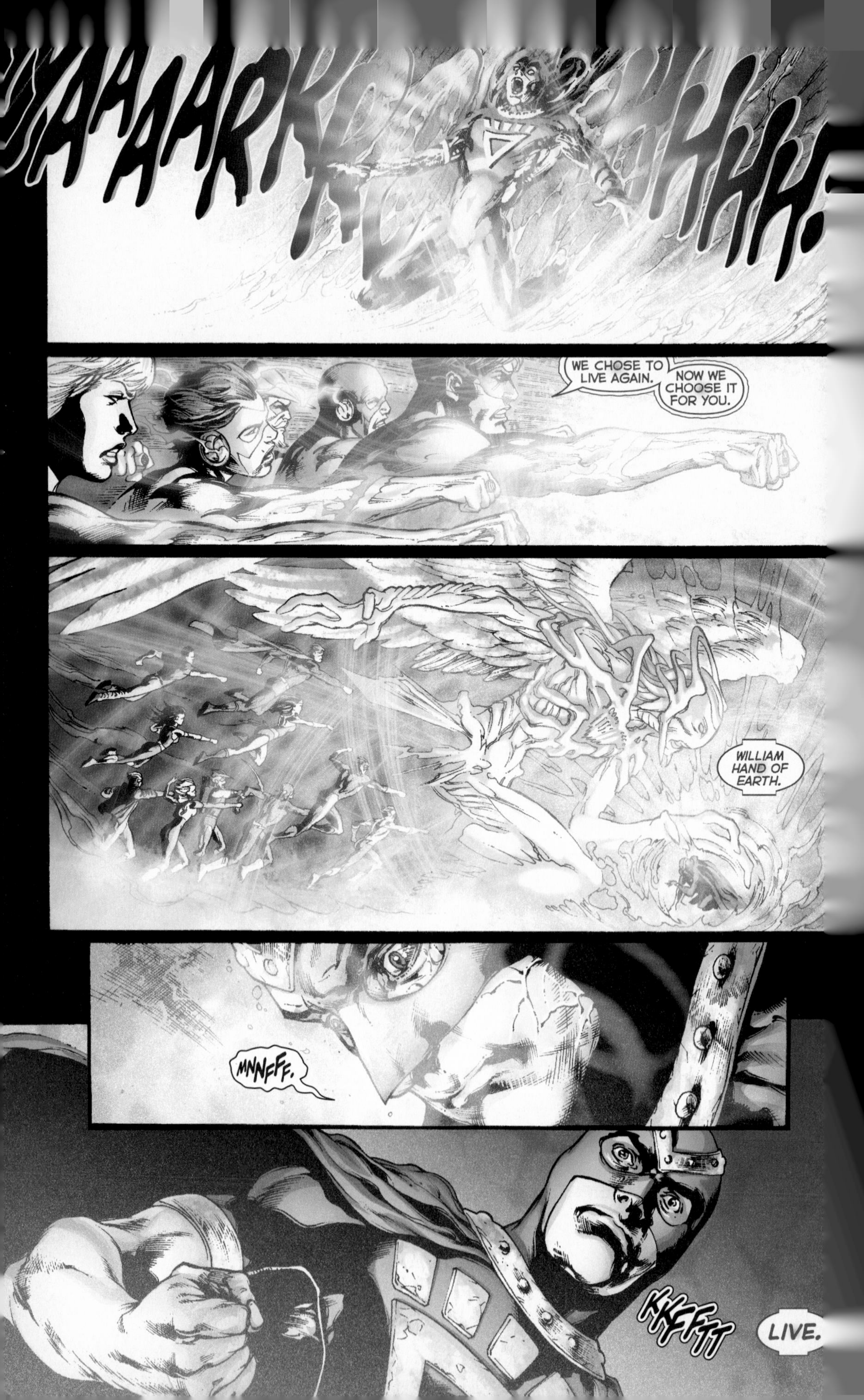
AAAAARK
OOOHHH!
WE CHOSE TO LIVE AGAIN.
NOW WE CHOOSE IT FOR YOU.
WILLIAM HAND OF EARTH.
MNNFFF.
KKFFTT
LIVE.

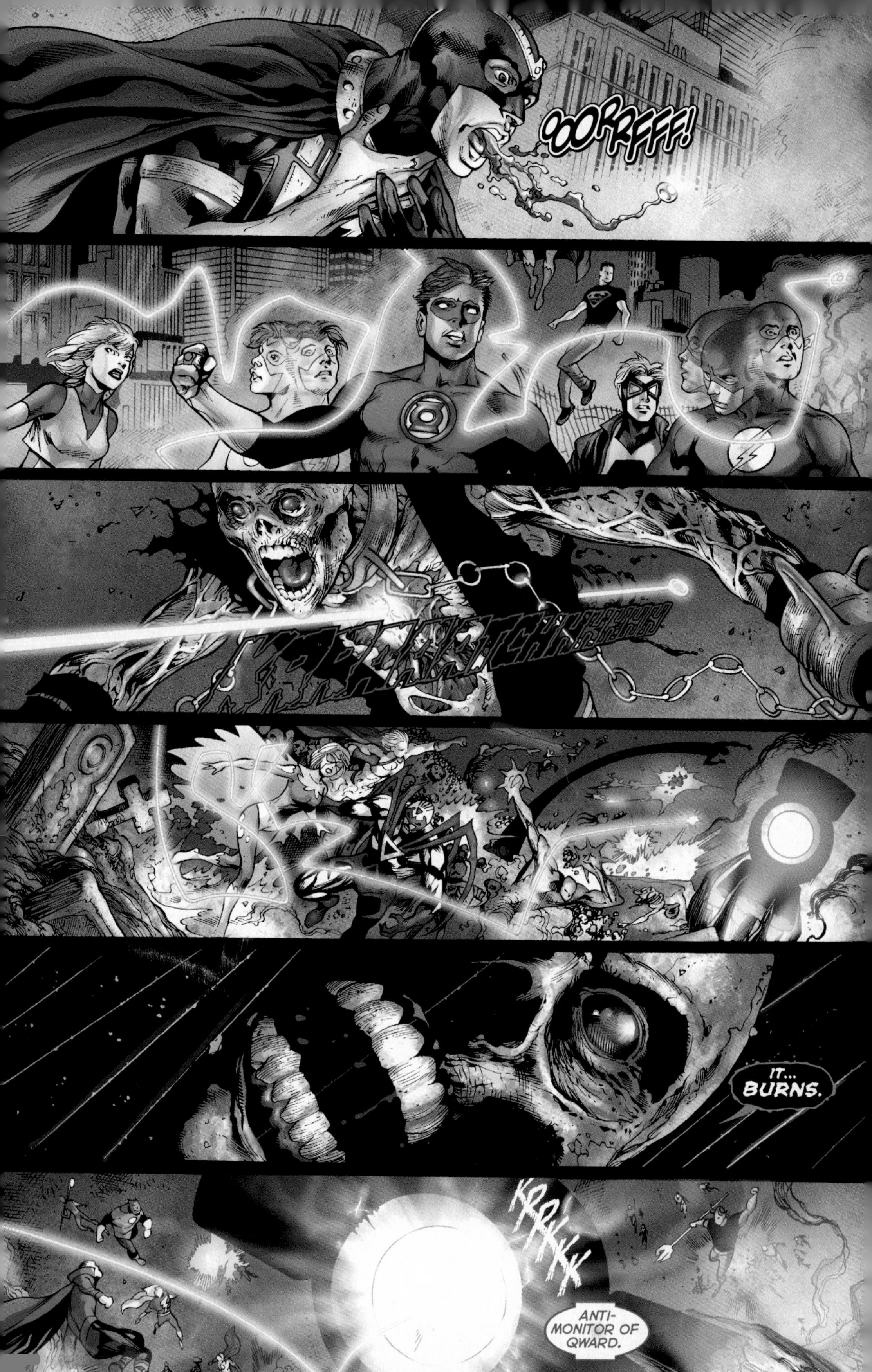
OOORRFFF!
IT... BURNS.
KRRKKK
ANTI-MONITOR OF QWARD.

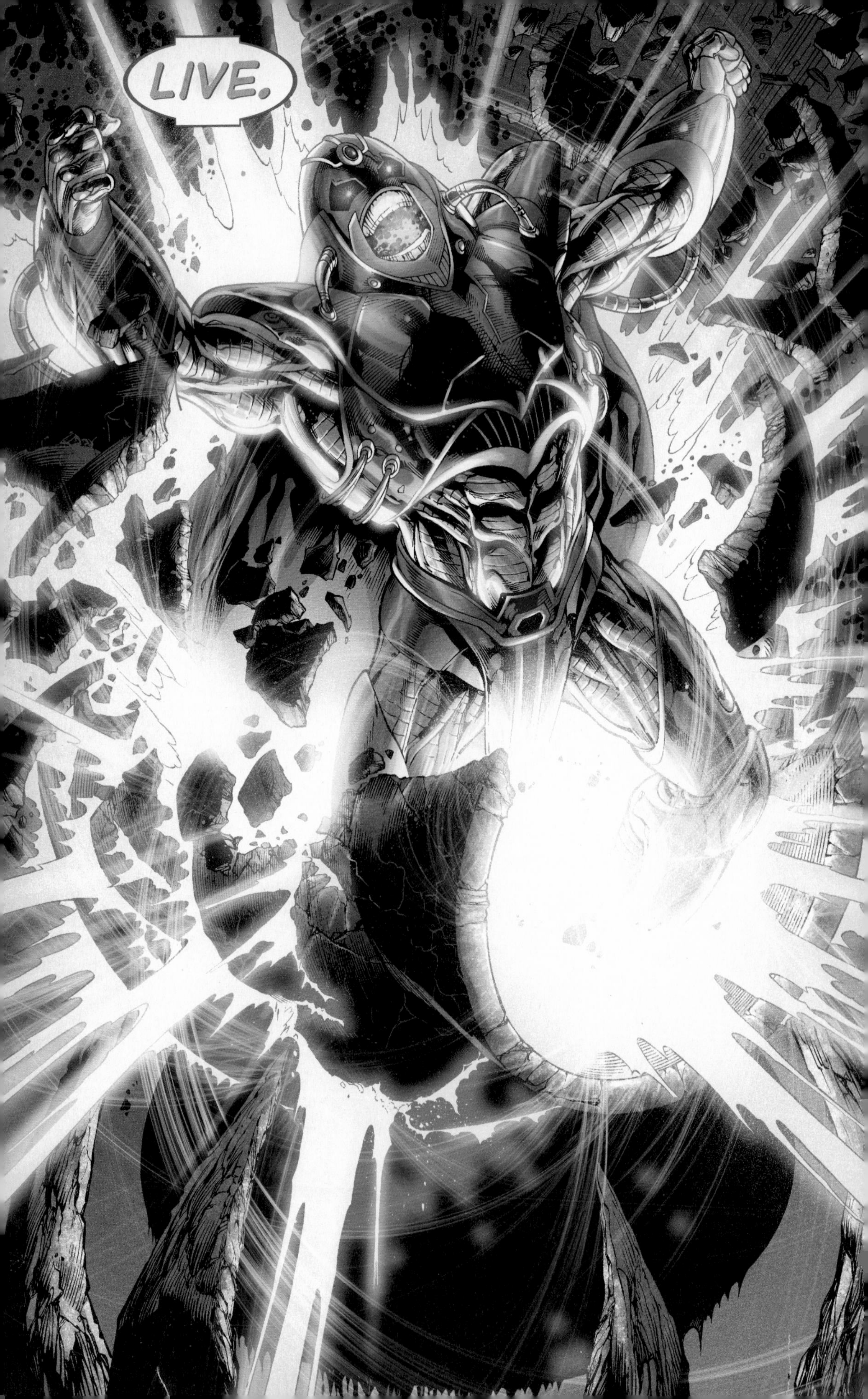
LIVE.

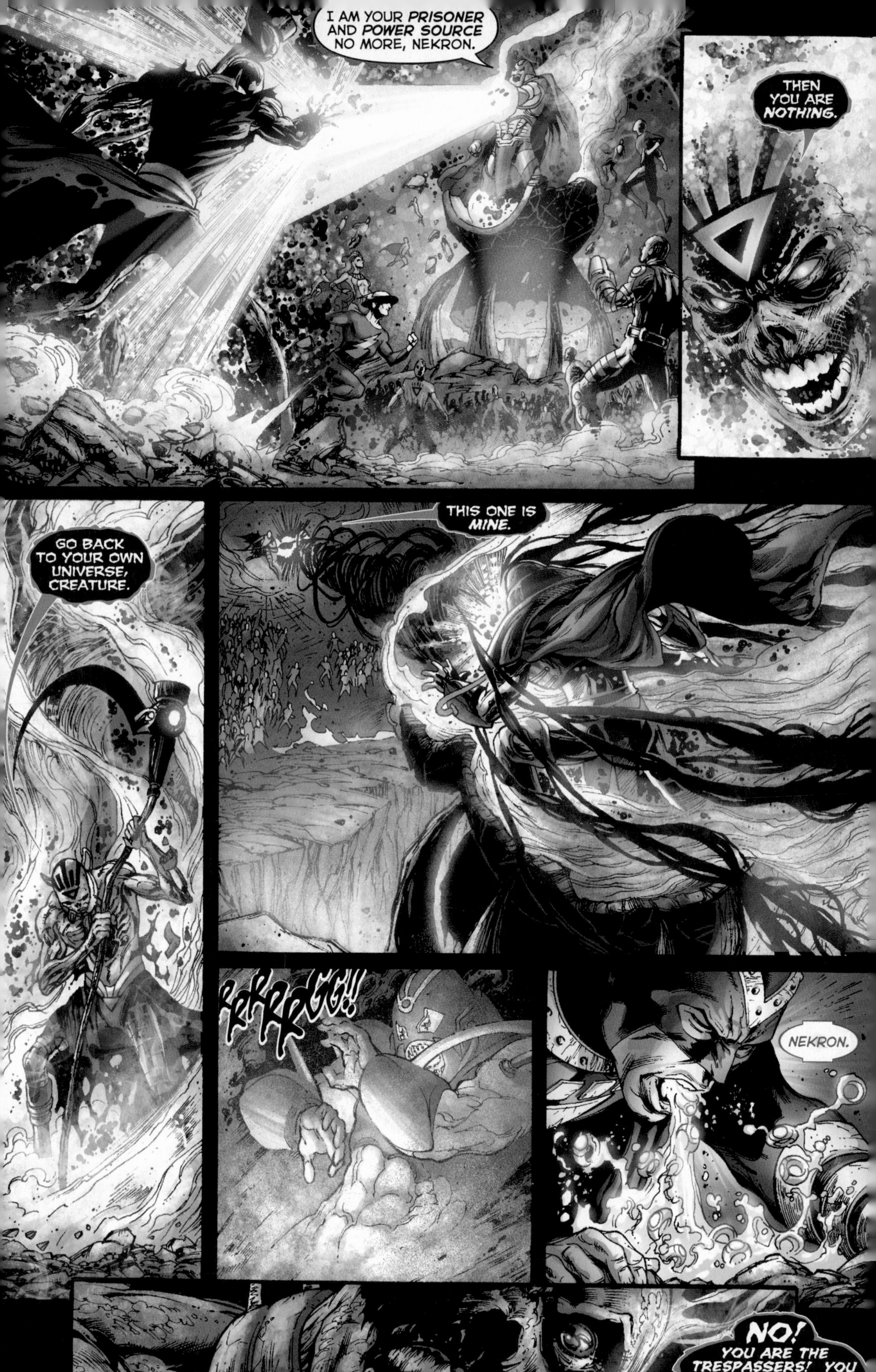
I AM YOUR *PRISONER* AND *POWER SOURCE* NO MORE, NEKRON.
THEN YOU ARE *NOTHING.*
GO BACK TO YOUR OWN UNIVERSE, CREATURE.
THIS ONE IS *MINE.*
RRKRGG!!
NEKRON.
NO! YOU ARE THE TRESPASSERS! YOU ARE THE ENEMIES TO EXISTENCE--!

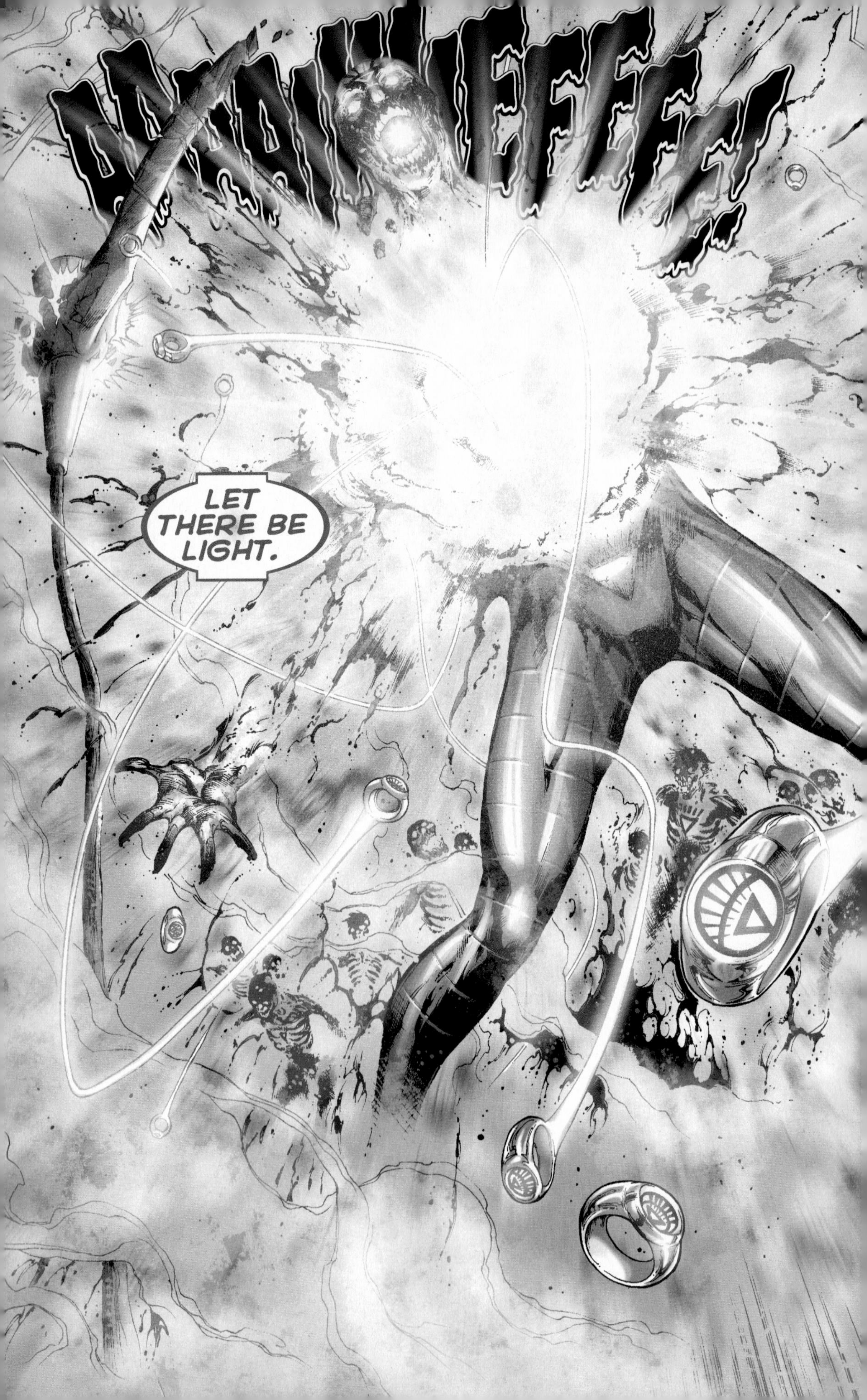
LET THERE BE LIGHT.

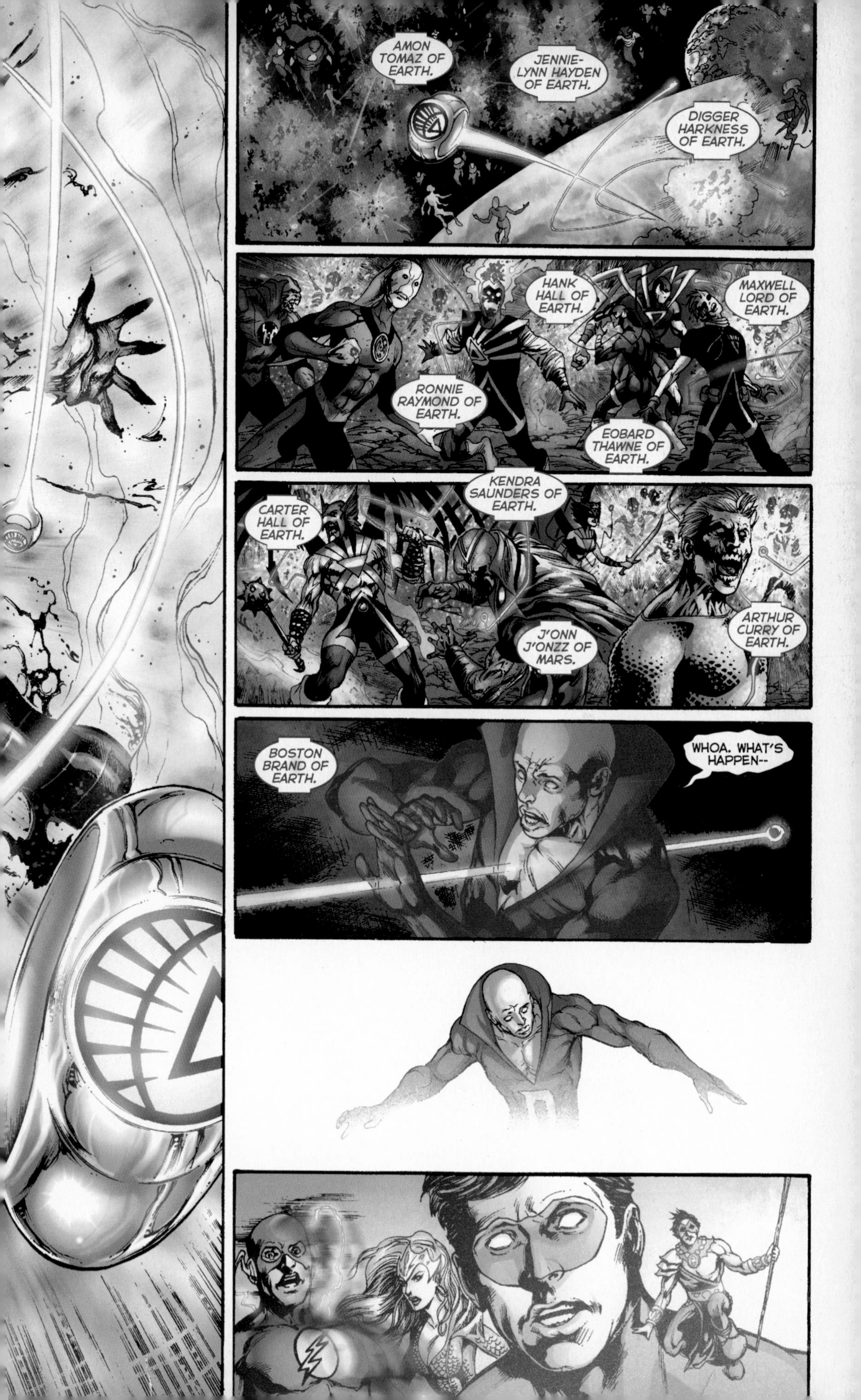

AMON TOMAZ OF EARTH.
JENNIE-LYNN HAYDEN OF EARTH.
DIGGER HARKNESS OF EARTH.
HANK HALL OF EARTH.
MAXWELL LORD OF EARTH.
RONNIE RAYMOND OF EARTH.
EOBARD THAWNE OF EARTH.
CARTER HALL OF EARTH.
KENDRA SAUNDERS OF EARTH.
J'ONN J'ONZZ OF MARS.
ARTHUR CURRY OF EARTH.
BOSTON BRAND OF EARTH.
WHOA. WHAT'S HAPPEN--

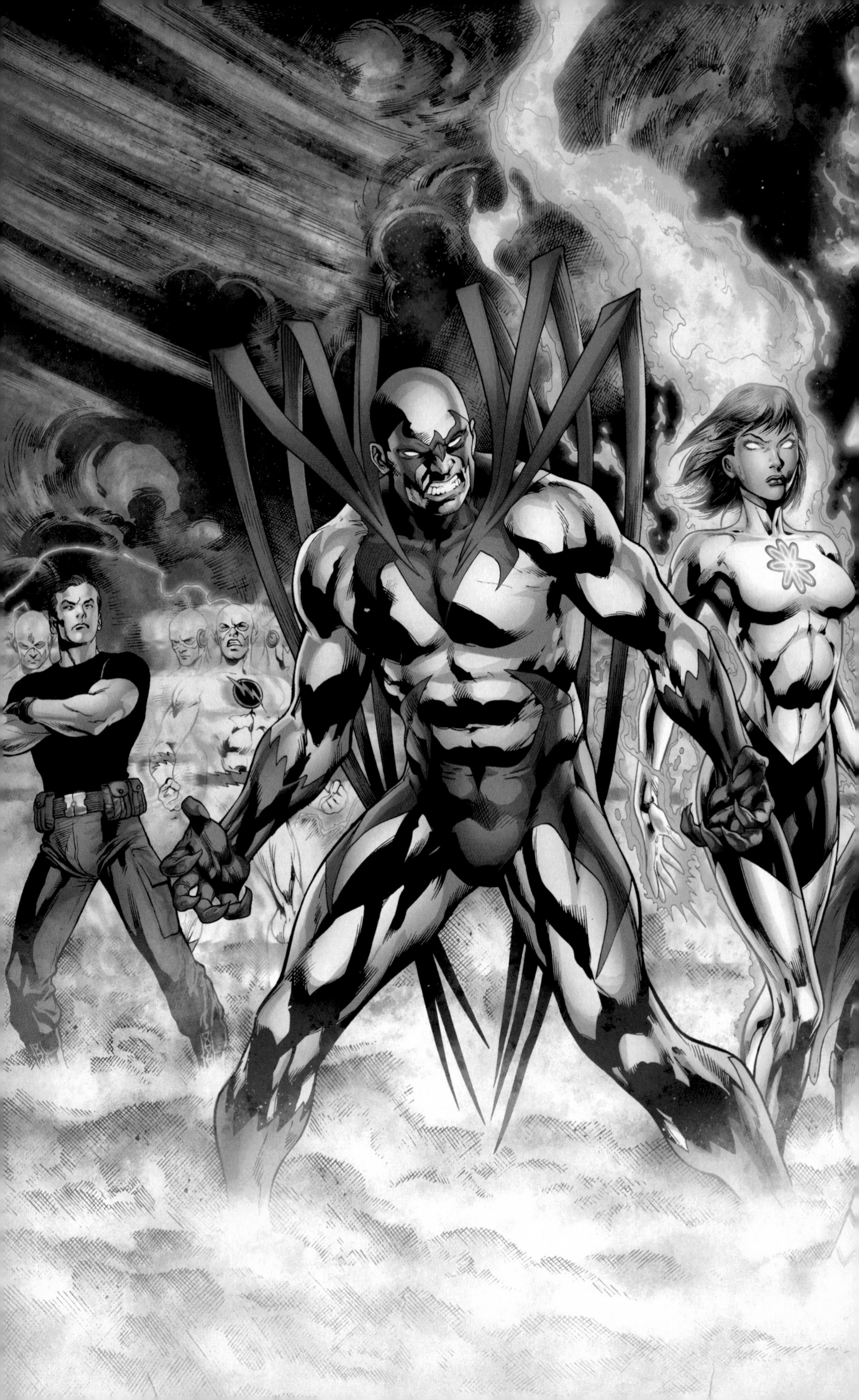

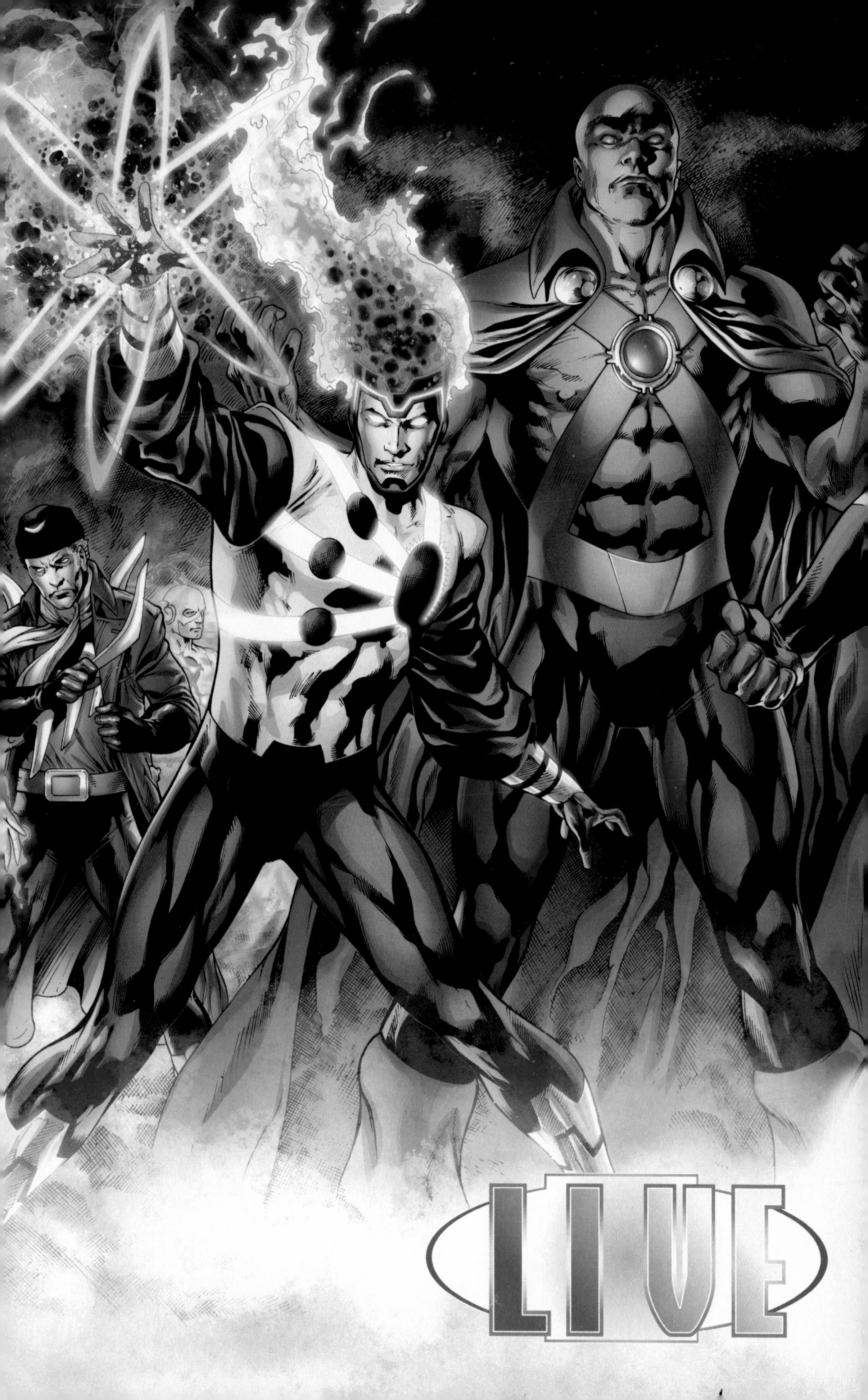
LIVE

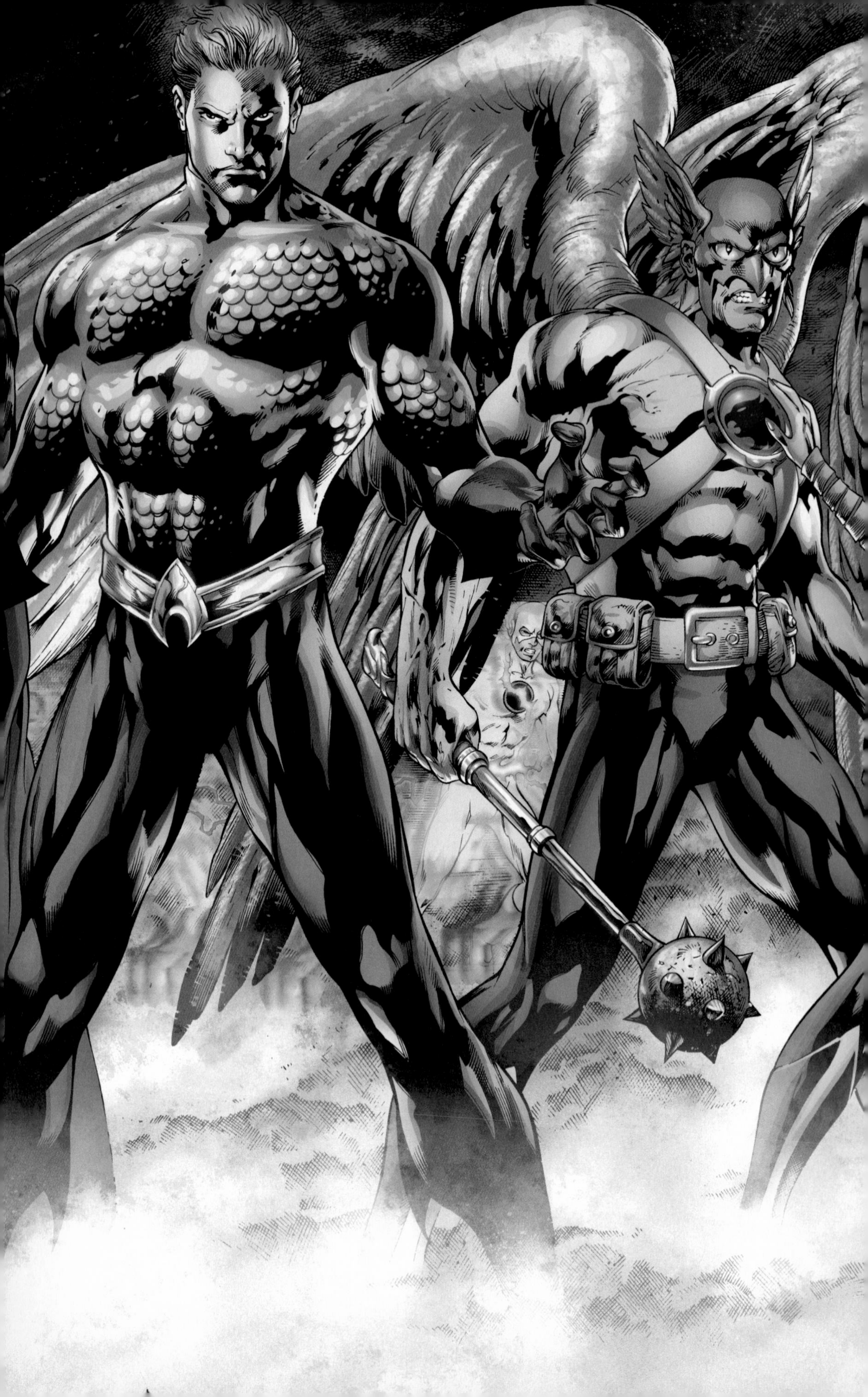

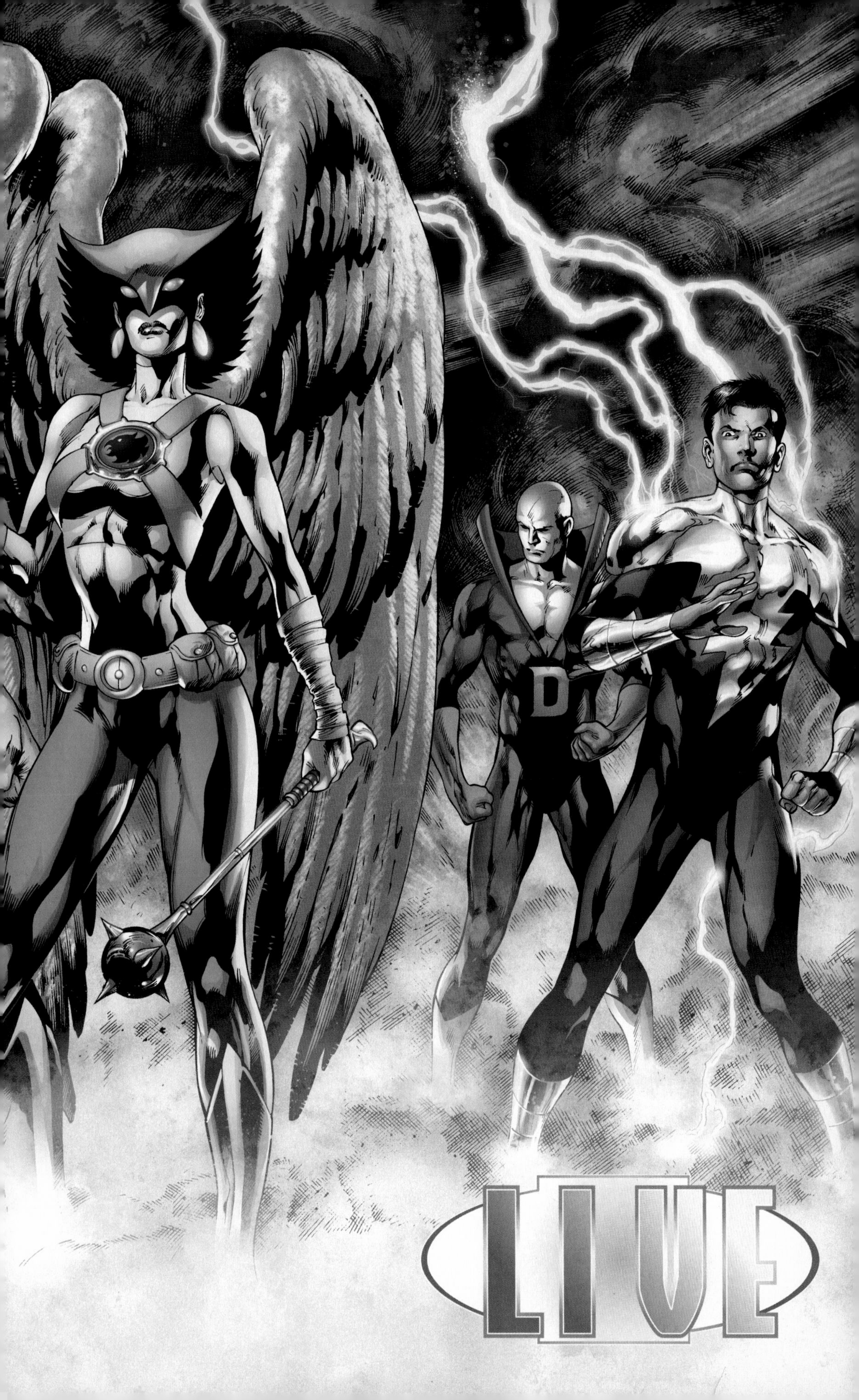
LIVE

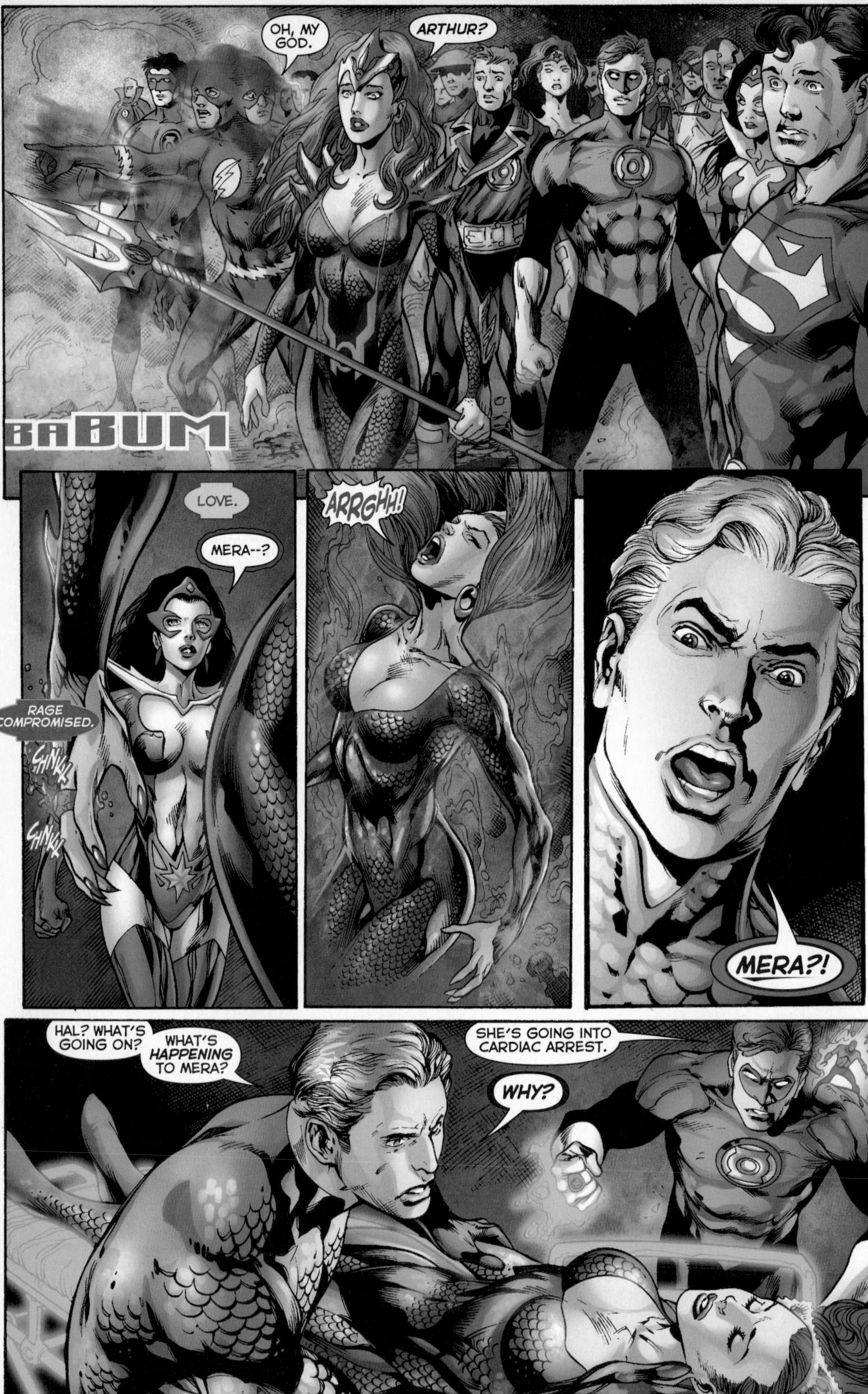
OH, MY GOD.
ARTHUR?
BABUM
LOVE.
MERA--?
RAGE COMPROMISED.
ARRGHH!
MERA?!
HAL? WHAT'S GOING ON?
WHAT'S *HAPPENING* TO MERA?
SHE'S GOING INTO CARDIAC ARREST.
WHY?

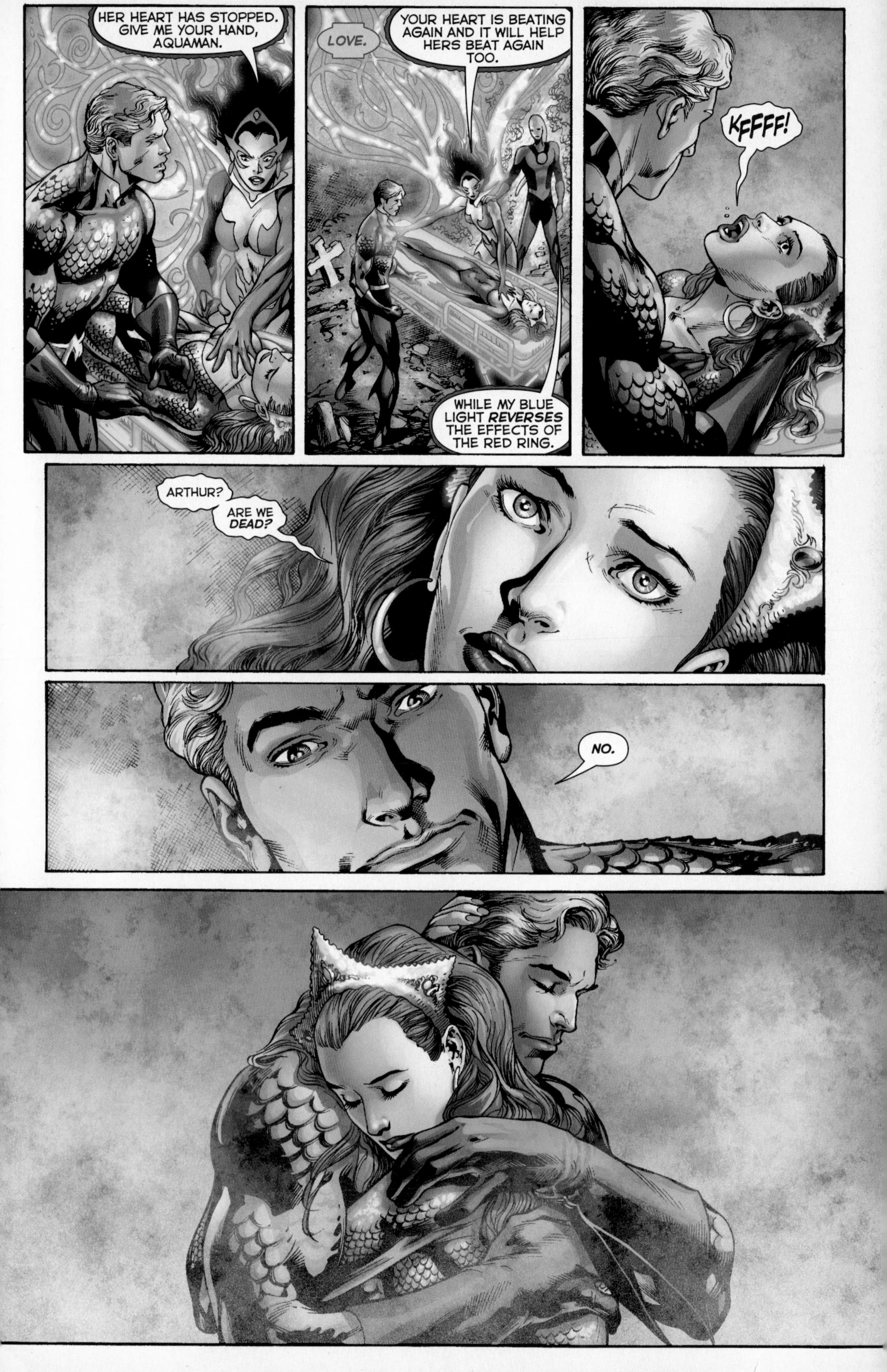
HER HEART HAS STOPPED. GIVE ME YOUR HAND, AQUAMAN.
LOVE.
YOUR HEART IS BEATING AGAIN AND IT WILL HELP HERS BEAT AGAIN TOO.
WHILE MY BLUE LIGHT *REVERSES* THE EFFECTS OF THE RED RING.
KFFFF!
ARTHUR?
ARE WE *DEAD?*
NO.

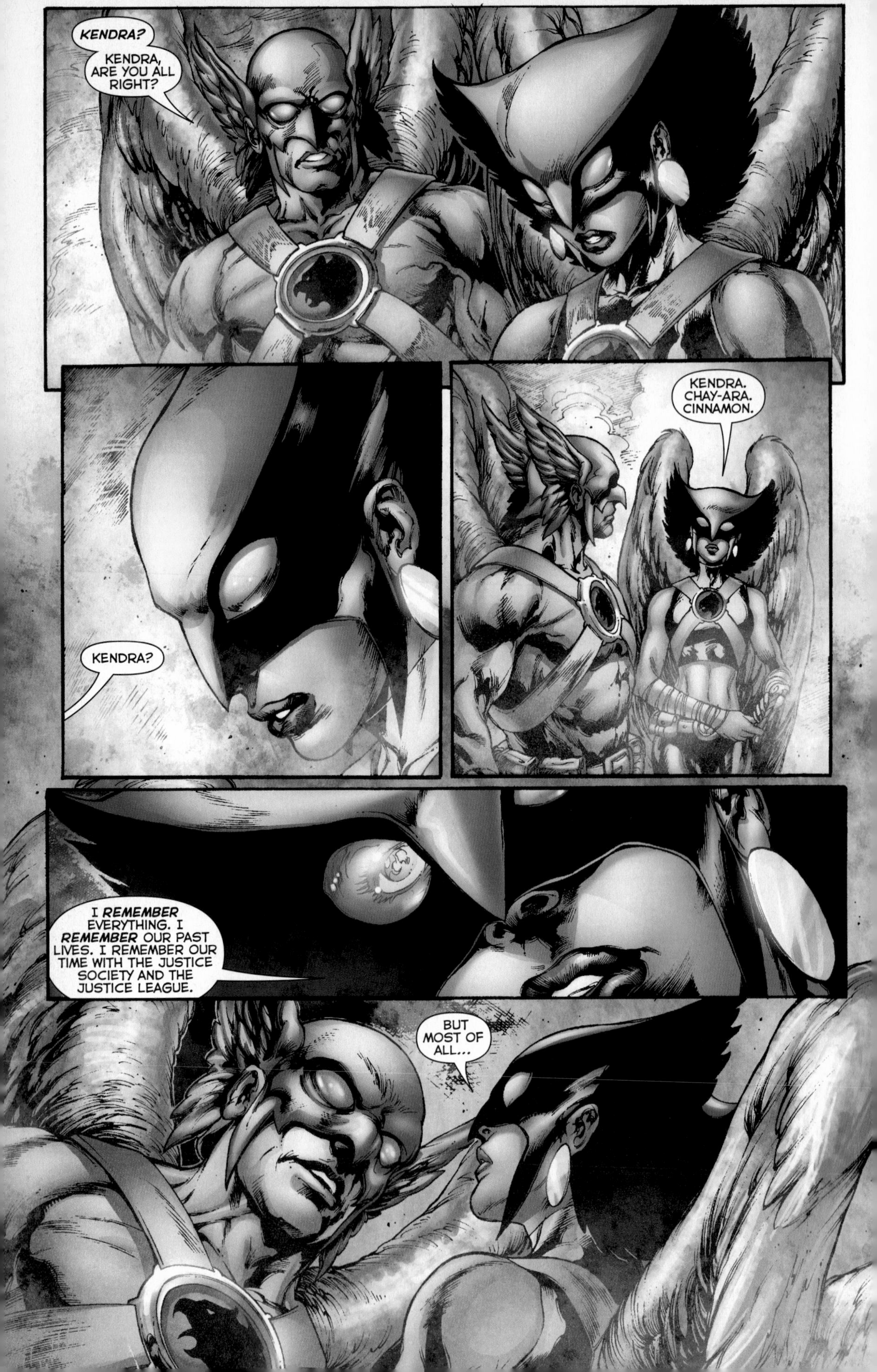
KENDRA?
KENDRA, ARE YOU ALL RIGHT?
KENDRA?
KENDRA. CHAY-ARA. CINNAMON.
I REMEMBER EVERYTHING. I REMEMBER OUR PAST LIVES. I REMEMBER OUR TIME WITH THE JUSTICE SOCIETY AND THE JUSTICE LEAGUE.
BUT MOST OF ALL...

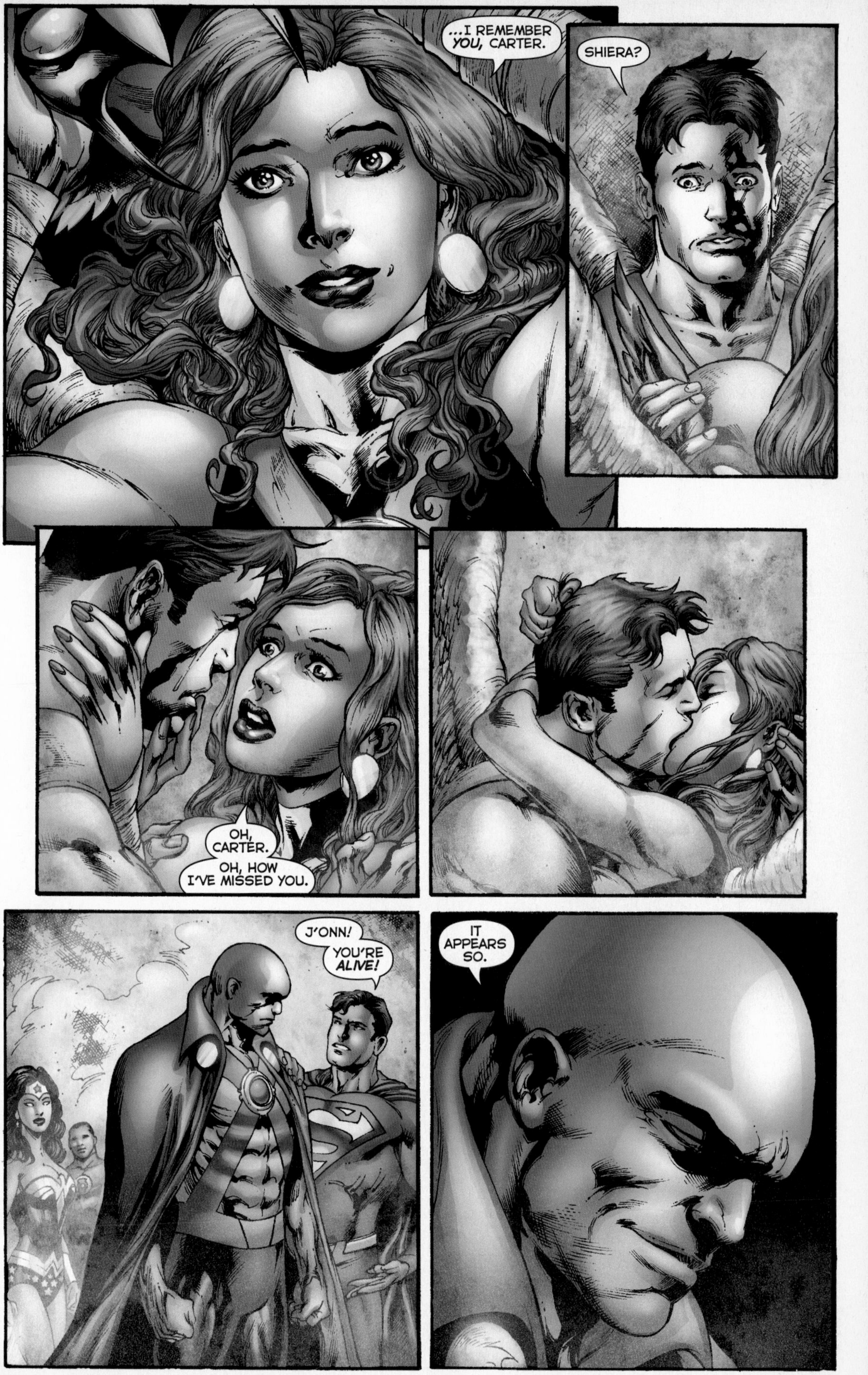
...I REMEMBER YOU, CARTER.
SHIERA?
OH, CARTER.
OH, HOW I'VE MISSED YOU.
J'ONN!
YOU'RE ALIVE!
IT APPEARS SO.

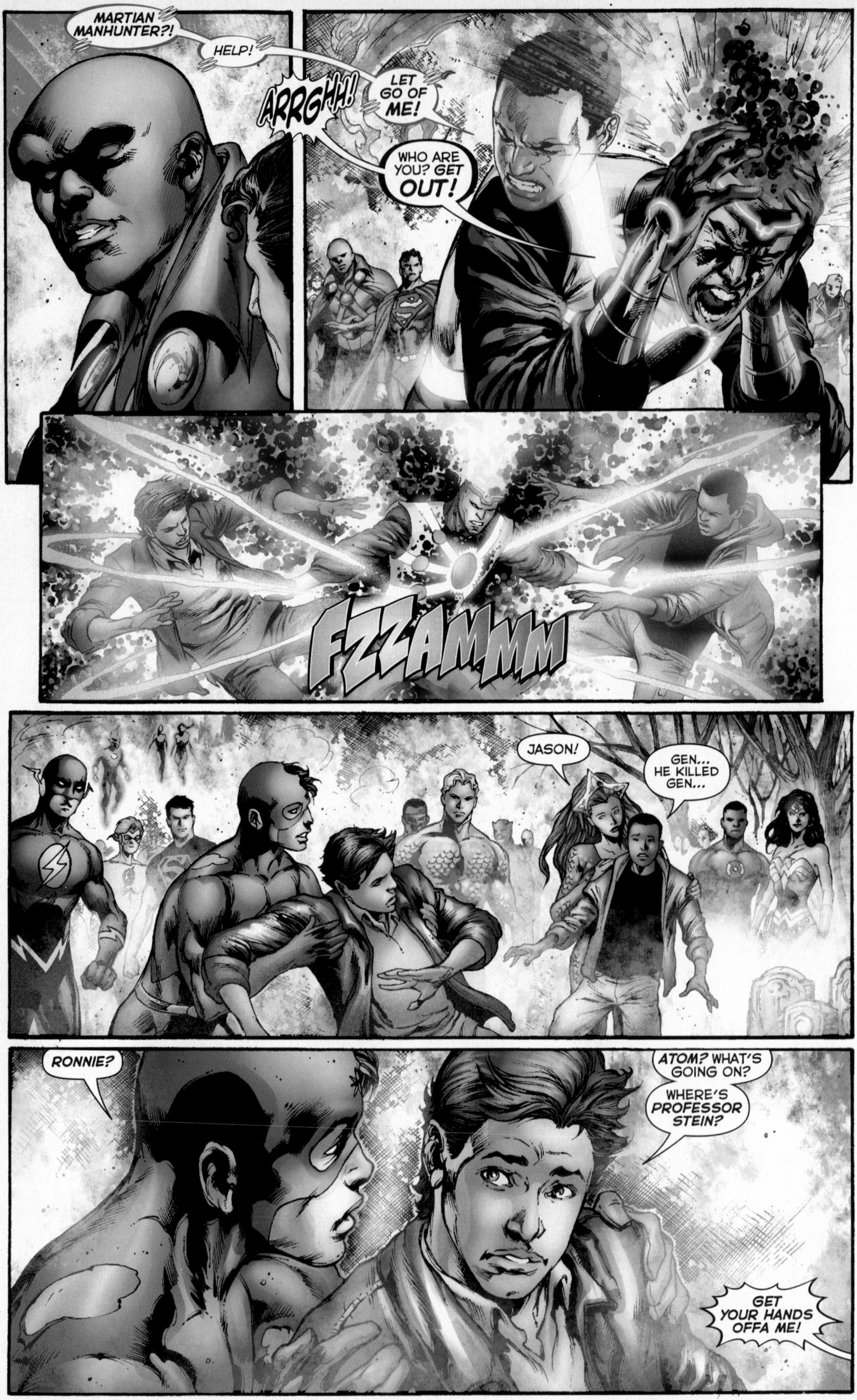
MARTIAN MANHUNTER?!
HELP!
ARRGHH!
LET GO OF ME!
WHO ARE YOU? GET OUT!
FZZAMMMM
JASON!
GEN... HE KILLED GEN...
RONNIE?
ATOM? WHAT'S GOING ON?
WHERE'S PROFESSOR STEIN?
GET YOUR HANDS OFFA ME!

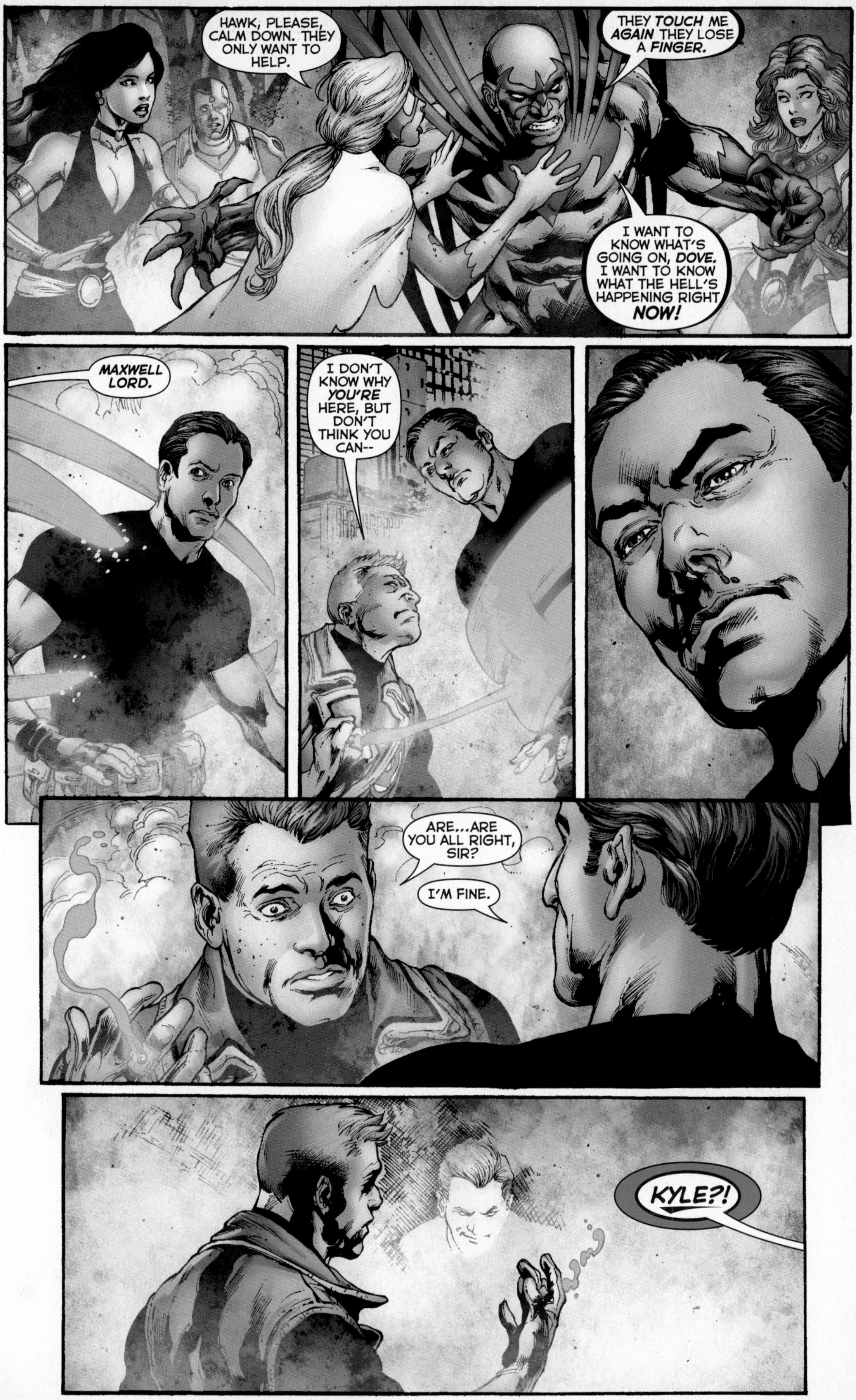
HAWK, PLEASE, CALM DOWN. THEY ONLY WANT TO HELP.
THEY TOUCH ME AGAIN THEY LOSE A FINGER.
I WANT TO KNOW WHAT'S GOING ON, DOVE. I WANT TO KNOW WHAT THE HELL'S HAPPENING RIGHT NOW!
MAXWELL LORD.
I DON'T KNOW WHY YOU'RE HERE, BUT DON'T THINK YOU CAN--
ARE...ARE YOU ALL RIGHT, SIR?
I'M FINE.
KYLE?!

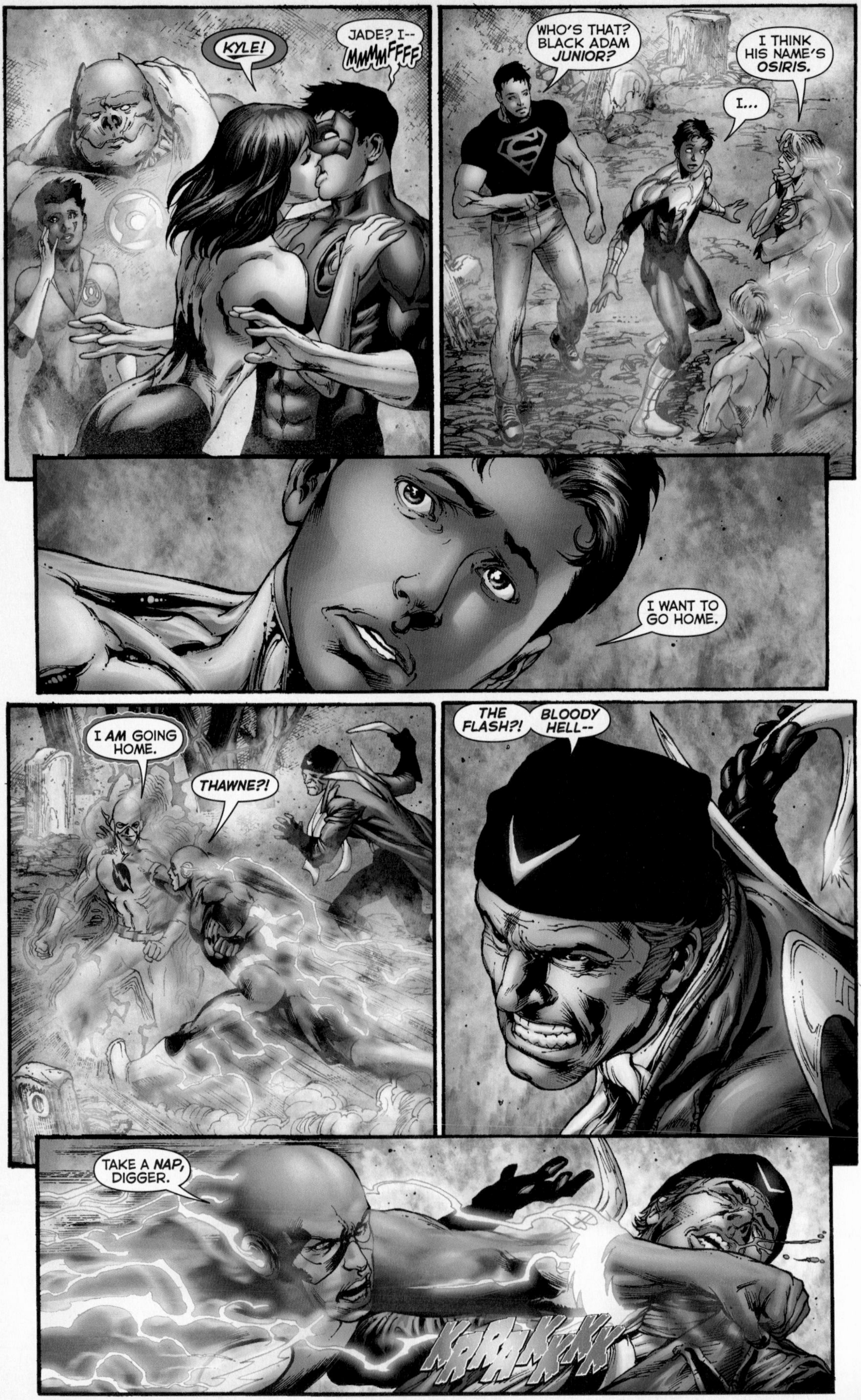
KYLE!
JADE? I-- MMMMFFFF
WHO'S THAT? BLACK ADAM JUNIOR?
I THINK HIS NAME'S OSIRIS.
I...
I WANT TO GO HOME.
I AM GOING HOME.
THAWNE?!
THE FLASH?!
BLOODY HELL--
TAKE A NAP, DIGGER.
KRRAKKKK

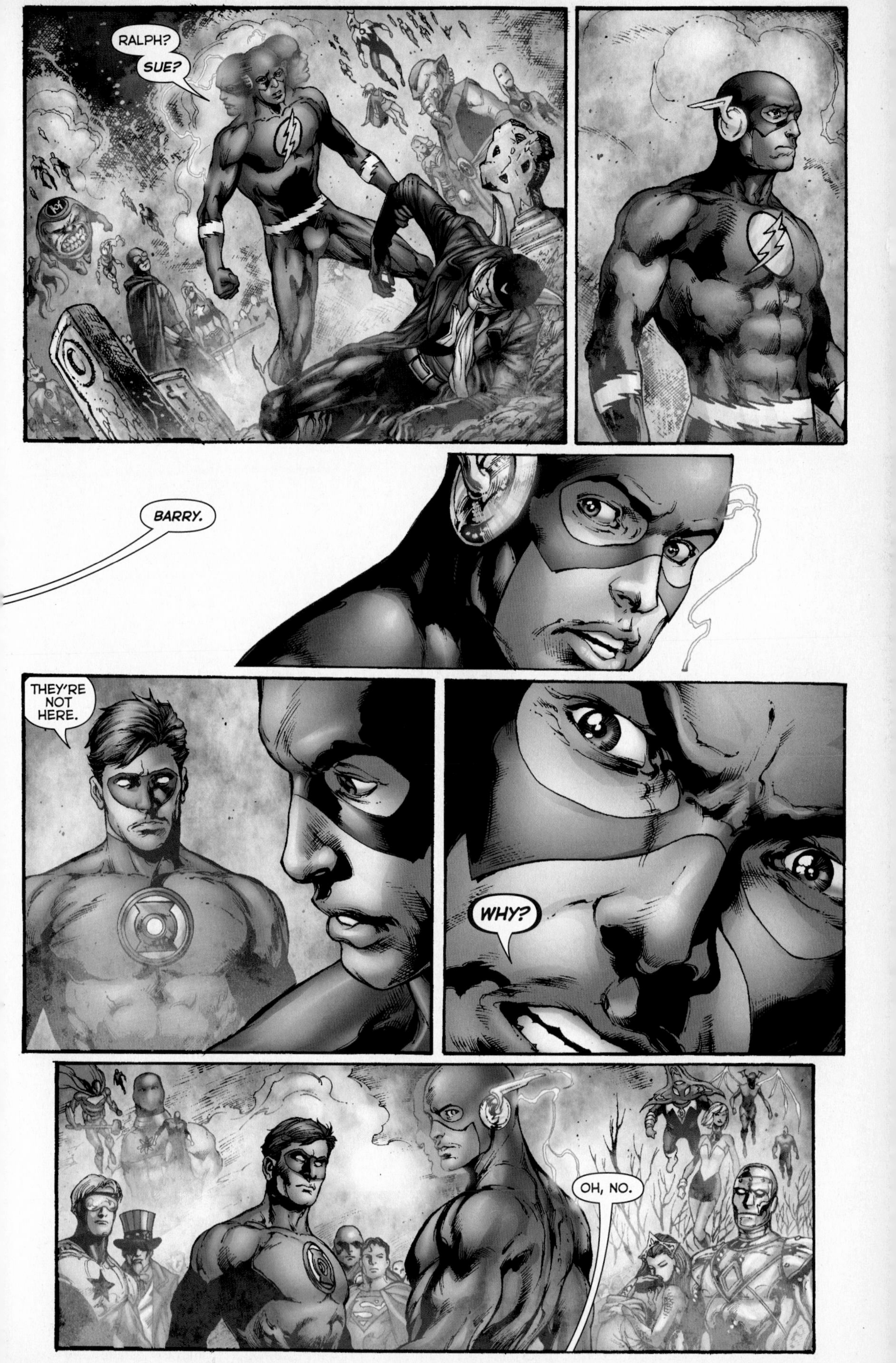
RALPH?
SUE?
BARRY.
THEY'RE NOT HERE.
WHY?
OH, NO.

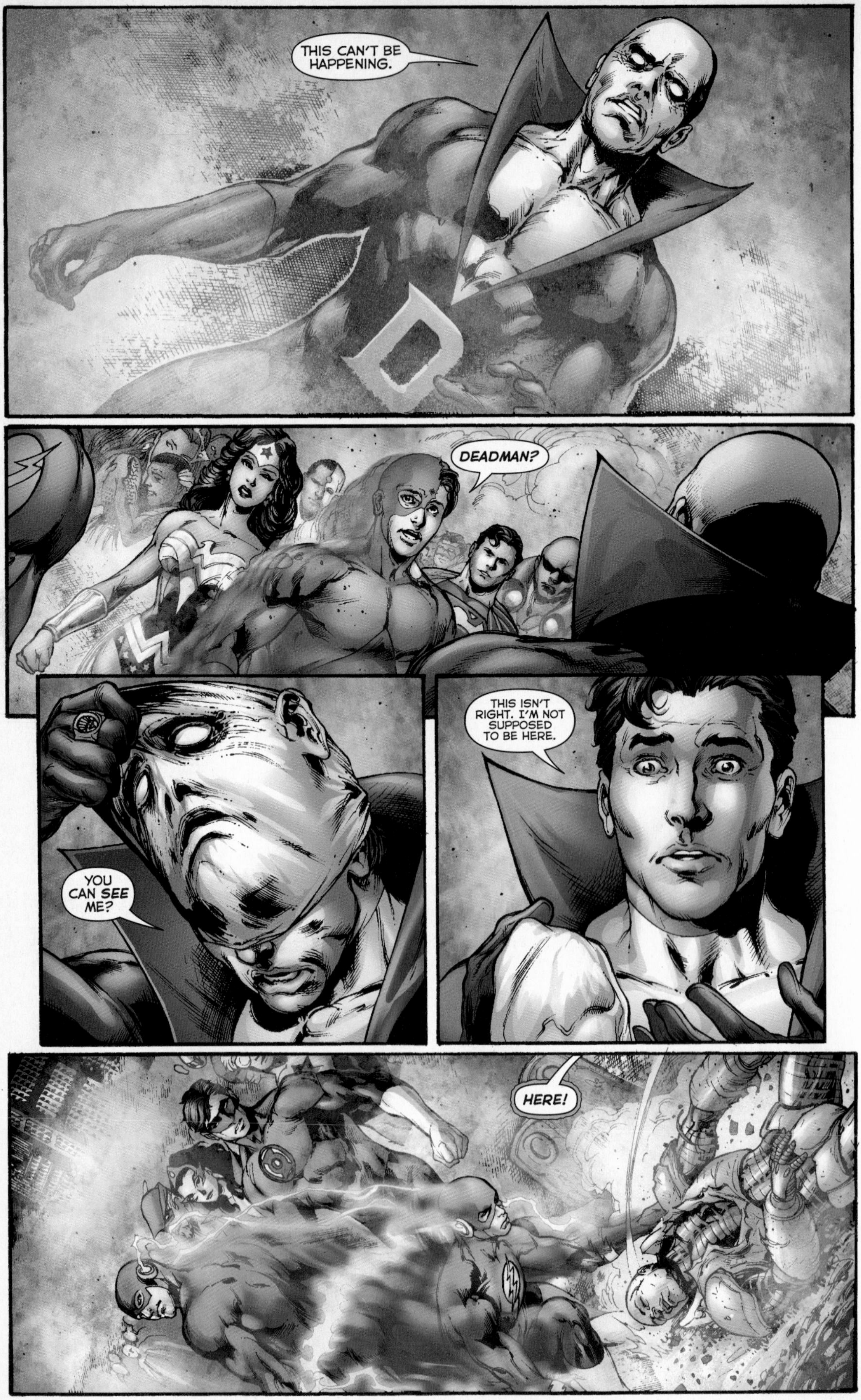
THIS CAN'T BE HAPPENING.
DEADMAN?
YOU CAN SEE ME?
THIS ISN'T RIGHT. I'M NOT SUPPOSED TO BE HERE.
HERE!

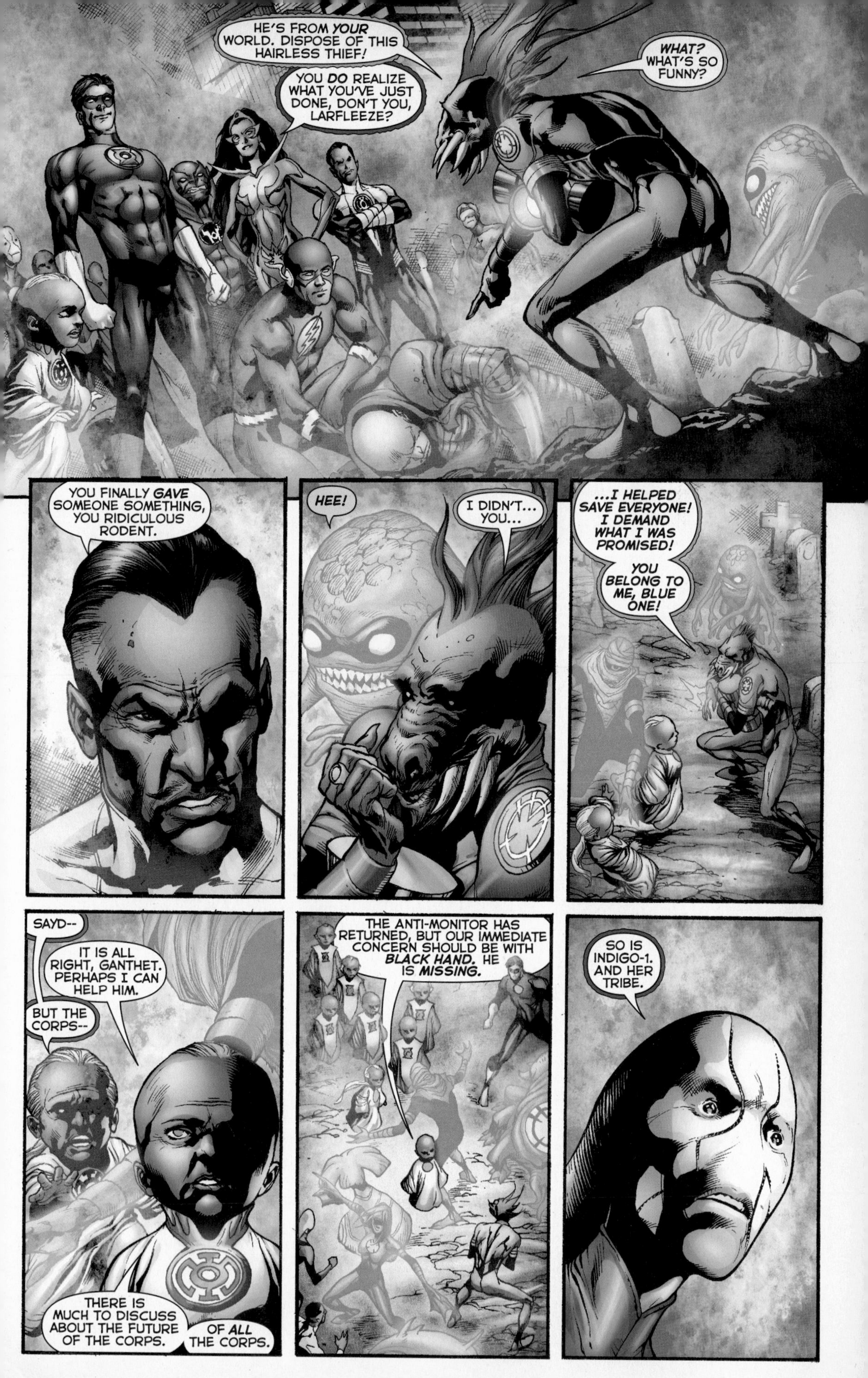

HE'S FROM *YOUR* WORLD. DISPOSE OF THIS HAIRLESS THIEF!
YOU *DO* REALIZE WHAT YOU'VE JUST DONE, DON'T YOU, LARFLEEZE?
WHAT? WHAT'S SO FUNNY?
YOU FINALLY *GAVE* SOMEONE SOMETHING, YOU RIDICULOUS RODENT.
HEE!
I DIDN'T... YOU...
...I HELPED SAVE EVERYONE! I DEMAND WHAT I WAS PROMISED!
YOU BELONG TO ME, BLUE ONE!
SAYD--
IT IS ALL RIGHT, GANTHET. PERHAPS I CAN HELP HIM.
BUT THE CORPS--
THERE IS MUCH TO DISCUSS ABOUT THE FUTURE OF THE CORPS.
OF *ALL* THE CORPS.
THE ANTI-MONITOR HAS RETURNED, BUT OUR IMMEDIATE CONCERN SHOULD BE WITH *BLACK HAND.* HE IS *MISSING.*
SO IS INDIGO-1. AND HER TRIBE.

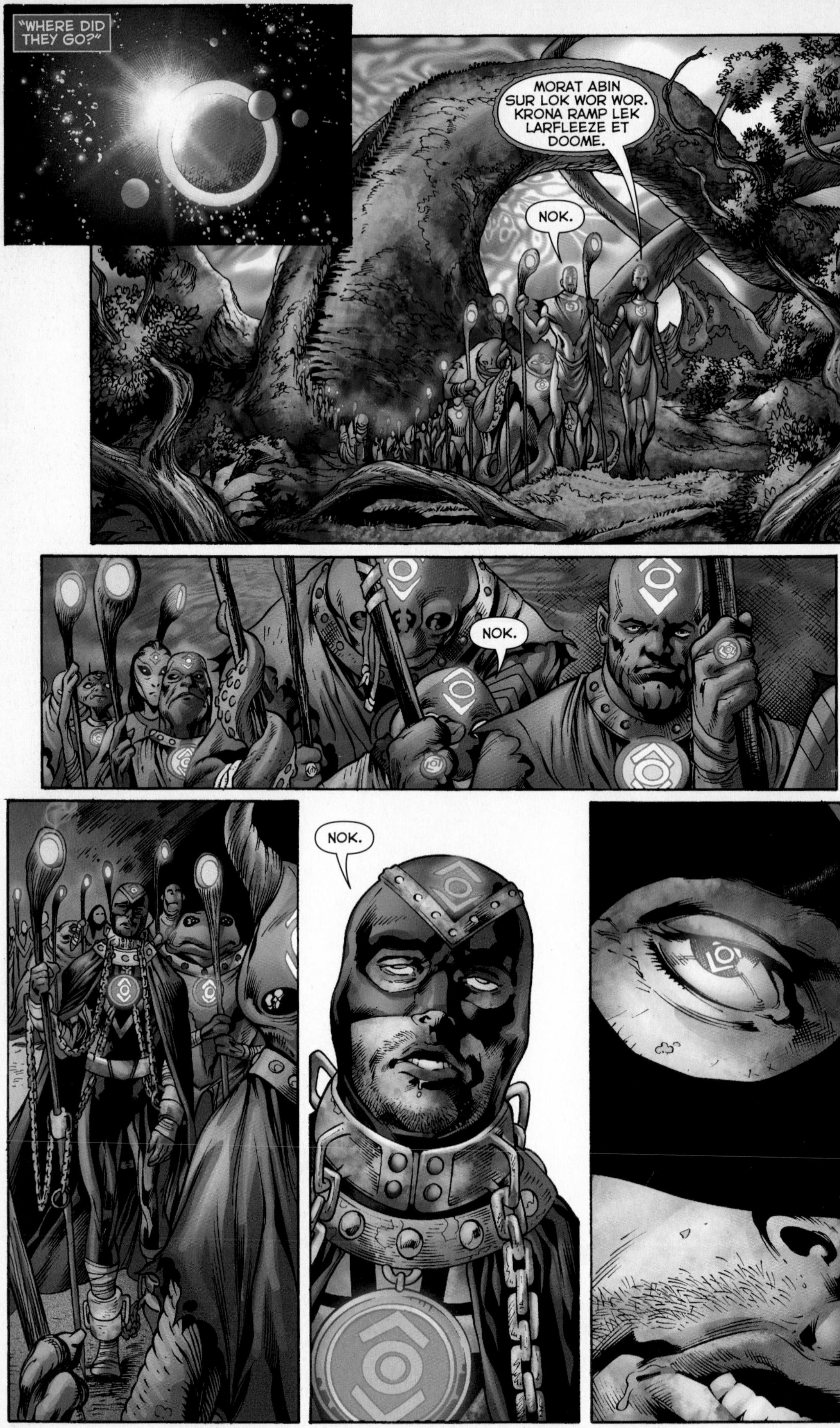
"WHERE DID THEY GO?"
MORAT ABIN SUR LOK WOR WOR. KRONA RAMP LEK LARFLEEZE ET DOOME.
NOK.
NOK.
NOK.

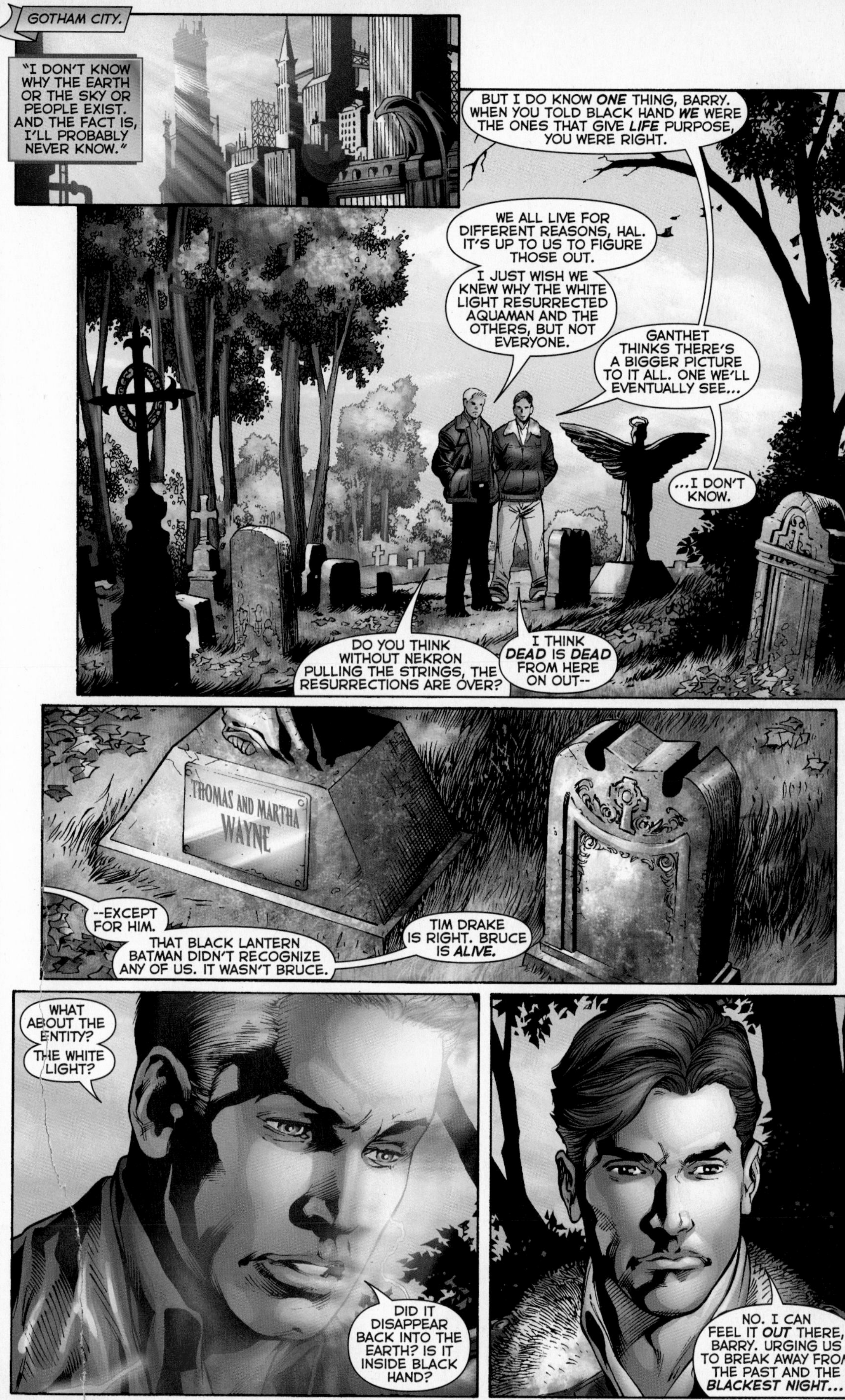
GOTHAM CITY.
"I DON'T KNOW WHY THE EARTH OR THE SKY OR PEOPLE EXIST. AND THE FACT IS, I'LL PROBABLY NEVER KNOW."
BUT I DO KNOW ONE THING, BARRY. WHEN YOU TOLD BLACK HAND WE WERE THE ONES THAT GIVE LIFE PURPOSE, YOU WERE RIGHT.
WE ALL LIVE FOR DIFFERENT REASONS, HAL. IT'S UP TO US TO FIGURE THOSE OUT.
I JUST WISH WE KNEW WHY THE WHITE LIGHT RESURRECTED AQUAMAN AND THE OTHERS, BUT NOT EVERYONE.
GANTHET THINKS THERE'S A BIGGER PICTURE TO IT ALL. ONE WE'LL EVENTUALLY SEE...
...I DON'T KNOW.
DO YOU THINK WITHOUT NEKRON PULLING THE STRINGS, THE RESURRECTIONS ARE OVER?
I THINK DEAD IS DEAD FROM HERE ON OUT--
THOMAS AND MARTHA WAYNE
--EXCEPT FOR HIM.
THAT BLACK LANTERN BATMAN DIDN'T RECOGNIZE ANY OF US. IT WASN'T BRUCE.
TIM DRAKE IS RIGHT. BRUCE IS ALIVE.
WHAT ABOUT THE ENTITY?
THE WHITE LIGHT?
DID IT DISAPPEAR BACK INTO THE EARTH? IS IT INSIDE BLACK HAND?
NO. I CAN FEEL IT OUT THERE, BARRY. URGING US TO BREAK AWAY FROM THE PAST AND THE BLACKEST NIGHT...

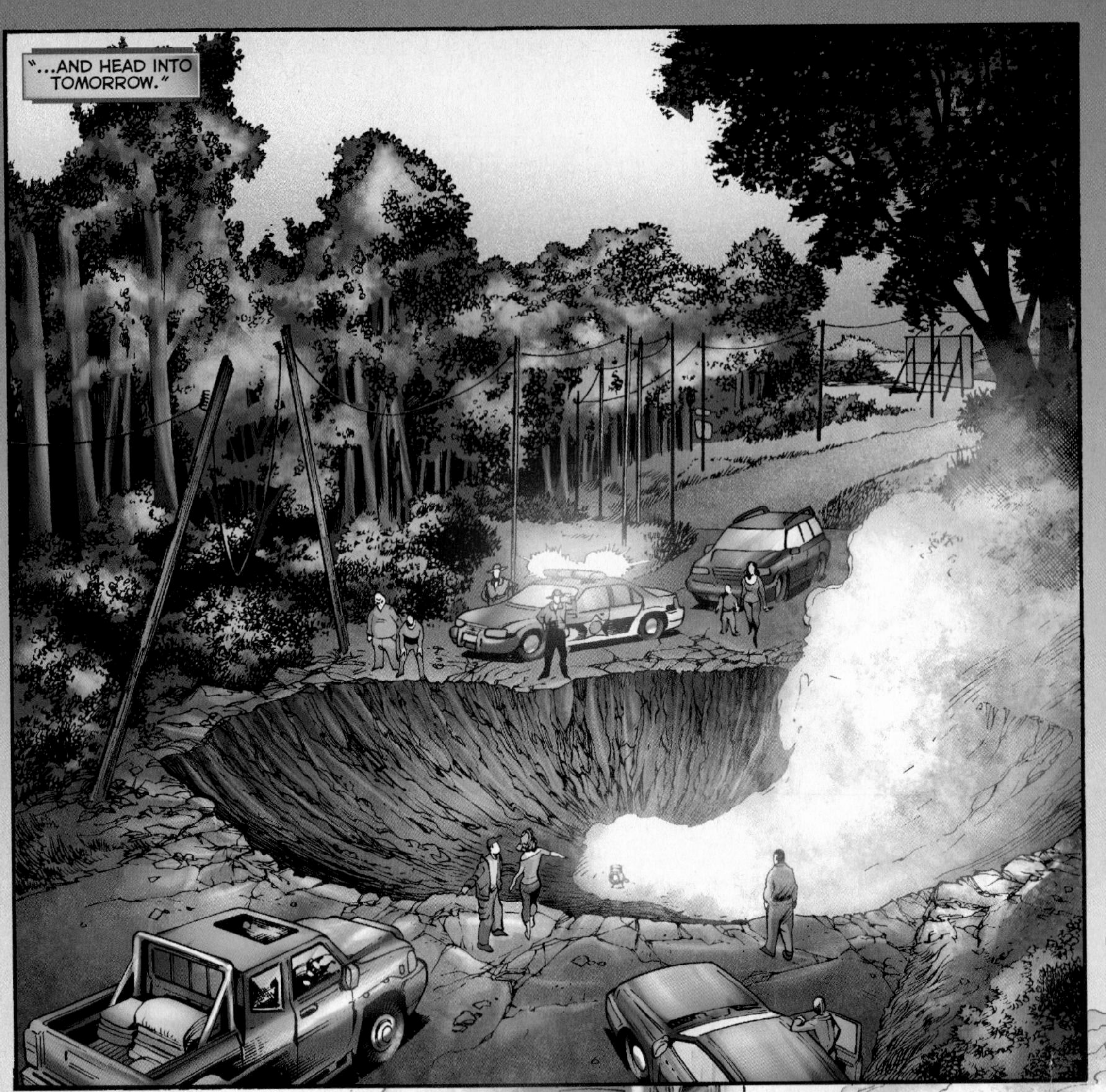
"...AND HEAD INTO TOMORROW."
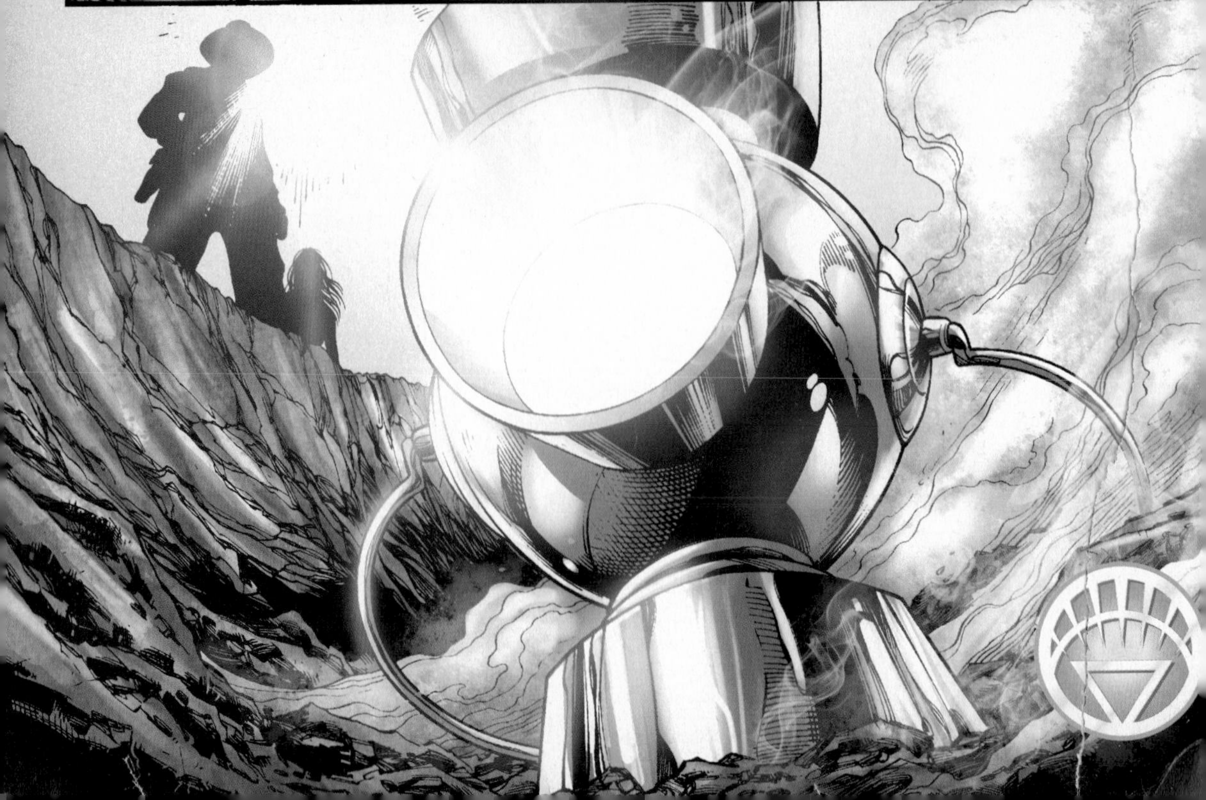

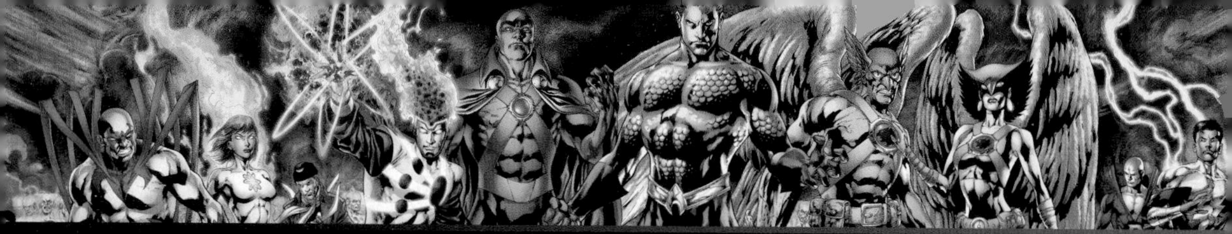

BLACKEST NIGHT
VARIANT COVER GALLERY

BLACKEST NIGHT 1A
by Ethan Van Sciver with Hi-Fi

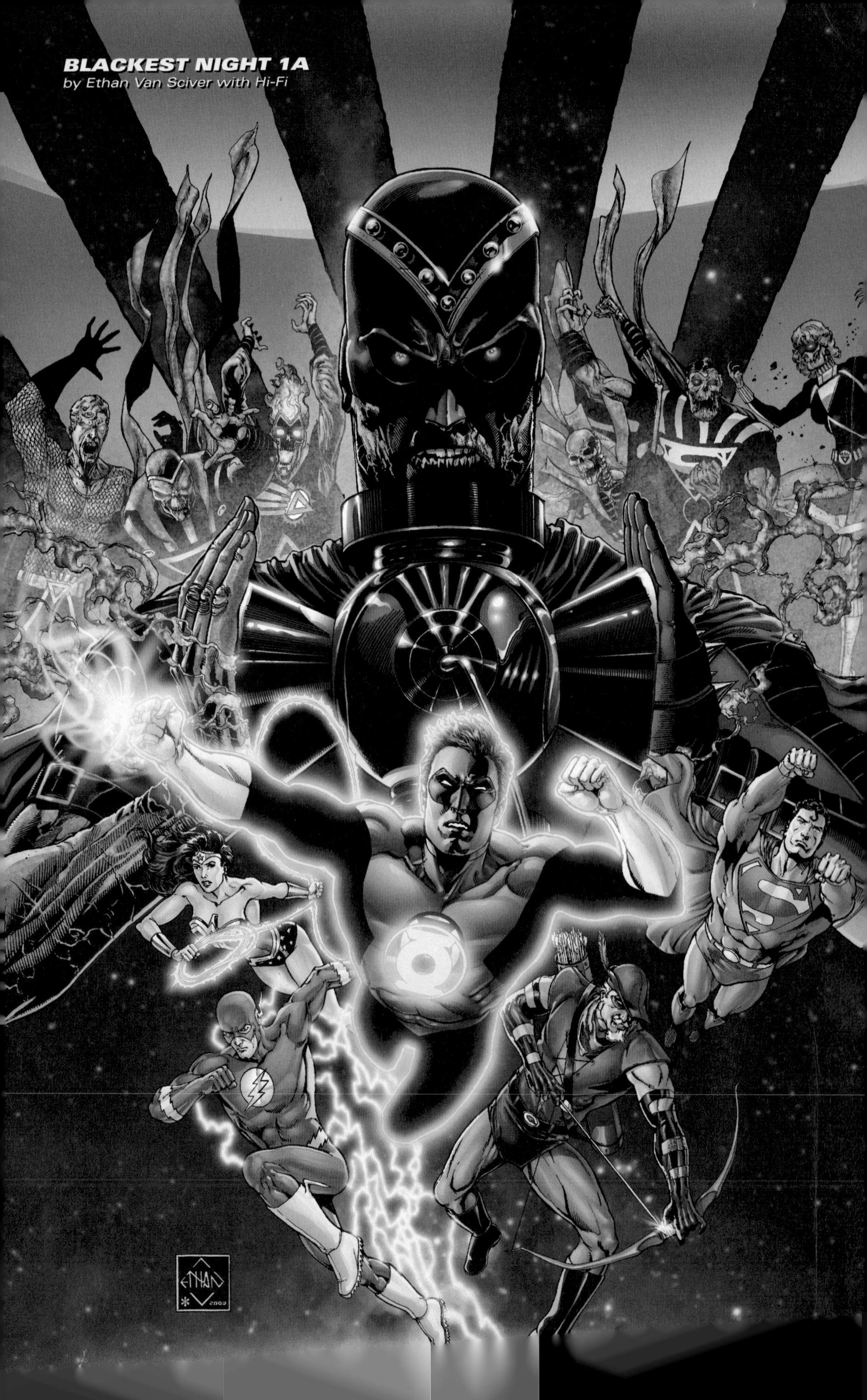

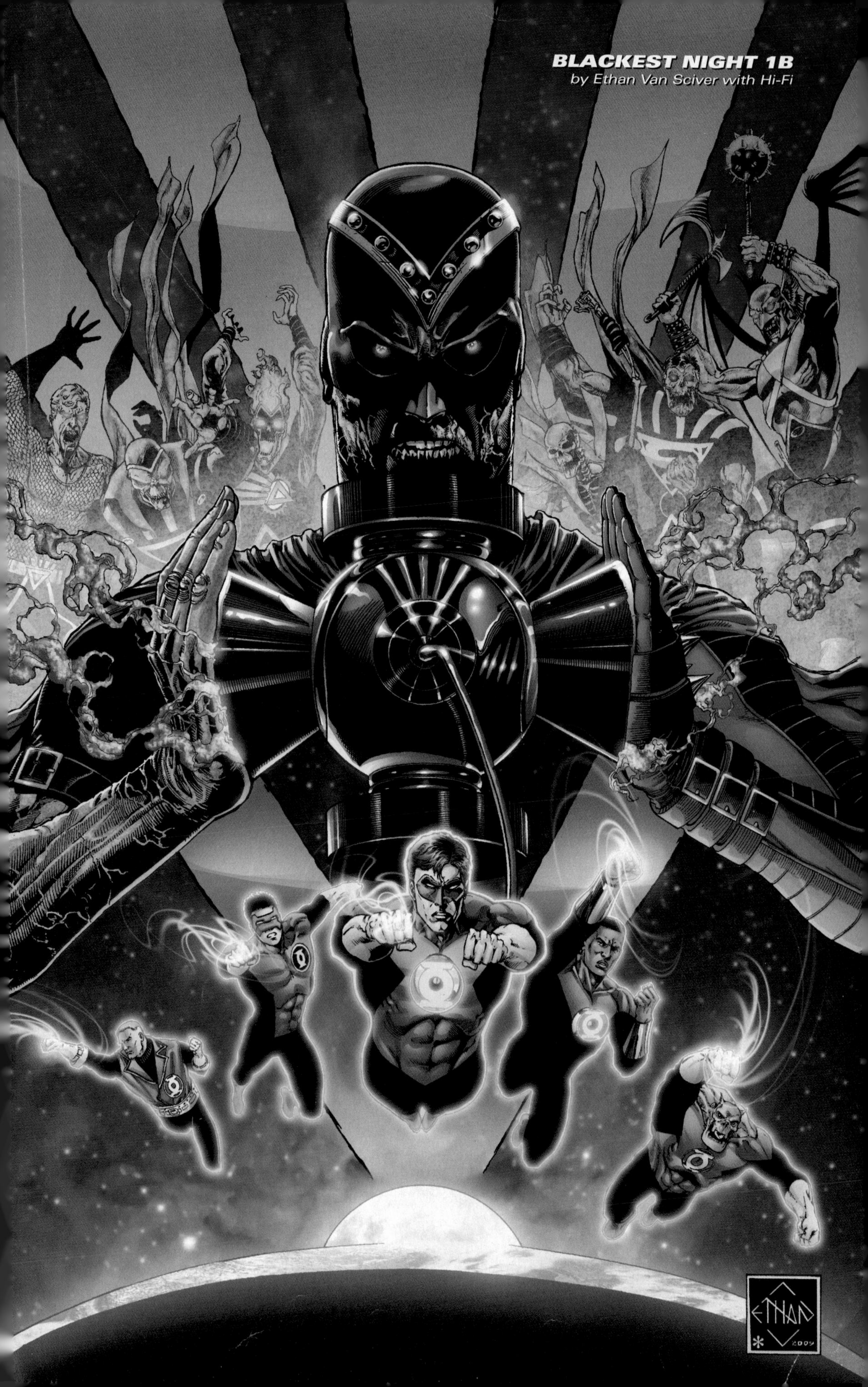
BLACKEST NIGHT 1B
by Ethan Van Sciver with Hi-Fi
ETHAN 2009

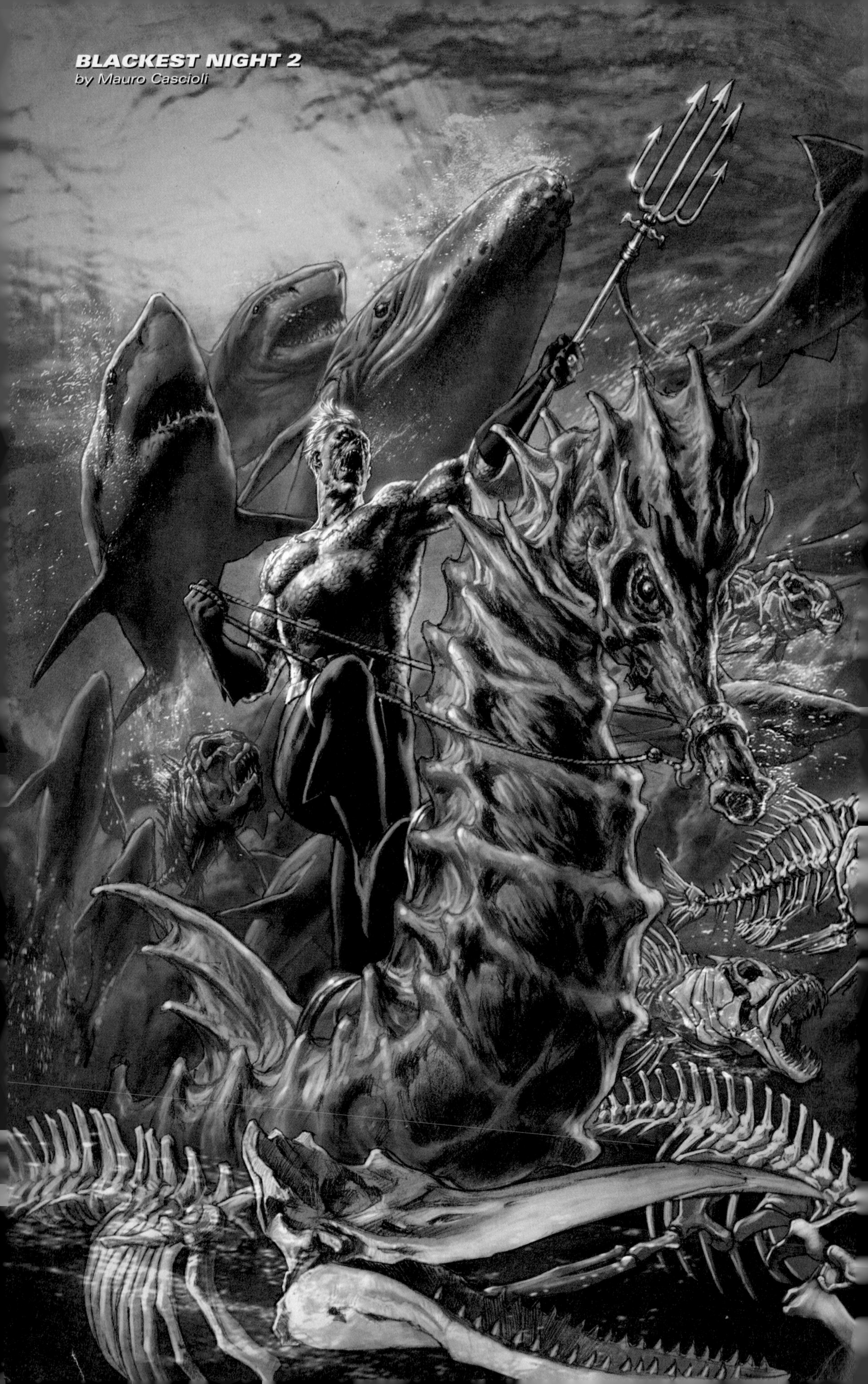

BLACKEST NIGHT 2
by Mauro Cascioli

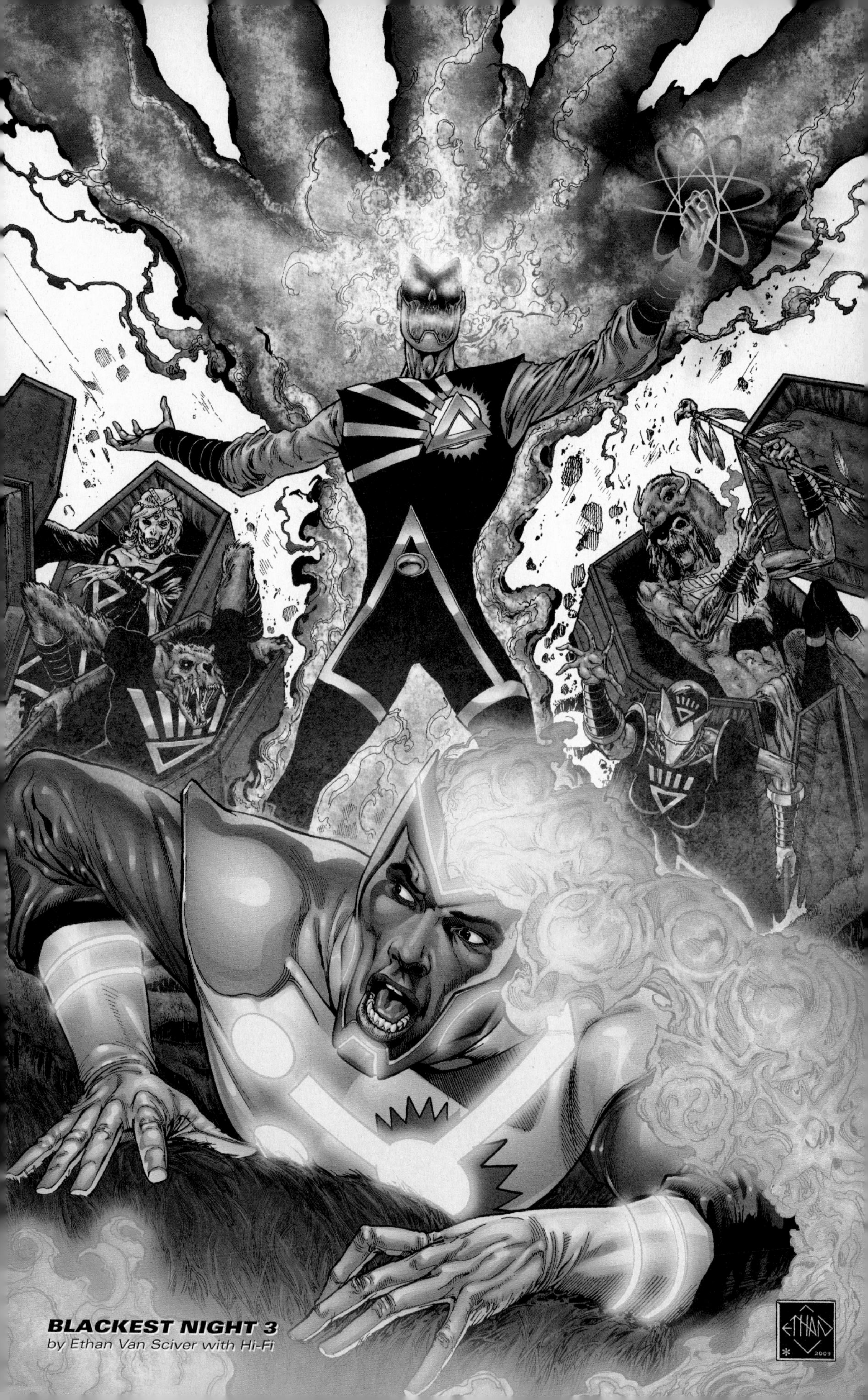

BLACKEST NIGHT 3
by Ethan Van Sciver with Hi-Fi

BLACKEST NIGHT 4

by Rodolfo Migliari

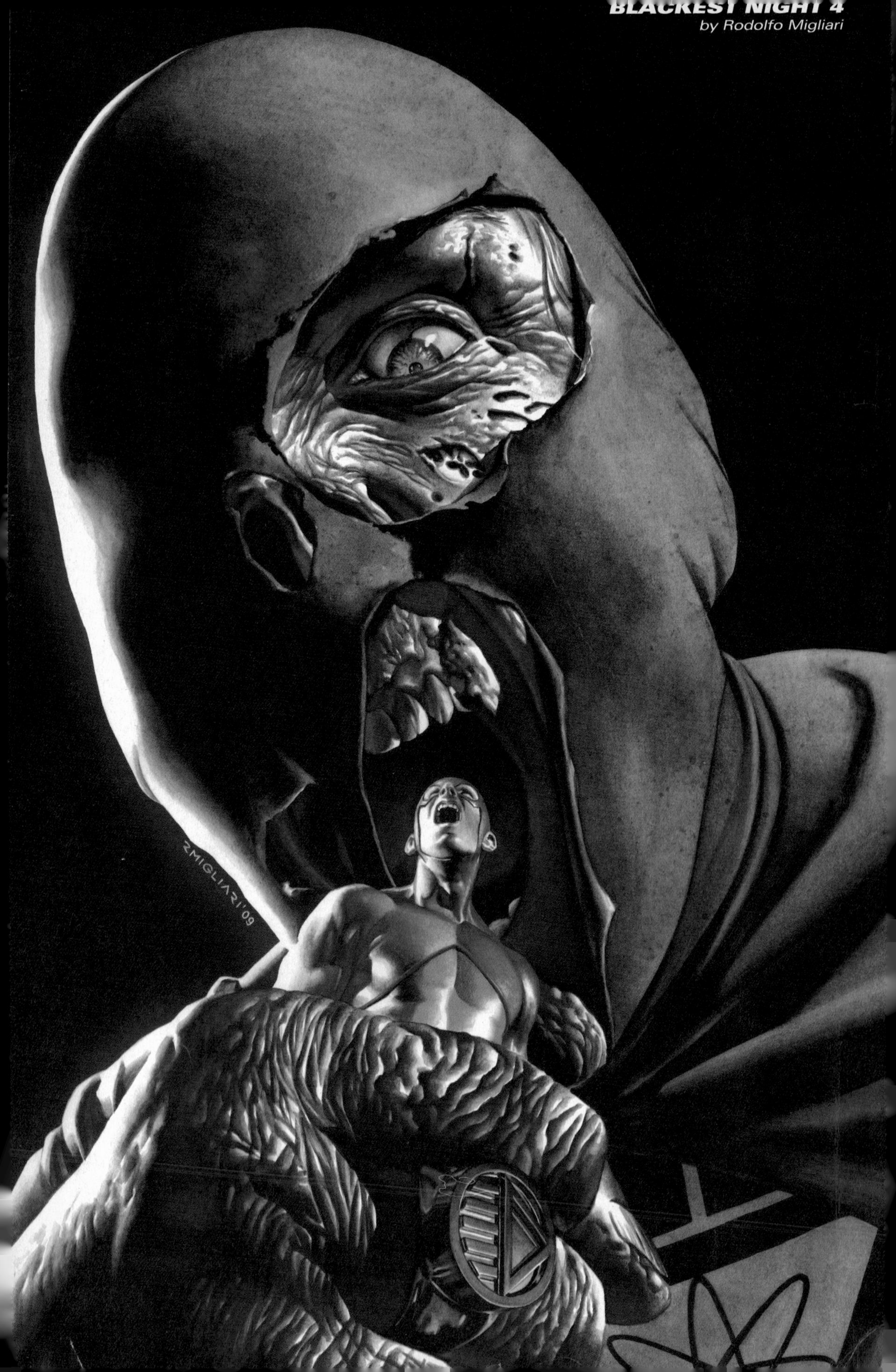
RMIGLIARI'09

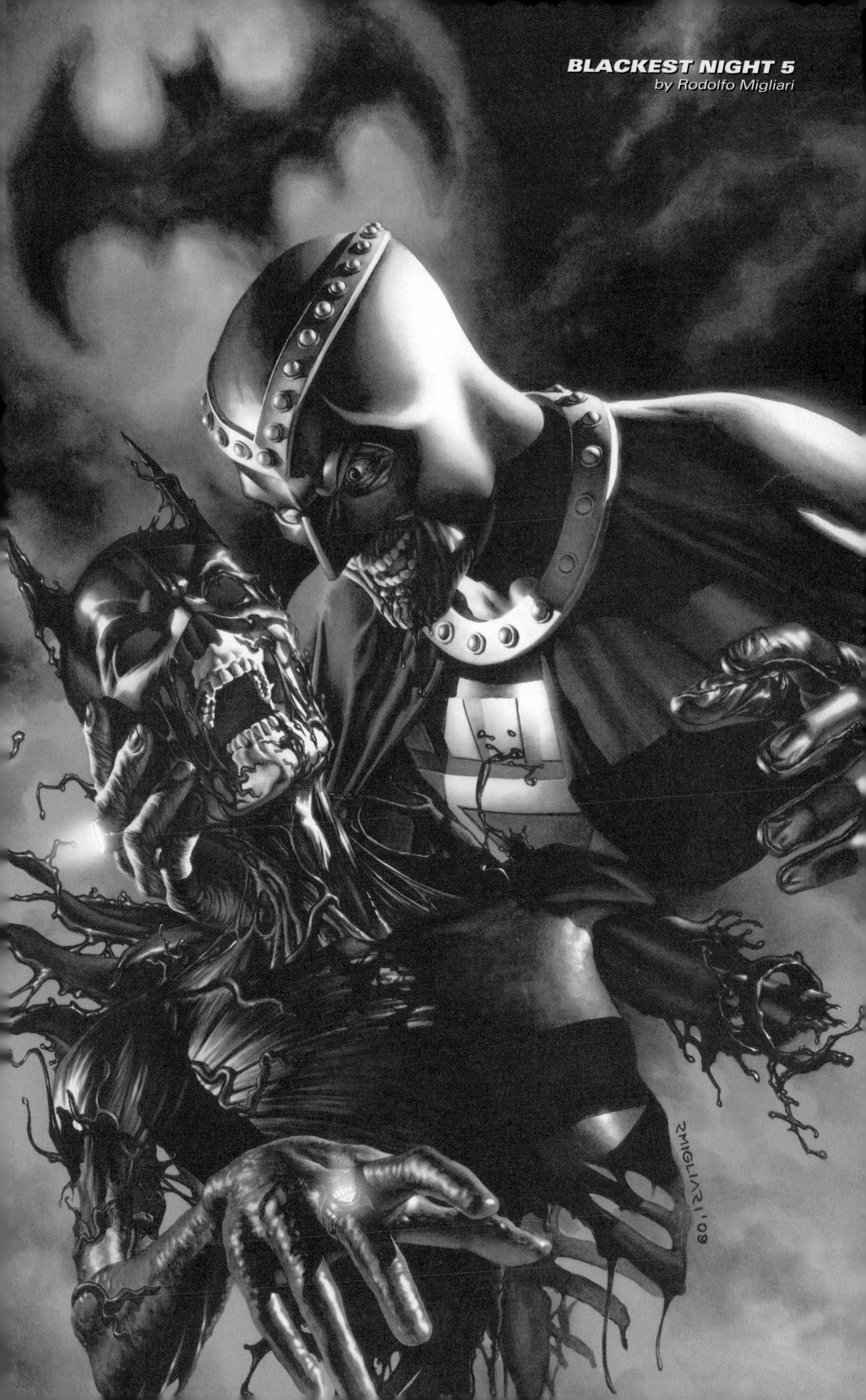
RMIGLIARI'09

BLACKEST NIGHT 5
by Rodolfo Migliari

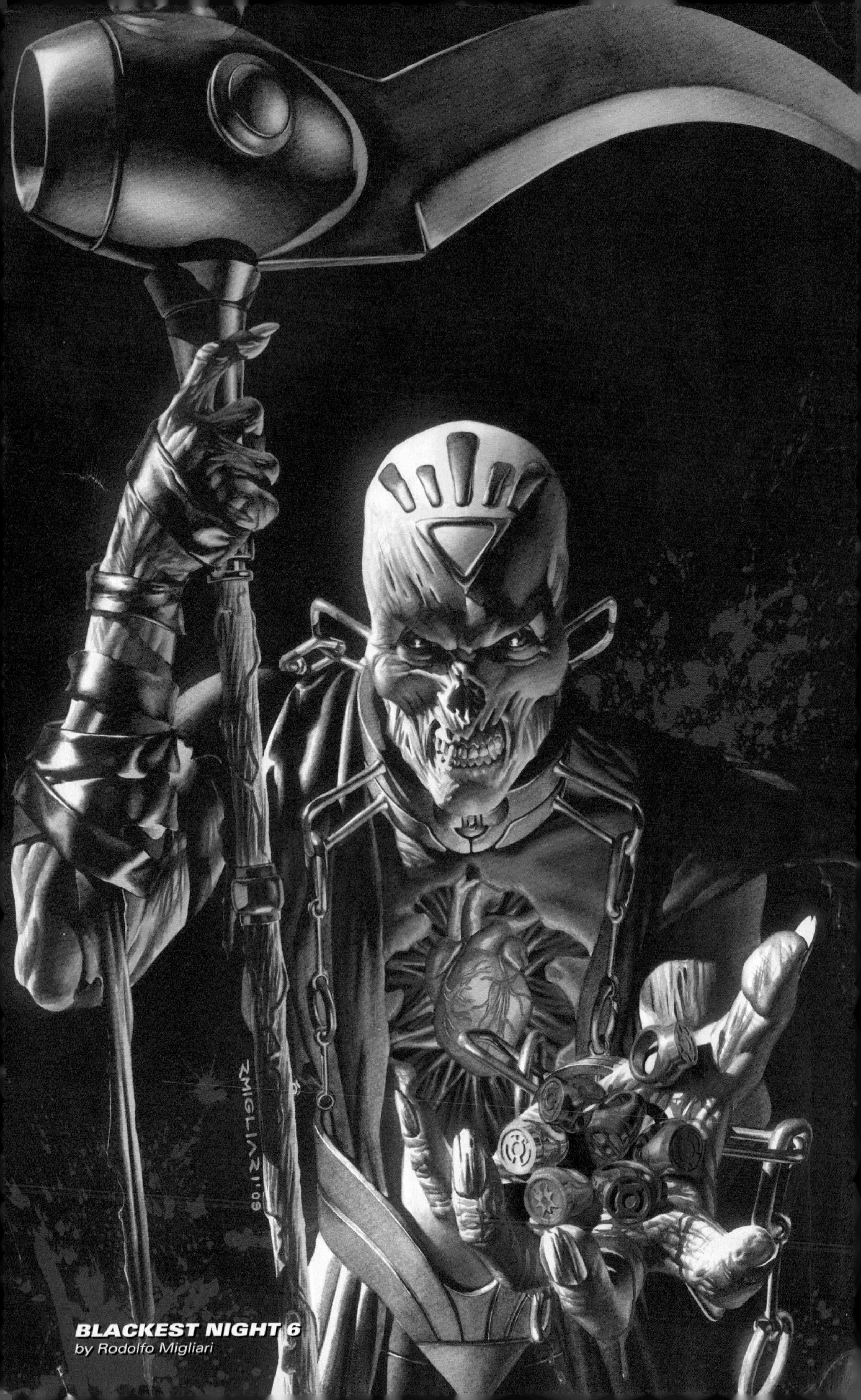

BLACKEST NIGHT 6
by Rodolfo Migliari

BLACKEST NIGHT 7
by Rodolfo Migliari

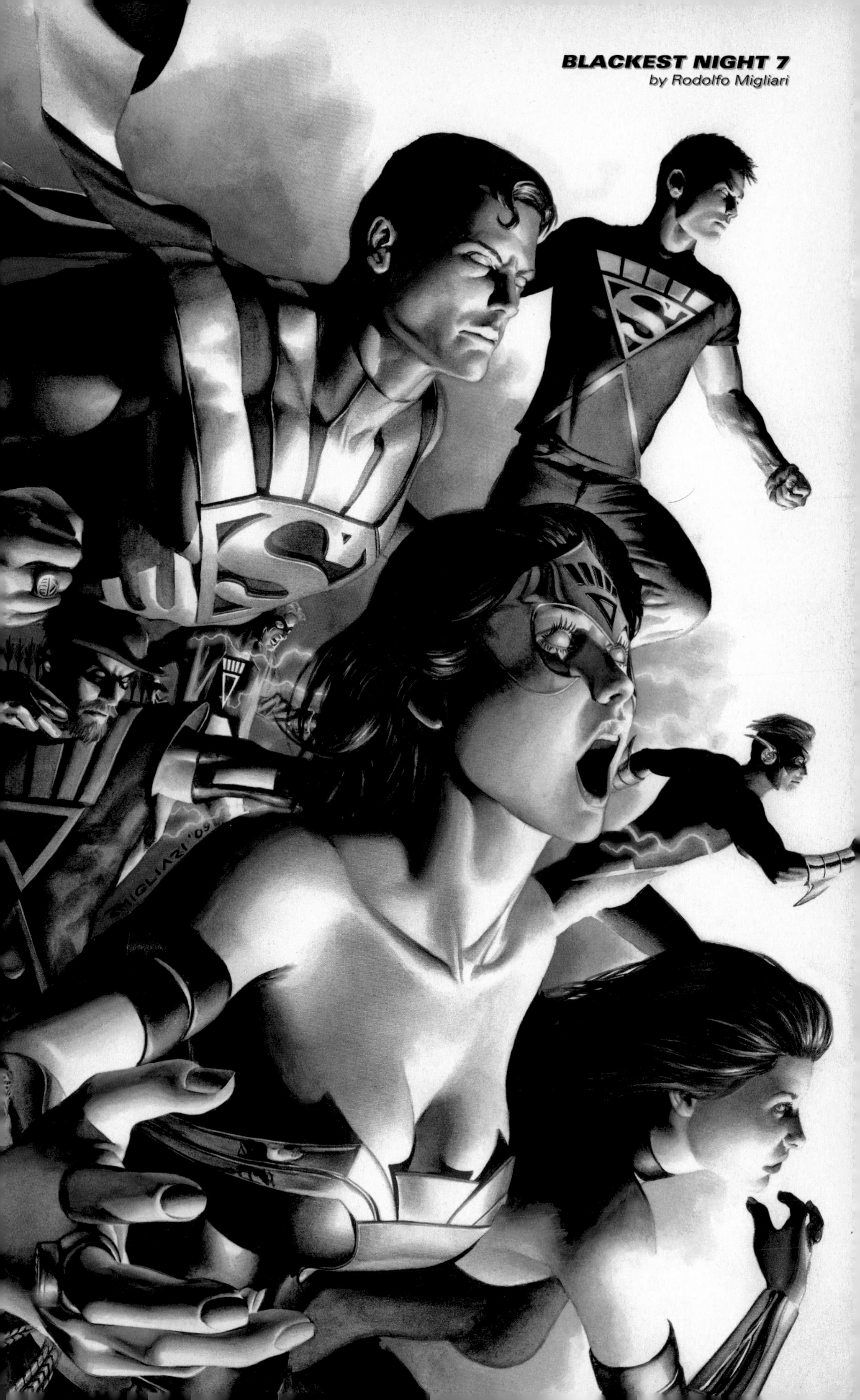
MIGLIARI '09

BLACKEST NIGHT 8
by Doug Mahnke & Christian Alamy with Randy Mayor

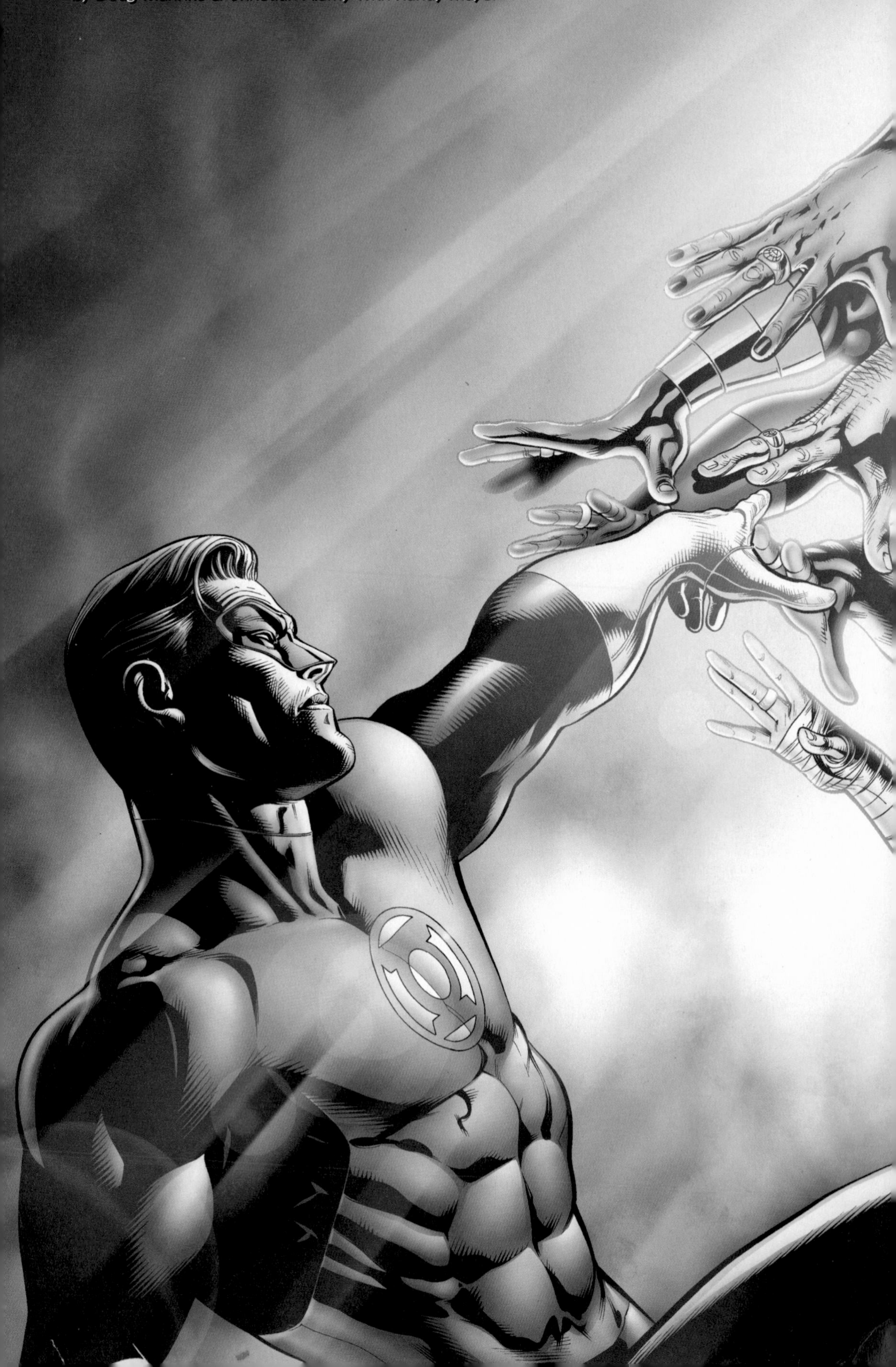

BLACKEST NIGHT DIRECTOR'S COMMENTARY

The creative team and the editors look back on their favorite moments from BLACKEST NIGHT.

GEOFF JOHNS/Writer IVAN REIS/Penciller OCLAIR ALBERT/Inker JOE PRADO/Inker
ALEX SINCLAIR/Colorist NICK J. NAPOLITANO/Letterer ADAM SCHLAGMAN/Associate Editor EDDIE BERGANZA/Editor

ISSUE #1

GEOFF: Ok, now, let's get into it.

PAGE 2/panel 1

ALEX: Still one of my favorite panels from the entire series. Thanks to this panel, I knew just how cool and how HARD it was going to be working on BLACKEST NIGHT.

PAGE 2/panel 2

EDDIE: You pretty much knew the tone of the book, when on the second page you had Black Hand licking the skull. It really would be like no DC series before it.

PAGE 4-5

ALEX: Here was the first of many Guy Gardner ring fixes.

IVAN: I started to do a different symbol for the GLs... now they have a 3-D symbol on their chests... and not a simple drawing... I'm not talking about the energy symbol.

PAGE 6/panel 4

ADAM: Heroes Day doesn't just honor super-heroes, but REAL heroes like firemen, cops and soldiers.

PAGE 6/panel 5

GEOFF: The entire thematic concept of Green Lantern, for me, is overcoming fear. In the original comics back in the '60s, Hal was chosen because he was without fear, but for me, really, the emotional reality is that he's able to overcome fear. No one is without fear unless they're crazy. We just work through it. So "NO FEAR" means a lot more than just leaping before looking...though Hal does plenty of that, too.

Diane Nelson, the new President of DC Entertainment, uses "NO FEAR" as the model for the company. Ironically, GREEN LANTERN is the first film DC Entertainment is fully involved in, which is going to be AWESOME!

IVAN: "Fear" is the key word to all GL mythology

PAGE 9/panel6

ADAM: "...but everything's DYING." What a great line foreshadowing what's to come.

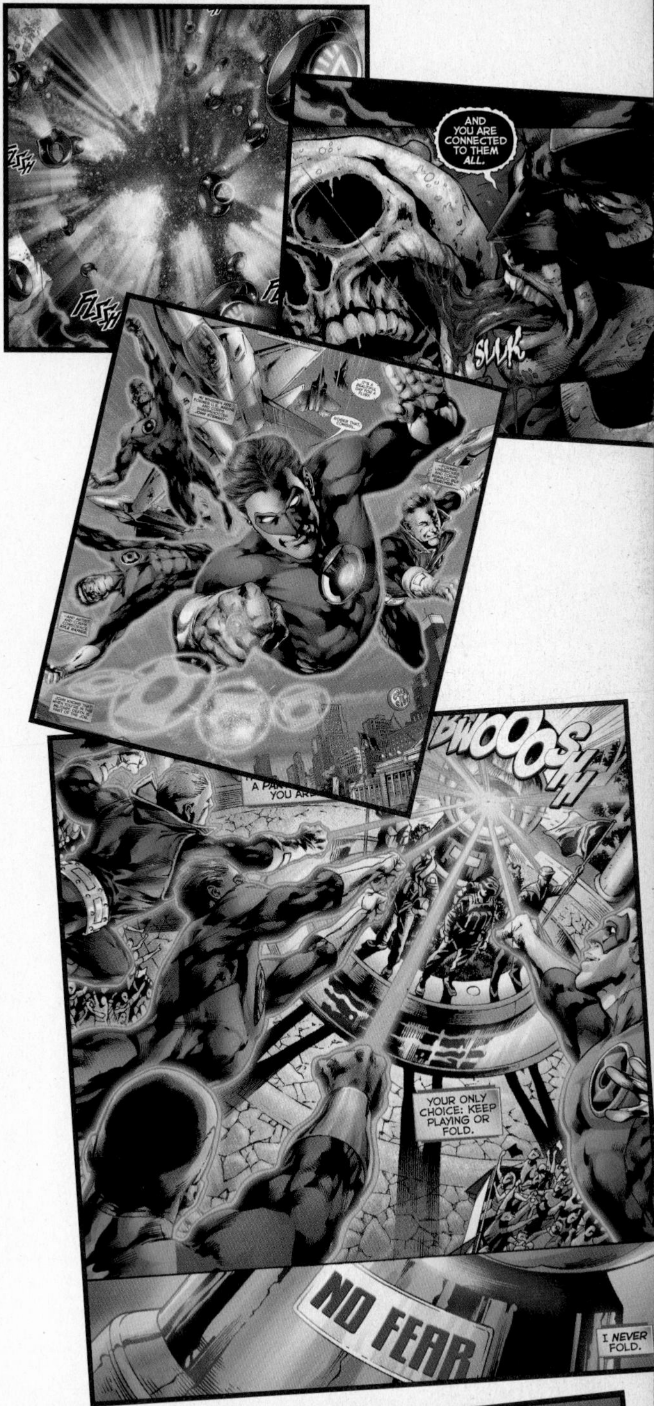

AND YOU ARE CONNECTED TO THEM ALL.
BWOOOSH
YOUR ONLY CHOICE: KEEP PLAYING OR FOLD.
NO FEAR
I NEVER FOLD.

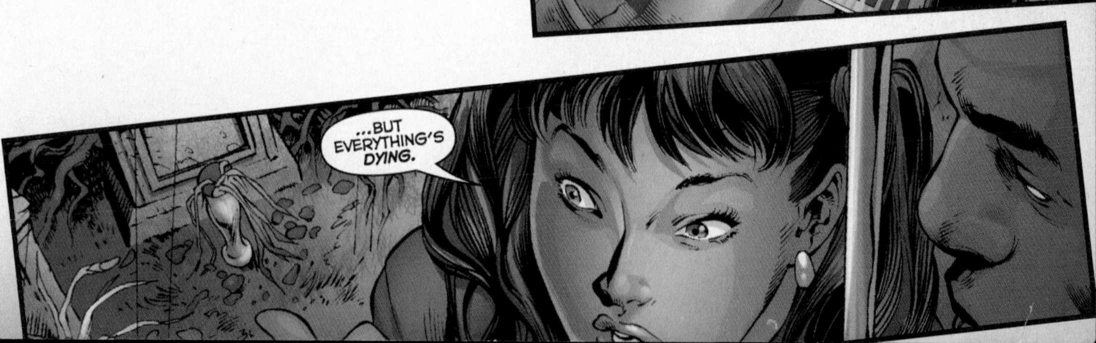

...BUT EVERYTHING'S DYING.

PAGE 11

GEOFF: I wrote JUSTICE SOCIETY OF AMERICA, and the previous series JSA, when I started writing comics and had just left the series when I was moving onto starting BLACKEST NIGHT. Recently, I had taken in Damage and he'd turned into one of my favorite and most complex characters on the team. Damage is the son of the Golden Age Atom, but unlike most of the sons and daughters of the JSA, he never met his father face-to-face or cared about carrying on his legacy. BLACKEST NIGHT give me the opportunity for Damage to finally meet his father.

ALIVE WITH A CRUSHED NASAL CAVITY AND A MANGLED PROFILE.
YOU WANT ME TO FACE MY FATHER, ATOM SMASHER?
HELL.

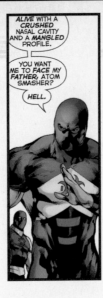

PAGE 12

GEOFF: Let me talk about Aquaman's wife and Queen of Atlantis, the enigmatic Mera. Her origin is a bit undefined. She's from "another water dimension" and she showed up early in the AQUAMAN series. She was the one character in the DC Universe that didn't appear to have any real connection or role in BLACKEST NIGHT, but I knew from the beginning that I didn't want to only focus on the obvious or focus on a smattering of everyone. But Mera, in my opinion, has the potential to be one of the strongest female heroes in the DC Universe. She was clearly the breakout of BLACKEST NIGHT...maybe next to Larfleeze.

LEADERS.
AMNESTY BAY.
THE GRAVE OF ARTHUR CURRY.
AQUAMAN SHOULDN'T BE BURIED ON LAND.
YOUR HUSBAND SHOULD BE WITH HIS PEOPLE, MERA. BENEATH THE SEA.
ARTHUR'S "PEOPLE" TRIED TO MURDER HIM WHEN HE WAS A CHILD, GARTH. THEY HATED HIM BECAUSE HE HAD BLOND HAIR.
THAT'S NOT WHY--
AND THEY HATED YOU BECAUSE OF YOUR VIOLET EYES. IF IT WASN'T FOR ARTHUR, THE ATLANTEANS WOULD'VE CUT THEM OUT.
THEY CAN BE A SUPERSTITIOUS AND VIOLENT PEOPLE.
ARTHUR'S MOTHER DIED BRINGING HIM TO THE SHORE, BACK TO HIS FATHER.
THIS IS WHERE HE FELT SAFE, GARTH.
THIS IS WHAT HE WANTED.
THERE'S A MAGNIFICENT TOMB WAITING FOR HIM IN ATLANTIS. IT'S AMONG THE MOST BEAUTIFUL CORAL FIELDS, SURROUNDED BY SEA LIFE OF ALL KINDS WAITING TO SEE THEIR SAVIOR.
THE TOMB IS SIDE-BY-SIDE WITH THE OTHER GREAT LEADERS OF OUR CITY...AND HIS SON.
YOUR SON.
MERA, PLEASE GIVE ME AUTHORIZATION TO HAVE HIS REMAINS MOVED.
THE DIRT IS NO PLACE FOR A KING OF THE SEAS.

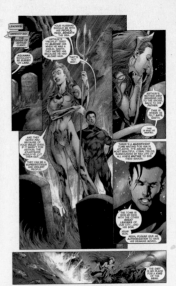

ALEX: Aquaman has always been one of my favorites, but I had never colored Mera before. I love textures so she became one of my favorite characters in the series and Ivan did an amazing job drawing her (and everyone else)!

PAGE 12/panel 1

NICK: Did a lot of tombstones during this series (might have a second career there :)), but Aquaman's was tough.

SO WHO ELSE?

PAGE 12/panel 5

IVAN: Death has already arrived to the sea.

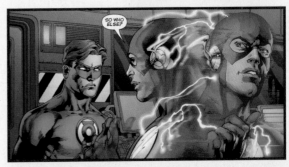

PAGE 14-15

IVAN: I love to draw multiple images of the Flash to show his fast movements... even to show the simple ones.

PAGE 16-17

ADAM: An incredible, overwhelming spread beautifully illustrated by Ivan Reis showcasing the many deaths that have occurred in the DC Universe.

IVAN: I think it was more than 55 characters.

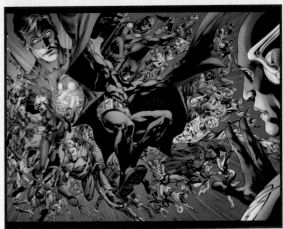

GEOFF: This and the following page are my favorite moments in the first issue, and they tie directly into my favorite moment in issue #8.

ALEX: I have a version of this without the Green Lantern construct effect over it because "you never know."

NICK: This is what a letterer calls a "gimme" page–SILENT–but man, I stared at this one a while. Are they all dead? Beautiful, Ivan!

NOT RALPH AND SUE TOO.
...NOT THEM
HOW, HAL?
WHY?

PAGE 18

EDDIE: This page is a testament of Ivan's artistic abilities. He totally sells how sad Barry is over the loss of his friends.

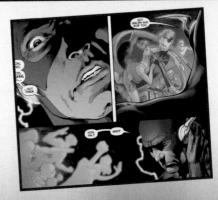

PAGE 19

IVAN: The first time we see Hawkman in the story... I love drawing Hawkman.

PAGE 22/panel 1 and 2

IVAN: This is the only moment that you can see Flash sitting down with no additional movement. He just learned about all his dead friends and he's devastated.

PAGE 26/panel 1

ADAM: My favorite panel possibly in the entire series. This is where things turn and really get bad. What an image! Scar takes a bite out of a Guardian and we're off to the races.

GEOFF: Definitely a horror moment but not the most heart-wrenching of issue #1.

PAGE 30-31

EDDIE: Pretty much Guy said it all. Things were gonna get nasty.

IVAN: Everybody in this spread is dressed in black costumes with heavy shadows on their faces and black borders on the page...I don't know how it was possible to discern all the characters =)

PAGE 30-31/panel 2

NICK: Man! This is when you say to yourself, "How can I put a huge piece of text on this freakin' magnificent piece of art"? The "RISE" was a big commitment for this page. Seems to have worked out.

PAGE 30-31/panel 3

NICK: THIS is when I realized that J'onn was coming back and not in a "feel good" way. I also realized there were no limits to where Geoff would take this story. I was HOOKED!

PAGE 33

NICK: "GET OUT OF THE HOUSE! THE CALL'S COMING FROM INSIDE THE HOUSE!!" Anyone who can place that quote knows how on the "edge of my seat" I was during this scene.

PAGE 33/last panel

EDDIE: The nascent "Black Lantern vision" that would become so prevalent over the series and give it a unique flavor.

GEOFF: Eddie, this is an important thing to pull out. The creative coordination that BLACKEST NIGHT required only worked because of Eddie and Adam. Eddie, in particular, really focused on ensuring that the "Black Lantern vision" was present in every tie-in and series. Plus it looked cool. We refined the look in the subsequent GREEN LANTERN issue that followed this one.

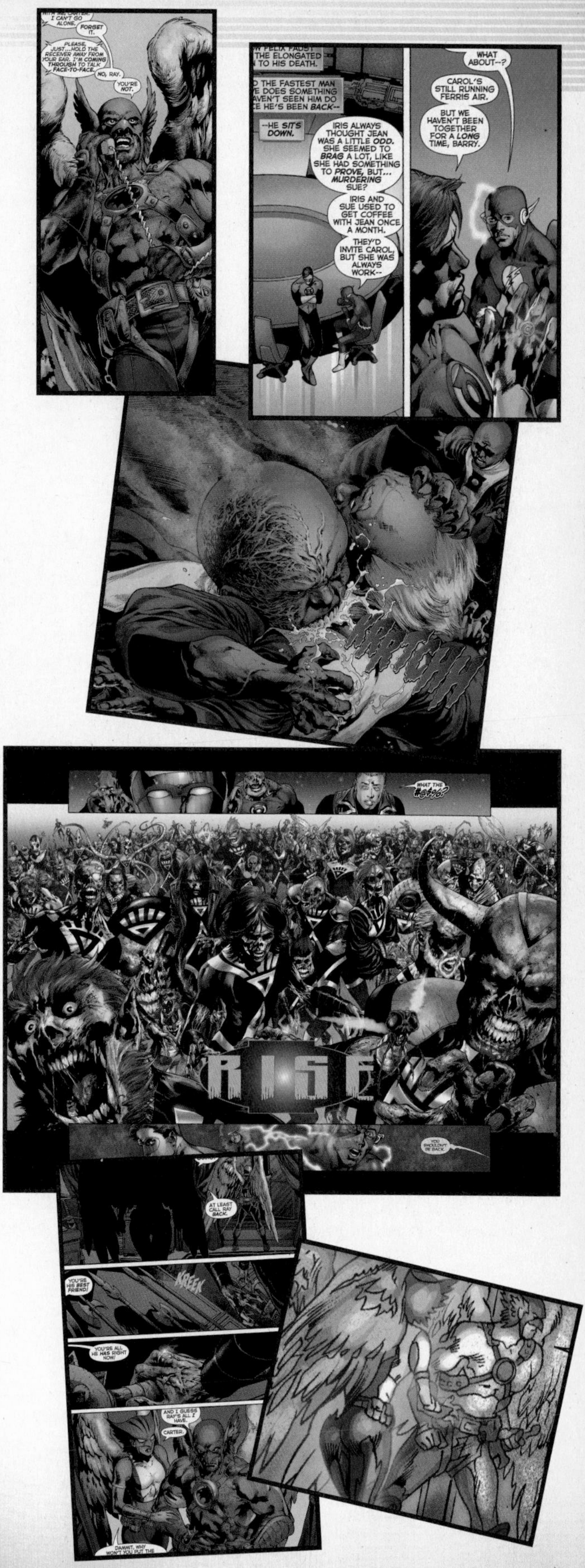
FORGET IT.
PLEASE, JUST...HOLD THE RECEIVER AWAY FROM YOUR EAR. I'M COMING THROUGH TO TALK FACE-TO-FACE.
NO, RAY.
YOU'RE NOT.
--HE SITS DOWN.
IRIS ALWAYS THOUGHT JEAN WAS A LITTLE ODD. SHE SEEMED TO BRAG A LOT, LIKE SHE HAD SOMETHING TO PROVE, BUT... MURDERING SUE?
IRIS AND SUE USED TO GET COFFEE WITH JEAN ONCE A MONTH.
THEY'D INVITE CAROL, BUT SHE WAS ALWAYS WORK--
WHAT ABOUT--?
CAROL'S STILL RUNNING FERRIS AIR.
BUT WE HAVEN'T BEEN TOGETHER FOR A LONG TIME, BARRY.
RISE
YOU SHOULDN'T BE BACK.
AT LEAST CALL RAY BACK.
YOU'RE HIS BEST FRIEND!
YOU'RE ALL HE HAS RIGHT NOW!
AND I GUESS RAY'S ALL I HAVE.
CARTER.

PAGE 35/panel 2

ALEX: My face looked just like Hawkman's when I opened this page. This whole sequence really stuck with me for a while after I finished it. Geoff and Ivan skillfully depicted so much emotion here.

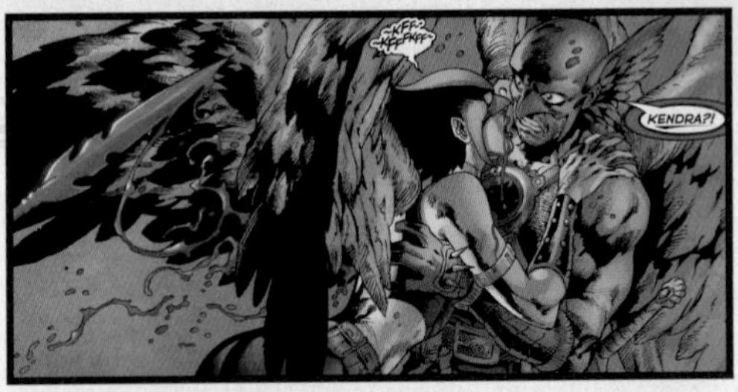
KENDRA?!

PAGE 40/panel 3

JOE: For me the most terrifying moment and the one that set the tone for the whole Blackest Night was the Hawks being attacked by Ralph and Sue Dibny. That was cruel, ruthless and heartbreaking at the same time. When at last Carter and Kendra are about to be together, they die! Just heartbreaking!

GEOFF: Originally, when I was first laying out the series, I had thought somewhere Hawkman and Hawkgirl would be killed by their own bodies, but when they became the first ones murdered by the Black Lanterns I knew the scene had to be more. I also knew how "evil" it was to have the corpses be the Elongated Man and Sue Dibny. But for me, it was more horrific because they were such a sweet couple who had such a tragic ending – which is what the Hawks unfortunately are cursed with: to meet and fall in love in every life and die at the height of it.

OCLAIR: Dude, I can't highlight a specific point that is my favorite here. The story develops at such a crazy pace, culminating on the last page! And then... we want MORE!

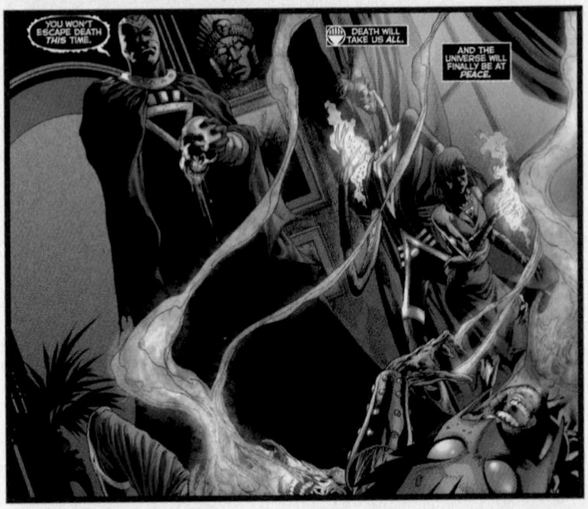
YOU WON'T ESCAPE DEATH THIS TIME.
DEATH WILL TAKE US ALL.
AND THE UNIVERSE WILL FINALLY BE AT PEACE.

ISSUE #2

PAGE 1

IVAN: With the dead rising, the story opens in widescreen.

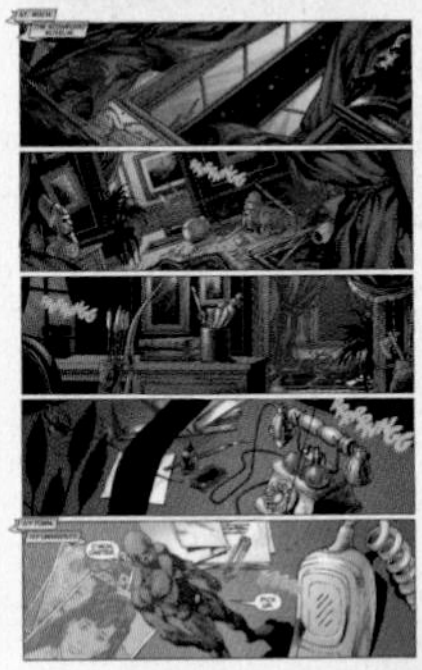

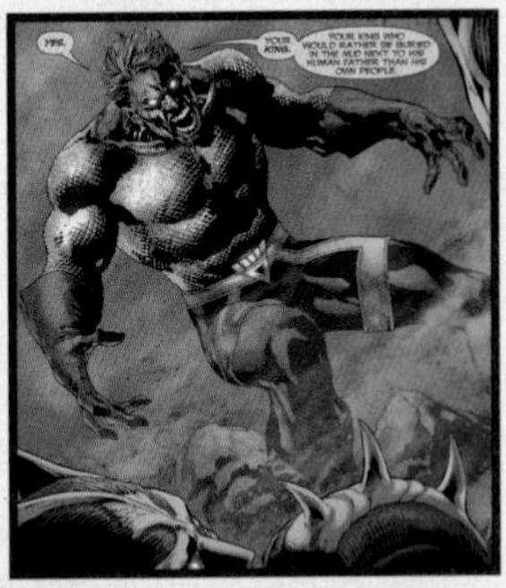

PAGE 6/panel 1

GEOFF: Issue #2 was an always going to be about building tension, dread and centered around Black Lantern Aquaman's reveal. I wanted to anchor the issue around who I considered our main dead hero. I see Aquaman as one of DC's toughest heroes, dead or alive.

ADAM: Here's our first shot of Black Lantern Aquaman and holy cow, he just ripped out the heart of one of his people. Our heroes are evil and they kill. ANYTHING can happen!

ALEX: He's undead, he's evil...but he is still sooooo cool looking.

OCLAIR: Again a crazy rhythm here that culminates in Aquaman's appearance! The carnage begins, and it ends with Garth's death! Even the "calm" (if that's an adjective I can apply here) parts, such as the Phantom Stranger/Black Lantern Spectre is crazy! Every page I inked got me looking forward to what would happen next!

PAGE 7

NICK: This page took a while... Second time I had to do the "Black Lantern Oath" (First was in the #0 issue) had to make sure to help bring the reader around the page as Geoff & Ivan intended-PLUS-C'mon! It's the Black Lantern Oath! DON'T CHOKE!

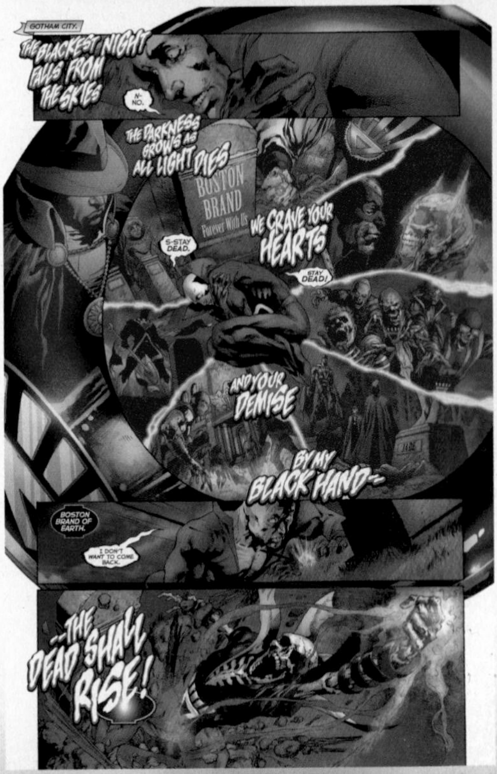
GOTHAM CITY.
THE BLACKEST NIGHT FALLS FROM THE SKIES
N-NO.
THE DARKNESS GROWS AS ALL LIGHT DIES
BOSTON BRAND
Forever With Us
WE CRAVE YOUR HEARTS
S-STAY DEAD.
STAY DEAD!
AND YOUR DEMISE
BY MY BLACK HAND--
BOSTON BRAND OF EARTH.
I DON'T WANT TO COME BACK.
--THE DEAD SHALL RISE!

PAGE 7/panel 2

NICK: Deadman in the fetal position, rocking (Oh! The page doesn't move but I know he's rocking!) repeating: "Stay Dead! Stay Dead!" MAJOR CREEPY! Nice scene, guys!

GEOFF: I've said it before (well, on Twitter) but Nick rocked it this whole series. Lettering is an art form all its own because it's incorporated into Ivan's art, especially scenes like this. Placement, font, size can make or break a page. Especially when I write too much dialogue!

PAGE 7/next to last panel

ADAM: "I don't WANT to come back." He doesn't know how correct he is but that's for another story.

JOE: I can't wait to see that!

PAGE 8/panel 3

GEOFF: This was another important moment for me. The only character that the black rings are unable to corrupt postmortem is Don Hall, Dove. Dove was the avatar of peace. He's content that he's lived his life and has fully accepted that he's dead. He also shares something in common with the white light, as Dawn Granger the second Dove does. Exactly what is another story we're telling in BRIGHTEST DAY.

PAGE 11/panel 3

ADAM: What a great idea to have Aquaman be able to control dead sea life. Great one, Geoff! And check out Ivan's amazing rendition. What an amazing fight scene. Check out that eel ripping off the Atlantean's lips.

GEOFF: Although BLACKEST NIGHT is dark, I still wanted it to be fun. And what's more fun than zombie sharks?

PAGE 12/panel 5

ADAM: I LOVE Pariah. You always knew something awful was going to occur when he showed up, so I knew Geoff had to put him in here and what a way to do so.

PAGE 14-15

ADAM: The double page vertical spread really showcases the immense size and power of the Spectre, and we know we're in massive trouble.

ALEX: I just love how Ivan drew him "muscles out" as if the skin has been removed. Great image!

IVAN: Yep! I took off his skin… just to show the muscle… he could join in the Body World Expo.

ADAM: Who's been pumping Crispus full of steroids?

JOE: Funny thing here was you guys asked me to design the Black Lantern Spectre and I thought… "Wow! Cool! Jim Corrigan as a Black Lantern!" I did the design and just then you told me it should be Crispus Allen!

GEOFF: Should it be…?

PAGE 18

IVAN: Here we discover that we can't kill the dead.

PAGE 19/ panel 1

EDDIE: This was an especially hard scene for me as a Titans fan and a fan of the underdog that Garth was. But these deaths had to mean something, and the demise of the original Aqualad had a big impact that will continue to affect the living characters.

GEOFF: I knew how much a fan Eddie was of Tempest and we also knew if someone died in BLACKEST NIGHT it was no longer going to be mean that they were coming back next issue. Although twelve do at the end (spoilers!), the rest are dead.

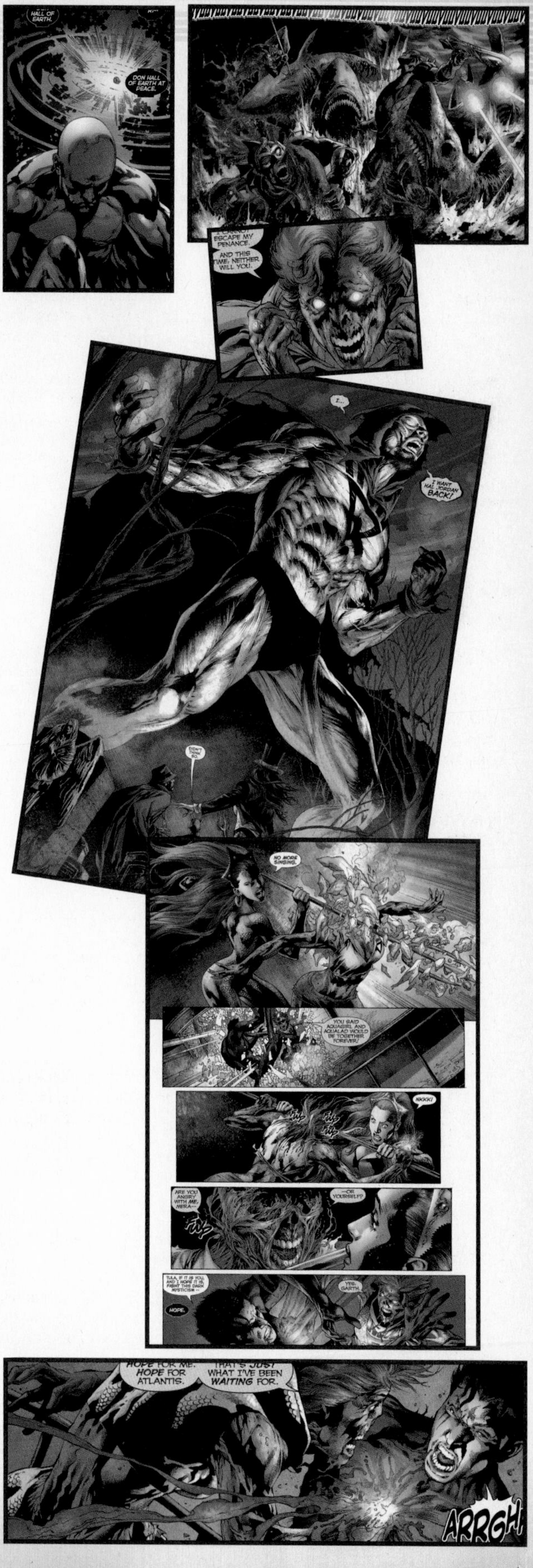
HALL OF EARTH.
DON HALL OF EARTH AT PEACE.
ESCAPE MY PENANCE.
AND THIS TIME, NEITHER WILL YOU.
I...
I WANT HAL JORDAN BACK!
NO MORE SINGING.
YOU SAID AQUAGIRL AND AQUALAD WOULD BE TOGETHER FOREVER!
NKKK!
ARE YOU ANGRY WITH ME, MERA--
--OR YOURSELF?
TULA, IF IT IS YOU, AND I HOPE IT IS, FIGHT THIS DARK MYSTICISM --
HOPE.
YES, GARTH.
HOPE FOR ATLANTIS.
WHAT I'VE BEEN WAITING FOR.
ARRGH!

PAGE 24

EDDIE: What can you say, but wow and look out, heroes.

ALEX: I did my best to keep scenes with regular heroes clean and slick and anything with Black Lanterns really textured and decayed—hard to look at. This page is a good example of just how much texturing I tried to get away with.

ISSUE #3

PAGE 1

EDDIE: Originally, this scene opened with Gen and Jason making out. I wanted more of a cliché teen horror movie opening with these two. We went back and forth on it. Ivan eventually drew the more serious version, which with everything else that winds up happening I think turned out for the best—this was just not a slasher flick.

GEOFF: Yeah, in all honesty, I think this was the one scene that was re-written to have them making out, but the revised script got lost and Ivan drew from the original. We all decided it worked best anyway.

PAGE 4/panel 3

ALEX: I just want to say how freaking cool this panel is. So chilling it's almost hard to look into his eyes.

PAGE 6/panel 1

ADAM: The Atom popping out of the black ring is a freakin' awesome idea, Geoff. And look at the ripped mask and black eye, he sure got in a massive scrape with Hawkman and Hawkgirl.

PAGE 10

EDDIE: OK, this is a perfect example of a cool character just breaking out. Mera was not intended to have such a huge part in this, but she started commanding every scene she was in.

PAGE 11/panel 4

ADAM: Some more foreshadowing here. Ray Palmer is glowing with Compassion. Hmm...

NICK: I hadn't figured out the emotional tether at this point. I figured Ray (The Atom) was gonna bite it here!

GEOFF: The Atom is another example of a character seemingly with no connection to BLACKEST NIGHT but ends up becoming a vital part of saving the universe from Nekron.

PAGE 12/panel 1

EDDIE: And here's Indigo! She just burst onto the scene. I don't think anyone ever considered how bad-ass compassion could be.

ADAM: Or how mysterious!

OCLAIR: Here we start to have a little hint of what's waiting for us ahead. And a little hope is installed in our little hearts!

NICK: AND – RAY LIVES!!

RADICAL!

I HATE THINKING TOO HARD ABOUT STUFF THAT SUCKS. BUT RIGHT NOW I DON'T HAVE A CHOICE.
THERE'S A BIG EMPTY SPOT IN MY HEAD WHERE THE PROFESSOR USED TO HANG. I'VE GOT A VACANCY THAT NEEDS TO BE FILLED.
I HATE BEING IN THE DARK.
HOW ABOUT YOU BE MY NEW NERD BRAIN, FLASH?

AAHHH!

COMPASSION.
--YOU STILL FEEL BAD FOR JEAN. SHE WAS A TERRIBLE PERSON, RAY. SHE LEFT YOU. SHE MURDERED MY WIFE.
IT WAS--NNN--AN ACCIDENT.

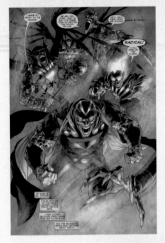

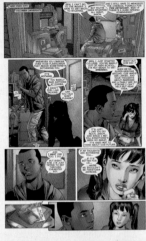

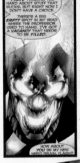

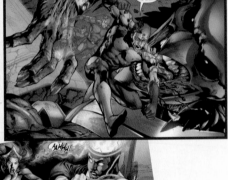

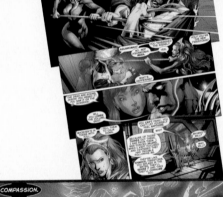

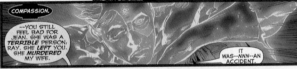

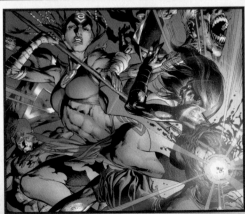

BLACKEST NIGHT DIRECTOR'S COMMENTARY

PAGE 14/panel 1

IVAN: And here we discover we CAN kill the dead. =)

GEOFF: I wanted to set up the rules clearly on how you kill a Black Lantern. After two issues of seemingly unstoppable undead heroes and villains, Indigo-1 revealed the secret behind it — it takes a combined force of two powers from the emotional spectrum. And with the Indigo Tribe able to channel others in the immediate area, they make strong allies in this fight. Their ultimate mission, however, remains a mystery.

NICK: As much as I love Ralph & Sue — after they slaughtered the Hawks in issue one I was still SOOOO ticked. They had to go—BIG TIME!

JOE: I loved that document you guys created for all creators working on BLACKEST NIGHT tie-ins. All the rules on how to kill those damn bastards!

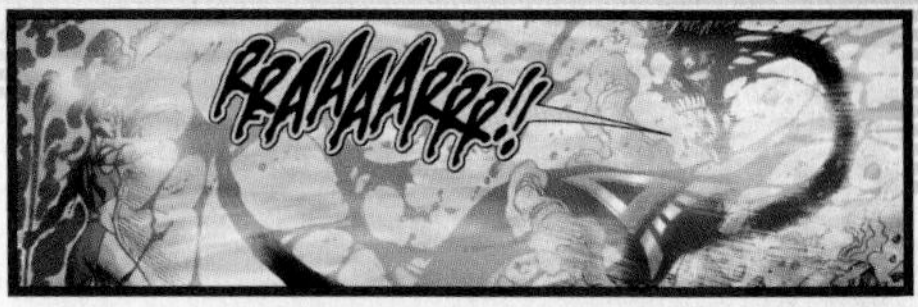
BRAAAARRR!!

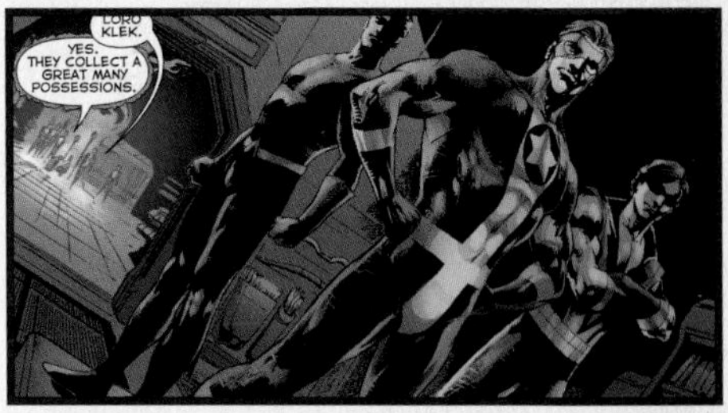
LORD KLEK.
YES. THEY COLLECT A GREAT MANY POSSESSIONS.

PAGE 15/panel 5

EDDIE: One little panel sets up the trouble the deceased Detroit League would be to the JLA in their book.

PAGE 16-17

EDDIE: Another of Ivan's amazing vertical spreads that would become the signature of the series. Our wonderful Brazilian artist would top himself with each one.

NICK: Agreed, Eddie. We worked really hard to get Indigo's dialogue to overlap with the relevant panels.

PAGE 16-17/panel 4

NICK: See those "Please Standby"s behind Hal? Eddie and Adam asked me to put them everywhere in this book! Obsess much, guys?!

ADAM: We love ya, Nick!

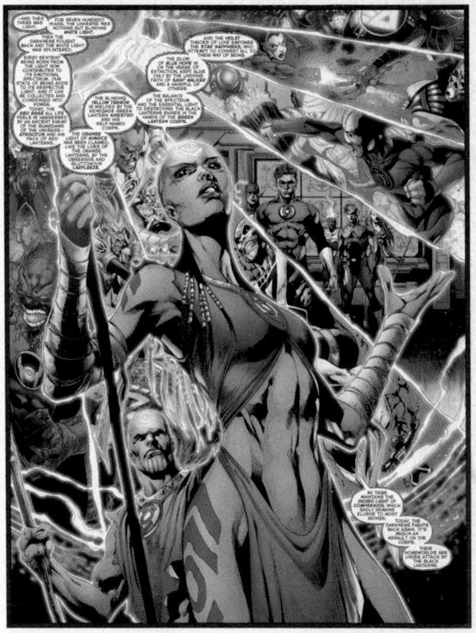

PAGE 24

EDDIE: Like I said, this was no simple zombies attack/slasher flick. Underscoring it was the emotional content that would also tear at the readers' heart too. Nice job, Geoff.

ADAM: A real gut-wrenching scene. Geoff wanted this to be a few pages long to really pull at your emotions and boy, did it work.

IVAN: And it was the same camera sequence for four pages... just with emphasis on the emotions of the characters and Geoff's terrific script.

NICK: TORE—MY—HEART—OUT!! Man, you guys are hard. Was kind of hoping we might see her at the (bright) end—didn't work out that way.

JOE: This issue was the one I started helping Oclair Albert on the inks. It was the testing ground for me on how to ink Ivan, and at the same time make it look as good as Oclair's inks. Tough job! I love this whole sequence because the emotional content was so heavy!

ADAM: What a terrific job you did on the series, Joe! Over 100 designs and the spectacular inks all made for an unbelievable BLACKEST NIGHT event.

GEOFF: This was the hardest death scene I ever wrote. The torture is not only on Gen, but Jason. I knew this was going to have major fallout well beyond BLACKEST NIGHT and into BRIGHTEST DAY after Ronnie Raymond returned. Firestorm, like Aquaman and Martian Manhunter, is one of DC's mainstays in my opinion and deserves some more spotlight in the center of the DCU.

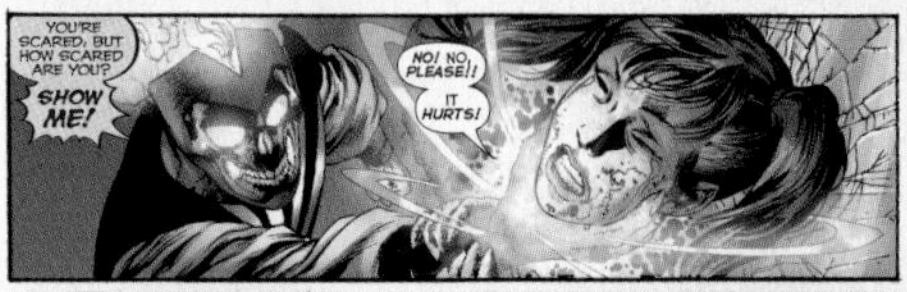
YOU'RE SCARED, BUT HOW SCARED ARE YOU?
SHOW ME!
NO! NO, PLEASE!!
IT HURTS!

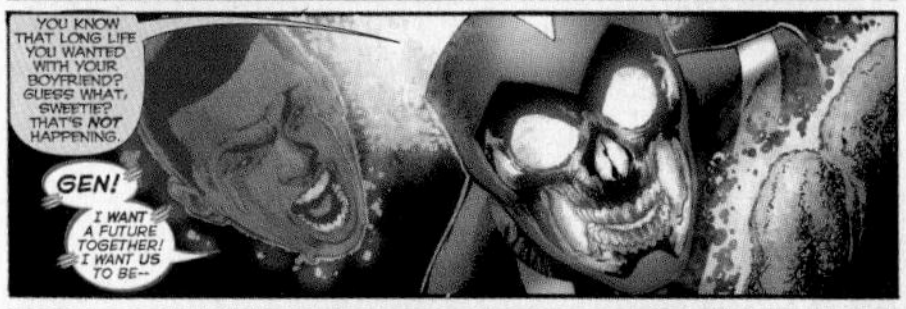
YOU KNOW THAT LONG LIFE YOU WANTED WITH YOUR BOYFRIEND? GUESS WHAT, SWEETIE? THAT'S NOT HAPPENING.
GEN!
I WANT A FUTURE TOGETHER! I WANT US TO BE--

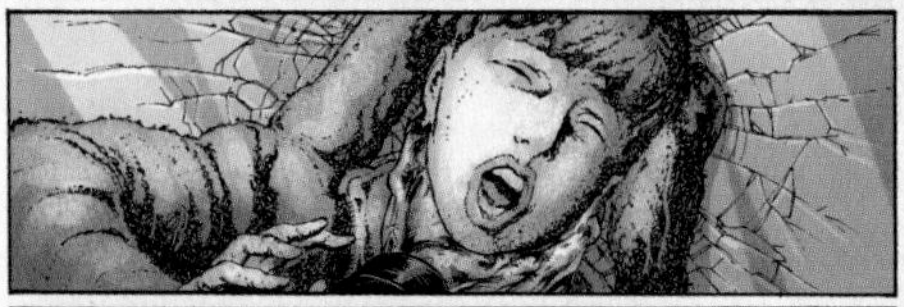

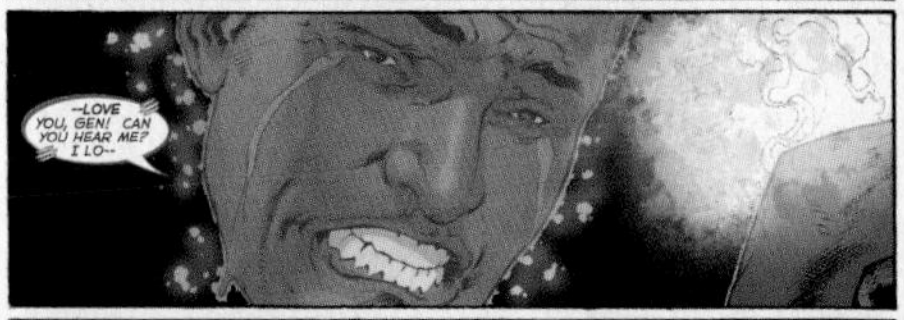
--LOVE YOU, GEN! CAN YOU HEAR ME? I LO--

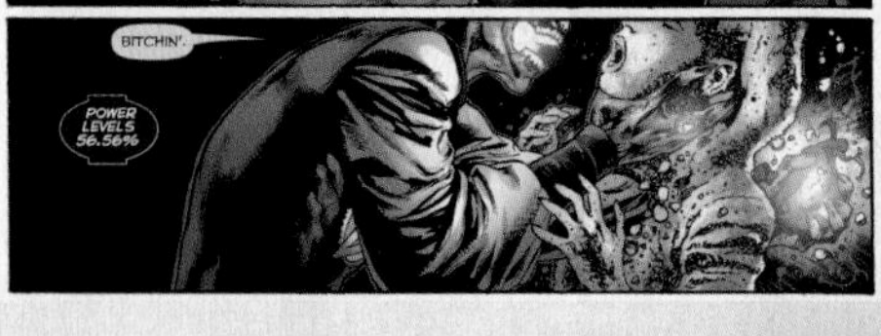
BITCHIN'.
POWER LEVELS 56.56%

ISSUE #4

PAGE 2-3

EDDIE: Ivan's take on Black Lantern Copperhead was so cool, we gave him the cover focus on this issue.

ALEX: Yeah, he's also the only Black Lantern with a tad more color on him than anyone else. Eddie had his favorites.

EDDIE: Yeah, but originally, I thought we'd have more color on the BLs like with Aquaman. You got off easy, Sinc.

NICK: NOT THAT WAY, BARRY!!

GEOFF: Hahahahaha!

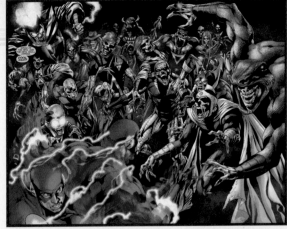

PAGE 4/panel 2

WITH JASON ON BOARD, I CAN TRANSMUTE ORGANICS--!
POWER LEVELS 93.88%
WILLPOWER NOW, JASON? PFFT. IT'S USELESS BANGING HEADS WITH ME, BUT I'LL TAKE IT.
NOW WHERE WERE WE, FLASH? I THINK I WAS ABOUT TO TAKE YOUR "BRAAAIIIINS," BUT I JUST GOT A NEW ONE, SO GIVE ME YOUR HEART--

ADAM: Notice that since Jason Rusch is inside Firestorm and his emotions are running rampant, that the power levels are still increasing. But what will happen when they reach 100%?

NICK: This scene was a classic "Indiana Jones running from the boulder"! AWESOME. Only difference is Barry's trying to save Mera and Ray along the way! OH—and the boulder is ZOMBIES!

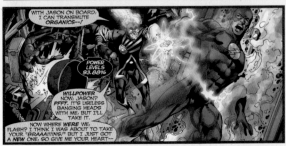

PAGE 8/panel 3

RRARRRR!

GEOFF: I knew that readers would feel like this scene was "out of place" initially until I revealed that both Scarecrow and Lex Luthor would play bigger rolls in the series later on. I wanted to set up Scarecrow's lust for fear and his inability to feel it because of his years of exposure to fear gas…unless hunted by the Batman.

ADAM: The Scarecrow shows no emotion in Black Lantern vision so Azrael cannot see him. This is due to the fact that he's immune to terror and sets up the role he'll be playing later on in this book. It'll be the greatest feeling he'll ever have.

ALEX: Black Lantern Azrael was one of my favorite BL designs—awesome job, JOE!

JOE: It was awesome designing Black Lantern Azrael!

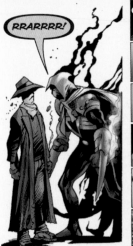

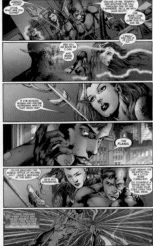

PAGE 12

AGREED, ATOM?
ATOM, WHAT ARE YOU DOING?
DIALING UP MR. TERRIFIC AND ROUTING THE CALL THROUGH ONE OF HIS T-SPHERES. HE'LL BE WITH ALAN SCOTT.
ONE MORE LONG DISTANCE JUMP FOR YOU AND ME.
I REALLY WISH ONE OF US COULD FLY.
SEE YOU AS SOON AS I CAN.
AND GOOD LUCK.
IF I'M WONDER WOMAN AND YOU'RE SUPERMAN, WHAT'S THAT MAKE HIM?
THE FLASH.
YOU'VE REACHED THE MOBILE OFFICE OF MICHAEL HOLT. LEAVE A MESSAGE AT THE BEEP.
HE'S NOT ANSWERING.
JUST MEANS THE RE-ENTRY WILL BE A LITTLE MORE TURBULENT.
DO YOURSELF A FAVOR AND TRY TO KEEP YOUR EYES OPEN THIS TIME, MERA.

EDDIE: This scene crystallized who our next big stars would be, but also reminded us that Barry Allen, The Flash is cool!

JOE: A whole new "Trinity" and they worked so damn well.

PAGE 20/panel 1 & 2

GRANT!
POWER LEVELS 100%
MY SWEET, SWEET RAY.
JEAN?

EDDIE: Another hero dies, and Ray Palmer is confronted with a ghost that has been haunting him for a very long time.

GEOFF: I went back and forth on who should kill Damage. The obvious idea was his father the Golden Age Atom for whom he had pent-up anger because he was absent in his life. It was a large part of the chip on Damage's shoulder. But instead I wanted a glimmer of hope. I wanted Damage to finally overcome that rage and grab onto hope for the first time maybe ever. And that, unfortunately, would not only be his downfall, but the return of Ray Palmer's greatest and strangest enemy…his ex-lover and murderer of Sue Dibny, Jean Loring.

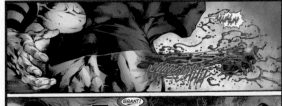

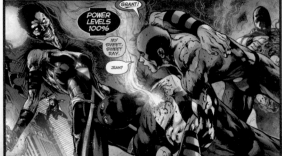

PAGE 22/panel 1

FLESH.
FLESH.
FLESH.
FLESH.

IVAN: Here starts Nekron's rise, and I changed all the borders on the pages to black.

ADAM: In case you're wondering who those two Black Lanterns are, they are Ash and Saarek, who are the two Green Lanterns that were tricked into going to Ryut where the Black Power Battery lay.

ALEX: This whole sequence was awesome, culminating with the big Nekron reveal. For the Black Lantern, I wanted it to look like spirits or something supernatural was coming out of it rather than just light.

PAGE 24-25/panel 1

OCLAIR: With all the deaths and Black Lanterns showing up, can it get any worse? YES! It can! The LORD OF THE DEAD appears! Damn!

EDDIE: A version of Nekron had appeared before, but he was nothing like this. Geoff and Ivan let the dark side of their imagination loose for this creation.

GEOFF: Originally, we had planned on creating a new character, but the concept of Nekron was already within the Green Lantern mythology, although he had rarely appeared.

JOE: I remember all of us trading emails almost 'til midnight until Ivan sent the final design. That day we talked on the phone for hours exchanging ideas.

ALEX: Each final splash was more amazing than the previous one, and this one is probably my favorite. I found myself getting caught up in all the detail Ivan put into every undead body coming out of the ground. I used some overlapping fractal filters and layers to create the effect.

ISSUE #5

PAGE 2-3

ADAM: The New Guardians have arrived, and they're here to stay. I'm so excited about all these brand new characters that Geoff, Ivan and others have created. They're such a part of the Green Lantern mythos now and have such incredible personalities. And the oaths are utterly fantastic! But check out Larfleeze on the side over there wondering why these fools are wasting their time and pondering how he'll get a hold of all their rings and power batteries.

IVAN: Alex was the star of this spread, keeping the dark tone of the story with a rainbow of colors.

ALEX: I too said, "Oooooooh...pretty," when I saw this, then I realized this was where I had to really earn my money. I had to use eight different light sources without allowing one to stand out over the others. It also couldn't look like someone just dropped a bag of Skittles on the page. Luckily Ivan drew them (unintentionally?) in cool-warm-cool-warm order so the final image did not feel unbalanced when it was colored.

GEOFF: A big part of the pride I really take in BLACKEST NIGHT as a whole is that we introduced all these new characters into the DC Universe that are here to stay. Along with reviving classic characters and reinventing ones like Black Hand and Nekron, creating characters that don't fade away is a real challenge, and with the help of my amazing artistic collaborators we did it. Obviously, I have a lot of fun writing Larfleeze, but Saint Walker may be the unsung hero and the most complex in my mind. I particularly love where we're taking him post-BLACKEST NIGHT.

PAGE 5/panel 2

WHAT YOU'VE DONE TO MY FRIENDS AND THESE POOR PEOPLE HAS GONE WAY BEYOND SACRILEGIOUS.

ALEX: I love the Flash. I've been dying to work on him for a long time because I have always wanted to make him look like he is moving so fast that you're not really sure where he is at. I am so grateful to Ivan for allowing me to explore this with his art in this series. This panel stands out to me as a good example of how I think the Flash should look.

GEOFF: I love the way you expanded on what Ivan did with the Flash, Alex. The speed blurs and lightning that crackled around him really stood out, especially against the often black backgrounds.

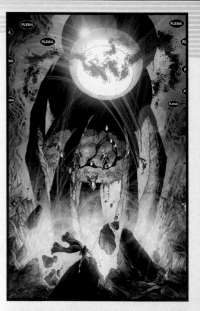

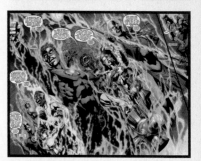

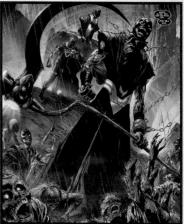

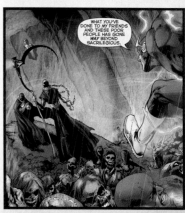

PAGE 14-15

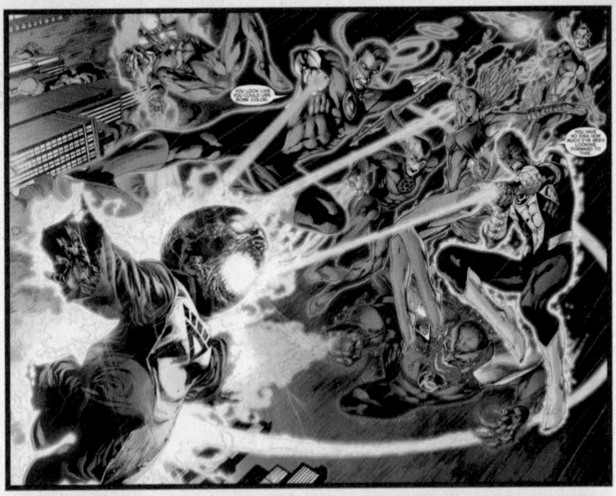

EDDIE: Ivan's contribution to Scar's final look.

IVAN: Here Scar is dominated by the scar...it's growing across her entire body...the blackness growing inside her.

EDDIE: I love this spread! Our New Guardians cutting loose on Scar. Geoff talks about moments you wanna hang up on your wall. This is one of them. Actually, with BN there's hardly any wall space left when the series is done.

ADAM: Ivan continues to blow me away. Every page that he sends in makes my jaw drop. And check out those colors from Alex Sinclair. All the light surrounding Scar rocks.

ALEX: Taste the Rainbow! C'mon, somebody had to say it. Great idea from Geoff to have the merging colored beams become pure white light. I added the multicolored streaks as a kind of color echo.

PAGE 20-21

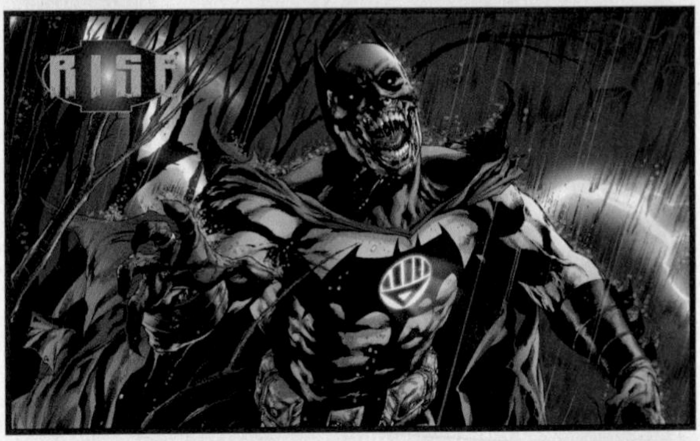

OCLAIR: And then Black Lantern Batman appears! Even if it was just for a few pages, THAT made us fear for our heroes!

EDDIE: I was in Brazil with Ivan when he showed me this page. It's a wonder it and I ever made it back to the States.

JOE: Cool thing was that back at San Diego Comic-Con '09 I was sketching out a Black Lantern Batman just for fun, then Eddie showed up out of nowhere, saying, "Oh, awesome, Joe! Now put that away! No one needs to see that now. C'mon!" One week or so later, Black Lantern Batman was born. I also love the fact that I inked this spread!

ALEX: The funny thing about the art on this series is that you'll open the book and say, "THIS is my favorite spread." Then you find yourself saying the same thing over and over again, page after page, issue after issue. THIS is my favorite spread...until I turn the page.

PAGE 22-23

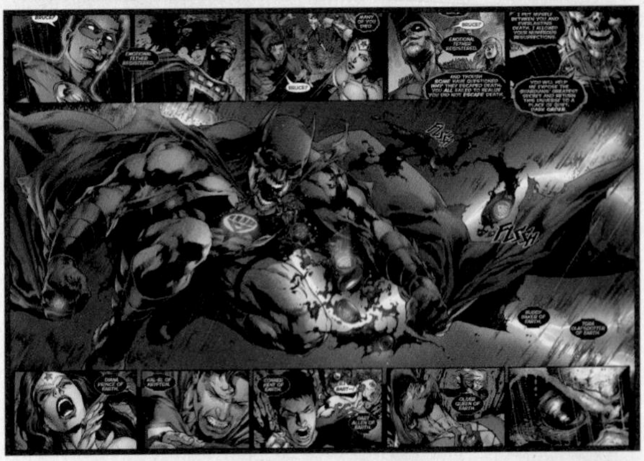

EDDIE: The emotional tether created by these pages was huge—it not only affected the characters but was visceral for all of us working on this project.

ALEX: I told you so.

PAGE 25-26

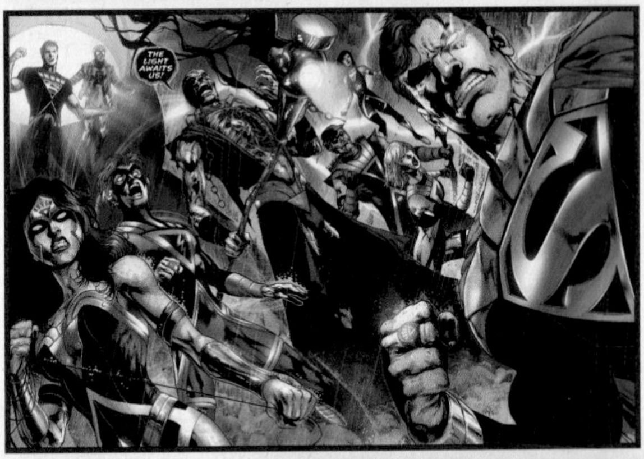
THE LIGHT AWAITS US!

EDDIE: Yeah, this caught people off guard.

ADAM: Things have turned from bad to worse. What a twist. Go Geoff!

GEOFF: Everyone expected it to be a simple combination of light that would destroy Nekron and the Black Lantern, but the true white light was something else entirely.

ALEX: Now run along and change your underpants.

ISSUE #6

PAGE 1/panel 1

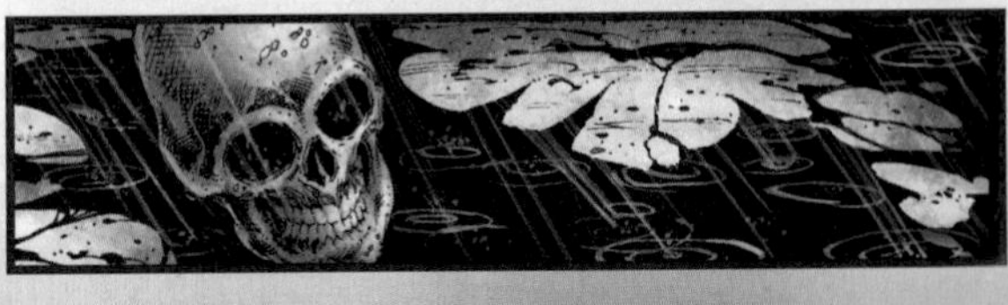

EDDIE: Love the subtle Bat-Signal shown here. A small thing, but the reason for the conflict this issue.

ALEX: And Eddie asked for more yellow on the ground to create it. I thought he was coo-coo until I tried it. Great call, Eddie!

PAGE 6/panel 2

ADAM: Ivan perfectly gets across the determination and confidence on Barry's face here as he runs forward into the future.

GEOFF: I wanted to emphasize that this was not an easy feat for the Flash...especially time-traveling without a cosmic treadmill to guide him. He and Hal could've been thrown two years into the future if he pushed himself too far.

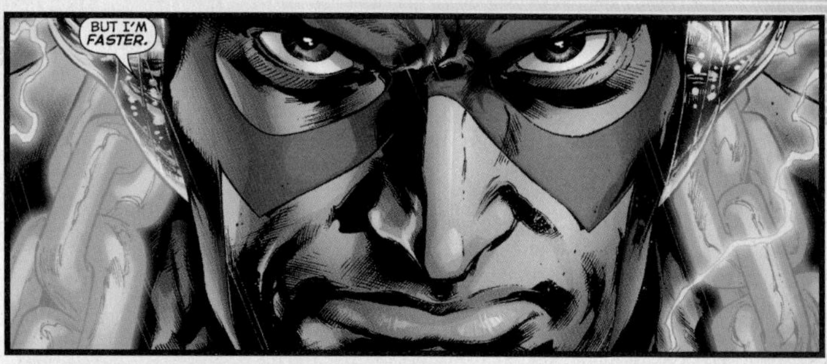
BUT I'M FASTER.

PAGE 10-11

EDDIE: I kept rushing our colorist Alex Sinclair on this one. "What's the holdup," I said. "The Black Lanterns chasing John are all grey and black, what's the hold-up?" Aren't we editors stinkers?

ALEX: I don't think we can print what I was thinking when Eddie kept asking me that...

IVAN: You could have said something like this to me..."What's the holdup...the Black Lanterns chasing John are all a black mass with no form or details..." but you didn't... you left me to draw each one with all the details.

ADAM: And those details are what make this project far superior than anything that's come before. This really is an instant classic!

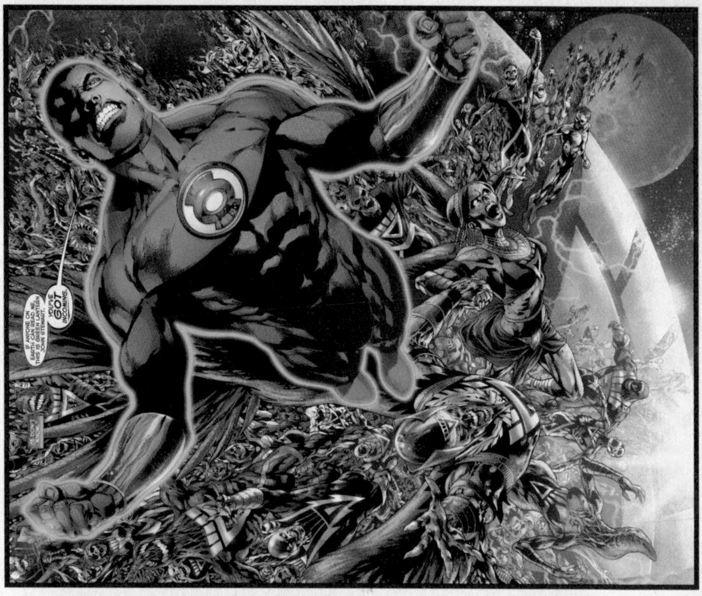

PAGE 14

EDDIE: Props to Adam for coming up with the idea of Ganthet becoming an actual Green Lantern deputy.

GEOFF: Originally, I had deputies for everyone, but I wasn't sure who would be a deputy for Green Lantern. It felt wrong to make one of our Earth heroes or villains another Green Lantern, but when we went through everyone and Adam threw out Ganthet...brilliant. This is why I love working with Eddie and Adam. Creative collaboration is the best.

PAGE 15/panels 4 & 6

ALEX: This set of panels here and on page 20 are incredible. The framing and composition Ivan used to focus on the deputy rings was so cool. I felt like I was watching a movie and the director suddenly slowed the camera down to capture that moment in time.

PAGE 19/last 3 panels

EDDIE: This could have gone different, we had other candidates for the yellow ring, but it worked out.

PAGE 20/panels 2, 4 & 6

ALEX: More of the cool framing from Ivan to emphasize those rings. Genius!

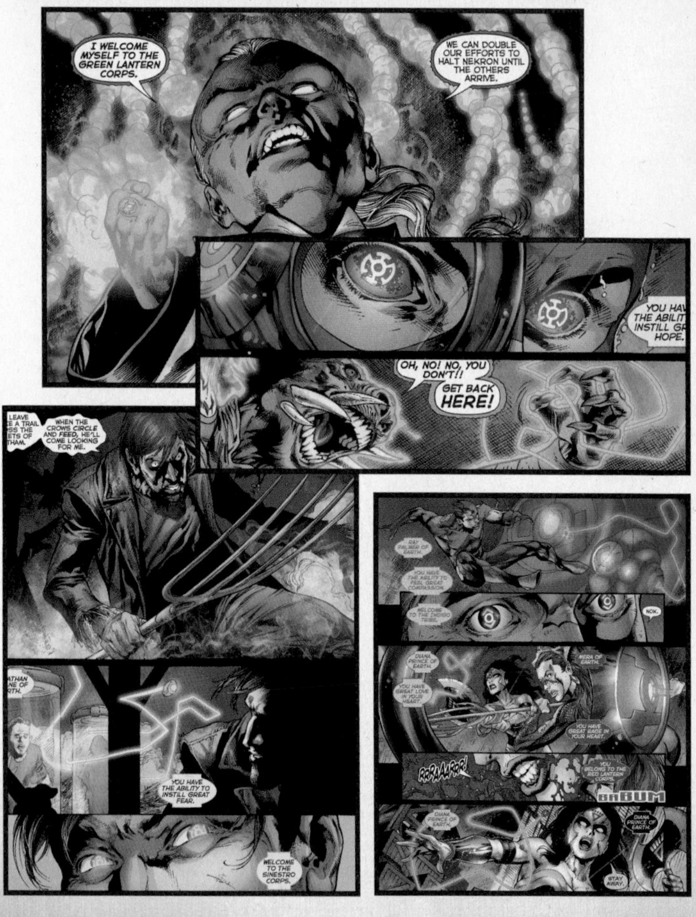
I WELCOME MYSELF TO THE GREEN LANTERN CORPS.
WE CAN DOUBLE OUR EFFORTS TO HALT NEKRON UNTIL THE OTHERS ARRIVE.
OH, NO! NO, YOU DON'T!!
GET BACK HERE!
WHEN THE CROWS CIRCLE AND FEED, HE'LL COME LOOKING FOR ME.
YOU HAVE THE ABILITY TO INSTILL GREAT FEAR.
WELCOME TO THE SINESTRO CORPS.

BLACKEST NIGHT DIRECTOR'S COMMENTARY

PAGE 22-23

EDDIE: And yet another shock ending. It was fun figuring out with Alex what the colors would be on these guys. Flash was hard because he looks like the Atom. Hence the huge blue lightning bolt over the Blue Lantern symbol.

ALEX: Yeah, I like the fact that we were able to incorporate colors other than their Lantern ones since they were deputies and not full-blown Lanterns. I also remember Wonder Woman's costume needed some serious surgery because the design changed after the page had been pencilled and inked.

NICK: EASTER EGG! There's art under that HUGE end caption! Show them!

OCLAIR: OK, how in hell does Luthor get an ORANGE ring??? C'mon! He's the greediest person on Earth! OK, at the end it made sense, but damn! LUTHOR???!!!

ADAM: It was also a blast figuring out which characters really embodied which emotions. We almost used the Joker.

JOE: It was awesome designing this character MONTHS before we even got the script. The Joker would have been sooo cool!

GEOFF: But it's great to give Scarecrow the spotlight. If anyone is about fear beyond Batman, it's Scarecrow, not the Joker. What's the color for insane?

ISSUE #7

PAGE 2-3

EDDIE: The penultimate chapter and all hell is breaking loose—this is why we read comics!!!!

JOE: HELL YEAH!!!

NICK: Scarecrow's having WAY too much fun with his new toy!

IVAN: And it is why the penciller doesn't sleep… I'm wrong…the spread on 10-11 is why the penciller doesn't sleep. LOL.

PAGE 7

EDDIE: Lex turns on the guys. Genius! Both on Lex's part and Geoff's for thinking of it. It should never be too easy on the heroes, and villains have to stay in character.

GEOFF: I always knew giving any kind of power to Lex Luthor was a bad idea…and I knew he had to betray the New Guardians, which was prophesized. Atrocitus even attacked Larfleeze and mentioned it in a previous GREEN LANTERN issue.

PAGE 10-11

EDDIE: Aw, hell YEAH! The colored Corps joined together. We've been talking about it for a while now and here is the moment finally. Thank you, Ivan!

NICK: Agreed! Guy's balloon should say: "Ivan makes us look GOOD!"

JOE: I remember Ivan yapping away about this for months!

GEOFF: How Ivan pulls this off, I'll never know. There is literally no one else in comics who has this kind of range. From the emotion of Carter dying and calling to Kendra to this epic spread.

IVAN: (starting to take a needed nap): ZZZZZZZZZZZZZZZZZZZ!!!!!!!!!!!

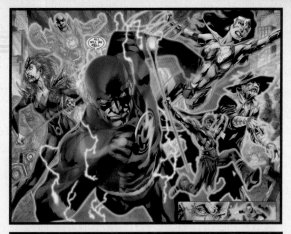

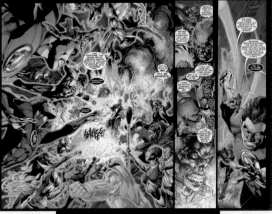

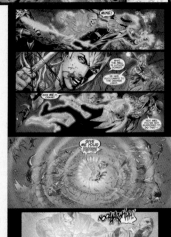

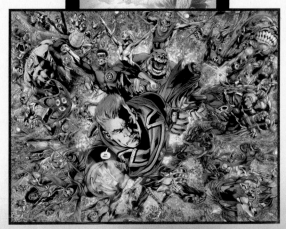

PAGE 14/panel 4

ADAM: The Anti-Monitor is being used to power the Black Lantern power battery and he's still in there. Uh oh!

PAGE 16/panel 5

ADAM: What insane ritual is Black Hand completing using the guts of a Guardian? Notice that the Guardian's insides make up all the colors of the spectrum, and also make note of the symbol drawn on the ground. Something is coming and it will remain in the DC Universe for a long time.

GEOFF: I wanted the Guardians' organs to literally be the seven emotions hardened like fossils inside their bodies. They had buried them so deep for so long, billions of years, they literally internalized them.

ALEX: This was a little tough to pull off. You have different colored organs—great idea by the way—covered in yellow blood and they kinda have to glow.

LET ME OUT.
CYBORG... SOMETHING... SOMEONE... IS IN THERE.

PAGE 18-19

EDDIE: Created over a weekend, our life Entity had to be unique.

PAGE 24-25

EDDIE: Now, this was the ending no one was expecting!

OCLAIR: Sinestro empowered by the life Entity!

ADAM: Most people believed a White Lantern would appear in BLACKEST NIGHT. Everyone thought it might be Hal Jordan who had already used some of the color rings, but lo and behold, it's the renegade Sinestro.

JOE: YEAH! Save for a few guesses here and there, almost no one was betting their chips on Sinestro. Plus it was a blast for me to create the design. After six to seven versions, we ended up going back to the first one I came up with. Fun times!

ADAM: I want to give a special shout-out to the "Greatest Letterer in the Universe" as Nick J. Napolitano has been dubbed. He's been able to create unique balloon designs for many of the characters and makes sure to highlight all of Ivan's art by taking up the least real estate as possible.

NICK: Thanks much—I'll tell ya—when this scene was building (from page 23) the way Geoff wrote it and Ivan drew it, it just swept you in. As Sinestro was imbued with the White Light, he seemed (REALLY) to be going mad. Before I even read the end caption (Beware his Power) I thought—WE—ARE—SCREWED!!

ALEX: Nick RULES!! Oh, and coloring the White Lantern for the first time was way cool. Had to mess with the logo too as the design changed over a period of time.

GEOFF: It's amazing how one TO BE CONTINUED caption can change the tone of the book – BEWARE HIS POWER.

IVAN: It was a beautiful moment... Alex was able to create a terrific atmosphere and he just used white color...all I needed to do was draw only one character.

I AM THE GREATEST LANTERN OF THEM ALL!
DESTINY AWAITS.
NEXT! BEWARE HIS POWER!

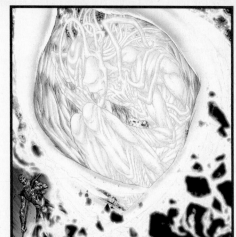

ISSUE #8

PAGE 2-3

IVAN: A classic fight of the good against the evil ...the black against the white.

ALEX: How cool is this spread? The classic good vs. evil/white vs. black (although with a twist since Sinestro's wearing white) image. There's so much energy and movement in this image. I had a blast on it.

GEOFF: I think, for me, this is where the entire purpose of life vs. death comes into view. It's more than just a concept to me personally; it's a personal struggle due to the loss I've had in my life. We have to embrace life the best way we can.

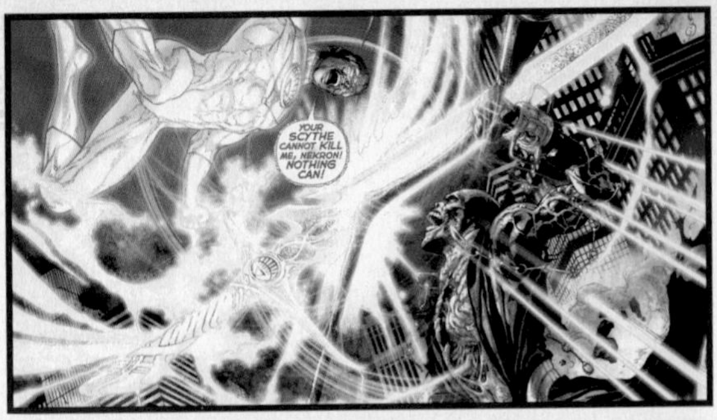
YOUR SCYTHE CANNOT KILL ME, NEKRON! NOTHING CAN!

PAGE 6/panel 1

ADAM: Nekron is not so easily killed. He can come back as any Black Lantern. Just how powerful is Nekron? The answer might never be known.

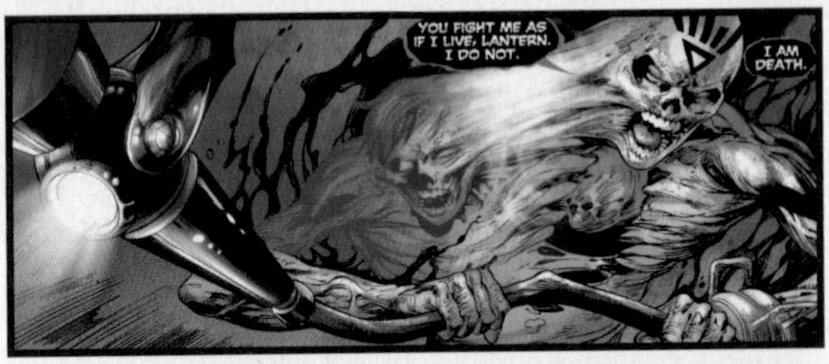
YOU FIGHT ME AS IF I LIVE, LANTERN. I DO NOT.
I AM DEATH.

PAGE 10-11

OCLAIR: Here all goes to hell! Everyone (I mean EVERYONE) fights against Nekron's army of Black Lanterns!

ADAM: SPEECHLESS! Just unbelievable. Ivan drew more characters on this spread than he's probably ever drawn. Let's hear from the mastermind behind it himself.

IVAN: I just didn't have the courage to count, Adam... But it was the most entertaining page I have ever done... I avoided making the aura energy around the GLs because this page had too much information and details...this way I could keep the atmosphere of the page intact.

EDDIE: At this point in any event, the artist starts to look for short cuts. Less backgrounds or none. Silhouettes. Not Ivan. He asked for more. He and Geoff would not relent!

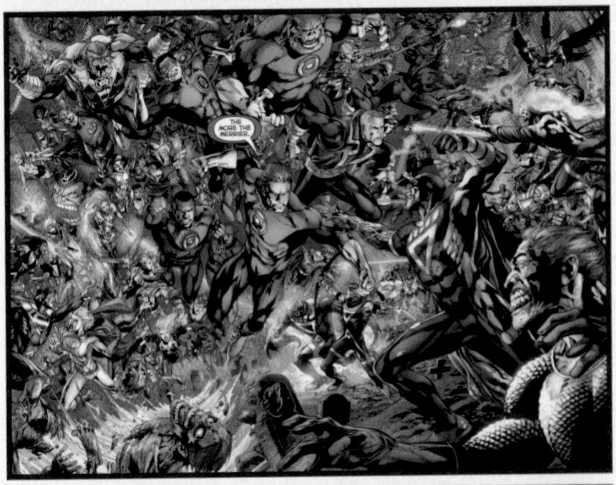
THE MORE THE MERRIER.

PAGE 16-17

ADAM: The heroes strike back! A hero never gives up, they always fight back and have the resolve to continue to keep fighting even through the toughest and darkest times. This is their moment!

ALEX: New problem—buncha heroes wearing white, shooting white beams in front of a white logo. I was starting to suspect Geoff and Ivan didn't like me...

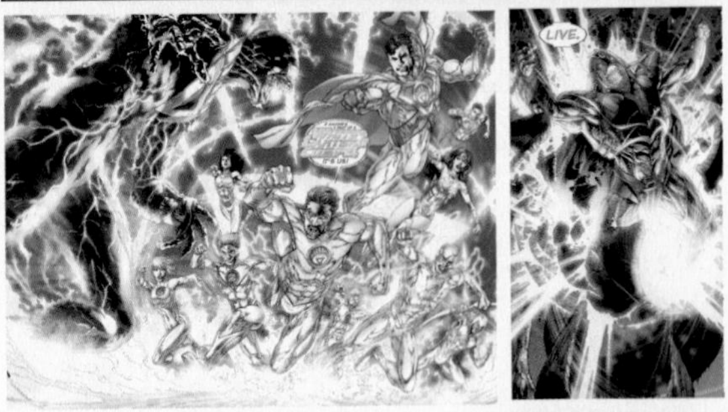
LIVE.

PAGE 20

ADAM: Crap! The Anti-Monitor's back. The power battery's been destroyed and there's no source powering it, but one of the greatest threats the universe has ever faced is back. When he will strike, we'll just have to wait and see.

GEOFF: Oh, you know where and when...

IVAN: ...but it was a terrific moment for the Anti-Monitor.

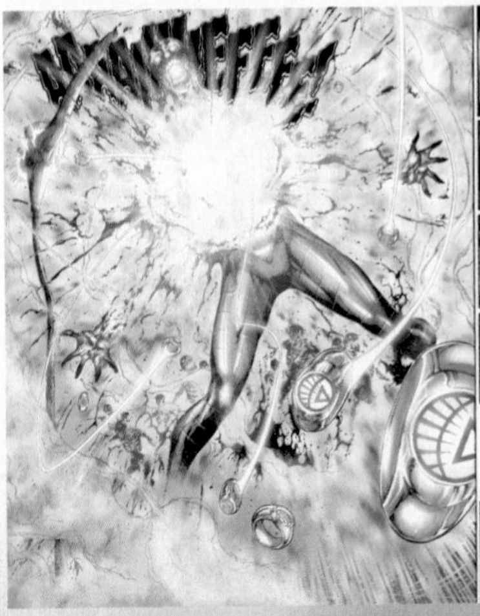

PAGE 22-23

IVAN: Now, the big evil was defeated and the borders of the pages return to white again as the widescreen panels end... the story returns to normal panels as it was at the beginning of the series.

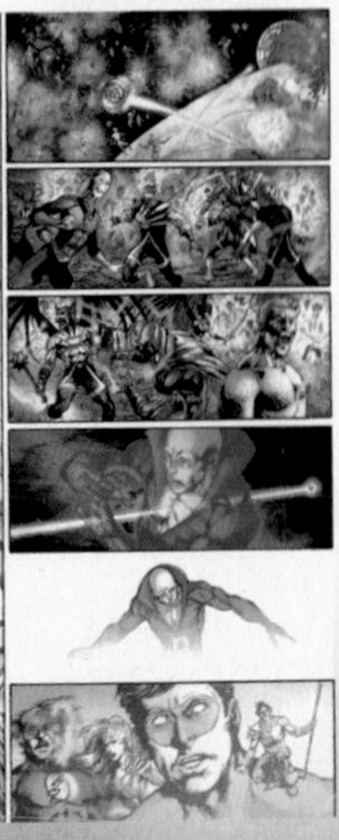

PAGE 24-27

ADAM: Now this warrants a gatefold poster shot! Twelve returning characters. What does this mean? Heroes and villains. Why were they chosen? What will they do with a second chance? Brightest Day is upon us, but it's not what you think.

JOE: So freakin' awesome! We've talked about a possible gatefold for months and Ivan, Oclair and Alex kicked ass on this! The hardest part for me was coming up with the designs for the heroes and villains. Tons of notes from Geoff, Pete, Eddie and Adam. These twelve characters were WAAAAY tougher to design than the 130+ Black Lanterns I came up with. Just J'onn J'onnz had fourteen different versions.

NICK: Kinda like I mentioned for issue #1—The "LIVE!" caption had a lot of weight for the narrative here (DON'T COVER IVAN'S ART) and with the heroes that were resurrected on this page it felt — historic. I was really happy with the end result. AND I didn't cover (too much of) Ivan's art.

IVAN: It was my first gatefold ever!

GEOFF: The fact that this could become a gatefold like this was wonderful – and it was Ivan's idea. We didn't have 60 pages, but when you have a moment like this that's this big, I felt extremely comfortable with 40 pages for the finale. Much to everyone's dismay, I love more pages! Many of our GREEN LANTERN issues were 24. (Sorry, guys!)

ALEX: For you techno enthusiasts, this file was a whopping 3.5 GIGs open. Took 15 minutes just to save. I was suddenly transported to the early '90s coloring on a Performa! To save time, I copied out each character, colored him/her on his/her own and pasted it back to the main file. Doing the special effects took an entire afternoon/evening.

EDDIE: It also had to be done before the rest of the book. Doing gatefolds like this is about as easy as killing Black Lanterns, but in both cases the result is well worth it.

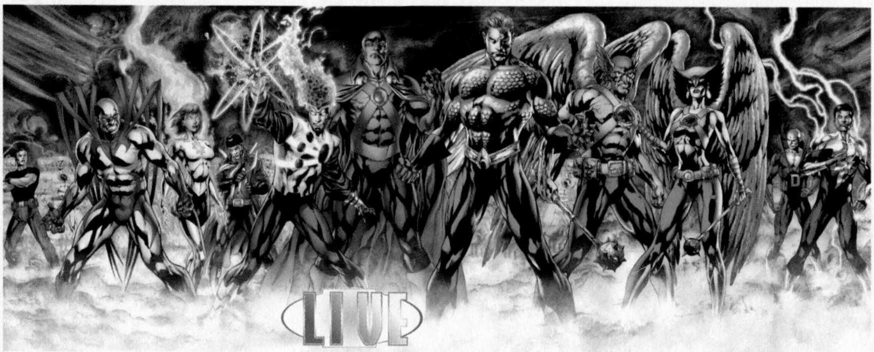
LIVE

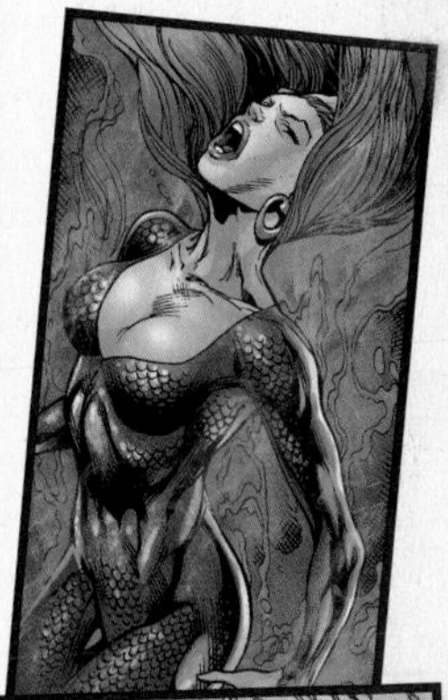

PAGE 28/panel 3

ALEX: I love how this panel turned out. The red disappearing as her true form emerges.

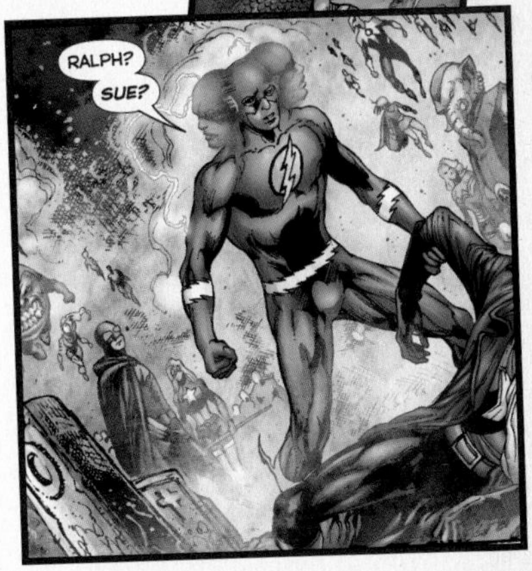
RALPH?
SUE?

PAGE 35/panel 1

ADAM: Barry searching for Ralph and Sue Dibny is an awful moment that just tears at your heart. Ivan perfectly portrayed it here. It's just so sad seeing some terrible people returned to the land of the living while some saints remain dead.

GEOFF: Tying right into that first moment of Barry realizing they're gone in issue #1. Despite everything, that pain is still there.

PAGE 40/last panel

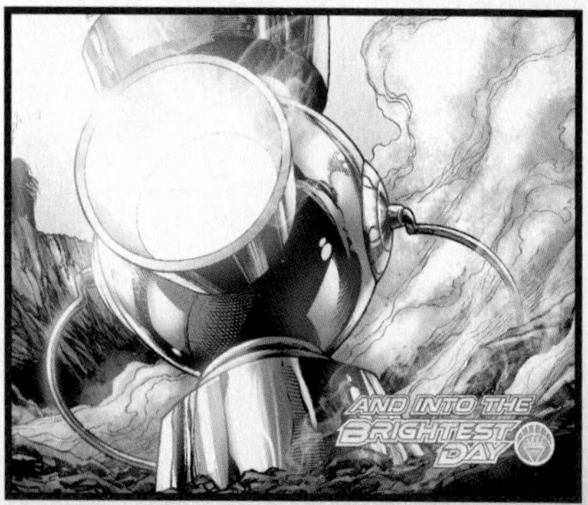
AND INTO THE BRIGHTEST DAY

JOE: Awesomely epic and inspiring... but what awaits our heroes in the future? Just keep reading!!!

EDDIE: Thank you, Joe, for helping with the "camera" angle here. Really makes the Lantern stand out.

ALEX: Can't wait to read what comes next!

GEOFF: It's in a vault in my office, but it'll be on stands soon!

EDDIE: I really HATE that it's over... this series had one of the best and hardest-working crews I've ever had the pleasure to be associated with!

IVAN: WOW... I hope all the readers enjoyed all the hard work spent on this story... there was so much energy and dedication put in from each of us to make sure it was the best it could possibly be... I wish the best to this team. Thanks guys... now if you'll excuse me... I'm going to slee ...ZZZZZZZZZZZZZZZZZZZ

BLACKEST NIGHT – Deleted Rainbow Raiders Scene
By Geoff Johns

PAGE ONE
PANEL ONE.
Cut to the hidden safe house of the D-grade super-villain group: the RAINBOW RAIDERS. They are all in a penthouse adorned with color artwork, most of which they stole, overlooking Keystone City. It's raining outside. Lightning streaking across the sky from right to left – like the Reverse-Flash's symbol.

RED is the leader here. All the Rainbow Raiders – ORANGE, YELLOW, GREEN, BLUE, INDIGO and VIOLET – are gathered together. They each hold a glass full of red liquid poured from a decanter at a nearby bar.

1. BANNER: Keystone City
2. CAPTION: The black market art gallery of the Rainbow Raiders.
3. YELLOW: We never even had a chance to take on any of the Flashes, Red. I never did.
4. RED: Do you really think we would've WON? We picked up and divided the gear of one of the most disrespected Rogues in the business, guys.
5. RED: We're LUCKY we're not rotting away in Iron Heights, but let's all face it, it was only a matter of time.
6. RED: If there WAS time left.

PANEL TWO.
The Rainbow Raiders all raise their glasses in a toast, high in the center of the seven low-grade villains.

7. RED: The dead are taking over the Earth.
8. RED: Here's to being on the winning side.
SFX: klink

PANEL THREE.
The Rainbow Raiders drink the cyanide-laced Kool-Aid.

[NO DIALOGUE.]

PANEL FOUR.
An overhead shot of the seven Rainbow Raiders all lying on the ground dead a la JONESTOWN.

[NO DIALOGUE.]

PANEL FIVE.
Same exact panel as panel four. No black rings are coming. These guys don't have any connections to anyone.

9. CAPTION (FLASH): "As far as we know, only the dead with emotional ties to us are rising. The rest are staying in their graves."

BLACKEST NIGHT – Deleted Ragman Scene
By Geoff Johns

DOUBLE PAGE SPREAD
PANEL ONE.
We're in Gotham City, opening on a large shot of THE RAGMAN racing frantically across the rooftops. Think of Ragman as a cross between Spider-Man, Spawn and rooted in Joe Kubert horror (who created him) rather than the clean super-hero version we've seen lately. Ragman's panicked and tired. He's in mid-leap here, off the edge of a building, over a barbed wire fence and into a massive trash yard. Something is chasing him.

1. BANNER: Earth.
2. CAPTION (BLACK HAND): I hear death call his name.
3. NEKRON (DISEMBODIED): Rory Regan.
4. CAPTION (BLACK HAND): The Ragman. He sees trash for treasure, lives in self-imposed poverty and clutches to the Kaballah in some misguided hope to cure our society of its inequity.
5. CAPTION (BLACK HAND): But despite what he believes, not everyone was created equal.

PANEL TWO.
Ragman lands hard on the huge piles of trash, losing his balance and toppling over.

6. CAPTION (BLACK HAND): It's called the food chain.
7. RAGMAN: NNFFGG
8. BLACK HAND (O/P): Your suit is an ancient patchwork prison of people stitched together by your vengeance. Each RAG a different TRANSGRES-SOR you've stolen.
9. BLACK HAND (O/P): You may be their jailer, Rory Regan –

PANEL THREE.
Ragman gazes up and we reveal a swarm of dozens of black rings flying over the edge of the building and down at him. They're like a crazed flock of birds, moving at odd angles, but then correcting their path as they lock back into Ragman and heading right for him. They burn through the barbed wire fence and any trespassing signage it might have. Nothing can keep them out.

Standing on the edge of the building where the rings are coming from is Black Hand, holding Bruce Wayne's skull.

10. BLACK HAND: -- but WE are their masters. And we want your inmates back.
11. BLACK RING: Flesh.
12. BLACK RING: Flesh.
13. BLACK RING: Flesh.
14. BLACK RING: Flesh.
15. CAPTION (BLACK HAND): Rory Regan is like the others the voice sends me after. Those who have manipulated and escaped death.

PANEL FOUR.
CUT TO the Black Lantern Hawks from pages 2 and 3 panel 2 from BLACKEST NIGHT #3. Any angle of them tackling Green Lantern Hal Jordan while the rest of the Black Lantern Justice League battle Barry Allen in the background.

16. NEKRON (DISEMBODIED): Carter Hall and Kendra Saunders.
17. BLACK LANTERN HAWKMAN: I'd rather be spilling Green Arrow's blood, but I'll settle for YOUR pompous ass, Jordan.

PANEL FIVE.
CUT TO an image from BLACKEST NIGHT: BATMAN #2 of BLACK LANTERN DEADMAN.

18. NEKRON (DISEMBODIED): Boston Brand.

PANEL SIX.
From BLACKEST NIGHT #2, the Black Lantern Spectre reaches his massive hand into the cemetery and tears it up, tossing Phantom Stranger, Zatanna and Blue Devil into the air.

19. NEKRON (DISEMBODIED): Crispus Allen.
20. BLACK LANTERN SPECTRE: You are not Hal Jordan. I have no interest in you.

PANEL SEVEN.
Black Hand approaches Ragman, but the focus is Ragman. Ragman is surrounded by the swarm of black rings like a swarm of killer bees. His rags react, shimmering and fluttering at the proximity of the black rings. There are so many balloons they should overlap one another (the names are actual DC characters, people Ragman has killed in his series).

21. NEKRON (DISEMBODIED): Cyrus Gold.
22. NEKRON (DISEMBODIED): Kit Freeman.
23. NEKRON (DISEMBODIED): Mitchell Shelley.
24. NEKRON (DISEMBODIED): Jim Craddock.
25. BLACK HAND: They will play with your essence no more.

PANEL EIGHT.
And like that, the black rings each shoot down into one of the patches on Ragman's uniform. Ragman buckles down in a standing fetal position in pain. The balloons should overlap a bit as these are not DC characters, just normal people that Ragman has incarcerated.

26. BLACK RING: Aaron Haaland of Earth.
27. BLACK RING: Jack O'Mullane of Earth.
28. BLACK RING: Jason Blanchard of Earth.
29. BLACK RING: Chaz Simmons of Earth.
30. BLACK RING: Dann McNerney of Earth.
31. BLACK RING: Lauren Howes of Earth.
32. BLACK RING: Andrew Westin of Earth.

PANEL NINE.
And then Ragman arches open as the tattered suit rips apart and the patches transform into dozens of Black Lanterns, revealing the naked, battered and smoldering Rory Regan underneath.

33. BLACK RING: RISE.
34. RAGMAN (BURST): AARRRRR!!

PANEL TEN.
VERY CLOSE ON Black Hand, pleasured from all of this.

35. CAPTION (BLACK HAND): All of this death.
36. BLACK HAND: Mm.

NEKRON

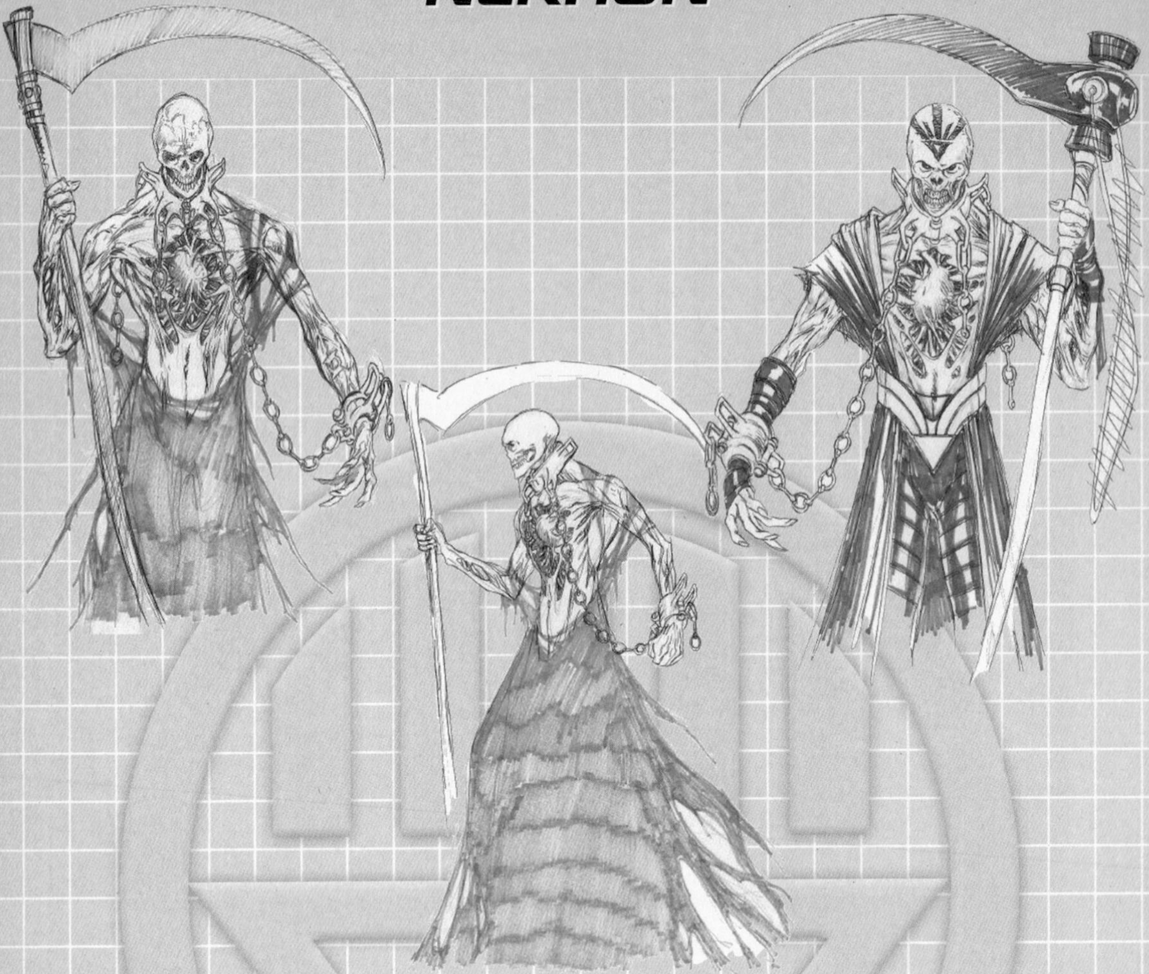

ALTER EGO: LORD OF THE DEAD
NEKRON, THE LORD OF THE DEAD, DRAWS HIS POWER FROM THOSE WHO HAVE PERISHED. HE IS THE CREATOR OF THE BLACK RINGS AND RULER OF THE LAND OF THE UNLIVING. HIS ULTIMATE GOAL IS TO DESTROY ALL LIFE, RETURNING THE UNIVERSE TO PURE DARKNESS.

Designs by Ivan Reis

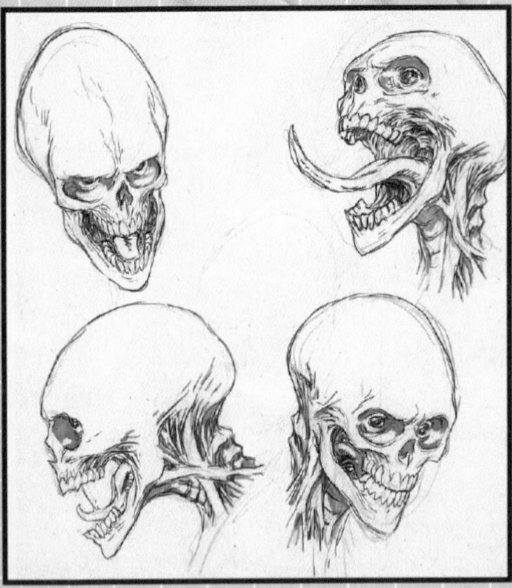

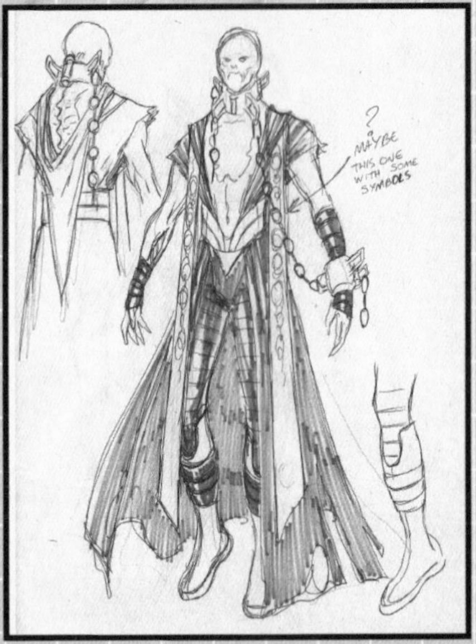
?
MAYBE
THIS ONE
WITH SOME
SYMBOLS

THE ENTITY

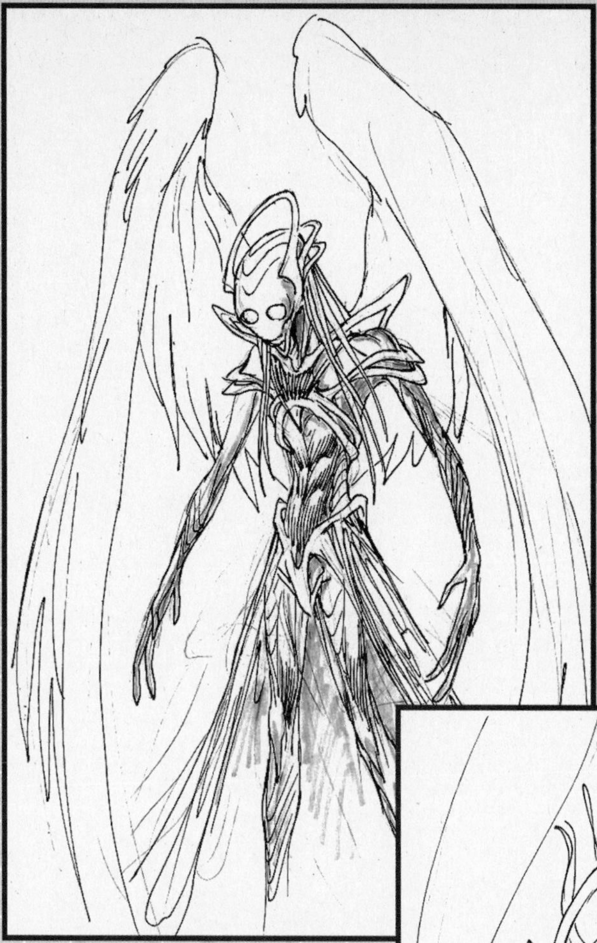

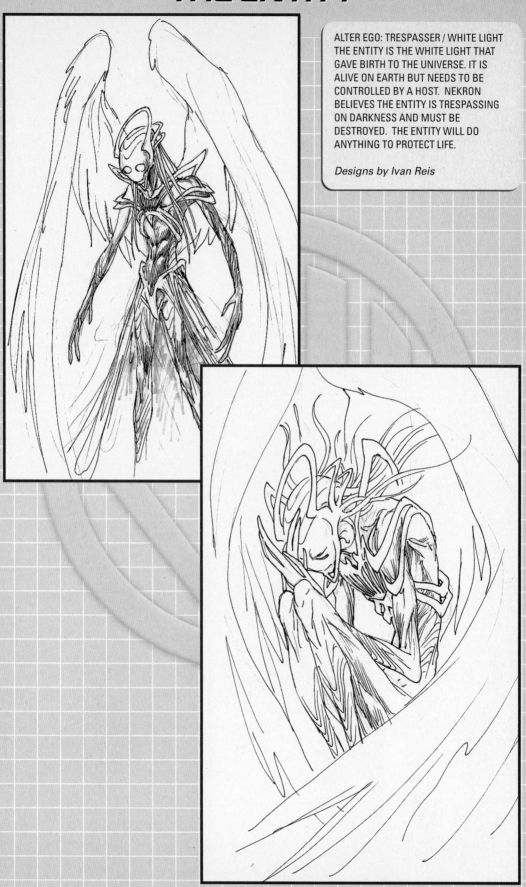

ALTER EGO: TRESPASSER / WHITE LIGHT
THE ENTITY IS THE WHITE LIGHT THAT GAVE BIRTH TO THE UNIVERSE. IT IS ALIVE ON EARTH BUT NEEDS TO BE CONTROLLED BY A HOST. NEKRON BELIEVES THE ENTITY IS TRESPASSING ON DARKNESS AND MUST BE DESTROYED. THE ENTITY WILL DO ANYTHING TO PROTECT LIFE.

Designs by Ivan Reis

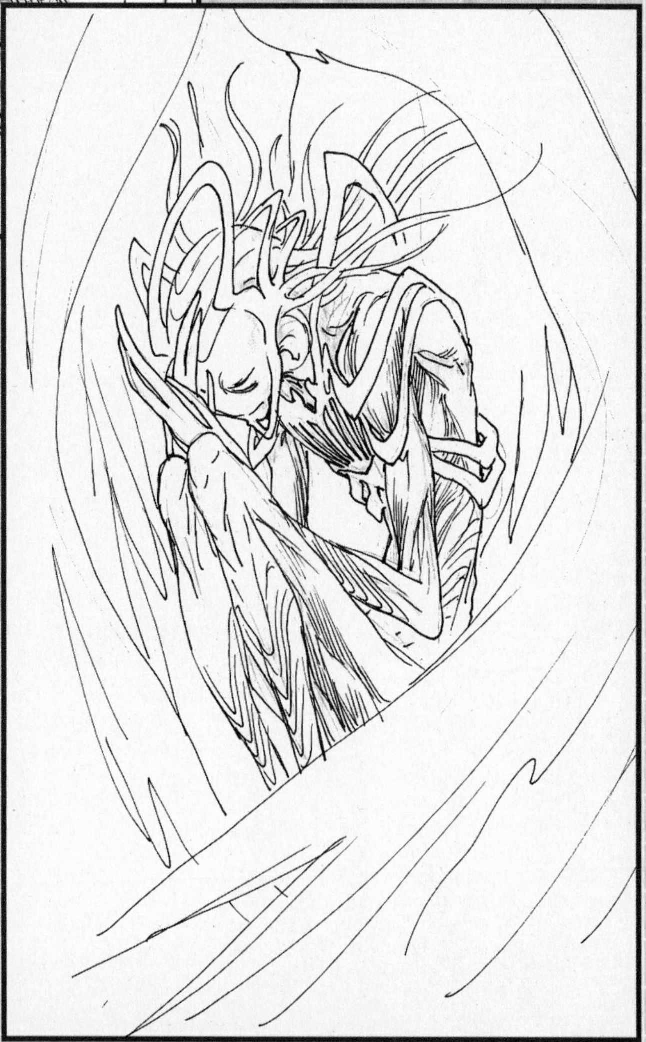

WHITE LANTERN SINESTRO

ALTER EGO: THAAL SINESTRO
ONCE THE GREATEST GREEN LANTERN, SINESTRO WOULD BECOME HAL JORDAN'S GREATEST FOE AND FOUNDER OF THE YELLOW LANTERN CORPS. WHEN SINESTRO REALIZES THE ENTITY REQUIRES A HOST, HE STEPS FORWARD SAYING THAT HE, NOT HAL JORDAN, WILL CLAIM THE ENTITY'S POWER. SINESTRO THEN ENTERS THE WHITE LIGHT AND EMERGES A WHITE LANTERN.

Designs by Joe Prado

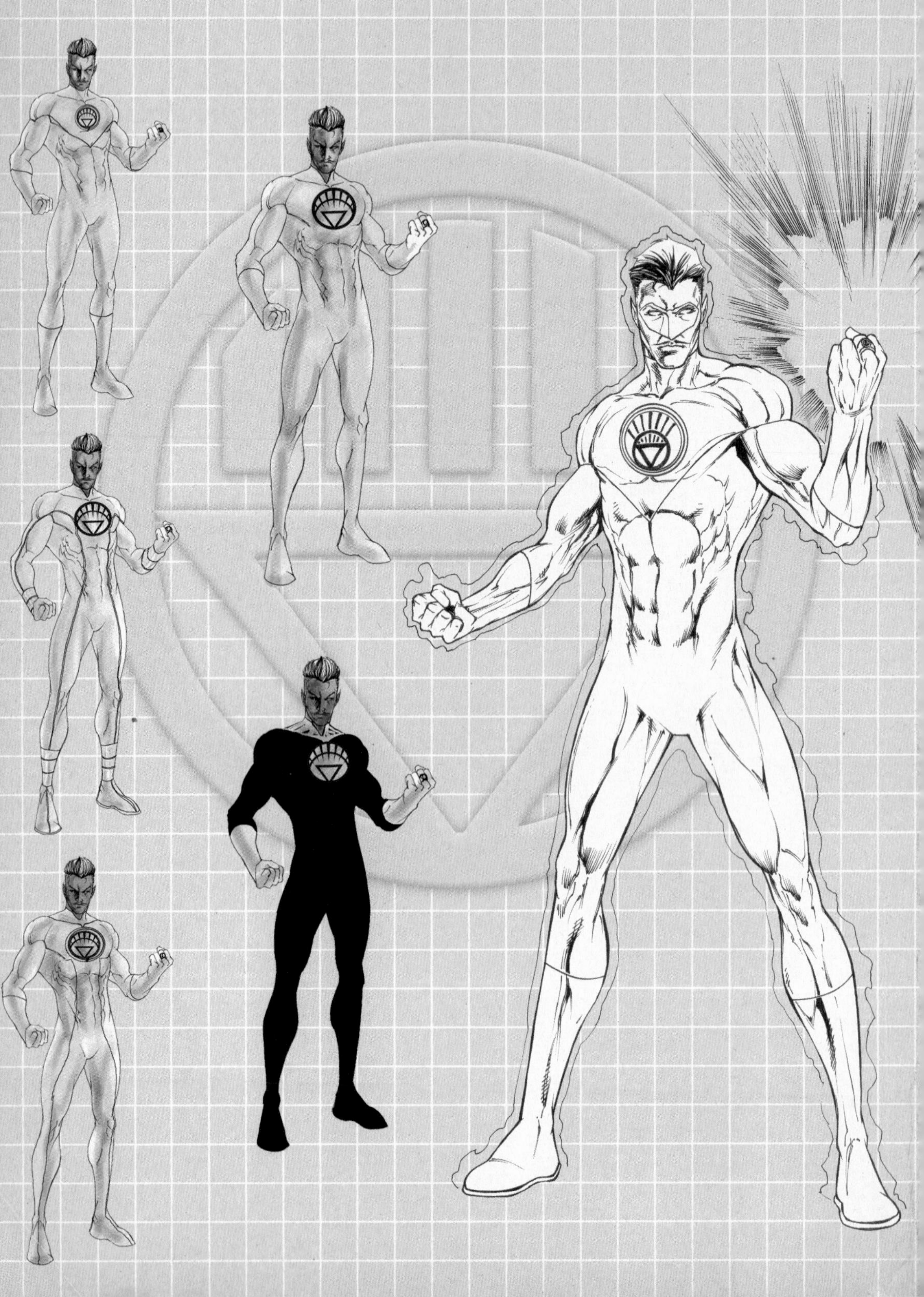

BIOGRAPHIES

GEOFF JOHNS

Geoff Johns is one of the most prolific and popular contemporary comic book writers. He has written highly acclaimed stories starring Superman, Green Lantern, the Flash, Teen Titans and the Justice Society of America. He is the author of the *New York Times* best-selling graphic novels GREEN LANTERN: RAGE OF THE RED LANTERNS, GREEN LANTERN: SINESTRO CORPS WAR, JUSTICE SOCIETY OF AMERICA: THY KINGDOM COME, and SUPERMAN: BRAINIAC.

Johns was born in Detroit and studied media arts, screenwriting, film production and film theory at Michigan State University. After moving to Los Angeles, he worked as an intern and later an assistant for film director Richard Donner, whose credits include *Superman: The Movie, Lethal Weapon 4* and *Conspiracy Theory.*

Johns began his comics career writing STARS AND S.T.R.I.P.E. and creating Stargirl for DC Comics. Geoff received the Wizard Fan Award for Breakout Talent of 2002 and Writer of the Year for 2005 through 2008 as well as the CBG Writer of the Year 2003 through 2005, 2007 and 2008, and CBG Best Comic Book Series for JSA 2001 through 2005.

After acclaimed runs on THE FLASH, TEEN TITANS and the best-selling INFINITE CRISIS miniseries, Johns co-wrote a run on ACTION COMICS with his mentor, Donner. In 2006, he co-wrote 52, an ambitious weekly comic book series set in real time, with Grant Morrison, Greg Rucka and Mark Waid.

Johns has also written for various other media, including the acclaimed "Legion" episode of SMALLVILLE and the fourth season of ROBOT CHICKEN. He is writing the story of the DC Universe Online massively multiplayer action game from Sony Online Entertainment LLC and has recently joined DC Entertainment as its Chief Creative Officer.

Johns currently resides in Los Angeles, California.

IVAN REIS

Ivan Reis is a comic book artist born in 1976 in São Bernardo do Campo, São Paulo, Brazil. He started his US career in the 90s, on *Ghost* and *The Mask* for Dark Horse. After pencilling an issue of THE INVISIBLES for Grant Morrison, he started a long run on *Lady Death* for Chaos Comics, then did *The Avengers* and *The Vision*, with Geoff Johns, for Marvel.

In 2004 Ivan began to work exclusively for DC. After illustrating high-profile series such as ACTION COMICS, INFINITE CRISIS and RANN-THANAGAR WAR, he started his now legendary run on GREEN LANTERN with his inker of choice, Oclair Albert, and Geoff Johns. Ivan is currently working on BRIGHTEST DAY for DC Comics.

OCLAIR ALBERT

Oclair Albert is a seasoned inker, active on the market since the early '90s. His credits include *The Avengers, The Vision*, ACTION COMICS, RANN-THANAGAR WAR, INFINITE CRISIS, and for the past four years has inked Ivan Reis's pencils on GREEN LANTERN.

JOE PRADO

Joe Prado started his career as a professional comic book artist in Brazil during the '90s, and has done hundreds of illustrations for RPG magazines and books. Six years ago he started to produce comics for the US market. His credits include ACTION COMICS, SUPERMAN, BIRDS OF PREY, GREEN LANTERN and THE WARLORD.

FOLLOW THE COMPLETE

BLACKEST NIGHT

SAGA IN THESE GRAPHIC NOVELS

BLACKEST NIGHT

Geoff Johns & Ivan Reis

BLACKEST NIGHT: GREEN LANTERN

Geoff Johns & Doug Mahnke

BLACKEST NIGHT: GREEN LANTERN CORPS

Peter J. Tomasi & Patrick Gleason

BLACKEST NIGHT: BLACK LANTERN CORPS Vol. 1

Peter J. Tomasi, James Robinson, J.T. Krul, Ardian Syaf, Ed Benes & Eddy Barrows

BLACKEST NIGHT: BLACK LANTERN CORPS Vol. 2

Geoff Johns, James Robinson, Greg Rucka, Scott Kolins, Eddy Barrows & Nicola Scott

BLACKEST NIGHT: RISE OF THE BLACK LANTERNS

Geoff Johns, Peter J. Tomasi, James Robinson & others

BLACKEST NIGHT: TALES OF THE CORPS

Geoff Johns, Peter J. Tomasi & others

BIOGRAPHIES

GEOFF JOHNS

Geoff Johns is one of the most prolific and popular contemporary comic book writers. He has written highly acclaimed stories starring Superman, Green Lantern, the Flash, Teen Titans and the Justice Society of America. He is the author of the *New York Times* best-selling graphic novels GREEN LANTERN: RAGE OF THE RED LANTERNS, GREEN LANTERN: SINESTRO CORPS WAR, JUSTICE SOCIETY OF AMERICA: THY KINGDOM COME, and SUPERMAN: BRAINIAC.

Johns was born in Detroit and studied media arts, screenwriting, film production and film theory at Michigan State University. After moving to Los Angeles, he worked as an intern and later an assistant for film director Richard Donner, whose credits include *Superman: The Movie, Lethal Weapon 4* and *Conspiracy Theory*.

Johns began his comics career writing STARS AND S.T.R.I.P.E. and creating Stargirl for DC Comics. Geoff received the Wizard Fan Award for Breakout Talent of 2002 and Writer of the Year for 2005 through 2008 as well as the CBG Writer of the Year 2003 through 2005, 2007 and 2008, and CBG Best Comic Book Series for JSA 2001 through 2005. After acclaimed runs on THE FLASH, TEEN TITANS and the best-selling INFINITE CRISIS miniseries, Johns co-wrote a run on ACTION COMICS with his mentor, Donner. In 2006, he co-wrote 52, an ambitious weekly comic book series set in real time, with Grant Morrison, Greg Rucka and Mark Waid.

Johns has also written for various other media, including the acclaimed "Legion" episode of SMALLVILLE and the fourth season of ROBOT CHICKEN. He is writing the story of the DC Universe Online massively multiplayer action game from Sony Online Entertainment LLC and has recently joined DC Entertainment as its Chief Creative Officer.

Johns currently resides in Los Angeles, California.

IVAN REIS

Ivan Reis is a comic book artist born in 1976 in São Bernardo do Campo, São Paulo, Brazil. He started his US career in the 90s, on *Ghost* and *The Mask* for Dark Horse. After pencilling an issue of THE INVISIBLES for Grant Morrison, he started a long run on *Lady Death* for Chaos Comics, then did *The Avengers* and *The Vision*, with Geoff Johns, for Marvel.

In 2004 Ivan began to work exclusively for DC. After illustrating high-profile series such as ACTION COMICS, INFINITE CRISIS and RANN-THANAGAR WAR, he started his now legendary run on GREEN LANTERN with his inker of choice, Oclair Albert, and Geoff Johns. Ivan is currently working on BRIGHTEST DAY for DC Comics.

OCLAIR ALBERT

Oclair Albert is a seasoned inker, active on the market since the early '90s. His credits include *The Avengers, The Vision*, ACTION COMICS, RANN-THANAGAR WAR, INFINITE CRISIS, and for the past four years has inked Ivan Reis's pencils on GREEN LANTERN.

JOE PRADO

Joe Prado started his career as a professional comic book artist in Brazil during the '90s, and has done hundreds of illustrations for RPG magazines and books. Six years ago he started to produce comics for the US market. His credits include ACTION COMICS, SUPERMAN, BIRDS OF PREY, GREEN LANTERN and THE WARLORD.

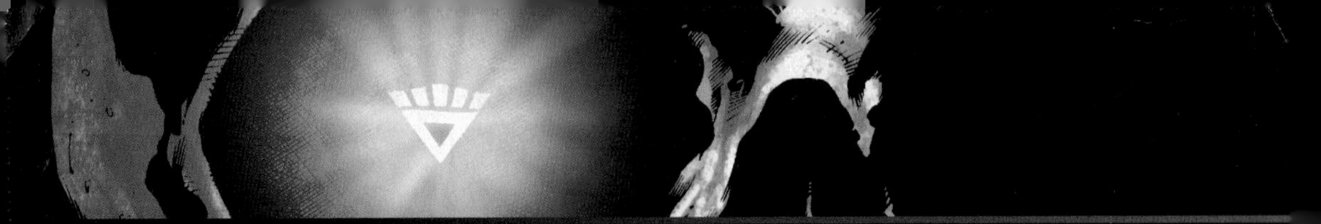